SLAV OUTPOSTS IN C
EUROPEAN HISTORY

SLAV OUTPOSTS IN CENTRAL EUROPEAN HISTORY

THE WENDS, SORBS AND KASHUBS

Gerald Stone

Bloomsbury Academic
An imprint of Bloomsbury Publishing Plc

BLOOMSBURY
LONDON · OXFORD · NEW YORK · NEW DELHI · SYDNEY

Bloomsbury Academic

An imprint of Bloomsbury Publishing Plc

50 Bedford Square	1385 Broadway
London	New York
WC1B 3DP	NY 10018
UK	USA

www.bloomsbury.com

BLOOMSBURY and the Diana logo are trademarks of Bloomsbury Publishing Plc

First published 2016

© Gerald Stone, 2016

British Library Cataloguing-in-Publication Data
A catalogue record for this book is available from the British Library.

ISBN: HB: 978-1-4725-9210-1
PB: 978-1-4725-9209-5
ePDF: 978-1-4725-9211-8
ePub: 978-1-4725-9212-5

Library of Congress Cataloging-in-Publication Data
Stone, Gerald.
Slav outposts in Central European history : the Wends, Sorbs and Kashubs / Gerald Stone.
pages cm
Includes bibliographical references and index.
ISBN 978-1-4725-9210-1 (hardback) – ISBN 978-1-4725-9209-5 (paperback) –
ISBN 978-1-4725-9211-8 (ePDF) – ISBN 978-1-4725-9212-5 (ePub)
1. Sorbs–History. 2. Kashubes–History. 3. Slavs–Europe, Central–History.
4. Slavs–Germany–History. 5. Europe, Central–Ethnic relations–History.
6. Germany–Ethnic relations–History. I. Title.
DD78.S6S76 2015
943'.00049188–dc23
2015007912

Typeset by Integra Software Services Pvt. Ltd.
Printed and bound in India

CONTENTS

LIST OF ILLUSTRATIONS

LIST OF MAPS

ACKNOWLEDGEMENTS

For their readiness to supply illustrations free of charge and for permission to publish them, I am grateful to the Sorbian Cultural Archive (Serbski kulturny archiw), Bautzen, the Wendish Museum (Serbski Muzej), Cottbus, and the Kashubian Institute (Instytut Kaszubski), Gdańsk. I am also indebted to Stephanie and Martin West for their help with Latin queries.

INTRODUCTION

Wends, Sorbs, and Kashubs

This is a history of the westernmost Slavs. It is set in the wide, fluctuating frontier area of contact between the German language and its Slav neighbours, extending, roughly speaking, from the rivers Elbe and Saale in the west to the upper Oder and lower Vistula in the east. In the latter part of the first millennium AD, these lands (referred to in this book as Trans-Elbia) were the home of a conglomeration of pagan Slav tribes. The Latin sources record them collectively as *Sclavi, Slavi* (and the like), or as *Winedi, Venedi* (and the like), but when Latin is replaced by German, they appear mainly as *Wenden* (rarely as *Winden*). The English equivalent *Wends* is the term used here.

The medieval habitations of the Wends were the western outposts of the Slavs. To their west they faced the Kingdom of the Franks. Along the Baltic coast they extended to the lower Vistula, where their eastern neighbours were the Prussians (*Prusai*), speakers of a Baltic language. Eventually, the fate of all the west Slav peoples was drawn, to a greater or lesser extent, into the vortex of German history, but the Wends lay in the direct path of Frankish (later German) expansion. In the east, they and the *Prusai* stood in the way of Polish access to the Baltic Sea. Today, what was once their homeland lies mainly in Germany and partly in Poland. Borders have been drawn and redrawn many times.

The Wends survive, even today, as the Kashubs in northern Poland (to the west of Gdańsk in the *Województwo Pomorskie*) and as the Wends and Sorbs in parts of Brandenburg and Saxony. They are among the European linguistic minorities of whom political frontiers take no account. One of the medieval Wendish tribes, located in 782 AD between the Elbe and Saale, was identified in Latin as the *Sorabi*. From this name, centuries later, the German analogue *Sorben* was devised and occasionally applied to those Wends in Brandenburg and Saxony who in their own language used the self-designatory noun *Serb*. In the late 1940s, *Sorben* was given official approval and in Saxony, at least, *Wenden* fell out of fashion, except in topography (e.g. *Wendische Straße*). In this book, therefore, the English analogue *Sorbs* is also used, when appropriate.

The Wends of the Baltic coast too were in German called *Wenden* until the eighteenth century, since when *Kaschuben* has prevailed. In this book, they are generally referred to as *Kashubs*, but in translations from German, *Wenden* is always conveyed as *Wends*. The Wends may be defined as those western Slavs who have never had their own state. Although it is clear from both translations and contexts that medieval Latin *Sclavi* and *Slavi* are usually the equivalents of German *Wenden/Winden*, in all the quotations in this book, Latin *Slavus/Sclavus* is translated as 'Slav'.

In present-day German, the variant *Winden* refers to the Slavs south of the Alps who are better known as Slovenes (and who regard the form *Winden* as derogatory). But it is only since the nineteenth century that the distinction between *Wenden, wendisch* (West Slavs) and *Winden, windisch* (South Slavs) has been stabilized. Before that usage was erratic. The history of the Slovenes is outside the scope of this book.

Trans-Elbia

Germany to the east of the Elbe and Saale is colonial territory, taken by conquest as part of the process that was once seen as 'the advance of culture toward the east during the Middle Ages, based upon the superiority of the older and higher culture...' (M. Weber 1906/1974: 384). The German colonization of the east (*Ostsiedlung*) was then regarded as 'the greatest exploit of the German people in the Middle Ages' (*Widu. Gesch.* 1935: 63). For the Wends, however, it was their downfall, and their subsequent history has been a tale of decline. Since their subjugation they have remained outside the mainstream of European history and have never succeeded in making a mark on the political map. At the same time, however, their history is a tale of survival.

The Wends still survive in the east German psyche. Opening the Wendish Museum in Cottbus on 3 June 1994, Dr Manfred Stolpe, prime minister of the state of Brandenburg, said that 'every true-born Brandenburger has a Wendish great-grandmother' (*NC* 1994: 4), and similar claims could be made about the other inhabitants of Trans-Elbian Germany. Centuries after the subjugation the Elbe-Saale line remained a cultural boundary. The condition of the peasantry beyond the Elbe, even as the feudal order approached its end, has been judged 'far more onerous and far more degrading than the vestigial serfdom of western Europe' (Blum 1978: 38–9), and this may have been so because Trans-Elbia was a zone of comparatively recent German settlement (Clark 2006: 161). The Trans-Elbian mind is said to have been perceptible even in the nineteenth century as a 'subservient mentality which passively accepted the actions and encroachments of the state', forming 'a kind of psychic pendant to the authoritarian political system' (Wehler 1985: 129). A special feature of the Trans-Elbian sociological landscape were the Junkers, endowed with land expropriated from the Wends (Taylor 1945: 28–9).

Before the Wends

The Slavs appear late in European history. Tribal names ostensibly referring to Slavs (*Sclaveni, Sclavini, Antes,* and *Veneti*) are found no earlier than the mid-sixth century in the works of the last historians of the ancient world, Procopius of Caesarea and Jordanes. Jordanes in his history of the Goths (c. 552 AD) places the Slavs (*Venethi, Sclavini/ Sclavi,* and *Antes*) in an area taking in the Black Sea coast, the eastern Alps, and the west Carpathians. It includes the upper Vistula, but says nothing of the space between the Oder and the Elbe (*MPH*, 1: 1–2). The Germanic tribes located by Tacitus (in his

Germania) and others in the first two centuries AD in the space between the Vistula and the Elbe had by the eighth century been replaced by Slavs, and, because there is no record of invasion or conquest by them, their arrival is presumed to have been a peaceful process. It is estimated to have taken place between 600 and 700 AD, as the Slavs moved into land which was unoccupied, having been deserted by its Germanic inhabitants before 500 AD (Blaschke 2003: 68–9).

The 'German colonization of the East' was once a prominent issue in German history textbooks and a matter of pride. It was claimed that the medieval incursions into Slav land were justified because the invaders and colonizers from the west were reoccupying land that had previously been theirs. They called it the German re-occupation (*deutsche Wiederbesiedlung*) of the east, a notion that eventually bolstered the idea of *Lebensraum*, affecting political policy (Blaschke 2003: 66). Reinforcement was provided by the anachronistic use of the term *Deutschland*, as in connotations like 'The immigration of the Slavs into north Germany' (*Die Einwanderung der Slawen in Norddeutschland*) (Montelius 1899: 127). The 1935 Nazi textbook *Widukind* (not to be confused with the tenth-century chronicler Widukind of Corvey) was merely repeating received opinion, when it referred to: 'The German east, land of the German people since time immemorial, having been surrendered to the Slavs after the time of the great Germanic migration [...]' (*Widu. Gesch.* 1935: 71).

The two assumptions (i) that the Wendish lands beyond the Elbe were re-occupied (rather than simply occupied) and (ii) that Germany existed before the Wends arrived are mistaken, because the Germanic tribes who are thought to have occupied these lands in the third and fourth centuries were not German (*deutsch*). By 500 AD, at which time Germany (*Deutschland*) did not yet exist, they had withdrawn to a position west of the Elbe-Saale line (Blaschke 2003: 68). The trap of equating *Germania* with Germany is always open and the task of explaining to tourists, for example, the presence in Germany today of the Wends and Sorbs is fraught with the temptation to oversimplify. A brochure for tourists, published in Bautzen, once wrote: 'From the sixth century Slav tribes colonized large parts of central and north Germany' (*Sorben* 2000: 1). This was corrected in later editions.

The notion of 're-occupation' is also present in the Polish term *Ziemie Odzyskane* 'Recovered Territories', the name given to the German territory east of the Oder-Neisse Line annexed by Poland in 1945, but the inhabitants of much of this land in the Middle Ages, before it fell victim to German expansion, had been not Poles but Wends. The history of the Wends therefore extends into parts of what is today Poland (Pomerania, eastern Lusatia).

CHAPTER 1
SUBJUGATION 800–1200

The Frankish Empire

Around 800, the year when Charlemagne was crowned emperor of the Holy Roman Empire, the limits of Slav settlement extended at least as far west as the lower Elbe and the Saale (see Map 1.1). They stretched northwards to a point close to where Kiel now stands, embracing what later became east Holstein. Along this frontier the heathen Slavs faced the Christian forces of the expanding Frankish Empire (Herrmann 1985: 10). The chain of events culminating in this situation leads us back to the decline of the Western Roman Empire. It was this that had first provided the Franks, a Germanic tribe originating in the region of the lower Rhine, with opportunities for expansion. Clovis or Chlodwig (c. 466–511), king of the Salian Franks from 481, succeeded in enlarging his domains to incorporate much of Roman Gaul, and his conversion to Christianity in 496 brought him the assistance of Roman bishops and officials in consolidating his gains.

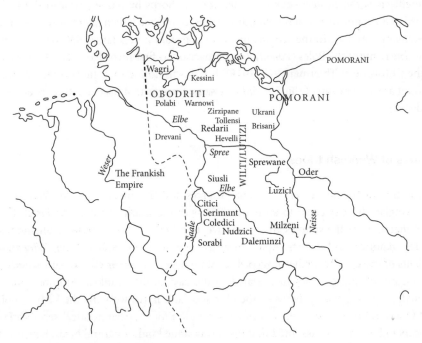

Map 1.1 Western limits of Wendish settlement c. 800 (shown by a broken line _ _ _ _) and names and locations of main Wendish tribes.

From a small tribal territory a great empire emerged, and throughout the reign of the Merovingian dynasty (c. 500–752) expansion continued (Scheuch 2001: 13).

To the east of the Frankish Empire in the early sixth century lay the territory of the heathen Thuringians (*Toringi*), a Germanic tribe, stretching as far east as the River Saale. Clovis's four sons continued their father's policy of expansion and, in alliance with the Saxons, conquered the Thuringians in 531, incorporating their land (Herrmann 1985: 36–7; Köbler 1999: 650; Scheuch 2001: 13). In the following century the Franks encountered the empire of Samo, a state created out of an alliance of Wendish tribes which around 625 had fought successfully against the Avars before coalescing as a political unit. Dagobert, king of the Franks, seeing himself threatened by Samo, embarked on a campaign against him, but suffered defeat at Wogastiburg (location unknown) (Labuda 1949: 23–4, 126–32; Herrmann 1985: 12, 37). It is in the context of Dagobert's defeat that we encounter the Sorbs, one of the Wendish tribes, and learn the name of their leader Dervanus. In 630 or 631, according to the chronicle of Fredegar, 'Dervanus too, a leader from the tribe of the Sorbs, who were of the clan of the Slavs and in times past had belonged to the kingdom of the Franks, consigned himself with his followers to the kingdom of Samo (...*etiam et Dervanus dux gente Surbiorum, que ex genere Sclavinorum erant et ad regnum Francorum iam olim aspecserant, se ad regnum Samonem cum suis tradedit*)' (Fredegar 1888: 155). Samo died in 658. The location of his kingdom is uncertain, but it may have been on the River Morava, on the site of the future Moravia (Magocsi 1993: 8–9).

Fredegar is the earliest source to mention the Sorbs by name and also the earliest record of the name of any of the Wendish tribes in the area which later became Germany (Herrmann 1985: 7). In the scheme of Slavonic tribal nomenclature 630/631 is an early date. The name of the Poles (*Poleni*), by comparison, is first recorded over 300 years later in the Chronicle of Thietmar (975–1018). It is worth noting that the *Surbi* in Fredegar's account are a subgroup of the *Sclavini* (the same form as that used a 100 years earlier by Jordanes).

Names of Wendish tribes

There are no further seventh-century sources for the history of the Wends. The Merovingian dynasty came to an end in 751 with the death of King Childerich III..In Carolingian times the sources are less elusive, but they still concentrate on alliances and battles, victories, and defeats. Apart from the generic terms *Sclavi, Slavi, Winedi*, and variants of these, early medieval records contain over sixty other ethnic names denoting the various Wendish tribes in the area to the east of the Frankish Empire. They are located, roughly speaking, between the Elbe and Saale in the west and the Vistula, Bober, and Queis in the east. Possibly out of consideration for modern political sensibilities, it appears to be generally assumed that there was some kind of natural break between the tribes that subsequently came under German control and those subsumed by Poland, but there is no evidence for this. The Poleni (who gave Poland its name) were a land-locked tribe, bounded to the north, between the Oder and the Vistula, by the Pomerani. To the east of the Bober and Queis were the ancestors of today's Silesians (Dadosani and Slezani).

Many of the Wendish tribes were small and insignificant and most of them were not independent but part of larger ethnic formations. The main significant groupings were as follows, proceeding from the Baltic southwards:

1. The Obodriti. These are first noted in connection with Charlemagne's Saxon campaign in 781. They were made up of the Wagri (also known as Travjani), who originated in east Holstein, the Polabi, between the Rivers Trave and Elbe, the Warnowi, on the upper Warnow and Mildentz, and the tautonymous Obodriti, located between Wismar Bay and south of Lake Schwerin.

2. The Pomerani between the lower Oder and Vistula.

3. The Velunzani, also called Lutizi. Their German name is Wilzen. They included the Kessini, on the lower Warnow, the Zirzipane, between the Rivers Recknitz, Trebel, and Peene, the Tollensi, to the east and south of the Peene on the Tollense, and the Redarii, to the south and east of Lake Tollense on the upper Havel.

4. The Rujane or Rani. These were the inhabitants of the island of Rügen. As Rugini they are mentioned in a reference datable to around 703 in Bede's *Historia ecclesiastica gentis Anglorum* 'Ecclesiastical History of the English People', which was completed in 731 (Herrmann 1985: 8).

5. The Ukrani. These were settled on the River Uecker and are first mentioned in 934.

6. The Murizi. Their presence is first recorded in 948, when they were living on the River Müritz.

7. The Linoni. Their main centre was Lenzen in the Altmark.

8. The Drevani (first mentioned in 1004) and the Lipani (first mentioned 956) inhabited land to the west of the lower Elbe. They lost their independence to the Franks around 780 during the reign of Charlemagne.

9. The Hevelli. The name they gave themselves was Stodorani. They inhabited an area to the south of a large expanse of primeval forest separating them from the Obodriti and Velunzani. The Hevelli are first recorded c. 850 as Hehfeldi. Closely associated with them were the Dossani (948), located on the River Dosse; the Zamzizi (948), inhabiting the Ruppin area; the Rezani (948), on the upper Havel; and the Neletici (948), Liezizi (948), and Zemzizi (948), all settled on the lower Havel and the Elbe-Havel pocket, as were also the Smeldingi and Bethenici (c. 850).

10. The Sprewane (948). Their homeland lay to the east of the Hevelli on the lower Dahme and the Spree. To the south of the Hevelli was an area recorded as Ploni. Westwards from here on the right bank of the middle Elbe opposite Magdeburg was the territory of the Marzane (850). The Hevelli, Sprewane, and Marzane

were separated from the Sorbian tribes to their south by the wooded and uninhabited hills of the Fläming and other forests.

11. The first reference to the Sorbs (*Surbi*), dated 630 or 631 (see above), does not locate them, but in the eighth and ninth centuries there are several sources which place them close to the Rivers Elbe, Saale, and Mulde. It is significant that Thietmar (975–1018), who describes the Spree landscape later associated with the Sorbs, does not record the name *Sorabi* (or anything like it).

12. The northernmost of the tribes who inhabited what later became Lusatia (Ger. *Lausitz*) were the Lusici (c. 850 as *Lunsici*). Their homeland became Lower Lusatia (Ger. *Niederlausitz*). To their south-east were the Milzeni (c. 850 as *Milzane*) in what eventually became Upper Lusatia (Ger. *Oberlausitz*). The earliest sources treat both Lusici and Milzeni as independent tribes (Herrmann 1985: 9). Near the Lusici and Milzeni were the Selpoli (948) and the Besunzane (c. 850). On the middle Oder at the end of the eleventh century the presence of the Leubuzzi is recorded. The Licicaviki are mentioned in this area in 929. Other constituents were the Citici, Serimunt, Colodici, Siusler, Daleminzi (or Glomaci), Chutici, Nisane, Plisni, Gera, Puonzowa, Tucharin, Weta, and Neletici (Herrmann 1985: 7–14).

We may assume that the Latin names are mostly based on words applied by the tribes to themselves. Occasionally we are told explicitly that that is so, but, in a few cases, the Franks had a name for a Wendish tribe that differed from that used by the Wends themselves. Thietmar von Merseburg, for example, refers to 'a district which we call Delemenci, but which the Slavs call Glomaci' (Thietmar 1992: 61), which establishes that the names Daleminci and Glomaci both refer to the same tribe. Similarly, Stodorane was the Wendish name for the tribe called Hevelli in Germanic (Herrmann 1985: 8–9).

Eighth century

Pippin the Younger (751–768), the first king of the Carolingian dynasty, was at odds with the Saxons, a heathen Germanic people inhabiting the lands to the north-east of the Franks in the same area, broadly speaking, as that known today as Lower Saxony. From here, in the mid-fifth century, the Saxons had begun their participation in invasions and migration to the Romano-Celtic island of Britain, which would one day be England. In Merovingian times (c. 500–752) the Saxons were not only consolidating their position in Britain but also making advances on the Continent, penetrating south into Frankish territory.

Pippin's son Charles, later known as Charlemagne, succeeded him in 768, and two years later the Frankish diet resolved on war against the heathen Saxons. The Saxon wars were at the centre of Frankish policy for nearly thirty years, during which time the Franks were sometimes allied with the Wends. In 748 several Wendish chieftains had supported Pippin in a campaign against the Saxons (Fredegar 1888: 181; Herrmann 1985: 328, 542).

In 782, according to the Frankish chronicler Einhardus, Charlemagne, hearing that the Sorbs, 'Slavs who inhabit the plains between the Elbe and the Saale', had carried out raids into the Saxon and Thuringian lands, ordered his officers 'to punish the insolence of the restive Slavs as quickly as possible'. No sooner had they entered Saxon territory to carry out this task, however, than they heard that the Saxons were arming for war against them. 'So they gave up the march against the Slavs and set out with troops of the East Franks for the place where the Saxons were said to have assembled' (*Annales* 1895: 61).

In 789 Charlemagne embarked on his first campaign against another Wendish tribe, the Wilti, whose great army also included Saxons, Friesians, Sorbs, and Obodriti. They were, nevertheless, no match for the Franks. Their leader, Dragavit, was obliged to surrender hostages and swear fealty to Charlemagne. Although alliances were made and broken without scruple, the Franks were steadfast in their main objective of taming the Saxons, and in 795, supported by the Obodriti prince Witzan, Charlemagne opened a new offensive against them. Crossing the Elbe, however, Witzan was ambushed by the Saxons and killed. He was succeeded by Thrasco, who three years later avenged Witzan's death. Standing fast in the Obodriti alliance with Charlemagne, Thrasco in 798, in a combined operation with Frankish forces, triumphed over the Saxons at Suentanafeld (near Bornhöved in Holstein) (Herrmann 1985: 328).

Ninth century

Thrasco needed Charlemagne's backing not only in hostilities against the Wilti but also to bolster his own position among the Obodriti. He appeared before Charlemagne in 804 at Hollenstedt, south of Harburg, whence the Franks were launching one of their last campaigns against the Saxons, presented gifts, and was confirmed by him as king of the Obodriti (Herrmann 1985: 328–9). For their services as the most faithful allies of the Franks in the Saxon wars, the Obodriti were rewarded with the land along the northern Elbe, including the area where Hamburg would later stand, from which Charlemagne had expelled most of the Nordalbing Saxons. The Obodriti thereby became a buffer between the Carolingian and Danish Empires. The Danes had been supporters of the Saxons and so now viewed the Obodriti with belligerence. In 808 Göttrick, king of the Danes, marched into Obodriti territory in alliance with the Wilti, the traditional enemies of the Obodriti. In the ensuing hostilities the Obodriti had great difficulty in holding their own, even with Frankish support. Thrasco's personal position was now precarious, but in 809, with the support of his old enemies the Saxons, he attacked the Wilti, devastated their settlements, and returned home victorious, laden with booty. He then attacked the Smeldingi (a subgroup of the Hevelli), captured their capital, and compelled everyone to accept his sway. Now at the height of his power, Thrasco was taken unawares by the Danes in Reric and assassinated. His people, the Obodriti, apparently because they had failed to give the protection expected of a buffer, were now deprived of their Nordalbing lands. The Franks tried another defensive expedient, establishing a *Limes Saxoniae*, a protective band of territory between Lauenburg and the Kiel Förde (Herrmann 1985: 329).

Until 800 (the year of Charlemagne's coronation) the Saxons had maintained their independence, but in the first part of the ninth century they were finally subjugated by the Franks. Having resolved their Saxon problem, the Franks no longer needed their alliance with the Sorbs, who were now merely standing in the way of their expansion, so in 806 the Sorbs became the victims of Frankish aggression:

> And thereupon coming to Aachen a few days later he sent his son Karl with an army into the land of the Slavs that are called Sorabi, who are situated on the River Elbe. In this expedition Miliduoch the leader of the Slavs was slain, and two strongholds were built by the army, one on the bank of the River Saale and the other near the River Elbe.

> (*Annales* 1895: 121)

Miliduch, who in another source is described as 'a proud king who was reigning among the Sorbs' (*rex superbus, qui regnabat in Siurbis*), is the second individual in Sorbian history to be identified by name (the first was Dervanus) and the first recorded as having fallen in battle. That is enough to ensure him a place in the encyclopaedias, though nothing else is known about him (*SSS*, s.v. *Miliduch*).

In the last years of Charlemagne's reign (died 814), the Franks were gaining a kind of control over all the Wends to their east. In his biography of Charlemagne, in a passage relating to around the year 806, Einhard claims:

> Thereafter he tamed (so that he might make them pay tribute) all the barbarian and savage peoples who are located between the River Rhine, the River Vistula, the sea, and the Danube, and inhabit Germania, who in language are fairly similar, but in customs and dress are very dissimilar. The most important among them are the Weletabi, the Sorabi, the Abodriti, and the Boemani. Against these he waged war; the others, who were far more numerous, submitted to him voluntarily.

> (*Einhardi Vita* 1911: 18)

Having installed an Elbe crossing and fortress at Höbeck (Hohbuoki) opposite Lenzen in 789, Charlemagne thought he had established Frankish authority, but in 810 the Wilti showed that they thought otherwise by destroying it. Two years later they were again defeated by a superior Frankish army and forced to hand over hostages (Herrmann 1985: 329).

The *Limes Sorabicus*

The emperor's representatives on the outskirts of the Frankish Empire had special responsibilities for defence. For this purpose the Frankish *Mark* 'march' was devised, a border-territory constituting a political and military unit ruled by a *Graf* 'count'. *Marken* 'marches' were set up at several points on the empire's frontiers. They were a way of streamlining the defence of the state's outer limits and in later centuries they provided bases for the formation of new German principalities. Just as the German word *Mark* may mean either 'frontier' or 'border-territory, march', so each of the Latin equivalents *marchia* and *limes* in medieval German sources has both senses. *Marken* as administrative units along the Saale and Elbe, where Frankish and Wendish lands met, were first created in the ninth century.

A capitulary of Charlemagne issued in Diedenhofen (Thionville) in 805 specified the points at which trading with the Wends and Avars was permitted along the Franks' eastern limits, a line stretching from Bardewik on the lower Elbe to Lauriacum (now Lorch) on the Danube. It was once erroneously thought that the capitulary in question used the term *limes sorabicus* 'Sorbian frontier' to refer to this eastern boundary, but in fact the term is not actually found in this source. It does, however, occur later in the *Annales Fuldenses* under the years 849, 858, 873, and 880, but here it has the sense 'borderland, march' not 'frontier'. This *Limes Sorabicus* was a Sorbian march, whose ruler (the *Markgraf* 'margrave') was simultaneously Duke of Thuringia. The ruler of this *Sorbische Mark* (as it is known in German historiography) in the years 847–873 was Takulf, Duke of the Sorbian March (*dux Sorabici limitis*), and after his death Ratulf (who is mentioned only once, in 874). He was followed from 880 by Boppo (or Poppo) (*SSS*, s.v. *marchia, limes sorabicus*).

Louis the Pious (r. 814–840)

Towards the end of Charlemagne's life, once the Saxons had been subdued, the Frankish policy of expansion was gradually replaced by one of consolidation (Scheuch 2001: 18). His son and successor Louis the Pious, however, was determined to maintain the empire's influence beyond the Elbe. He exploited intrigues and rivalries among the Obodriti aristocracy. Following the assassination of Thrasco in 809, Charlemagne had transferred the royal power not to Thrasco's son Cedragus, who was still a child, but to Slawomir. In 817, three years into his reign, Louis the Pious, realized that he could use Cedragus, who was now a man, to manipulate Slawomir. He ordered Slawomir to share royal power with Cedragus, but Slawomir would not comply. Instead, he showed his resentment by allying himself to the Franks' most bitter enemies, the Danes, and with them began military action in the north-Elbe region, attacking the fortress built by Charlemagne at Esesfelth near Itzehoe. He was unable to take it, however, and a Frankish expedition against the Obodriti succeeded in taking Slawomir prisoner.

It was now 819. Slawomir together with several other Obodriti leaders was taken before the Imperial Court at Aachen, where he was condemned to banishment. Cedragus, who now reigned over the Obodriti in his stead, at first showed no more inclination than Slawomir to conform to Frankish control and conspired with the Danes. Eventually, however, renewed conflict with the Wilti persuaded him that he could not afford to be at loggerheads with the Franks. Louis too wanted to have the Obodriti on his side and finally, at an Imperial Diet at Compiègne in 829, an accommodation was reached. With the majority of the Obodriti princes behind him, Cedragus was confirmed by Louis as king of the Obodriti (Herrmann 1985: 330).

Louis also aspired to exert his power over the Wilti. In 809 Dragovit had been succeeded as king of the Wilti by Liub, but after Liub fell in battle against the eastern Obodriti, he was succeeded by his elder son Milegost. Milegost's royal authority, however, was not universally accepted. He was therefore deposed and replaced by his younger brother Cealadrag; but Milegost would not accept dethronement and fighting broke out between them. In 823 Milegost and Cealadrag appealed to Louis for a ruling as to which of them should reign. Louis favoured Cealadrag, who also had the support of the Wilti nobility, and at an Imperial Diet at Frankfurt in 823 confirmed him as king and imposed an obligation of fealty on both the brothers. Cealadrag is the last recorded king of the Wilti (*Annales* 1895: 160; Herrmann 1985: 330).

Sorbs in the ninth century

The Sorbs, despite the defeat they had suffered at the hands of Charlemagne in 806, were still ensconced as far west as the Saale, which divided them from the Germanic Thuringians, and they were continuing to assert their political independence (*Einhardi Vita* 1911: 18). The Annals of the kingdom of the Franks refer under the year 816 to Sorbian insubordination, sedition, and mutiny. A Frankish army was dispatched to besiege and conquer Sorbian strongholds. Once this objective had been achieved, the inhabitants of the areas surrounding their strongholds also submitted. As among the Obodriti and Wilti, so among the Sorbian nobility there was constant feuding and contention for superiority. One Sorbian noble, named Tunglo, was denounced by his peers before Louis the Pious at an Imperial Diet held at Ingelheim in June 826 and accused of treachery to the emperor. He was thereupon commanded to appear before the next Diet to answer for himself. Otherwise he would be condemned as a traitor. He did appear and somehow managed to justify himself (Herrmann 1985: 330–1).

Louis's difficulties with the Danes encouraged the Wends to revolt again in 830 and 839. In the latter year the small Sorbian tribe of the Colodici was conquered by a Frankish-Saxon army, their main fortress Kesigesburch and eleven further strongholds were taken, and their king, Cimusclo, was killed. A new king was elected before the fighting was over and he made peace and surrendered hostages (Herrmann 1985: 331). When Louis the Pious died in June 840, a process of disintegration among the rulers of the Franks was already far advanced, and in 843 Charlemagne's three grandsons in the Treaty of Verdun divided up the Frankish Empire. Lothar, Louis the Pious's eldest son, took the central part, stretching from Friesland to central Italy, and was given the title of emperor. Charles the Bald was lord of the western part. The East Frankish Empire was now ruled by the king known to German historiography as Louis the German (*Ludwig der Deutsche*), though this anchronistic title was given to him only centuries later, thanks to a tendentious translation of *Ludovicus Germanicus*. The East Franks called their country (in Latin) *Francia*. Germany (*Deutschland*) did not yet exist (Herrmann 1985: 332; Scheuch 2001: 19; Geuenich 2004: 185–7).

Louis the German's expansionist aims were mainly directed towards Lorraine (to his west) and the Great Moravian Empire (to his south-east), but he did not overlook the Wendish lands lying due east and he continued to harry the Obodriti and the Sorbs. In early 840, however, just before the death of Louis the Pious, the Sorbs (despite their defeat the year before) had exploited the dissension between father and son to free themselves from Frankish control. At that time Louis the German, being in revolt against his father and in danger of attack by the Imperial forces, was obliged to withdraw into Sorbian territory and pay the Sorbs to allow him to pass through to Bavaria, where he had his political power base. Throughout the 840s the power struggle between Louis the Pious's sons gave the Sorbs years of relief from Frankish attention. In 851, however, when his political base was better established, Louis the German undertook a new campaign against the Sorbs. He resolved on punishing them not only by force of arms, but also by starvation. Having invaded their land with a large army and 'after destroying their crops and depriving them of all hope of a harvest', he subdued them 'more by hunger than by the sword' (Brankačk 1964: 225; Herrmann 1985: 331–2).

Slav prospects of victory continued to be diminished by discord and treachery in their own ranks. When in 856 Louis the German attacked the Daleminci (a Sorbian subgroup), several Sorbian princes attempted to strengthen their own positions by fighting on the side of the invaders. Two years later (858) the Sorbs, after 'perfidiously murdering Duke Ciscibor, who was faithful to him [Louis]', were planning to defect, whereupon Takulf, the Duke of the Sorbian Mark, 'who was well acquainted with the laws and customs of the Slavs', marched against the turbulent Sorbs. There were several further Sorbian risings before the end of the ninth century, the last being in 880. Although the Sorbs were now entrapped in the feudal system of tribute and dependency, the Franks were as yet unable to influence the social structure of the Sorbian tribes. The most powerful of the Wendish tribes were still the Obodriti, but in a war of 844 against the Franks, their king Gostimysl was killed and the kingdom broke up. In its place there appeared various smaller political units, each ruled by a *regulus*, some of whom were quite capable of inflicting damage on the Franks. By 858 they were reunited and headed by King Dobemysl. Frankish successes against them were limited (Herrmann 1985: 332).

The Saxon kings – Heinrich I (r. 919–936)

Following the death of Ludwig the Child in 911, the hereditary principle was dropped and Konrad I (911–918) was elected king of the East Franks. Significantly, he was elected not only by the Frankish dukes but also by rulers of other Germanic tribes. This may be regarded as a critical stage in the progress of the East Frankish Empire towards becoming the German state. On his deathbed Konrad charged his brother to offer the throne to Heinrich, Duke of the Saxons (Scheuch 2001: 24).

Heinrich I, known as Henry the Fowler (*Heinrich der Finkler*), was the first Saxon king and first of the Ottonian dynasty. He is generally considered to be the founder and first king of the German state, which had hitherto been the East Frankish Empire. However, the state was not yet called German (*deutsch* or *teutonicus*). Reference to the king as *rex teutonicorum* and the use of *diutsch* in an ethnic sense were to appear only in the late eleventh century. Before this both *diutsch* and *teutonicus* were applied to language, but it is sometimes hard to distinguish between the general sense 'vernacular (not Latin)' and the specific sense 'German' (König 1985: 59; Henry the Fowler 2014). Nevertheless, German historians conventionally refer to the state as Germany (*Deutschland*) from Konrad's time onward and that practice is followed here.

Heinrich had his seat in Merseburg and from here he carried out raids against the Deleminci/Głomaci. Meanwhile, near Merseburg, but to the east of the Saale, he made arrangements for terrorizing the Slavs by creating a band of militarized marauders:

> This unit was composed of robbers, for King Heinrich was very severe against foreigners, but in all things very kind to his own countrymen; so whenever he saw that a thief or a robber was strong of arm and fit for war, he released him from the due penalty and, stationing him in the outskirts of Merseburg and giving him land and arms, ordered him to spare his compatriots but against the barbarians to carry out predatory raids as much as they dared.

(Widukind 1971: 90–1)

Under Heinrich eastward expansion of the Reich and the incorporation of Slav territory became a central objective. Even before becoming king, he had, in 905/906 at the command of his father Duke Otto of Saxony, been 'sent with a great army into the land which we in German call Delemenci, but the Slavs name Glomaci, whence he returned the victor, having inflicted much devastation and burning' (Herrmann 1985: 335; Thietmar 1992: 6).

In the early years of Heinrich's reign the weight of the Hungarian invasions began to be felt. The Hungarians had settled in Pannonia in 906. During the course of an armistice with them, which appears to have come to an end in 926, Heinrich had had new castles built and reinforced his army. But it was not the Hungarians he was preparing to attack. Having annexed Lorraine in the course of two campaigns in 925, he now began to focus on the Wends. His campaign against the Hevelli in the winter of 928/9 was probably undertaken to test his new army, which had been built up primarily to fight the Hungarians. Taking advantage of freezing weather to cross the frozen lakes and reaches of the River Havel surrounding the main stronghold of the Hevelli at Brandenburg, Heinrich overcame its garrison and took them prisoner together with Tugumir, their Prince, who was taken home to Saxony as a hostage (Widukind 1971: 68; Herrmann 1985: 335).

Immediately after this Heinrich was engaged in further fighting with the Deleminci/ Glomaci and succeeded in taking their stronghold at Gana, thought to have been near where Hof in Kreis Oschatz now stands. All the Slav men capable of bearing arms were killed; the women and children were carried off (Herrmann 1985: 335 and 544n.). The year 929 was extremely busy. In the spring, Heinrich, in alliance with Duke Arnulf of Bavaria, attacked Bohemia and captured Prague, including King Wenceslaus I, who thus became his vassal. According to Widukind, Heinrich had now pacified all the neighbouring Slav tribes (Obodriti, Wilti, Hevelli, Deleminci, Redarii, and Czechs), but in August the Wilti revolted. The revolt started among the Redarii, who managed to cross the Elbe and take the fortress of Walsleben on the Uchte north of Stendal. All the inhabitants were slaughtered. This encouraged other Slav tribes to join the revolt, but retaliation came quickly. A Saxon army laid siege to the fortress of Lenzen, east of the Elbe facing the Höhbeck, an important crossing on the frontier of the empire (Widukind 1971: 70). In the Battle of Lenzen, which took place on 4 September 929, the Wilti were numerically superior, but they could not withstand Heinrich's heavily armed cavalry and were forced to retreat. Some fled, but most of them were driven into a swamp and drowned. The garrison, facing defeat and having been granted a guarantee of safe conduct, surrendered. Despite the guarantee they were all slaughtered (Herrmann 1985: 336).

It was also in the year 929 that Heinrich set about building a citadel on the Elbe in order to subjugate the Deleminci/Glomaci and Milceni: 'He cleared a hill, standing beside the Elbe and at that time densely covered with trees, and here he created a castle, giving it the name Misni from the stream which flows to the north of it. As is the custom today, he fortified it with a garrison and other defences. From here he compelled the Milzeni, when they had been subdued to his authority, to pay tribute' (Thietmar 1992: 20). The stream later became in German the Meisa and the town Meissen. The foray into the land of the Milzeni, implicit in Thietmar's last sentence, is dated by Herrmann (1985: 337) to 932. This is the territory to the east of Meissen which five centuries later would come to be known as Upper Lusatia and where the Wends would survive (as the Upper Wends or Upper Sorbs). Heinrich also went on to attack the Lusici and destroyed their stronghold Liubusa, which thereafter remained deserted (Thietmar 1992: 20) and is thought to have stood in the region where subsequently the town of Luckau would be built (Herrmann 1985: 337). Here too the Wends were to survive (as the Lower Wends/Sorbs).

Otto I the Great (936–973)

After the death of Heinrich I in 936, his successor Otto I the Great (936–973) continued the policy of expansion and the steady annexation of Wendish territory into his dominions. In the year of his accession and coronation, Otto responded to a revolt by the Redarii by sending an army led by Herrmann Billung, who managed to reimpose imperial control. Billung was rewarded with honours and appointed margrave on the lower Elbe with responsibility for defence against the Redarii, Obodriti, Wagri, and Danes. To further his expansionist policy Otto I revived the system of Marches (Herrmann 1985: 338).

In 937, Gero, who had hitherto held a small county on the Bode south of Magdeburg, was appointed margrave of the middle Elbe and Saale and charged with the responsibility for dealing with the Wends (Herrmann 1985: 338). Otto ran into conflict with the Saxon nobility. He took no account of their concerns, but pursued single-mindedly his aim of keeping them under control and of strengthening the kingship. He ignored demands regarding the recently instituted margraviates made by Wichmann I, brother of Herrmann Billung. Growing dissatisfaction with Otto resulted in a conspiracy against him, in which Wichmann I participated before going over to the Wilti and the Wolini.

Gero, who was now carrying out Otto's command to subdue the Wends between the Elbe and the Oder, has acquired a special infamy in Wendish history for his duplicity in inviting a large number of the Wendish chieftains (*principes*) to a gathering and 'after they were drunk with wine following a luxurious banquet', having about thirty of them murdered during the night. According to Widukind (1971: 106–7), this was a pre-emptive action, taken to forestall a planned assassination. Whatever its motivation, Gero's trick resulted in a new offensive by the Wends, including the Obodriti.

Meanwhile, the king of the Hevelli, Tugumir, who had been captured by Heinrich I in 928/929 (see p. 14), had by now been a prisoner for nearly ten years. In 939 he was allowed to return to his people, but, seduced by rewards and promises, he had agreed to pretend that he had escaped. The Hevelli accepted him as their ruler and he made use of his newly regained power to have his rival (his nephew) murdered. He then surrendered the stronghold of the Hevelli at Brandenburg, together with all its territory, to Otto (Widukind 1971: 108–9; Herrmann 1985: 339). The suppression of the Wendish offensive of 939 and the capture of Brandenburg tipped the balance irrevocably in favour of the invaders. Before long most of the Slav tribes as far as the Oder had submitted to Otto as overlord. Only the Obodriti, a contingent of the Wilti, and the tribes centred on the Spree (Lusici and Milzeni) remained independent (Herrmann 1985: 339).

The church

In Otto I's time the first churches were built in the Wendish lands. Bishoprics were founded in Havelberg and Brandenburg in 948, subordinate to the Archbishop of Mainz. This was the beginning of a new chapter in the history of the German eastward expansion. The two missionary bishoprics together covered an area corresponding roughly to Gero's margraviate and so purported to include the lands of the Wends on the Havel and the Spree, in addition to territory of the Wilti. In the 950s Margraves Gero and Billung undertook campaigns to break the last remnants of Slav opposition and to effect the authority of both church and state. They encountered opposition, however, not only from the Wends but also from dissident Saxon nobles, who were hoping to establish a privileged position for themselves in the lawless marches and would therefore sometimes fight in alliance with the Wends (Herrmann 1985: 340). In his 954 campaign against the Uckri, Gero was supported by Duke Konrad of Lorraine (Widukind 1971: 150–1), Otto's son-in-law, who in 953–954 had participated in an unsuccessful revolt against the king and been deprived of his duchy. He was now trying to rehabilitate himself by proving his worth in the east.

Gero's campaign against the Uckri ran into difficulty, when it was discovered that resistance was also coming from the Obodriti, who were theoretically subjects of Margrave Herrmann Billung. It turned out that they were being incited to revolt by Saxon Counts Wichmann II and Eckbert, who eventually defected to the Obodriti altogether and encouraged the Obodriti princes Nakon and his brother Stoignew to make incursions into Saxony. At the beginning of 955 Margrave Billung launched an all-out attack on the Obodriti, but failed to achieve a decisive result (Widukind 1971: 158–9, 164–5). Led by Wichmann II, the Obodriti appeared again in Saxony just before Easter 955. Billung's forces were too weak to repulse them and a Saxon fortress referred to as 'urbs Cocarescemiorium' (unidentified) was surrendered and the garrison slain (Widukind 1971: 158–61). Women and children were taken prisoner. When Count Thiedrich, acting on behalf of Margrave Gero, advanced into Wendish territory and destroyed a castle, he found himself on swampy ground, where he 'had neither room to fight nor opportunity to flee' (Widukind 1971: 154–5). Fifty of his elite, armoured cavalrymen were killed. In 929 under Heinrich I the deployment of the same number of armed cavalrymen had decided the Battle of Lenzen.

The Obodriti were encouraged by their success to extend their operations into a full-scale campaign, in which they were joined by the Wilti. Margrave Billung began to wonder whether he could hold out and called on the king for help (Widukind 1971: 160–3; Thietmar 1992: 46–7). Otto, who had just achieved his great victory over the Hungarians in the Battle of the Lechfeld, immediately marched against the Obodriti and Wilti, and on 16 October 955, before daybreak, the Battle on the Raxa (Recknitz) began. Prince Stoignew was killed. Widukind is unrestrained in his gruesome narrative:

> The same day the camps of the enemy were attacked, and many people slain or captured, and the slaughter lasted until deep into the night. The next morning Stoignew's head was set up in the open field. All around about 700 prisoners were beheaded. Stoignews's counsellor had his eyes gouged out, his tongue torn out, and then they left him lying helpless among the corpses.

> (Widukind 1971: 164)

Nakon, who was residing in the fortress of Mecklenburg, south of Wismar, surrendered on hearing of his brother's death. Wichmann II and Eckbert, who had expected to use the Wendish offensive to strengthen their own positions vis-à-vis the king and the margraves, but had stayed away from the scene of the hostilities, fled to France to pursue their plans there. Otto had inflicted a shattering defeat, but the will of the Wilti to resist was not broken. Until 960 Otto I continued to launch offensives against the Wends in Gero's march. Wichmann II had by now returned from France and for a time continued to resist, but in the end he had no choice but to submit and swear allegiance to Otto.

Around 963 the Redarii, led by Wichmann II, marched against Mieszko I of Poland and defeated him (Widukind 1971: 170–1). Mieszko must have now been hard pressed, for at about the same time he was under attack from Gero (Thietmar 1992: 66–7). It was in 963 too that Gero invaded the land of the Lusizi. Heinrich I had been active here before him in 932, but had been unable to establish superiority. Now, according to Widukind (1971: 170–1), the Lusizi were forced into total servitude (*in ultimam servitutem*), but only after desperate fighting in which Gero himself was wounded and many of his men were killed, including his nephew. Gero's march had grown and after his death (in 965) Otto I decided to break it up. To the north Herrmann Billung remained responsible for keeping the Obodriti, Wagri, and Lutizi in check, but to the south six new, smaller units came into being under the control of commanders who had already proved their worth in Trans-Elbian campaigns. The area between the Elbe and the Peene in the north and the land of the Lusizi in the south was given to Margrave Dietrich von Haldensleben. South of him was Margrave Hodo, who held the Saxon Ostmark, subsequently to become the nucleus of the Wettin lands (Herrmann 1985: 342).

Along the lower Saale and the middle Elbe Thietmar, a nephew of Gero and son-in-law of Herrmann Billung, ruled over the Serimunt, Neletici, and Siusli. Also lying almost exclusively in Wendish land were the new marches of Merseburg, Zeitz, and Meissen. To the end of Otto I's life this distribution remained unchanged, but later these six districts were re-arranged as three marches: the Nordmark, the Ostmark, and Mark Meissen. Nakon, Prince of the Obodriti, died in 965/7. He was succeeded in 967 by Mistav, who immediately went to war against the Wagri, because Selibur (Želibor), their leader, had rejected his overlordship (Herrmann 1985: 343). Herrmann Billung gave judgement in the dispute between Mistav and Selibur, ordering the latter to pay a fine of fifteen pounds of silver. Selibur rejected the judgement and, in alliance with Wichmann II, attacked Herrmann Billung. However, Billung and his ally Mistav proved too strong for Selibur, who, once his castle had been taken, was forced to allow his rule over the Wagri to pass to his son, whom Mistav was prepared to acknowledge (Widukind 1971: 170–1; Herrmann 1985: 343; Thietmar 1992: 48–9).

Wichmann II was now forced to flee and went to the land of the Wolini on the Baltic, whose capital Wolin in the Oder Estuary was an important trading port. Before long, in alliance with the Wolini, he was marching against Mieszko I of Poland, who was aspiring to capture the Oder Estuary. Mieszko sought the assistance of his son-in-law, Boleslaw of Bohemia, and in alliance with him managed to defeat the Wolini. In the course of this campaign in 967 Wichmann II was killed. On 18 January 968 Otto I, who at the time was in Italy, wrote a letter to Herrmann Billung, Margrave Dietrich, and all the Saxon nobility, alluding to the recent defeat of the Redarii and ordering their annihilation, 'for you know how often they have broken faith and what injuries they have inflicted'. Despite Otto's clear command, however, at a meeting at Werle, where the letter was read out, a decision was taken to give priority instead to a planned attack on the Danes and to maintain peace with the Redarii, because the Germans knew they were not strong enough to fight two wars at the same time (Widukind 1971: 174–5; Herrmann 1985: 343).

The Archbishopric of Magdeburg (962/968)

The title of emperor, first bestowed on Charlemagne in 800, was subsequently held for a time by rulers of the West Frankish Empire, but then fell out of use. It had been vacant for thirty-eight years when Otto I revived it. He was crowned emperor in Rome on 2 February 962, and while there he sought and obtained from Pope John XII authority to arrange church administration in newly conquered territory. On 12 February Pope John XII approved the establishment of a new bishopric, that of Magdeburg, which was to cover all the Slavs already subjugated or yet to be subjugated. Five years later, at a synod in Ravenna which gave its approval to a report from Otto I on his missionary activity among the Slavs, Pope John XIII raised Magdeburg to the status of an archbishopric, made the bishops of Brandenburg and Havelberg subordinate to it, and permitted the institution in Merseburg, Zeitz, and Meissen of further bishoprics for the Slavs. The foundation of the Archbishopric of Magdeburg was finally completed in early 968. It was given seniority over all other churches to the right of the Rhine (Herrmann 1985: 344).

However, whereas in 962 Pope John XII had provided for the incorporation into the Ecclesiastical Province of Magdeburg of all Slavs already subjugated or yet to be subjugated, John XIII in 968 gave the Province a fixed border in the east, contiguous with the western border of the new Diocese of Poznań, which he had also founded in 968 as a consequence of the conversion two years earlier of Prince Mieszko. If Otto had plans to go further in the east (which can scarcely be doubted), they were now halted by the episcopal frontier set before him. By marrying Dobrava, daughter of Boleslav I, king of the Czechs, and accepting Christianity in 966, Mieszko had subtly ensured that his realm would be assigned to a newly established Diocese of Poznań, outside the Holy Roman Empire. This distinction between Mieszko's subjects and the Slavs to their west ensured the eventual acquisition of statehood by the part of Europe later known as Poland. No ethnic terms relating to Poland or the Poles are recorded in Mieszko's time. To further his missionary activity in the east and, in particular, to bring the Wagri (inhabitants of east Holstein) and the Obodriti into the Christian fold, Otto I set up the Diocese of Oldenburg, subordinate to the Archdiocese of Hamburg-Bremen. The date of its foundation is not recorded. It may have been as early as 948, but the first Bishop of Oldenburg, Egward, was consecrated in 968, according to Adam of Bremen (II/26) (Herrmann 1985: 344).

Otto II (973–983): The Lutizi federation

Otto I the Great died in 973 and was succeeded by Otto II. During Otto I's lifetime the political centre of Germany had moved from Aachen (where he had been crowned king) to Magdeburg, which was described by Bruno of Querfort in the eleventh century as 'a new metropolis of the Germans' (*MPH*, 1: 191). When Otto I died, all was quiet on the empire's eastern borders and here there now followed ten years of peace, for

Otto II was more concerned with his campaigns in Italy. The peaceful interlude all but coincided with his ten-year reign, but it was a few months before his death (in Rome on 7 December 983) that a new conflict broke out following the formation of an unprecedented system of alliances among the Wendish tribes. A federation was formed, consisting primarily of the Kessini, Zirzipani, Tollensi, and Redarii, which were all component tribes of the Wilti. From this time on the chroniclers west of the Elbe usually refer to them collectively as Lutizi. Otto's diversion of resources to Italy had provided the Wends with the opportunity for a new offensive against the invaders (Herrmann 1985: 344; Thietmar 1992: 112–13; Scheuch 2001: 22).

The Slav offensive seems to have been triggered by some hostile act by Duke Thiedrich, margrave of the Nordmark, the home of the Redarii, Hevelli, and Wilti. 'The peoples who, having accepted Christianity, were liable to pay tribute to the kings and emperors, provoked by the arrogance of Duke Thiedrich, took up arms in unanimous temerity' (Thietmar 1992: 104). On 29 June 983, the Lutizi appeared outside Havelberg, defeated the garrison, and destroyed the Bishop's palace. Three days later they took Brandenburg. Folkmar, the third bishop of Brandenburg, had already fled. Margrave Thiedrich's defence was useless and he was lucky to escape with his life. The priests were taken captive and the body of the second bishop Dodilo, who had been strangled by his own followers three years earlier, was exhumed. His vestments and all the church's treasures were plundered. Heathen rites were performed 'and this lamentable change was praised not only by heathens but by Christians too' (Thietmar 1992: 104–5).

In the westward advance into the Altmark (west of the Elbe) the Obodriti were also involved. They attacked the St Laurence Monastery at Kalbe on the Milde and 'they chased our men like fleeing deer, because our sins made us afraid and gave them a strong mind' (Thietmar 1992: 104). The Obodriti did not pause until they reached the Tanger, a little tributary of the Elbe, north of Magdeburg; but here they were met by an army led by Bishop Giseler, Bishop Hildeward of Halberstadt, Margrave Thiedrich, and others, who defeated and dispersed them. Brandenburg, however, remained in the hands of the Lutizi and was successfully defended by them. It was not until September 991 that a German army regained it. The Obodriti also made persistent attacks on Oldenburg and Bishop Folcvard was forced to abandon his castle (Herrmann 1985: 348).

Otto III reigned from 983 to 1002. Between 990 and 995 the Obodriti under Mstivoj made several incursions into Nordalbingia and Denmark. They managed to destroy Hamburg, the seat of the archbishop. The Quedlinburg Annals in the year 995 record that Otto III 'was totally incapable of subduing' the Slavs (Herrmann 1985: 348). As the millennium and Otto's reign neared their ends, German aspirations beyond the Elbe seemed increasingly quixotic. The Lutizi, Obodriti, Hevelli, and other Wends continued to maintain their heathen independence, while bishops continued to be consecrated for the imaginary sees of Brandenburg, Havelberg, and Oldenburg. In the Nordmark margraves continued to hold office without being able to exercise real political power (Herrmann 1985: 349).

Eleventh century: Thietmar of Merseburg (975–1018)

Thietmar of Merseburg was born in 975, consecrated Bishop of Merseburg in 1009, and died in 1018. In 1012 he began writing his chronicle, which begins in the early tenth century (the reign of Heinrich I) and covers the course of German eastward expansion and the Christianization of the Wends up to the time of his death. The first Bishop of Merseburg was Boso (died 970) and Thietmar recounts a story, which was probably handed down to him by people who had known Boso personally, concerning Boso's use of the Wends' language in his missionary work. Thietmar, it should be noted, refers to members of his flock as *Sclavi*, never *Sorabi*, although *Sorabi* is the form used in other sources to refer to the Wends of the Merseburg diocese in the tenth and eleventh centuries.

To Thietmar we are indebted for the first recorded Wendish sentence, which appears in the following anecdote:

> So that he might more easily instruct those entrusted to him, he wrote down Slavonic words and invited them to sing *Kyrie eleison*, explaining to them the benefit of this. They changed this mockingly into a wicked *vkrivolsa*, which in our language means 'the alder is standing in the thicket', saying 'that is what Boso said', whereas he must have said something else.

(Thietmar 1992: 74)

This is the earliest record we have of anyone committing a string of Sorbian words to writing, but it does not exactly prove that Boso had any real command of the language. Slightly more persuasive as evidence that Boso knew Wendish is Thietmar's observation that he had found the emperor's favour because 'by assiduously preaching and baptising in the east he had claimed innumerable people for Christ' (Thietmar 1992: 74). Thietmar too knew at least a little Wendish, as we may deduce from comments here and there in his chronicle, especially his explanations of the meanings of Wendish names, but it is impossible to say whether he knew it well.

From the facsimile edition of Thietmar's manuscript it is easy to see that *vkrivolsa* has been altered (*Chronik* 1905: fol. 31Bb) and Holtzmann, who saw the autograph, tells us it has been changed from an earlier *kriolosso* (Thietmar 1992: 74n.). Whatever the composition of the original record, however, it is actually easier to reconstruct an early Slav sentence meaning 'the alder stands in the thicket' from the phonetic components of the phrase *Kyrie eleison* than with either *vkrivolsa* or *kriolossa*. *Kyrie* must have sounded exactly like **kъri je* 'in the thicket is' (locative of *kъrъ*) and *eleison* may well have suggested **el'ša* 'an alder', though the match is not perfect (Stone 1986: 339–41). The mention of the alder in a charm would have fitted the world view of a tenth-century Wend, for a belief in its magical properties survived until the nineteenth century (Veckenstedt 1880: 441; Schneeweis 1953: 128) and its medicinal potential (as a source of aspirin) is no mere superstition. In Thietmar's estimation, however, the sacred formula had been desecrated by association with nature worship.

Thietmar does not say whether he was able to preach to the Wends in their own tongue, but later in the eleventh century the sermon was a significant part of religious observance in the conquered territories. In the cathedrals in Magdeburg, Merseburg, and Meißen, where there already was a German-speaking population, preaching was probably carried out in German, but everywhere else the Slav vernacular must have been used. Bishop Eiko of Meissen (992–1015), who proudly stated that he often preached out in the country, must have used Wendish (Schlesinger 1962, 1: 224). Werner (1059–1093), Bishop of Merseburg, though he knew no Wendish, is said to have caused sermons and books to be written in it, which he then read aloud to the people himself or had them read aloud by the clergy. Whether anyone could understand him is not reported, but the chances of the clergy being understood were no doubt better. Those who were not Wends must have been compelled to learn the vernacular, if they worked in rural parishes. But how they did it and with what success is not known (Schlesinger 1962, 1: 127).

Heinrich II (1002–1024)

Otto III had aimed, broadly speaking, to maintain alliances with the Poles against the Lutizi and this had been generally to the Polish advantage. Under Mieszko I (died 992) and his son and successor Bolesław Chrobry (r. 992–1025) the Poles had become powerful. Emboldened by the existence of the independent archdiocese of Gniezno, Bolesław now refused to pay homage to Heinrich II and supported various German dukes and margraves who disputed his claim to the German crown. The balance of power was changing. Faced with this new powerful neighbour beyond the Oder, Heinrich sought to make an alliance with the Lutizi, who had been the victims of Polish expansionist policy. On 28 March 1003, in Quedlinburg he received ambassadors of the Lutizi and Redarii. As Thietmar reports with disapproval: 'He also received mercifully ambassadors from the Redarii and those that are called Liutici, calmed the hitherto rebellious men with flattering gifts and pleasant promises, and made bosom friends out of enemies' (Thietmar 1992: 226). And so it came about that the Christian emperor, in alliance with the heathen Lutizi, fought Christian Poland. This did not escape theological censure in the works of, for example, Bruno of Querfurt (Herrmann 1985: 356).

Heinrich was disquieted by the concentration of power resulting from the Polish annexation of Bohemia. He therefore in 1004 marched against Bolesław and managed to drive him out of Bohemia, reinstating Duke Jaromir. Bolesław was compelled to concede not only Bohemia but also the lands of the Luzici and Milzeni. Success notwithstanding, Heinrich felt that his victory had been less than decisive and in 1005 embarked on a new campaign against the Poles. Thietmar is the main source for these events, but his testimony is problematic, because as a bishop he so clearly disapproved of Heinrich's alliance with the pagan Lutizi. 'These warriors, once slaves and now for our sins free men, came in such an assembly to the king's aid. Shun their company and their cult, dear reader! Hear and follow rather the commands of Holy Scripture!' (Thietmar 1992: 270). It is unlikely that the Lutizi really wanted Heinrich to achieve outright victory over Bolesław. From their point of view, a balance of power between Germans and Poles was preferable (Herrmann 1985: 357). At the request of Heinrich's generals the advance of his army came to a standstill outside Poznań and peace was made with the Poles. Its terms are not known, but according to Thietmar, 'Our men went homewards full of joy' (Thietmar 1992: 272). This is strangely at variance with the Quedlinburg Annals, which record: 'The King however returned home with a badly mauled army in sorrow, because he had not achieved a good peace' (Herrmann 1985: 358).

Bolesław soon set about restoring his position. At Easter 1007 ambassadors of the Lutizi and of Duke Jaromir of Bohemia appeared before Heinrich at Ratisbon and informed him that Bolesław had attempted with words and money to induce them to undertake actions hostile to the empire. They made the future support of the Lutizi and the Czechs conditional on an immediate war against the Poles, but subsequent events make it clear that the reaction of the Saxon leaders to this prospect was unenthusiastic. 'Our men knew everything that was going on, but appeared on the scene hesitantly and took up the pursuit all too slowly,' wrote Thietmar (1992: 278). Archbishop Tagino of Magdeburg, in particular, dragged his feet in reacting to Bolesław's hostile actions (Herrmann 1985: 359). Tagino 'did not make adequate preparation, although he was fully informed', says Thietmar, who was with Tagino at the time, and continues: 'I found myself with him. When we reached Jüterbog, the prudent ones therefore thought pursuit of the enemy with so few troops was not advisable; so we turned back' (Thietmar 1992: 278).

The Lutizi evidently did not take part in this campaign. They are not mentioned again in the sources until 1013, when by the Treaty of Merseburg Bolesław was enfeoffed with the lands of the Luzici (later Lower Lusatia) and of the Milzeni (later Upper Lusatia). Peace with Heinrich relieved him of danger on his western flank, so he turned his sights eastward and attacked Kievan Rus'. Heinrich meanwhile was free to embark on an Italian campaign. After the Treaty of Merseburg, Bolesław aimed for a Polish–Bohemian alliance and sent his son Mieszko to negotiate with Udalrich, Duke of Bohemia. Udalrich, however, wary of incurring Heinrich's displeasure, took Mieszko prisoner and handed him over to Heinrich, who was thus provided with a surety in future dealings. In 1014 Heinrich was crowned emperor. He was eager to find a solution to his Polish question, but there were always voices at court, mainly among the Saxon lords, opposing hostilities with the Poles. Bolesław himself encouraged this with bribery (Herrmann 1985: 359–60).

The same voices urged Heinrich to return Mieszko to his father and eventually Heinrich acquiesced, hoping that with this sign of goodwill he might be able to dissuade Bolesław from further military action and possibly even induce him to acknowledge his status as a vassal. With such hopes in mind Heinrich summoned Bolesław to appear before him, but the Polish leader rejected the summons. He also refused a request to surrender the lands of the Lusici and the Milzeni and threatened to take even more. And so in summer 1015 hostilities broke out again. This time the Lutizi did participate in alliance with Heinrich. Three divisions were directed by Heinrich to proceed east from different starting points and to aim to converge at a point beyond the Oder. At a location near Krossen the division led by the emperor himself succeeded in crossing the Oder and defeating an army led by Bolesław's son Mieszko, but neither the northern division, which was commanded by Herrmann Billung and contained a 'contingent of heathen Lutizi', nor the southern division, consisting of Bohemians and Bavarians, was able to reach Heinrich's forces, who were soon forced by the Poles to withdraw, suffering heavy losses (Herrmann 1985: 360).

In 1017 Heinrich embarked on his last great campaign against the Poles. The traditional assembly point for forces massing to march against the Poles was Leitzkau, near Magdeburg, and it was here in July 1017 that the German army gathered, shortly to be joined by the Bohemians and the Lutizi. The combined force marched into Silesia and besieged the castle at Nimptsch, but failed to take it despite repeated assaults including the use of siege engines. Relations between the allies were always erratic. One of Herrmann Billung's attendants threw a stone at a banner carried by the Lutizi, portraying one of their heathen goddesses, and damaged it. 'The Lutizi returned home in anger and complained at the insult done to their goddess' (Thietmar 1992: 424). The emperor's lack of success in his war against Bolesław only increased the degree of discontent among the Lutizi and they were further discouraged when, crossing the River Mulde in spate at Wurzen, they lost not only the idol of their goddess but also an elite unit of fifty men. 'Under such evil omens the remainder went home and, incited by wicked men, urged others to quit the Emperor's service,' wrote Thietmar (1992: 424).

From Heinrich's point of view, the campaign of 1017 was a failure. The Treaty of Budissin in 1018 was no better for him than the Treaty of Merseburg had been five years earlier. Bolesław had cause to be content. He kept the lands that later would be Lusatia (then populated by the Lusici and Milzeni) and the emperor was even constrained to aid Bolesław with 300 cavalrymen in his campaign against Yaroslav of Kiev. Peace between the Germans and the Poles released the Lutizi for other escapades, including attacks on their Wendish neighbours, the Obodriti (Herrmann 1985: 361).

For the period immediately after the Treaty of Budissin the sources on the Lutizi and the Obodriti are scanty. Thietmar's chronicle breaks off with his death in 1018. The same year there was some hostile action from the Obodriti, of which there is an account in an Anglo-Saxon source on a campaign in 1019 by Canute the Great against the Wends (*Wandali*). This unlikely location for a report on a purely Continental conflict is explained by Canute's success in uniting England and Scotland with Denmark and Norway at a time when Denmark held sway over the Obodriti and Wagri (Herrmann 1985: 362).

Around 1021 Heinrich held court in his fortress at Werben on the Elbe, in the Altmark, in order to ascertain the mind of the Slavs. He learned from their princes that they were now ready to live in submission and peace. The Obodriti, Polabi, Wagri, Kessini, and all other Slavs in the Oldenburg diocese agreed to pay tribute; but they were only bluffing. 'But their promise was full of hypocrisy and falseness. As soon as the Emperor adjourned

the Court and turned his mind to other things, they cared no more for their promises'
(Helmold 1963: 94). For many years to come, the Obodriti would repulse all attempts to
rule them.

Wars of Konrad II (r. 1024–1039) against the Lutizi

Heinrich II died in 1024 at the age of 52. He was the last of the Saxon kings, the dynasty
(also known as Ottonen or Liudolfinger) which had begun to rule more than a century
earlier with Heinrich I. There ensued a brief period of uncertainty, because Heinrich II
had no son, but the grandees of the empire before the end of the year elected Konrad II
from the Frankish line of the Salier, a new dynasty. Meanwhile, during the brief hiatus of
power, Bolesław Chrobry, early in 1025, used the opportunity to have himself crowned
king of Poland. Later that year he died and was succeeded by his son Mieszko II, who like
his father refused to pay homage to the German king (Herrmann 1985: 363).

The Lutizi soon found themselves threatened by the Poles and consequently sought
support from Konrad II, who decided, for the time being, at least, to continue the
alliance with them established by his predecessor. In 1028 Mieszko carried out an attack
on the Germans and advanced as far as the Saale, inflicting substantial destruction,
which also affected the Lutizi, especially the Hevelli. The Lutizi therefore, according to
the Hildesheim Annals for 1028 and 1029, appeared before Konrad in Pöhlde in the
Harz and asked for help against the 'tyrant Mieszko', promising in return to render 'true
service' (Herrmann 1985: 363). His reply is not recorded, nor is it known whether the
Lutizi participated in Konrad's wars against the Poles that followed from 1029 to 1032,
but their outcome – the defeat of Mieszko – was undoubtedly of significance to them, for
Mieszko was consequently obliged to cede the lands of the Lusici and Milzeni which his
father had acquired. They became the Saxon Ostmark, with which Count Dietrich von
Wettin was now enfeoffed (Herrmann 1985: 364).

Furthermore, at the Treaty of Merseburg in 1033, Mieszko was forced to renounce
the title of king and submit to the emperor. The ensuing suspension in German–Polish
hostilities brought German–Lutizi friendship to an end and introduced over twenty
years of warfare between the former allies. The focus of military activity moved to the
vicinity of the stronghold at Werben on the Elbe, where in 1033 a Saxon army was
defeated by the Lutizi and over forty knights perished. Konrad, preoccupied with the
question of the Burgundian succession (Burgundy was incorporated into the empire
that year), did not counter-attack, but merely reinforced the Werben fortifications. This
did not hinder the Lutizi in attacking Werben again in 1035, overrunning the fortress
'as a result of treachery', and killing the greater part of the garrison. Konrad responded
by launching a comprehensive campaign into the lands beyond the Elbe, supported
by Břetislav, Duke of Bohemia. The outcome, though there were heavy losses on both
sides, was indecisive. Only a further offensive, waged primarily by the Saxon nobles,
ended in the subjugation of the Lutizi, who were then made to pay tribute and hand over
hostages. In internal matters, however, they still remained independent. There was as yet

no question of re-establishing the episcopates of Brandenburg and Havelberg, which had both been destroyed in 983 (Herrmann 1985: 364–5).

The empire of the Obodriti: Decline of the Lutizi federation

Udo, Christian Prince of the Obodriti, was murdered by a Saxon in about 1028. His son, known to history only by the Germanized name Gottschalk (Latin *Godescalcus, Gadescalcus, Godeschalcus,* and *Goscalcus*) though he must have had a Wendish name too, was then attending a school at Lüneburg. When he heard of his father's death, he abandoned his studies, rejected Christianity, and returned to his people. He raised a band of armed followers and carried out reprisals for his father's death against the Saxons and other Christians in Holstein and Stormarn. Following a chance meeting with a Christian Saxon, however, he repented of his cruelty, and later he joined the court of Canute the Great, who then ruled over an empire consisting of Denmark, England, Norway, and Scotland. He participated in Canute's military campaigns in Normandy and England, gaining a reputation for bravery. He married Sigrid, the daughter of Sven Estridsen, Canute's nephew (Helmold 1963: 96–8).

Following the death of Canute in 1035 and the collapse of his empire, Gottschalk, with the support of Sven, king of Denmark, managed to master the Obodriti and regain his father's throne. He also subdued some of the Lutizi, exacted tribute from them, and united them with the Obodriti (Herrmann 1985: 365). Heinrich III died in 1056 and was succeeded by his son, also Heinrich (b. 1050), who was still a child. Affairs of state were managed by his mother Agnes as regent, until, at the age of fourteen, he began to reign as Heinrich IV (Scheuch 2001: 27).

Because alliances between Christian and pagan armies were routinely contracted, the Christian mission was often superseded by purely mercenary considerations. In 1057 war broke out between one coalition of the Redari and Tollensi and another of the Zirzipani and Kessini. The Redari and Tollensi secured the support of Ordulf, Duke of Saxony, Sven Estridsen, king of Denmark, and Gottschalk, Prince of the Obodriti. The power of this united front soon overwhelmed the Zirzipani and Kessini, who, having suffered heavy losses, managed to purchase peace at a price of 15,000 marks. 'The princes divided the money between them', writes Helmold, and continues:

> There was no mention of Christianity, nor did they give honour to God who had brought them victory in the war. In this the insatiable avarice of the Saxons can be recognized, who, though they are superior in the art of war to the other peoples contiguous to the barbarians, are always more eager to exact tribute than to win souls for the Lord. For respect for Christianity would have already long been greater among the Slavs, if the avarice of the Saxons had not hindered it.

(Helmold 1963: 102–4)

The work of Gottschalk, on the other hand, who some years earlier had re-introduced Christianity among the Obodriti, met with Helmold's approval: 'And the work of God prospered in his hands so much that an endless stream of heathens flowed to the grace of baptism. Also the churches once destroyed were rebuilt everywhere in the land of the Wagri, as well as of the Polabi, and Obodriti' (Helmold 1963: 100).

The Wendish rebellion of 1066

Victory over the Zirzipani and Kessini was followed by nine years of peace, but the conversion of the Obodriti was only superficial and Saxon avarice, as Helmold acknowledged, was a constant irritant. Gottschalk was an ardent Christian and would himself often speak in the churches, explaining in simple Slav words what the bishops and priests could only express in obscure terms. A new see in the land of the Obodriti, that of Mecklenburg, was founded. Bishop Johann of Mecklenburg was consecrated in about 1055–1057. He was said to have come from Scotland. At first his mission was successful and he converted the Obodriti in their thousands (Helmold 1963: 100–4). In 1066, however, an anti-Christian revolt broke out, beginning with the assassination of Gottschalk on 7 June that year. There were many more casualties, especially among the clergy. Bishop Johann was taken prisoner in Mecklenburg. The old man was then beaten with sticks and led through various Slav settlements as a laughing stock. His hands and feet were cut off and his body was thrown into the street. Then his head was cut off, fixed to a pole, and offered to the God Radigast. This happened on 10 November 1066. Gottschalk's wife Sigrid, daughter of the Danish king Sven Estridsen, was thrown out of the town of Mecklenburg, naked, together with other Christian women. Taking her young son Heinrich with her, she found refuge with Sven (Helmold 1963: 106–8).

The Wends now reverted to their heathen beliefs. Ordulf, Duke of the Saxons, who had succeeded his father Bernhard in 1056, was incapable of any kind of military success against them. Gottschalk should have been succeeded as Prince of the Obodriti by his elder son Budivoj (Butue), but he was rejected by his people because they feared he would follow in his father's footsteps, seek to avenge his death, and collaborate with the Saxons. The throne was seized by Kruto. Budivoj turned to the Saxons for support and with their help managed to regain the throne, but his Christian pedigree was against him and his position was always uncertain. Within a few years the Wends 'with an armed hand had shaken off the yoke of servitude and were striving with such obstinacy to defend their liberty that they would sooner die than resume the title of Christianity or pay tribute to the princes of the Saxons' (Helmold 1963: 110). Budivoj continued the struggle, but in 1074 or 1075 with a large band of supporters he was forced to surrender to Kruto outside the fortress of Plön. They were all put to death (Helmold 1963: 118).

Gottschalk's younger son Heinrich (Heinrich von Alt Lübeck) in 1090 attempted to return from his Danish exile, but Kruto denied him entry, so he changed tactics. With an army of Danes and Wends he attacked from the sea and captured Oldenburg. After a number of such raids Kruto, who was now an old man, decided to sue for peace and was forced to concede to Heinrich the right to return to his homeland. Kruto had a young wife named Slavina. She entered into a conspiracy with Heinrich, who invited Kruto to a banquet and there contrived to make him drunk. As he was unsteadily leaving the banqueting hall, a Dane struck him with a battleaxe, decapitating him in one stroke. Heinrich seized power, married Slavina, and took revenge on his enemies. His attempts, in alliance with Duke Magnus of Saxony, however, to reimpose a Christian regime and exact tribute were met with fierce resistance, especially from the Polabi and Obodriti. They decided to fight him and elected in his place a leader whose name is not recorded, 'who had at all times been opposed to the Christians' (Helmold 1963: 140–2).

In 1093 a great and decisive battle was fought between a large and well-armed formation of Wends and an army of Nordalbingians, the Saxon tribes living adjacent to the Wends (Bardi, Holzati, Sturmari, and Thetmarci), which had been assembled and was led by Magnus, Duke of Saxony. They met in the land of the Polabi at a place called Smilow (Schmilau), near Ratzeburg in East Holstein (Map 1.2). The armies came within sight of each other early in the morning, but Magnus, conscious that he was facing a formidable enemy, used delaying tactics. Battle was joined only in the early evening, shortly before sunset, by which time Saxon reinforcements were approaching and the Wends, dazzled by the glare of the setting sun, suffered a crushing defeat (Helmold 1963: 144).

Map 1.2 Sites of events covered in this chapter.

Following the Battle of Smilow, Prince Heinrich reigned over the Obodriti, Polabi, and Wagri, and by the end of the century he was also receiving tribute from the Rani, Kessini, Zirzipani, Lutizi, Brisani, Hevelli, and Pomerani. Some of these tribes are frequently subsumed under the name of the Obodriti. In all his military operations against other Wends, Heinrich was supported by the Saxon Dukes. By maintaining friendly relations with both Saxons and Danes, Heinrich managed to preserve the integrity of his domains and reigned over not only Wends but also some Saxons. He was referred to as 'king in all the land of the Slavs and the Nordalbingians' (Helmold 1963: 145, 150). He was now able to impose his will on all the Wends north of the Havel between the Elbe and the Oder, but he desisted from his Christian mission, so as not to provoke further hostility (Helmold 1963: 150; Herrmann 1985: 367, 379).

The Magdeburg appeal (1108)

At the southern edge of the lands ruled by Prince Heinrich, in the region of Havelberg and Brandenburg, lived the Hevelli (or Stodorani) and the Brisani. In about 1101 he received intelligence of an impending mutiny in these parts and, apprehensive lest this lead to a general revolt, set out with his Nordalbingian friends for Havelberg and laid siege to it. The town managed to hold out for several months. Meanwhile, Heinrich's son Mistue (Mstivoj) assembled a company of 200 Saxons and 300 Slavs and attacked an unconnected Wendish tribe living in the vicinity, named the Lini or Linoges. They were a peaceful people, not thought to be mutinous, but they were prosperous and seen as a source of booty. Laden with spoils, Mistue's unit then joined Heinrich's army and a few days later the Brisani and the other rebels sued for peace (Helmold 1963: 150–2).

The Emperor Heinrich IV died in 1106. He was succeeded by his son Heinrich V, under whom policy was broadened to include the colonization of Wendish land.

The German migration eastwards is said to have been spread mainly over the 150 years from the mid-twelfth century to the end of the thirteenth (Herrmann 1985: 407), but evidence of the new frame of mind comes as early as 1108 in a celebrated letter from Adelgot, Archbishop of Magdeburg, written in the name of various potentates of Merseburg, Naumburg, Meissen, Havelberg, and Brandenburg, and also of 'all the great and small of east Saxony' (universi orientalis Saxoniae maiores et minores). It was addressed to their counterparts in the West, led by the Archbishop of Cologne, including the bishops of Halberstadt and Minden, the Abbot of Corvey, the Duke of Lorraine, and Count Robert of Flanders. Its intended recipients extended all the way down the social ladder to 'all the faithful in Christ, bishops, abbots, monks, hermits, recluses, priests, canons, curates, princes, knights, servants, apprentices, and all the great and the small', urging them to participate not only in fighting the heathens but also in colonizing their land (Helbig and Weinrich 1968: 96–101).

The letter is an appeal from the frontiersmen of the east to their western kinsmen to come and defend the Christian communities on the outposts of Christendom against the heathen Wends. 'Long weighed down by manifold oppressions and calamities of the pagans, we sigh for your mercy to alleviate with us the ruin of your mother church' (Helbig and Weinrich 1968: 98). Designed to incite hatred of the pagans, the letter dwelt on the harrowing details of atrocities committed against Christians:

> Glorying in the malicious idolatry of their inhumanity, they have profaned the churches of Christ, they have destroyed altars, and they do not fear to perpetrate against us things which the human mind shudders to hear. They often betake themselves into our region and, sparing no one, rob, kill, destroy, and inflict excruciating tortures; some they behead and sacrifice the heads to their idols. Some they disembowel, cut off their hands, tie their feet together, and, insulting our Christ, say 'Where is their God?'

> (Helbig and Weinrich 1968: 98).

The originators of the call are said to have been the king of the Danes and other neighbouring princes, but '[o]ur King too, the author of this war, with all those he can summon, will be a most ready helper' (Helbig and Weinrich 1968: 100). This is a reference to King Heinrich V, who was crowned emperor only in 1111. Finally, the appeal raises the prospect of material rewards in the form of fertile land:

> The heathens are most wicked, but their land is very good in flesh, honey, flour,...and birds, and, when it is cultivated, abundant in all the products of the earth, so that none can be compared to it. Thus say those who know it. Therefore, o Saxons, Franks, men of Lorraine and Flanders, famous men and tamers of the world, here you can both save your souls and, if it please you, acquire the best of land to inhabit.

> (Helbig and Weinrich 1968: 102)

Duke Lothar von Supplinburg

When in 1123 the margrave of Meissen and Lusatia died, Emperor Heinrich V granted the fief to Wiprecht von Groitzsch (d. 1124), but simultaneously Lothar von Supplinburg, Duke of Saxony, nominated Albrecht the Bear as margrave in Mark Lausitz and Konrad von Wettin in Mark Meissen. By force of arms and with the support of Lothar, Konrad was able to hang on to his new possession despite the efforts of the emperor. The Wettins were to hold sway in these lands until 1918 (Herrmann 1985: 381; Scheuch 2001: 20–30, 202).

Towards the end of the reign of Emperor Heinrich V (probably in 1123 or 1124), King Heinrich of the Obodriti (Heinrich von Alt Lübeck) led a campaign against the Rani or Rugiani, the inhabitants of the Island of Rügen, who had killed his son Woldemar. He raised a great army of his own followers and also requested help from the Saxons, who sent 1,600 warriors. The attack took place during a hard winter, when it was possible to reach the island on foot across the frozen sea. The Saxons led the assault and burned the villages close to the shore, whereupon the Rani promptly opened peace negotiations. They agreed to pay 4,400 marks for peace, but they had no coinage, so it was agreed they might pay with gold and silver objects. When it came to the point, however, they could only raise about half the sum agreed. Consequently, the invasion was repeated the following year, but this time the invaders, after they had been on Rügen three days, discovered that the ice was melting. They were only just able to return to the mainland without suffering disaster. With the death of Heinrich von Alt Lübeck in 1127, attempts to punish the Rani were abandoned (Helmold 1963: 152–8).

Pribislaw-Heinrich (c. 1075–1150)

At the beginning of the twelfth century the land of the Hevelli and its fortress Brandenburg were absorbed by the Obodriti state under Heinrich of Alt Lübeck, who lived until 1127. Under him a *comes* named Meinfried had reigned over the Hevelli, but in the year of Heinrich's death Meinfried was overthrown and succeeded by Pribislaw, scion of a princely family of the Hevelli, who on baptism had taken the name Heinrich. Pribislaw-Heinrich's realm was remarkably well developed economically, as may be seen from the fact that he minted his own coinage (Herrmann 1985: plate between 262 and 263). He is referred to as *rex* 'king', which may mean that he had received this title from the emperor. At all events, he collaborated with neighbouring German princes and consequently faced opposition from the heathen priests and nobility among his own people. To the west of his domain lay the Altmark, ruled over by Albrecht the Bear, who was of the Ascanian dynasty. Pribislaw-Heinrich must have believed in total collaboration with the Germans, for he decided to make Albrecht the Bear his heir, thus ensuring that he was the last Slav ruler of Brandenburg and the Hevelli (Herrmann 1985: 266, 387).

Pribislaw-Heinrich's realm was unaffected by the Wendish Crusade of 1147, but after his death in 1150, Albrecht asserted his right of inheritance with the assistance of Pribislaw's widow Petrissa. Against heathen resistance he destroyed the shrine of the God Triglav on the Brandenburg Harlungerberg and expelled the Slav heathens from the castle. In 1153, however, it was taken over with Polish assent by Knes Jaxa von Köpenick, who, as Pribislaw-Heinrich's nephew, had a good claim to this important stronghold and already held lands in the Spree area around Köpenick, where he was a vassal of Poland. Finally on 11 June 1157, Albrecht the Bear, aided by the Archbishop of Magdeburg, who like him wished to rid the area between the Elbe and the Oder of Polish influence, conclusively conquered the Brandenburg fortress (Herrmann 1985: 266, 397).

From now on Albrecht called himself margrave of Brandenburg. But since Ottonian times Brandenburg had been considered a royal possession and half of it had been given to the bishopric founded in 948. After 1157 the Bishop of Brandenburg, who had been driven out of his diocese by the Wendish rebellion of 983, was able to re-assume his seat in Brandenburg and to introduce an ecclesiastical administration. Between 928 and 1157 this strategic centre of the Havel and Spree region had had thirteen owners. Now it was firmly in the hands of the Ascanians (Herrmann 1985: 397–8). German settlers were introduced. The Wendish population was enslaved (Scheuch 2001: 163).

Emperor Lothar III von Supplinburg (1125–1137)

Emperor Heinrich V died childless in 1125 and was succeeded by Lothar von Supplinburg, who in 1134 enfeoffed Albrecht the Bear with the Saxon Nordmark (or Neumark). The Ascanian dynasty thus gained great power in the Wendish lands. In 1136 Lothar enfeoffed the Wettin Konrad von Meissen with the lands of the Luzici, the Budissin land, and the Elbe basin around Dresden. The Wettins thus united the future Lusatia with Mark Meissen and became rivals of the Ascanians and the Bishops of Magdeburg in the scramble for possessions in the Wendish lands (Herrmann 1985: 381). It was of significance that Lothar, during his reign as king and emperor (1125–1137), also remained Duke of Saxony, and so, with the power of central authority, could pursue his Saxon expansionist policy. After the death of Prince Heinrich of the Obodriti on 22 March 1127, the succession was disputed between his sons Knud and Sventipolk, but their rivalry was merely academic, for before the end of 1128 they had both been murdered. Helmold hints that Lothar and the Danes were behind this sudden extinction of the dynasty. Despite the loyalty of the Obodriti, their dynasty no longer fitted in with Lothar's policy and in 1129 he enfeoffed his ally the Danish Prince Knud Laward with what he still called 'the Kingdom of the Obodriti' and crowned him (Helmold 1963: 188).

On January 1131, however, Knud Laward was murdered by a Danish kinsman. Power in the Obodriti lands was now divided between the two Wendish princes, Pribislaw, a nephew of Heinrich, and Niklot, scion of another noble line. Pribislaw ruled over the Wagri and Polabi. Niklot's rule took in the Mecklenburg territories as far as the Peene. In Pribislaw's title of 'regulus' and in his choice of Alt Lübeck as his main residence there is more than an echo of Heinrich's regal tradition (Herrmann 1985: 382). It is important to distinguish between this Pribislaw (a nephew of Heinrich) and a later Pribislaw, the son of Niklot. Nor should either of them be confused with Pribislaw (Pribislaw-Heinrich), the last ruler of the Hevelli.

The client status of the two Wendish princes (Pribislaw and Niklot) is demonstrated by the emperor's decision to build a castle in their territory. While staying at Bardowick in 1134, Lothar received a suggestion from the missionary priest Vizelin that there was a certain hill in the land of the Wagri which would be a suitable site for a fortification 'for the salvation of the Slavs' and for defence. The hill had once earlier been used as a fort by Knut, king of the Obodriti, but in 1130 the garrison there had been overcome and taken prisoner by a band of robbers at the instigation of Adolf I (the Elder), Duke of the Holsati (Helmold 1963: 198). In 1134 Lothar went to inspect the site. He commanded the Nordalbingian population to assemble and participate in the construction of the castle.

The two Wendish princes were also obliged to make an appearance and to provide help. With a sense of foreboding, they complied.

On completion, the structure was manned by a strong garrison and given the name Sigeberg (later Segeberg). At the foot of the hill the emperor founded a church and allotted some six villages to subsidize the divine office and support the needs of the clergy posted there to perform it. Vizelin was placed in charge first of the construction and then of the administration of the church. Similar arrangements were made for a church in Lübeck and Lothar charged Pribislaw with the duty, on pain of losing favour, to protect Vizelin and his deputies, an odd commission for a heathen.

In 1137 Emperor Lothar died and Pribislaw exploited the ensuing conflict between Margrave Albrecht the Bear and Lothar's son-in-law Heinrich the Proud to re-assert his independence. In late summer 1138 he seized and destroyed Segeberg and all the surrounding villages inhabited by Saxons. The Segeberg oratory and monastic buildings went up in flames. One monk, named Volker, was killed; the others fled to Neumünster. Father Ludolf, the priest in Lübeck, and others with him, lived in constant fear of their lives and witnessed atrocities inflicted on Christians daily, yet Pribislaw did not abandon his commitment to protect men of the cloth (Helmold 1963: 204–6).

Emperor Konrad III (r. 1138–1152)

The following winter there was a massive Saxon campaign of retaliation. Following the expulsion of Adolf II von Schauenburg (1130–1164), Graf Heinrich von Badwide had been given the county of Holstein-Stormaren, including the castle at Segeberg, by the new Duke of Saxony, Albrecht the Bear (Duke 1138–1142). An army of Holzati and Sturmari led by Graf Heinrich von Badwide wrought havoc throughout the land of the Wagri. They gave full rein to their desire for vengeance, leaving behind them a desolate and derelict landscape in the Wendish lands of Plön, Lütjenburg, and Oldenburg, and also in the area between Schwale, the Baltic, and the Trave (Herrmann 1985: 383). The castle at Plön, which had managed to withstand the onslaught, was taken a few months later (summer 1139) in a renewed campaign. The destruction and slaughter were taken to unusual extremes, because there was no commanding hand to restrain them. As Helmold notes in a revealing aside: 'For the princes are accustomed to protect the Wends, to augment their tribute' (Helmold 1963: 208).

The devastation was such that, when hostilities between Graf Adolf II von Schauenburg and Graf Heinrich von Badwide ended and Adolf began the reconstruction of the land of the Wagri, the country was deserted. He therefore sent messengers to Flanders, Holland, Utrecht, Westphalia, and Friesia with a general invitation to come and settle in the land taken from the Wends. He also invited the Holsati and Sturmari:

Was it not you who subjugated the land of the Slavs and paid for it with the deaths of your brothers and fathers? So why should you be the last to come into possession of it? Be the first to migrate into this pleasant land, inhabit it, and enjoy its delights, for you deserve the best of it, you who took it from the hand of the enemy.

(Helmold 1963: 210–12)

What remained of the Slav population was pushed back into the Oldenburg and Lütjenburg lands, the Wagri coast, and the island of Fehmarn. Between 1140 and 1143 the Wendish chiefs in most of Wagria were replaced by a new Christian nobility. The latter were followed by colonists brought in to clear new land for agriculture and increase the revenues of their landlords, who in turn were compelled to pay Adolf tribute and perform services. The break up of traditional Wendish political structures and colonization by a new peasantry from the west was a watershed, for until now the conquerors had only demanded tribute and military service from the conquered (Christiansen 1997: 52–3).

Pomerania

Emperor Lothar had also had plans for expansion into the territory of the Pomerani west of the Oder. At the beginning of the twelfth century, Duke Wartislaw of the Pomerani was extending his influence westwards into the Peene and Tollense region as far as Demmin and in the south along the Oder and Uecker, incorporating Lutizi land which later became part of Inner Pomerania (*Vorpommern*) and Mecklenburg. At the same time Bolesław Krzywousty (1102–1138), Prince of Poland, was also beginning to expand into the land of the Pomerani. During 1121–1122, Bolesław captured Stettin, overthrew Wartisław, imposed Polish overlordship, and compelled Wartisław to accept Christianity for himself and his people (Herrmann 1985: 384). Further campaigns against the Lutizi brought Bolesław as far west as Lake Müritz. Evidence for this is in Ebbo's biography of Bishop Otto of Bamberg, who in 1128 on his second mission to the Pomerani met a fisherman who for seven years had lived on an island in the lake, where he had fled after the conquest of this region by the Prince of Poland (Herrmann 1985: 385; *MPH*, 2: 54). A result of this Polish westward expansion was the foundation of the bishopric of Lebus on the Oder during 1123–1124.

Bolesław could not afford to delay the conversion of the Pomerani, because he had to forestall any claims that might be made to this region by the Archbishop of Magdeburg or the Bishop of Havelberg. He subordinated the Pomerani to the Archbishop of Gniezno. Bolesław also secured the services of a Spanish monk, who preached in Wollin during 1121–1122 but without success. More successful was the preaching there of Otto of Bamberg, who for a long time was chaplain to the Polish court. His conversion of Domiszlaus, a member of the aristocracy of the Pomerani, was crucial. In 1128 the leaders of the Lutizi in the Peene region on the island of Usedom also accepted Christianity. In 1140 a Polish bishopric was established at Wollin in the Oder Estuary; later it was moved to Kammin (Map 1.3). It came under neither Gniezno nor Magdeburg but directly under the Pope (Herrmann 1985: 385).

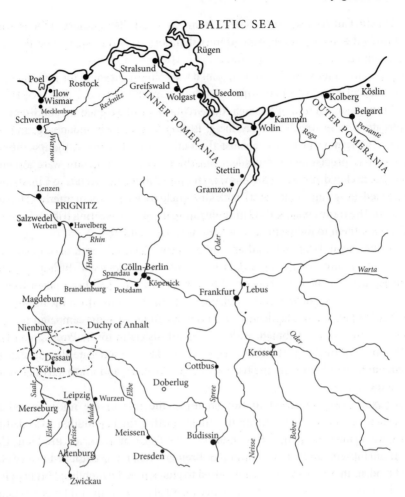

Map 1.3 Sites of events covered in Chapters 1 and 2.

The Wendish Crusade of 1147

In the course of his efforts to raise an expedition of knights to go to Jerusalem and conquer the heathens (to be known later as the Second Crusade) Bernard, Abbot of the Cistercian monastery at Clairvaux, travelled to Frankfurt on Main, where in December 1146 he met the emperor. In March 1147, he was present at the Imperial Diet in Frankfurt which made arrangements for the expedition. Here he discovered that the Saxons felt that fighting the Wendish heathens on their own eastern borders was preferable to fighting the Muslims in south-east Europe and the Middle East, so he put the matter to the Pope, Eugenius III. A month later the Bull *Divina dispensatione* was issued, sanctioning the conduct of a war on European pagans by European Christians, to be led by Bishop Anselm of Havelberg, as an alternative to fighting the Turks (Helmold

1963: 214–16; Christiansen 1997: 53). As Helmold noted: 'The authors of the expedition saw fit to send one part of the army to the orient, the second to Spain, and the third to the Slavs who dwell next to us' (Helmold 1963: 216).

The emperor, after some hesitation, joined the columns heading for Jerusalem, while the Saxon secular and spiritual princes, led by Heinrich the Lion, Adolf II of Holstein, Albrecht the Bear, Konrad of Meissen, the Archbishops of Magdeburg and Bremen, the Papal legate, Bishop Anselm of Havelberg, Bishop Wigger of Brandenburg, and Abbot Wibald of Corvey went to war against the Lutizi and Obodriti. Although the Saxon campaign was proclaimed a crusade, even the Christian Pomerani were among the quarry. The declared aim of the Saxons was either to subdue the Wends to Christianity or (as the Magdeburg Chronicle put it) 'with God's help to destroy them utterly' (Herrmann 1985: 388). The traditional method of subjugating them and exacting tribute from them, while leaving them to follow their own faith, was now outdated.

From the accounts of Helmold and other chroniclers, however, it is apparent that the motives of some of the crusaders were not those professed. Bishop Anselm of Havelberg saw a chance of recovering his bishopric, which had been taken from him by the Wendish rising of 983, and acquiring the Lutizi lands to which the bishopric laid claim. The Archbishop of Magdeburg, to whom the initiative in the campaign against the Christian Pomerani is attributed, wished to assert his claim to the Pomeranian Duchy and Bishopric. Albrecht the Bear's ambitions in the Havel region were already realized or assured, but he had his eye on the territory of the northern and north-east Lutizi in the Peene and Oder areas.

The Saxon army advanced in two columns: the one in the north sallied forth against their old allies, the Obodriti; the other, starting further south, proceeded from Magdeburg against the Lutizi. The Obodriti were faced by Heinrich the Lion, Count Adolf II of Holstein, and the Archbishop of Bremen. When news reached Prince Niklot of the Obodriti that an army was being raised to attack him, he mobilized his people and started building a great fortress at Dubin between Lake Schwerin and Döpe (Nebensee) as a shelter and refuge. He sent envoys to Count Adolf to remind him that there was a treaty between them and to request a meeting. This request was rejected on the grounds that such a meeting might offend the other princes.

Niklot's reply, sent by messenger, was as follows:

I had resolved to be your eyes and ears in the land of the Slavs that you had begun to inhabit, lest you suffer molestation from the Slavs who once owned the land of the Wagri and complain that they have been unjustly deprived of their patrimony. Why then do you deny your friend in time of need? Is it not need that tests friendship? Hitherto I have restrained the hand of the Slavs from harming you, but now I shall withdraw my hand and leave you to your own devices, since you reject your friend, ignore our treaty, and deny me a meeting in time of need.

(Helmold 1963: 222)

To this Adolf's envoys replied: 'Our lord is prevented from speaking to you by difficulties of which you are aware. Remain faithful, therefore, and keep your promise to our lord. If you should observe the Slavs secretly making preparations for war against him, warn him.' And Niklot promised that he would do so (Helmold 1963: 222). When he realized that invasion was imminent, however, he mobilized his fleet for war and set sail into the Bay of Lübeck and up the Trave. Keeping his promise to Adolf, he sent a messenger to Segeberg to warn him that war was imminent. He then attacked Lübeck and the suburbs of Segeberg, but spared the Holsati west of the Trave. The victims were mainly recent immigrants to Wagria from Westphalia, Holland, and elsewhere. Niklot's army, 3,000 strong, then headed north-east towards Süsel, where they set on a Friesian settlement of 400 men before returning to their ships and sailing away laden with prisoners and booty (Herrmann 1985: 389).

When the news reached the Crusaders that the Wends had started the war without waiting to be attacked, they immediately set out eastwards into the land of the Obodriti to punish them. The two Slav fortresses Dubin and Demmin were besieged. A Danish army appeared on the scene and joined the besiegers of Dubin close to Lake Schwerin. It was a long siege. One day unexpectedly a detachment of the besieged army came out of Dubin, attacked and killed many of the Danish besiegers, and escaped back into the fastness. At this point the commanders of the Crusading army, vassals of Duke Henry the Lion and Margrave Albrecht the Bear, paused for thought. Recalling that the land they were laying waste was already held in fealty to their lords, who received tribute from its agricultural surpluses, they began to say to each other: 'Is not the land we are devastating our land, and the people we are fighting our people? Why then are we behaving as our own enemies and squanderers of our own income? Do not these losses rebound on our lords?' (Helmold 1963: 228). Very soon peace negotiations were opened. The Slavs accepted the condition that they be baptized, but subsequently reverted to their traditional beliefs (Helmold 1963: 229).

The other Saxon Crusader column marched from Magdeburg against the Lutizi stronghold at Demmin and carried on from there until it reached Stettin, where Christianity had already been imposed by Bolesław Krzywousty during 1121–1122. They encircled the town and laid siege to it. The inhabitants hung crosses from the walls to demonstrate their Christian credentials and asked the besiegers 'why they had come to them with military forces. If it were to confirm them in their Christian belief, this could be achieved by bishops preaching rather than by force of arms' (Vincent of Prague, quoted in Herrmann 1985: 388). The Saxons, says Vincent, had brought such a great army to Christian Stettin 'more to take away their land than to strengthen the inhabitants in their Christian faith' (Herrmann 1985: 388).

After the crusade

The crusade was broken off in autumn 1147. There was uncertainty as to its value even then. Its objectives were poorly defined and resistance was strong. Bishop Anselm, however, was now able to take possession of his diocese and there followed a period of colonization. German government was established in the Prignitz and Rhin territories. The Magdeburg diocese continued its expansionist policy by establishing monasteries in Stolpe, Grobe, and Gramzow. The Bishop of Wollin/Kammin, however, continued to come directly under Rome. East of the lower Elbe the episcopates could be refounded: Mecklenburg and Oldenburg in 1149, Ratzeburg in 1154 (Herrmann 1985: 390).

Count Adolf II now aimed at reconstruction. He again made alliances with the Wendish nobility and exacted tribute. In 1151 the Kessini and Zirzipani revolted against Niklot and he was able to re-establish control only with the assistance of Adolf, who supplied him with over 2,000 Holsti and Stormari. Now squeezed into the north-east corner of Wagria, the Slavs were made to pay 1,000 marks to Heinrich the Lion and 100 marks to Adolf (Herrmann 1985: 390).

By 1154 there were not many Wends left in this area. Helmold describes their end:

> So God's work grew in the land of the Wagri and the count [Adolf] and the bishop [Gerold] helped each other. Around this time the count rebuilt the fortress of Plön and made there a town and a market. And the Wends who inhabited the surrounding villages receded, and Saxons came and lived there; gradually the Wends disappeared from the land.

> (Helmold 1963: 298)

Only in the name Wagrien would their erstwhile presence here be commemorated. Prince Pribislaw, whom Helmold continues to call *regulus* as late as 1156, and the Wagri chiefs were made beholden to Adolf by gifts. This assured the smooth implementation of Adolf's colonization policy. He insured himself against attack from the south by means of a treaty with Prince Niklot, who undertook to protect the settlers from the natives (Herrmann 1985: 383).

The independence of the Wagri was now severely limited, but they continued to maintain their pagan religion, and near Oldenburg at their most sacred site the God Prove was still worshipped (Herrmann 1985: 391). In the end, however, Pribislaw, Prince of the Wagri, accepted Christianity, and in 1156 he and Thessemar, a member of the Wendish nobility, were hosts to the Bishop of Oldenburg and his retinue on their missionary visit to the vestiges of Slavdom in East Holstein. Helmold was one of the Bishop's companions and he recalled:

> As we drew close to that grove and refuge of unholiness, the Bishop summoned us to proceed with violence to the destruction of the shrine. He sprang from his horse and demolished with his staff the finely decorated fronts of the gates. We pressed into the court, piled up all its fences around those sacred trees, threw fire into the pile of wood and made it into a bonfire, fearing all the time that we might be stoned by a mob of the inhabitants. But we were protected by heaven.

> (Helmold 1963: 288–90)

After listening to an edifying speech by the Bishop, Pribislaw, Prince of the Wagri, complained that his people were being treated with such severity that,

> because of taxation and the cruelest slavery, death seems better than life.... What is left to us but to abandon our land, to set sail, and to live among the waves? What guilt is it of ours if we, expelled from the land, make the sea unsafe, taking our subsistence from the Danes and the merchants who sail the sea? Will that not be the fault of the princes who drive us to such lengths?

> (Helmold 1963: 290)

The piracy of the Wends of Oldenburg and Lütjenburg, referred to here by Pribislaw, was directed mainly against the Danish coast and Danish shipping, while Heinrich the Lion and Adolf were away in 1159, busy fighting in Emperor Friedrich I's second Italian campaign.

In the late 1150s Heinrich the Lion began harrying Niklot, ruler of the Obodriti and the final blow was struck in 1160, when Niklot stood his ground with his sons Pribislaw and Wertislaw in his stronghold at Werle and here he met his death while on a sortie. In the settlement now imposed on the Wends only Werle itself and the lands belonging to it were left in the hands of Niklot's sons Pribislaw and Wertislaw (Helmold 1963: 310). Elsewhere new settlers and the church administration moved in. 'The tithes in the land of the Slavs grew, because Germans came streaming in from their own country to settle the spacious land, fertile in grain, rich in abundant pastures, and well supplied with fish, flesh, and all good things' (Helmold 1963: 312).

It was not long, however, before the new regime was threatened. In 1163 the Obodriti rose again in a revolt led by Pribislaw and Wertislaw. Werle was besieged. Wertislaw and many Slav nobles were taken prisoner by Duke Heinrich. Pribislaw, however, fought on in an attempt to regain his birthright. With a great army he besieged castles that had formerly belonged to the Obodriti and recaptured a number of them. In February 1164, outside the walls of Mecklenburg, he declared to its Flemish defenders: 'A great atrocity has been committed against me and my people [...] we have been driven from our homeland and robbed of our patrimony. You have increased this injustice by invading our land and occupying the castles and villages which belong to us by right of inheritance' (Helmold 1963: 340). The fortified town was taken and all the men killed, while the women and children were taken prisoner. The Obodriti then turned towards the fortress of Ilow, where Pribislaw appealed to the Wends inside the castle:

> You all know how much harm and oppression our people has suffered from the power of the Duke which he inflicted on us, taking from us the inheritance of our fathers and installing in them all immigrants, Flemings and Dutchmen, Saxons and Westphalians, as well as people of other origins. This injustice my father felt bitterly until his death. That is the reason why my brother is in perpetual imprisonment and why there was no one left to think of the welfare of our people

and call it back to life from the ruins, except for me alone. Consider then, you men of the surviving relics of the Slavs, take courage and surrender to me this castle and its illegal occupiers, so that I may punish them, as I have punished those who invaded Mecklenburg.

(Helmold 1963: 342)

The Wendish inhabitants of Ilow, however, were terrified by thoughts of the consequences, and declined to surrender the fortress. The besiegers too now began to have second thoughts and decided to camp for the night. The next morning they set off for home (Helmold 1963: 342–4).

Despite this setback Pribislaw had many successes. He managed to capture further castles, including those of Malchow and Quetzin. Heinrich the Lion, however, responded without delay to the Obodriti revolt and suppressed it with great cruelty. First he had his prisoner Wertislaw hanged near Malchow. He then concentrated a great army in the vicinity of Demmin. The king of the Danes was standing by to come to his aid with a fleet. The final battle took place on 6 July 1164 at Verchen, not far from Demmin, ending in victory for Duke Heinrich. Adolf II was killed. The Slavs, fighting under the leadership of Pribislaw and the Pomeranian Dukes Bogisław I and Kasimir I, lost 2,500 men (Herrmann 1985: 393).

The land of the Obodriti had been ravaged, and its population decimated. Many of them fled to Pomerania or Denmark. Pribislaw took refuge with the Pomeranian princes and later led several raids into the counties of Schwerin and Ratzeburg. In 1167, however, when Heinrich found himself threatened by the Saxon princes, he restored to Pribislaw the greater part of the conquered Obodriti lands as a fief, hoping by this action to ensure for himself the support, or at least neutrality, of Pribislaw in his imminent struggle. Only Schwerin stayed in the hands of Heinrich's vassal Count Gunzelin.

Thus the epic story of Obodriti independence and resistance under the family of Niklot came to an end. But, whereas the Obodriti state around Alt Lübeck disappeared, a partially Obodritic state in Mecklenburg merged with the German Duchy of Mecklenburg. Niklot and his son Pribislaw were the ancestors of the Dukes of Mecklenburg, a dynasty that came to its end only in November 1918 with the abdication of Grand Duke Friedrich Franz IV (*Mecklenburg* 2014: 3). In 1167 or shortly thereafter, Pribislaw accepted Christianity. In 1171 he founded a monastery at Doberau, endowed the episcopate of Schwerin, and in 1172 accompanied Heinrich the Lion on his pilgrimage to Jerusalem. His son Borwin married one of Heinrich's daughters (Herrmann 1985: 393).

The Wendish component in the population was now in terminal decline, so Helmold's pro-German chronicle ends on an upbeat note. Its closing words reveal a state partitioned along ethnic lines with the Wends reduced to the status of outlaws outside their territory:

Pribislaw [...] stayed peaceful and content with the part of his inheritance allowed him, built up the towns of Mecklenburg, Ilow, and Rostock, and settled within their territory the Slav population. And because Slav robbers were molesting the Germans who lived in Schwerin and its territory, Gunzelin, the prefect of the fortress [Schwerin], a strong man and a vassal of the Duke, ordered his men to seize and hang immediately any Slavs they might find in out-of-the-way places without evident reason. And so the Slavs in one way or another were restrained from their thieving and robbery.

(Helmold 1963: 382)

In the further history of these Wendish regions the Wends play no significant role. Events are dominated first by the conflict between Heinrich the Lion and his opponents among the Saxon princes and second by the struggle between the Welfen and the Staufer dynasties. For a long time the emperor was interested only in his Italian policy and left the princes of Holstein, Mecklenburg, and Pomerania to counter Danish expansion (Herrmann 1985: 394).

However, Heinrich the Lion's obsession with expansion into Slav lands was his downfall. He unwisely refused to give the Emperor Friedrich I Barbarossa (1152–1190) assistance in his Italian campaign, as a result of which he was banished and deprived of most of his lands. It was in direct fealty to the emperor that both Niklot von Rostock, Prince of the Obodriti and son of Wertisław (and a rival of Pribisław's son Borwin), and Bogisław, Duke of Pomerania, held their lands (Herrmann 1985: 394; Scheuch 2001: 30, 149).

German settlers between Saale and Oder

The area to the south of Magdeburg had been under German rule since the tenth century. In the twelfth century the Wettins under Konrad I the Great (b. 1098/1099, r. 1127–1157) and Archbishop Wichmann of Magdeburg (1116–1192) supported agricultural development as a means of increasing both income and control. The first record of German settlers here tells how Wiprecht von Groitzsch (c. 1050–1124), who controlled the Elster-Mulde region, allotted land in 1104 to immigrant Frankish peasants between the Mulde and the Pleiße. They settled in family groups, receiving with hereditary title land cleared in the forest and giving their names to the villages they founded (Herrmann 1985: 408, 558). Around 1109 Bishop Walram of Naumburg was settling peasants in the land of the Zeitz Cathedral Chapter in villages near Taucha, which had been cleared from the forest (Herrmann 1985: 409, 558). During 1145–1146 newly cleared land in the Pleiße area is mentioned which had just been settled or was being settled. The tithes were allotted to the Monastery at Bosau, nr. Zeitz. Many Wendish villages continued to exist, retaining their old names, but underwent economic restructuring. They retained their traditional, circular layout (Herrmann 1985: 409, 558).

Under the new regime many of the old social structures were retained. Some Wendish princes were left to reign under German supervision. Vestiges of the old order may be seen in the retention of old words relating to political power or social status, such as *wićaz* 'vassal', *župan* 'headman', and *starosta* 'elder' (Schuster-Šewc 1986: *passim*). The settlers lived according to German law, but for a long time this was not imposed on the Wends, who continued to live according to their own legal system. Problems arose when legal cases arose involving both Wends and Germans, but German law envisaged this possibility and laid down procedures to handle it, including the question of the languages to be used before the courts (Schulze 1980: 358–60).

The fate of the Wends following their subjugation and the colonization of their land is a matter of debate. One view is that they were the victims of a policy of eviction and extermination. The 1147 Crusade had promised either to convert them or 'with God's help to destroy them utterly' (cf. section The Wendish Crusade of 1147 earlier in the chapter). A sinister interpretation of events is to be found in the works of several Slav historians of the nineteenth century, and the theme was taken up and developed as part of the class struggle in the scholarship of the German Democratic Republic. Another is that the Wends were gradually and peacefully assimilated, a view sometimes bolstered by the claim that they were, in any case, greatly outnumbered by the colonists.

There are certainly sources which refer without explanation to Wends leaving their land, but they are neither numerous nor particularly ominous. In 1123 Otto, Bishop of Halberstadt, ordained that the tithes of virgin land in the parish of Wiederstedt (south of Aschersleben) made arable by Wends and Saxons should be paid to Ulrich, archpriest of that parish. 'But if it should happen in that parish that the Slavs, abandoning the previously cultivated land (as happened in the case of the Slav village Warwize), compelled by some necessity, should depart thence, and Saxons should come in to settle it, the tithes should be paid as stated above' (Helbig and Weinrich 1968: 102–3). A document of 1149 bestowing on Arnold, Abbot of the Nienburg Monastery, the tithes of the Burgward of Kleutsch (south-east of Dessau) on the Mulde, reveals that the Abbot, 'having driven out the old heathen Slav peasants, settled there new peasants of the Christian faith' (Helbig and Weinrich 1968: 136–8, no. 30). Eviction may also be suspected in the formulation of an 1159 allusion to two villages in the vicinity of Magdeburg as 'hitherto in the possession of Slavs (*hactenus a Sclavis possessas*)' (Helbig and Weinrich 1968: 62–5) and in an 1160 transaction whereby Count Herrmann von Warpke conveyed to the church in Diesdorf (Altmark) eight Wendish villages 'whose inhabitants hitherto were Slavs (*quarum incole adhuc Sclavi erant*)' (W. Vogel 1960: 51n.).

Because Wends lived under their own legal system, their land was not tithable, but there were other taxes to which Wends, and only Wends, were liable. In the land and tithe records we frequently encounter entries of the type 'they are Slavs, there is no tithe' (*Sclavi sunt, nullum beneficium est*). It is thus generally safe to conclude that untithable land was inhabited by Wends, even if this is not specified. Land vacated by Wends or from which Wends had been evicted could be settled by German or Flemish immigrants, thereby becoming tithable. Clearly, financial interests were involved. The taxes to which the Wends were liable included the general Wendish levy, which was called *kuritz* (*census Sclavorum*), and the *wogiwotnitza* (*census ducis*), payable to the margrave.

A decree of Heinrich the Lion, endowing the diocese of Ratzeburg in 1158, ordains:

The tax of the Slavs, however, throughout all parts of these three dioceses shall be per hide three measures of corn, which is called a *kuritz*, one shilling, one pot of linseed oil, and one hen. Out of these the parish priest shall have two pence and the third gallon. After the land has become tithable, however, the Wends having been evicted (*Sclavis eiectis*), the entire tithe shall be available to the bishop…

(*MUB*, 1: 58, no. 65)

The same formula is repeated in a further edict of Heinrich the Lion of 1174, confirming and extending the privileges of the Diocese of Ratzeburg (*MUB*, 1: 110, no. 113). The three dioceses in question are those of Ratzeburg, Lübeck, and Schwerin.

Wendish language

The earliest surviving Wendish texts date from the sixteenth century, and knowledge of the languages spoken by the Wends before that is fragmentary. Evidence of medieval Wendish comes only in the form of individual words dispersed here and there in the Latin sources. Most of them are names – personal names (anthroponyms) or place names (toponyms) – but a few common nouns, adjectives, prepositions, and verbs are also attested. To these we may add the short sentence imperfectly recorded by Thietmar (see earlier).

Some of the heathen Wends appear in the sources under German names, but the names by which most of them are identified are unmistakably Slavonic, like *Boliliut, Budislav, Jaromir, Jaroslav, Miliduoch, Mistivoj, Dobremir, Pribislav, Selibor, Svantibor, Sventipolk, Wartislav, Wertislav*, in which the components can often be recognized by comparison with other Slav languages as: *bol* 'more, better', *bor* 'fight', *duch* 'spirit', *lut* 'fierce', *mil* 'gentle', *mir* 'peace, world', *slav* 'fame, glory', *svęt* 'sacred'. They are quite distinct from the names of the Germanic protagonists like *Adelheid, Eberhard, Friedrich, Heinrich*.

More eloquent, however, and more numerous than personal names are Wendish place names. They are a keystone of Wendish history, because they establish the Slav character of the Trans-Elbian landscape and have remained in place long after the departure of the Wendish inhabitants. The Slav elements of which they are composed can usually be identified and the earlier the source the easier it is to recognize the components. For example, in *Thobragora* (952) the components *dobra* 'good' and *gora* 'hill' can be detected, although by 1207 this place is recorded as *Godenberge*, the earlier senses 'good' and 'hill' being retained under a German exterior (Eichler 1985–2009, s.v. *Dobragora*). Occasionally the sources explain in Latin the sense of the components. Helmold, for example, writes (c. 1167): 'There is, however, Aldenburg, the one that in the Wendish language is called *Starigard*, that is old town' (*Est autem Aldenburg, ea quae Slavica lingua Starigard, hoc est antiqua civitas, dicitur*) (Helmold 1963: 68), attesting the Wendish words *stary* 'old' and *gard* 'town, castle'. From the same source (c. 1167) comes the gloss: 'So they call the evil god in their language *Diabol* or *Zcerneboch*, that is black god' (*Unde etiam malum deum lingua sua Diabol sive Zcerneboch, id est nigrum deum, appellant*) (Helmold 1963: 198), revealing Wendish *diabol* (a German borrowing), *černy* 'black', and *bog* 'god'. When Thietmar (1012/1018) writes: 'A meeting was held in *Belgern*, which means fair hill' (*Fit conventus in Belegori, quod pulcher mons dicitur*) (Thietmar 1992: 304), he not only reveals the etymology of Belgern but also attests the Wendish words *gora* 'hill' and *bělъ* 'beautiful, fair'. In no other Slavonic language does *bělъ* have this sense (elsewhere it means 'white'), but the sense is corroborated elsewhere in Thietmar.

The foundation deed (1180) of the Cistercian Abbey at Lehnin, south-west of Berlin, records: 'And he bestowed on the monastery the name *Lenin*, which is said with the Slav word *lanie* or hind' (*Et imposuit nomen monasterio Lenin, quod slovanico vocabulo lanie vel cerva dicitur*) (Helbig and Weinrich 1968: 150, no. 3). This is evidence of the Wendish word *lanie* 'hind' (cf. USo. *łanjo* 'fawn' (J. Kral 1927, s.v.), Pol. *łania* 'hind'). A deed of endowment issued by Kasimir of Pomerania for the Cistercian monastery at Dargun in East Mecklenburg in 1174 quotes the Wendish names of several landmarks, including: 'to a certain great oak [which] from its great size gets the name *wili damb*...' (*in quandam magnam quercum, [...] a sua magnitudine nomen accepit wili damb...*) (*MUB*, 1: 112, no. 114) and so attests the Wendish words *wili* 'great' (OCS *velij* 'great') and *damb* 'oak' (Pol. *dąb* 'oak').

Latin glosses are used to explain not only place names. The Wendish bushell *kurica* has been mentioned earlier, which, as a unit of the taxation system under Wendish law, appears regularly: 'But a bushell of the Slavs is called in their language *kuritsa*' (*Modius autem Slavorum vocatur lingua eorum 'curitce'*) (Helmold 1963: 312). Another measure of volume was the *wusyp*: 'excepting that payment which is called *wuzop*' (*excepta ea pensione que wuzop dicitur*) (1197) (W. Vogel 1960: 60). The *wićaz* 'vassal, tenant' was a specifically Wendish social rank, whose rights and duties varied with the passing of time, but originally had a military role. Thietmar in his almost contemporaneous account of Bolesław Chrobry's assault on Budissin in 1002 describes the east gate as being: *in parte, qua satellites habitant dicti Sclavonice Vethenici* 'in the part where the guards live who are called *Vethenici* in Slavonic' (Thietmar 1992: 202). Later they were engaged in agriculture, but held tenancies which were dependent on providing a service, as: *in equis servientes, id est withesi* 'those who serve with horses, that is *withesi*' (1181).

CHAPTER 2
COEXISTENCE AND EROSION 1200–1500

Survival

In the thirteenth century, the two ethnic communities, Wendish and German, after centuries of warfare, were living at peace, though in the main they lived separately and there were occasional minor conflicts. There were still broad expanses of Trans-Elbia, where the Wends predominated, but in them further German churches, monasteries, and fortresses continued to be constructed. In colonial seclusion the Wettins at Meissen aspired to follow the customs of western courts. The wandering poet Walther von der Vogelweide (c. 1170–c. 1230) arrived here in 1210 during the reign of Dietrich I (r. 1198–1221). The works he composed during his three-year stay here contain only one hint of the Wendish environment: a reference to the monastery (founded 1165) at Doberlug, fifty kilometres north of Meissen. In a poem sighing for the return of summer, he says that rather than continuing to languish in the grip of winter, he would become a monk at Doberlug. It has been suggested that the allusion is to a local joke, known only to the Meissen court (Lemmer 2002: *passim*).

Wendish villages were designated as such by the adjective *slav(ic)us*, as in the following examples from the vicinity of Stendal (west of Berlin): 'In Insel, a Slav village' (1238) (*In Insula, villa slavica*); 'Möhringen, near Stendal, a Slav village, afterwards laid waste by Werner, Count von Veltheim' (1201) (*Morunge prope Stendal, slavitica villa, postea deserta facta a Wernero, comite de Veltheim*) (W. Vogel 1960: 59n.).

There are still occasional references to evictions, but the fate of the Wends evicted from their land remains obscure, as in the case of the inhabitants of the island of Poel in the Bay of Wismar, where in 1210 half the corn tithes to be collected from the newly installed German settlers on the island were allotted by Dietrich, Bishop of Lübeck, to Prince Heinrich (Borwin I) of Mecklenburg. Poel had been 'hitherto inhabited by Slavs', but 'on account of destitution and scarcity of men of that nation able to cultivate it, Prince Heinrich of Mecklenburg settled German peasants there' (*MUB*, 1: 187, no. 197). The Wends of Böbelin, a village granted to the monastery of Neukloster (south-east of Wismar) in 1236, had evidently resisted eviction, according to Brunward, Bishop of Schwerin: '… nor were we able for many years to make allocation to farmers inhabiting it on account of the devastation of the Slavs evicted thence at one time or another' (*MUB*, 1: 452, no. 454).

Wend(e) was not yet a surname, but still only an ethnonym capable of translation as *s(c)lavus*, as in *Wilhelmus Sclavus* (1233), *Johannes Slavus* (1266). In thirteenth-century Stendal, bearers of these names are often prominent citizens, or members of the town council or guilds: in 1285 *Jacobus Sclavus* was a town councillor, in 1266 *Johannes Slavus* joined the tailors' guild. In the following century *Werneker Went* was received by the guild of merchants (1330). Stendal even had a *platea Slavorum* 'Street of the Slavs' in 1475, which later became *Wendstraße* (W. Vogel 1960: 57). In the Schwerin area there are references to Wendish bailiffs (*Slavorum advocatia*), though their duties are not revealed (e.g. *MUB*, 3: 652, no. 2421, dated 1296). In 1267 in Rostock the Wendish bailiff Hermann issued loans to two men against the security of their house (*MUB*, 4: 218, no. 2692).

The town of Salzwedel in the Altmark, west of the Elbe, was in a Wendish zone, as may be seen from the provision in its 1247 statutes to admit both German and Wendish peasants (*rustici teutonici sive sclavi*) to citizenship (W. Vogel 1960: 48). Twenty-six years later Salzwedel confirmed the non-discriminatory principle without specifying ethnicity: 'Whoever wishes to be a citizen of Salzwedel, shall enter freely and come and go without difficulty or impediment' (1273) (W. Vogel 1960: 48). Salzwedel lies on the south edge of the Hanover Wendland where the Wends were to survive into the eighteenth century (see Chapter 5).

Language was not the only feature whereby Wends were distinguished. They retained their old legal system. Their villages were laid out to a different plan. Their conversion to Christianity was recent and sometimes only superficial. Anyone described as pagan or a barbarian in the thirteenth century, whether or not the word *sclavus* is used, is obviously a Wend. A document of 1235, without using the word *sclavus*, reports that the inhabitants of certain villages in the Altmark had not yet fully accepted Christian doctrine and that therefore Bishop Dietrich of Halberstadt had decided to erect a church in one of them to facilitate full conversion:

> Let it be known to all that, because certain men in certain villages, namely Cuzeresdorp, Honlege, and Modenborg, and another Modenborg, belonging to the Distorp church, have not yet fully accepted the Catholic faith, but are still held ensnared by certain pagan rites, Dietrich [...], having a proper wish to bring those who dwell in the villages to the truth of the true faith, has decided to build a church in one of the villages themselves, so that from this their devotion to accepting the faith may be the more inspired.

> (W. Vogel 1960: 53)

The suspicion that the recalcitrants were Wends is confirmed in 1245, when Bishop Meinhard confirms his predecessor's decision, but adds a threat:

> If, however, the aforementioned men, namely the Slavs, are unwilling to renounce their rites, let German peasants of the Catholic faith be substituted for them.

> (W. Vogel 1960: 53)

By the thirteenth century organized resistance to the invaders was over, but the Wends in their scattered settlements preserved a separate way of life and occasionally made their presence felt. The sporadic references in the sources usually relate to fairly trivial matters, but are occasionally sufficient to indicate that below the surface there was unrest. An incident in the villages of Zechlin and Repente north-west of Berlin in 1256 suggests an abiding Wendish propensity to recalcitrance. The construction of a mill in Zechlin on the shores of a lake had resulted in a rise in the water level, causing damage to the pastures of the nearby Wendish village of Repente. In a settlement with Johann von Havelberg (lord of Repente) the Doberan Monastery (lord of Zechlin) agreed to make compensation by giving him '10 marks in Slav coins for the damage caused, 5 being paid on St John's day and the other 5 next St Michael's day'. The monastery was anxious to preserve the peace, so the settlement was made on condition that von Havelberg 'should not waver in restraining from turmoil the Slavs of his village called Repente by amicable settlement of their complaints'. Also revealed here is the fact that the silver coins minted by Wendish princes were still in use (*CDB*, 2: 367–8; W. Vogel 1960: 117).

When Margraves Otto and Johann in 1258 made a gift of land to the Lehnin Monastery, its limits were described as reaching 'as far as the burial place of the Slavs situated on the left side of the Vinowe road'. This is revealing insofar as the heathen Slavs are known to have cremated their dead. Burial was a Christian innovation, so it would appear that the Wends, even after conversion, still had their separate cemetery (W. Vogel 1960: 97 and n.). In 1273 the Chorin Monastery was endowed with the Wendish village of Ragösen (south of Brandenburg) with 26 hides of land (*villam slavicalem Rogosene cum 26 mansis*) (*CDB*, 13: 206; W. Vogel 1960: 102), but the following year the same village was described as 'formerly Slav' (*quondam slavicalem*) (*CDB*, 13: 217; W. Vogel 1960: 102n.), suggesting that the Wends had been transplanted to another location or evicted. In 1285 Helmold, Count of Schwerin, sold to the Reinfeld Monastery (in Holstein) the village of Lositz, near Uelitz (south of Schwerin). He undertook, as part of the deal, 'to evict all the Slavs and natives (*omnes Slavos et Cives*) now inhabiting the village and without all hope of return to proceed with them in such a way that they, voluntarily departing, would not remember that they had ever had any title or property in the village, and if by chance (which God forbid) anyone of their number in the future should on this account molest the said church, we shall help them [sc. the monks]' (*MUB*, 3: 188, no. 1809; Habel and Gröbel 1989, s.v. *cives*).

Two hundred or so miles to the south from here the church was already taking account of the Wendish language, as emerges from a 1293 document issued by Heinrich, Archbishop of Magdeburg, granting forty days indulgence to congregations present at sermons preached 'in German or Slav' (*theutonice seu slauice*) by the priest of the parish church of Budissin (St Peter's), or his curate (*CDLS*, 1: 139, no. 87). Similar evidence of Wendish sermons at St Peter's is found in records of 1294 and 1299 (*CDLS*, 1: 145, 163). Less than a mile from St Peter's, at the church of St Mary, just outside the town walls of Budissin, a specification of the duties and rights of the parish priest, dated 21 March 1293, stated:

The one called will hear confessions, especially in Lent and Advent, and also he will have care of the sick in the hospital. In time of need he will care even at night for the sick outside the town and in neighbouring villages. Therefore the aforementioned priest must know German and Slav (*tevtonicum scire debet et sclauicum*). But if he does not know Slav, he will keep with him a Slav curate (*Si uero sclauicum nesciret, sclauicum socium secum obtinebit*) [...].

(CDLS, 1: 137–8, no. 86)

For many years after their subjugation the Wends retained separate laws and institutions. When Heinrich, Prince of Mecklenburg, in 1315 renewed the jurisdiction of the Doberan Monastery (Mecklenburg) over the Wendish villages of Stülow and Hohenfelde, he specified that this was to be according to Wendish law:

> Moreover, we wish that all implementation of jurisdiction in the aforementioned villages Stülowe and Hohenfelde shall be and shall be made by Slav law (*iure slavicali*), as Slav practices have been from antiquity (*prout antiquitus Slavi usi fuerunt*).

(MUB, 4: 154, no. 3759)

Under the new jurisdiction the Wendish nobility and gentry retained their social status within the Wendish sphere. Mentions of Wendish lords (*wendische Herren*) are not uncommon in the thirteenth (1295) (*MUB*, 3: 601, no. 2352B) and fourteenth centuries. In a document of 15 August 1334, the German lords of Putlitz (north-east of Wittenberge) and other knights promised to place their castles at the disposal of the margrave and not to fraternize with the Wendish lords (*mit den Wendeschin herren*), promising: '...that we shall not be reconciled with the Wendish lords and their helpers with our castles and houses, and not lend them unless it be our lord the margrave's counsel and his will' (*MUB*, 8: 460–1, no. 5533). When, on Christmas Eve 1351 Ludwig, margrave of Brandenburg, signed a document in Luckau dividing his patrimony between his brothers Ludwig the Roman and Otto, it was still necessary to include the specific condition 'with all sovereign authority over the Wendish lords' (*MUB*, 13: 130–1, no. 7550).

There is no evidence from the fourteenth century of any limits on Wendish residence in towns. In Rostock there was a Slav street (*fovea Slavorum*), which is mentioned frequently in the municipal records between 1324 and 1335. In 1333 a Slav (*Slavus*), Henneke Cruze, sold a house there to a Nicolaus Pozewolk (*MUB*, 6: 286, no. 3917n.) (Map 1.3).

The *Sachsenspiegel*

Written down by Eike von Repgow (ca. 1180–ca. 1235) between 1225 and 1235, the *Sachsenspiegel* is a compilation of legal customs and conventions at that time. It is not a statute but a record of customary legal practice. For centuries its influence continued to be felt in German legal systems and in some areas, such as Prussia, it remained valid until 1794 (Dobozy 1999: 1). The original version is lost, but its contents are known from hundreds of manuscript copies, the oldest of which date from the beginning of the fourteenth century. There are four particularly valuable fourteenth-century illuminated versions. The home of Eike von Repkow's family was the village now known as Reppichau, between Dessau and Köthen (Cöthen), in the Duchy of Anhalt (Gau Serimunt), an area where in Eike's time, to judge from references in the *Sachsenspiegel*, the Wendish element was still strong.

Eike was a *Schöffe* of the court of the county of Wörbzig which covered the *Gaue* of Serimunt, Coledici, Zitici, and Nudzizi (H. K. Schulze 1980: 358). The main function of a *Schöffe* was as a juror or lay assessor in a court of law, a position needing extensive knowledge of the law of the area. *Schöffen* came from land-owning families of long-standing and belonged to the rank of the fifth level of knighthood (Dobozy 1999: 196). From the *Sachsenspiegel* something can be learned of the legal practices affecting the Wends in the thirteenth century. They still had their own legal system (III. 73), but the German courts Eike describes were competent to deal with both Saxons and Wends. Wends are mentioned specifically only in Book III, in several of the very short chapters (III. 69–73). Of significance for the Wends are principally Chapter III. 71, which describes procedures for litigants whose native language is not German, and III. 72, dealing with inherited social status.

Book III. 69–70. In the courts held under royal authority, the judge and the lay assessors (*Schöffen*) could pass judgement on defendants of either ethnic group: 'They must have gowns on their shoulders. They must be without weapons. They must pass judgement soberly on any man, be he German or Wendish, servile or free (*he si düdesch. oder wendesch. oder egen. oder uri*)' (Sachße 1848: 287, III. 69 §2). However, they did take the ethnicity of the defendant into account and, in the lower courts, a Wend could not judge a Saxon nor a Saxon a Wend. The judge and lay assessors (*Schöffen*) were bound to be of the same nationality as the defendant: 'When not sitting under royal authority, any man who is not accused of legal incapacity may pass judgement on another, except a Wend on a Saxon, or a Saxon on a Wend (*ane de wend uppe den sassen. unde de sasse uppe den wend*)' (Sachße 1848: 288, III. 70 §1). However, Dobozy's supposition that medieval concerns extended to 'the protection of the rights of ethnic groups such as the Wends' is before its time (1999: 24).

The ethnic rule did not extend to courts sitting under the king's authority and, even in the lower courts, it did not apply when a defendant had been caught red-handed and was immediately taken before the court: 'But if the Wend or the Saxon has been caught red-handed in the crime and with hue and cry is brought before the court, a Saxon testifies against a Wend and a Wend against a Saxon, and either of them who has been caught in this way must suffer the judgement of the other' (Sachße 1848: 288, III. 70 §2).

Book III. 71. Everyone had the right to be tried in his own language. The earliest version of the *Sachsenspiegel* therefore says: 'Every man who is charged may refuse to answer, unless he is charged in the language which is native to him (*an der sprake de ene angeboren is*)' (Sachße 1848: 288–9, III. 71 §1). As time passed, however, in response in the gradual increase in the number of Wends who could speak German, in addition to their native language, the courts modified this rule. The second version, revised by Eike von Repkow himself (Schulze 1980: 359), added the proviso: '...if he does not know German and makes claim to this right. If he is charged in this language he must answer, or his advocate must answer on his behalf, so that the plaintiff and the judge can understand it' (Sachße 1848: 289, III. 71 §1). And continues: 'But if he has appeared as plaintiff or defendant or delivered a judgement before a court using German, and this can be proved by witnesses, he shall answer in German; except before the [...] Empire [sc. a court under the Emperor's authority]. For there everyone has law according to his birth (*wente dar heft manlik recht nach siner bord*)' (Sachße 1848: 289, III. 71 §2). These provisions arose not from a desire to protect 'the rights of ethnic groups' but from the medieval principle of personal law, whereby each individual was subject to the laws of his tribe. The legal customs described by the *Sachsenspiegel*, though by now based on territorial law, continued to respect personal or tribal law in certain instances (as in III. 69, III. 71, and III. 73) (Dobozy 1999: 17).

Book III. 72. It deals with the status of children of marriages between persons of unequal social status. In particular, it explains that when a woman of the *Schöffen* class marries a man of lower status, their children inherit the father's status. This rule is subject, however, to the overriding proviso given in Book III. 73 that the children of a free woman always inherit her free status. This leads on to the question of the status of the children of Wends:

> §1. Since the beginning of the law, it has been the law that a free woman never gets a servile child. Since Bishop Wichmann's time, however, the law has existed that sons and daughters of a German mother obey [sc. are serfs of] whomever she belongs to, whether the father is German or not German. And a Wendish woman's child obeys according to the father if he is Wend. But if he is German, it obeys according to the mother. §2. It is said that all Wendish women are free, because their children obey according to the Wendish father, which is not so, because she pays her lord the marriage fee every time she marries. If she leaves her husband, as Wendish law provides, they must give her lord the heifer-money (*Färsenpfennig*), that is three shillings, and in some places more, depending on local custom. (Sachße 1848: 291–2, III. 73 §1–2)

The rule that, if the mother was a Wend, the child of a Wendish father belonged to its father's owner, whereas the child of a German father belonged to the mother's owner, will surely have had demographic implications. In many cases, no doubt, both parties were owned by the same lord, but in other cases it appears to have been advantageous to the owner of Wendish serfs, if his women married Germans but his men married Wendish women. There are many imponderables here, but there seems to have been an economic inducement towards mixed marriages.

There are four illuminated and illustrated versions of the *Sachsenspiegel*. The purpose of the illustrations was to help illiterate litigants. For the historian, in view of the general shortage of sources of any kind on the Wends in the Middle Ages, let alone pictorial sources, they are an unexpected windfall. The outward appearance of Wendish men and women in the thirteenth and fourteenth centuries is otherwise hidden from us. The four manuscripts in question are located in Oldenburg (dated 1336), Heidelberg (1294–1304), Dresden (1295–1363), and Wolfenbüttel (1358–1362). The pages are divided into two columns with the text on the right and the pictures on the left. The number of pictures per page is usually between four and six. Close links between the text and illustrations are provided by coloured capital letters in the text which are repeated alongside the relevant pictures.

In the illustrations to Chapters III. 69–73 (and possibly elsewhere in the manuscripts), Wends can usually be identified and distinguished from other ethnic groups. Their distinctive features vary from one manuscript to another. In the Heidelberg Codex they are portrayed with shorter hair than the Saxons and with straps around their lower legs (puttees) (Figure 2.1). In the Dresden and Wolfenbüttel Codices they wear a tricoloured kilt.

Figure 2.1 Folio 24v of the Heidelberg *Sachsenspiegel* showing Wends in litigation. Universitätsbibliothek Heidelberg, Cod. Pal. germ. 164, Seite 24v. Reproduced by permission.

Wendish banned 'on pain of death'?

How the Wends were so quickly removed from the landscape and replaced by German settlers has been much debated. They may have been the victims of genocide or they may have been gradually assimilated. Seeing there is no record of an overall Imperial policy, it is likely that there was much local variation in the behaviour of the conquerors. Since the nineteenth century, however, one school of historians has striven to present the Wends as victims of persecution, another to suggest that there was a period of peaceful coexistence accompanied by a process of assimilation. In the German Democratic Republic, where the class struggle was held to be the main driving force of history, the emphasis was on oppression. Among representatives of both schools, however, there has long been a tradition in Wendish historiography of alluding to various official bans imposed on the use of the Wendish language from the thirteenth to the fifteenth centuries. Most commonly, they are said to have applied to courts of law, but it has also often been claimed that the prohibitions were more general and were accompanied by punitive measures. As Richard Andree put it:

> Forbidding the Wendish language on pain of death was a frequent practice in the thirteenth century. [...] In Anhalt in 1293 Bernhard II forbade Wendish as the language of the law courts, and the abbot of Nienburg Monastery proceeded with a similar ban. In Altenburg the Wendish language melted away from the time when the Landgrave Friedrich banned it in 1327 on pain of death and declared every Wend to be incapable of holding public office. In the same year Wendish was banned in Leipzig, and similarly we find a ban on it in the Zwickau courts. In Meissen it lasted a century longer, for here it was banned from the courts only in 1424.

(1874: 143)

Although he gives no sources, Andree is a reputable scholar, and his assertions have been accepted on trust and repeated frequently. One credulous writer after another has reproduced them, partially or in full, each citing the authority of his predecessor (e.g. Bogusławski 1861: 158, 206; E. O. Schulze 1896: 94; Frinta 1955: 15; Šołta 1976: 34–5; *Stawizny*, 1: 135; Wukasch 2004: 12). In this game of Chinese whispers the dates and locations have varied slightly. Only Kötzschke (1935: 171), noting the lateness of the sources, betrays a tinge of scepticism.

In 1970 Brankačk explained that the bans on the Wendish language were part of a deliberate discriminatory language policy: 'On the lower Saale, around Altenburg, Zwickau, Leipzig, and Meißen the ruling strata of the German feudal nobility in 1293, 1329, and 1424 issued discriminatory language bans "deeply wounding to Wendish nationality"' (Herrmann 1970: 392). The words 'deeply wounding to Wendish nationality' are taken from Huth (1829: 164) and the date 1329 (for 1327) stems from a misreading of the same source. Notably absent from Brankačk's account, moreover, is any reference to courts of law, an omission which implies a general ban.

This version clearly did not fit the view of peaceful coexistence between Germans and Slavs in the area in question, so H. K. Schulze (a proponent of that view) was prompted by it to check the sources. He concluded that only one case (that of Anhalt 1293) was capable of corroboration from a source contemporary to the events described (1980: 354–5).

Bans (i): Anhalt 1293

The source in question is the report of an agreement, reached by Counts Albrecht I and Bernhard II of Anhalt with Abbot Konrad of Nienburg on 10 April 1293, that henceforth in the courts under their jurisdiction the Wendish language would not be permitted and that Wends would be obliged to use German. The agreement was the result of an application made by the Abbot to the Counts of Anhalt arising from his concern at certain court proceedings which had turned out to the disadvantage of certain Wendish peasants, serfs of the Nienburg Abbey. As a result of unfavourable verdicts much of the Abbey's land had been left uncultivated for long periods. For the location of Nienburg, see Map 1.3.

The idea that the change to German was part of a discriminatory or oppressive language policy is not born out by the record. In the first place, the change was motivated by mercenary, not ethnic, considerations, inasmuch as it was initiated by the Abbot, who was dismayed to see potentially profitable land lying unused, and his petition was only conceded (*indulsimus*) by Albrecht and Bernhard on payment of forty marks. Second, the reform was introduced not to obliterate the Wendish language, but to save the Wendish peasants from a disadvantage which was attributed to their ignorance not of German but of their own language (H. K. Schulze 1980: 361).

A crucial concept arising in the agreement is expressed by the Middle High or Low German word *vare* 'risk, entrapment' (Kluge 1963, s. v. *Gefahr*) in the phrase 'multas varas'. It is defined as: 'The danger of the disadvantage, which accrues to the parties from an infringement of the rules of procedure, e.g. the form of oath' (Schiller and Lübben, 5 (1880): 199, s. v. *vare*). The document opens with a reference to the Tower of Babel, as a result of which:

[…] in one and the same region one man cannot understand the speech of another without an interpreter, or can understand him only with difficulty; it is for this reason that the men of the Wendish tongue belonging to the Nienburg Monastery and to our jurisdiction, of which some on account of inexperience and ignorance of their [own] language have suffered for quite a time many dangers of disadvantage accruing from infringements of the rules of procedure (*propter inpericiam et ignoranciam sue lingue in nostris iudiciis pertulerunt aliquamdiu multas varas*), so that consequently many fields have been deserted for long periods, we have conceded (for forty marks in Stendal coin), at the urgent request of the honourable lord abbot Conrad and of the whole community of the aforementioned church, so that the said properties may be reformed to advantage, that they shall henceforth be content with the German language, the Wendish language having been totally dropped in the presence of us or our representatives in the courts.

(Siebert 1904: 190–1)

How a Wend could suffer disadvantage from ignorance of his own language becomes clear if we recall that by the provisions of the *Sachsenspiegel* (III. 71, see earlier in the chapter): 'Every man who is charged may refuse to answer, unless he is charged in the language which is native to him.' It is only reasonable to suppose that in Anhalt by 1293, owing to the recent expansion of German, not everyone who was born a Wend was still capable of speaking Wendish in court. Forensic procedure was changed to accommodate this development (H. K. Schulze 1980: 360–3).

Bans (ii): Anhalt, Leipzig, Zwickau, Altenburg 1327 (1329)

The trail followed by Schulze in his unsuccessful quest for a primary source attesting a language ban 'on the lower Saale, around Altenburg, Zwickau, Leipzig, and Meißen' in the 1320s took him back no further than Spangenberg, who had reported in conjunction with events of 1327: 'In this year a change also took place on the Saale in the lands of the princes of Anhalt, whereby the serfs had to present their cases to the courts only in German and not in Slavonic or Wendish, as they had done hitherto' (1572: 332). He also found T. Schmidt, who had noted that in 1327 the Wends, bringing their causes before the courts 'in Zwickau and in the whole land, but above all in Leipzig', were ordered 'on pain of heavy penalty' to use not 'the Slavonic or Wendish language' but German. This was because 'positions of authority were all held by Germans and they either could not understand the Wendish language well or else had a horror and loathing of it' (1656: 159–6).

On the basis of textual similarities Schulze concluded that Spangenberg, directly or indirectly, was the source for Schmidt. He further theorized: 'Spangenberg evidently knew of the document of the Counts Albrecht I and Bernhard II of Anhalt, but incorrectly allocated this event to the year 1327. [...] Schmidt then, retaining the wrong date, extended the language ban to Zwickau and Leipzig and heavily embellished Spangenberg's concise account in the verbose way of the early-modern chroniclers' (1980: 366). Whether we accept Schulze's theories or not, it is a fact that a language ban in the Leipzig area, dated 1327, also appears in another seventeenth-century source, which is probably a little earlier than Schmidt and free of his embellishments:

In the year 1327 in and around Leipzig in the neighbourhood the Wendish language was done away with, and so the people had to present their cases in and outside the courts in the German language.

(Heydenreich c.1635: 50)

Several further details (or, perhaps, embellishments) appear in Pölitz (1809: 87), who refers to the Wendish character of several villages in his own time in the Altenburg, Zwickau, and Leipzig area, adding:

Only their language was lost after the Landgrave Friedrich in 1327 banned the Wendish language on pain of death, and at the same time declared all Wends to be incapable of holding public office.

The idea that Wendish in the fourteenth century was forbidden on pain of death and that Wends were barred from public office is no older than this.

Huth (1829), in the context of the investiture of Friedrich the Serious (*der Ernsthafte*) (1310–1349) with the Burgraviate of Altenburg in 1329, alludes to 'a decree of the latter from the same time period (*aus derselben Zeit*), by which in all the law courts of the Pleißenland the Wendish language, where hitherto it had been customary, was abolished and German introduced in its place' (1829: 163–4). This, presumably, explains Brankačk's 1329 (for 1327).

Bans (iii): Meissen 1424?

There remains the reference in Andree (1874) and his followers to the year 1424. Schulze, in conclusion, was forced to admit: 'The basis for the report of the abolition of Slavonic as the language of law courts in Meissen in 1424 remains unexplained' (1980: 367). The explanation is, however, as follows. There is little doubt that Andree's source was K. A. Jenč (1849–1850: 132), who wrote: 'A hundred years later in 1424 the Sorbian language was thrown out of the law courts in Meissen.' Jenč's footnote on the same page, however, purporting to quote from his source, gives the date as 1427: 'Weisse: antiq. Misn Saxon. 1727 p. 98 –: "in 1427 the Wendish language was abolished from the court and replaced by German" ' (*anno 1427 a foro ejecta est lingua Vendica, in cujus locum Germanicae successit usus*).

'Weisse: antiq. Misn Saxon. 1727' can be deciphered as the book: *Antiquitatum Misnico-Saxonicarum singularia duobus libris exposita, quorum alter antiquissimorum misniae incolarum, Hermundorum, Thuringorum ac Venedorum; alter Saxonum veterum […] auctore M. Christiano Henrico Weissio, Gymnasii Altenburgensis Directore* (Chemnitz, 1727). Unfortunately, page 98 contains nothing of relevance, but on page 71 we find:

In our Meissen (*In Misnia nostra*) finally in 1327 (*anno demum quarti decimi seculi vicesimo septimo*) the Wendish language was abolished from the courts and was replaced by the use of German.

In other words, the references to 1424 as the date of the abolition of Wendish from the courts of Meissen, noted in K. A. Jenč (1849–1850: 132), Andree (1874: 143), Brankačk

(Herrmann 1970: 391), Stone (1972: 12), Kunze (1993: 11), Wukasch (2004: 12), and others, all stem from a mistranslation of Weiss. Further fifteenth-century variants (Bogusławski 1861: 158, 206, Bogusławski and Hórnik 1884: 71) are also spurious.

Since Weiss is not known to have had any particular association with the city of Meissen, his 'in Misnia nostra' is more likely to refer to the margraviate as a whole (*Meißnerland*).

In the new, revised edition of Herrmann (1985), Brankačk acknowledged Schulze's contribution, but made no concessions. It would have been unthinkable to compromise the axiom that the history of all hitherto existing society is the history of class struggles. He therefore reaffirmed his claim that: 'On the lower Saale, around Altenburg, Leipzig, and Meissen in 1293, 1329 [*sic*], and 1424 the ruling classes of the German feudal nobility issued discriminatory [...] language bans.' He again cited Andree, protesting in despair that 'the ruling class by no means always had its oppressive practices recorded in writing' (Herrmann 1985: 463, 571).

The question whether there ever was a 1327 decree banning Wendish in Anhalt or the Meissen Margraviate or both, remains imponderable. If there was, however, it is more likely to have been a consequence of the decline of the language (as in the case of the 1293 decree) than a cause. Evidence of a language ban as an instrument of ethnic oppression has yet to be revealed.

Union of Wendish towns

From the thirteenth century onwards the attributive *wendisch* is found referring to a group of towns within the Hanse. The group, known as the *wendische Städte*, was led by Lübeck and consisted of Lübeck's neighbours to east, west, and south: Hamburg, Kiel, Wismar, Rostock, Lüneburg, Stralsund, Greifswald, Stettin, and Anklam. They formed a maritime union, an inner circle for mutual trade advantage within the Hansa and concluded secret commercial treaties. They also issued their own coinage. Some of these towns still had a Wendish element in their populations in the thirteenth century, but in no case can it have been large or influential. The reason for the adoption of the adjective *wendisch* therefore remains a mystery. Rostock, for example, continued to bear the title 'urbs vandalica' long after its Wends had disappeared, and in the case of Hamburg there is no known historical association at all with the Wends.

In 1379 the Wendish towns concluded a monetary union (*Wendischer Münzverein*) and each minted its own coins based on the Lübeck Mark. The union remained in force until the sixteenth century. In 1541 Lüneburg minted the *Wendentaler*, showing the arms of the Wendish Towns (Daenell 2001: *passim*; Scheuch 2001: 180; *Münzverein* 2014).

The fourteenth century

Several changes of sovereignty during the course of the fourteenth century affected the area which would later become the Wendish heartland. The Budissiner Land had passed in 1253 as the dowry of Princess Beatrix, daughter of the king of Bohemia, to the margraves of Brandenburg. Half a century later (1303 and 1304), their domains were further extended to include the Lusatian March (later Lower Lusatia), which hitherto had been held by the House of Wettin. In 1319, however, the king of Bohemia managed to recover the Budissiner Land for the Czech Crown. He similarly acquired the Görlitz Land in 1329 and Lubań and Zittau in 1346. The king of Bohemia's representative in the Budissiner Land was the *Burggraf*, who resided in Budissin in the castle. Both he and the *Landesvogt* were always members of the Bohemian aristocracy. The further acquisition for the Czech Crown of the Lusatian Mark was effected by the Emperor Charles IV in 1367. This expansion was part of a policy of the Luxemburg-Bohemian dynasty, which led to wars with Brandenburg. A passage in the Magdeburg Chronicle expresses the opinion that the Lusatian Mark was sold to Bohemia 'on the advice of wicked people' and threatens the guilty parties with retribution (Lehmann 1968: 606; *Stawizny*, 1: 117–18).

There is nothing to indicate that in these territorial adjustments the ethnicity of the general population was ever taken into account. Few documents in the late Middle Ages denote the ethnicity of the population, but it would be rash to conclude that the unspecified are Germans. Regions described in one source as having a Wendish population may be unspecified in another. The ethnicity of both individual villages and individual persons, however, continues to be recorded. A document of 1302, from Schollene (north-east of Stendal), granted permission for 'natives and Slavs (*Cives et Sclavi*) in Schollene to cut firewood in the Molkenberg woods' (W. Vogel 1960: 65). In 1306 the Crucemann brothers sold the whole village of Banzow to the Hospital of the Holy Ghost in Salzwedel (in the Altmark) 'but excepting two Slavs' (*CDB*, 12: 49). At the end of the century (1398) Duke Otto of Brunswick made a gift of six Slavs, living in Banzen, to a knight named Crucemann (*CDB*, 25: 288). A document of 1319 alludes to two Wends in Winkelstädt (Kr. Gardelegen in the Altmark): 'In the village of Winkelstädt our two Slav subjects, that is Bernard and Richard, living there on two farms...' (*CDB*, 22: 114; Vogel 1960: 61; Habel and Gröbel 1989, s.v. *cives*).

That there were still Wends in the vicinity of the town of Templin in the Uckermark (north of Berlin) in 1320 emerges from a document issued that year by Dukes Otto and Wartislaf of Pomerania concerning the town's jurisdiction: 'They shall henceforth judge the peasants, be they Wendish or German, in our town and in our land' (W. Vogel 1960: 104n.). Of the village of Liepe in the Uckermark a document notes in 1375: 'Liepe is a Slav village (*villa slavica*), it has 23 houses, every house gives 4 shillings and 8 pence' (W. Vogel 1960: 101). In 1354 an oath of allegiance to Duke Barnim of Pomerania includes a note of 'Wendish villages on the Oder, Tzutzen and Krywen, and other Wendish villages lying between Zcweyt and Stolp, Margrevendorph and Bismarow and Dobertyn, excepting only by name the village of Vlemyschdorph' (*CDB*, B 2: 351). In 1330 Heinrich Holstein, Bailiff of Penzlin (north of Neu-Strelitz), recorded completion of a settlement between the Broda monastery and a group of Wends, led by members of the de Jazeke family, who claimed to have hereditary rights to property on the de Jazeke estate. The monastery managed to buy them off but only to the tune of forty-five marks. The names of the 'Slavs called de Jazeke' (*Slavos dictos de Jazeke*) are listed (*MUB*, 8: 145–6, no. 5161).

The prefix *de* indicates social status (= *von*). In 1370 Rostock town council granted 'the Slavs' the privilege of using a road suitable for wheeled traffic (*per quam currus potest pertransire*) (*MUB*, 16: 636–7, no. 10125).

Collections and analyses of the evidence of the Wends between the Saale and Bober during the Middle Ages are in shorter supply than those covering the territory further north. By 1376, at the Budissin collegiate church of St Peter there was a Slav curacy (*vicaria Slavica*) whose holder was charged with caring for the souls of the Slavs (Reuther 1953a: 123; Schlesinger 1962, 2: 258–9). Jatzwauk (1912: 61) estimated that in 1400 nearly 36 per cent of the inhabitants of the town were Wends (Reuther 1953a: 122–3). Knauthe, although, as a Protestant, he was at pains to emphasize the neglect of the Wendish language by the church before the Reformation, estimated that in the pre-Reformation cathedral chapter in Budissin the majority of the canons were Wends (1767: 209).

The *Kietz*

A particular type of Wendish settlement which appears to have emerged in the period during and following the German colonization was the *Kietz*. A suburban village, situated close to a fortified town, the *Kietz* was there to provide the town with certain services, especially the supply of food, and the villagers were Wends. The word is German, but in origin it is probably a borrowing from a Wendish word which has not been recorded. The closest cognate forms known from other Slavonic languages are Old Polish *chycz* 'peasant's cottage' (*Słownik staropolski*, s. v.) and Kashubian *chëč* 'house' (Sychta 1967–1976, s. v.). See also Eichler (1960), who, however, notes only the longer variant *chycza*, a less likely model for the German masculine *Kietz*.

The *Kietz* was typically located beside water, and the food it supplied to the town was mainly fish. The most common employments, therefore, were catching and selling fish. The fortress, to whose laws the inhabitants of the *Kietz* were subject and which they were bound by feudal obligations to serve, provided protection (Ludat 1936: 200). By the end of the fifteenth century most *Kietze* had been Germanized, but the word lives on in dialectal German as a derogatory term denoting a run-down quarter of a town. Although *Kietz* is a common noun, occasionally it has been adopted as part of the name of an originally Wendish location. In medieval sources its status (as common noun or place name) is sometimes uncertain.

There were many *Kietze* in the Havelland. The fortress of Brandenburg had four, two of which together bore the name Woltitz (W. Vogel 1960: 71). In 1319 Margrave Woldemar sold to Neustadt Brandenburg 'ownership of a village which is called the *Kietz* or Woltytz' (W. Vogel 1960: 71n.). In this instance the ethnic identity of the villagers is not specified, but frequently it is stated expressly that the inhabitants of a particular *Kietz* were Wends. In 1321 Rudolf of Saxony sold to the Brandenburg cathedral chapter a stretch of the River Havel with fishing rights and 'with the Slavs holding out on the right bank in the village, which is called the *Kietz*' (W. Vogel 1960: 72). There are also several mentions in the fourteenth century of a *Kietz* serving Schorin (now Marquardt, part of Potsdam), such as: '...four Wends in the *Kietz* at Schorin' (*vir Wenden up deme Kytze to Schoryn*) (1358) and 'with two Wends in the *Kietz* at Schorin' (*met twen Wenden up deme Kytze to Schoryn*) (1381) (W. Vogel 1960: 73n.). The *Kietz* serving Potsdam itself is first mentioned in 1349, when Margrave Woldemar conferred on the von Torgow family 'the Kietz at Potsdam with full rights' (*den kytz zu Postamp met allen rechte*) (W. Vogel 1960: 72n.). It preserved its Wendish character until at least 1375, when there is a reference here to 'the Slavs of the village or Kietz' (*Slavi de vico vel Kietz*) (W. Vogel 1960: 73n.).

Spandau too was served by a *Kietz*. It is first mentioned in 1319 in an allusion to 'the Wends there in the Kietz' (*die Wende uff dem Kitze doselbst*) (W. Vogel 1960: 74n.). In the Uckermark (north-east of Berlin) the presence of a Wendish village called (the) *Kietz* near the town of Lunow was noted in 1315: 'That we have given to the church of Chorin...the old manor, lying beside the town of Lunow, and the Slav village, which in the vernacular is called the Khycz' (*Quod antiquam Curiam, prope villam Lunowe sitam, et vicum Slavicalem, qui vulgariter Khycz vocatur,...dedimus...ecclesie Chorin*) (W. Vogel 1960: 100n.).

As we move into the fifteenth century the use of the words *wendisch, slavus*, and so on to denote villages and their inhabitants diminishes. In 1407 the occupants of the Spandau *Kietz* are referred to as 'my gracious lord's poor people' (*myns gnedigen heren arme lude*) and the designation of Wends as 'poor people' seems to have been a convention. At all events, a further reference to the same people, this time specifically as 'our Wends here in the Kietz just outside Spandau' (*unser Wende uff dem Kycze hie fur Spandow*), is found in 1431, and in 1515 the Brandenburg Elector Joachim I confirmed the ancient privileges of the Spandau Wends (W. Vogel 1960: 74n.). A further confirmation of privileges dated 1562, now by the Elector Joachim II, refers to them as 'our dear faithful ones, the common Kietzers in the Kietz of our town Spandow' (*liebe getruwen die gemeine Kietzer ufm Kietze von unser Stadt Spandow*) (W. Vogel 1960: 74n.).

To the north-east from here at Wriezen on the Oder the *Kietz* and its Wendish fishermen are mentioned by Margrave Friedrich in 1420 as 'our dear faithful Wends, our fishermen in the Kietz at Wriezen on the Oder' (*unser lieben getruuen di wende, unse vischern uff dem kycze czu Wretzin an der Oder*) (Vogel 1960: 94n.). In 1421 one Heinz Donner is recorded as being responsible for collecting for the margrave 'all money, rent, and duty from the Kietzer and, from the Wends in the marsh, yarn-duty...' (*alle gult, Rente, Czinsze von den kiessern und von den wenden uff dem bruche, Garnczinsse*) (*CDB*, 12: 433; W. Vogel 1960: 94n.). It is thus evident that there were, in addition to the Kietzer, other Wends living in the Oderbruch in the vicinity of Wriezen. Relations between the town and its *Kietz*, however, were not always cordial. In 1510 the Elector had to intervene, following a complaint from the townspeople that the Kietzer were guilty of practices they considered unfair competition (W. Vogel 1960: 94n.).

In 1430 the revenue from the fishing industry of Oderberg and Lunow came to 94 shillings and 16 groschen, to which the record adds: 'Also received from the Wends 3 shillings' (*Item von den wenden ingnommen III schilling*) (*CDB*, 12: 363; W. Vogel 1960: 101n.). From this Vogel deduces that the fishing here was by now mainly in the hands of

Germans and that the Wends lived only in the *Kietz*. Over a century earlier (1308) there had been a reference to a common fishery between Oderberg and Liepe (then a Wendish village) and the Kietzer of Oderberg (W. Vogel 1960: 101n.).

Exclusion from guilds

By the early thirteenth century the German craftsmen in the towns in the Wendish lands were already organizing themselves in guilds. An applicant for membership was normally required to show that he was a citizen of the town in question. Sometimes an undertaking to acquire citizenship within a year and a day was acceptable. However, economic factors usually made it desirable to control the number of members and so further hurdles were introduced, notably requirements that the applicant be a freeman (not *eigen* 'in feudal bondage') and a German. In Wendish territory this condition was sometimes directed specifically against Wends.

The statutes of the Schwerin guild of wool weavers, for example, states (4 October 1372): 'The first privilege is this: who wishes to be a brother of our guild here in Schwerin must be genuine and true, German and not Wendish, free and not in bondage, and of good reputation with written testimonials, as is a usual custom in all towns' (*Dyt erste privilegium is dit: de wil wesen eyn medebruder vnses amptes her to Swerin, schal wesen echte unde recht, Dudes unde nicht Wendes, vry unde nicht eyghen unde wol beruchtet myt bryuen tuchnisse, alzo id ys eyne wonlike wonheith in allen steden*) (*MUB*, 18: 642). In Löbau (20 kilometres south-east of Budissin) on 19 December 1448, the town council ratified the statutes of the guild of butchers, including the custom 'not to accept any Wends, shepherds, pipers, or other people of the greedy kind, but pious, legitimately born, and of the true German sort' (*Item keinen Wendischen, Schäffers, Pfeifers noch andere begehrender Leute Art aufzunehmen, sonder fromme, ehrlich geborne und von rechter deutscher Art*) (*CDLS*, 4: 555–6).

The earliest known guild statutes excluding Wends date from the fourteenth century, beginning with a 1323 statute of the drapers' and clothmakers' guild in Brunswick and followed in 1353 by that of the shoemakers of Beeskow (Vogel 1960: 121–2). The relatively late appearance of the anti-Wend paragraph, almost a century after the first known statute prescribing conditions for entry to a guild, may be evidence that it was not an old tradition but an innovation made to meet new circumstances. The Wends, in other words, had once not been a problem but were now gradually becoming one for some guilds. This view is supported by two surges in the frequency of inclusion of the paragraph, first in the first half of the fifteenth century and second in the mid-sixteenth century. The Wends were even in the sixteenth century, it seems, still moving from the country into the towns and in appreciable numbers (W. Vogel 1960: 128–9).

In the towns of Brandenburg in the period from 1231 to 1652 (according to Vogel's analysis) the total known number of guild statutes specifying conditions of entry is 120 (1960: 122–5). For most of these towns more than one set of such statutes is known, so the number of towns with at least one guild whose entry conditions are known is much smaller, namely twenty-four. In exactly half of them one guild at least had a paragraph excluding Wends (1960: 125–6).

The surviving records, however, show that in a given town it was possible for one guild to exclude Wends and for another at the same time not to do so. In Spandau in 1536, for example, the shoemakers' statute excluded Wends, while that of the tailors did not (W. Vogel 1960: 124). Although it is hard to draw general conclusions from the evidence available to date, it is clear that, whatever new discoveries are made, the once widespread claim (up to and including Hopp 1954) that from the mid-fourteenth century there was a ban on Wends in all Brandenburg guilds is now untenable (W. Vogel 1960: 125).

It has been suggested that the exclusion clause was a mere formula which in practice was ignored (Ludat 1936: 98n.) and it is hard to prove a negative. Nevertheless, Hopp managed to do precisely that (1954: 80, 85) and Vogel (1960: 127) concurs. The evidence comes in the form of communications (admittedly not numerous) from one official body to another, attesting to the true German and not Wendish birth of particular applicants. That the guilds took the matter seriously is well demonstrated by a complaint of 1516 to the city fathers of Frankfurt/Oder that they were ignoring all the rules by granting citizenship to Wends, while the guilds were doing their best to maintain the ethnic barrier (W. Vogel 1960: 127–8).

Upper and Lower Lusatia: Nomenclature

In early records the Latin word *Lusizi* referred only to the northern part of what later became Lusatia. By the fourteenth century the usual Latin forms were *Lusatia* and *Lusacia*, corresponding to German forms such as *Lawsicz* (1371) and *Lussitcz* (1390). They denoted only the territory that was subsequently to be known as Lower Lusatia (*Lusatia inferioris*/*Niederlausitz*) (Lippert 1894: 43–51). To the south, centred on Budissin, lay the land that had once been the home of the Milzeni. From the twelfth to the fourteenth century the terms 'Terra Budissinensis' and 'Provincia Budessinensis' were in use (Kavka 1978: 141). In the thirteenth century the margraves of Brandenburg had made a division into the Budissiner Land in the west and the Görlitzer Land in the east (*Stawizny*, 1: 116; Kavka 1978: 142). It was not until the early fourteenth century that the sense of *Lusatia*/*Lausitz* expanded to cover the whole of what is now Lusatia. The earliest unambiguous record of the wider meaning is in the matriculation records of Leipzig University, where a list dated 23 April 1410 and headed 'The following originating from Lusatia...' (*Infrascripti de Luzasia exeuntes...*) is found to contain students not only from Guben and Senftenberg but also from Kamenz and Budissin. A year later the new meaning is confirmed by a list headed 'De Lusacia' and consisting exclusively of students from Kamenz, Bautzen, and Görlitz (Lippert 1894: 51, 57–8). The earlier meaning, however, also survived for a time. A report of the Hussite army's movement towards Cottbus after the siege of Budissin in 1429 says: 'then they made another sharp right-hand turn and came into the Lusatian land' (*und quomen yn Lawsitczer lant*) (Jecht 1911: 238).

Later still in the fifteenth century the practice grew up in the princely chanceries of referring to the northern part as *Lusatia inferioris* or *Niederlausitz* and the southern part by the new name *Lusatia superioris* or *Obere Lusatz*, then finally *Oberlausitz* (Blaschke 1997/2000: 56; *Stawizny*, 1: 116). Simultaneously, however, the names *Land der Sechsstädte* and *Sechsstädteland* continued be used, reflecting the importance of the royal towns of Upper Lusatia. Even in the sixteenth century in the usage of the Dominican Johann Lindner, known as the Monk of Pirna (writing around 1530 – see Chapter 3), *Lausitz* clearly is still capable of having the meaning 'Lower Lusatia', though he is inconsistent and, in addition, uses the terms *Ober-Lausitz* and *Nieder-Lausitz* to avoid ambiguity.

The Six-Town Union

In the Middle Ages, economic development began gradually to give an advantage to those whose income was in money over those whose income was in kind. The nobility had few opportunities for making money, yet they needed it to maintain their social position. The towns, meanwhile, became ever richer through manufacturing and trade. The nobles in the lands of Budissin and Görlitz (later to be called Upper Lusatia) reacted with a well-known money-making method, consisting of waylaying and robbing the merchants as they progressed along the main highways between the towns. The town archives contain many examples of complaints about the dangers on the roads. It was obviously in the interest of the towns and their commerce that there should be security on the roads, and it was up to their overlord to provide this, but there was no resident overlord and the robber barons thrived. On 21 August 1346, however, at the express behest of the *Landvogt* appointed by the king of Bohemia the five royal towns, Budissin, Görlitz, Kamenz, Lauban, and Löbau, combined with Zittau (which then belonged to Bohemia) to form the Six-Town Union (Blaschke 1997/2000: 52–3). The towns then collaborated to ensure internal peace and protect trade, primarily by maintaining safety on the roads against attacks by members of the nobility (Bahlcke 2001: 99).

The Union was able to raise detachments of armed men and with them to curb the activities of the robber barons. Particularly advantageous to those engaged in robbery were their castles standing at conveniently remote locations well away from the towns. In 1355 King Charles IV gave the Union licence to 'smash and burn the pernicious courts and strongholds' of the noble robbers and in case of resistance to declare them outlaws and pass sentence (Bahlcke 2001: 106). Rebuilding them was forbidden, which explains why Upper Lusatia became and remained a land without castles (Blaschke 1997/2000: 53). There was in fact a pact between the king of Bohemia and the Six-Town Union against the local nobility. The nobles were forbidden to build towns, so the towns achieved a remarkable degree of independence and self-confidence. In their ability to own land, villages, and serfs, the towns had a status similar to that of feudal lords. A town's feudal holdings were known as its *Weichbild*. Nevertheless, the nobility formally still had the upper hand and the Estates were always led by a *Landeshauptmann* who was a noble.

Budissin revolt of 1405

In May 1405 there was a revolt by the craftsmen of Budissin, led by the head of the cloth-workers, Peter Preußelwitz. Master craftsmen were demanding the right to seats on the town council. They also resented the council's restrictions on the right to brew beer. Having armed themselves and intending to arrest the town councillors, they entered the Town Hall, but the councillors had fled to the castle, seeking refuge with the *Landvogt*. The insurgents occupied the Town Hall and elected a new council, under whose leadership they managed for a time to defend themselves against the attacks of other towns of the Union. They attempted to take the Ortenburg, the seat of the *Landvogt*, but without success. Reinforcements arrived from Görlitz and by the end of August the revolt had been suppressed. The same year and during 1406–1407 there were further disturbances in Görlitz, Zittau, and Kamenz (Czok 1961: 108–13; *Stawizny* 1: 125).

It was not until 1408 that King Wenceslas came to Budissin with an army, promising to investigate complaints against the original deposed town council. In the course of the proceedings, however, it became clear that he was not on the side of the craftsmen but of the merchants. He had several men put in irons and thirteen members of the new council including the mayor were put to death in the market square. Certain others were also found guilty and expelled from the town, though they later were able to return on payment of a large fine. The town was temporarily deprived of the right to elect its own councillors (Reymann 1902: 21–3; Czok 1961: 115).

Nowhere in the sources is the ethnic identity of the participants in these events mentioned. It is worth recalling, however, that Budissin is exceptional, inasmuch as it is the only Lusatian town known to have been a town before the Wends were subjugated. There is no reason therefore to link its origins to the German colonization, and it has been calculated that at the end of the fourteenth century about 35 per cent of its population were still Wends (Jatzwauk 1912: 60f.). The ethnicity of individual inhabitants of Budissin is rarely specified, however, and, in the absence of evidence one way or the other, Peter Preußelwitz has been adopted by the Sorbs as Pĕtr Pruzlica with an entry in the Sorbian dictionary of national biography (*NBS*, s.v.).

One contemporary Budissin Wend whose ethnicity is known is a certain Jacoff, who is recorded as 'the Wendish goldsmith' (*der Windische goltschmid*). The town was famous for its goldsmiths, of whom there were twelve. In 1399 he had his workshop in Brüdergasse, but a year later he moved to larger premises in Lauenstrasse. From the record of the taxes he paid, it is clear that he was one of the richest inhabitants. He died in 1407. His case proves that social advancement for Wends in Budissin was quite possible. He was not only admitted to a guild but also became a prominent citizen (*NBS*, s. v. *Jacoff*). It may be surmised that among goldsmiths (though not among the general population) Wends were rare and that therefore it was convenient, for purposes of identification, to specify his ethnicity.

The Hussites

When Luther appeared on the scene in the sixteenth century, the western church had already been seeking reform for a century and more (Chadwick 1984: 11). In England an early contribution had been made by followers of John Wycliffe (c. 1330–1384), known as the Lollards, who in the late fourteenth century condemned such practices as clerical celibacy, indulgences, and pilgrimages, and rejected the belief in transubstantiation (*ODCC*, s. v. *Lollardy*). Wycliffe's writings were influential far beyond the shores of England, and, following the marriage in 1382 of Anne, sister of King Wenceslas IV of Bohemia, to Richard II of England, they found a Bohemian audience. This influenced the two great Czech reformers Jan Hus (c. 1372–1415) and Jerome of Prague (c. 1370–1416). The University of Prague, where Hus was Dean of the Philosophical Faculty from 1401, became a stronghold of the Wycliffite doctrine.

In 1411 Pope John XXIII excommunicated Hus and placed his followers under an interdict. Having appealed against this decision, he was invited in 1414 to attend the Council of Constance where, travelling under a safe conduct of the Emperor Sigismund, he arrived in November. Here he was arrested and put on trial. Despite the emperor's efforts to free him, he was condemned to death for heresy and, on 6 July 1415, burned at the stake. The following year his friend and follower Jerome of Prague suffered the same fate. Most Czechs were by now Hussites and the Czech nobles protested against these atrocities and took up arms. They urged the Lusatian Estates to support them, but in vain. Following the death of King Wenceslas on 16 August 1419 his brother Sigismund, king of Hungary, laid claim to the Czech Crown. The Hussite nobles, however, rejected him and refused him allegiance. The Estates of Upper Lusatia, taking a different view of the situation, decided to accept his claim and sent a deputation to Hungary to assure him of their loyalty (Reymann 1902: 24).

The ethnic (anti-German) element in the Hussite movement is unmistakable. The Czech nobility was still predominantly Czech-speaking. On 17 January 1420, Sigismund was in Breslau, where he received the Upper Lusatian Estates' deputation and confirmed their ancient privileges (Reymann 1902: 24). Present with the deputation, reputedly, was the Town Clerk (*Stadtschreiber*) of Budissin, named Prischwitz or Preischwitz (Reymann 1902: 24). The king now issued a document calling on the Six Towns and nobles of Upper Lusatia to assist him in punishing the rebel Hussites in Bohemia and Moravia. He assured them that their participation in his campaign would not prejudice their rights and privileges. Possibly this is to be interpreted as a threat. If so, it is in contrast to the promise made by King Wenceslas to the Upper Lusatian Estates in 1390 that if they ever rendered him assistance outside their own territory they would be rewarded financially (Reymann 1902: 24). The Upper Lusatians dispatched their auxiliary forces to Moravia and thence to Bohemia. It has been calculated that the Six-Towns Federation supplied about 400 men and that the nobility provided a considerably smaller number (Jecht 1911: 24), but Upper Lusatian help for Sigismund achieved nothing. In fact, the entire campaign was unsuccessful for Sigismund's army.

Meanwhile, on the home front in Upper Lusatia there was constant fear of invasion and preparations were made. For one or two days a week from May to July 1421 the lords of the villages in the vicinity of Budissin sent their serfs (numbering as many as 1,243 and predominantly Wends) to work on the town's defences, digging trenches and raising ramparts. The Cathedral Chapter sent 98, the Marienstern Nunnery 240 (Jecht 1911: 26). At the end of 1421 the Upper Lusatian forces returned home, but from Kremsier, on 22 March 1422 Sigismund issued a new order for the Six Towns to build defences in readiness for a Hussite attack. Budissin Town Council and its citizens again set about constructing walls and trenches, supported by the nobility and the church, whose contribution came in the form of days of human labour carried out by their serfs (Reymann 1902: 24–5). These can only have been Wends. The Abbess of the Marienstern Nunnery, for example, donated 170 workers for the Thursday after St John's Day 1422 and for the following day. The Council had eighteen cannon cast (Reymann 1902: 25).

News came of Hussite attacks in other parts of Upper Lusatia, but Budissin remained unaffected. Years passed, but the tension remained. On 16 May 1427, Lauban and its nunnery were plundered and burned by the Hussite army (Jecht 1911: 132). Two years later Kamenz suffered the same fate. Fortress Budissin kept itself in a state of readiness and on 12 October 1429, a Hussite army of 4,000, commanded by one Molesto or Mielasko (thought to be a distorted record of Mikulášek, according to Jecht 1911: 236), appeared outside the town. Submission having been demanded and the demand been rejected, Budissin was stormed from three sides for three days, but held fast. The heaviest fighting was near the southern precipice overhanging the River Spree. The garrison commander Thimo von Colditz here enlisted the help of women and girls in preparing and carrying boiling water, molten pitch, and sulphur to drop on the enemy. After three days fighting the besieging army gave up and moved on, heading for Meissen before turning east again into Lower Lusatia. Their leader Mikulášek had been shot by two arrows and died of his wounds, which led to dissension among the attackers (Jecht 1911: 238).

Further north Cottbus and Luckau held out against the Hussite attacks and Calau and Drebkau saved themselves by paying ransom, but Guben, on 27 October 1429, was destroyed (Jecht 1911: 239). From Guben the invaders moved on to Neuzelle, where the monastery was destroyed and the monks killed with extreme savagery. Many cases of espionage and treachery were reported and there was a suspicion that the population was well disposed to the invaders (Jecht 1911: 240). We may speculate that the Wends, who outside the towns in Lusatia were in the overwhelming majority, may have felt an affinity with the Czechs, but this cannot be substantiated. Nowhere in his detailed account of the Hussites in Lusatia does Jecht (1911) even mention them.

In late 1430 Hussite armies were again devastating parts of Upper Lusatia and in February 1431 they carried out another attack on Budissin. Approaching this time from the east, they took up positions behind the church of Our Lady and fired their cannon on the town, inflicting severe damage, but after a nine-hour engagement they were thrown back. Relief came on 26 February, when the attackers withdrew eastwards and occupied Löbau. The following year in April they were back in Lusatia and on 1 May they were outside the Wendish townlet of Wittichenau. By 8 May 1432, however, they had returned to Bohemia, never again to enter Upper Lusatian territory (Reymann 1902: 26–7; Jecht 1914: 43, 63, 124).

Peter Preischwitz

The success of the Hussite armies resulted largely from their innovatory military thinking. Firearms were still in their infancy, but the firearms that the Hussites had were advanced for their time. Their tactics too broke new ground, particularly their use of the *Wagenburg*, a stronghold on wheels consisting of a circle of waggons joined by chains. They were also helped by sympathizers among their enemies. The historiography of the GDR cast the Hussites in a progressive role and advanced the wishful view that the poorer people of Budissin sided with them (*Stawizny* 1: 133). A case in point from the 1429 siege is the treachery of Peter Preischwitz, the Town Clerk.

When they attacked Budissin on 14 October 1429, the Hussites were depending on his collaboration. By previous arrangement with them he had started a fire in the Reichengasse to confuse the defenders and had wetted the town's gunpowder supplies. So that the invaders could identify his house and spare it, when they sacked the town, he laid new tiles over each window. During the assault he communicated with the attackers by shooting arrows to which messages had been attached, but one of them was found by a loyal citizen and Preischwitz was arrested by the garrison commander Thimo von Colditz. Preischwitz had promised the Hussites that he would open the town's gates for them and for his services he was to receive a payment of 6000 Groschen and a pension of 600 Groschen (Reymann 1902: 25–6; Jecht 1911: 237; Needon 1930: 12). The fire he had started had consumed a quarter of the town. In Budissin on 3 February 1431, Preischwitz was dragged from the Market Square on a cowhide through the streets before being cut open, his heart flung in his face, and his body quartered. One quarter was hung over each of the town's four main gates. There is a tradition that his head was hung over the Nikolai Gate and that he is depicted in the carved stone head that may still be seen there (Reymann 1902: 26).

Such is the traditional account, but none of the sources for these events is older than the sixteenth century, except one original document, which records Preischwitz's confession. From this it emerges that the discovery of his treachery cannot date from 1429, but must have occurred later. It also shows that there must have been some second act of treason and that it was only during the investigation of this (probably under torture) that the earlier betrayal of October 1429 was revealed. This revelation also solves the mystery of the delay between the attack (14 October 1429) and the execution (3 February 1431). The confession reveals the names of some of Preischwitz's accomplices, including Friedrich von Hakenborn and Georg von Bieberstein, who, like some other noblemen, especially those hostile to the towns, sided with the Hussites on their progress through Upper Lusatia (Needon 1930: *passim*; Ruske 2002: *passim*).

Nowhere do the early records indicate whether Preischwitz was a German or a Wend, but a tradition has sprung up that he was a Wend. Since 1954 it has been claimed that he was Pětr z Přišec and came from Preuschwitz (Přišecy) on the southern outskirts of Budissin (*NBS*: s.v. *Přišec*). It is certainly true that he is nowhere described as a German and that, if he came from the Wendish village of Preuschwitz/Přišecy (as is surmised), he is likely to have been a Wend. In 1968 Jurij Wjela published an historical novella woven round the sparse data available (*Pětr z Přišec*).

The absence of the Wends from the minds of contemporary chroniclers and thus from the view of historians who have succeeded them is well demonstrated in the historiography of the Hussite movement. Much of the military action recounted by Richard Jecht in his history of the Hussite wars (Jecht 1911/1914) took place in villages that must have been populated predominantly or entirely by Wends, yet he never mentions them. Consideration of the ethnicity of the protagonists, however, is not fruitless. Although we know nothing of the Wends' feelings towards the Czechs, Czech solidarity with the Wends is revealed in a manifesto of the Prague Utraquists issued in 1420:

> Moreover, this group around the Pope has everywhere all around commanded our hereditary enemies the Germans to do unjust battle against us, and with false indulgences from suffering and sins has ingratiatingly provoked and inflamed them. Some, though they have no cause, are yet always enraged against our nation; and what they have done to our nation in the Rhin Basin, in the Meissen lands, and in Prussia, where they have evicted them, they mean to do to us and occupy the places of the evicted (*a jako sú našemu jazyku učinili w Rýnu, w Míšni, w Prusech, a jej wyhnali, takéž nám mienie učiniti a obsesti miesta wyhnancóv*).
>
> (*Akta* 1844: 212–13; Bartoš 1933: 254).

The allusion to the fate of the Czechs' northern neighbours, the Wends on the Rhin (a tributary of the Havel), in Mark Meissen, and further north in Prussia (the *Ordensstaat*), whom they call 'our nation', is unmistakable.

Because the story of the Hussites in Lusatia is haunted by rumours of spies, treachery, and the invaders' ability to find sympathizers in the territories they overran, the relative weight of ethnic and religious motives among the Hussites should not be underestimated. The case of Peter Preischwitz should be considered in this context.

The church before the Reformation

After he became a Christian, the Obodrite prince Gottschalk is reported to have often spoken in the churches, explaining in simple Slav words what the bishops and priests could only express in obscure terms (Helmold 1963: 100) and the church might well have learned from his example that there was something to be said for the use of the Wendish vernacular in its missionary activities. It is only among the Wends further south, however – the Sorbs – that we find specific references to linguistic considerations in the appointment of priests, and even here facts are scarce.

Whether the first priests in the parish of Göda, founded in 1076 by Bishop Benno (1066–1106), were Wends is not recorded, but the name of one Pribizlaus 'sacerdos de Godowe', mentioned in a document of 12 January 1216 suggests he was a Wend (Pietsch 2006: 38). Göda has the second oldest church in Lusatia. The oldest is in the capital of Upper Lusatia, Bautzen (called Budissin until 1868, though spellings with -au- are found as early as 1409) (Eichler 1985–2009, s. v.). Here the church of St John is said to have been founded by Bishop Eido I in 999. Bishop Bruno II, however, had the original church demolished and in 1213 began rebuilding it at his own cost. A collegiate chapter, incorporated with the church, emerged between 1213 and 1218. On 24 June 1221, the building had progressed sufficiently for it to be dedicated by Bruno to the Apostle Peter and John the Baptist, but since the end of the thirteenth century it has been known simply as the church of St Peter (Schlesinger 1962, 2: 257).

The collegiate church of St Peter was for centuries the town's only church. The existence of the church of Our Lady, built outside the town walls and intended for the rural population, is attested from 1293. The church of St Nicholas, also just outside the town walls, is known to have existed since the fifteenth century, but it was originally used only for funerals. The church of St Michael in Bautzen/Budissin, which has been the home of the Wendish Protestant congregation for nearly 400 years, was founded in the fifteenth century. According to legend, during the Hussite attack on Budissin in October 1429, the Archangel Michael was seen hovering over the defenders, assuring their success. Near this commanding spot, just outside the town walls on a bluff overlooking the Spree, a chapel was erected and consecrated by the Bishop of Meissen. It was dedicated to St Michael in gratitude for his intervention. The first documentary record of the chapel dates from 1473 (Reymann 1902: 347). In 1541 the Town Council started using the building for the town school (now Protestant) which had formerly been in the Franciscan Monastery.

In Cottbus it is only in 1451 that the existence of Wendish priests comes to light in a minor item in the will of Bishop Johann IV Hofmann of Meissen: 'Let the book *Katholicon*, which was prepared for me in Leipzig, be placed in some public place in Cottbus for the sake of the poor Slav priests, who, as they are generally ignorant or inexperienced, can thus have access to the said book for words and to improve their Latin' (*CDS*: 88, no. 1004).

The church in the Spreewald village of Briesen is first recorded in 1346, but there is no mention in pre-Reformation records of the ethnicity or language of either the priest or his parish, though the village was later revealed to be solidly Wendish and remained so to the end of the nineteenth century. The church preserves some remarkable medieval wall paintings, constituting precious evidence of religious life among the Wends before the Reformation. Discovered during restoration work during 1952–1956, they were probably executed in 1486, to judge by the date revealed on the north wall. Apart from Biblical scenes (including Judgement Day, Christ's Passion, and the Crucifixion), they portray

St Christopher. Contemporary figures, including monks, are also depicted. Of especial interest are the lay personages, among whom are an archer and two musicians. One of these is a Wendish bagpiper, the other a naked female playing a lute (Krautz 1974: 20–7).

Pomerania – Pomerelia – Cassubia

After 1181, when the Dukes of Pomerania swore fealty to the Holy Roman Emperor, German settlers began to cross the Oder into their domains. To their south, Konrad, Duke of Mazovia, was suffering from incursions by the heathen Prusai (speakers of the Baltic language, Prussian), who inhabited the land to the east of the lower Vistula. To help him in dealing with this problem he called on the knights of the Teutonic Order and by the 1230s an extensive military operation was under way. As the war proceeded, great fortresses (Marienburg, Elbing, Thorn, Allenstein, Marienwerder, and Königsberg) were founded and built by the knights in the wilderness where the Prusai roamed, leading to the formation of a new German state on the eastern Baltic. Though properly named the *Ordensstaat*, it soon came to be referred to by words derived from the name of its earlier inhabitants, the Prusai. In 1243 it was divided into four dioceses, those of Kulm (Chełmno), Pomesania, Warmia, and Sambia (Davies 2011: 342).

The *Ordensstaat* also occupied territory to the west of the lower Vistula, called *Pommerellen*, including the port of Gdańsk (Danzig). This is the area which since the nineteenth century has been associated with the Kashubs and we may surmise that they were already here in the time of the Teutonic State, though their presence is recorded only centuries later. When the light of history first shines on the Kashubs they are located further to the west in Pomerania. Their name is first recorded in its Latin form in a Papal Bull of 1238, where Duke Bogisław appears as 'dux Cassubie'. Thereafter, the feminine singular form *Cassubia*, denoting a territory, occurs regularly: 'regnum Datie, Cassubiam et Pomoraniam...' (1245). In 1289 Duke Przybysław is described as 'dominus terre Belgarth in Cassubia', indicating that the Kashubs were located as far west as Belgard on the River Persante (Labuda 2006: 38).

The interrelationship of the people and lands referred to by the terms *Cassubia* (*Cassubi*) and *Pomorania* (*Pomorani*) is uncertain. *Pomorani* is found earlier than *Cassubia*. It is possible that they both referred to the same people and area, but that *Cassubia* was the word used by the natives, whereas outsiders derived the descriptive *Pomorani* 'sea-side dwellers' from Slav *po* 'by, along' and *more* 'sea'. Polish chroniclers, by a process of loan translation, sometimes call them *Maritimi* (Labuda 2006: 38). The Dukes of Pomerania in the thirteenth and fourteenth centuries commonly included the words *Slavi/Wenden* and *Cassubia/Cassuben* in their titles. This is true, for example, of the trio Otto I (1279–1344), Wartisław IV (before 1290–1326), and Barnim III (c. 1300–1368). 'Nos Otto, Wartislaus et Barnym dei gracia duces Slavorum, Cassubiae atque Pomeraniae...' (1321) (*PUB*, 6: 33, no. 3495) is paralleled by 'Wy Otto, Wartislaff und Barnim von gotts gnadenn hertzogen der Wende, Cassuben und Pommeren' (1321) (*PUB*, 6: 63, no. 3535) (Labuda 2006: 39).

After around 1180 the land between the lower Vistula and the Leba formed a duchy ruled by Sambor I. Called *Pommerellen* 'Pomerelia', it was independent of *Pommern* 'Pomerania' and had its capital at Gdańsk. After 1294, when the house of Sambor died out, *Pommerellen* became the victim of aggression by Poland, Brandenburg, and Bohemia (whose king was a contender for the Polish throne). The Teutonic Knights were throughout most of the thirteenth century engaged in subduing the *Prusai* east of the Vistula, but they successfully completed these operations in 1283. Their newly conquered land, retaining the name of its inhabitants (the *Prusai*), became in Latin *Prussia* and German *Preussen*. The knights now turned their attention westwards and in 1308 seized *Pommerellen*. The aggressive policy of the Teutonic Order (or Prussians) motivated Poland and Lithuania to form an alliance and at the Treaty of Krewo in 1385 the two countries were united under Władysław Jagiełło.

In 1410 the power of the knights suffered a serious setback when they were defeated by the Polish–Lithuanian forces at the Battle of Grunwald (Tannenberg). Thus began the decline of the Order. In 1454 the noble and urban estates of Prussia rebelled against the Order and accepted Kazimierz Jagiellończyk, king of Poland, as their overlord (Köbler 1999, s.v. *Pommerellen*). The Thirteen Years' War (1454–1466) ended with the Second Peace of Thorn, whereby the Teutonic Order was forced to cede *Pommerellen* (the land between the lower Vistula and the River Lupow/Łupawa and home of the Kashubs) to Poland. The *Ordensstaat* (from now on Prussia) was divided into two. The western lands, called Royal Prussia, came under the Polish Crown, while those in the east with their capital in Königsberg continued to be ruled by the Order.

The death of the last speaker of the Wendish language on the island of Rügen occurred around 1404, as we know from the chronicler of Pomerania Thomas Kantzow (ca. 1505–1542):

> And around this time [1404] an old woman called Gulitzin is said to have died in the country on Rügen who was the last in the land there who could speak Wendish. For although this land long before was already wholly German, a few Wends had remained until this time who were in no hurry to die out. Now, however, and from this time on Pomerania and Rügen have been totally German and Saxon, and there is not a single Wend therein except for a region in Outer Pomerania (*Hinterpommern*) towards Prussia and Poland, where there are still a few Wends and Kashubs; but quite commonly they can speak German as well.
>
> (Kantzow 1908: 316, quoted by Olesch 1989a: 134).

Place names (toponyms)

In the thirteenth and succeeding centuries the sources continue to disclose reminders of the Wendish linguistic background. There are still no Wendish texts, but the language remains perceptible, though partly veiled, in the place names and personal names. They are still predominantly in the forms the invaders had adopted from the natives they had subdued, but after 1200 a growing tendency may be observed for the settlers to create new place names from German roots. In 1217 a *Friderichesdorf* is noted near Doberlug (subsequently *Friedersdorf*), named after a *Friedrich*. Another German personal name appears in *Witherholdeshagen* (1234), later *Werenzhain*, near Finsterwalde. *Lyndenowe* (1228) is derived from Ger. *Linde* 'lime-tree', *Frankynow* (1229), from the ethnonym *Franken* 'Franks' (Eichler 1975: 19 and s.v.). Some German names may be translations of earlier Wendish versions.

The Wendish word *gora* 'hill' is remarkably common. The capital of Rügen (today *Bergen*) is first recorded in 1289 as *Gora sive Mons in Ruya* 'Gora or the Hill on Rügen' (Trautmann 1949: 5). Of Gork (east of Oppelhain, south-east of Dobrilugk) the scribe writes:... *usque ad locum, qui Slavica lingua Gork, quod Theutonice Horst vocatur* 'as far as the place which in the Wendish language is called *Gork*, because it is *Horst* in German' (1298) (Eichler 1963: 72–3). Cf. Ger. *Horst* 'wooded hillock'. Common nouns denoting features of the landscape, such as hills, rivers, streams, ponds, lakes, fords, valleys, fields, meadows, villages, groves, stones, birds, and animals, appear regularly. The Wendish components are easily recognized, as in *Doberoztrowe* (1296), composed of *dober* 'good' and *ostrow* 'island' (Eichler 1985–2009, s.v. *Dobristroh*). Prepositions and prefixes are often perceptible, as in *Sabrod* (1380) < *za brodъ* 'beyond the ford', *Salesen* (1350) < **za lĕsъ* 'beyond the wood'.

The scribe's explanation of Prösa, south of Friedersdorf:... *usque Brüse quod apud nos Vort interpretatur* '...as far as Brüse, which by us is interpreted as Vort' (1298) (Eichler 1963: 72) conveys the locative case of the Slav word *brod* 'ford' (cf. LSo. *w broźe* 'in the ford'). This has been translated by Ger. *Furt* 'ford'. In another example the scribe interprets *prom* 'ferry': *navis quae archa vel prom dicitur* 'a ship which is called *arca* (vessel) or *prom*' (1325) (Eichler 1985–2009, s. v. *Promnitz*).

Particularly abundant in East-Elbian topography are names embodying the Wendish suffixes *-itz*, *-witz* (patronymics), or *–ow*, *-in* (possessives). A patronymic is a name with the sense 'son (or daughter) of' derived from a given name. For example, from the nickname *Krak* (*Wilhelmus Crac*, cf. Kash. *krak* 'raven', 1331, PUB, 8: 8) the patronymic *Krakewic* is derived (1392 *Johannes Krakeuitzen*, MUB, 22: 170) (Schlimpert 1978: s.v.); from the Christian name *Petr* the patronymic *Petrovic* (1233 *Wsemir Petricouic*, PUB, 1:160) (Schlimpert 1978: 100). The scribe may even elaborate, as in a 1335 record from Köslin: *Paulus miles dictus Barthcevitz* [...] *dilecti patris nostri Barthi militis* 'Paul the knight called Bartkewitz [...] of our beloved father the knight Bart' (Schlimpert 1978: 197). From its original sense 'son of', the patronymic ending grew to include 'followers of' and eventually could form derivatives to denote inhabitants of a particular place. The suffix *–witz/-itz* is thus also found in place names derived from appellatives, such as Ger. *Cunnewitz*, cf. So. *Konjecy* (< *koń* 'horse').

Names ending in *-itz* may alternatively come from feminine singulars ending in *-ica*: *Chemnitz* < **kamenica*, cf. So. *kamjeń* 'stone'. The town takes its name from the river *Chemnitz*, attested as feminine in 1174 in the context 'usque ad Kamenizam fluvium'. The same suffix may also come from the Slavonic masculine diminutive suffix *-c*, as in Ger.

Daubitz = So. *Dubc* (< *dub* 'oak'). The patronymic suffixes *-witz* and *-itz* appear in such place names as *Görlitz, Colditz, Drewitz, Oelsnitz, Ostritz, Strelitz, Dahlewitz, Tschernitz, Zschornewitz*, and many more. With few exceptions they are a sign of Slav origin.

The possessive adjectival suffixes *-ow* and *-in* are exemplified in *Gatow* (Gotowe 1351), *Beeskow* (Bezekowe 1263), *Pankow* (Panckow 1438), *Berlin* (Braline 1215), and *Schwerin* (Zverin 1171). These are formed from both personal names and appellatives and are usually fossilized in their masculine nominative singular form. Thus *Beeskow* is formed from *bezk* 'elder-berry (diminutive)'. Since medieval times both these suffixes have been subject to sporadic modification, Wendish adjectival *-in* being reinterpreted as the German plural ending *-en*, while *-ow* has often been equated with Ger. *-au* 'meadow'. *Cottin* (1374) became *Kotten*, *Lubin* (1150) became *Lübben*, *Turgowe* (1243) became *Torgau*, and *Spandowe* (1232) became *Spandau* (Eichler 1985–2009, s. v.; Trautmann 1948: 85). Conversely, the suffix *-ow* was capable of attachment to a German root, as in *Lyndenowe* (1228) from Ger. *Linde* 'lime'.

In the ending *-ow* in modern German, the *w* is silent. *Gatow, Pankow*, and *Wustrow*, for example, are pronounced as if they were written respectively *Gatoh, Pankoh*, and *Wustroh*. This discrepancy requires a special note in the rules of German spelling: 'in most German names ending in -ow the w is silent: Bülow ['by:lo], Teltow ['tɛlto]' (Duden 1974: 102). There is a Wendish explanation. Despite the German change from bilabial /w/ to labio-dental /v/ in the thirteenth century (Kienle 1960: 119) and the consequent disappearance of the diphthong *-oŭ* from the sound system, traditional spellings with *-ow* were retained. German phonetic *-oŭ* became *-ō*. Wends in their own language naturally continued and continue to pronounce *-ow* as *-oŭ*, and even as late as the mid-twentieth century, in the German spoken by Lusatian Wends, the substitution of diphthongs for long vowels could still be observed: for example, *Browt* for *Brot* 'bread', *Mownat* for *Monat* 'month' (Michałk and Protze 1967:28, [1974]: 50).

Because the Wendish components in place names remained largely incomprehensible to Germans, there has since the Middle Ages been a tendency to massage ostensibly senseless Slav components until they begin to make sense. As we have seen, the Slav adjectival ending *-in* makes less sense to a German speaker than the German plural ending *-en*; the Slav ending *-ow* gains meaning if replaced by German *-au* (cf. *Aue* 'meadow'). Similarly, Wendish *dober* 'good' may make better sense as German *ober* 'upper'. A village to the north-east of Merseburg, first recorded in 1246 as *Dobertawe*, had by 1545 become *Obertau*.

The German medieval diphthongizations (*i* > *ei, u* > *au*) naturally affected not only German but also Wendish place names previously adopted by German. The town first recorded in the phrase *in urbe Libzi vocata* 'in the town called Libz' (1012/18) is later noted in *usque Liptzk Slavorum civitatem pervenit* 'he went as far as Liptzk, a city of the Slavs' (1193). In the fifteenth century the diphthong appears: *Leipczke* (1430) and *Leipczigk* (1459) (Eichler 1985–2009: s.v.); today it is *Leipzig*. The name of the *lipa* 'lime-tree' is well represented in East German toponym: also in *Leipa* (north of Torgau), *Leippe* (USo. *Lipoj*, west of Hoyerswerda). Although *Budissin* retained this form of its name officially until 1868, when it became *Bautzen*, colloquial diphthongal variants had been in use since the fifteenth century (*Bawdissin* 1419).

Scholarly interest in the Slav etymologies of the place names of East Germany goes back at least to the seventeenth century, but the definitive twentieth-century treatises on the subject are Trautmann (1948/1949/1950) and Eichler (1985–2009), which complement each other. Trautmann covered the Polabian names (*Elb- und Ostseeslavisch*) in the north and established a boundary between them and the Sorbian names further south. Sorbian names are dealt with by Eichler. The border runs along the northern perimeters of Kreise Oschersleben, Wanzleben, Schönebeck, Zerbst, Roßlau, Wittenberg, Jessen, Herzberg, Luckau, Lübben, Beeskow, and Eisenhüttenstadt (Eichler 1985–2009, 1: 9).

Personal names (anthroponyms)

Whether Wendish or German, a medieval inhabitant of Trans-Elbia normally had only one name, a baptismal name. A patronymic or a nickname might be added to facilitate identification, but these were not inherited. Eventually, patronymics, nicknames, and even baptismal names developed into surnames, retained from one generation to the next, but there is no evidence of this before the seventeenth century (Wenzel 1987–1994, 1: 15). Names of the pre-Christian type remained predominant until the fourteenth century (Schlimpert 1978: 181–5): for example, Budislav (1374–1382 *Bodeslaw*), Luboslav (1276 *Lubezlao cellerario nostro de Lukkowe*), Dobromysl (1430 *Dobermußel*), and they were often abbreviated: for example, Buda (1416 *Bude*, 1430 *Buda*). Eventually, only the abbreviations survived. By the fifteenth century the full form *Budislav* is no longer attested, but the short forms are common: Buda (1416 *Bude*, 1417 *Buden*, 1432 *Bauda*, 1433 *Buda*, 1430 *Buda*), Budach (1465 *Bawdach*), Budak (1456 *Bawdag*), Budaš (1411 *Budaczsch*), and Budiš (1359 *Budisch*). Bronisław survives both in full (1550 *Bruntzlaw*) and abbreviated as Broniš (1440 *Bronis*, 1445 *Bronis*, 1449 *Bronisch, Dy Brönischynne*).

Isolated cases apart, it is only after 1300 that names of saints or Biblical figures become traditional among the Wends (Meschgang 1973: 155). With the adoption of Christian names and the imposition of a German church and secular administration many of the traditional Slav names disappeared; but Wendish Christian names were still distinct. Examples (mostly in abbreviated or hypocoristic form) are:

1. From Georgius: Jurik (1359 *Juryg von Molysschewicz*, 1400 *Jurig*), Juriš (1407 *Guritzsch*, 1426 *Jurisch*, 1429 *Ghurisch*, 1431 *Jurisch, Jhurisch Kunrad* 1455), Joriš (1374–1382 *Joriz*, 1440 *Jorisch Hommack*), Jorš (1374 *Jorz*), Jurk (1474 *Jurge*, 1482 *Jurg*).

2. From Elisabeth: Betka (1414 *Betka von Egenitz, Äbtissin*), Habeta (1476 *Habeta Gelnitz*).

3. From Johannes: Hanuš (1358 *Hannus Selege*, 1359 *von Hannus Hunlyn*), Jan (1359 *Jane, der do wonyt in Tichnicz hofe*, 1363 *Jan Zeysch*, 1393 *Jan Wudenik,*

1416 *Jan Czornag*), Jank (1374–1382 *Janc et Matei*, 1374–1382 *Matei der Jankinne*, 1473 *Jank Rademacher*), Jenč (1359 *Pecz Gencz brudir*, 1359 *Jentsch Pistori*), Jenš (1334 *von Jenschen von Rebsitz gekauft*, 1424 *scabini Jenschin*).

4. From Katharina: Kača (1437 *Kaßſche Jorynne*, 1439 *Kasche Jorin, Katczsche Jorin*, 1440 *Katczsche Mythawa*).

5. From Martinus: Měrćin (1440 *Mertczschin Raßig zu Rademeßdorff*), Měrćink (1451 *mit Mertschincken*).

6. From Stephanus: Šćěpan (1381 *Szepan Radeken son*, 1453 *Tschepan*, 1474 *Zczepan*, 1485 *Czyepann Sowa*, 1494 *Schipan Sowa*).

After 1400, as the sources increasingly reveal the existence of people low in the social scale, the use of bynames and nicknames grows more apparent (Wenzel 1987–1994, 1: 19). They can be categorized as patronymic, occupational, habitational, descriptive, toponymic, anecdotal, and so on and may provide early evidence of Wendish common nouns and adjectives. Occupational names, for example, reveal a specific slice of the Wendish vocabulary: Čolmar (1432 *Colmer*, 1439 *Ilße Czolmerynne*, 1463 *Czolmer*; cf. LSo. *cołmaŕ* 'waterman'), Ćěsla (1423 *Tscheschla*; cf. USo. *ćěsla* 'carpenter'), Kmeć (1466 *Kmetz*; cf. USo. *kmjeć* 'farmer'), Krawc (1374–1382 *Kraucz*; cf. USo. *krawc* 'tailor'), Kuchar (1489 *Kuchar*; cf. USo. *kuchar* 'cook'), Kowal (1371 *Kobal*; cf. LSo. *kowal* 'blacksmith'), Kupc (1463 *Kupczs*; cf. USo. *kupc* 'merchant'), Rybak (1376 *Rybag*, 1475 *Ribagk*, 1488 *Rybagkynne*; cf. USo. *rybak* 'fisher').

Among bynames denoting social status are Budar (1433 *Budar*; cf. Uso. *budar* 'cottager') and Starosta (1359 *Starast, Staras*, 1374–1382 *Starasta*, c. 1400 *Thomas starasta*; cf. LSo. *starosta* 'elder, headman'). Habitation names are Brězan (1374–1382 *Presan*, 1448 *Bresan*; cf. USo. *brěza* 'birch'), Delan (1416 *Delan*; cf. USo. *delan* 'lowlander'), Kerk (1434 *Kergk*; cf. USo. *kerk* 'bush').

The following are nicknames related to physical attributes or character: Baran (1443 *Peter Paran*, 1474 *Baran*; cf. LSo. *baran* 'ram'), Baranic (1400 *Baranicz*; 'son of Baran'), Bobr (1420 *Bober*, 1484 *Bober*; cf. USo. *bobr* 'beaver'), Broda (1426 *Broda*, 1436 *Broda* 1463 *Brode*; cf. LSo. *broda* 'beard'), Jagoda (1381 *Jagede*, 1487 *Jagoden*; cf. LSo. *jagoda* 'berry', Kuźer (1414 *Kuser*, 1451 *Kuser*; cf. LSo. *kuźeŕ* 'curl', Kwič (1405 *Quitzsch*, 1470 *Quicz*, 1471 *Qwitscz*; cf. USo. *kwič* 'cloak'), Kij (1457 *Kye*; cf. USo. *kij* 'stick'), Kuna (1420 *Kuna*, 1489 *Kuna*; cf. USo. *kuna* 'marten'), Rak (1359 *Rag*, 1381 *Raken*, 1451 *Ragk*, 1498 *Raack*; cf. LSo. *rak* 'crab').

CHAPTER 3
REFORMATION 1500-1600

Town and country

By the beginning of the sixteenth century the tide of German colonization had risen far and wide over the former area of Wendish habitation. There now remained only a diffused scattering of Wendish settlements – a Wendish archipelago in an ethnically German ocean. The largest and most robust of the Wendish islands was located roughly between Cölln-Berlin and Dresden (north to south) and Wittenberg and the River Oder (west to east). Covering about 15,000 square kilometres, it was centred on Lower Lusatia and embodied the whole of that margraviate, including the Cottbus Circle (*Kreis Cottbus*), a Brandenburg exclave. This compact Wendish heartland further included the greater part of Upper Lusatia, portions of the Electorates of Saxony and Brandenburg, and a small slice of the Duchy of Silesia. Each of the two margraviates was ruled by its Estates under the overlordship of the king of Bohemia. The parts of the heartland in Saxony were in the Meissen Circle (*Meissener Kreis*) and the Electoral Circle (*Kurkreis*) (the latter so named by the Elector Friedrich III the Wise because it included his residence at Wittenberg) (see Map 3.1).

Map 3.1 Main compact Wendish zone in the sixteenth century.

The Slav inhabitants of most of the compact zone were the people we would now call Sorbs. They called themselves in their own language by versions of the noun *Serb* and its corresponding adjective *serbski* (as we know from the few occasions when it appears in sixteenth-century Wendish sources). Although their homeland is denoted in Latin sources as *Sorabia* and in German as *die Wendei*, these two terms are not synonymous, for not all Wends were Sorbs. On their western and northern peripheries the Sorbs had in the Middle Ages been bounded by other Wendish tribes (Lutizi, Veleti, Obodriti, Hevelli), whose languages differed from Sorbian, as is revealed by the place names. This linguistic type (called Lechitic) included all the Wendish languages except Sorbian. For this reason we shall resist the temptation to apply the adjective Sorbian to the whole zone and call it instead the compact Wendish zone. In the east in the vicinity of Krossen, the Wendish language was contiguous with Polish. Outside the compact zone there were further Wendish islands and atolls (all Lechitic) strewn across north Germany between Lüneburg and the lower Vistula.

In the compact zone in the sixteenth century there were more than 600 Wendish rural communities (*Landgemeinden*). The Germans lived mainly in the towns, but all the towns were small, and many had substantial numbers of Wendish inhabitants. The capital of Lower Lusatia, Lübben, had a population of between 1,500 and 2,000 (*Stawizny*, 1: 152). Its largest town, Guben, was perhaps twice that size. It is estimated that at this time 80 per cent of the population of Lower Lusatia was Wendish. Faced with a native population of these proportions, the German colonial authorities were not yet ready to contemplate its Germanization. It was only in the mid-seventeenth century that things in this respect began to change (Mětšk 1969: 46 n. 55).

A few miles beyond the northern edge of the Wendish heartland, in the land-locked Electorate of Brandenburg, stood Cölln, an urban settlement on an island in the lower Spree, where in the closing years of the fifteenth century the Elector, Johann Cicero (1455–1499), had established his residence. On the opposite bank lay Berlin, a similar settlement, which since 1432 had formed a single municipality with Cölln. Together they constituted the embryonic capital of Brandenburg, but until 1732 it was not from Berlin but from Cölln-an-der-Spree that electoral edicts were issued and dated. The number of inhabitants of the conurbation in the sixteenth century was between 10,000 and 12,000. By European standards it was small. For comparison, Cologne in the sixteenth century had around 40,000 inhabitants, London about 150,000, and Paris about 210,000 (Clark 2006: 4; *Cologne* 2014; *Paris* 2014).

Relative to other Transelbian towns, however, Cölln-Berlin was not particularly small. The second largest in Brandenburg was Frankfurt-an-der-Oder, whose population at this time was around 5,500. In the neighbouring electorate of Saxony the Elector resided until 1547 at Wittenberg, where the number of inhabitants was a little in excess of 3,000. In Dresden, where the Elector moved his residence that year, it was no greater (Mětšk 1962c/1981: 95; *Dresden* 2014; *Frankfurt* 2014). The description of Berlin as 'an overgrown military camp – till the eighteenth century not even overgrown' (Taylor 1945: 26) is only a slight exaggeration; it was in the sixteenth century still a small, remote colonial outpost. The shades of the Hevelli were still evoked by the proximity of living Wendish communities.

That the Elector of Brandenburg at the end of the sixteenth century still lived within walking distance of Wendish territory emerges from the travelogue of the student Michael Francus, who on 9 August 1591 rose from his bed in Berlin at 4 am and walked south for some 32 kilometres (20 miles) until he arrived at Zossen on the River Notte. He noted in his diary: 'beyond the little river Notte the German language is replaced completely by the Wendish' (Mětšk 1965a: 12).

An earlier affirmation of the Wendish presence on the south-east outskirts of Berlin is a 1565 autobiographical note of the Wittenberg ordinand Valentin Molitor (i.e. *młynik* 'miller'), stating that in October that year he 'was called by Mr Christopher Schenken to the office of pastor of the Wendish-language church in the village of Gräbendorf' (Buchwald 1895: 53 no. 545; Muka 1896: 125). In the twentieth century, Gräbendorf lay only 25 kilometres (15 miles) south-east of Berlin's perimeter. To the west of Cölln lay Spandow (later Spandau), a townlet grown out of a fortress, where the continuing presence of Wends is clearly implied by the recurrent inclusion in the guild statutes of the shoemakers and tanners (1536, 1540, 1585) of a paragraph banning Wends from membership (W. Vogel 1960: 124). The Wends here were linguistically Lechitic and thus (we may deduce) not Sorbs.

Having evolved, in most cases, out of German camps or fortresses planted in recently subdued Wendish territory, the Transelbian towns were generally slow to expand. Economic conditions favoured urban growth, but immigration from nearby villages was hindered, in the first place, by the rigidity of the feudal order and, second, by attempts to exclude Wends from trade guilds and citizenship. Some towns consequently remained German outposts in a Wendish landscape, beleaguered by morose Wendish peasants, on whom they were dependant for food and other supplies. Most towns, however, did not fit this picture. They did not all have anti-Wendish regulations and even those that did usually interpreted them liberally. There is thus ample evidence of the presence of Wends among the inhabitants of most towns inside the compact Wendish zone. Sometimes they even predominated. That it was possible to become a citizen of a town without even being able to speak German is demonstrated by the surviving sixteenth-century Sorbian texts of oaths of allegiance to be sworn on admission to citizenship (of Budissin 1532 and of Lieberose c. 1550) (Schuster-Šewc 1967a: 33, 415). The terms *wendischer Flecken* and *wendisches Städtlein* 'Wendish townlet' are commonly encountered in the sources.

Where the German townsmen were in a minority, they were prone to assimilation by the Wendish majority and so found it increasingly difficult to enforce the regulations intended to keep the Wends in their place. Conflicting motives resulted in inconsistent decisions. In 1516 the city fathers of Frankfurt/Oder received a complaint from the local guilds, reproaching them for granting citizenship to Wends, while the guilds were doing their best to maintain the ethnic barrier (W. Vogel 1960: 127–8). The dividing line between the ethnic categories 'Wend' and 'German' was sometimes blurred. A Wend unable to speak German was called *stockwendisch*, but in some towns, where the presence of Wends was taken for granted, the words *wendisch* and *Wende* might alone be sufficient to mean 'ignorant of German'. In Schlieben, for example, where there is not much doubt that most inhabitants were Wends but could speak German, the gratuitous use of the adjective in a reference to a 'wendischen Brose' (Ambrosius) implies ignorance of German, as does an allusion to the burial of 'eine alte Wendin' in Sonnenwalde (Mětšk 1962d/1981: 160). A clear example comes from the church visitation to Wahrenbrück in 1529, which left the following instruction: 'Because there are some women who are Wendish and belong to the parish, and the pastor cannot speak Wendish, he shall take pains to obtain the ten commandments, the creed and the Lord's Prayer in Wendish and to read the same aloud and teach them' (Sehling 1902: 687).

In the bigger towns (Budissin and Luckau are examples) the Wends resided in separately designated Wendish streets and Wendish quarters (*Wendische Viertel*), but whether this reflects a system of ghettoization is unclear. Neither Wendish citizens nor inhabitants of the Wendish quarters suffered any civil disabilities, so far as is known, and cases are recorded even of residents of the Wendish quarter who became town councillors. Ethnic conflicts occurred from time to time, but grievances and disturbances were usually settled by legal process, and by no means always to the disadvantage of the Wends. Among the surviving documents related to ethnic tension is a treaty of 1542 between the Wendish and German citizens of Luckau (Mětšk 1968: 57–62). The topography of many Transelbian towns (including Dresden) retained the word *wendisch* centuries after their Wends had disappeared.

The employment of interpreters in Wendish towns is significant. The accounts of wages paid to the gatekeepers of Wahrenbrück and Liebenwerda in the first half of the sixteenth century took into account their duties as Wendish interpreters (*wyndische Interpreten*) and for translating (*vor Tolmetschungk*). Their services may have been needed in connection with the role of towns in supplying escorts for travellers (Mětšk 1962d/1981: 160). Most Wends, however, did not live in towns, and in the country the contrast between the life of a Wendish serf and his German lord was stark. Wendish peasants were habitually regarded by their masters as pig-headed, rebellious, and barely human. An impression of this attitude can be gained from a discussion between representatives of the church authorities and the local junkers, during a visitation to the Herrschaft of Baruth in 1555, as to whether 'their serfs were not swine and cows but human beings' (Mětšk 1962d/1981: 168).

Inside the margraviate of Lower Lusatia and surrounded by it on all sides was the Brandenburg exclave of Kreis Cottbus (see Maps 4.1 and 6.1). Here the German component in the population – between 10 and 15 per cent, including towns – was even smaller than in the margraviate (Mětšk 1962a: 17). The town of Cottbus had about 3,000 inhabitants, including a large number of Wends. Further south, however, in Upper Lusatia, German settlers already outnumbered the Wends. Budissin, the capital, which had 5,800 inhabitants in 1568 (Bahlcke 2001: 112), was very unusual in having a history as a town going back to the time before the German conquest (it is mentioned in Thietmar's Chronicle). Although predominantly German, it had a sizeable Wendish minority, as did Kamenz (about 2,600 inhabitants) and Löbau (1,500 inhabitants). Whereas around the year 1450 settlers had still constituted almost half the population of the margraviate (Mětšk 1968: 100), by the mid-sixteenth century, when it had a total

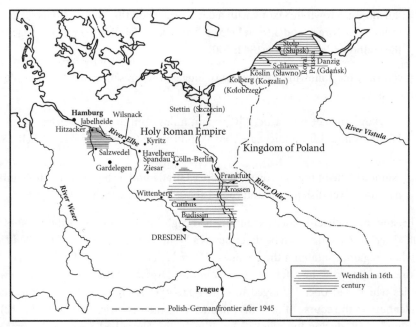

Map 3.2 Zones of Wendish survival in the sixteenth century.

population of approximately 146,000, no more than 50,000 (little more than a third) were Wends (Blaschke 1967/2000: 120–1). In the south-west the compact Wendish zone extended into the Electorate of Saxony to within about 15 miles of Dresden. The eastern extremity of their territory reached beyond Upper Lusatia into Kreis Priebus of the Silesian Principality of Sagan (Mětšk 1968: 20–1) (Map 3.1).

In the predominantly German eastern part of Upper Lusatia lay Görlitz, its largest town, with 8,685 inhabitants in 1586 (Bahlcke 2001: 112), almost all of whom were Germans. The populations of the townlets (*Städtlein* or *Flecken*) were often measured not in thousands but hundreds. Such were, for example, Peitz (700–800 inhabitants) in Kreis Cottbus (Mětšk 1962a: 17), Liebenwerda (850) in the Kurkreis (Mětšk 1962d/1981: 157), and in Upper Lusatia: Hoyerswerda (550) (Blaschke 1998/2000: 229), Wittichenau (under 1000), and Muskau (under 1000) (Blaschke 1967/2000: 130).

The picture of the German town in a setting of Wendish villages is exemplified in the account of Johann Lindner (or Tilianus; *Linde = tilia* 'lime-tree'), also known as Monachus Pirnensis (the Monk of Pirna), recording his travels in Upper and Lower Lusatia and parts of Saxony around 1530. The Wends were not of particular interest to him, but in his laconic sketches of the towns they occasionally put in cameo appearances.

1. 'Ruhland, a townlet and castle in the Wendland, 2 [German] miles from Senftenberg' (Schelz 1842: 329). (A German mile is approximately five English miles.)

2. 'Guben…has surrounding it much wine-growing and many Wendish people' (Schelz 1842: 303).

3. 'Eilenburg, a town in Saxony with a decent castle on the Mulde, 2 [German] miles from Torgau and 3 from Leipzig, has many Wendish people in villages in the countryside...' (Schelz 1842: 300).

By contrast, the following formulations suggest the presence of Wends inside the town walls:

1. 'Storkow, townlet and castle, 2 [German] miles from Beeskow, 3 from Fürstenwalde, 3 from Luckau,...has Wendish and German people' (Schelz 1842: 334).
2. 'Kamenz, one of the Six Towns in Upper Lusatia under the Crown of Bohemia... has many Wendish people and round about in villages' (Schelz 1842: 296–7).

The student Michael Francus spent the first night of his journey as the guest of the Bailiff (*Vogt*) in Zossen, which he describes as a Wendish townlet (*wendisches Städtlein*). The whole region, containing the counties (*Herrschaften*) of Zossen, Teupitz, Bärwalde, Storkow, and Beeskow, he refers to as the Wendish District of the Kurmark. These were counties which had once belonged to Lower Lusatia, but had gradually come under Brandenburg in the course of the fifteenth and sixteenth centuries (Mětšk 1965a: 12).

Around 1568, during the reign of Joachim II, the Notte had been made navigable and locks had been constructed, but the landscape remained uninviting. 'This Wendish District is a swampy and sandy land with meagre villages and a few meagre Wendish towns' is Francus's verdict (Mětšk 1965a: 28, Anhang 4). Legal status rather than size was the main distinguishing feature between townlets and villages. The populations of Zossen, Teupitz, Bärwalde, and Storkow are estimated in hundreds, but Beeskow may have had as many as 1,600 inhabitants (Mětšk 1965a: 42). Zossen, Teupitz, Storkow, and Buchholz were, according to Francus, 'all of them completely Wendish', though the Monk of Pirna had sixty years earlier recorded Storkow as ethnically mixed, the home of 'windisch und dewczß volk'. The discrepancy suggests that the Germans had been prone to assimilation.

Francus discovered that members of the Beeskow guilds were quixotically still clinging to the paragraphs in their statutes requiring members to be of German birth, 'though their wives can barely understand a word of German'. On the other hand, there was no doubt about the ethnicity of the landowning class or of their attitude to the natives: 'Totally German in this Wendish District, however, are the nobility and the junkers, who look on their Wendish serfs as so many head of cattle and they hate them very much' (Mětšk 1965a: 34–5, Anhang 5). After more conversation over a midday meal in the Bailiff's house Michael Francus resumed his journey south and by nightfall, having crossed the border into the Saxon Electoral Circle, he reached Baruth, another Wendish townlet, where he found an inn to spend the night (Mětšk 1965a: Anhang 5).

The following year (1592) Francus was again travelling in the Wendish zone to the south of Berlin, this time in the Brandenburg exclave Kreis Cottbus. He first visited the townlet Peitz, which he found inhabited by poor, brutalized people, whose livelihoods had been ruined by the presence of the fortress. The latter, built (or re-built) some thirty years earlier by the forced labour of some four or five hundred people, was the only imposing building. The church was a simple structure, to which, he said, less industry and expense had been devoted than to the castle and fortress. Setting out from Peitz for Cottbus, Francus found he could make progress through the marshes only by keeping to the dikes (Mětšk 1962a: 24).

Cottbus had been previously described by the Pirna Monk as being surrounded by Wends (*hat... vil Windisch volk vmher*), but Michael Francus merely characterized it as a Wendish town. This discrepancy too suggests a recent assimilatory shift. Francus found that the town contained a church where preaching took place in Wendish. The preacher turned out to be his old friend Martinus am Ende, who provided him with accommodation. From here Francus passed through various Wendish villages and the townlet Drebkau before arriving in the Wendish village of Bahnsdorf, where he put up for the night (Mětšk 1962a: 25).

A persistent bone of contention in the towns was guild membership. A 1525 decree of the Elector Joachim I (1499–1535) aimed to reconcile the conflicting claims of the four German guilds (cloth-makers, shoemakers, bakers, and butchers), on the one hand, and 'our citizens of the Wendish nation', on the other. It confirmed the ancient statutes of the guilds, but also ordained that the Wends had the right to see and read the 'letters and privileges' of the guilds. It dismissed Wendish challenges to the guilds' statutes, but sought reconciliation, first, by ordaining that they be permitted to see the guild's books 'as often as necessary' and, second, by declaring that the Wendish wives of guild members should have the same status as their husbands. Consequently, their sons should be deemed qualified for entry to one of the guilds (Mětšk 1962a: 22). Fourteen years later (1539) Margrave Johann of Brandenburg removed restrictions on the entry of Wends to the Cottbus linen-weavers' guild without regard to parentage but subject to payment of special fees. Even in 1549, however, there were still disputes in Cottbus between Germans and Wends over entry to the guilds of furriers and tailors, as well as over the right to brew beer (Mětšk 1962a: 22–4).

Maps

The sixteenth century saw the publication of the first printed maps showing the location of Wendish habitation. The best known and most instructive of them is that of Bartholomäus (or Barthel) Scultetus, a Lusatian townsman, born in Rabenberg on the outskirts of Görlitz. In 1557, at the age of seventeen, he matriculated at Wittenberg University and moved in 1559 to Leipzig University, where he was taken under the wing of Johannes Humelius (or Hommilius), from whom he learned geodesy and cartography. He took the degree of magister at Wittenberg in 1564 before going on to lecture on geometry at Wittenberg and Leipzig. Among his pupils was Tiho Brahe, who became his firm friend and was destined for fame as an astronomer.

Scultetus returned to Görlitz in 1567 and three years later became a teacher of Mathematics at the Görlitz Gymnasium. He had discussions with Bishop Johannes Delphinus, the Apostolic Legate, and with Bishop Lambert on the proposed reform of the calendar. He held various municipal offices. The successful introduction (at Emperor

Rudolf II's command during 1583–1584) of the Gregorian calendar in Upper Lusatia and the other Bohemian lands is attributed to Scultetus. Because the reform had originated in Rome, Saxony decided against it, and, as her border with Upper Lusatia sometimes ran through Wendish parishes (e.g. Göda), the resultant chronological hiatus must have brought new doubts to parishioners still struggling with the new religion. In 1584 Scultetus resigned his post at the Gymnasium to devote himself to municipal matters and died in 1614 at the age of 74 (Reuther 1955/1956: 1147).

The suggestion that Scultetus should make a map of Upper Lusatia came from his friend Christoph Manlius (1546–1578). The Upper Lusatian Estates also expressed an interest and Jakob von Salza provided 160 thalers from the municipal exchequer. During the years 1581–6 Scultetus carried out eleven field trips in Upper Lusatia, each lasting several days, but it is thought likely that he also gathered some of his data indirectly from informants. The map, entitled 'Lusatia Superior', appeared as a woodcut in 1593. Only a few copies have survived into the twenty-first century. It was the first map of Upper Lusatia based on empirical observations. Among its most valuable features is a dotted line, labelled 'Deutsch/Wendisch', dividing German from Wendish territory.

When a few gaps in the line are made good, it may be seen to follow the following route: from west of Ruhland, where the Sieggraben joins the Schwarze Elster, going south-westwards through Kroppen (Reichanau near Königsbruck, Brauna), Liebenau, Zschornau, north of Kamenz and Elstra, Glaubitz, Potschapplitz, Medewitz, Gaußig, (Rodewitz, Bederwitz, along the Cunewald valley, north of Schönbach), into the Upper Spree area as far as Wendisch-Kunnersdorf, northwards past Ebersdorf, south of Wendisch-Paulsdorf, along a northwards-stretching S-shaped bow through Sohland am Rotstein, Dobschütz, Arnsdorf, Krischa, Gebelzig, Maltitz, including Großradisch, past Uhmannsdorf, Daubitz, Kleinpriebus to Priebus, along the Neisse north-westwards to Wendisch-Mosta, Dubrau, to Zeisdorf (Reuther 1953b: 158–9). Because the main purpose of the map was evidently to warn German travellers of areas where an interpreter might be needed, partly Germanized (hence unproblematic) Wendish villages were often shown on the German side of the ethnic line (Mětšk 1960b: *passim*).

There is no Lower Lusatian equivalent of the Scultetus map. Though maps of some other Wendish areas were published during the sixteenth century, none of them contains anything approaching the degree of detail supplied by Scultetus. The second edition of the *Kosmographie* of the Basle professor Sebastian Münster, published in 1550, contains a high-quality map of the Baltic coast between Rügen and Danzig, showing Pomerania's borders with the Altmark, the Neumark, and Poland. An area called 'Vandalia' is shown between the rivers Stolp and Leba, and a 'Cassubia' further to the west, but of Wends in Royal Prussia there is no indication at all (Bugenhagen 2008: 10–11).

Reformation

The mood of the age, embodying an appetite for learning, led to the foundation of schools, as well as two universities of particular significance for the Wends: Wittenberg

(1502) and Frankfurt/Oder (1506). The new hunger for knowledge was one of the germs of the Reformation, whose history, from its very beginning, was interwoven with the history of the Wends. Martin Luther (1483–1546) was born at Eisleben, west of the Saale, in the Duchy of Mansfeld. His childhood passed in Mansfeld (1484), Magdeburg (1497), and Eisenach (1498). From 1501 he attended the University of Erfurt and in 1505 entered the Augustinian monastery there.

All these locations were to the west of the Main Wendish Compact Zone, but in 1508 the 24-year-old Luther moved east and became a teacher at the University of Wittenberg. When the stronghold on the Elbe named Wittenberg was first recorded in 1180, it lay well inside Wendish territory, which at that time extended west as far as the Saale. Since 1293 it had been the residence first of the Dukes, then (from 1355) the Electors, of Saxony. At the end of the fifteenth century, the Elector Friedrich III the Wise (1463–1525; r. from 1486) built his palace here, constructed a bridge across the Elbe, and in 1502 founded a university, giving it the name Leucora (a Greek translation of *Witten-* 'white' and *-berg* 'hill'). Here in 1517 Martin Luther issued his 'Ninety-Five Theses upon Indulgences', allegedly by nailing them to the door of the church of All Saints, which served both palace and university (Cameron 1991: 100, 452–3; Scribner and Dixon 2003: 1). Situated close to the edge of the forest, Wittenberg, the cradle of the Reformation, was a frontier town inhabited mainly by German settlers. As the home of Lutheran doctrine, it thrust itself to the forefront of European politics, but the population of the town was still very small, and on the outskirts of the town there was still a Wendish presence. David Chytraeus (1530–1600), a leading light of the Reformation, who first came here in 1544, attended lectures by Luther, and lived in Melanchthon's house, wrote: '[...] at the present day along the whole course of the Elbe, in both Lusatias, near Meissen and Wittenberg (*prope Misnam & Witebergam*), and in the Duchy of Lüneburg there remain peoples who use the Wendish language' (Chytraeus 1593: 39; Mětšk 1963/1981: 73-4n.).

The area surrounding Wittenberg, notwithstanding its dignified title of 'Electoral Circle' (*Kurkreis*), commemorating the Electoral association, was sparsely populated and notoriously poverty-stricken. Only in the immediate vicinity of the town itself were there signs of a slight mitigation of the general economic misery. It had gained the official status of a town in 1293, but even at the beginning of the sixteenth century it was still 'more like an old village than a town' (Myconius 1543, cited in Mětšk 1962c/1981: 95). By 1520, however, the population had grown to around 3,000 and the presence of the university and the Electoral court imparted a modest distinction (Mětšk 1962c/1981: 95). Friedrich III in spring 1505 had engaged Lucas Cranach the Elder (1472–1553), one of the great artists of the Northern Renaissance, as court painter.

The German craft-guilds in Wittenberg, as in many other frontier towns, had rules excluding Wends from their membership. They were probably located in the southern and eastern suburbs, living partly from arable farming, but mainly from bee-keeping and fishing in the Elbe. Their presence in the nearby village of Kemberg is attested in 1513 by the existence here of separate German and Wendish tribunals in conformity with the rule in the *Sachsenspiegel* that Germans should not pass judgement on Wends and vice versa

(Mětšk 1962c/1981: 95–7). Wittenberg even had a Wendish name. On 11 August 1591, as the wandering student Michael Francus approached Wittenberg from the north-east, on the road from Zahna, passing 'through various German and Wendish villages', he noted that 'this town Weißenberg or Wittenberg – called Wytparck, however, by the Wends – lies more in the dale than on the hill, is finely built yet not very big, [and] is longer than it is broad' (Mětšk 1962c/1981: 96–7, nn. 9 and 20; Mětšk 1965a: Anhang 5).

The first Wends to be touched by Luther's doctrine will no doubt have been those standing below his pulpit in Wittenberg, but the news travelled fast to their compatriots further east in Upper Lusatia. On 24 January 1520, the Bishop of Meissen issued an order to his diocese condemning the new doctrine, but that same year in the Wendish parish church of Postwitz, just south of Budissin, the priest Paul Bosak was already preaching it and shortly thereafter he gave Communion to his parishioners in both kinds (Knauthe 1767: 218–19). This was notably early in the progress of the Reformation.

In 1527 the Lutheran Church was established as the state church of Saxony, and visitations of parishes throughout the Electorate were initiated. A visitation to the Wendish parish of Baruth in the Electoral Circle in 1529 found a pastor who had accepted the reformed religion but had little sympathy for his Wendish flock. He complained 'that in the villages there were many Wendish peasants, who were pig-headed, uncouth people, and although the gospel of the Lord had been preached in Baruth for some four years, the people nevertheless opposed it and refused to take the sacrament in both kinds'. The visitors instructed the pastor 'that henceforth he was to give no one the sacrament except in both kinds' (Sehling 1902: 524).

Wendish speakers were under-represented among the pre-Reformation clergy, so the new insistence on the vernacular meant that, in reformed Wendish parishes, there was an immediate shortage of Wendish-speaking pastors. The new university at Wittenberg proceeded to supply them. Some of them were ordained by Luther himself (Buchwald 1894: 4–12; Muka 1896:113). The sudden need for Wendish clergy and also the connection between the reforms and developing attitudes to education are revealed in a decree issued by the Upper Lusatian Estates after their St Elizabeth's Day Assembly in 1538:

> Particularly since in the country and in the towns hitherto we have had to suffer a great shortage of pastors and clergymen on account of the Wendish language, every serf shall be diligently admonished by his masters, and from the pulpit too, so that if anyone has a friend or sons who are proficient at school-work and quick to learn, then he or they should with the utmost diligence be kept at school and not be suffered to lack any possible financial support and promotion.

> (Knauthe 1767: 235; *Kurzer Entwurf* 1767: 9–10)

There was a good response from both the nobility and the urban patriciate. The Upper Lusatian Estates also decreed a lenient application of the laws of servitude in suitable cases, including release from the *adscriptio ad glebam* (*Kurzer Entwurf* 1767: 10).

In 1546 Luther died and the following year the Protestant forces of the Schmalkaldic League were defeated by the Emperor Charles V. Johann Friedrich the Magnanimous (*der Großmütige*), Elector of Saxony, who had led the League, was deprived of the electoral title (after being condemned to death and reprieved). Moritz, Duke of Albertine Saxony, in reward for having supported the emperor was promoted to Elector. During his Electorship (1547–1553), Moritz and his church council endowed four places for Wendish students as servitors at the Electoral School at Meissen and one place for the son of a Wendish clergyman (*Kurzer Entwurf* 1767: 10). In 1575 (during the reign of Elector August), further scholarships were established at the Electoral Schools (*Fürstenschulen*) at Meissen and Grimma for Wends aiming for a university education (Knauthe 1767: 238; Muka 1897b: 129).

Of the kind of men who responded to the call for new Wendish clergy in the reformed church something can be learned from the ordination records in the town parish church at Wittenberg, beginning in 1537, which often specify the ethnicity of the ordinand or of his parish (Buchwald 1894, 1895: *passim*; Muka 1896, 1897a, 1897b: *passim*). Most ordinands already had a profession before their arrival in Wittenberg, often a lay position connected with the church, such as sexton (*editus*), verger (*custos*), schoolmaster (*Schulmeister*), or scribe (*Schreiber*). Some reformist pastors, however, had been ordained before the Reformation, but converted to the new doctrine, such as Paul Bossack (at Postwitz by 1520), Johann Axt (Reichwalde by 1527), Bartel Span (Prietitz by 1532), Nicolaus Poster (Kittlitz by 1535), and Gregorius Kirst (Baruth by 1537) (Knauthe 1767: 218–22; *Kurzer Entwurf* 1767: 42, 54, 124). In Budissin the reformed doctrine was first preached in German by Michael Arnold in 1523, but he was replaced in 1527 by two (unnamed) 'new, but bold, learned preachers', one preaching in St Peter's in German, the other in St Nicholas's in Wendish. They are reported to have triumphed over the Franciscans in a disputation on the subject 'whether the mass is a sacrifice' (Knauthe 1767: 194). In Neschwitz the Reformation was introduced around 1550 by Peter Pelck, who had been Catholic priest here since 1536, but was evidently slow to make his mind up (*Kurzer Entwurf* 1767: 79). The last Wendish parish in Upper Lusatia to accept the new order was Gaußig, where the last Catholic priest Lucas Jentsch was still in office as late as 1575 (*Kurzer Entwurf* 1767: 46).

Many of the Wendish ordinations were carried out by Martin Luther, Johannes Bugenhagen, and other luminaries of the Reformation, including Paul Eber, who kept his own records with personal notes on individual ordinands. Explicit statements that the ordinands are going out to preach the gospel in Wendish are not uncommon. Simon Kschink of Cottbus, for example, is noted on 9 November 1561 as having been called to Ruhland 'to teach the gospel in the Wendish language (*ad docendum Euangelium lingua vandalica*) in the office of a deacon' (Buchwald 1895: 9, no. 155, XV; Muka 1896: 122).

It is obvious from the Wittenberg records that many of the ordinands were not graduates of Wittenberg University, or of any university, but had merely come there to be tested and ordained. In the case of those that are Wittenberg graduates, this fact is specifically stated, as in this 1543 entry: 'Sebastianus Matisschintz from Strade near Vetschau. Summoned from this University to Teupitzk to the priestly office' (Buchwald

1894: 34, no. 522). Some were graduates of other universities (Frankfurt/Oder, Leipzig, etc.). Comments of the type 'having studied at no university' (*in nulla versatus Academia*) or 'has not been at any university' (*in nulla academia fuit*) are common and may imply disapproval. The usual explanation was poverty. As Burchardus Leschka Cotbusianus in 1567 was forced to admit, 'after starting at Wittenberg, [...] when owing to lack of the necessities of life I could not continue my studies, I was called [...] to preach the gospel in the town of Elsterwerda. And after that I was sent to seek ordination [...]. On the day of Christ's Ascension in 1567 I was ordained' (Buchwald 1895: 79, no.706; Muka 1896: 127).

Some of the Wittenberg ordinands called to parishes in Brandenburg had studied at the University of Frankfurt/Oder, as did the majority of the Brandenburg clergy after the Elector's conversion became public knowledge in 1563 (Mětšk 1965a: 73). Once Frankfurt University had ceased to be a bastion of Catholicism, it found itself in competition with Wittenberg and, consequently, could not remain indifferent to the needs of Wendish parishes. The first known case of a Wendish Wittenberg ordinand who had studied in Frankfurt is that of Paulus Kuschius, who in 1566 was called 'that he might preach the gospel in the Wendish language' (*ut Evangelium doceat lingua vandalica*) in Teupitz (Buchwald 1895: 71, no. 666, XXVI; Muka 1896: 126; Mětšk 1965a: 73).

Records for graduations and ordinations from Frankfurt University are poor, but evidence that Wendish linguistic exercises were being conducted there around 1560 for ordinands expecting to work in Wendish parishes comes in a 1656 document announcing the revival of 'the Wendish-language training begun almost 100 years ago in this university by Gregorius Schwarmius of Senftenberg and protected then by the most illustrious professor Mr Andreas Musculus and continued afterwards with the authority of Mr Pelargus by Andreas Tharaeus of Muskau, Solomon Nicolaus, Andreas Clemannus, and many others' (Mětšk 1965a: 73, 1976; Teichmann 1998: 169; cf. Chapter 4, p. 139).

In view of the emergency, academic standards were relaxed. For instance, to the record dated 21 March 1562 of the ordination of Peter Steffen and Marcus Adam, both from Wittichenau, this note has been added by Eber:

> These two men, Wends by birth, mere youths, and having attended no university and not well taught, were nevertheless admitted to ordination, since it had been explained to us that very few priests skilled in the Wendish language can be had there, and they themselves had promised to return at Michaelmas so that they might be examined again and their progress tested.

> (Buchwald 1895: 11, nos. 186–7, XVII; Muka 1896: 122)

One entry suggests that for a Wendish ordinand even knowledge of Latin was dispensable, so long as his German was adequate: 'he could not reply in Latin, but [did so] fluently in German – to the office of deacon' (Buchwald 1895: 8, no. 151, XV; Muka 1896: 121). Another says that the ordinand's work should be limited to dealing with Wends. To an entry beginning 'I Lucas Schimantz from Reppen, called to the ministry as a deacon in

Vetschau a. d. 1564 on the day of the purification of St Mary' this note has been added by Eber: 'having attended the University of Leipzig for three years and a further five years the school at Vetschau, a townlet in Lower Lusatia – to the office of deacon to teach in Wendish only – a young Wend and badly taught' (*ut tantum vandalice doceat. – Vandalus iuvenis et male informatus*) (Buchwald 1895: 29, no. 367, XXI; Muka 1896: 123). The qualification 'to teach in Wendish only' suggests Schimantz has been reluctantly ordained as a concession to the pressing needs for Wendish clergy. Candidates qualifying for ordination despite being poorly prepared are not uncommon.

It is surely significant that the occupations of the ordinands are never agricultural. The profession most commonly recorded is *Schulmeister* 'schoolmaster', but seeing that schools were under the control of the church and that *docere Evangelium* meant 'to preach the gospel', it is possible that the borderline between teacher and pastor is blurred. Next in frequency come church offices, such as *custos* 'sacristan', *edituus* 'sexton', *Kirchendiener* 'verger', *cantor*. There are also handicrafts and trades, including *Setzer* 'compositor', *Tuchmacher* 'cloth-maker', *Büttner* 'cooper', *Seiler* 'rope-maker', *Fenstermacher* 'window-maker', *Kürschner* 'furrier', *Buchbinder* 'bookbinder', and *Buchdrucker* 'printer'. If the Upper Lusatian Estates' intention 'to mitigate the severity of the *adscriptio ad glebam*' resulted in anyone being released from feudal servitude (see above), there is no evidence of it here. In entries such as that for 'Johannes Agricola Sprembergensis' (1567) (Muka 1896: 127), we are dealing not with a profession but a byname (presumably *Bur* 'peasant').

Saxony was at the forefront of the Reformation and the Lusatias were close behind, but Brandenburg was a little slow to follow. The Peace of Augsburg in 1555 acknowledged the existence of Lutheran states and the right of Lutheran princes to impose confessional conformity on their subjects, establishing the principle of *cuius regio, eius religio* 'whose realm, his religion'. In Brandenburg, however, the Hohenzollerns were chary of harming relations with the emperor, and Joachim I (1484–1535) never accepted Luther's reforms. Joachim II (r. 1535–1571) was converted in 1539, but he avoided total alignment with the Protestant camp and did not publicly acknowledge his conversion until 1563. It was only under his son Johann Georg (r. 1571–1598) that Brandenburg became wholeheartedly Protestant (Mětšk 1965a: 72; Clark 2006: 7).

The Wittenberg records show that by 1545 Wendish ordinands were being dispatched to Upper Lusatia, Electoral Saxony, Lower Lusatia (including the Cottbus exclave), and the Brandenburg Kurmark (Muka 1896: 113–15). There is also evidence at the parish level of the substitution of Wendish for Latin. A directive of the visitation of 1555 in Senftenberg promoted the use of the Wendish (Sorbian) language in all the Wendish parishes under the Superintendent of Hayn (subsequently Großenhain) including Senftenberg, Fürstenwalde, Bockwitz, Mückenberg, Lauta, Necksdorf, Bethen, and Kletitz. Because these parishes were remote and scattered, and the Superintendent was not competent in the Wendish language, one of the Senftenberg pastors was to be his coadjutor to ensure preaching, singing, and holy communion were held 'in the Wendish language, according to God's word, in a Christian way, properly, in orderly fashion, and in conformity with the liturgy in the Senftenberg church'. The Senftenberg parish itself, however, was divided over the language question, and the visitors ordained that provision should be made for both Wendish and German services in the parish church. The Wends were, in addition, to have their own church, where they would hear their own Wendish sermons, epistles, and gospels, and sing their psalms, and hymns. Every second Sunday a Wendish communion service would be held in the parish church (Sehling 1902: 672).

To be ordained at Wittenberg to preach the Gospel in Wendish (*ad docendum Evangelium lingua Vandalica*) will have been seen by many Wends as a mark of distinction, and the emergence of a literate class must have raised the status of the Wends and their language. The following ordinand's biographical note of 1574 leaves no doubt as to the importance, in his estimation, of his Wendish qualifications:

> I Georg Berger of Petershain in the Margraviate of Lower Lusatia, the son of the venerable Simon Berger, Pastor of Petershain, have studied eight years at Cottbus and have with great zeal learned the Wendish Catechism and Wendish hymns of Dr Martin Luther. Being thus of the Christian religion and of the true Wendish nation I was called by the noble and honourable Kunze von Loben zu Geissendorf and also by the noble and honourable, the virtuous Lady Margarete von Zabelitz, deceased, to be a Wendish sacristan. Then I was called by the Christian congregation to be a Wendish minister and clergyman at Spreewitz, lying near Spremberg, and ordained on 19 June 1574.

(Muka 1897a: 47)

Towards the end of the century the Wendish church in Cottbus had a linguistic problem. On 9 February 1594, the Cottbus town council wrote to the Elector Johann Georg (b. 1525, r. 1571–1598) concerning the appointment of a new Wendish pastor to replace Matthias Deutschmann, who had resigned four days earlier. The councillors were embarrassed by the fact that, having already appointed a successor, they had received news that the Elector also had a candidate, namely, one Johann Muscovius from the Storkow region. They asked the Elector to reconsider his proposal. Their choice had fallen on the previous deputy pastor, Martin am Ende, and there were a number of other local people hoping for preferment as a result of his promotion. So, to the office of deputy vacated by Martin am Ende they had promoted a man who had attended the local school, a Martin Zernigk. He had a year's experience of preaching, was a native of the place, and competent in the local variety of Wendish (*welcher der hiesigen Sprach geläufig, ein eingeboren Kind*). As for the Elector's preferred candidate, Johann Muscovius, the councillors did not doubt his virtues, but considered his regional provenance a disadvantage, because 'he does not know our language, for there is a great difference between that of Storkow and that of Cottbus'. They concluded with the hope that the Elector would excuse their action and be satisfied with the result (Mětšk 1962a: 26).

Johann Georg consented, but a little over a year later (9 March 1595) he wrote to the General Superintendent of the Neumark to elucidate the problem underlying the Cottbus council's objection to his candidate, Johann Muscovius. He had meanwhile asked for the opinion of Andreas Tharaeus of the University of Frankfurt as to 'whether a non-native pastor could not be well understood' (Mětšk 1962a: 26) and had been informed that there were indeed substantial differences between the dialects of the Wendish language, although within the Cottbus exclave they were not as great as between the same and the dialect of the Pomeranian and Kashubian Wends or between the Wends of Krossen and the Poles on the Oder (*Oderpolen*). (The Elector's allusion here to the dialect 'of our Pomeranian and Kashubian Wenden' (*unserer pommerschen und kassubischen Wenden*) ignores the settlement of Grimnitz 1529, which had established that the Duke of Pomerania was a direct vassal of the emperor.) He summarizes:

> So a subject of the Cottbus Circle can understand the language of the whole Wendish Krossen Circle, which are under both the government and consistory of the Neumark at Küstrin, and especially the dialect of the Sommerfeld area and the Bobersberg land, no less well than our Wends of the Beeskow diocese, whose dialect, moreover, varies not inconsiderably from that of Amt Zossen on its Wendish side and its Schenken land [sc. Teupitz]. The variation is no less in the case of the dialects of Wendish under the Crown of Bohemia, to the extent that the Wends not far from our town of Frankfurt under the Neuzelle monastery can understand those under the lordships of Sonnenwalde and Dobrilugk much better than those between the Görlitz *Weichbild* and the villages of the Königsbrück lordship.

> (Mětšk 1962a: 27)

Lest the General Superintendent should have felt he was being blinded by science, the Elector concludes with a clear instruction: 'If therefore no native is available for the office of pastor, you are to prefer a native of our land of a different Wendish dialect to an outsider. Where, however, our Wendish subjects understand German well enough, you are obliged obediently to impose the same to the edification of the Christian church' (Mětšk 1962a: 27). This letter provides us with a useful outline of the dialectal divisions in the area between Zossen (just south of Cölln-Berlin) and Königsbrück (just north of Dresden), including the area in the east where Wendish met Polish.

Andreas Tharaeus, who matriculated at Frankfurt University in 1588, seems to have enjoyed Johann Georg's favour, because we next find him at the beginning of the seventeenth century as the incumbent of Friedersdorf (south of Berlin), a Wendish parish to which the Elector himself had the right of presentation (Mětšk 1965a: 85–6). The adjective *Muscoviensis*, which Tharaeus was in the habit of appending to his name, means he came from the townlet of Muskau on the Neisse. Of Johann Muscovius, the Elector's favoured candidate for the Cottbus vacancy, nothing more is known, and the question of a link between Andreas Tharaeus Muscoviensis and Joannis Muscovius is imponderable.

Luther's testimony

Michael Francus and David Chytraeus are not the only providers of evidence of Wendish inhabitants in the vicinity of Wittenberg in the sixteenth century. Our prime witness is Martin Luther himself. Called to Wittenberg by the Elector in 1508 to teach theology, he spent the rest of his life there. Thanks to him and the other reformers the town was raised to prominence between 1512 and 1546. Among members of Luther's circle, however, opinions of the town were not high. They wondered why a university had been founded at all in such a remote place and why God had chosen it to be the starting point for the dissemination of his word (Malink 1983: 68, nos. 6 and 9). Even the Rektor of the University, Christoph von Scheurl, called Wittenberg a backwater (*Winkel*) and complained of its 'drunken, coarse people, given to gluttony' (Malink 1983: 61). Luther is reported in his *Table Talk* to have said 'I have often marvelled that our God gave his word among the treacherous Wends near Wittenberg. I think he gave it to Jerusalem [and] to Wittenberg and its neighbourhood so that at the last judgement he might reproach them with their ingratitude' (Malink 1983: 68, WA TR 2, 236, Nr. 1847). (Quotations from Luther are here taken from Malink (1983), who uses the *Weimarer Ausgabe* (WA). TR=*Tischreden* 'Table-talk').

Luther's poor opinion of the town stemmed above all from its location and proximity to the Wends. He is reported to have said: 'Wittenbergers are on the frontier of civilization; if they had progressed a little further, they would have come into the midst of barbarity' (Malink 1983: 58, WA TR 2, 669, Nr. 2800b). He harboured a sense of the vulnerability of the Wittenbergers in their exposed outpost, realizing that they were dependent on Wendish peasants for food: 'Were it not for the good Elector, and him alone, the university could not remain here for one year because of the Wends; they would starve us out' (Malink 1983: 69, WA TR 4, 606, Nr. 4997). The Wends of Wittenberg were, according to Luther, 'different from other Wends, especially in appearance, just as a beast differs from a man in specific nature, essence, and, of course, in reason. Thus all the features of the Irish have been thrown into this Wendland, stupidity, loutishness, etc. [...]. Indeed, to judge from their deeds and desires they are stupid and loutish. Standing during the sermon, they do not wish to pay attention or understand, but with head bowed like tree-trunks they stand, blind and deaf, etc.; afterwards, on leaving the church, they ridicule or at least laugh at the word and its teachers' (Malink 1983: 67–8, WA TR, 411, Nr. 8545).

For Luther, however, Wendish turpitude was all part of God's great purpose, as may be seen in his reported attempt to identify the Wends with the Biblical 'worst of the nations', specified in Ezekiel 7.24, namely, 'I will bring the worst of the nations to take possession of their houses' (RSV). He explained the allusion as follows:

Of the Wends. But the worst of all the nations are the Wends, among whom God has cast us. For God always turns aside to all the worst peoples, just as there was no more obstinate a people than the Jews. They killed their prophets and the son of God, so that neighbouring peoples prophesied, as it says in Ezekiel, that the Jews would not go unpunished. So Christ comes here too among the Wends to destroy the work of the Devil and to drive out the devils that have their abode here among the peasants and townsmen. For Christ reigns in the midst of enemies. If there were a worse people than the Wends, that is where the gospel would have dawned.

(Malink 1983: 69, WA TR 4, 606, Nr. 4997)

Most of Luther's observations on the Wends come from the *Table Talk*, which was compiled by Joannes Aurifaber (1519–1575) from a variety of collections of Luther's remarks recorded by his friends, and it must be conceded that its value as a source for details of history is compromised (Malink 1983: 56–7; Chadwick 1984: 75). For evidence of the Wends, however, we are not limited to the *Table Talk*. There is, for example, the manuscript biography of Luther, written by his friend Mattäus Ratzeberger (1501–1559), where he is reported as saying: 'But when I step up into the pulpit, I see what kind of listeners I have; to them I preach what they can understand. For most of them are poor, untutored people and simple Wends' (Malink 1983: 56).

Reform in Budissin and Radibor

As we have seen, Lutheran ideas had reached Upper Lusatia by 1520. In 1522 there was a demonstration in Budissin against the sale of indulgences. The town council appointed the Lutheran preacher Michael Arnold in 1523 and by 1524 the town council and the majority of the inhabitants had accepted the Reformation (Reymann 1902: 239; Mahlink 2002: 122). During Advent 1525 a mob attacked the churches of St Nicholas and St Peter and plundered them, stealing pictures, flags, and 'the great Easter candle which was 15 ells high and the thickness of a man' (Vitzk 1857: 202).

Even before the Reformation, although mass was always said in Latin, the vernacular was not wholly absent from religious observances, and the question whether mass would be accompanied by a sermon and, if so, whether it would be in Wendish, had always been a matter of concern to Wendish congregations. Not far from St Peter's Church in the centre of Budissin stood a Franciscan monastery with its own church, and here preaching took place in Wendish. This was naturally the church most commonly attended by the city's Wendish inhabitants. In the turmoil of the Reformation, however, the monks soon fell on hard times and began to abandon the monastery. After most of the German inhabitants of the town had already accepted the new doctrine, their opponents in the Cathedral chapter still hoped to prevent the Wends going the same way and accordingly made provision in 1527 for preaching in Wendish in the church of St Nicholas (Reymann 1902: 301, 309). By this time the Franciscans were in disarray. St Nicholas's remained true to the old religion, so for a time it seemed that the Wends would do so too. Both sides were anxious to avoid conflict and were prepared to negotiate. There was a series of treaties between the two confessions in the town.

Apart from the Franciscans' church and the chapel in the *Ortenburg*, there was only one parish church in Budissin, the Cathedral of St Peter, to which all the other churches

(St Michael's, St Nicholas's, and the churches of Our Lady, of the Holy Ghost, and of Mary and Martha) were subordinate. The Cathedral Chapter was headed by a Provost, who, however, resided in Meissen (in Saxony) and took little part in Budissin affairs. Its real leader, therefore, was his deputy, the Dean. The last Dean under the old order was Hieronymus Ruperti, who in 1556 concluded a *Simultaneumsvertrag* with the Town Council, an agreement whereby the church building of St Peter's could be used by both confessions at separate, agreed times (Seifert 2002: 110–11).

Budissin was a predominantly German town with a Wendish minority, most of whom were concentrated in the Wendish quarter, but the town was surrounded by Wendish villages, which belonged to the Budissin parish. When, a few years later, application was made to the Chapter for the reformist Wends of the parish to have their own Wendish pastor, it was refused on the grounds that 'the Wends, as they are allocated to the parish of St. Nicholas, should adhere to the confession of the same' (Reymann 1902: 348). It was conceded that they might take Communion from the Protestant clergy of St Peter's, but the Chapter was in effect compelling the Protestant Wendish inhabitants of Budissin to attend Roman Catholic mass in St Nicholas's.

Many Wends found it easier to make their way to a reformed church in one of the neighbouring parishes outside the town (Knauthe 1767: 225). The Town Council therefore made provision for the Protestant Wends by appointing to St Peter's deacons who could speak Wendish and who would hold Wendish services there. The Chapter agreed to this, but required of the Council under article 4 of the Organ Treaty (*Orgelvertrag*) of 17 May 1583 that they would not put pressure on the 'Wendish peasant people' of St Nicholas's parish, who were already allocated to their own (sc. Roman Catholic) clergy and their own church (Reymann 1902: 348).

The principle *cuius regio, eius religio* 'whose country – his religion', agreed at the Peace of Augsburg in 1555, meant that every prince (*Landesherr*) of the empire was free to settle the confessional question in his own lands, but the Lusatias were constitutionally anomalous. They were both ruled by their respective Estates. They owed allegiance to the king of Bohemia, it was true, and he was sometimes called their *Markgraf* (e.g. Knauthe 1767: 206, 247), but he was not resident. The principle of *cuius regio, eius religio* therefore operated at the level of *Grundherr* 'lord of the manor' (Blaschke 1961/2000: 34–6). Among the lords of the manor, however, were the religious houses of Marienstern, Marienthal, Lauban, and Neuzelle, and the Cathedral Chapter in Budissin. These all remained Catholic and fully expected that the churches in the villages they owned or of which they were patrons would do so too. With the exception of Neuzelle in Lower Lusatia (where the monastery remained Catholic, but its villages converted), this is indeed what happened; but parish boundaries did not always coincide with secular boundaries, and the geography was often so complicated that adjustments had to be made and compromises reached.

The parish of Budissin was considerably larger than the town itself, because it included many surrounding villages, which were predominantly (if not totally) Wendish. Those owned by the Cathedral Chapter now became part of the new Catholic parish; the rest became part of the new Lutheran parish. To the north-west of Budissin stretching almost as far as Hoyerswerda lay the three parishes Crostwitz, Nebelschütz, and Wittichenau. These were all the property of the Marienstern Nunnery and so remained Catholic (see Map 4.1).

The parish of Radibor is an hour's walk north of Budissin. The lord of the manor here and patron of the benefice stood fast in the old religion, as did the parish priest, even though the people of the parish wanted to accept the reforms (Knauthe 1767: 253, 335). The Cathedral Chapter claimed the right of presentation, but there was no doubt as to the ownership of the land (Blaschke 1961/2000: 36n.). In 1575 a new landlord, Hans von Plaunitz, attempted to introduce Luther's doctrine, but this was immediately prohibited by the intervention of the Emperor Maximilian II. Two years later, after the death of the parish priest Jurij Andrea, the question of Radibor's confessional allegiance was reopened. There were two churches in the village, St Mary's (the parish church) and St Cross. In his negotiations with the Dean of Budissin regarding the vacancy in 1577, von Plaunitz said he was prepared to compromise and proposed the appointment of a Roman Catholic priest to St Mary's and of a Lutheran to the smaller church of St Cross. Meanwhile the parish was without a priest, but the mass continued to be celebrated in Radibor by priests sent out individually from Budissin, until on 26 November 1577 the Emperor Rudolf II, who had succeeded Maximilian in 1576, decreed that both churches be assigned to a Catholic priest.

Hans von Plaunitz appears to have accepted failure with resignation, and Father Bosćij Zacharias, the new incumbent, was for some twenty years able to discharge his office unmolested. Even after 1585, when von Plaunitz had sold the manor of Radibor to Christoph von Haugwitz auf Putzkau, Zacharias was left in peace. It was only a matter of time, however, before efforts to Lutheranize the parish were renewed, and when Christoph von Haugwitz died and was succeeded by Kaspar von Haugwitz, life was made difficult for the priest. Moreover, the new lord of the manor's ambitions went further than introducing the reformed religion; he also coveted the traditional judicial rights held by the priest in the village of Camina, part of the parish. In 1598, having subjected Zacharias to a year of persecution, von Haugwitz drove him out of the parish and appointed a Lutheran in his place. From July 1598 to August 1600 the Lutheran doctrine prevailed in Radibor and the Catholic authorities were helpless. The Dean in Budissin continued to send a priest out regularly to celebrate mass, but von Haugwitz regularly made trouble for him (*Wosady* 1984: 35–6).

The Sequestration (1547)

In 1546 King Ferdinand and his brother the Emperor Karl V were preparing for war with the Schmalkaldic League. As overlord of Upper Lusatia, Ferdinand demanded support from the Upper Lusatian Estates, and, despite misgivings, at the beginning of 1547 the Six Towns undertook to provide him with a contingent of 500 men for a period of two months. The nobles promised 1,000 cavalrymen (Blaschke 1999b/2000: 89). On 23 April the Imperial army was encamped west of Meissen and ready for battle with the forces of Johann Friedrich, Elector of Saxony. Realizing that the two-month period agreed with the Estates was about to run out, Ferdinand wrote to the Six Towns requesting an extension of two months. The Towns, however, also anticipating the expiry of the two-month commitment, had already ordered their men to withdraw, so that they would be at home by the date originally agreed. The contingent supplied by the nobles had remained with the emperors' forces.

On 24 April the emperor was victorious at the decisive battle of Mühlberg-on-the-Elbe, in which the Towns' contingent was not a participant. Johann Friedrich, Elector of Saxony, had been defeated. His cousin Moritz, who had fought with the emperor, was accordingly rewarded with the electoral title and most of the electoral domains. The day after the battle, the Towns received the king's letter of 23 April and were thrown into confusion. They did all they could to make amends by sending newly raised infantry and provisions, but his was a futile gesture, seeing the battle was over, so the king, in ungracious mood after the Imperial victory, refused to accept them (Blaschke 1999b/2000: 90). The new Elector Moritz, having fought on the emperor's side for only one reason, soon rejoined the Protestant camp (Ludwig and Hennen 2002: 37).

Ferdinand punished the towns by imposing a huge fine and depriving them of all the privileges they had acquired in the course of the centuries, including the right to administer justice. They were required to surrender all their artillery and to secede their possessions in land to the king. These and other measures taken against them are known as the Sequestration (*Pönfall*) of 1547 (Blaschke 1999b/2000: 90–1). Most of the confiscated land was transferred to Upper Lusatian nobles, the principal beneficiary being Ulrich von Nostitz. Its loss not only deprived the Towns of income, but also stripped them of social rank as landowners. They were humiliated and impoverished.

The king evidently realized that, in their ruined and demoralized state, the Towns would be incapable of making their wonted contribution to the general well-being of the body politic. It was not long, therefore, before he made possible a degree of recovery. As early as 1548, it seems, the Wendish villages Strehla, Oberkaina, Niederkaina, Preuschwitz, Stiebitz, and Kleinkunitz were restored to Budissin, and similar restitution was made to the other five members of the Six-Town Union (J. Schneider 1961: 184). The nobility meanwhile remained satisfied, because the balance of political power had moved in their favour.

For the rural population as a whole, however, including the Wends, the Sequestration marked a serious setback. The Towns' loss of the right to administer justice, both summary and superior, meant the protection from the nobility afforded to the serfs by the towns and their relatively unbiased courts was removed. In 1562 the emperor restored to the Six Towns their right to administer justice, both summary and superior, but only on the territory of the town itself and its villages (known as the *Weichbild*). Landowners were now given the right to administer superior justice on their own estates. They were admonished not to allow prisoners in their gaols to starve to death, nor to employ torture or carry out executions without instruction from the *Landvogt* or the court of appeal in Prague, but in reality the landowner now had power of life and death over his serfs (Knothe 1885: 246–7).

Feudal order and peasant revolts

The social antagonism between lord and serf, inherent in the feudal set-up, was compounded in the Wendish lands by an ethnic dimension. The legal status of Wendish serfs, allotted to them following military conquest in the Middle Ages, was generally inferior to that of German serfs, who had voluntarily come to the east as settlers on favourable conditions. Every serf, of course, whether Wendish or German, was obliged to perform services for his lord and also to pay him a small annual rent.

The economic status of a peasant was correlated with the size of the plot he occupied and worked. A plot of a size so small that its occupant with his family could barely make a living was known as a *Gärtnernahrung*, its occupant as a *Gärtner*. In Wendish villages such plots had existed since the earliest times. In German villages, on the other hand, they had originally not existed. Even smaller than a *Gärtnernahrung* was a *Häuslernahrung*, occupied by a *Häusler*. Here there was no arable land apart from a little garden surrounding the house. The *Häusler* eked out a living by working for other peasants or for the lord, but for the latter he was obliged in addition to perform unpaid services. For all serfs, Wendish and German, the quantity and nature of these services was always a sore point. Originally, they had usually amounted to no more than a few days a year, but from the end of the fifteenth century landowners started to increase them arbitrarily. The expression 'daily, full services', which meant six days' service a week, is first encountered in the sixteenth century, but it is impossible to tell whether in Wendish villages it was not older than that. In German villages, however, it was not original and attempts to impose it on them provoked resistance and unrest (Knothe 1885: 159, 184–98).

The economic fate of the trans-Elbian peasant depended substantially on the conditions of tenure of his plot. In Wendish villages everyone was a leaseholder (*Lasse*) and was required to pay rent. He could at any time be evicted. In German villages many peasants were freeholders, whose land could be inherited (Knothe 1885: 200–1, 221). The landowners were not all of the nobility. A town within its walls was an oasis, separate in most respects from the rural order of subservience, but it could own villages or parts of villages, known collectively as its *Weichbild*. Individual citizens of towns could also be landowners. There were ecclesiastical lords too, such as the Marienstern Nunnery and the Budissin Cathedral Chapter.

The towns and ecclesiastical lords, on the whole, were less inclined than the nobles to impose unreasonable demands on their villages and reluctant to use violent measures to seek compliance. Consequently, runaway serfs from nobles' estates often sought refuge in villages owned by the towns. In retaliation the nobles managed to have a paragraph included in the Second Prague Treaty of 1534 whereby both sides agreed not to assist fugitives, but to return them to their owners. In a document drawn up in 1544, in an attempt to resolve some of the tension between towns and nobles, known as the *decisio Ferdinandea*, King Ferdinand I acknowledged that there was more misery in the nobles' than in the towns' villages and that this was caused by the imposition by the nobles of daily services and other burdens on their peasants.

There is nothing in the accounts of mistreatment to suggest any difference between Wendish and German villages, but accounts of events in Wendish areas are rare. An unknown quantity in the narrative are the separate Wendish courts held in Budissin and Göda, for which no records survive. Exceptionally, a record of an incident in the Wendish village of Petershain (Hóznica), west of Niesky, in 1540 has defied the ravages of time. Here fourteen serfs resisted their lord (von Gersdorff) over the issue of services. They were imprisoned, but released after nine months on the condition that they would appear again before the king in Prague, bareheaded and barefoot, unarmed, and in a white smock. Following their release from gaol, however, many of them fainted and one died (Knothe 1885: 245–8). It is not surprising that rural restlessness was never far below the surface throughout the century.

The German Peasants' War of 1524–1526, arising from economic distress in south Germany and stimulated by the Reformation, spread north into Thuringia and Saxony, but stopped short of the Elbe (Scheuch 2001: 55). Such evidence as can be found of mutinous events in the Main Compact Wendish Zone at this time relates to small-scale incidents. One took place in 1527 in the Estates-governed domain (*Standesherrschaft*) of Hoyerswerda, encompassing some forty Wendish villages. The root of the trouble is not known, but military assistance was quickly summoned from nearby towns and twelve ringleaders were taken to Budissin and imprisoned there. Before long they escaped. Meanwhile, the other rebels made their way to Prague, to exculpate themselves, but in this they were unsuccessful, and their leaders were executed. An enquiry into the cause of the rebellion established that it had been provoked not by the Reformation but by distress arising from extreme conditions of servitude (Knauthe 1767: 214–15).

In 1528 there were disturbances in the Wendish District of the Kurmark. A Wendish shepherd fled from Heinrich von Queiß, the junker of Blossin in the *Amt* of Storkow, sought refuge in Friedersdorf, and found supporters in the nearby village of Dolgenbrodt. A raiding party of serfs from both villages then invaded the von Queiß estate and stole some sheep. Instead of retaliating, von Queiß chose to manipulate the situation to charge his feudal superior the Catholic Bishop of Lebus (who was also mortgagee of the Storkow Manor) with failing to perform his duty to help to crush the rebels. Exploiting the anti-popish sentiments of the time, Queiß now raised a band of noblemen to attack the Bishop. Von Queiß's men were led by Nickel von Minckwitz, lord of Sonnewalde, owner of two estates in the *Amt* of Beeskow, and a Lutheran. Circumstances had thus put the Bishop and his ally the Catholic Elector of Brandenburg on the same side as the Wendish rebels (Mětšk 1965a: 45).

A further Wendish incident (referred to as 'die Windischen hendel') in *Amt* Schlieben (Saxon *Kurkreis*) took place during 1545–1546. Wolf von Schönberg, *Amtmann* of Dobrilug, was having a watch kept on the border with *Amt* Schlieben 'on account of the rebellious Schlieben Wends'. About the same time a Wendish serf had escaped from gaol in Dobrilug and it was feared he would find refuge among his fellow Wends (*Mitwinden*) in the *Amt* of Liebenwerda. Whether this amounts to a mutiny is questionable (Mětšk 1962d/1981: 164–5),

To the west of Luckau lay the village of Uckro, where in 1546 the lord of the manor, the junker Franz von Minckwitz, was resorting to sheep-rustling. The elected spokesmen of the people of Uckro and other villages, sent to remonstrate with him, forced their way into the manor house and threatened him with retribution. He sent a message to the *Landvogt* of Lower Lusatia asking for help. The rebellion spread to further villages, as more serfs united in revolt and drove their lords out of their manor-houses, and by mid-1548 Luckau was half surrounded by rebellious villages. The rebels denied all allegiances, claiming to be subjects of the emperor alone, but in the end they were defeated by the *Landvogt*'s forces. One of the sources for the Uckro rebellion is the 1668 Modest Admonition (*Ohnvorgreifliche Monita*) (see Chapter 4), which recalls that 'because the general revolt, which came to an end in 1548, against Herr Franz von Minckwitz, made only too apparent the malignant obduracy of the Wends in the Luckau Circle, the *Landvogt* of Lower Lusatia, Herr Jaroslav von Kolovrat, finally, as a result of many complaints and pressure from the nobility, made an order to the head of the Lower Lusatian Lutheran Church in Lübben on 21 July 1592 that the German language should be introduced in the entire Margraviate' (Mětšk 1969: 15–16). The names of the chief rebels in Uckro in 1548 and the names of the other villages involved in the rebellion were discovered early in the twentieth century in the Uckro Manor Register (*Schloßregister*), but this was destroyed during the Second World War (Mětšk 1976–7/1981: 238).

Writing in Wendish

In the colonized lands beyond the Elbe and Saale German culture arrived late. It came through the towns, but here the towns were of recent foundation and small. So far as literary culture is concerned, it is obvious that the lands to the east, while under Wendish control, could not have participated in the Old High German period (which ended in 1050). Even in the Middle High German period (1050–1500) literature was still predominantly a western and southern affair. While such poets as Hartmann von Aue (c. 1165–1215), Walter von der Vogelweide (c. 1170–1230), and Wolfram von Eschenbach (c. 1170–1220) were writing, the lands beyond the Elbe had only recently been subdued and colonization was not yet complete. Walter von der Vogelweide's visit to Meissen (see Chapter 2 above) was an exceptional exploit, but the first German poet to have originated in the east is the Minnesinger Heinrich (Frauenlob), who was born in Meissen between 1250 and 1260.

Beyond the Elbe, therefore, the question of German intellectual or cultural decline on the eve of the Thirty Years' War (postulated by Wedgewood 1961: 46–7) does not arise, for here the settlers' culture was still evolving, and what had not yet bloomed could not be fading. Beyond the Elbe, literary culture, both German and Wendish, begins with the Reformation. Its first exponents wrote mainly in Latin, sometimes in German, and hardly ever in Wendish. They include Joannes Rhagius Aesticampianus (1457/1460–1520), Adam Puschmann (1532–1600), Bartholomaeus Scultetus (1540–1641), Casparus Peucerus (1525–1602), Casparus Janitius (c. 1550–1597), Albin Moller (1541–1618),

Joannes Bocatius (1569–1621), and Jakob Böhme (1575–1624). The ethnicity and native language of some of these early writers is uncertain. There is no reason to doubt that Moller, who was born in Wendish territory and wrote in all three languages (Latin, German, and Wendish) was a Wend or that Böhme, who was born in the German village of Alt Seidenberg (now Sulików) near Görlitz and wrote in Latin, was a German, but not all cases are so clear cut. The ethnic affinities of Rhagius Aesticampianus, Peucerus, and Bocatius will be considered below.

The sixteenth century brings us an expanding supply of texts in Wendish, beginning with a sentence on a page of a Latin manuscript dated 1510, the only surviving book from the library of the former Dominican monastery in Luckau, which was dissolved in 1555. It has been transcribed as:

Ach moyo luba lupka/biß weßola thy sy/my luba

and interpreted as:

Ach moja luba lubka, by(d)ź wjesoła, ty sy mě/mi luba

'Oh, my dear love, be joyful, you are dear to me' (*Najstarši* 2011: 45; Wornar 2011: *passim*).

The oldest text longer than one sentence is the Budissin Citizens' Oath (*Der Burger Eydt Wendisch*), dating from 1532 and consisting of sixty-two words. It is the formula of an oath to be sworn by newly initiated citizens of Budissin, promising obedience to the king of Bohemia and the town authorities. It is strongly infiltrated with Czech elements (Wornar 2012: *passim*). The existence of a Wendish version of the citizens' oath suggests that it was possible to be a citizen without being capable of taking it in German. From the townlet of Lieberose in Lower Lusatia we have the text of an oath of loyalty to the town council, datable to 1536–1537 (Roggan 2011: 65), and from Zossen, south of Berlin, comes a brief manuscript baptismal formula of 1543 in Wendish (Mětšk 1965a: *Anhang* 3; Petr 1967: 10–13).

By 1548, however, only two years after Luther's death, a complete Wendish translation of the New Testament had been made by Mikławuš Jakubica, pastor of Laubnitz in the administrative district of Sorau, in the far east of Sorbian territory, beyond the Neisse. The manuscript, which is written in the local dialect of the Laubnitz and Sorau region, is today in the *Deutsche Staatsbibliothek* in Berlin (Ms. Slav. fol. 10). It was written 'to the glory and praise of God, who is all-powerful, true, and just, and for all the faithful, especially for those of the Sorbian tongue and nation (*wosebnie Jasikowy a Narodu Serpskemu*)'. These words in the colophon reveal for the first time that the Wends in this area called their language *serbski*.

Jakubica was expecting his translation to be printed (Schuster-Šewc 1967b: 415), but it remained a manuscript, neglected or forgotten, and had no influence outside its parish. It is signed: 'Vandalicus interpres Nicolaus Jakubiky Anno christi 1548'. Almost nothing is known of the translator, who has been identified as Nicolaus Kubike or Kubke, apart from the fact that he was pastor of Laubnitz/Lubanice in the years 1523–1525. The adjective *serbski* occurs several times, not only in the colophon, but also in the New Testament itself (Schuster-Šewc 1967b: 144; Šewc 1997: 47).

Albin Moller (1541–1618)

A further twenty-six years were to pass before the appearance of the first Wendish printed book. This is Albin Moller's *Ein Ewigwerender Kirchen Calender [...] Auch ein Wendisches Gesangbuch [...] Auch der Kleine Catechismus mit dem Tauff und Träwbüchlein* ('An Everlasting Church Calendar [...]. Also a Wendish Hymnal [...]. Also the Little Catechism with the Book for Baptisms and Weddings'). Published by Michael Wolrab in Budissin in 1574, it contains 314 pages. The only surviving copy is in the Sorbian Central Library in Budissin. It contains 122 Wendish metrical hymns, psalms, and canticles, most of which (if not all) are translations from German or Latin. In the one surviving copy there is no sign of the everlasting calendar mentioned in the title, though Moller's preface, addressed to the *Landvogt* of Lower Lusatia, also refers to it. It is reasonable to assume that most of the texts are Moller's own work, but two of the hymns published here are translations made as early as 1545 by Simon Gast, the first Lutheran pastor in Lübben, at the request of the *Landvogt* Albrecht Schlieck. Moller's primary aim in producing a printed version was to promote uniformity in church practice throughout Lower Lusatia. He writes:

> For I have seen how muddled things are in the villages concerning the hymns and the catechism, so that to express the same meaning some Wendish hymns have too few syllables and others too many, also that the same hymn is sung in one church with one set of words and in the next with another set, so that there is no uniformity in accordance with an agreement, but only the confusion of the simple Christians. Therefore I wished to serve the ordinary churches in the villages with my talent and this translation in the conduct of the Christian office, in view of the difficulty and of St Paul's admonition that everything in God's churches should proceed decently, properly, and with respect. For people, especially the simple Christians, may become more assured and confident in their belief and religion if everywhere in neighbouring churches there is a united consensus in doctrine, preaching, baptism, singing, and the like...
>
> (Moller 1959: 5v=12)

The disparity between texts used in different parishes and the need for uniformity are habitual themes in early Wendish books.

Moller gives insights into the order of service in his time, and by his references to 'Sunday gospels which are explained by hymns which are therefore sung before them' (Moller 1959: 6r=13) and to hymns that are to be sung 'after the epistle' (Moller 1959:

58v=118), he reveals that services included passages read aloud from the New Testament. Yet the only New Testament of which we know at this time was that of Jakubica (1548), which existed in only one manuscript copy.

The publication of Moller's hymnal was an isolated incident. It might well have been expected to be influential in bringing uniformity into liturgical practice, as the author intended, but such textual influence as can be perceived in manuscript hymns of the next century, including some found in Upper Lusatia (Wölkowa and Šěn 2001: 51), is meagre. It is not without significance, however, and when the Wittenberg ordinand Georgius Berger of Petershain in Lower Lusatia recorded in 1574 that he had learned the Wendish Catechism and 'the Wendish hymns of Dr Martin Luther' (see above, p. 88), he may well have been referring to Moller's book.

It was not until 1749 that the next hymnal in the Wendish of Lower Lusatia appeared in print, but during the intervening 175 years there are scattered allusions to the existence of Moller's book. Warichius, Tharaeus, and Martini all knew it, as did the compiler of the 1749 hymnal, Johann Ludwig Will. It is unlikely that many copies would have found their way into the hands of Wendish serfs, who usually could not read, but we do not even know how many were printed. That some copies did, however, reach some Wendish churches, may be concluded from the instruction issued the following century to have them removed thence. In the words of the 1668 Modest Admonition (*Ohnvorgreifliche Monita*) (cf. Chapter 4, p. 145):

> Wendish singing in church shall be completely stopped. Therefore church patrons are to have all manuscripts with old Wendish hymns etc. that may still be present in the churches removed, also any books printed in that language, such as Magister Moller of Straupitz's hymn book and Little Catechism translated into Wendish, as being idolatrous and not conducive to the true fulfilment of servile obligations.

> (Mětšk 1969: 15–16)

Albin Moller was born in 1541 in Straupitz, 7 miles (12 kilometres) to the east of Lübbenau (Figure 3.1). He attended a Latin school in Calau, and then studied theology, first at Frankfurt/Oder, later at Wittenberg. At Wittenberg he matriculated on 2 February 1568 as Albinus Mollerus Straupicensis (Krausch 1978: 161). By February 1572 Moller was living in Tornow (Kreis Calau) – one of the villages destroyed in the twentieth century by opencast mining – and was probably the pastor there. He was already busy with astrology and published a *Prognosticon Astrologicum* for the years 1573 and 1574. By the time he signed the preface to his *Hymnal and Catechism* on 6 September 1573, he was pastor of Straupitz. He stayed here until Michaelmas 1574, after which he was often on the move, perhaps not always of his own volition, for in the postscript to his hymnal he was openly critical of the church authorities. He was evidently a strict Lutheran at a time of conflict with, on the one hand, Calvinists and, on the other, followers of Melanchthon, known as Philippists and Cryptocalvinists. There are sporadic derogatory allusions in his publications to the Calvinists.

Figure 3.1 Albin Moller (1541–1618). Woodcut in *Die grosse Practica Astrologica* (Leipzig, [1611]). Reproduced here by permission from a copy in the Herzog August Bibliothek Wolfenbüttel: Xb 1721 (2).

In 1582 he was in Groß Döbbern, 8 miles (12 kilometres) south of Cottbus and inside the Cottbus Circle. The Elector of Brandenburg, Johann Georg I (1571–1598), was, like him, an orthodox Lutheran. It appears that Moller had fled to Groß Döbbern and was living here in reduced circumstances (Krausch 1978: 164). However, he was now in touch with Leonhard Thurneysser, electoral physician in Berlin and entrepreneur, who had his own laboratory and printing press. Prominent among Thurneysser's many profitable activities was the publication of almanacs, a field in which Moller too had some expertise, having published several prognostications. From two surviving letters from Moller to Thurneysser, written in 1582 on 4 March and 6 July, it is clear that Moller was then working for Thurneysser as an astrologer. Thurneysser was also in course of publishing a huge herbal, which was to provide plant names in many languages, including Wendish. The first volume appeared in Berlin in 1578, the Wendish names having been provided by *Landphysicus* Johann Teckler, but Thurneysser now decided to replace him with Moller, who drew up a list of the Wendish names for 240 medicinal plants (Stone 1991: *passim*).

Moller seems to have found his true calling in the almanac business. Almanacs composed by him appeared regularly from 1584 onwards in Leipzig, Frankfurt/Oder, Breslau, Prague, and Wilna. They even came to the notice of the Imperial Court in Vienna. Almanacs must have been the source of a small but steady income for Moller, but, although their appearance can be followed year after year, his place of residence between 1582 and 1601 is unknown. He achieved celebrity as one of the leading astrologers of his time, and his fame lingered on long after his death. As he grew older, his eccentricities increased until finally he had the reputation of a crank who was to some a figure of fun but to others a person to be feared. His ambiguous reputation is demonstrated in an anecdote recounting his appearance at a provincial shooting match in Guben in 1600, to which crowds of people came streaming from near and far. Moller was there probably to sell his almanacs and horoscopes. A prominent figure at such gatherings was the *Pritschmeister*, a master of ceremonies and jester who carried a wooden ferule (*Pritsche*) which he wielded to maintain order. The *Pritschmeister* at the Guben gathering teased Moller and was encouraged by 'certain gentlemen' to beat him with his ferule. Shortly afterwards, when shooting at birds took place, a sudden gale blew up and broke the frame set up as a perch for the birds, making it necessary to erect a new one. The superstitious people saw in this a sign of Moller's revenge for the disrespect shown to him and attributed to him the power to control the wind.

He is reported to have written to the Emperor Rudolf II, complaining that both young and old were making fun of him and calling him a stargazer. The emperor (himself no mean stargazer) is said to have replied sympathetically, promising him protection. By 6 August 1607, Moller was living in Altdöbern in Lower Lusatia and here he remained until his death on 26 December 1618 (Krausch 1978: 173). This date is likely to be reliable, although doubt has been cast on it, largely because the annual appearance of his almanacs did not come to an end at this time. The continuing use of a name for commercial purposes, however, even after the bearer's death, was not unusual (Krausch 1978: 173). Finally, a Czech almanac in the Moller tradition dated April 1622 stated that it was 'composed by his heirs'.

Who Moller's heirs were is not known, but the business, as it may be termed, was taken over by his pupil Johann Fischbach, an Alsatian, and even when Fischbach issued almanacs under his own name he styled himself 'disciple and imitator of Magister Albinus Moller of Straupitz' (Urban 1993: 90–1). This continued until at least 1647 and until 1646 the almanacs were still adorned by Moller's portrait. The Moller brand name and logo thus survived the originator by some twenty-eight years.

Wenceslaus Warichius (1564–1618)

Jakubica and Moller wrote in varieties of the Wendish spoken in Lower Lusatia (though neither of them specified the local provenance of his language). Of religious texts in the Wendish of Upper Lusatia there is no sign until the 1590s, though, writing in the eighteenth century (and referring exclusively to Upper Lusatia), Christian Knauthe said he had seen Wendish manuscripts dating from the sixteenth century containing Protestant forms of service for baptism, marriage, confession, communion, and prayers (Knauthe 1767: 230). Of these not one has survived, but there exists a manuscript containing ten hymns in the Wendish of Upper Lusatia, translated from German or Latin and bearing the fragmentary title 'Ein Wendisch [...] Geschrieben 159[3]' and the names 'Gregorius B[...]' and 'Georgius'. It is dedicated to the Dean of the cathedral chapter in Budissin, Gregorius Leisentritt (c. 1550–1594). Four of the hymns have pre-Reformation origins, four are by Luther, and two from other authors (Wölkowa 2007: 7–9). This, the first Wendish text of devotional content from Upper Lusatia, is only 2 years older than the first printed book in this linguistic variety.

The modern concepts of Upper Wendish (Sorbian) and Lower Wendish (Sorbian) as distinct varieties (or even languages) did not yet exist, though the obstacles arising from dialectal fragmentation were already on the minds of the authors of the first printed books, beginning with Moller. When Wenceslaus Warichius (1564–1618) published his version of Luther's *Little Catechism* in 1595 in Budissin (the second Lusatian Wendish printed book), he founded a separate tradition from Moller. He was aware of the existence of Moller's hymnal and was (so far as we know) right in thinking that it was the only Wendish printed book older than his own. Like Moller, he saw that the manuscript translations being produced piecemeal by pastors in their various parishes were resulting in confusion. He writes:

> For it is manifest how the fundamentals of Christian doctrine, the Sunday epistles and gospels, are being translated quite unevenly by some people, sometimes into an altogether alien, illegitimate sense. For during divine service they have only the German text before them and they are forced to give it to the people impromptu, as the mouth guides them, which arises partly from a lack of Wendish books and partly from ignorance and lack of experience in the grammar of this language. But the harm that results from these disparate translations is as follows: the poor, simple listeners, especially the servants that must move from one place to another almost every year, are perplexed thereby and taken aback, when in one place they hear one and in another place another version and translation of the Catechism and other texts.

(Warichius 1595: [8r-8v]=Schuster-Šewc 2001: 29–30)

One of his intentions was to encourage other pastors to write and print Wendish books (Schuster-Šewc 2001: 9r=31), thereby establishing uniformity. When he writes of 'Christian unity' as one of his objectives (Schuster-Šewc 2001: 9r=31), he was thinking not of reconciliation with the Roman church, but of attaining consistency between the various Wendish Lutheran parishes. Like Moller, however, he wrote in the dialect of his own parish, which did nothing to promote the consistency he advocated.

Warichius, born in Gröditz in 1564, was the son of a landowner's steward. He attended the Budissin Gymnasium from 1576 to 1584 and studied theology at Wittenberg 1584–1586. He served as deacon (assistant pastor) at Göda from 1587 to 1598 and was from then on pastor of Göda until his death there in 1618.

Göda was on the south-west edge of Upper Lusatia, bordering Electoral Saxony (Mětšk 1968: 26). The border, in fact, ran through the parish. Fourteen villages, including Göda itself with the parish church, were thus outside the jurisdiction of the Upper Lusatian Estates (Knauthe 1767: 359). As pastor of Göda, Warichius was subordinate to the Bischofswerda superintendent and responsible for the little Latin school in Göda, which prepared Wendish boys for advancement to free places at the Electoral high schools in Meissen and Grimma. In 1580 the school had twenty-four pupils (Muka 1897b: 129; Mětšk 1968: 75). The original syllabus, which survived until the 1870s and was seen and copied by Liška, ordained that:

The school in Göda shall be so constituted that Wendish boys shall therein learn German and Latin, and also the fundamentals of grammar, so that Wendish boys may be educated who can be assisted to enter the high schools known as Electoral Schools, as our most gracious lord the Elector of Saxony has decreed.

(Liška 1876: 33)

The boys were to be taught for three hours in the morning and three hours in the afternoon, one hour in the afternoon being devoted to music. The rest of the time all the lessons were devoted to German and Latin (Liška 1876: 33–4).

By the end of the sixteenth century the number of Lusatian Wendish printed books in existence was two: Moller's Hymnal (1574) and Warichius's Catechism (1595). A second edition of the latter appeared in 1597. Pomeranian Wendish books will be considered below.

Wends writing in Latin

It is only in the sixteenth century that we get to know the biographical details of individual Wends. It is not always easy to identify individual writers as Wends, however, especially if they write exclusively in Latin and German. A case in point is that of Caspar Peucer (1525–1602), a prominent polymath and son-in-law of the reformer Philipp Melanchthon. Born in Budissin on 6 January 1525, Peucer came from the class of urban craftsmen. He attended Latin schools in Budissin and Goldberg, Silesia, after which he matriculated at the University of Wittenberg on 26 March 1543, signing the register there as Caspar Beutzer Budissinensis. He studied philology, astronomy, and medicine, and found lodgings and patronage in the house of Philipp Melanchthon. In 1547, during the Schmalkaldic War, when Wittenberg was threatened by the army of the Emperor Charles V, he fled to the University of Frankfurt/Oder, where he continued his medical studies until 1548. After the defeat of the Elector Johann Friedrich at the Battle of Mühlberg, Wittenberg was replaced by Dresden as the Electoral residence, but the Elector Moritz safeguarded Wittenberg University. The dominant position in theology, once held by Luther, was now assumed by Melanchthon, who in 1548 recalled Peucer to Wittenberg as a university teacher. In 1550 Peucer became a professor in succession to Aurifaber. In February that year Melanchthon gave his permission for the marriage of his daughter Magdalena (1531–1575) to Peucer, and the wedding took place on 2 July. They had ten children.

On Melanchthon's death in 1560 the Peucers inherited his house and other property in Wittenberg, and the same year Elector August appointed Peucer professor of medicine. He was held in high regard at the Elector's court and in Wittenberg he was a prominent citizen. As Melanchthon's assistant and adviser in Slavonic matters (Kühne 1983: 153), Peucer corresponded with Bishop Jan Blahoslav, author of the first Czech translation of the New Testament from the Greek. In this correspondence evidence of Peucer's Wendish birth comes to light. Writing on 8 January 1566 to Blahoslav he says: 'The young nobleman Daniel, when he found out that I took delight in the Wendish language (*lingua Heneta*), gave me as a gift his copy… [of] the New Testament translated by you into our language' (*FRA* 1859: 287; Frinta 1952: 147). In another letter of thanks, dated 19 June 1566, he writes: 'sometimes for amusement I attempt to recall also the Wendish language, in which I was born (*in qua natus sum*)' (*FRA* 1859: 289; Frinta 1952: 147). As German was not Peucer's first language, it is not surprising that he once said: 'I will listen, but I would sooner speak Latin, for I can express my thoughts better in the Latin language than in the German' (Kühne 1983: 160) (Figure 3.2).

As Melanchthon's heir he supervised the Melanchthon legacy and attempted to preserve his doctrine. In 1561 he published Melanchthon's *Corpus doctrinae christianae*. In all these activities there were hidden dangers, for the sectional Lutheran party of Flacius Illyricus was plotting against the followers of Melanchthon. In 1570 Peucer was appointed physician to the Elector August and his family, but in 1574 he was one of group accused of Crypto-Calvinism. He was tried and imprisoned, first in Rochlitz, then in Zeitz, and finally in the Pleißenburg in Leipzig. Altogether, he spent twelve years in gaol. His wife Magdalena died in 1575. At length, thanks to the pleas of influential friends, on 8 February 1586 he was released, arriving the next day in Dessau. He was prohibited from returning to Wittenberg and to the house he had inherited from Melanchthon, but

Figure 3.2 Caspar Peucer (1525–1602). Engraving by Balthasar Jenichen, Museum Bautzen, Inv.-Nr.: R 10497. Reproduced by permission.

in Dessau he was able to live in peace and in 1587 he remarried. He died in Dessau on 25 September 1602 (Kühne 1983: 156).

Eight years after his release, he published his *Idyllium Patria* (Budissin 1594), most of which had been written in prison, but had subsequently undergone revision. Consisting of 1,080 lines of Latin verse, it constitutes in the first place a history of Upper Lusatia, but it is also a hymn of praise to his native land. He recalls his happy childhood and the time when the Reformation was new in Budissin:

> This town received me new-born with the light and air of its sky:
> It fed me and educated me with good studies.
> At that time in the mists of error, in almost the whole
> World the radiance of the Gospel shone.
> (Peucer 1594/2001: 16/38, ll. 275–8)

The Wends appear in their historical contexts, but here the author's Wendish identity is not revealed. He makes a distinction between the generic *Henetus* and the specific *Sorabus*:

> Whatever is now still left from the Wendish race (*Heneta de stirpe*)
> Is called by name and by voice the fatherland of the Sorbs (*patria Sorabum*).
> (Peucer 1594/2001: 36/78, ll. 749–50)

He recalls how in his prison cell 'surrounded by uncouth soldiers on guard' he meditated on his fate and the consequences of his friendship with Melanchthon, which had brought him first great honours, then great suffering.

The Latin writer Johannes Rhagius Aesticampianus (1457–1520) is identified as a Wend solely from his place of birth, Sommerfeld in Kreis Crossen in the Neumark. That this was a Wendish-speaking area at the time of his birth is proved, first, by a document of the Küstrin Consistory referring to the Inspectorate of the Crossen Superintendent in 1775:

> Formerly it was only in the towns that the churches under this Inspectorate were German too. Otherwise, those under the Lordship of Rothenburg and beyond the Forest of Griesel and Cunersdorf and [under] Schlesisch Drehnow were Polish. The others and those under the Provost were Wendish. Now all the churches of Kreis Crossen are German.

> (Mětšk 1958: 24)

Secondly, there is a 1683 record of the appointment of a Wendish sacristan (*des Windischen Küsters bestallung*) in Sommerfeld (Mětšk 1958: 5). Since 1945 these lands have been part of Poland and what was once Sommerfeld is now Lubsko. Its Wendish name is recorded as Žemŕ.

It is surmised that Johannes Rhagius's Wendish name was Jan Rak (from *rak* 'crab'). Aesticampianus means 'of Sommerfeld'. He was a prominent humanist scholar and well travelled. On 14 May 1491, when he was in his early thirties, he matriculated at the Jagellonian University in Cracow, and here he was taught by the well-known Humanist and poet Conrad Celtis (1459–1505). On graduation Rak left Poland and travelled via Vienna to Italy. After a stay in Bologna he moved on to Rome and here his poetic gift, demonstrated in his *Carmina* (Straßburg 1501), was recognized by Pope Alexander VI, who bestowed on him the title of *Poeta laureatus*.

From 1501 he was Professor of Rhetoric and Moral Philosophy at the University of Mainz, but in 1506 he was summoned by the Elector of Brandenburg, Joachim I (1499–1535), to teach Greek at the newly founded Viadrina, the University of Frankfurt/Oder. After only one year, however, he left the Viadrina, which he described as a 'ruin' (*in se praecipiti eadem ruina*), and moved to the University of Leipzig, where his *Epigrammata* were published in 1507 (Irmscher 1983: 41–3).

Rak returned to Rome in 1511, where in 1512 he was awarded the degree of doctor. For a brief period he taught Greek in Paris, whence he moved on to Cologne, but in 1513 he was forced to move again, driven out by his Dominican opponents. After brief stays in Cottbus and Freiberg (Saxony) he came to Wittenberg in 1517 and taught here until his death on 31 May 1520. In Wittenberg he became a friend of Luther and Melanchthon and accepted the Lutheran doctrine, though he was considerably older than them (Irmscher 1983: 44–5).

In a Sapphic hymn of praise to Saint Barbara in the *Epigrammata* (1507), Rak reveals a few biographical details. He implies that he had experienced travel by sea and thanks the saint for protecting him on more than one occasion. He dedicates the poem to her for saving his life from attackers on the way home after taking a bath:

Quod tibi (thermis rediens amoenis
Salvus et turma iuventum madente
Qui meum nudo iugulum petebant
Ense) dicavi.
[…] which (returning safe from a pleasant warm bath
and from a drunken mob of youths
who sought my throat with a naked sword)
I have dedicated to you.

(Udolph 2004: 14)

Another Renaissance poet whom we deduce to have been a Wend, despite the fact that his published works contain nothing in Wendish is Johannes Bocatius. Referred to usually by his Latin name (though there is a German document in which he calls himself Hans Bock), he was born of Wendish parents in 1569 in the Wendish townlet of Vetschau, west of Cottbus. He matriculated at the University of Frankfurt/Oder (the Viadrina) as Joannes Bocacius Wetzoviensis in 1588 and in 1594 he was appointed Rector of the Gymnasium in Eperies (now Prešov, Slovakia). The same year he was married to the 15-year-old Elisabeth Bels. The title *poeta laureatus* was bestowed on him in 1596 by the Emperor Maximilian I and two years later he was elevated by Rudolf II to the nobility (Teichmann 1998: 174, 186–7).

Bocatius left Eperies in 1599 to take up the position of Rector of the Gymnasium in Kaschau (now Košice, Slovakia), where he became involved in the conflict arising from the emperor's attempts to re-Catholicize this hitherto Lutheran area. With the majority of Protestants in Siebenbürgen and Upper Hungary Bocatius joined the resistance led by Stephan Bocskay, who in 1605 sent him as envoy to seek the help of the Protestant princes of Germany. On the way from Heidelberg to Brandenburg in February 1606 he was arrested, taken to Prague, tortured, and condemned to death, though the death sentence was later commuted to life imprisonment. On 30 November 1610, his wife and brother-in-law managed to engineer his escape, and on 10 January 1611, he was back in Kaschau, where in April his citizen's rights were restored. In 1613 he was reinstated as Rector (D. Teichmann 1998: 202–11).

In 1618, at the time of the Prague defenestration and revolt, Bocatius was librarian and court historian to Gabriel Bethlen, Prince of Siebenbürgen, who in 1620 was crowned king of Hungary, and he was still in the king's service at the time of his death in Ungarisch Brod in 1621 (D. Teichmann 1998: 238). His works fill many volumes. They include not a single word of Wendish, but the self-designation 'M[agister] Iohannes Bocatius Sorabus, poeta laureatus caesarius, ludirector Epperiessinus' is persuasive (Mokoschinus 1599, quoted in Bocatius 1990, 2: 847 and Bocatius 1990, 1: 41).

Where Wendish met Polish

To the east of Lower Lusatia, in the Neumark, the immediate neighbours of the Lusatian Wends (Sorbs) were Poles. This is where the Bober joins the Oder in the Krossen Circle. Sorbian territory reached not only as far as but even a few miles to the north of the Oder and to the east of the Bober. Although by 1775 they were German, all the churches in the Inspectorate of the Krossen Superintendent had once been Wendish or Polish. As late as 1683 there is a report of the appointment of a Wendish sacristan in Sommerfeld (see p. 106 earlier in the chapter).

Evidence of the Wendish ethnicity of this region in the sixteenth century comes mainly from entries in the *Erb Register des Ambts Croßen* (now in the *Landeshauptarchiv* in Potsdam) (Mětšk 1958: 9). For example, regarding the villages belonging to the church of St. Andreas, am Berg vor Krossen the *Erb Register* under the year 1550 notes:

> From the Polish or the Wendish villages the pastor has half of the eggs, the sexton has the rest. Polish villages are Pommertzigk and Blumbergk. At Easter the sexton gets eggs from the six Wendish villages Rädtnicz, Goßkar, Khämen, Mortzig, Lochwicz, and Bilow. These he must share with the pastor. At Christmas he gets cakes from the aforementioned six villages. Those he alone keeps. From the three

German villages Mertzdorff, Hundsbelle, and Berge he gets from each household 4 florins and nothing more.

(Mětšk 1958: 21–2)

Further recorded here from the same date are the obligations and remuneration of two chaplains at the parish church of St. Georg in Krossen itself:

Each of the two chaplains at Krossen shall receive in money and other considerations as follows: 60 florins money, 2 florins-worth of wood, 1 malter of corn from the Church of St Georg because he gives a Wendish sermon there every Sunday.

(Mětšk 1958: 22)

The linguistic situation in the Krossen Circle was later referred to by the Elector of Brandenburg Johann Georg (1525–1595; r. from 1571) in instructions to the General Superintendent of the Neumark regarding the qualifications of Wendish preachers. The mayor and council of Cottbus had objected to the appointment of a pastor there from the Storkow area who was not familiar with the Cottbus dialect. The Elector had therefore sought the opinion of Andreas Tharaeus, of the University of Frankfurt, on dialectal variation. See para on the Cottbus Circle above (Mětšk 1962a: 26–7) (Map 3.3).

Map 3.3 Brandenburg, Saxony, and the margraviate of Lower Lusatia in the Wendish area south of Berlin (sixteenth century).

Pomerania

Though it was still ruled by members of the native, originally Wendish, Greifen dynasty, the demographic and linguistic complexion of the Duchy of Pomerania by the sixteenth century was predominantly German. By adopting the German language and German ways, the Pomeranian Dukes had become part of the network of princely houses of the empire and of Europe. They contracted dynastic marriages with other ruling families. How far they retained a familiarity with the Wendish language is uncertain, but Szymon Krofey assumed they could at least read it (see below), and they never lost a sense of their Wendish roots, as may be seen from their attachment to Slav names, such as Barnim, Bogislaw, and Wartislaw, which not only marked them out as Slavs but also distinguished them from Poles. A similar message was conveyed by the persistent Kashubian and Wendish references in their titles.

Evident too is the Slav ethnicity of some members of the Pomeranian nobility at this time. Although competence in the Wendish language must have varied a good deal regionally as German advanced, there still are a number of references to noblemen speaking Wendish or Polish. (In some secondary sources *polski* 'Polish' may correspond to *wendisch* in the original. I have not checked all the primary sources. Scepticism is advised. Cf. Chapter 7.) At a trial in 1525 one of the witnesses deposed that, riding towards Stettin, he met the Stolp nobleman Lukas von Putkamer, who asked him 'in Wendish' when he intended to return (Ślaski 1959: 40). In 1552 in preparation for negotiations between Pomerania and the kingdom of Poland regarding their borders, Duke Barnim IX put forward the names of several noblemen from the Stolp Kreis whom he considered qualified for participation in the Pomeranian delegation owing to their command of Polish (Wielopolski 1954: 96).

In the report of a trial of 1566 resulting from a confrontation over a disputed meadow it was recorded that Jacob von Zitzewitz of Jannewitz (Janiewice) in the vicinity of Schlawe (Sławno) had urged his men on with cries in Polish of 'Thrash 'em, lads!' (*Bijće, chłopcy!*) (Ślaski 1959: 50). The Chancellor to Dukes Barnim XI and Philipp, Jacob von Zitzewitz (c. 1507–1572), whose ancestral estate lay in Muttrin, south-east of Stolp, is reported to have been regarded by the Inner Pomeranian nobility as a 'Wendish interloper' (*wendischer Eindringling*) (Zitzewitz 1927: 46–7).

An order of 1514 prohibiting the admission of Wends to guilds in Stettin reflects a lingering Wendish presence here, and there is a similar ban dated 1539 relating to Kolberg (Ślaski 1959: 35) (Map 3.4). A little further east, the following ban of 1516 on the use of the Wendish language in the town market of Köslin attests its survival here:

> Nor shall anyone buying from the Wendish people use the Wendish language, so that the ordinary citizens shall not fear to be caught out by difficulties of language, on pain of three pounds.

> (Berghaus 1867: 213)

BALTIC SEA

Map 3.4 Brandenburg, Pomerania, and Poland before 1648.

Dated 1548, an account of Bartłomiej Sastrow referring to his visit in 1546 to Jacob von Zitzewitz on his estate at Muttrin/Motaryzno, near Stolp, records: 'Where the Zitzewitzes have their seat is Kashubian and Wendish (*Casubisch und Wendisch*). When the children are old enough they learn Wendish and German together simultaneously' (Zitzewitz 1927: 47; Ślaski 1959: 47). It is impossible to say whether the implicit distinction between Kashubian and Wendish is of any significance.

In 1517, the year when Luther nailed his ninety-five theses on indulgences to the door of the castle church in Wittenberg, Bogislaw X (1454–1523; r. from 1474), known as Bogisław the Great, engaged Johannes Bugenhagen (1485–1558) to write a history of the Duchy, a task which he completed with extraordinary alacrity. Born in Wollin in 1485, Bugenhagen, after studying at the University of Greifswald from January 1502 to summer or autumn 1504, became the rector of the town school in Treptow on the River Rega. In 1509 he was ordained priest. Early in 1517 he came to the notice of Duke Bogislaw, who summoned him to Rügenwalde, where the court was then resident, to give him his commission. Bugenhagen immediately set off on a tour of Pomerania, visiting monasteries and other likely places in search of suitable documents to use as sources for his history. Returning to Treptow in the autumn, he set about writing his *Pomerania*, and by May 1518 it was complete (Bugenhagen 2008: 13–16).

It is primarily based on medieval sources, but follows events up to the author's lifetime. He saw Pomeranian history as a gradual process of Germanization resulting from the conversion carried out by Otto of Bamberg rather than from conquest and colonization. It gives prominence to the Wendish origins of the Duchy, but says little about the activities of the Wends in the author's own time. Nevertheless, his occasional

Wendish allusions are valuable. Bugenhagen was to become one of the leading lights of the Reformation and its chief architect in Pomerania.

The *Pomerania* is helpful with terminology. It refers to 'The Winiti, whom we nowadays call *Wende* in the vernacular tongue, but more formally *wandali* or *Slavi*' (*Vt sunt Winiti quos vernacula lingua Wende hodie dicimus, honestiore autem vocabula wandalos vel Slavos*) (Bugenhagen 2008: 40). Bugenhagen, unlike Luther, was not hostile to the Wends. He respected their traditions of hospitality and care of old people (Bugenhagen 2008: 127). He was fascinated by the fact that the Dukes of Pomerania retained the formulae referring to the *Wenden/Slavi* in their titles and was at pains to explain why. In his interpretation of Pomeranian history German-speaking immigrants from other parts of the Holy Roman Empire receive scant attention. The fact that by his time the native tongue of most of his countrymen was German, he attributed to the influence of Christianity. In the chapter entitled 'The Pomeranians were once called Wends' (*Pomerani quandoque Slavi dicti*) (Bugenhagen 2008: 78–85) he quotes manuscripts going back to the thirteenth century to justify the conventional formula in the title of the Dukes (*Barnim et filius Bugslaus dei gratia duces Slavorum* 'Barnim and his son Bugislaw, by the grace of God Dukes of the Slavs'). He was nevertheless mystified by it, however, because, as he says, not all Slavs are Pomeranians. It is

> …as if only the Pomeranians were Slavs, which they call Vandals or, as now, Wends (some are not loath to write Windi); they were once called Winiti and Winuli. Although I have not read of a cause for this, I shall still place before the readers a conjecture which, if I am not mistaken, is not be despised. First, it is certain that the Pomeranians, who are the first of the Winiti, were the last to turn to Christ and that all the Winiti at one time used only the Slav language, which gradually was changed by believers in Christ into German, especially by those inhabiting towns. Then all rejoiced, the superstitions of their ancestors having been rejected and their speech having changed, to be called not Slavs but Germans (*non Slavi sed Teutones*). Thus it happened, we believe, that the Pomerani, who were the last of the Winuli to believe, especially rejoiced in the name of the Slavs (*Slavorum*), although the Slav name (*Slavicum nomen*) remained not only among them. For it becomes clear from the histories that the Pomeranians still spoke Slav at the time of their conversion. Otherwise, why did the holy Otto, a German, speak to the Pomeranians through an interpreter?

Bugenhagen took an enlightened view of the Wends' language and disapproved of those who mocked their imperfect German. He regarded them, apparently, as his fellow countrymen:

> If, however, we now consider the language, then the Slavs in our land are few in number and they live close to the Poles, whose language they can more or less

understand. They live in the countryside, it is true, but owing to traffic with towns they speak both languages. They nevertheless so cherish the Slav tongue (*Slavica*) that if one of our people accosts anyone [of them] in his own neighbourhood, whether by supplications or admonishments, he rejects the German language. But to admit the truth, this is our fault, because we are too ready to laugh at those whose language we do not know, when they speak ours. Indeed, they hardly ever learn German perfectly, if they have once imbibed the Slav language (*Slavicam linguam*) perfectly. The German language has articles just as Greek does; Wendish is spoken without articles like Latin (*Slavica absque articulis loquitur, Latinis similiter*).

If we accepted that this fault, if such it is, arises not from ignorance but rather from knowledge of a different way of speaking, then we might not, in such an unchristian way, laugh at this people, who are already very pious and cultured, but rather respect them like the rest of our people. On account of these Slavs and the neighbouring towns and the others which were the last to give up speaking Slav, our princes still describe themselves as Dukes of the Slavs or Wends (*Duces Slavorum sive Wandalorum*). We hear that princes of other lands are accustomed to act similarly, because they have a number of Slavs in their territory.

(Bugenhagen 2008: 84–5)

The distinction drawn here between *Slavi* and *Poloni* implies that *Slavi* was a translation of vernacular *Wenden*.

Another prominent historian of Pomerania is Thomas Kantzow (1505–1542), who was born in Stralsund and studied at the University of Rostock (founded 1419). His works were written only a few years after Bugenhagen's *Pomerania*. Some are in Low German and some in standard German. Coming from Stralsund, he was naturally well informed about Rügen and Inner Pomerania (*Vorpommern*), but his allusions to the Wends of his own time in Outer Pomerania (*Hinterpommern*) are not very revealing:

The people are now wholly German and Saxon, except that there are still a few Wends and Kashubs (*etliche Wende und Cassuben*) living in the country in Outer Pomerania. They are much more refined and pious than they were in the time of the Wends. Yet they still have in them, both from the Wends and from the severe climate where they live, much coarseness. For they think little or nothing of studies or the liberal arts. Therefore they do not have many learned people either, although there are some fine brains among them, as may been seen in many, when someone takes them in hand.

(Kantzow 1897: 413)

In Kantzow's view the word *Wend(e)* was a term of abuse:

> These peoples and lands were, according to the testimony of all German, Polish, Bohemian, Danish and other histories that deal with them, from their first origins until Christianity and some years thereafter, everywhere Wendish, as even now a whole region in Outer Pomerania is, where no one but Wends live. Therefore we are unable to derive their origin from anywhere else but from the tribe of the Wends. And although among us now the name and tribe of the Wends is so despised, that we call someone a Wend or a Slav (which is a thing) (*einen Wend oder Slafen (welchs ein Dinck ist)*) as an insult, we should not at all be ashamed of our origin.

(Kantzow 1897: 3)

He was consequently puzzled by the uninhibited use of the word *wendisch* by the Hanse towns (cf. Chapter 2, p. 56):

> ...as the seven main towns of the Hanse, namely Lübeck, Hamburg, Lüneburg, Wismar, Sund, Rostock, and Danzig, are not ashamed of the name, but in all their dealings and honours call and sign themselves the seven Wendish towns (*die sieben wendische Stette*), notwithstanding that Hamburg and Lüneburg were Saxon from their beginning and that the other towns too are now all German.

(Kantzow 1897: 419)

When Bogislaw the Great was succeeded in 1523 by his sons Georg I (r. 1523–1531) and Barnim IX, the status of the Duchy vis-à-vis the Holy Roman Empire was in dispute, because Elector Joachim I Nestor of Brandenburg (r. 1499–1535), who was eager to expand his land-locked territory and acquire a stretch of Baltic coast, laid claim to the overlordship. The Dukes, for their part, were in no doubt that they were the vassals only of the emperor, not of Joachim. Their case was expounded by Bugenhagen in his history of Pomerania (2008: 84–93).

However, they were anxious to avoid a crisis and in a mood for compromise, so eventually, following negotiations, a treaty was drawn up and agreed at Grimnitz, nr. Eberswalde, in 1529, whereby the Dukes' direct imperial fief (*Reichsunmittelbarkeit*) was established and agreed. This was very satisfactory for Georg and Barnim, but they, realizing that Joachim could not be expected to leave the negotiations empty-handed, conceded an older claim that if the Greifen line should become extinct, the Elector of Brandenburg would inherit. In view of the dynasty's unfathomable antiquity, however, that eventuality was thought unlikely.

The Treaty of Grimnitz was confirmed by the Emperor Charles V at the Diet of Augsburg in 1530. The following year Georg I died and was succeeded by his son Philipp I (1515–1560). Barnim IX now reigned jointly with his nephew Philipp I, but in 1532 they again divided the Duchy into two: Barnim ruled Pommern-Stettin and Philipp

Pommern-Wolgast. They agreed not to oppose the propagation of Luther's doctrine in their domains and in 1535 a new *Kirchenordnung* was published, composed by Johannes Bugenhagen and accepting the Confession of Augsburg. In 1536 in Torgau, Philipp was married by Martin Luther to Maria of Saxony, daughter of Johann Friedrich I, Elector of Saxony. The first General Synod, held in Greifswald in 1541, assured the independence of the Lutheran Church and restricted the role of the Dukes in church matters (Szultka 1991: 48–9; *Pommern* 2014).

The new church, to judge from the records of its deliberations, took no account at all at first of the special linguistic needs of the Wends in Outer Pomerania. There is no mention of them before the Fourth General Synod, held in Stettin in 1545. Even here there is no more than a marginal allusion to them in a discussion on 'Poor-houses for poor schoolchildren and students', which concluded 'That various houses may be built, where poor boys and students may be given instruction, who later may and can be used as pastors, preachers, and other clergy' and that 'At Stargard and Stolp there could also be such a house, as is especially necessary at Stolp on account of the Wendish language' (Balthasar 1725: 42). Recommendations as to the books which should be held in churches and parsonages throughout the Duchy, beginning with 'die Teutsche Biblia', as well as advice on books to be avoided, contain no mention of the needs of the Wends (Balthasar 1725: 35).

It is not until 1594 that the first evidence emerges of a concern for teaching and preaching in the language of the indigenous population. In that year Duke Johann Friedrich of Pomerania issued his *Leges Praepositis Ecclesiarum* (Laws for the General Superintendents of the Churches), containing the following instructions:

> He [the General Superintendent] shall command the Wends' preachers (*Vandalorum Concionatores*), if there are any, to express in Wendish (*Vandalice*) the same things which they have got to know in Latin or German, and to take notice of those who know the language well.

> (Szultka 1991: 67–8)

The point of taking 'notice of those who know the language well' can only have been to facilitate the recruitment of competent clergy. Whether any General Superintendents did in fact ever issue such commands is not recorded, but there is some evidence that at a local level in eastern Outer Pomerania Wendish was used by the church.

Allusions to entire Wendish congregations are significant, as in a sermon delivered at the dedication of a new church in Schmolsin at Whitsun 1582, by David Croll, a native of Stolp, who had been appointed Superintendent of Stolp in 1574. In his 1582 sermon he said:

> For although Outer Pomerania (*Hinterpommern*) is still for the greater part inhabited by old Slav Wends and we on account of them at times have to hear disparaging talk that we live here at the end of the world, where the Lord's Prayer comes to an end, supposedly, that we here in this Wendish place are so brutal,

barbaric, and stuck in such deep obscurity that we have no perception (or very little) of the truth of the Gospel, yet things are really (praise God) quite different. For we thank the Lord God for permitting the light of the Holy Gospel to arise in this place too, and very early, whereby not only people of rank, but also many poor Wendish peasants and their dear children have come to such an awareness of the pure, salutary doctrine and piety as you may ever find among the Germans. For it is clear that the town of Stolpe, which in other ways too is richer in talents than the other nearby towns, was the first in Pomerania to reject, through the grace of God, the unchristian Popery, as soon as the Holy Gospel had been revealed by Luther, and to accept the pure evangelical doctrine. Therefore, it was soon spread into the neighbouring Wendish churches among the nobility and their poor serfs, and has borne manifold fruit, as [we see] before our eyes.

(Croll 1586: [3–5])

The assertion that Outer Pomerania was 'for the greater part' (*zum mehren theil*) still inhabited by Wends is surely significant and Croll's tone is by no means unfriendly to them. The burden of his message is that despite imputations of backwardness the Wends have been at least as quick as the Germans to accept the reformed doctrine. Perhaps too eager to bolster the anti-Slav stereotype, Szultka (1991) perceives in Croll a hostile attitude to the Wends. He accuses Croll of saying that 'Germans are compelled to listen to their "foul" language' and that in Wendish parishes 'brutality and barbarism reign', while 'Protestantism is very weakly spread' (1991: 68). In actual fact, nothing of the kind is to be found in the sermon.

The century was not out before the subject of the Ducal succession, raised at Grimnitz in 1529, returned to haunt the Greifen. In 1577 Duke Johann Friedrich (1542–1600) of Stettin-Pomerania had married Erdmuth of Brandenburg (1561–1623), daughter of the Elector Johann Georg of Brandenburg. Thirteen years later there were still no children, and Elisabeth von Dobschütz (or Doberschütz), a Pomeranian noblewoman, was accused of having made Erdmuth barren by means of witchcraft. Accompanied by her husband Melchior, Elisabeth fled to Krossen, but she was caught and taken back to Stettin, where she was imprisoned, tortured, and condemned to death. On 17 December 1590, she was decapitated and her body burned outside the gates of Stettin (Bauer 1911, 1: 493–5; *Dobschütz* 2013).

Pomeranian Wendish in writing

The arrival of the Reformation in Pomerania must have led to an increase in the use by the clergy of the Wendish vernacular, yet there are no surviving Wendish or Kashubian texts from this time. The history of Wendish in Pomerania is thus quite different from its history in Lusatia and its environs, where (as we have seen) several substantial texts have survived from the sixteenth century.

There is nevertheless one book printed in the sixteenth century which reveals something of liturgical practice in Wendish churches in Pomerania at that time. The only surviving copy was found in the parsonage in Schmolsin by F. Tetzner in 1896. The title is *Duchowne piesnie D. Marcina Luthera y ynßich naboznich męzow. Zniemieckego w Slawięsky ięzik wilozone Przes Szymana Krofea sluge slowa Bozego W Bytowie. Drukowano w Gdainsku przes Jacuba Rhode. Roku Panskiego 1586* ('Spiritual songs of Dr Martin Luther and other pious men. Translated from German into the Slav language by Szymon Krofey, servant of God's word in Bütow. Printed in Danzig by Jakob Rhode. In the year of our Lord 1586').

The language into which the book has been translated is described in the title as *Slawięsky ięzik* (ostensibly 'Slav language'), but it can by no stretch of the imagination be identified with the Slav language of Pomerania (whether this be called Wendish, Slovincian, or Kashubian) recorded in later sources. Krofey's language is in fact a kind of Polish, but Polish with a distinct Wendish (Slovincian or Kashubian) admixture. For example, it shows such Kashubian phonological features as *i* (for Polish *ę*) as in *dzikuiemy* 'we thank' (Pol. *dziękujemy*), Kashubian *dz* (for Polish *dź/dzi*) in *bądze* 'will be' (Polish *będzie*), and *iol* (for Polish *eł*) as in *piolny* 'full' (Polish *pełny*). Examples of the Kashubian vocabulary are *cierkiew* 'church' (for Polish *kościół*), *zob* 'cradle' (Polish *żłób*), *gwisno* 'surely' (Polish *pewnie*), *brutka* 'maiden' (Polish *panna*), *ziemko* 'hard, heavy' (Polish *ciężko*), *ninia* 'now' (Polish *teraz*) (Olesch 1958a: *passim*; Popowska-Taborska 2001: *passim*). Krofey's designation of the book's language as 'Slawięsky ięzik', distinguishing it from Polish, is significant.

It is likely that Krofey's word *slawięsky* was the local self-designation, the equivalent of German *wendisch*. This is also implied by the fifteenth-century use of Polish *słowieński* in the term *słowieńska gryzwna* (=Latin *Sclavonica marca*) (*Słownik staropolski*, s.v.), probably denoting the *Wendentaler* or another coin of the *Wendischer Münzverein* (see Chapter 2, p. 56). The interpretation of *slawięsky* as having the generic sense 'Slavonic' has been persuasively rejected by Treder (2003: *passim*; 2006: 231, 275). For one thing, there is no reason why the Pomeranian Wends, any less than the Slovaks and Slovenes, should not have used a self-denotation based on the root *slov-*, and, for another, there is no evidence that Krofey (let alone his readers) had a sense of the Slavonic languages as a group. Moreover, the adjective *słowiński*, denoting the local language, was to be found still in use in this area 300 years later (see Chapter 6).

Krofey's book was published with the support of the Dukes Barnim X and Johann Friedrich and with the hope, expressed by the author in his foreword, that they might be *pobudzona* 'stimulated' and *nawiedzona* 'visited, haunted' by it (Ślaski 1959: 45). These are strange words, unless Krofey believed that they were able to read and understand it. Krofey also translated a catechism (*Cwicżenie Kathechismowe*), but this has not survived and is known to have existed only from a later edition (1758), which survives in a single copy (Ślaski 1959: 45–6). Whether it was printed in Krofey's time is not known. It is significant that, although he was the pastor of Bütow, his *Duchowne piesnie* was published and printed in Danzig (Gdańsk), across the border in Royal Prussia. Danzig in the sixteenth century had a thriving book-publishing industry, but there is no evidence in the Duchy of Pomerania at this time of any publishing in Polish at all (with or without Wendish features).

It is thus a mystery how pastors with Wendish parishes managed to care for their congregations without the help of the printed word. Many of the faithful will have been unable to read, it is true, but certainly not all. Schools in both towns and villages were in the care of the church, which after the Reformation was placing a new emphasis on literacy (Figure 3.3).

The need for devotional literature may have been satisfied, to a limited extent, by the use of books from Poland, printed in Polish. A few copies of such books are said to have survived here and there in east Pomeranian parishes, but the evidence is sparse. A church visitation in 1590 reported having found a Polish bible in Glowitz, south of

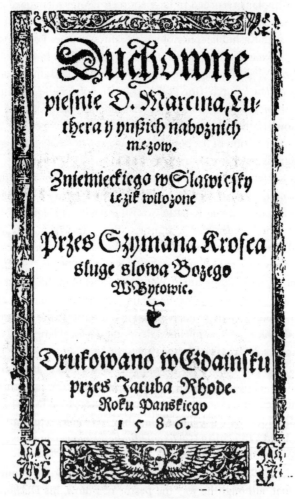

Figure 3.3 Title page of Simon Krofey, *Duchowne pieśnie* (Gdańsk 1586), showing use of the adjective *Slawięski*. Instytut Kaszubski, Gdańsk.

Lake Leba, in addition to a Latin bible and Luther's *Hauptpostille* (Tetzner 1899: 151). In Budow (Budowo) the visitation approved the purchase of a Polish Lutheran bible (Ślaski 1959: 44). Polish books are also reported to have been found in the libraries of the Dukes and members of the nobility, which is clearly of relevance to the question of the survival of the Wendish language among the social elite (Ślaski 1959: 44).

Wends in Royal Prussia

In 1466 in the Second Peace of Thorn, the Teutonic Order had been forced to cede Pommerellen (the home of the Kashubs between the lower Vistula and the River Lupow/Łupawa) to Poland. The *Ordensstaat* (from now on called Prussia) was divided into two. The western lands, called Royal Prussia, came under the Polish Crown, while those in the east with their capital in Königsberg continued to be ruled by the Order. Thanks to the Reformation, however, the Order's rump state lasted only until 1525, when its Grand Master, Albrecht of Hohenzollern, accepted the reformed doctrine, secularized his organization, and created the Duchy of Prussia as a fief of the Polish Crown. The price he had to pay for ducal autonomy was fealty to the king of Poland, first confirmed at a ceremony in the Market Square of Cracow in 1525 and re-confirmed on the coronation of every new Polish king or the succession of every new duke until 1648 (Friedrich 2000: 23).

Paradoxically, very little is found in sixteenth-century sources relating to Wends or Kashubs in Royal Prussia, the territory between the Rivers Leba and Vistula, which, from a later perspective, we might regard as the Kashubian heartland. Until the nineteenth century much more is known of the Slav population to the west of the Leba (in the Duchy of Pomerania) than to the east of it (in Royal Prussia). In sixteenth-century sources relating to Royal Prussia, every occurrence of the word *kaszubski* or *Cassubius* is precious. If the Slavs here are not referred to by the term *wendisch*, that is probably because they are not mentioned in German sources at all before the nineteenth century.

Of the Kashubs east of the Leba in the sixteenth century very little is known. The political history of Royal Prussia is well documented, but the Kashubs play no part in it (Friedrich 2000: *passim*). In the Duchy of Pomerania, the Wends were still fairly numerous, particularly in the region from Cöslin eastwards. The westernmost part of the *Ordensstaat* was formed by the Lands of Lauenburg, and Bütow and after the Thirteen Years War these would have become part of Royal Prussia (hence part of Poland), had Poland not promised them to Duke Erik II of Pomerania in return for his support in the war. Nevertheless, the status of the area remained uncertain until 1526, when Zygmunt the Old gave it to Duke Georg I of Pomerania as an almost unconditional fief. It remained part of Pomerania until the end of the Griffin dynasty in 1637 (*Lauenburg* 2014).

Royal Prussia consisted of the Bishopric of Warmia and the three voivodeships: Culm (Chełmno), Marienburg (Malbork), and the Pomeranian voivodeship (west of the Vistula and including Danzig). The biggest, richest, and most populous of these was the Pomeranian Voivodeship (here always referred in full to avoid confusion with the Duchy of Pomerania). However, its population in the late sixteenth century (about 150,000) was considerably less dense than that of either of the other two voivodeships (Friedrich 2000: 23–6). The standard of living in Royal Prussia as a whole was somewhat higher than in the rest of the Polish Commonwealth (Kromer 1984: 194).

The Royal Prussian provincial diet (*Landesrat*) was modelled on the Polish *Sejm*, and in 1569, when the parliamentary union of the kingdom and the Grand Duchy of Lithuania took place, places were provided in the Polish *Sejm* for Prussian deputies. A degree of separate law and self-government was maintained, however, and the Union of 1569 was not the end of the Prussian diet. It continued to protect Prussian legal traditions, including a *jus indigenatus*, which meant only natives could be office-holders. The definition of 'native', however, was vague and much disputed. According to one view, an *indigena* 'native' meant nothing more than a land-owning nobleman (Friedrich 2000: 29–35). Although until 1570 knowledge of the German language was a condition of being an *indigena Prussiae* 'native of Prussia', there is no known case of a non-German speaker being denied this status, provided he had been born in Royal Prussia, was of legal birth, and owned land (Friedrich 2000: 38). Until 1600 the *jus indigenatus* was valid in both Prussias (Royal and Ducal); an *indigena* of one was automatically an *indigena* of the other. But this changed, as an increasingly critical view was taken of Ducal Prussia's political system (Friedrich 2000: 39).

The *jus indigenatus* was a cardinal feature of the identity of Prussian burghers and nobles, regardless of native language. There was among them a strong sense of solidarity and Prussian identity, uninfluenced by language (German or Polish). There was a high degree of bilingualism. Royal Prussia recognized the king of Poland as its lord and master, but the relationship was often problematic. The ruling class of Royal Prussia saw itself as a society superior to the rest of the Polish Commonwealth.

In the proceedings of the Royal Prussian *Landestag* (*Sejm*) and local parliaments of lower status (*sejmiki*), all three languages (German, Polish, and Latin) were used. German predominated, however, and on the rare occasions when a speech was made in Polish, deputies sometimes complained that they could not understand it. At times they also objected to Latin for the same reason. The complaints appear to have been made purely on practical grounds without nationalistic connotations. None the less, the linguistic implications of the link with Poland were not overlooked. Speaking at an assembly of the Marienburg *sejmik* in 1573 Jan Działyński, Voivode of Culm, and Jan Kostka, Castellan of Danzig, not only dismissed the idea that ignorance of German disqualified a candidate from election to a local *sejmik*, but also went further and said that subjects of the king of Poland should learn Polish ('... so sollte man sich polnisch reden lernen' (Gerlach 1959: 166n.). It was only in the next century, however, that Polish really began to gain ground in the debates of local parliaments. The three languages were also used in public records, by the bureaucracy, in the law courts, and in publishing (Gerlach 1959: 167–85).

The Royal Prussian national identity was based not on language or ethnicity, but on a shared history and political culture. The national identity revealed to us by the sources, however, is solely that of the governing and writing classes. Of the identity of the peasants who tilled the land or of the fishermen who gathered the harvest of the lakes and sea we know next to nothing, but there is no reason to doubt that they were Kashubs. Martin Cromer named them separately from the Poles:

> [...] both the origin and the language of the Polish people is shared with the Czechs, Ruthenians, Muscovites, Croatians, Moravians, Silesians, Kashubians, Bulgarians, Rascii, Serbs, Illyrians, and the general name of Slavs or Wends (*universo nomine Slavico seu Venedico*). Nevertheless, it is so varied that some of these peoples scarcely and with difficulty understand each other.

> (Cromer 1577: 49)

He is also referring to the Kashubs, though not by name, when he writes:

> Yet the inhabitants of Prussia, though predominantly Germans or of German origin and using the German language mainly in writing court records, generally speak in a language in which Polish words are mixed with German.

> (Kromer 1984: 55)

Some historians are certainly in the habit of taking for granted the presence of the Kashubs in Royal Prussia in the sixteenth century. Odyniec, for example, in a meticulous study of the *Starostwo* of Putzig, says 'The population of the Castellany of Putzig consisted of Kashubians', yet among his sources there is only one that names them, a document of 1599 (referring once to 'Poloni aut Cassubae' and once to 'Poloni...seu Cassubii' (1961: 43, 45).

The first mention of Kashubs in the Polish language seems to be in the literary work *Dworzanin polski* 'The Polish Courtier' (1566) of Łukasz Górnicki (1527–1603). Inspired by Baldasare Castiglione's *Il Corteggiano* 'The Courtier', it consists of conversations between cultivated gentlemen concerning the behaviour of the ideal courtier, the court in this case being that of Bishop Maciejowski at Prądnik, near Cracow. In Chapter 1 the subject under discussion is languages. In the course of an examination of the ideal courtier's linguistic attributes and attainments one of the participants, Pan Kryski, expresses his views on the use of archaic and foreign words:

> But if there is no present-day word for the thing the courtier would like to describe, then not only am I not offended by an old word, but prefer it to a foreign one. Finally, I would not wish a courtier to despise even a Prussian Kashubian word (*Pruskiem Kászubskiem słowem*) – words which we laugh at so readily – for he will find there many a word that describes the thing so exactly that it is impossible to be more exact.

> (Górnicki 1566: [41v-42r])

This unambiguous reference to the Kashubs of Royal Prussia (as opposed to those of Pomerania) reveals that among Poles there existed a stereotypical perception of Kashubian speech as comic. Górnicki himself, however, regards Kashubian as a useful source of Polish neologisms. Górnicki came from Little Poland, but he worked in the service of the king of Poland (Zygmunt August) and accompanied him on a visit to Danzig in 1552, where he must no doubt have met Kashubs, or at least heard of them and their strange language.

The last Wends in Mecklenburg (1521)

The death in 1404 of the old woman called Gulitzin, in all probability, brought to an end the story of the Wendish language not only on Rügen, but also in the whole of Inner Pomerania. A little further west, however, in Mecklenburg, the language survived into the following century. A document of c. 1521 reveals that the Mecklenburg Wends and their language still lived on in the Jabel Forest. This is a history of medieval Mecklenburg written for Duke Heinrich V by Nicolaus Marschalk (also known as Thurius), who was born in Roßla (Harz) in 1470 and came to Mecklenburg only towards the end of his life. In 1505 he was employed at the Mecklenburg court and from 1510 he was lecturing at the University of Rostock. He died in Rostock in 1525.

In his *Vitae Obetritarum* (c. 1521) Marschalk Thurius alludes to: '... Wends still in both essence and language, who inhabit the forest of Jabel, they have changed nothing in their way of life' (...*qui Gabellarum saltus incolunt, tam re, quam sermone adhuc Sarmathae, nihil de moribus mutavere*) (Nicolaus Marescalcus Thurius, *Vitae Obetritarum*, printed from the manuscript by Westphalen 1740: 1510; Lisch 1837: 177). The use here of the noun *Sarmata* to denote a Wend rather than a Pole is unusual, but any ambiguity is removed by an entry in a glossary (*En vocum elucidarium*) appended to the work, which says: '*Sarmatha & Vandalus & Sclavus*, ein Wende [...] yet it means not only Poles but all Wends' (*non tamen significat solos Polen, sed omnes Wenden*) (Westphalen 1740: 1576). Situated in south-west Mecklenburg, the Wends of the Jabelheide were separated by little more than the Elbe from the Wends of the Duchy of Brunswick-Lüneburg (see below).

Two further sixteenth-century Wendish allusions are found in the accounts of the Mecklenburg ducal exchequer, perhaps both referring to the same person. The first (1512) notes a sum of money paid 'to the boy who beats the drum, the Wend' (...*dem Jungenn der die trome sleit der wende*), and the second (1514) records an item of clothing given 'to the Wend, the drummer' (...*dem wendt trumsleger*) (Lisch 1837: 177). After Thurius, only memories of the Mecklenburg Wends lingered on, notably among the Dukes of Mecklenburg, who could trace their lineage back to Pribislav, Prince of the Obodrites.

A set of sentences purporting to be a version of the Lord's Prayer in the language of the Mecklenburg Wends was published in 1557 in Basle by the Emperor Ferdinand's historian Wolfgang Lazius in his book *De gentium aliquot migrationibus, sedibus fixis, reliquis, linguarumque initiis et immutationibus ac dialectis libri XII* (Lisch 1841: *passim*). Although portions of it are not beyond recognition as Slavonic, it has been grievously distorted in copying and is scarcely of any philological value as a record of Mecklenburg Wendish.

The Duchy of Lüneburg and western Brandenburg

The history of the Wends in Mecklenburg thus comes to an end, but on the opposite bank of the Elbe at this time, owing to the haphazard nature of the sources, Wendish history has barely begun. Not much is known of the Lüneburg Wends before the seventeenth century, though they must have been there and the history of the town and principality of Lüneburg is well documented. The fortress of Hliuni on the Ilmenau, first mentioned in 795 AD, grew into the settlement of Lüneburg, which was incorporated as a town in 1247. Then the principality of Lüneburg grew up, bordered by the Elbe, the Weser, and the Altmark. It was joined to Brunswick in the Duchy of Brunswick-Lüneburg, which in 1692 developed into the Electorate of Hanover (Köbler 1999, s.v.). It is a mystery how or why the Wends for centuries managed to survive here as a separate ethnic community while under German state and church authority.

The presence of Wends here in the Middle Ages is sporadically attested by, among others, Thietmar (1018), Helmold (1172), and Arnold von Lübeck (1212) (Olesch 1968: 1), but Frankish incursions into this region began at least as early as the ninth century, and by the eleventh century at the latest the Slavs here had been subjugated. Seven hundred years later, however, they still survived. Very little is known of them in the Middle Ages, though sporadic, laconic documentary references are enough to assure us that they were there. The existence of the counties of Dannenberg (1303) and Lüchow (1320) is documented, and in the course of the fifteenth century there are occasional allusions to antagonism between the Wendish inhabitants and their German neighbours (Schwebe 1960: 9, quoting Manecke 1858: 764).

The Reformation was introduced to the Principality of Lüneburg by Ernst I the Confessor in 1527. With what success the pre-Reformation Church grappled with the linguistic situation in the Wendland is not known, but the emphasis placed by the Reformers on preaching and the vernacular might have been expected to reveal the German–Slav linguistic divide. Evidence at this stage is still extremely sparse, but one significant observation is found in a letter dated 9 January 1536 from Clemens Wendel, Pastor of Hitzacker, to the master builder Gabriel Buering in Boitzenburg (about 20 miles away on the opposite bank of the Elbe and so in Mecklenburg). He wrote: 'The Wendish people are so ignorant that I can achieve few results with my sermons' (*Nu synth de wendischen lude szo vnnuorstendich, dath ick weynich fruchth dorch myne predicacien kan don*) (*Briefsammlung* 1837: 207–8). In 1570 an agreement between the citizens of Lüchow and their town council was reached to the effect that 'although the

Wends in former times were declared to have forfeited citizenship, access to citizens' rights should in future no longer be denied them totally' (Schwebe 1960: 9, quoting Jacobi 1856: 92).

Hitzacker, Wendel's parish, was one of the villages included in General Superintendent Hildebrand's visitation of 1671, by which time he concluded that there were no longer any Wends in the county (*Amt Hitzacker*), though the population still shared some of the unorthodox observances he had observed in neighbouring Wendish villages (Olesch 1967: 239). Of these villages in the sixteenth century, however, we know nothing. To their immediate south, on the other hand, in the Altmark (Brandenburg) lies the little town of Salzwedel, where the Wendish presence had been documented since the Middle Ages. They were still there in 1512, when the Elector Joachim instructed the town, not for the first time, to withdraw the right to brew beer from the 'Wendish and improper people' (*wendische und unechte lewthe*) (W. Vogel 1960: 48, 130). Salzwedel was one of the towns whose guilds' statutes excluded Wends (1512 and 1527) and it is striking that in the sixteenth century there were to the east and south-east of Salzwedel several other towns where the guilds made similar anti-Wendish provisions, namely, Kyritz (1569, 1580), Havelberg (1563), Gardelegen (1555), and Ziesar (1555) (W. Vogel 1960: 126). These five towns all lie within a circumference of 100 km, and between Kyritz and Salzwedel lies Bad Wilsnack (see Map 3.2), a place of pilgrimage in pre-Reformation times and a favoured destination for local Wends, as we learn from a native of the town, Matthäus Ludecus (1517–1606) (also Lüdke, Luidtke, or Lüdecke), who became Dean of the collegiate church of St Nicholas here.

In Wilsnack on 13 August 1383, a disastrous fire had occurred. In the burnt ruins of St Nicholas's Church the parish priest had found three consecrated wafers, unharmed but stained with blood. After Dietrich II, Bishop of Havelberg, had certified the miraculous nature of this event, Wilsnack had become a place of pilgrimage. Although there were some who even before the Reformation questioned the cult, pilgrimages to the 'Miraculous Blood' (*Wunderblut*) or 'Holy Blood' (*Heiliges Blut*) of Wilsnack flourished and its reputation attained international proportions. Visitors included the English mystic Margery Kempe (c. 1373–1439) (*OCEL*, s.v.). It was only after the first Protestant pastor arrived here in 1552 and burned the relic that the pilgrimages came to an end (*CDB*, 2: 128).

Ludecus's account was published in Wittenberg in 1586 with the title *Historia von der Erfindung, Wunderwercken und Zerstörung des vermeinten heiligen Bluts zur Wilsnagk*) 'History of the Discovery, Miraculous Works and Destruction of the Supposedly Holy Blood at Wilsnack'). He is a well qualified witness, who had seen with his own eyes the hordes of pilgrims flooding into the little town, some of them having come great distances on foot. Among them there were people who were said, on a sudden impulse, while working in the fields or elsewhere, to have been moved to set off for Wilsnack, bringing with them the forks, spades, or other agriculture implements they had been using at the time, and these they then left there as gifts. By the time of the Reformation the town consisted almost entirely of lodging houses for the accommodation of pilgrims.

Ludecus significantly distinguishes the Wends and other local people from the pilgrims. He writes:

> In the church there also, in a segregated place, a false and fraudulent pair of scales of considerable size was kept, on which the pilgrims – first and foremost, however, the superstitious Wendish folk and other people from the neighbourhood – men, women, and maidens, whose animals or crops were not thriving, or else had lain sick for a time, would have themselves weighed, so that the sacrificing priests might better establish the magnitude of their sins.

(Ludecus 1586: [18])

CHAPTER 4
CONFESSIONS 1600–1700

The Thirty Years' War

The defenestration

In 1608 Matthias, the brother of the Emperor Rudolf II, was designated as the future king of Bohemia. Rudolf continued to reign in Bohemia, thanks only to the support of the Protestant Estates, in return for which he was in 1609 compelled to concede to them a *Majestätsbrief* guaranteeing religious freedom. With the exception of the representatives of the Budissin Cathedral Chapter and of the nunneries of Marienstern and Marienthal, the Upper Lusatian Estates were also Protestant and feared the possible reimposition of Catholicism. They were made uneasy by their inability to obtain from Rudolf the same guarantees he had given the Bohemian and the Silesian Estates in 1609. In April 1611 Matthias was elected king of Bohemia in place of Rudolf – who, however, remained emperor – and an acknowledgement (*Revers*) was obtained, guaranteeing the Upper Lusatian Estates the continuing practice of their Protestant religion (Wedgwood 1961: 67; Chadwick 1984: 143; Blaschke 1994b/2000: 110; Blaschke 1999a/2000: 94–6; Scheuch 2001: 53). For the Wends, although they had no representation at these events, these were matters of great significance.

The new king decided to travel to Lusatia to receive the homage of the Estates. On 3 September 1611, as the royal retinue approached Budissin from the south, passing through Wendish Protestant villages, it was met in Postwitz by the *Amtshauptmann* von Gersdorf at the head of 500 mounted noblemen (Reymann 1902: 59). In Postwitz, the village where as early as 1520 the parish priest, Paul Bosak, had given communion in both kinds (see Chapter 3), the king was entertained to luncheon by the Estates. Confessional scruples were put to one side, as grace was said by the Protestant pastor, Michael Schwach. Invited by Matthias to ask a boon, Schwach begged him to allow the Postwitz church to continue to give the people the chalice, and the king promised to permit and protect its use. On arrival in Budissin, Matthias attended mass, and then proceeded to the Ortenburg, where on 5 September the act of homage took place, and a further assurance of the maintenance of the religious status quo was issued. Neither this, however, nor the *Revers* granted in April had the legal force of a *Majestätsbrief* (Knauthe 1767: 247–8; Reymann 1902: 59; Blaschke 1999a/2000: 96).

In 1612 Emperor Rudolf died and was succeeded by Matthias, leaving the confessional question unresolved. In Bohemia there was continual friction and antagonism, usually arising from disputes over church buildings and land. On 17 June 1617, Ferdinand, Archduke of Styria, was pre-elected king of Bohemia, ready to succeed Matthias, and the following day the Bohemian Estates – with the exception of the two Royal Governors (*Statthalter*) of Prague, Vilém Slavata and Jaroslav Martinitz, who were Catholics – demanded from the king-elect a guarantee of the *Majestätsbrief*. He complied, but the confessional peace, if it had ever existed, was nearing its end. On 5 March 1618, the Protestant Estates, through their *Defensores*, demanded from Matthias a settlement of their grievances. This was refused (Wedgwood 1961: 71–2).

On 23 May the infuriated Protestants threw Slavata and Martinitz (together with their secretary) from an upstairs window of the royal castle, the Hradschin, into the courtyard below. They survived the defenestration, but the assault was an act of sedition marking the beginning of a coup d'état. The Protestant assembly appointed a provisional rebel government of thirty *Directores* and voted to raise an army of 16,000 men (Reymann 1902: 349; Wedgwood 1961: 74–5). Thus began the Thirty Years' War.

Upper Lusatian participation

The Bohemian *Directores* immediately informed the Upper Lusatian Estates of the May rebellion in Prague and in the course of the following winter the Bohemian Estates offered to obtain a *Majestätsbrief* for Upper Lusatia. They proposed a union of Bohemian, Silesian, and Upper Lusatian Estates. This was a temptation the Upper Lusatian Estates could not resist, for they had always aspired to full equality among the lands of the Bohemian Crown, and at their diet at the end of March 1619 they decided to join the Bohemian rebellion.

On 20 March 1619, Emperor Matthias died and towards the end of July the Electors gathered in Frankfurt-am-Main. On the last day of that month Silesia, Moravia, and Upper Lusatia signed the terms of membership of a Federation with Bohemia in the name of national integrity and the Protestant religion. On 27 April a delegation from the Upper Lusatian Estates arrived in Prague and on 15 May Upper Lusatia was received into the Confederation of all Habsburg lands that had united to resolve the religious conflict (Wedgwood 1961: 84, 88; Blaschke 1999a/2000: 97). On 19 August the Confederate states issued a declaration that Ferdinand had ceased to be their king and on 26 August they elected as their new king Friedrich, the Elector of the Palatinate, a Calvinist. Upper Lusatia was thus fully participant in the revolt. Two days later in Frankfurt/Main Ferdinand was elected emperor, just as the news arrived that he had been deposed as king of Bohemia (Wedgwood 1961: 88–90).

In the constant bickering between the confessions in Upper Lusatia, the Catholic party was led by the Dean of the Budissin Cathedral Chapter, while the Protestants were represented by the Budissin Town Council. August Widerin von Ottersbach (1577–1620), who became Dean in 1609, was a particular target of Protestant abomination, notably because he had opposed the efforts of the Estates to obtain a *Majestätsbrief* (Seifert 2002: 112). In Budissin on 27 August, the day after Friedrich's election, the Protestant authorities, under the aegis of the Bohemian *Directores*, set about evicting the Catholic clergy from the Cathedral (which since 1543 had been used by both confessions as a *Simultankirche*) and assigning them to the church of St Nicholas. Things quickly got out of hand and degenerated into a sectarian riot. Desecration of the mass in the Catholic part of the church by the rioters was followed by an attack on the Deanery and the Chapter House, which were (as they still are) located just a few steps across the road from the Cathedral. The buildings were plundered. The fleeing priests were chased into the Cathedral, which the rabble then proceeded to smash up. The municipal authorities, with the help of a number of armed citizens, managed to drive the mob out of the church and Dean Widerin von Ottersbach was provided with a carriage, in which he was conveyed in safety to the Ortenburg, guarded by a detachment of soldiers, preceded by the *Landeshauptmann* von Gersdorf mounted on horseback. The Ortenburg and Chapter House remained under armed guard for ten days (Reymann 1902: 240; Blaschke 1999a/2000: 97) (Figure 4.1).

Figure 4.1 The biconfessional church (*Simultankirche*) and Cathedral of St Peter, Bautzen, *c.* 1920. Serbski kulturny archiw, Bautzen.

The *Directores* invited the Upper Lusatian Estates to submit a list of complaints in ecclesiastical and political matters. The reply included the disadvantages suffered by the Wends in and around Budissin, who were still prevented from attending Protestant church services and obliged to attend mass (Knauthe 1767: 250). The terms of the Confederation signed on 31 July included in paragraph 10 the provision 'that in all the united lands, including all towns, market townlets, and villages thereof, the free exercise of the Protestant religion should be permitted and allowed in every local language' (Reymann 1902: 349). The local language provision was of especial significance to the Wends, giving them a new prominence. In immediate compliance, the town council now allotted to them the chapel of St Michael with the right to hold Wendish services there and to appoint a Wendish pastor. On 1 September 1619, it was consecrated as the parish church of the Lutheran Wends by Antoni Gommer, Archdeacon of St Peter's, who on that occasion also delivered the first Protestant sermon there to a congregation of Wends who had hitherto attended mass at the church of St Nicholas. Peter Bräuer was appointed pastor of St Michael's and on 29 September (St Michael's Day) he preached his first sermon (Knauthe 1767: 251–2; Reymann 1902: 349–50).

A group of Budissin citizens wrote to the town council on 2 September 1619, pointing out that – with the exception of one stalwart Catholic named Philipp Schönborn – the citizens of the town were now all Protestants. It was therefore unjust that they should be dominated by the Catholic Dean and Chapter, particularly by exclusion from the chancel of the Cathedral (Reymann 1902: 240). On 31 January 1620, Dean Widerin and his clergy took the oath acknowledging the Articles of Confederation and on 1 February he was able to move back into the Deanery. He declared that for the sake of peace he would surrender the Cathedral to the town council and would be satisfied with control of St Nicholas's Church. The new agreement came into force on 18 May 1620. In the Cathedral, the council had the railing removed and the Catholic altars, font, and so on were transferred into St Nicholas's Church, where Dean Widerin first held mass at Whitsun (7 June 1620). His parishioners (if, as claimed in the letter of 2 September 1619, the citizens of the town were now, apart from Philipp Schönborn, all Protestants) can only have come from the surrounding Wendish villages owned by the Chapter. On 27 June 1620, however, Dean Widerin died, aged 42 (Reymann 1902: 240–1; Neander 1920: 58; Seifert 2002: 112).

By May 1620 in the Wendish townlet Wittichenau, owned by the Marienstern nunnery, the Protestant congregation had grown to 300 and a pastor had been installed. In the Wendish village Radibor, whose ecclesiastical patron was the Budissin Cathedral Chapter, the Catholic priest was removed and replaced by a Protestant pastor. In Gaußig, where for several decades a dispute had been raging over the use of the church and the appointment of a priest, a Protestant pastor was installed. The Catholic *Landvogt* Carl Hannibal von Dohna was deposed. He abandoned the Ortenburg and was replaced on 2 May 1620 by the Protestant Count Schlick, appointed by King Friedrich (Blaschke 1999a/2000: 98).

As the military struggle gained momentum, the Protestant belligerents might well have expected to receive the support of the Protestant Elector of Saxony, Johann Georg

I, but he disappointed them. When it came to the point he put loyalty to the emperor first. His loyalty, however, did not come cheap. Ferdinand soon realized he was too weak militarily to regain Bohemia alone, so he made a proposal to Johann Georg, promising to compensate him for military expenditure. The most important of the Elector's conditions for acceptance were that the emperor must promise not to oppress Lutherans in Imperial lands, including Bohemia, and, as surety for military expenditure, must mortgage to the Elector the margraviates of Upper and Lower Lusatia. Ferdinand accepted and on 22 April 1620 appointed the Elector Imperial Commissioner in both Lusatias and in Silesia with a mandate to dissuade the Estates from their rebellion and restore them to obedience. He was authorized to use military force, but he was to assure those ready to submit of an imperial pardon (Blaschke 1999a/2000: 99–101).

A written guarantee of reimbursement of the costs of military action was signed on 6 June 1620 and the Elector immediately set about executing his assignment. On 5 September his envoy announced the contents of the Imperial commission to the town council and Estates assembled in Budissin, and they were ready to submit. Before they could do so, however, the vanguard of Friedrich's army reached the town and occupied it, taking the envoy prisoner. A few days later the Saxon army with 12,000 men under the command of Count Wolf von Mansfeld arrived outside Budissin and besieged it. The citizens, under occupation by Friedrich's forces, were forced to swear allegiance to him (Blaschke 1999a/2000: 101).

The commandant of the Protestant forces in Budissin, *Gouverneur* Dick, ordered the roof of St Nicholas's Church to be removed and an artillery battery erected inside it. The building was totally destroyed. It was less than three months since the Catholics had taken possession of it. On 13 September the Saxons began an artillery bombardment. As a result, on 2 October fire broke out and on 5 October Budissin capitulated. In the fire 1,136 houses and five churches were destroyed (Reymann 1902: 310; Blaschke 1999a/2000: 102). The Elector entered the town on 9 October, maintaining a hostile posture but ready for reconciliation. The council and population received a full pardon and restitution of their privileges. No punishment was imposed (Blaschke 1999a/2000: 102).

On 8 November Friedrich's army was defeated at the Battle of the White Mountain in Bohemia and on 3 March 1621 Johann Georg concluded the Dresden Accord with the Upper Lusatian Estates, restoring their full allegiance to the emperor and granting a full pardon. The Imperial Commission of 22 April 1620 now came into effect, transferring executive power in Upper Lusatia to the Elector. At the emperor's command, the Cathedral in Budissin was restored to its state before the rebellion. By 31 October 1622, the *Simultankirche* was again in operation. It was now time for the costs to be reckoned, and in January 1623 Saxony presented to the emperor its account for four million gulden. Ferdinand could not pay. Because he had mortgaged the two margraviates to Johann Georg as security for the costs of the imperial commission, he was obliged on 23 June 1623 to issue a document (the *Immissionsrezess*), confirming the Elector as the proprietor (*Inhaber*) of these lands. At the next Upper Lusatian diet the Elector, as mortgagee, received the homage of the Estates and so became the feudal overlord and beneficiary of the revenue (Reymann 1902: 241–2; Blaschke 1999a/2000:102–3).

The Peace of Prague (1635)

The destruction of 1620 was only the first of a series of catastrophes suffered by Budissin during the Thirty Years' War. In 1634 Johann Georg, having changed sides and joined the Protestant alliance, was again besieging Budissin, which this time was held by the emperor's forces. On 2 May the besiegers set fire to the town, quickly reducing it to ashes again (Reymann 1902: 101). The Cathedral was badly damaged and remained out of use until 1640. For six years its congregation had the use of the Wendish church of St Michael, the Protestant Wends meanwhile being left without Wendish services. The Catholic church of St Nicholas, having served its predominantly Wendish parishioners for less than three months before its destruction in 1620, was destined to remain a permanent ruin (Reymann 1902: 310–11, 350–51) (Figure 4.2).

On 30 May 1635, in Prague a treaty was signed between the Elector and the emperor. The Saxon bill (including interest) had meanwhile risen to 72 tons of gold. He therefore transferred the two Lusatias to the Elector of Saxony irrevocably. The transfer was

Figure 4.2 Ruins of the church of St Nicholas (*Mikławšk*), Bautzen, *c.* 1920. Serbski kulturny archiw, Bautzen.

made not to Saxony but to the Elector personally and was hereditary. Nevertheless, the margraviates remained a male fief of the Crown of Bohemia. The protection of the Catholic religion and its spiritual institutions were specifically confirmed and the Augsburg Confession was also to be protected with its traditions. The conditions of the transfer were recorded in a treaty (the *Traditionsrezess*), which was approved by the Estates in December 1635. The final formality was the Imperial enfeoffment of Johann Georg on 16 August 1638. The emperor, as king of Bohemia, retained supreme rights over the Catholic Church in Lusatia. This was no mere formula. In the years to come, as we shall see, he intervened on a number of occasions to maintain the Catholic position, and most of the Catholics of Lusatia, it should not be forgotten, were Wends (Blaschke 1999a/2000: 104).

The Lusatias were not incorporated into Saxony and continued to be governed by their Estates. The Dresden authorities had no power in either Upper or Lower Lusatia and Saxon laws had no validity there unless they were expressly accepted by the Lusatian Estates. Upper Lusatia was now a Lutheran country with a Roman Catholic minority, whose existence was constitutionally guaranteed. The confessional symbiosis was demonstrated most graphically in the *Simultankirche* of St Peter in Budissin. The Upper Lusatian governing class scrupulously maintained the confessional status quo and the Saxon Elector was generally reluctant to interfere in Upper Lusatian affairs (Blaschke 1999a/2000: 105). For the rest of the seventeenth century the independence of the Lusatias from Saxony even extended to the calendar, for whereas both Lusatias in 1584, while under the Czech Crown, had adopted the Gregorian calendar, Saxony did not do so until 1700 (Map 4.1).

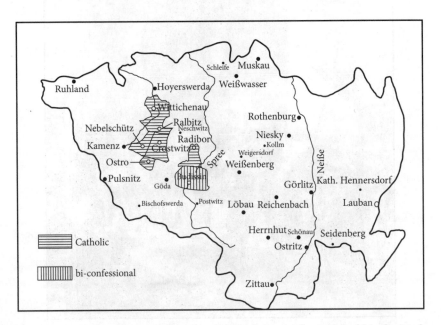

Map 4.1 Upper Lusatia, showing the six Wendish Catholic parishes and the biconfessional parish of Budissin after 1635.

Confessional conflict in Wittichenau

A prominent scene of interdemoninational turbulence was the Wendish townlet of Wittichenau. It had traditional links with Hoyerswerda, another small Wendish town lying a few miles to its north. Until the Reformation it was customary on Easter Sunday morning for the men of Wittichenau to ride on horseback round their fields singing hymns to bless the sprouting crops. They would then ride to Hoyerswerda to visit the church and congregation there before returning home to Wittichenau. The men of Hoyerswerda would meanwhile reciprocate the courtesy by making a similar visit to Wittichenau. Analogous rituals took place in and between other parishes. In 1540, however, the reformed religion was introduced in Hoyerswerda, while Wittichenau, being subject to the nunnery of Marienstern, remained Catholic. Reformed Hoyerswerda, regarding the Easter Ride (*Osterreiten*) as a piece of popish superstition, immediately abandoned it, thereby breaking a traditional link with Wittichenau (*Wosady* 1984: 63–4) (Figure 4.3).

To the south of Wittichenau lay the similarly unreformed village of Ralbitz and on Easter Sunday 1541 Wittichenau sent its riders there and received the Ralbitz riders in return, thereby establishing a new and lasting tradition. Some of the inhabitants of Wittichenau, however, were turning to the new religion, and by the early seventeenth century plans were afoot there for the comprehensive introduction of the Reformation.

Figure 4.3 Easter Riders setting out from Wittichenau *c.* 1865. Serbski kulturny archiw, Bautzen.

A favourable opportunity occurred in 1620, when the town was occupied by Protestant troops, who were lodged in the church of St Cross. There were by then about 300 Protestant inhabitants (largely foreign soldiers), so a Protestant pastor was sought. The choice fell on a deacon in Hoyerswerda, named Matej, but in view of the hostile atmosphere he was reluctant to accept the call until he was promised protection by both the *Landvogt* Adolf von Gersdorf and the junker Rudolf Ponikowski auf Hoyerswerda (Neander 1920: 64).

The following year the Protestants lost power in Prague, and the soldiers left Wittichenau. As soon as they had gone, Catholics broke down the locked doors of the church and repossessed it. Father Maćij Schaden, the Catholic priest who had recklessly allowed the soldiers to hold the keys, was accused of disloyalty and run out of town. In his place Jan Haša (Hasius) was appointed and he remained until 1630, when the town was visited by the plague and he fled to Rumburk in Bohemia. The loss of life from the disease was such that by 1632 the number of surviving married couples was no more than five. At Easter one year only five horsemen rode to Ralbitz (*Wosady* 1984: 63).

The emperor's role as defender of the Catholic Church in Lusatia was put to the test in 1668, when the Saxon Elector Johann Georg II, in response to the request of several Protestant citizens of Wittichenau, gave permission for Protestant services to be held in the church of St Cross. This caused grave concern among the Catholics. The parish priest was Bosćij Njekela, but it was his assistant Ferdinand Serbin (1635–1682) who resolved on appealing directly to the Emperor Leopold I. In late 1668, in wintry conditions he covered on foot the 250 miles (400 kilometres) from Wittichenau to Vienna, crossing Bohemia from north to south through mountains and forest, thereby gaining a place in Catholic legend. He demanded an audience with the emperor, put his case, and obtained an edict guaranteeing the rights of Catholic parishioners in St Cross's Church. The emperor also rewarded Serbin financially and offered him a place at court, but he declined the honour (*NBS*, s.v.; Schneider 1864: 4; *Wosady* 1984: 54–5).

Confessional conflict in Radibor

The confessional conflict between the Protestant lord of the manor and the Catholic parishioners in Radibor rumbled on through the closing years of the sixteenth century (see Chapter 3) until, eventually, Rudolf II in April 1600 decreed that Radibor should again have a Catholic priest and that no one should obstruct the Dean in admitting the new incumbent. In the summer that year Jurij Kokla (Coculus) was sent out from Budissin to take up this uninviting office, but before the end of the year he had left to be priest of Crostwitz, his native parish. Following this brief Catholic interlude Lutheran services were now resumed and maintained until 1603. At the same time the spiritual needs of the adherents of the old faith in Radibor were met by priests who continued to make the journey from the Deanery in Budissin, while the wrangling over a permanent solution continued (Neander 1920: 66).

Lutheran continuity was again briefly broken in 1603 by the appointment of Father Handrij Glaws, who stayed less than a year and was replaced by another Lutheran introduced by von Haugwitz. Like all the other Lutheran pastors in this story (written by Catholics) he remains anonymous. In January 1605 the emperor again intervened, commanding the removal of the Lutheran and his replacement by a Catholic priest. This time the Catholics gained control for a good number of years despite the appearance in 1606 of a new owner, Christoph von Minkwitz auf Pietschwitz, another fierce opponent of the Catholic Church. However, Father Jurij Młynk (Molitor) managed to serve the parish from 1605 to 1620, overcoming all the obstacles put in his way by von Minkwitz, who unsuccessfully demanded of the emperor permission to appoint a Lutheran to St Mary's (which up to now had been used by the Catholics), while conceding that the smaller church of St Cross (which had hitherto accommodated the Lutherans) might have a Catholic (Neander 1920: 66–7). After the formation of the Confederation in 1619, however, the Catholic party in Radibor was at a disadvantage. The Lusatian Estates now obtained from the Directorate a resolution directing the removal of Father Młynk and his replacement with a Protestant (Knauthe: 335, 253–4). Młynk was driven out, but received the Catholic parish of Crostwitz, under the patronage of the Marienstern nunnery. The Protestant Andreas Martini was admitted to office in late 1619 (Knauthe: 253; Neander 1920: 67).

Now the Reformation in Radibor began in earnest. St Mary's Church was cleared of all reminders of papist times. The altar was thrown out, ornamentation and vestments were destroyed, and the sacred vessels were sold. Pews and pulpit were renovated and a new font was installed. The account eventually written by the victors in this struggle asserts that, because services were poorly attended when Martini was preaching, von Minkwitz had the parishioners (most of whom were serfs and thus at his beck and call) summoned to the manor house and driven thence with whips through a gate into the church (Neander 1920: 67). In July 1622 a message from the Emperor Ferdinand II arrived, instructing von Minkwitz to get rid of Martini. According to one account, it was actually the people of the village of Camena, which was in the Radibor parish, who drove him out. Each new priest of Radibor was entitled by custom to receive a fine bullock from the peasant holding the office of village mayor in Camena. When Martini came to collect this perk, however, he was unlucky. The people of Camena, it is said, threw stones at him and drove him out of the village and back to Budissin, never to return (Neander 1920: 68).

Von Minkwitz, despite many attempts, never again succeeded in installing a Protestant minister. Faced now with the emperor's command that he present a Catholic to the living, he first asked the previous incumbent, Jurij Młynk, to return, but Młynk declined. Eventually, in January 1623, Jan Wjacsław Wołenk (Johannes Olenius), until now a curate in Crostwitz, was presented by von Minkwitz and instituted by Dean Gregorius Kattmann von Maurick (Knauthe 1767: 335–7; Neander 1920: 68). Although he stayed twenty-seven years, Wołenk was to have many disagreements with the lord of the manor and to suffer grievously at his hands.

Trouble came at Easter 1623, when the horsemen assembled for their traditional ceremony and ride. This should have concluded with a service in the parish church, but while the riders were following their route encircling the fields and the St Cross church, von Minkwitz's huntsmen and other servants barricaded the gates to the parish church and were standing guard with drawn swords. The Easter riders demanded to be allowed to ride, in the traditional way, round the church singing their hymns, but von Minkwitz refused. In his eyes the tradition was an offensive piece of popery. The riders' leader, Dučman of Basankwitz, told them to dismount and a few of them managed to run through the school into the church tower and ring the bell for help. Everyone came running and a brawl ensued. Dučman's horse was stabbed. Finally, the riders were victorious and drove the lord's men into the manor house. They then attended vespers in the church. Some of them got into the squire's brewery and either drank his beer or let it drain away. Von Minkwitz managed to send a messenger to Budissin to fetch armed help, but when the soldiers arrived, they found all was quiet. Everyone had gone to bed. The soldiers, however, were not tired, so they made their way to the village tavern, where they made merry at the lord's expense, leaving him with a bill for 144 thalers. For many years after this the Easter Ride did not take place (*Wosady* 1984: 37).

Ehrenreich (Ehricus) von Minkwitz, who took over the lordship in 1637, was another zealous Protestant. He wrote to the Estates claiming that he could not be compelled to support a Catholic priest, because the church was primarily for the gentry. If the people would not listen to the Lutheran pastor, they could attend mass in Budissin, which was not far away. Ehrenreich von Minkwitz realised that forcing the villagers to attend Lutheran sermons on Sundays was beyond his power, but on other days he could summon them to perform their feudal obligations and drive them into the church instead of sending them to their work. He revived the tradition of whipping them into the church through a gate in the churchyard wall (Neander 1920: 37).

In 1641 Radibor fell into the hands of Swedish forces and von Minkwitz used them against Father Wołenk. They subjected him to the torture known as the *Schwedischer Trunk*, holding him on the ground and forcing liquid manure down his throat. They then stamped on his belly until the liquid squirted back out of his mouth. He survived, but was crippled and incapable of performing his duties. Although he continued to live in the village, the pastoral care of his parishioners was now handled only irregularly by priests from Budissin. It was not until 1650 that the Dean recalled him to Budissin (*Wosady* 1984: 37–8; Winarjec-Orsesowa 1996: 70). Although von Minkwitz now had the upper hand, he could not find a Lutheran pastor willing to accept the parish (*Wosady* 1984: 38).

One of the first acts of the new Dean Martin Saudrius (installed late 1650) was to complain about the situation in Radibor to the Saxon Elector, by whose order it proved at last possible to appoint Father Jurij Lok as parish priest. Despite continued harassment by von Minkwitz, he was able to hold his ground and eventually relative peace ensued. When, in 1675, Lok died, the Dean appointed Adam Augustin Hałš (Hawš) as his successor (M. Kral 1937: 71–2). Although there had been constant resistance from the villagers to the lord's attempts to introduce the reformed religion in Radibor, the number of Lutherans had steadily grown and by 1679 (or 77) they were actually a majority (Neander 1920: 70; M. Kral 1937: 72). Yet the Catholics eventually triumphed. All the other parishes in Lusatia that remained Catholic were under the protection of either the Budissin Cathedral Chapter or one of the Cistercian nunneries (Marienstern or Marienthal). Radibor is the only parish in Lusatia under a secular lord that could not be moved from the old faith (Neander 1920: 66–72).

Brandenburg

A Wendish composer – Johann Crüger

One of the Wendish celebrities whose ethnicity can be established only by their place of birth (cf. Chapter 3) is Johann Crüger (1598–1662), composer of many well-known hymn tunes, including several sung regularly in English churches. The hymns 'Hail to the Lord's Anointed' (AM 142), 'Now thank we all our God' (AM 205), 'Praise to the Lord, the Almighty' (AM 207), and 'Deck thyself, my soul, with gladness' (AM 257) are usually sung to his tunes. He was born on 9 April 1598 in Breesen, then a Wendish village, close to the little town of Guben on the Neisse. Breesen was still recorded as 'German and Wendish' as late as 1775. Today, as Großbreesen, it is part of the German town Guben. On the opposite bank of the Neisse, now in Poland, lies Gubin, on the site of the Guben Crüger knew. His father, Georg, was a citizen of Guben and an innkeeper in Breesen (Mětšk 1962a: 108, 1965a: 120).

After studying music in Regensburg, Freiberg, and Berlin, at the end of 1616 Crüger entered the Berlin Gymnasium, located in the former monastery of the Grey Friars. From 1620 to 1622 he studied theology at Wittenberg, where he matriculated as Johannes Crügerus Gubinensis Lusatus. In 1622 his first hymnal *Paradisus Musicus. Musicalisches Lustgärtelein* was published in Berlin. He was invited by the Berlin town council to become a teacher at the Berlin Gymnasium and cantor at the church of St Nicholas in Berlin. He usually described himself as Director of Music at St Nicholas's Church (Hoffmeister 1964: 15–28, 44).

His hymnal *Neues vollkömmliches Gesangbuch Augsburgischer Konfession*, which appeared in Berlin in 1640, contained the words and music of 248 new and traditional hymns. The second edition, published in 1647, bore the new title under which it was to become famous: *Praxis Pietatis Melica*. It included several hymns to words by Paul Gerhardt, the well-known hymnwriter, whom Crüger had first met in 1643. They remained friends for life. *Praxis Pietatis Melica* reached its tenth edition in 1661 (Hoffmeister 1964: 64–5, 68–70). These were times of tension between the Lutheran and Reformed (Calvinist) parties in Brandenburg. The Elector Friedrich Wilhelm (known as the Great Elector) was a Calvinist, but the Estates were mainly Lutheran. At the beginning of the 1650s Crüger came to the attention of the Elector, who was planning to reorganize the music of services in the Cathedral of the Holy Trinity (which was Calvinist). He asked him if he would be willing to take on the task and become musical director of the Cathedral. Musically and professionally, this was a very attractive proposition, but in the eyes of Crüger's Lutheran friends at St Nicholas's acceptance would compromise him. Although he expressed a willingness to pursue the matter, in the end the projected preferment came to nothing owing to the resistance of the musicians already employed at the Cathedral. The Elector instead engaged Crüger to produce a revised edition in two volumes of the Calvinist hymnbook used in the Cathedral. It included a selection of Lutheran hymns and was published in 1658 with the title *Psalmodia sacra*. Crüger died on 23 February 1662 (Hoffmeister 1964: 72–7, 80). Crüger's ethnicity has engrossed Wendish musicologists. The German name Crüger or Krüger (from Ger. *Krüger* 'taverner') is common among the Lusatian Wends. Johann Crüger appended to his name the Latin epithets 'Gub. Siles[iensis]' and 'Lusatus' (Guben lies on the border between Silesia and Lusatia), but not 'Sorabus'. It is asserted that among his hymn tunes there were 'many of a Sorbian character, because in his childhood years he will surely have heard and sung Sorbian folk-melodies' (Raupp 1978: 41–2). Of indirect relevance is the fact that on his mother's side he was the second cousin of Georgius Kohlheim, a contributor to a 1656 book of Bible extracts in Wendish (see below) (Mětšk 1965a: 122–3; Mětškowa 1987: 1–2).

Wends at the University of Frankfurt/Oder

In Brandenburg's second city Frankfurt, in the seventeenth century there was still a Wendish presence. The University (*Viadrina*) was preparing ordinands for the ministry in Wendish parishes, and the Wendish-language training (*exercitationes linguae Vandalicae*), which had been introduced there in the mid-sixteenth century, but had been followed by a long period of inactivity, was resumed in 1656. The announcement was made in the following document (which survives):

> The undersigned announces and consigns to the knowledge of the Wendish students of this Academy of the Oder and of all desirous of ministering in the Wendish church and makes it known that after an interval of long duration with the permission of Mr Rector and the Theological Faculty he intends to continue the Wendish-language training begun almost 100 years ago in this university by Gregorius Schwarmius of Senftenberg and protected then by the most illustrious professor Mr Andreas Musculus and continued afterwards with the authority of Mr Pelargus by Andreas Tharaeus of Muskau, Solomon Nicolaus, Andreas Clemannus, and many others. Participants in the Wendish group are expected tomorrow at 6 o'clock in the evening before the Great Gate by Georgius Crüger of Lieberose, Student of Theology. Signed in the year of the Lord 1656, the second day of the month of October.

(Mětšk 1976: 3; Teichmann 1998: 169)

Georgius Crüger Liberosensis, as he styles himself here, is evidently identical with the M. Georgius Krüger Liberosensis Lusatus, who in 1675 in Wittenberg defended and published a dissertation entitled *De Serbis, Venedorum Natione vulgo dictis die Wenden*. Of the names mentioned here, Andreas Musculus, Christoph Pelargus, Gregorius

Schwarmius, Andreas Tharaeus, and Salomon Nicolai can all be identified in other sources. Whether the Crügers of Lieberose were related to the Crügers of Breesen is not known (Mětšk 1976: 3).

Located on the Oder, to the north of Guben and on the edge of Wendish territory, Frankfurt was an important centre of book-production. Printing had begun here in 1502 (Kind-Doerne 1973: 947n.) and it was here in 1610 that the next Wendish book was printed (the third, chronologically). It bore the title *Enchiridion Vandalicum* 'A Wendish Handbook' and was written by the Andreas Tharaeus named by Georg Crüger in 1656. Despite the Latin title, the text is predominantly Wendish.

Andreas Tharaeus was pastor of Friedersdorf, about 20 kilometres south-east of Köpenick (a south-east suburb of Berlin). He describes himself as *Muscoviensis*, meaning that he came from the townlet of Muskau on the Neisse. He studied theology at the University of Frankfurt and, before the end of the sixteenth century, had been appointed Lutheran pastor to the Wendish parish of Friedersdorf. It was here that he wrote his *Enchiridion*, which consists mainly of prayers, forms of worship, and guidance on how to conduct religious instruction. It was intended for the use of lay readers (*Küster*), deputizing for the clergy at a time when many ministers had to rely on assistants to cover the two or three churches in their care. Wendish texts of the sixteenth and seventeenth centuries, as a rule, consist of translations, but Tharaeus's book is exceptional, for though it includes extracts from the Bible and other religious works, it is otherwise his own composition. It occasionally reveals something of the secular concerns of the congregations. Within the form of marriage ceremony, for example, there is a specimen sermon, which makes use of a blunt, earthy imagery, strangely juxtaposed with the predominantly devotional tone. He cautions young men against assuming that it is easy to find a suitable bride and recommends prayer as the key to making the right choice. It is true, he says, that the world is full of women.

But I also know that they are not all the same and that they are not all of one mind. One is a dishonest self-admirer and has already kicked off a few horseshoes. Another is pig-headed, cannot and will not be silent, thrashing about and biting all round her like a guard-dog. A third is a lazy swine who constantly lies in the space behind the stove or stands in the window or in the doorway, wears white hands and attends to nothing. A fourth likes to raise a jug or tankard and carries off everything out of the house in search of beer and wine. Now if he gets one like that, whose fault is it but his own? Why did he not turn his lips to God? Why did he not ask Him for a good woman? Likewise, many a young woman may get a drunkard, a gambler, a reveller, a lazy work-shy oaf, an obstinate ruffian and brawler, who always clothes her in black and blue. That comes from her not wanting to ask God for a good and devout husband. Now, whoever wants to avoid all this should fear God and not forget his prayers.

(Tharaeus 1990: 187–93)

Calvinism

The decision in 1613 of Johann Sigismund, Elector of Brandenburg since 1608, to become a Calvinist opened up a lasting confessional breach between the Hohenzollern dynasty and its Lutheran subjects. The sectarian conflict affected not only Germans but also the Wends in the Wendish District of the Kurmark and the Kreis Cottbus exclave. The Elector promised to respect the guarantee of tolerance already conceded by statute, but changes in ecclesiastical politics were inevitable. Lutheran professors were compelled to refrain from attacks on the Reformed (Calvinist) Church. The Estates' right to appoint clergy to parishes was confirmed but made subject to the supervision of the Elector's ecclesiastical officials, the General Superintendents and Inspectors (Mětšk 1965a: 117; Clark 2006: 116–18).

In the Beeskow area the predominantly Wendish population was Lutheran and remained so even after the appointment of Calvinist Church Inspectors. In 1631, against all the odds, the combined efforts of the nobility, the towns, and the lower priesthood of the area succeeded in having a Lutheran inspector appointed. This was Gottfried Treuer. When he died in office in 1666, the Elector's faction managed to fill the vacancy with a Calvinist named Paul Prieffer (or Prüfer) (Mětšk 1965a: 117–18, 126).

On 9 December 1667, Friedrich Wilhelm (the Great Elector, r. 1640–1688), issued a rescript addressed to Prieffer as Inspector of Beeskow. It alludes to reports of

> what abominable things the inopportune zeal and blasphemy of the Lutheran pastors in the years of the inspectorate of Gottfried Treuer had until now attributed to His Electoral Highness and His kin in religion, also how the Wendish books, which his Electoral Highness himself had once deigned to have printed and published, had in such places through the action (*auctore*) of the quarrelsome and recently fugitive Paul Gerhardt, formerly Pastor of St Nicholas's Church, decried the wholesome doctrine as heresy and changed the true religion into abominable blasphemy.
>
> (Mětšk 1969:14, 45, 1965a: 126–8)

In order to prevent in future any 'unusual work of this kind, of which this is such a pernicious example', the Elector issued the following four commands, enumerated under four paragraphs:

1. As already ordained in 1662, the installation of clergy from Wittenberg is to be prevented, so far as possible.

2. All clergy in the villages and elsewhere, 'but especially Deacon Gotthelf Treuer' (nephew of Gottfried), are to be earnestly reprimanded and admonished.

3. 'You are to confiscate from the churches and schools and thereafter totally liquidate the Wendish books specified under letters a to e, which aim to instil into young people hatred for the true religion and its adherents equally:

a. Christian Schmeer's Psalter from the year 1653,

b. the Catechism and Articles of Faith by Adam Thilo from the year 1654,

c. the hymnbook in Wendish translation of Johann Henning and Ernst Julius Coccius from the year 1655,

d. the extracts from the Holy Scripture of the Old and New Testaments, provided by the former Inspector Treuer assisted by Joh. Lupinius, Christian Friedhelm, Georg Kohlheim, Joh. Crüger, and Caspar Janosch from the year 1656,

e. the Enchiridion Vandalicum of Tharaeus from the year 1610, and Wendish manuscripts, if any are still in existence.'

4. 'You and your successors are to aim for the total removal of Wendish pastors, but in such a way as to treat his Electoral Highness's Wendish subjects with great gentleness and patience in the exercise of their religion for the sake of peace and unity, to avoid untimely unrest, and to refrain herein from any impetuosity.'

(Mětšk 1969: 14–15)

The 1667 rescript reveals a strange confusion of confessional and ethnic issues. Most remarkably, however, paragraph 3 shows that the Elector was now ordering the destruction of Wendish religious books whose publication he had himself once supported. With the exception of Tharaeus's *Enchiridion Vandalicum*, not a single copy of any of the books mentioned has been seen since Friedrich Wilhelm's time. We might doubt whether they ever existed but for the following corroborative evidence:

1. Reporting conversations that took place in March 1687, Jacobus Tollius, Professor of Latin and Greek at Duisburg University, states: 'The good Elector used to say moreover that he had caused the Bible and songs from psalms, [...] and the Catechism to be translated into their [the Wends'] language and published' (Tollius 1700: 42; Mětšk 1965a: 118n.).

2. A contemporary register of public funds for Beeskow notes that in 1653 Inspector Treuer received 1 florin and 5 argents 'for the printing of Schmeer's Wendish Psalter' (Mětšk 1965a: 119).

3. A similar record shows that in 1655 Deacon Coccius was paid 4 bushels and 5 pecks of rye 'for work on the Wendish hymnal' (Mětšk 1965a: 119).

4. A 1656 account of the church coffers records the expenditure of 4 groschen 'for 2 quires of paper for indexes to the Wendish extracts from Holy Scripture' (Mětšk 1965a: 119).

5. The authors of all four books specified in paragraph 3 (a–d) (Thilo, Schmeer, Henning, Coccius, Lupinius, Friedhelm, Kohlheim, Crüger, and Janosch) can be identified as pastors in nearby parishes (Mětšk 1965a: 124).

The existence of the last item in the list (Tharaeus's 1610 *Enchiridion Vandalicum*) is corroborated by the single specimen which survived the Elector's destruction order until

1945. Its contents, which had been copied by hand before the First World War and were published in 1990, are described above (Tharaeus 1990: 8–9).

The 'quarrelsome and recently fugitive' Paul Gerhardt referred to in Friedrich Wilhelm's rescript is the prominent late-Reformation hymnographer, mentioned earlier as a friend of the Wendish composer Johann Crüger. Although Gerhardt's biography is generally well documented, the Electoral Rescript of 1667 is the only direct evidence of his involvement in Wendish affairs. How through his action 'the Wendish books, which his Electoral Highness himself had once deigned to have printed and published', came to decry 'the wholesome doctrine as heresy' and change 'the true religion into abominable blasphemy' is not known. Gerhardt's connection with Wendish religious controversy, however, is not surprising.

He was born on 12 March 1607 in Gräfenhainichen, between Wittenberg and Halle, in an area which by this time was German, but he must have come into contact with Wendish students at Wittenberg University, where he began his studies on 15 December 1627. After graduation he appears to have lived for some years in Berlin, where he met Crüger. Gerhardt's first published poems, set to music by his friend, appeared in Crüger's *Praxis Pietatis Melica* (Berlin, 1647) (Hoffmeister 1964: 68; Hesselbacher 1999:15, 18, 21). From 1651 to 1657 Gerhardt was Provost of Mittenwalde, south of Berlin, very close to Wendish territory and adjacent to Gottfried Treuer's parish (Mětšk 1965a: 41, 51, 127). As Provost, Gerhardt was responsible for the supervision of several Wendish parishes. It may be significant that Gerhardt's stay here included the period 1653–1666, when the four phantom books were published (Mětšk 1965a: 127). In 1657, however, Gerhardt was called to serve as a priest of the church of St Nicholas in Berlin, where Crüger was Director of Music (Hesselbacher 1999: 59).

The Electoral Edict of Tolerance, issued in September 1664, ordered both Calvinist and Lutheran clergy to refrain from disparaging each other. All pastors were required to state their acceptance of the edict by signing and returning a document called the Acknowledgement (*Revers*). Some refused to sign and were deprived of office. Others, having signed, immediately found themselves shunned by their parishioners and their sermons boycotted (Clark 2006: 121). Gerhardt was among those who refused. His position at St Nicholas's Church and his poems/hymns published in Crüger's books had by now brought him a certain renown and he was, in any case, not one of those preachers who were known for their use of abusive, sectarian language. Friedrich Wilhelm, therefore, was anxious to avoid conflict with him and sought reconciliation. Nevertheless, in February 1666 Gerhardt was relieved of his office. There were protests from the people and the Estates. Friedrich Wilhelm sought a middle way. He ordered him to be reinstated, saying he was confident Gerhardt would refrain from maligning the Reformed Church, even if he did not sign the Acknowledgement. Gerhardt, however, feeling he was still under moral pressure, declined the offer, whereupon on 4 February 1667 the Elector issued instructions for his place to be filled. A year later, on 5 March 1668, Gerhardt's wife died and in October that year he was elected Archdeacon of Lübben, capital of Wendish Lower Lusatia, where the overlord was Duke Christian of Saxony-Merseburg, a Lutheran. Gerhardt died in Lübben on 27 May 1676 (Hesselbacher 1999: 91–8, 126–33).

According to Mětšk, Gerhardt left Berlin in 1667 and, before moving to Lübben, stayed for a time in Lübbenau, also in Lower Lusatia (1965a: 127; 1969: 14, 45–6, n.46). Mětšk also alludes to another tradition which places Gerhardt in Wendisch Buchholz (1965a: 130). Hesselbacher (1999: 100–26) omits this episode and appears to place him in Berlin until his move to Lübbenau, but in view of the Elector's description of Gerhardt as a 'fugitive' (*entlaufen*), either of Mětšk's versions makes better sense.

Further light on the unstable disposition of the Elector towards the Wends may be shed by the record already mentioned of a conversation he had in 1687 with Jacobus Tollius. Although the twenty-two volume collection of documents relating to the reign of Friedrich Wilhelm contain not a single direct reference to the Wends (Mětšk 1965a: 18), there are a few sources (of which this one) pointing to the Elector's cognizance of his Wendish subjects and to his policies affecting them. Tollius writes:

The most Serene Elector [...] said there is no prince in the Roman Empire who rules over more peoples. Having enumerated them, as well as their languages, he said something about the Wends, well worth knowing and not uninteresting. They still use the Slav language; they are a most unsteady people, unfaithful, disposed to rebellions, seditious; they inhabit populous settlements of five hundred or six hundred heads of families. They have a king of their own race, but secretly, who lacks neither crown nor sceptre; to him they contribute an annual tax of one silver coin each; the Elector had seen this king once with his own eyes – a young man, powerful equally in both body and mind. When He had looked at him more closely and had been observed by an older man of that people and without doubt of no mean authority, this same older man, in order to disperse His suspicion, had poked the king with a stick and driven him away like a base slave. The good Elector said he had furthermore commanded the Bible and songs from the Psalms for singing in church and the Catechism to be translated into their language and published; but he considered it unsafe to open schools on account of their fickleness of disposition and the inaccessible forests and swamps they are wont to inhabit, for they do not lack firearms even, but hold them secretly. Once, moreover, being surrounded by four or five thousand of them, he had eventually and with difficulty extricated himself with the help of eight hundred soldiers armed with flintlocks, and so routed them. Hence in birth certificates or documents of the neighbouring Germans it is clearly added that he of whom they testify is not a Wend nor quarrelsome.

(Tollius 1700: 42)

There had clearly been a time in the 1650s when Friedrich Wilhelm had considered it right to provide the Wends with religious books in their own language. He did not merely permit their publication. As he himself said twice (first in the 1667 rescript and later to Tollius), he had actually caused them to be published. Their publication dates, moreover, are spread over a period of four years (1653–1666). Yet eleven years later he ordered their destruction. The reasons for this extraordinary volte-face are not known, but from the rescript it is clear that Paul Gerhardt and Lutheran-Calvinist polemics were somehow implicated. From the conversation with Tollius (more than twenty years after the books had been published) it is evident that the Elector now regarded the Wends with grave suspicion, even fear, and was not disposed to do them any favours. It is not impossible that the Elector's wife Luise Henriette was involved in this mystery, for she was a Lutheran and may have influenced the Elector's decision during 1653–1666 to have the books published. She died in June 1667, six months before the rescript was issued. As a Lutheran hymnwriter, she is known to have been in touch with Johann Crüger, who set some of her poems to music. From 1653 she was ruler of Amt Stahnsdorf, where Pastor Christian Schmeer had his parish (Mětšk 1965a: 120, 129–30).

Lower Lusatia (Saxony)

Calau

By the Peace of Prague 1635 both Lusatias were transferred to the Elector of Saxony, and in Lower Lusatia, after the death of Johann Georg I in 1656, there were significant innovations. By the terms of the Dresden General Agreement (*Hauptvergleich*), which administered the Elector's estate, Lower Lusatia went not to the new elector but to his brother Christian I, Duke of Saxony-Merseburg. The electoral line retained control only of foreign policy, military affairs, and a few other areas. Internal matters were left entirely to the cadet line. Christian I broke with tradition by residing in Lower Lusatia and striving to replace gradually the traditional rule of the Estates with an administration by officials in the spirit of feudal absolutism. By 1667 he had induced them to transfer the administration of cultural policy (church and schools) to a newly created Supreme Consistory (*Oberkonsistorium*), located in Lübben (Mětšk 1965b: 77).

The new Supreme Consistory announced to the Estates an unprecedented policy for the Germanization of the Wends in a document known as the Modest Admonition (*Ohnvorgreifliche Monita*). The text survives and can be dated to 1668. It opens as follows:

A modest admonition as to how the total abolition of the Wendish language in this Margraviate might best be promoted, how such [might] be announced to the Estates of the *Land* in this Margraviate by the newly instituted Supreme Consistory at the serene intention of the most noble, most illustrious, and high-born prince and gentleman Christian, Duke of Saxony [...] Margrave of Lower Lusatia [...]

(Mětšk 1969: 15)

Among the localities where the Modest Admonition foresaw particular difficulty in imposing the German language was Kreis Calau, whose administrative centre, the townlet Calau, had over a thousand inhabitants, almost all Wends (Mětšk 1969: 17;

see Map 3.3). Their numbers were regularly replenished by immigration from the surrounding countryside, and there is ample evidence that the normal spoken language of the town until the end of the eighteenth century was Wendish. The official language, however, was German and it was in this language that the municipal records were kept. Merbach, who was able to read the originals, noted: 'Even in official records of the fifteenth and sixteenth centuries unmistakable traces of the Slav character of their writers are to be found. They wrote in German, it is true, but they thought and construed in Wendish' (1833: 173; Mětšk 1965b: 75).

Taking account of the need for the liturgy in the vernacular following the Reformation, Calau had acquired a new church, in which services were held in Wendish, and most of its clergy were native speakers. Traditional procedures for presentation to the parish demanded proof of proficiency in Wendish, but the new Supreme Consistory, which was responsible for the appointment of the Calau superintendent, now had another agenda. Since 1566 the office of Superintendent of Calau had been held almost continuously by Wendish speakers, but in 1677 Superintendent Christian Knittel, scion of an old family of Calau merchants, died. An opponent of Germanizing policies, he had held office since 1644. The vacancy presented the authorities with an opportunity to promote the new policy by appointing a successor who was ignorant of Wendish.

David Andreas Teuerlein fitted the bill. He had been born in Altenburg and was not a Wendish speaker. His appointment, as might have been expected, provoked protests. Teuerlein himself wrote: 'Because I am not familiar with the Wendish language, when I gave my trial sermon here in 1677, there were protests against me by the incorporated parishioners of the nobility (*von denen Eingepfarrten von Adel*)' (Mětšk 1965b: 79n.). These noble protesters were the owners of adjacent estates, belonging to the parish of Calau, though administratively outside the municipal limits. Protests were also made by the majority of the citizens.

That the citizens should protest is not unexpected, seeing the native language of most of them was Wendish, but the behaviour of the nobility is more interesting, for it is commonly supposed that the landed class consisted of German speakers and supporters of Germanization. The motive for their uncharacteristic attitude on this occasion may have been the desire to avoid provoking unrest among their serfs (Mětšk 1965b: 79, 83n.), but the rural nobility of old standing at this time were, in any case, not always hostile to the Wendish language, though they were hostile to innovation (Mětšk 1969: 47, n.78). This is not the only instance in the seventeenth century of support for Wendish by the landed class (cf. Leuthen below).

The protests were not merely verbal and are described in one Consistory source as *turbationes* 'riots'. Although the Consistory would not be diverted from its goal of appointing its favoured candidate, it was prepared to compromise. Teuerlein remained Superintendent, but it was agreed that his Wendish-language duties be transferred to the incumbent Wendish deacon G. Churisius, who was relieved of certain existing duties by creating the new post of sub-deacon. The right of the town council to appoint to this office was acknowledged and they chose a Wend, Joachim Schmidt, born Calau 1633. This was a substantial concession on the part of the Teuerlein party, because it involved making the Superintendent responsible for the financial support of the sub-deacon, thereby avoiding any new monetary burden on the citizens.

Although the use of Wendish in church services was unaltered, the presence of the new, linguistically incompetent, Superintendent was a constant cause of irritation and he was not allowed to forget it. The townspeople, according to the record, 'made life very hard for him' (Mětšk 1965b: 80). Five years after Teuerlein's appointment a new crisis arose. Deacon Churisius had been called away to become pastor to the Wendish village of Sallgast, leaving the deacon's office vacant. Sub-deacon Schmidt was the obvious candidate. The council, exercising its traditional right, named him as their chosen candidate and required him to give a trial sermon in Wendish, so that the opinion of the congregation might be heard. The congregation had no objection and in August 1682 Duke Christian finally gave his consent. The fact that the council had to ask him twice before he agreed suggests that he acceded only reluctantly. Schmidt's preferment left vacant the office of sub-deacon, which was automatically held jointly with the headship (*Rektorat*) of the municipal school.

For this vacancy the council favoured Benjamin Roscius, a theology student and son of Pastor Georg Roscius in Laasow, Kr. Cottbus. It was ascertained that he had the support of the unloved Superintendent Teuerlein. Arrangements were made for Roscius to deliver a trial sermon in the presence of a priest competent in the Wendish language. This was Deacon Joachim Schmidt, who reported favourably on Roscius's Wendish speech and pronunciation. His German trial sermon also met with approval, but before the procedures could be completed, a letter objecting to the proposed appointment was received, signed by a large number of citizens. On examination, these objections were found to be groundless, and it eventually transpired that the group opposing Roscius, led by a man named Beyer, had its own candidate, one Gottfried Pötsch, a man born in the town in 1652. Beyer's group recalled that they had invested in Pötsch's education – he had studied at the University of Frankfurt/Oder – and they did not wish to see him outdone by an outsider. Pötsch, however, though a native of Calau, had only an imperfect command of Wendish, because he had spent most of his childhood outside the Wendish area. For this reason his candidacy the previous year for the office of precentor in the Calau church had failed, but his supporters now (September 1682) stated that he had given an undertaking to achieve the necessary standard in the language within six months or so (Mětšk 1965b: 81–2).

The successful candidate in the competition for the precentorship had been Christian Kubitz, a Wend. The precentor's duties included delivering twenty Wendish sermons a year. It was now suggested that Pötsch, if elected, might take over Kubitz's German sermons and Kubitz take over Pötsch's Wendish sermons. Kubitz, moreover, could help Pötsch to perfect his Wendish. Alternatively, Kubitz could be given the post of sub-deacon and headmaster, leaving the precentorship vacant for Pötsch. Kubitz, under financial pressure exerted by Pötsch's supporters, was ready to accede to this proposal. The difficulty faced by the monolingual Teuerlein in a hostile Wendish environment is at this point revealed in an admission by him that he has realized that without Wendish 'hardly any ecclesiastical or school function here could be carried out'. He therefore proposed that Pötsch, who had declined in writing the invitation to deliver a Wendish trial sermon, be offered a new deadline. The view of the council that Roscius should be appointed without more ado was unchanged. They rejected as absurd the idea that Pötsch should learn Wendish after he had been appointed: 'For if a man will only learn when he already holds an office what he needs to perform that office, how then shall the office in the meantime be performed?' (Mětšk 1965b: 82).

The resolution of Pötsch's supporters was beginning to flag. Their first submission had born 41 signatures, the second 56, but the third (of 30 September 1682) only seven. Eventually Pötsch himself realized the hopelessness of his candidature and withdrew. His letter to Joachim Schmidt, who now turns out to have been his brother-in-law, reveals a number of significant aspects of the affair and also of Wendish–German relations more generally in seventeenth-century Calau:

Most honourable and highly respected brother-in-law,

Although I, at a tender age, was no different from the other children of this town in that I spoke only Wendish and first of all began to learn spelling with the help of the Calau ABC booklet (*ABC-kniglitzki*), published by Herr G. Ermelius, yet, when in my eighth year my mother's brother took me to live with him in Torgau, I soon became so German that I now frame my thoughts only in the latter language, though I can still understand everything well in Wendish. I was this time planning to deliver a Wendish sermon next Sunday, and had taken great pains to prepare it, partly on my own and partly with the help of others [*ope aliorum*]. Yet I still find it excessively difficult to memorize it. I can, it is true, retain very well what I have translated myself, but the rest, prepared with the help of others, it is impossible for me to get it into my head, and that makes me anxious lest, if I should take it upon myself to deliver the sermon and actually appear, I should either have to withdraw from the pulpit or start preaching in German. If that happens, you yourself or the Precentor will have to think about how to get the sermon done. Although Master Beyer and many friends of my poor parents among the citizens here faithfully support me, I must nonetheless fear that not only the parochially incorporated peasants through their lords but also the majority of the citizens, who make life very hard for Pastor Primarius Teuerlein, because he cannot speak Wendish, and who five years ago at the time of his investiture extorted from the Most Worshipful Consistory an adequate observation of the Wendish language, would put me into outlawry and excommunication, which misgivings I, dear brother-in-law, wish kindly to report and remain

Your willing servant

Gottfried Pötsch

Though undated, the letter clearly relates to the events of September and October 1682. An official hand has appended the following note:

Ermerius's [*sic*] Wendish spelling-book was already confiscated at the Calau school by the Consistory in 1669, yet not without the untimely resistance of the citizens and the late Primarius [sc. Superintendent] Knittel, who was a zealous Wend (*ein eifriger Wende*). We should not allow such disturbances as happened in 1677 to be repeated now in Calau on account of Pötzsch, particularly as even the nobility have come over to the opinion that Roscius, who certainly is a good Wend, could bring German step by step and, as it were, by degrees to greater acceptance, which is truly of great importance in a regional centre (*Kreisstadt*) of our Margraviate.

(Mětšk 1965b: 83)

The revelation that until 1669 reading and writing in Wendish were taught in the Calau municipal school raises the question: why were they learning to read Wendish when there were hardly any Wendish books? To be precise (if we ignore the Great Elector's phantom books), there were in 1669 only two Lower Sorbian printed books in existence, namely, Albin Moller's *Hymnal and Catechism* (1574) and Tharaeus's *Enchiridion Vandalicum* (1610). The third Lower Sorbian printed book, chronologically, is an ABC book dated 1671, but this obviously cannot be the book confiscated in Calau in 1669. All this suggests that by 1671 some eight Lower Sorbian books had been printed (three actual, five phantom) and that teaching Wendish children to read in their native tongue was more widespread than we might otherwise suppose.

Forbidden to preach in German: Leuthen

To the north of Lübben, in the watery and wooded glades of the Spree Forest, lies the village of Groß-Leuthen. Until the twentieth century it was simply Leuthen. In 1646, when the owner and lord of the manor, Freiherr Otto Wilhelm Schenck von Landsberg, was raised to the rank of *Standesherr*, Leuthen became a *Standesherrschaft* consisting of seven villages. The *Standesherrschaft* had only one church, which was situated in the village of Leuthen, close to Lake Leuthen. Schenk von Landsberg was patron not only of the church in Leuthen, but also of that in the adjacent parish of Groß Leine, and the pastor of Leuthen was similarly responsible for both the churches (Mětšk 1970: 153–4 and 155 (map)).

The new measures to promote German at the expense of Wendish, envisaged in the 1668 Modest Admonition, were not to the liking of all the landowning nobility. Many of them had been born and brought up in Wendish villages and were capable of at least understanding, and possibly speaking, the vernacular, which they heard all around them. Some of them were content with existing church practices in their villages, whereby sermons were delivered in Wendish. Neither they nor their family members felt excluded when attending Wendish church services and pressure from on high to impose German in their churches infringed their autonomy. Tradition demanded that before a new pastor could be appointed, he must meet with the approval of his prospective flock. By custom, a candidate put forward by the church patron was called upon to give a test sermon, once in German and once in Wendish. A candidate who could not give a sermon in Wendish was unlikely to meet with the approval of a congregation that could not understand German. There is evidence that every new pastor of Leuthen went through this procedure up to and including Johann Christoph Dahlitz in 1781, but not after him (Mětšk 1970: 166–7).

Although the Groß Leine church was under the patronage of the Leuthen *Standesherr* and the pastoral care of the pastor of Leuthen, the lord of Groß Leine, Henning von Zittwitz, holder of the high office of *Landesältester* of the Lübben District, fancied that he had certain rights over the Groß Leine church, because it stood on his land. The *Standesherr* of Leuthen, Schenck von Landsberg, resented and resisted Henning von Zittwitz's interference. Their differences of opinion on church matters involved the pastor of Leuthen (who preached at Groß Leine too), because they extended to his sermons. It was a matter not of doctrine but of language (Mětšk 1970: 162). The peasants of both parishes had little contact with German and few of them could speak it. The pastors were always Wends too. Had they not been able to speak Wendish, they would have been incapable of performing their duties. They could obviously speak German too, however, for all clergymen were university-educated. Among the names and incumbencies of the seventeenth-century pastors of Leuthen that can be discovered are those of Jacob Roscius 1632–1677, Daniel Reizig 1678–1679, and Michael Peuzner (or Püzner) 1679–1704 (Mětšk 1970: 166 and n.).

In 1692 Henning von Zittwitz complained to the Lübben Consistory about Pastor Michael Peuzner's habit of preaching only in Wendish: 'For the previous pastors H. Jacobus Roscius and H. Daniel Reizig always mixed in some German [*deuzsch mit untergeprediget*] with the usual Wendish sermon. It affects Herr Baron Schenck neither one way nor the other, whether the pastor preaches in German or Wendish. When the hour is spent, the sermon comes to its end.' He requested that 'the pastor be meanwhile emphatically instructed, subject to penalty, that in Gr. Leine he shall preach in German as well as Wendish' (Mětšk 1970: 163).

As soon as he became aware of von Zittwitz's interference, Schenck von Landsberg reacted by forbidding Peuzner to preach in German, and in a letter to Duke Christian, dated 11 July 1692, he protested:

In respect of my villages belonging to the manor of Leuthen I can in no way condescend to [permit] preaching in the German language, because this has never happened previously. And although the previous owner [sc. of Gr. Leine] von Zabeltitz more than seventy or eighty years ago asked for the same sort of thing, his request was totally rejected. This [request] too would develop in such a direction that bit by bit from a small portion a whole sermon would develop, which in our neighbourhood has already happened, so that in the place of a German *exordium* [introduction], no Wendish sermon at all is given, which is to the detriment of many hundreds of souls, who are ignorant of the German language. Therefore I too, on behalf of my subjects, seeing we have never had any sermons preached in German, cannot give consent in this matter. And although the Herr *Landesältester* refers to his German lady daughter-in-law (*Schwäher-Tochter*), yet in as many as nineteen years we have heard no complaints from her until now; only now is she demanding such unjustified things as this. And there are plenty of German sermons for her to enjoy in our neighbourhood, if this has now become such a serious matter for her.

(Mětšk 1970: 163)

Disagreements between *Standesherr* Schenck von Landsberg and *Landesältester* von Zittwitz were of old standing. This was not the first time von Zittwitz had meddled in church affairs in Groß Leine. He had already attempted in 1677 to establish himself as 'co-patron' of the Groß Leine church and had failed. The Lübben Consistory confirmed then that the right of presentation was exclusively the prerogative of Schenck von Landsberg and documents of that time allude to an even earlier dispute 'some time ago relating to German preaching in the church in Groß Leine'. In 1693 an agreement was drawn up, dated 18 November that year. Von Zittwitz was able to make one small gain: on Sundays when afternoon services were held, worship was to begin with an introductory German sermon lasting for a quarter of an hour. This procedure had been restricted hitherto to Christmas, Easter, and Whitsun, 'when the nobility (*Obrigkeit*) were taking communion there'. But the new arrangement still prescribed a Wendish sermon lasting three quarters of an hour.

Moreover, the extreme reluctance with which the concession of a fifteen-minute German introductory sermon had been granted by the *Standesherr* (and his pastor) was commemorated in a specific gratuity for the pastor, emphasizing that he was being asked to do something beyond his proper duty. Should von Zittwitz omit to deliver annually the perquisite of three bushels of rye and three of buckwheat specified in the agreement, the German mini sermon would lapse 'and there would be only the Wendish sermon as before' (Mětšk 1970: 163–4).

In the course of the deliberations a delegation from the Leuthen congregation visited Lübben. There they testified on oath that the people of the Leuthen parish could not understand German and begged to be allowed to continue to hear sermons in Wendish. They said: 'that the members of the congregation understood only Wendish and not German. Nor could they speak it and that was the only reason why preaching must done only in Wendish'. They further indicated that the *junker* of Groß Leine (von Zittwitz) and his family had a good command of Wendish. In their final expression of despair it may be possible to detect a veiled threat: '... for surely under this [proposed change] over one hundred souls would be put in danger. For we poor people cannot say how we might conduct ourselves under this innovation' (Mětšk 1970: 165 and n.).

The people of the parish had no doubt been emboldened by the uncompromising stance taken by their *Standesherr* towards the Consistory (of which he had recently been the chairman) and von Zittwitz. Pastor Michael Peuzner appears to have been particularly recalcitrant in linguistic matters. He had after all, by failing to 'mix in some German' in his preaching, departed from the tradition set by his predecessors. He gladly followed the course set by Schenck von Landsberg. When charged by von Stutterheim, the Director of the Supreme Consistory in Lübben, '...that you are supposed to have said you would still not [*doch nicht*] preach in German', he did not deny it, explaining that his patron Herr Baron von Schenck had forbidden him to do so (Mětšk 1970: 166–7 and n.).

Upper Lusatia (Protestants)

Michael Frentzel and censorship

Little or nothing is known of the legal formalities Moller (1574), Warichius (1595 and 1597), Tharaeus (1610), and Martini (1627) had to undergo to get their books printed and published. That censorship was a serious problem for authors, however, may be concluded from the vicissitudes of the next Wendish book, a translation of the gospels of St Matthew and St Mark made by Michael Frentzel. Published in Budissin in 1670, it was a significant milestone on the long road leading to the publication of the Upper Sorbian Bible.

Frentzel was born on 21 February 1628 in Pietschwitz (nine kilometres/five miles west of Budissin), in the parish of Göda. His father Michael was a titheman and peace officer employed by Rudolph von Bünau auf Pietschwitz, Provost of the Budissin Cathedral Chapter (Röseberg 1930: 44; Petr 1989: 11). Young Michael received his first education from his parents at home, then in the Göda village school. In 1641, at the age of thirteen, he was sent to the gymnasium in Budissin, where he lived in lodgings. On 11 June 1643, thanks to the intervention of von Bünau, he gained a free place at the Electoral School in Meissen. He completed six years here before matriculating at the University of Leipzig, where he held the Electoral Scholarship. Following ordination at Wittenberg in 1651, he was installed on 24 July that year as pastor of Kosel (eastern Upper Lusatia) and here on 30 April 1652 he married Anna Maria Donat (1638–1715), aged 14, from Luppa, near Radibor. He remained in Kosel for nearly twelve years. Then he was called as pastor to Postwitz, seven kilometres (four miles) south of Budissin, where he took up residence in February 1663. The patron of the Postwitz church being the town council of Budissin, he was introduced at the installation ceremony by two councillors (Frentzel 1688 in Schuster-Šewc 1993: 233–5). The parish of Postwitz (later Großpostwitz) was large and populous.

Like other Lutheran pastors, Frentzel will have had his manuscript Wendish versions of the Ordinal, the Catechism, and the epistles and gospels, but he felt it was time for Biblical texts to be published in print and began work on a complete translation of the New Testament intended for publication. By 1669 it was complete. It was now forty-two years since the publication of the last Wendish book in Upper Lusatia (Martini 1627). Meanwhile the production and use of manuscript translations, which varied from one parish to the next, had continued.

The *Traditionsrezeß* of 1635 prohibited any innovation in religious matters, and Frentzel was at pains to observe the legal niceties. Having no reason to doubt that the Protestant authorities would support his efforts to spread the word of God among the Wendish population, Frentzel wrote to the Elector Johann Georg II in Dresden, presenting him with a copy of his manuscript. The letter is not known to have survived, but Frentzel refers to it in a letter of 6 December 1670 to the High Consistory in Dresden as having been written 'last year in the eleventh week after Trinity', which must mean late August 1669. As Upper Lusatia was governed by its Estates, not by the Elector, Frentzel discreetly decided to write in his capacity as a former alumnus of the Electoral School at Meissen and of Leipzig University rather than as the pastor of Postwitz (Röseberg 1930: 83).

The matter was delegated to the Chief Court Preacher Martin Geier (1614–1680), who was encouraging. 'He also gave me this fatherly advice that I should dedicate and attribute my translation to the honourable Estates of the Country and Towns of this margravate of Upper Lusatia and they, as fathers of the fatherland, would without doubt promote this work for the good of their Wendish subjects' (Röseberg 1930: 84). His confidence was raised further by comments on the translation by his brothers of the cloth. Frentzel decided to go ahead with the printing of a small volume, containing the gospels of St Matthew and St Mark together with his versions of the Apostles, Nicene, and Athanasian Creeds. Several hundred copies were printed by Christoph Baumann of Budissin. The cutting of new type increased the cost of the job, which was carried out at Frentzel's own considerable expense (Knauthe 1767: 295; Röseberg 1930: 84).

Thirty copies bound in red were submitted to the Estates at their assembly on St Elizabeth's day (19 November) 1670. The book was dedicated to the Estates and the foreword signed in Postwitz with the date 10 November 1670 (Röseberg 1930: 78; Frentzel 1670: [v]). Even before this date, however, a complaint had been received at a meeting of the Budissin town council on 30 October 1670 from Christian Wilhelm von Watzdorf, lord of Bederwitz in the parish of Postwitz, against the pastor of Postwitz 'in respect of a prohibited publication without the prior knowledge of the authorities'. One month later (1 December) the council minutes reported:

> The Pastor of Postwitz Herr Michael Frentzel was summoned to appear at this place and in the name of the council a severe reprimand was delivered to him for having without the foreknowledge of the Council as his governor caused to be issued and printed here in Budissin a treatise in the Wendish language on the Gospels of Matthew and Mark, wherewith entirely the same reprimand was delivered to the bookbinder of this place, from whom 400 copies have been confiscated pending further order.

> (Röseberg 1930: 81)

The anticipatory nature of von Watzdorf's complaint is not its only surprising feature. It is hard to see how Frentzel's book could be referred to as a 'prohibited publication', nor how it could reasonably be called 'a treatise in the Wendish language on the Gospels of Matthew and Mark'. A possible explanation of both chronological and descriptive discrepancies is that von Watzdorf knew only that the printing of something related to the gospels of Matthew and Mark, unauthorized and in Wendish, was in progress in Budissin.

Frentzel, having received his reprimand in person in Budissin on 1 December, went straight home to his parsonage in Postwitz and started composing a letter to the High Consistory in Dresden. Dated 6 December 1670, it shows that a century and a half after Luther's excommunication the propriety of translating the Bible into Wendish was still not self-evident. Frentzel found it necessary to remind the High Consistory: 'that the Holy Bible has now been translated into almost all the languages spoken under the sun [...]. Only our Serbi or Wends in Upper and Lower Lusatia have nothing of God's word published in print (apart from Luther's Catechism and a hymn book)'. He warned them that improvised translations would lead to 'the extreme confusion and perplexity of poor Wendish folk', the proximity of Catholic parishes making them particularly vulnerable. This was demonstrated by his own parish Postwitz, 'almost on the Bohemian border', where, 'as a good part of my parishioners are subjects of the [Catholic] collegiate priests, for them it is particularly necessary that Christ with his bloody merits be portrayed and impressed with total clarity and comprehensibly before their eyes, yea into their hearts'. He had, he said, as an alumnus of the Electoral School in Meissen and of the University of Leipzig, submitted copies to the Elector, Johann Georg II, and also to the Elector's Court Preacher, Dr Martin Geier. Geier had responded by advising Frentzel to dedicate his work to the Upper Lusatian Estates. This he had done. Nevertheless, the Budissin town council had 'found themselves highly offended', issued a severe reprimand, and had all the copies confiscated ('apart from a few'). He was now petitioning the High Consistory to seek the return of the confiscated copies and to cause the book to be published 'with the grace and privilege of the Most Serene Elector', because 'I, as a simple fool, did not understand, let alone know, that I should have reported such an undertaking to my most highly esteemed lords in advance' (Röseberg 1930: 83–5).

Geier, as a member of the High Consistory, forwarded Frentzel's letter to the Elector with a letter of his own. Röseberg (1930: 81–5), who first retrieved these letters from the Saxon Chancery, took their dates at face value and so put Geier's letter chronologically before Frentzel's, overlooking the fact that Lusatia had adopted the Gregorian calendar, whereas Saxony had not. Geier's letter, dated 30 November 1670 (OS), corresponding to 11 December 1670 (NS), was written in reaction to the receipt of Frentzel's letter dated 6 December 1670 (NS). Because Lusatia was not part of Saxony, the Elector's personal involvement was constitutionally inevitable. As Geier put it:

[...] we hesitate to ordain anything in Upper Lusatian affairs of this kind without Your Electoral Majesty's gracious special command. Thus we submissively ask whether Your Electoral Majesty graciously pleases to write to the aforementioned Council and to desire it most obediently to report the reasons why it took from him the copies of the book, to demand the delivery of the translation, and then to command sufficiently qualified persons conversant with the Wendish language above all diligently to read the translation and to examine it lest it contain anything contrary to the analogy of faith, whereupon it would remain at your

Electoral Majesty's gracious pleasure whether you wished to allow the book to be published or not.

Geier gave his own version of the advice he had given Frentzel:

I told him that he should above all communicate with the worthy gentlemen of the Estates so that the work could appear with their foreknowledge and approval, and also with their support for the necessary costs; this I felt I should add for my exculpation before Your Electoral Majesty.

(Röseberg 1930: 82)

There is another letter to the Elector on the same subject, written in Dresden on 12 December 1670 (OS)=23 December 1670 (NS) by the Upper Lusatian *Landeshauptmann*, Count Vitzthum von Eckstädt (who is known to have attended meetings of the Budissin Town Council) and containing no mention of Frentzel's petition (Leszczyński 1963: 68). It seems, in fact, to be written in ignorance of the Elector's previous acquaintance with the case. Enclosing copies of the *Matthew and Mark* translation, he expresses guarded approval of Frentzel's intentions but uncertainty as to his competence. Von Eckstädt has therefore, 'owing to the negligent supervision of the aforementioned Council at Budissin', taken the matter in hand and, 'as it has as yet not undergone censorship' put a stop to it. The confiscated copies will be stored securely in the Budissin Town Hall until the Consistory has examined him on the project and decided if he is equal to the task. Then it would be open to the Elector to show the book to other Protestant Wendish preachers and seek their opinion of it (Röseberg 1930: 85–8).

The Elector Johann Georg II dealt with the matter expeditiously. On 5 January 1671 (OS)=16 January 1671 (NS) he wrote to the *Landvogt*, telling him about Frentzel's work and giving instructions:

Whereas the work has not been censored and there is no certainty as to whether the translation is to be trusted, it is now our most gracious desire that you make arrangements, so that a few clergymen in Budissin, experienced in the Wendish language, and also in the original Bible text, and also two equally skilled preachers from the country, be assembled, to study the work diligently and to examine whether the intended purpose of the above-mentioned pastor has been reached in such a way that there is nothing contained in it that is contrary to the analogy of faith, or whatever else there is to be mentioned, to make a written report, and thereby to reveal their opinion, so that we may then expect further most dutiful action.

(Röseberg 1930: 88)

Censors were appointed and eighteen months later they reported favourably. On 3 August 1672 (OS) (14 August 1672 NS), Johann Georg II wrote from Schneeberg to the *Amtshauptmann* in Budissin, lifting the prohibition and ordering the printed copies to be returned to Frentzel. The only reservation was 'that the copies be not distributed until he attaches on a separate sheet printed at the end of the work under his name the observations which were made by the censors concerning certain hard phrases in the main creeds (amendations and additions of this kind being not unusual)'. The question of further translations was raised:

> Should the dutiful Estates of our Margraviate of Upper Lusatia consider a translation of the New Testament possible, you are to make such disposal that this be entrusted not to a single person alone, especially on account of the attached notes, on which matter an experienced judgement will be needed. And as the censors of the above-mentioned work consider it not inadvisable that a Wendish Church Agenda, as well as the Catechism and a Gospel Book be translated (so that every pastor should not read the text as the fancy takes him), you are to present this matter to the most dutiful Estates and, if it is their pleasure, make provision for it to be prudently expedited.

> (Röseberg 1930: 88–9; Schuster-Šewc 1993: 10)

In deference to the delicate constitutional relationship between Upper Lusatia and Saxony, the Elector's letter to the *Amtshauptmann* contained proposals rather than commands and used terms like 'if it is their pleasure'. For their part, the Estates probably felt they must take cognizance of the Elector's wishes, but they were not disposed to be hurried.

Meanwhile, Frentzel remained active.

Postwitzscher Tauff-Stein (1688)

A bone of contention between the old and new religions was the status of the saints. The celebration of saints' days was often connected to old customs which were originally pagan feasts. One such case was the feast of St Walburga on 1 May coinciding with the pagan celebration of the beginning of summer and the revels of witches (*Walpurgisnacht*). Lutherans repudiated the veneration of saints, but old habits died hard and lighting fires and firing guns in the night before 1 May continued in Lusatia long after the Reformation in both Catholic and Protestant parishes.

In 1676 on the night before 1 May, the foresters of Budissin town council were celebrating in the Postwitz inn. They had brought their guns with them and shortly after midnight, to ward off witches, they went out into the garden and began to fire their guns into the air. A piece of paper wadding, still glowing, fell onto the thatched roof of the inn, setting it alight, and the fire immediately spread to Frentzel's house. Both the inn and the parsonage were burnt down. Frentzel must have disapproved, in any case, of *Walpurgisnacht*, and now, 'owing to the mischievousness of a few wicked people', as he put it, it had resulted in disaster. The Frentzel family was unharmed, but the house and its contents, including all Frentzel's papers, were destroyed. Materials for its reconstruction were provided by Budissin Town Council, as the church's patron, and by 1678 the new parsonage was complete.

In the 1680s the town council carried out alterations and improvements to the Postwitz church, including the provision of a new altar and font, and these events prompted the appearance of Frentzel's second book, the *Postwitzscher Tauff-Stein* ('Postwitz Font'), based on his sermons on baptism, delivered in 1687. He was now in touch with Philipp Jakob Spener, the founder of German Pietism, who had recently been appointed Court Preacher to the Elector at Dresden. On 2 January 1689, Spener wrote to Frentzel expressing his pleasure at the publication of the *Postwitzscher Tauffstein* and his sadness that the Wends had no Bible in their language, nor even a complete New Testament. Evidently unaware that in 1672 proposals for further translations had been made by the censors and conveyed by the Elector to the Estates, he promised to raise the question in the appropriate places, so that at least a Wendish New Testament or, at the very least, the Epistles might be published, 'lest we, who rebuke the Papists for preventing the laity from reading Holy Scripture, suffer the reproach that this cannot be so important or useful, seeing we take little care to ensure that our people can attain to read it' (Frentzel 1688 in Schuster-Šewc 1993: 194–5). Although the letter was directed to Frentzel, parts of it have an air of being addressed to a wider audience, so it is not surprising that he contrived to have it published as a preface to his *Tauffstein* (which nevertheless shows 1688 as its publication date).

In Spener the Wends now had a friend at Court and it is surely no coincidence that the question of a Wendish Bible, having lain dormant since 1668, suddenly reappears in the agenda of the Estates' assembly in August 1689, only months after Spener's letter to Frentzel. In the proposed new church regulations approved by the Estates in 1690 it was noted: 'Of the Wendish language. Whereas hitherto the policy here in Upper Lusatia has been directed towards the total extermination of this language, henceforth it shall, in the wholly Wendish communities for the time being in little towns and in village parishes, be retained, lest the Wendish serfs relapse into unchristian superstition and Catholicism' (Mětšk 1960d/1981: 40–1).

The Prätorius committee

Assemblies of the Estates were held three times a year in the Ortenburg in Budissin, on the third Sunday in Lent (known as *Oculi*), on 24 August (St Bartholomew's Day), and on 19 November (St Elizabeth's Day). The agenda of the Estates' assembly held in Lent 1668 had included the item: 'Various clergymen have translated the Gospels and Epistles into the Wendish language. Gentlemen will debate what is to be done about this.' The possibility of having these translations printed was considered, but delaying tactics ensued, and there followed an interval of twenty-one years, during which manuscript versions of Biblical texts continued to be in use.

Finally, at the St Bartholomew's Day assembly in 1689 the following item was on the agenda:

Translation into Wendish of the gospels and catechism. A memorandum has been prepared by various clergymen of the Wendish church to the effect that, whereas almost every parish has a different version of the customary prayers and hymns as well as of the Catechism and consequently, when labourers move from one parish to another to take up employment, they become not a little confused in their Christianity, steps might be taken for the Catechism and the prayers and hymns customarily used in the churches to be translated into a form of the Wendish language used equally everywhere. And since in this connection various complaints are made about neglect of monthly penitential sermons, catechismal examinations, and prayer-meetings, the Estates may wish to consider a possible remedy for this.

At their Oculi assembly in 1690, they agreed to seek an understanding with Pastor Paul Prätorius in Budissin, who was to be asked to propose 'some learned Wendish clergymen for translating' (Röseberg 1930: 95; Mětšk 1960d/1981: 27–9).

The minutes of the Oculi assembly the following year (1691) record that the clergymen proposed by Prätorius for the translation of 'the Sunday Gospels, Epistles, Catechism, and the like' had been approved. Following a meeting held in his house in Budissin on 25 April 1691 Prätorius reported that he considered the following three points necessary: '1. That four other Wendish clergymen apart from him be appointed for correspondence and consultation; 2. That such persons be chosen as could tolerate me [Prätorius] and each other, lest the good work reach deadlock owing to the caprice of one or another; 3. That because of dialectal variation they be selected from various regions.' The names he put forward were: '1. From the Kamenz and Hoyerswerda region: Tobias Zschuderley, Pastor of Lohsa; 2. From the Field and Muskau region: Johann Christoph Richter, Pastor of Milkel; 3. From the Görlitz and Löbau region Georg Matthaei, Pastor of Colm; 4. From the Budissin and Hill region Michael Rätze, the Wendish Deacon here [sc. Budissin].' These proposals were accepted by the Estates (Röseberg 1930: 96).

The five clergymen met many times in Budissin to discuss their work, and their efforts resulted in three printed books, namely:

1. *Luther's Little Catechism* (1693),
2. *The Epistles and Gospels* (1695),
3. *The Lutheran Order of Service* (*Agenda*) (1696).

They conducted widespread consultations, writing to all the Protestant pastors in Upper Lusatia with a list of particularly difficult words and phrases, requesting their opinions (Röseberg 1930: 97). Their spelling system was that recently published in Zacharias Bierling's *Orthographia Vandalica* (Budissin, 1689), based on that of German and diverging from the orthographical doctrines of both Frentzel and Catholic writers. From the bookbinder's bill, which has survived, it is known that 400 copies of the *Catechism* were printed, 500 of the *Epistles and Gospels*, and 500 of the *Agenda* (Röseberg 1930: 99).

Thanks to the mediation of Spener, Frentzel now had a patron who enabled him to publish from the existing manuscripts his translation of the epistles of St Paul to the Romans and Galatians. This was Henriette Katharina von Gersdorff (1648–1726), wife of *Landvogt* Nikolaus von Gersdorff (1629–1702). The latter appears to have been instrumental in the Estates' decision to appoint the Prätorius Committee. The book appeared under the title *Apostolischer Catechismus* in Budissin in 1693, the same year as the Prätorius Committee's *Catechism*. Freifrau von Gersdorff's grant covered not only the cost of production but also provided for two copies to be given free of charge to every Wendish church in both Upper and Lower Lusatia. She also commissioned Prätorius, Frentzel, and Michael Rätze to translate the *Book of Psalms* into Wendish, which duly appeared in 1703, the Freifrau again paying for the costs of publication, as well as for two copies to be donated free of charge to every Wendish church in both Upper and Lower Lusatia (Röseberg 1930: 104; Mětšk 1940/1981: 14–15).

As early as 1689, Spener had recommended to her the publication of Frentzel's New Testament. By 1702 she was ready to proceed with this too and in July that year the printing started in Budissin. By this time, Frentzel's sight had begun to fail and in a few years he became almost totally blind, though remaining otherwise in full command of his faculties (Röseberg 1930:105–6). His eldest son Abraham, pastor of Schönau auf dem Eigen and already an outstanding scholar and author of repute, took over some of the responsibility (Röseberg 1930: 107). On 22 September 1704, in Zittau (not in Budissin, as previously) printing was resumed in the shop of Michael Hartmann. The bilingual text in parallel columns was not easy to set and progress was slow. On 29 June 1706 Frentzel died. Printing was completed on 6 October. Once again Freifrau von Gersdorff paid for the book to be distributed free of charge to all Wendish churches. This time, in addition, it was given to schools and many poor people.

Abraham Frentzel (1656–1740)

The successful publication of Michael Frentzel's Upper Sorbian, New Testament in 1706 was due in no small measure to the intervention of his son Abraham, but apart from this Abraham does not appear in the history of the Sorbian Bible. His scholarly interests were of a different kind, leading him to make significant contributions to Wendish history, anthropology, and lexicography. He is the author of several books, but the greater part of his work has remained in manuscript, although it constitutes one of the main sources for the history of the Lusatian Wends in the early modern period.

Born in the parsonage at Kosel on 19 November 1656, while his father was pastor there, he was barely six years old when the family moved to Postwitz, but Kosel remained part of him and he sometimes gave his name as 'Abraham Frencel Koselâ-Lusatus'. When he was not yet ten, his parents sent him to the Budissin Gymnasium. He lodged with his uncle Abraham (Michael's brother), a master tailor. Throughout his time at the gymnasium (21 June 1666 to March 1679) the headmaster was Johann Theill (1608–1679), a graduate of the University of Jena, who was famous for the reforms he introduced, bringing the school an outstanding reputation. Theill was cognizant of the

Wendish presence in his school. He gave his Wendish pupils support and encouraged them to enter the clergy (Petr 1989: 12–13).

In 1679 Frentzel entered the University of Wittenberg, where he completed his theological studies in April 1682, hoping to find a position as pastor in a Wendish parish. Meanwhile, he accepted the post of domestic tutor at Spreewiese, near Klix, in the house of the *Oberamtshauptmann* Caspar Christoph von Nostitz (Petr 1989: 17; Fröde 1999: 4–5). On 12 July 1684, with a recommendation from von Nostitz, he was called to the pastorate of Gaussig, the parish adjoining Postwitz to the west. He gave his inaugural sermon in the Gaussig church on Rogation Sunday (*Cantate*) 20 May 1685. On 25 September that year he was married to Susanna Theill, the daughter of his old headmaster. Although she was a local lady, there is no evidence that she ever learned Wendish.

Early in 1686 the Abbess of the Marienstern Nunnery, Catharina Benadin, was contemplating the question of presenting a new pastor to the German-speaking parish of Schönau auf dem Eigen, the previous incumbent having died. Schönau lies in the fertile valley of the Pliessnitz, a tributary of the Neisse. Though Lutheran, the parish was the property of the Nunnery, which also retained the right of presentation. For the Schönau vacancy the Abbess chose Abraham Frentzel. By the terms of the Abbess's mandate Frentzel was bound to preach the word of God according to the unvaried Augsburg Confession, not to slander the Roman Catholic faith, and not to harm neighbouring clergy in their pastoral activities. This last provision may have a confessional explanation, although by the time of Frentzel's incumbency all the adjoining parishes were Lutheran. On 19 May 1686, in the presence of Caspar Burkart, as the Abbess's representative, Frentzel was solemnly installed. His inaugural sermon was preached on 23 May. From his manuscripts, notably the *Historia Ecclesiae Schoenaviensis*, as interpreted by Petr (1989: 22–8), we gain an impression of the Schönau pastor's daily life at the end of the seventeenth century. On assuming office he received ten thalers, ten bushels of rye (in sacks), ten bushels of oats, unspecified quantities of straw and manure, a tin washbin, two sieves, a table, benches and chairs, two cows, a vat for brewing, and various other vessels and utensils (Petr 1989: 23–4).

The Schönau peasants planted mainly rye, wheat, oats, barley, peas, flax, and vegetables, and kept fruit trees. Frentzel kept careful records, noting the yields and prices of crops. He attached much importance to recording the weather. His arrival in May 1686 was immediately followed by a disastrous drought. Not a drop of rain fell from 16 May to 29 June. The harvest was meagre and there was hunger. From Frentzel's letters to the Abbess in the years 1686–1699, preserved in the Nunnery's archives, emerge some of the problems encountered by a Lutheran clergyman responsible, in secular matters, to a Roman Catholic authority (Petr 1989: 26). Schönau had 197 hearths, (the taxation unit). This number corresponded to the number of families and of inhabited houses. The inhabitants were all engaged in agriculture or ancillary trades: of the heads of family five were millers, 102 were described as *Häusler*, forty-five as *Gärtner*, and forty-five as *Bauer*. The pastor too was a *Bauer*, for he had to work his glebe and bring the harvest home (Petr 1989: 36).

The native population of Schönau was entirely German, but there were seven Wendish serfs who had moved in from the predominantly Wendish villages to the north-west and west of Schönau. There were also Wends working in neighbouring villages, but they too had migrated from Wendish villages lying to the north-west. In the Schönau church books there are records of the death and funerals of Wendish immigrants. On 26 May 1699, Frentzel was called to Zittau to offer spiritual comfort to a Wend condemned to death for theft. The condemned man came from Kosel, Frentzel's birthplace, and had known Frentzel's father Michael, when he was pastor there (before 1662). Frentzel pleaded for the life of the man and succeeded in having his sentence commuted to forced labour (Petr 1989: 27). On 2 May 1700 in Schönau Frentzel was called upon to conduct the funeral service of a Wendish serf from Huttberg. Present at the funeral were the man's relatives from the Kittlitz parish, who 'knew not a word of German'. At the request of the parents Frentzel preached in Wendish (Petr 1989: 27).

In 1734, in the bosom of his large family, Frentzel celebrated fifty years as pastor of Schönau. By this time he was assisted in his office by his son Johann Christoph Frentzel (born 1712) and the following year Johann Christoph was presented by the Abbess (now Cordula Sommerin) to succeed his father. Abraham Frentzel died on 15 April 1740 and was buried in the Schönau churchyard. A writer of prodigious zeal, he is the author of fourteen printed books and over twenty fat folio manuscript volumes. The manuscripts are, for the most part, in the Christian-Weise-Bibliothek, Zittau. For the history of the Wends his most valuable work is the 1436-page manuscript *Historia populi et rituum Lusatiae Superioris, das ist kurzgefaßte Erzählung von der Oberlausitz Einwohnern und derselben Gewohnheiten* ('A history of the people and customs of Upper Lusatia, that is a brief account of the inhabitants of Upper Lusatia and their habits'). It is mainly in German, but contains many Wendish words. His main contribution to the study of the Wendish language is his four-volume book *De originibus linguae sorabicae*, vol. 1 (Bautzen, 1693), vol. 2. (Zittau, 1694), vol. 3 (Zittau, 1695), and vol. 4 (Zittau, 1696), which is in Latin with numerous Wendish quotations. This is the first Wendish dictionary and contains some 4,000 Upper Sorbian words with their German and Latin equivalents.

Historia populi et rituum is unparalleled as a source for everyday Lusatian life at the end of the seventeenth century it. The descriptions of clothing help us to picture the Wendish figures in the Upper Lusatian pre-industrial landscape. On weekdays the men usually wore a little shaggy black fur cap or a rough old hat, coarse shirt, and a sheepskin, sometimes with a tail dragging along the ground. They had wide black linen trousers with big pockets and shabby boots, though it was not unknown for them to go barefoot or in shoes and stockings. On Sundays and feastdays, however, and at weddings or other grand occasions they would don a hat (black or grey) or a tall round cap edged with fox's fur, wear a clean white shirt, a waistcoat (usually green), long black leather breeches, long boots of oiled leather with heels, a leather belt decorated with white shells, and a coat. An unmarried man might wear a grey, green, brown, or red coat, a finely embroidered belt, and sometimes a peaked cap edged with fox's fur with a stiff white feather stuck in the back. The feather, according to Frentzel's account, was becoming rarer.

Following the breakdown of social order during the Thirty Years' War the landed class in the years immediately following struggled to reassert control (Wedgwood 1961: 452). Only a little before his own time, as Frentzel reveals, the Estates had noted a new impudence among the Wends, reflected both in their inclination to carry weapons and in their dress sense. At their St Elizabeth diet in 1651 (he says) the Estates legislated:

> Whereas in the recent hostilities the Wendish peasants have become not a little insolent and some of them, particularly the youngest, sturdy peasant-lads, hang about in beer-houses and inns, if not with swords then with staffs and lead-filled cudgels, and thereby often provoke and cause much misfortune, even death and murder. Therefore, henceforth no one either in the towns or the villages is to frequent beer-houses and inns with weapons of that kind on pain of punishment of 2 Schock, which shall be paid for every infringement. Also, if any person be caught with a musket or with other dangerous weapons, all these penalties shall be doubled.

This decree was published by the *Landvogt* with an instruction that it be read from every pulpit in Wendish and German. Consequently, says Frentzel, in his time the Wends, with the exception of a few old men, would not carry a staff, even when on a journey. Perversely, however, in Frentzel's account, the Wendish man 'under his left arm carries a long double-edged sword with a silver basket hilt, but without a sword-belt. Only when he rides, he has a strap from his right shoulder to under his left arm, from which the sword hangs' (A. Frentzel, *Historia populi et rituum*, Chap. 5, quoted by Muka 1882: 23).

At their *Oculi* diet the following year (1652) the Estates had acceded to accusations concerning the length of Wendish hair:

> Whereas serious complaints have been received that those Wendish peasants who wear long hair scorn those who do not have hair of that kind, and that therefore often great fights are provoked and caused. Therefore, in order to counter such and other evils ensuing therefrom, all peasants, whether master or servant, shall be forbidden to wear hair differing from the ordinary peasant's crop on pain of whatever arbitrary punishment shall be imposed by the lord of that place, and men of rank shall be earnestly exhorted to maintain a firm hand in this matter.

(quoted by Muka 1882: 24)

In 1654 at their August assembly the Estates banned peasants, 'to subdue their increasing arrogance', from wearing costly ribbons and feathers in their hats or boots with heels and trimmed down-turns. Long hair was again banned. By the end of the century, however, the Wends would no longer suffer having their hair cropped and trimmed (Frentzel, *Historia populi et rituum*, Chap. 5, quoted by Muka 1882: 24). It is unlikely that this was a new problem in Frentzel's time. Since the Middle Ages wearing long hair had been a sign of the free man; the right to do so was denied to serfs (Grimm, 5, 1873, s. v. *Kolbe*).

Upper Lusatia (Catholics)

Jakub Xavier Ticin (1656–1693)

Lutheran lip service to the need for the faithful to have access to the word of God was sometimes matched by action only as a reaction to Catholic initiatives. The Catholics stole a march on the Protestants in 1679, for example, by publishing the first Wendish grammar. This was the work of the Jesuit Jakub Xavier Ticin, who was born in Wittichenau on 1 August 1656, the son of a coppersmith. He was taught in the Latin school in Wittichenau and entered the Society of Jesus in Prague on 17 October 1673, aged 17. Here he wrote a Wendish grammar, which on 24 July 1679 he defended as his MA thesis. With the official approval of the Jesuit General it was published that year in Prague as *Principia linguae wendicae, quam aliqui wandalicam vocant* (Michałk 1986: 61; Michałk 1992: 71). On 21 September 1679, Ticin was transferred by his order from Prague to Neiße, where he taught grammar until 1682, but from 1683 to 1687 he was back in Prague and here on 2 February 1687 he was ordained priest (Michałk 1986: 52). After four years at Komotau (1688–1692), in January 1693 he returned to Prague. Later that year he was a chaplain in the Imperial Army under the command of Prince Eugene of Savoy, fighting the Turks, and on 17 August 1693, during the siege of Belgrade, he was killed (Figure 4.4).

Ticin's most influential teacher at the Jesuit Seminary (*Clementinum*) in Prague was Bohuslav Balbín, a prominent figure in Czech history, who in his *Dissertatio apologetica pro lingua Slavonica praecipue Bohemica*, written c. 1672 (though not published until 1775), anticipated the Czech national revival. Balbín was the inspiration for all Ticin's works (Michałk 1992: 70). In his correspondence with other Catholic divines Ticin discusses plans for his grammar. His correspondents included representatives of both the Wittichenau and Crostwitz dialects, but there was never any question of arriving at a compromise norm. In this detail the story of the creation of a literary language for Catholic Wends is quite different from that of the work of the Praetorius committee, which was deliberately made up of representatives of various regions and aimed for a supra-dialectal amalgam. Ticin's correspondence is almost entirely in Latin. Now and again, however, as if to show that such things are possible, one or two Wendish sentences appear. That these men were capable of corresponding in Wendish also emerges from a letter dated 19 April 1685, in which Ticin reports having recently received a Wendish letter from J. H. Swětlik (Michałk 1988a: 51–2).

More or less regular postal services came into existence in Upper Lusatia in the seventeenth century and they were monopolized by an *Oberamstpatent* of 1678. The monopoly was put in the hands of Christoph Sillig, a citizen of Budissin who established a regular service between Budissin and Görlitz and beyond into Silesia (Bahlcke 2001: 151). The Budissin Cathedral Chapter was a Catholic island in a Protestant sea.

Figure 4.4 Jakub Xavier Ticin (1656–1693). Artist unknown. Reproduced from the original in the Prague Wendish Seminary by permission of the *Společnost přátel Lužice*.

Communication with the Catholic mainland (Bohemia) had to pass through Protestant territory and the postal service in Lusatia was in Protestant hands. For this reason Ticin did not trust it, tried to avoid using it, whenever possible, and often mentions the services of a messenger or the practice of asking reliable travellers to take letters with them. The prices charged by the post office (payable by the recipient) seem to have been arbitrary. 'I recently received your kind letter through the regular messenger, the reply to which I postponed until now, because I thought to save [you] the fee which is paid to the postman for letters to be released; for I do not doubt that a fairly high price is demanded by the Budissin heretics, whenever a letter is delivered to a Catholic' (Ticin to Fabricius 29 August 1682, Michałk 1987: 70–1). Whenever a letter was lost in the post, there was an intuitive assumption that the explanation was to be found in the confessional struggle. 'I wrote to you on 26 July, but I fear that owing to the impressed seal of the Society the letter may have been lost in the heretical post', wrote Ticin to Dean Martin Ferdinand Brückner à Brückenstein (1650–1700) on 13 August 1679 (Michałk 1986: 61–3).

It is significant that Ticin published his grammar ten years before the Estates even discussed whether the time was ripe to reverse the policy of 'total extermination' of the language (see above). He saw his grammar as a preliminary to a steady flow of religious books in the vernacular that would spread throughout the Lusatias (Upper and Lower) calling the people back to the Roman way. He felt that he was faced with a great opportunity to publish books in Wendish, while his opponents were doing nothing. He wrote: 'My book, I hope, will open the gates for the publication of many books in our mother tongue [...]. The lack [of a spelling system] is the reason why hitherto no book has been published by a Catholic.' After a few misgivings he had decided that Czech spelling could serve as a model for Wendish. When he wrote to Jan Ferdinand Serbin on 29 March 1678, he was not yet quite sure: 'As for the characters of our language, I would be glad if they could be expressed conveniently with German or Latin letters, but there are many words which (so far as I can judge) cannot be written perfectly and properly with these letters' (Michałk 1986: 54). A few months later he was discussing these questions with Donatus Josephus Fabricius (1614–1690), who was forty-two years older than him and had evidently already devised a way of writing Wendish (*mea[m] Wandalice scribendi ratione[m]*) (Michałk 1986: 57). Fabricius told him: 'The words of our language cannot be better expressed by any other letters than those of Czech, its sister language' (14 September 1678, Michałk 1986: 57). Eventually, Ticin wrote in the preface to the grammar: 'I have made an effort to find a universal orthography, also for the sake of avoiding cost, so adjusted to the Czech, that we can use Czech letters almost without changing or adding anything' (Ticinus 1679: A3r).

A central objective of the Society of Jesus was the conversion of heathens and heretics (Protestants), and Ticin saw his work as an integral part of the Vatican's general policy of re-Catholicization. He likened it to the work of Jesuit missionaries not only in India (converting the heathen) but also in Holland and England (converting heretics). Any overt plan for reconversion, however, could easily have been interpreted as infringing the *Traditionsrezeß*. When the *Principia* were ready for the press, Ticin decided to include a preface dedicating the work to Dean Brückner à Brückenstein. He sent him a draft for his approval, including the words: 'I hope that you will fairly and kindly consult this little gift, which in size is certainly insignificant, yet is great in its purpose to restore my errant countrymen (whose well-being you so ardently have at heart) back into the bosom of the Roman church' (Michałk 1986: 63). The Dean evidently regarded such a blatant reference to reconversion as risky and deleted the offending words (Michałk 1985: 21–32), so that the printed version read: 'I hope that you will fairly and kindly consult this little gift, which is certainly small in size, yet in its purpose scarcely to be scorned' (Ticinus 1679: *Dedicatio* [6]).

Georg Franz Sende (1652–1706)

Naturally, Brückner must have shared Ticin's hopes for the restoration of the Roman church, but he was more diplomatic. As Dean of the Budissin Chapter, moreover, he was in an exposed position. Ticin was in Prague and could say what he liked, but in Upper

Lusatia the Jesuits were not permitted to operate (Michałk 1991: 68, n. 36; Michałk 1994: 33, 39, n. 20). Another of Ticin's correspondents, however, appears to have thrown caution to the winds. On 6 April 1690, Ticin wrote to Father Georg Sende, the parish priest of Crostwitz, congratulating him on his missionary prowess: 'I have received two replies from you, and therefore with double comfort. Great as it may be from the first, it is far greater from the second, for you have in a short time with God's help brought in such a substantial harvest of confessed and converted little sheep. May God confirm what you have achieved. May He multiply the tiny flock of our countrymen into something immense, above all by the work of you who (to my mind) are effecting in the Six-Towns Land the same thing as our missionaries with apostolic courage are working to achieve in their arduous missions in India, Holland, and England' (Michałk 1990: 85).

In February the following year, in a letter alluding to material provided by Sende for Ticin to use in his *Epitome historiae Rosenthalensis*, he returned to the question of Sende's reconversion activity: 'Solely for my personal information and reassurance I should like to know how many you have led back into the bosom of the Catholic Church.' But the need for confidentiality is also reflected here: 'I promise not to make the slightest mention of this matter in this history book or any other' (Michałk 1991: 67–9). Ticin's correspondent, Georg Franz Sende (1652–1706), became parish priest of Crostwitz in 1680. In 1680 too, it is recorded, twenty-four former Lutherans in the village were received back into the Catholic faith. The earliest inventory of the confessional distribution in the parish was made by Sende in 1703, when there were 3,179 Catholics and 296 Lutherans (*Krajan 3*: 87; Michałk 1991: 53, 55–63).

As parish priest of Crostwitz, Sende had responsibility for the pilgrims' church at Rosenthal, which he habitually visited at least once a week on Fridays. He consequently became involved in a long-running dispute (in which the emperor played a part) between the Marienstern Nunnery's visitor, Abbot Andreas Troyer of Plass, and the Budissin Dean, Brückner à Brückenstein, as to their jurisdiction over the shrine (Magirius and Seifert 1982: 24; Michałk, 1987: 74–5; Michałk 1989: 76–80; Michałk 1991: 55–6).

The Gospels and Catechism for Catholics

Ticin was barely thirty-seven when he was killed. He had hoped that his *Principia* would 'open the gates for the publication of many books in our mother tongue', but from 1679 he was working on his history of the Rosental shrine, which he wrote in Latin and published in 1692. Meanwhile, however, he never ceased to think about the need for religious books in the vernacular and on 19 December 1684 wrote to the Dean in Budissin:

> I have myself often considered how necessary it is, in order to preserve the majesty of the gospel, to have the gospels printed in the vernacular, so that many priests would not be obliged to be extempore interpreters of the word of God before the sacred pulpit, translating it from the German or Latin into Wendish, not without grave danger of irreverence and of material heresy. So now your zealous solicitude

has brought about or is preparing to effect [a measure] whereby the holy reading of the gospel may be instituted in parish churches without the danger of this method.

(Michałk 1987: 72–5)

Apparently at Brückner's instigation, Ticin had already made detailed enquiries of two printers in Prague as to the cost of printing the gospels. The lower quotation was for 56 thalers to print 500 copies. As the price of printing 300 copies was not much lower, he was thinking of procuring 500, 'if you see fit'. He writes as if the translation were already at an advanced stage or even complete. It was evidently envisaged that Ticin would collaborate in seeing the work through the press. He asks that the copy be as clean and legible as possible, punctuated, and written in accordance with his *Principia*. 'If such a manuscript is already prepared, we shall begin printing in a few weeks. But if it has not yet been written in the way mentioned, I earnestly beg you through your great authority to have suitable scribes do it, who can read Czech and speak Wendish.' From the same letter it transpires that there were also plans for the publication of a Catechism and hymns, but there is no suggestion here that the translation of the Catechism is to be undertaken by Ticin himself: 'The same opinion applies to the Catechism, which one of our priests will easily be able to translate on at most one sheet from another language into ours. The same goes for the hymns. But nothing is more useful than the gospels…' (Michałk 1987: 72–5).

In 1685 Fabricius submitted to the Dean for approval a translation he had made some years earlier of the *Catechism* (1555) of Peter Canisius (1521–1597). Three years earlier Fabricius had sent a handwritten copy to Ticin, who cannot therefore have been surprised, when the Dean sought his opinion on its suitability for publication (Michałk 1988a: 48–50). Ticin recommended a printing of 300–500 copies in duodecimo, but suggested that certain dialectal features be changed 'with the author's agreement'. He went on: 'For if this book is to be the forerunner of future vernacular publications, it seems fitting, in order to avoid the mockery and ridicule of our adversaries, that it should conform to the recommended rules of the *Principia linguae wendicae*, lest the variability of this already not particularly esteemed language provoke aversion from the readers. So the author's Wendish will remain; only his Crostwitz or Budissin dialect will be slightly changed, as appropriate, into that of Wittichenau' (letter of 19 March 1685, Michałk 1988a: 48–50).

From Ticin's comments it appears that, to the ears of the Wittichenau Wends, there was something slightly comic about the Crostwitz or Budissin dialect. The dialect of Wittichenau, on the other hand, was evidently of high status, especially once it had been recorded in black and white in Ticin's *Principia*. The Dean, who was also from Wittichenau, seems to have agreed, but before making a final decision he sought two further opinions, which were both supplied by natives of Wittichenau. The next recorded event in this story is the publication before the end of 1685 of a translation of the Canisius Catechism made not by Fabricius but by Ticin. It is hard to avoid the conclusion that, outnumbered and outranked by speakers of the Wittichenau dialect, Fabricius withdrew or was replaced.

By 1690, when he read Spener's words in Frentzel's *Tauffstein* (1688/9), Ticin realized that the question of the gospels for Catholics was urgent. 'I request therefore that the priests will so arrange things that in the matter of printing the gospel-book the pseudo-Christians and monkey-preachers of the gutter do not steal a march on us. That is certainly their intention, as I perceive from the preface to Frentzel's *Font*' (25 May 1690 to G. F. Sende, Michałk 1990: 88). He also raised the question of censorship:

The law must be obeyed which says that nothing written in the Wendish language may be published. [...] On the pretext of this decree [...] – it is perhaps to be feared – the preachers [sc. Protestant pastors] and other bad Catholics might make difficulties and trouble, if our gospel-book should appear only in the Wendish language without the addition of the German. If we were to add the German version, then, in my opinion, they could not cause any unpleasantness for us, especially as Frentzel too, several times, and a certain Brandenburger c. 1609, have published books written in our language. It is helpful to know that. Perhaps through the mediation of Herr Vitzky [a Wend, then chaplain to the Imperial envoy in Dresden] the Papal envoy should with proper emphasis be asked to obtain from the Elector a mandate, in which a Budissin printer would be commanded to print the Wendish gospel-book; for we Catholics until this very day are in full possession of our rights in Lusatia.

(25 May 1690, Michałk 1990: 88)

Jurij Hawštyn Swětlik (1650–1729)

The task of further developing Wendish Catholic devotional literature in the mother tongue had already been taken up, well before Ticin's death, by another son of Wittichenau, who naturally had no difficulty in following the Ticinian tradition of basing the linguistic standard on the Wittichenau dialect. This was Georgius Augustinus Swotlik (Jurij Hawštyn Swětlik). He was born on 23 January 1650, educated at the local Latin school, and sent at the age of sixteen to the gymnasium in Český Krumlov. In 1670 he was admitted to the seminary at Olomouc and ordained priest in 1675. From 1683 to 1707 he was parish priest in Radibor, then for the last twenty-two years of his life at the Cathedral Chapter, first as resident canon and from 1717 as senior canon. He died there on 23 February 1729 (Michałk 1988b: 10).

By the end of the seventeenth century the number of people able to read Wendish was no longer negligible, but Ticin's translation of the Canisius Catechism may have been found difficult by the laity, even if they were literate, so a new version for 'the simple-minded and children' was produced by Swětlik and published in 1692 (probably). Swětlik's translation of the epistles and gospels for reading during mass, published as

Swjate Sćenja, lekciony a epistle na te njedźele a swjate dny toho cyłoho lěta ('The Holy Gospels, readings and epistles for Sundays and feastdays of the whole year'), which includes a supplement of 32 pages containing fifteen hymns, bears the date 1690, but the true publication date of this too was probably in 1692 (Michałk 1988b: 10). He is also the author of the Catholic hymnal *Serbske katolske kěrluše, kiž so na te s. s. róčne časy... spěwaju* (1696). Swětlik's hymns thus antedate those of the 1710 Protestant hymnal. The *Swjate Sćenja*, published in small octavo, contains over 400 pages and thirty-seven engravings. Between 1688 and 1707 Swětlik was working on his translation of the entire Bible into Wendish (from the Vulgate), based on the Catholic standard language devised and codified by Ticin's grammar (1679). His manuscript survives to this day in the archives of the Cathedral Chapter, but it has never been published. When Swětlik began his translation, there were no Wendish dictionaries of any kind in existence, but during the course of his work he composed his own Latin–Wendish dictionary, which he saw published in Budissin in 1721 as *Vocabularium Latino-Serbicum*. It complemented the Ticin grammar.

Pomerania

The Thirty Years' War

The political history of the lands inhabited by the Pomeranian Wends is well documented in the seventeenth century, but news and views of their lives, or even their precise whereabouts, remain scarce. The continuing presence of their language comes to light momentarily in 1621, when Bogisław, as yet merely Duke of Stettin-Pomerania, renewed the instruction to General Superintendents to instruct the Wends' pastors 'to express in Wendish the same things which they have got to know in Latin or German, and to take notice of those who know the language well' (cf. Chapter 3; also Ślaski 1959: 42). From 1625, as Duke Bogisław XIV (1580–1637), he reigned over the whole of Pomerania (*MSHP*: 41).

During the Thirty Years' War the attempts of the Dukes to remain neutral were unsuccessful. Both Imperial (Catholic) and Swedish (Protestant) forces ravaged the Duchy and by 1630 it was controlled by the Swedes. That Bogisław XIV would die childless and that the House of Griffin would thereby come to an end was obvious well before the actual date of his death on 10 March 1637. The forthcoming extinction was believed to have been devised by witchcraft. There were implications for the lands of Lauenburg and Bütow on the eastern border of Pomerania, for it was clear that they would now revert to the Polish crown. King Władysław IV Waza made plans accordingly. Under the Pomeranian Dukes the Lauenburg and Bütow Lands had accepted the Reformation, evidence of which among the Wendish inhabitants of Bütow comes in the form of Pastor Krofey's hymnal of 1586 (see Chapter 3).

The reversion to the Polish crown presented an opportunity for the Counter-Reformation and demands were made immediately by the Bishop of Kujawy for the restitution of the churches and parishes. Although there were by 1637 no Catholics living in either of the lands, the argument was used that the churches had been built before the Reformation (by the Teutonic Knights) and had therefore been taken from the Catholic Church. All the pre-Reformation churches were recovered by the Catholic Church and Catholic priests were installed. The Protestants resisted but managed to retain only a few churches that had been built after the Reformation. A notable case was that of St George's Church in Bütow, which was said to have been built in 1551 on municipal land and since consecration to have been used only by Protestants. Services there were 'in two tongues: in German for the townspeople and in Polish (Cassubian) for the people from the country' (Cramer 1858, 1: 277). At the Peace of Westphalia in 1648, the House of Griffin being extinct, Inner Pomerania (*Vorpommern*), including Stettin, was taken by Sweden. Outer Pomerania (*Hinterpommern*) went to Brandenburg (Scheuch: 181).

Nine years later, by the 1657 Treaty of Bromberg (Bydgoszcz), incorporating decisions of the earlier Treaty of Wehlau (Welawa), the king of Poland granted the lands of Lauenburg and Bütow to the Elector of Brandenburg in fief on the same favourable conditions as had been enjoyed by the Griffins, a state of affairs which prevailed until the First Partition of Poland in 1772. By the Treaty of Wehlau, however, the Elector could not reimpose the Protestant religion and Catholic property was guaranteed. On the other hand, the establishment of new Protestant parishes and the installation of pastors did not infringe the pact. The Protestants made a comeback, but from now on the simultaneous existence of Protestant and Catholic parishes was a feature of the Lauenburg and Bütow landscapes. How the ethnic and confessional factors here were correlated has yet to be studied dispassionately. The Kashubian language was to survive here until the twentieth century (Siebke 1940: 9; Ostrowska and Trojanowska 1974: 48, s.v. 'Bytów'; *Lauenburg* 2014).

A little further west, a good example of the continuing vigour of the Wendish language in eastern Pomerania at the time of the Thirty Years' War is supplied by the parish of Freist/Wreście, between Stolp and Lake Garde. Archival research by Szultka (1991) has disclosed reports of the difficulties encountered by the patrons in appointing a pastor here. It was a long-drawn-out affair extending throughout the 1630s and into the 1640s, the main point at issue being the Wendish-language competence of the candidates. The patrons of the Freist church were two noble families, the Gutzmer(ow)s of Freist and Gabel (Kępno) and the Bandemers of Kuckow (Kukowo) and Beckel (Wiklino). In 1630 they jointly presented to the parish one Peter Stuväus (Stücker) and noted his specific duty of teaching in 'both German and Wendish'. Six years later (17 September 1636) Jakob and Lorentz Gutzmer(ow) came to an agreement with Peter Bandemer that in future they would cooperate in appointing pastors and 'secondly, in every future appointment it will be ensured that the new encumbent knows not only German but also Wendish'. The parishioners, it transpires, were dissatisfied with their current pastor, who was himself conscious of his linguistic deficiencies and therefore eventually left Freist to become a deacon of the church in his native Rügenwalde, whence he wrote on 4 July 1639 in explanation of his departure: '...the main reason was indeed my ignorance of the Wendish language'. The Gutzmer(ow)s now proceeded to fill the vacancy by appointing Niklaus Krause, but in doing so they acted independently and so incurred the displeasure of the Bandemers. The Bandemers wrote complaining to the Consistory and asking whether they did not have the right to participate in the procedure, seeing 'how many Wendish villages belong to it [the parish] and is it not a Christian necessity that the pastor understands Wendish and can speak it?' (Szultka 1991: 81).

Despite the efforts of the Dukes to stay neutral Pomerania was now embroiled in the Thirty Years' War and under Swedish occupation. The last Duke had died on 10 March 1637. General Superintendent Dr Jakob Fabricius, who was a supporter of the Swedes, on 22 August 1639 summoned a committee to adjudicate in the Freist dispute, headed by the Stolp Superintendent Daniel Rubenow, and including P. Zimmermann and the pastor of Glowitz/Główczyce P. Grüneberg. The Gutzmer(ow)s were supporters of the pro-Brandenburg party (led in eastern Pomerania by the Stolp Landvogt Georg von Zitzewitz and Duchess Anna) and did not recognize the competence of Fabricius, considering that following the Duke's death all office-holders had lost their authority. But the Bandemers in October 1639 asked the committee again to make clear 'whether it was not necessary for the new appointee, on account of the parish children, to understand the Kashubian language well and be able to speak it' (Szultka 1991: 82).

The committee on 28–30 November reported that, after examination of all the circumstances, it 'considered that the preacher in Freist must know the Slav language, just as his predecessors had known it fluently with the exception of Peter Stuväus, who did not know that language and, although he tried to learn it without success, therefore resigned'. The committee had examined peasants from Beckel (Wiklino) and Kuckow (Kukowo), and also servants from the Kuckow grange. In reply to questions put to them they had replied that no one among them knew the German language with the exception of Joachim Mohn, who in his youth had been in Ziegnitz/Ściegnica and understood German, but his wife and children did not. 'They all answered similarly that their children could not understand German.' When asked if they would be able to understand Niklaus Krause, if he read them the Catechism in Wendish, they replied that they would not, because he had never yet read anything in Wendish, not even from the gospels. They said it was of utmost necessity for the pastor of Freist to know Wendish and that if Krause's appointment were confirmed, they would be compelled to go to neighbouring churches where services were held in Polish (Szultka 1991: 82).

Members of the committee also interviewed Krause, who was already performing pastoral duties in Freist, and he asked them to support his candidature, assuring them that he would learn Wendish within a year. The committee then reported to the Consistory, recommending against Krause's appointment, bearing in mind the difficulties caused by the previous encumbent's inability to learn the language and the unfavourable effect this had had on his pastoral work with children. On this basis the Consistory resolved on 10 December 1639 that the appointment of any new pastor to this parish must have its approval and that it was 'essential for him to be able to understand and speak Wendish'. Pastor Krause failed utterly to fulfil the conditions, because 'his ability to understand Wendish is so weak'. Therefore a new candidate must be sought (Szultka 1991: 82–3).

The Guztmer(ow)s were not impressed. They ignored the Consistory's decision, proceeded to hold trial sermons by Krause and Michael Brüggemann (son of the author of the 1643 *Mały Catechism*, see below), and sent a report on the trials to the Consistory in which they contradicted each one of its conclusions. They said Krause was capable of singing, reading, and pronouncing the absolution in the Slav language, so that 'the whole parish unanimously had supported his candidature'. The Bandemers protested, but both they and the Consistory were helpless. Without official confirmation Krause continued to perform pastoral duties in Freist. Still hoping for official approval, in September 1640 he sent the Consistory two testimonials from pastors of the Stolp Synod saying that he could speak Kashubian. The Consistory found the testimonials unreliable and ruled that another pastor should take over the care of the parish for one year, during which Krause must master the Slav language. In autumn 1641 Krause sent them a testimonial from the pastor of Budow (Budowo) saying that 'in both reading and speaking the Slav language he had made moderate progress'. Owing to the death of Fabricius on 11 August 1641, the affair appears to have ended in Krause's favour (Müller 1912: 564; Szultka 1991: 82–3).

There is further evidence of the Protestant church's interest in Wendish in eastern Pomerania. In 1623 Lady Erdmuta, who held authority in the Stolp District, nominated Paul Mantey to assist at the church of St. Peter in the Old Town of Stolp in the following terms:

> …we recall that under the church statutes an ordained sexton is to be maintained, especially in the Wendish region, who is fluent in the language of the Wends, for the better instruction and cultivation of the salvation of souls and holiness among the faithful and that furthermore the nobles of this parish have humbly petitioned us to this end; therefore we, as patron of the church in question, consider it necessary to nominate and appoint, to assist the said Rev. J. Hartwig, a qualified person who would preach Wendish sermons on Sundays in the local chapel and would, in addition to him, carry out and administer the holy sacraments; also he must diligently teach the young their catechism and prayers in the Wendish tongue.

Mantey performed his duties until 1635, when he was transferred to the office of pastor in Rowe, being replaced in Stolp by Jerzy Juris, who was followed in 1644 by Michael Pontanus. In 1678 Pontanus was succeeded by Sebastian Peter Silvestri until 1681 (Ślaski 1959: 43–4).

Polish or Wendish

In Pomeranian sources a distinction is generally made between Wendish and Polish (e.g. Bugenhagen, Krofey, Pontanus). We have also visited an area where Lusatian Wendish and Polish were distinguished from each other, near the point where the Bober joins the Oder in the Neumark (Chapter 3). Referring to the Pomeranian Wends, Bugenhagen says they live close to the Poles and 'more or less understand their language' (*quorum & linguam fere intelligunt*, see Chapter 3). It is clearly essential to distinguish between Wendish and Polish.

Wendish (*Vandalice*) was the language specified by Duke Johann Friedrich in his *Leges Praepositis Ecclesiarum* in 1594 (see Chapter 3) and the sources contain frequent allusions to the use of Wendish by the clergy in their parishes. Szultka (1991: 81–3), in his study of Freist, based on archival research in the State Archives in Szczecin, several times refers to the 'Wendish language' (*język wendyjski*). It is reasonable to infer from this that the original documents are in German and that the word used there is *wendisch*. It is, after all, doubtful if the Polish word *wendyjski* has any function other than as a translation of German *wendisch*.

It is uncertain whether any of the adjectives *polski, polnisch*, or *polonus* is ever attributed in contemporary sources to the vernacular of the Duchy of Pomerania. Also belonging to the same semantic field are *kaschubisch* and *slavisch* as well as their Polish and Latin equivalents. Our insights into the linguistic and ethnic relationships in Wendish areas are dependent on knowing the precise terms used in the sources in the original languages, for in translation the original distinctions are sometimes lost. Thus, for example, the same 'sexton…, who understands Kashubian' (*ein Küster…, der kaschubisch versteht*) mentioned by Tetzner (1899: 126) reappears in Ślaski (1959: 47) as 'a sexton knowing Polish' (*kościelny znający mowę polską*). On the basis of the discussion at the Fourth General Synod in Stettin in 1545 on houses for poor boys capable of becoming pastors and the need of such a house at Stolp 'on account of the Wendish language' (*umb der Wendischen Sprache willen*, Balthasar 1725: 42; cf. Chapter 3), Szultka concludes (1991: 73–4) that 'the education of pastors able to speak Polish was debated' (*umiejących mówić po polsku*). The fact that the Polish language was also used at times in Pomeranian contexts underlines the importance of being able to distinguish between the two languages. In the absence of access to the original documents, it may be prudent to take *polski* 'Polish' used in secondary sources with a pinch of salt.

Michał Pontanus (Mostnik/Brückmann)

In 1643 a second Pomeranian Wendish printed book appeared, following the precedent set by Krofey's *Duchowne piesnie* (1586) (see Chapter 3). The trilingual title is *Parvus Catechismus D. Martini Lvtheri Germanico-Vandalicus. Der kleine Catechismus D. Martini Lutheri/Deutsch vnnd Wendisch gegen einander gesetzt/Mit anhange der Sieben Bußpsalmen König Davids. Mały Catechism D. Marciná Lutherá Niemiecko Wándalski ábo Słowięski/to jestá z Niemieckiego języká w Słowięski wystáwion y ná jáwnosc wydan/z Przydatkiem Siedm Psálmow Pokutnych krolá Dawida y ynßych Potrzebnych rzeczi: osobliwie Historiy Passiy náßego Páná Jesusa wedlug Ewángelistá Matthevßá/y niektorych Piesn duchownych. Drukowány w Gdaińsku przez Jerzego Rhetá/Roku Pánskiego/1643* (The German portion says: 'The Little Catechism of Dr Martin Luther in German and Wendish printed opposite each other with the Seven Penitential Psalms of King David attached.' The Polish repeats this and adds 'and other necessary things, particularly the story of the Passion of our Lord Jesus according to the Evangelist Matthew and several hymns. Printed in Gdańsk by Jerzy Rhet in the year of the Lord 1643'). As in the case of Krofey's book, the only known copy was found in the Schmolsin parsonage in 1896 by F. Tetzner, and like Krofey, it is written in a language which might be called Polish mixed with a generous sprinkling of Kashubian features. The Catechism ends on p. 144. The Penitential Psalms begin on p. 145. The *Passya* 'Passion' has a separate title page repeating *Drukowány w Gdaińsku przez Jerzego Rhetá/Roku Pánskiego/1643* and is numbered separately from p. 1 to p. 68. There follows an errata slip and (in the only known copy) 31 pages of manuscript German and Polish–Wendish hymns (Figure 4.5).

In nomine JESU.

PARVUS CATE-
CHISMUS
D. MARTINI LVTHERI
Germanica - Vandalicus.

Der kleine Catechismus D. Martini Lutheri/
Deutsch vnnd Wendisch gegen einan=
der gesetzt/
Mit anhange der Sieben Bußpsalmen König
DAVIDS.

Maly Catechism D Marciná Lutherá Niemiecko
Wándalski ábo Słowieski/ to jestáz Niemieckiego jezyká
w Słowieski wystáwiony y ná jáwnosc wydan/

3 Przydatkiem Siedm Psálmow Pokutnych kro,
lá DAwIDA y inßych potrzebnych rzeczi: osobliwie
Historíy passíy náßego páná JESVSA weblug
Ewángelistá MATTHEVßá/ y niektorych
piesn duchownych.

Drukowány w Gdaińsku przes
Jerzego Rhetá/ Roku Pánskiego/ 1643.

Figure 4.5 Title page of Michael Pontanus, *Der kleine Catechismus* (Gdańsk, 1643). Instytut Kaszubski, Gdańsk.

174

Examples of the Kashubian lexical features are *ga* 'when' (Polish *gdy*), *le* 'only' (Polish *tylko*), *witro* 'morning' (Polish *jutro*), *cierkiew* 'church' (Polish *kościół*), *gwisny* 'certain' (Polish *pewien*), *Jastry* 'Easter' (Polish *Wielkanoc*), *nawożenia* 'bridegroom' (Polish *pan młody*), *ninio* 'now' (Polish *teraz*), and *ogord* 'garden' (Polish *ogród*). There are many Kashubian phonological features (*bądze* 'will be', *pisc* 'fist', etc.). The present tense of 'to be' begins *jem* 'I am', *jes* 'you are (sg.)', and the grammatical dual is well demonstrated (Olesch 1958b: 12, 15, *Passya* 37–8). The author clearly considered the language he was writing to be not Polish, but Wendish. He applies to it variously the adjectives *Vandalicus, Wendisch, Wandalski*, and *Słowięski*). On the last page of the Catechism (p. 206) is printed a note stating that it was written, translated, and published by 'MICHAŁ MOSTNIK/alias PONTANUS álbo Brückmann Sluga Slowá Bożego w Smołdyznie' in 1643.

Unlike Krofey, the book is bilingual, each page being divided into two columns, one Polish–Wendish and one German. The title page is trilingual: Latin, German, and Polish. As in Krofey, the word *polski* and its Latin and German equivalents have been studiously avoided. The Catechism is described in Latin as 'Germanico-Vandalicus', in German as 'Deutsch vnnd Wendisch', and in the Slavonic language we may call Wendish–Polish as 'Niemiecko Wándalski ábo Słowięski'. The word *Słowięski* occurs at least six times in the book, as in, for example: *Golgothá/to jestá po slowięsku mieysce lysinie ábo trupich głow* ('Golgotha is in Wendish the place of bareness or of skulls') (Olesch 1958b: *Passya* 35; Popowska-Taborska 2001: 311). Although the word *polski* never occurs, there is an errata slip mentioning those ignorant of *linguae nostrae Polonico-Vandalicae* ('our Polish-Wendish language') (Olesch 1958b: *Passya* [69]). This is the only concession to the possibility of a Polish component in the book.

In addition to being the home of the only surviving copies of Krofey and Pontanus's books, the parsonage of Schmolsin also preserved several important manuscripts written in the same type of language (Lorentz 1898: *passim*).

Royal Prussia

As in the sixteenth century, mentions of the Wends in sources from Royal Prussia are rare, and since none of them is in German, we have no direct evidence of the use here of the word *Wende*. Even Polish *Kaszuba* is extremely rare. Odyniec (1959) reveals many details of the social structures and rural economy of the *starostwa* of Kościerzyna, Mirachowo, Puck, and Skarszewo in the seventeenth century (later revealed as the core of Kashubian habitation), but his sources, so far as we can tell, reveal nothing of the language or ethnicity of the inhabitants. The only three known seventeenth-century instances of the Polish word *Kaszuba* are all linked to Royal Prussia.

The first is in an anonymous drama, completed in Danzig in 1643, which remained unpublished until 1999. In this drama there is a character named Sobieraj, who is referred to as *Kaszuba*. He speaks Polish, but in both his speech and that of another character, the *Kuchmistrz* 'chef', a few possibly Kashubian features can be identified (*sarn* 'stag', cf. Kash. *såren*; *knarz* 'boar', cf. Kash. *knârz* (Pol. *kiernoz*); *tyrzy* 'hauls', cf. Kash. *turzëc* 'gallop') (Treder 1999: 168). There is however no systematic Kashubian stylization in the speech of these or any other characters.

The second occurs in a poem of Wespazjan Kochowski (1633–1700), written to celebrate the Peace of Oliwa in 1660 (*Traktaty oliwskie*), where the Kashubs are found among the lowest social groups who will benefit from peace:

> Gbur, Żyd i Cygan, i Kaszuba gruby
> Zna pokój luby.
> Churl, Jew and Gypsy, and uncouth Kashub
> Knows cherished peace.

(Bystroń 1960: 23)

The third is in a work by Jakub Teodor Trembecki (1643–1720), with the title *Wotywa do wielmożnego Imci pana Aleksandra z Baucendorf na Kęsowie Kęsowskiego, starosty borzechowskiego, chorążego cesarskiego JW. Imci Pana Władysława Denhoffa wojewody pomorskiego in A. 1683 napisana, kiedy król Jmość szedł z wojskiem na cesarską pod Wiedeń* ('A votive offering to the honourable gentleman Alexander von Bauzendorf of Kensau, *starosta* of Borzechowo, imperial standard-bearer to the gracious Władysław Denhoff (Dönhoff), Voivode of Pomerania, written in the year 1683, when his Majesty the King was marching with his army to Vienna on imperial [service?]'). Anticipating victory and a safe return, Trembecki pictures a scene in the future when von Bauzendorf will regale his friends with tales of the Battle of Vienna, to the astonishment of his Kashubian servants:

> And so with your mellifluous tones you will give me a new report of it all, and I shall drink to your health, and approving everything, deep in thought, I shall catch sight of the uncouth Kashubs listening to you like me, open-mouthed.

(Brückner 1911: 289)

Of Bauzendorf's fate nothing further is known, but Voivode Władysław Denhoff (Dönhoff) (1639–1683) fell in the Battle of Párkány 1683.

Lüneburg

West of the Elbe

Sources of information on the Wends are so capricious that lack of evidence can never be taken to mean that they are not there. Nevertheless, an ominous silence in most of Transelbia in first half of the seventeenth century carries a suggestion that the only remaining survivors at this time are in Pomerania and the area centred on the Lusatias.

Unexpected evidence that this is not the case, however, now appears suddenly from the least likely direction, the western extremity of the Wendish world, west of the Elbe, in the Duchy of Brunswick-Lüneburg. And the evidence is plentiful, including texts in the Wendish language. Some sources are little more than lists of words, but several also record details of social conditions, history, customs, traditions, and superstitions (notably Hennig von Jessen, Parum Schultze, and Jugler).

To refer to these particular Wends, the scholarly literature has devised a variety of terms. Commonly preferred by English-language commentators is *Polabian* (e.g. Polański and Sehnert 1967: *passim*), applied to both language and people. In German *polabisch* and *Polaben* are often used, but the compounds *Drawänopolaben* and *dravenopolabisch*, which are no less common, remove any risk of confusion with the medieval *Polabi* (who were located further north) and links them securely to the *Drawehn*, the name of the part of the *Hannoversches Wendland* where they were found in the seventeenth century. The equivalent Polish terms are *połabski*, *Połabianie*, and *Drzewianie (połabscy)*. Another variant is *Lüneburgisch-Wendisch* (used by J. H. Jugler). These Wends themselves (when speaking German) and their German neighbours simply used the words *wendisch* and *Wenden*.

The sources on the language and customs of the Lüneburg Wends all date from the period 1663–1756 and result partly from an antiquarian curiosity about the language during its death throes on the part of several local clergymen; but the first thing about these Wends that attracted the attention of outsiders were their unusual religious rituals, which indicated that the Lutheran church had never managed to impose its norms here. The disapproval of the church authorities may well have been of long-standing, but it was brought to the fore as a result of changes in the secular government of the Duchy in 1671.

In that year the district of Dannenberg, following a long period of dispute between the Lüneburg and Wolfenbüttel lines of the Guelph dynasty, devolved on Georg Wilhelm, Duke of Brunswick-Lüneburg, residing in Celle. Even before the transfer of the Wends to his care, however, Georg Wilhelm had heard rumours of their ungodly ways. In his rescript of 13 July 1671, he instructed *Ober-Superintendent* Dr Joachim Hildebrand to hold a general visitation in the counties (*Ämter*) of Dannenberg, Lüchow, Hitzacker, Wustrow, and Scharnebeck. He explained as follows:

> Frequent complaints have been brought to our government of the foolish customs and ungodly living of the Wends inhabiting Wustrow, Lüchow, and other such places, especially in the institution of certain drunken feasts, and since then it has been our will to consider whether these [complaints], having been delayed by those disputes between us and the Wolfenbüttel line as to superiority (which are for the time being restrained), could not be effectively stopped; the obstacle [sc. dispute], however, having now by God's grace been removed: therefore, you are to instruct the pastors diligently to admonish the serfs to abandon such ungodly abuses [...].

(Olesch 1967: 221–2, n. 2)

Hildebrand proceeded to draw up a long list of questions (at least 99 in number) to be put to the pastor and schoolmaster in each parish. The visitation took place between 4 and 22 August 1671 and Hildebrand appears to have visited each parish in person to carry out the interviews. The original manuscripts of the records made at the time have not survived, but copies are accessible and have been published by Olesch (1967: 5–28 and 221–59) (Map 4.2).

Hildebrand discovered that his was not the first visitation to the area. The parish of Rosche-Suhlendorf (west of Uelzen), it transpired, had been inspected in 1663, revealing that 'because the people of this place are sprung from the Wends (*Wendenthumb*), they are still full of Wendish superstitions, all of which we can neither mention nor consider'. Despite this qualification the report on the 1663 visitation does reveal the essence of a number of unusual traditions among the Wends. Almost all the villages had what the report calls 'guilds' (*Gilden*), each of which held its assembly on a particular day of the year, though the days varied from one village to another. Some met on days

Map 4.2 Habitations of the Lüneburg Wends (late seventeenth century).

connected with the Virgin Mary, others on Ascension Day, and some at Whitsun, and so on. The objective of the assembly was to avert misfortune from the guild members, their animals, and fields during the coming year. The ritual consisted of the ceremonial slaughter of several sheep, cattle, and pigs, followed by the opening of several barrels of beer, which the members would drink until they were all drunk. That this cult of extravagant beer-drinking as part of religious observance lay at the heart of Wendish piety was corroborated by the 1671 visitation.

Another ritual noted in 1663 was that of erecting a great pole surmounted by a cross and above the cross a carved wooden cock. Below the pole the people would gather and drink together in a ceremony solemnly initiated by the village mayor (*Schultheiss*). Then they would dance and drink until the barrel was empty, regarding this as a kind of divine service. Pastors had repeatedly condemned the practice in their sermons, but no one cared. It was still widespread in 1671. Some of the Wends, according to the 1663 report, regarded certain days, including, the day after Ascension Day, the Ascension of the Virgin, and All Saints' Day as more important than Christmas. In the chapel at Daldorf there was an image of the Virgin, before which the people would kneel and pray, making offerings of new linen to it, and seeking divine intervention to cure sick people or animals (Olesch 1967: 252–3).

Apart from place names, the 1663 report is the first manifestation of a Wendish presence in the Lüneburg region since 1570. And for six years it remained the only indication of their existence. Then, in 1669, reports on another church visitation in the villages of Satemin, Plate, and Breese im Bruch, all of which came under the inspectorate of Uelzen, showed that the local pastors there were isolated from their parishioners by a language barrier. The report on Satemin dated 24 August 1669 states: 'The old people, because they are Wendish, do not understand [...] the German language, let alone the Catechism'. The record of the visitation in Breese im Bruch, dated 22 August, notes: 'The Pastor states that the people hereabouts are Wends and do not understand the German language well. If he had a Wendish Catechism [he said] and could understand it, he would be better able to impart its contents to them' (Olesch 1989b: 151–2).

The fullest account of the religious practices of the Lüneburg Wends is given in Hildebrand's report of 1671, often corroborating and expanding the observations of 1663 and 1669. The 1663 ritualistic pole surmounted by a cross and a cock is in the 1671 account more precisely described as a tree called the *Kreuzbaum* 'cross tree'. This is distinguished from the *Kronenbaum* 'crown tree': 'Peculiar to these Wends are two trees, one is the *Kronenbaum*, the other the *Kreuzbaum*. The *Kronenbaum* is a long straight alder-tree, from which they remove the branches and bark, so that it becomes white. Only at the top they leave the crown, which is green and round like a crown or a wreath.' The report says that on St John's Day, when they bring home the *Kronenbaum*, the young women sing joyful songs in Wendish, and when the new *Kronenbaum* is erected 'they dance and jump around like the children of Israel around their golden-idol calf' and 'they sing all kinds of superstitious songs in the Wendish language, believing this to be a divine service thanks to which they and their cattle will thrive [...]'.

When the feast of Christ's Ascension approaches, they go into the forest, choose a strong, tall oak and fell it with special blows. They chop it square and take it into the village or just outside it. They make holes in it crosswise and insert plugs or sticks, and set a wooden cock on the top and above the cock a cross, from which it is called the *Kreuzbaum*.

(Olesch 1967: 229)

Although both types of tree were found in most villages and both held sacred, the *Kreuzbaum* attracted greater veneration. It was believed to be the home of a spirit called the *Stete*. Whether this is to be read as a name or as the German word *Stätte* 'abode' and thus the spirit's abode is not clear (Olesch 1967: 5). There is an evident similarity to the custom of the *meja* or *Maibaum* 'may-tree', found among the Lusatian Wends (Sorbs), though this is only recorded as a harmless piece of folklore and did not incur ecclesiastical condemnation (Schneeweis 1953: 138).

The schoolmaster in Küsten (Lüchow County) complained to Hildebrand in 1671 'that he had a great deal of trouble before he could get the children to give up the Wendish tongue' (Olesch 1967: 244). In the parish of Bergen there were no Wends, and in Damnatz and Quickborn (Dannenberg County) it was reported: 'They have none of the Wendish recalcitrance here, because the true Wends live in Amt Lüchow' (Olesch 1967: 238). The recalcitrance of the true Wends was manifested primarily, it would seem, in their stubborn use of the Wendish language, whereby the content of their religious observances was concealed from the monolingual German church authorities. There is no evidence that any of the pastors in the Wendish villages had even the slightest knowledge of the Wendish language. Consequently, there was a clear-cut gap between the pastors and their flocks. In Predöhl (Lüchow County) the pastor, describing what seems to be a *Kreuzbaum* (though he calls it a *Kronenbaum*), reported:

...on it there stand a cock and a cross; they consecrate it with beer and drive their animals round it, thinking they are thereby blessed. They also sprinkle their stalls with beer. At certain times too they walk around with a candle, and say something; but being ignorant of the Wendish language, one does not know what it is. An old man is said to be always kneeling before the pole saying his prayers, especially on rogation days.

(Olesch 1967: 242)

There are no figures for Wendish church attendance, but there is no suggestion that it was anything but regular. Their conduct during services, on the other hand, occasionally attracted comment. The pastor of Presilentz and Wibbese said he had admonished his parishioners not to drink alcohol (*sauffen*) during the sermon. In Hitzacker too the pastor complained 'that the people would fill themselves with brandy before the sermon and leave the church before the blessing', but he also reported that no Wends resided in Hitzacker County (Olesch 1967: 238-9).

News that a few Wends still survived in the Lüneburg region attracted the attention of the philosopher Gottfried Wilhelm Leibniz (1646–1716), who from 1673 was in the service of the Duke of Brunswick-Lüneburg. Leibniz took a broad interest in the fate of the Slavs, and it was at his instigation that Privy Councillor (*Hofrat*) Chilian Schrader, in Celle, sought information from his brother-in-law Georg Friedrich Mithoff, magistrate in Lüchow, a village where the Wendish language and way of life were still alive. A surviving letter from Mithoff to Schrader dated 17 (27) May 1691 contains several Wendish texts, which he describes as prayers, accompanied by German translations. They reveal an unusual (by Lutheran standards) degree of devotion to the Virgin Mary and appear to preserve non-Biblical legends, as the following three examples show:

1. Pilate took a switch of thorn. He struck the Lord God on his right cheek. However many drops of blood God shed, Mary shed as many tears. Kyrie eleison.
2. Today is Mary's day, the day Jesus was born. The second day they baptized him. The third day he separated (*abgesteuert*) stones, water, and earth. All this our Jesus separated. Thus may he separate war from the whole world. Kyrie eleison.
3. Mary walked around the church with three candles; she was seeking God. She could not find him anywhere. The Jews break black thorns; they wanted to flog God. My God did not deserve this, to suffer all this suffering for us sinners.

(Olesch 1967: 52–3, 269–76)

If so many Wends as late as the 1660s were still monolingual, it is unlikely that knowledge of German among them at the time of the Reformation or earlier was any better. The communication to them of Christian doctrine must consequently have been difficult. It is significant, however, that Olesch's searches in the church archives at Hanover, Celle, and Lüchow revealed no sign of this difficulty, or, for that matter, even of a Wendish presence in the region before 1663. But there are indications that the Wendish language was ridiculed and even outlawed. Hildebrand (Olesch 1989a: 136) says the Wends were forbidden to speak Wendish in the presence of clergymen or officials and that they tended to keep their affairs as secret as possible. This is corroborated by Eccard (see Chapter 5). There is no suggestion that there were ever any Wendish-speaking pastors, so evidence of deviation from the official church line, including certain pre-Reformation practices, such as the veneration of the Virgin and other saints, is not unexpected.

In the parish of Predöhl each village celebrates particular days of the dead saints, which otherwise are not celebrated in our churches, when the pastor must preach and with the sexton is invited by the village mayor (*Schultheiss*) to dine. After the sermon the peasants drink until they cannot stand. They get through many barrels of beer and fight so terribly it is a wonder no one is killed.

(Olesch 1967: 228)

Veneration of the saints clearly conforms to Roman Catholic practice, but the cult of inebriation is more reminiscent of Bacchanalia.

In the light of these accounts, the fears of the Upper Lusatian Estates in 1690 that their Wendish serfs might 'relapse into unchristian superstition and Catholicism' (see above) become easier to understand. The sudden change that year from a policy 'directed towards total extermination of this language' to a readiness to let well alone in Lusatian Wendish-speaking parishes and even provide them with religious texts in Wendish may well have arisen from acquaintance with conditions among the Lüneburg Wends. The friendship between Leibniz and Spener (from 1675) could have provided a channel of information.

CHAPTER 5
FROM PIETISM TO ENLIGHTENMENT 1700–1800

Upper Lusatia

The Moravian Brethren

The Czech *Unitas fratrum* or Society of Brethren (also known as the Bohemian Brethren and later as the Moravian Brethren or Moravians) was an offshoot of the Hussite Movement. After the Protestant defeat at the Battle of the White Mountain (1620) they were exiled, but a century later, in 1722, they were invited by the Pietist Count Nikolaus Ludwig von Zinzendorf (1700–1760) to refound their community on land donated by him in the parish of Berthelsdorf, to the south-east of Löbau. Here they made a clearing and built their settlement close to the Löbau-Zittau road, naming it Herrnhut 'the Lord's shelter'. They practised a simple and unwordly form of Christianity with a strong emotional element. Their numbers grew and before long they set about bringing their version of the gospel to their neighbours in the surrounding villages of Lusatia. Their activities quickly developed into a worldwide missionary undertaking. Before von Zinzendorf died in 1760, they had sent 312 missionaries to many distant parts of the world (Hickel 1967: 25–34).

In the eighteenth century Herrnhut was less than six miles from the nearest Wendish village, Tiefendorf on the south-eastern outskirts of Löbau (Muka 1886: 75). The Moravians would become famous for spreading the gospel in the remotest corners of the world, but their first mission was to the people who lived within walking distance, including the Lusatian Wends. Like Spener and Frentzel, von Zinzendorf felt that the Wends were in great spiritual need and he had before him the example of his grandmother Henriette von Gersdorff (1648–1726), who had contributed significantly to their enlightenment by supporting the publication of Frentzel's New Testament (*NBS*, s.v. Gersdorf, H.; Zinzendorf). In 1728 the whole Bible in Upper Wendish was published, facilitating the missionary task, and the Herrnhut doctrine appealed to Wendish peasants.

Wends began to visit Herrnhut, treating the journey as a pilgrimage. First they came from nearby villages, such as Kittlitz and Hochkirch, but the message spread quickly and soon reached Hoyerswerda and even the Spree Forest. They naturally came on foot, marching towards Herrnhut, singing hymns as they went, sometimes spending as much as twenty hours on the journey (R. Jenč 1954: 180). On arrival they were greeted as brothers and sisters. They joined in the devotions, which consisted of Bible study, prayer, and hymn singing. Herrnhut opened a new world to them.

As the word spread, new branches of the brethren sprang up. The first was in Sornßig, near Hochkirch, led for many years by a serf smallholder named Jan Hastink (died 1795). From far and near Wends travelled to his house. Another centre was in Döhlen at the foot of the Czorneboh, where for twelve years meetings were held in the house of Handrij Bjenada (1709–1789). In Seidau, on the edge of Budissin, the Wendish brethren gathered around Marćin Foerster (1692–1759), who only late in life had learned to read, so that he might read the Bible to his illiterate compatriots (Jenč 1954: 181).

An important figure in the development of the Wendish branch of the Herrnhuter was Matthäus Lange (Matej Dołhi). Born in Doberschütz on 24 May 1704, he attended the school in Malschwitz; he then worked on the land as a labourer in Doberschütz and Seidau. Under the influence of Jan Pjech and Johann Gottfried Kühn he joined the Herrnhut brethren and, encouraged by Friedrich Caspar Graf von Gersdorff, he travelled the Wendish countryside, expounding to anyone who would listen the recently published Wendish Bible (*NBS*, s. v. Dołhi). Lange's activities attracted the attention of the pastor of Malschwitz, Adam Zacharias Schirach (Šěrak), a consistent opponent of the Herrnhuter, who even had him briefly arrested. By 1740 Lange had, by some unexplained means, acquired sufficient wealth to purchase a run-down estate in Temritz, and four years later he was appointed overseer of the von Gersdorff estate at Teichnitz, where there was a concentration of Wendish Herrnhuters under von Gersdorff's patronage (M. Kral 1937: 12). In 1746 at the invitation of von Gersdorff, a young German named Ernst August Hersen arrived in Teichnitz from Herrnhut. Having learned Wendish, he began to preach among the Wendish brethren. He translated a number of the Herrnhuters's hymns and published them in 1750 in a hymnal with the title *Tón hłós teje njewjesty Jezusoweje* 'The Voice of the Bride of Jesus'. Their strange baroque imagery caused offence among a number of Wendish clergymen, which was forcefully expressed by Christoph Gabriel Fabricius (1684–1757) in the preface to the third edition of his *Dźěćace modlitwy* 'A Child's Prayers' (1756). Hersen died young in 1750. Fabricius's objections to the Herrhut doctrine are further elaborated in his *Das entlarvte Herrnhut* 'Herrnhut Unmasked' (Wittenberg-Zerbst, 1745) (K. A. Jenč 1875: 14; Wićaz 1922: 8–9; *NBS*, s.v. Fabricius).

When von Gersdorff died in 1751, Teichnitz was inherited by his uncle, who did not approve of the Brethren and required them to leave. Fortunately for them, four years earlier Matthäus Lange, having sold his estate in Temritz, had purchased the neighbouring village of Kleinwelka and here in the little manor house he placed at their disposal a suitable room for their meetings. They continued to meet here until 1758. Meanwhile, in 1756 Lange had sold the village to Countess Agnes Sofija Reuss, who was herself a Herrnhuter (M. Kral 1937: 13). She supported the Brethren in Kleinwelka and gave them sites on her estates for building. They erected two communal buildings (one for men and one for women) and a school (M. Kral 1937: 13). There were further similar societies springing up in various parts of Upper and Lower Lusatia (R. Jenč 1954: 182).

Kleinwelka, Teichnitz, and Temritz are all in the parish of St Michael, Bautzen and lie close together to the north-west of the city. Furthest out (though still less than three miles away) is Kleinwelka, where the Wendish Moravian community found its home. In time a small amount of manufacturing grew up here, including a tannery, a coppersmith, a soap factory, a bell foundry, and a tobacco factory using tobacco grown locally (M. Kral 1937: 14). Whether among the original brethren from Moravia there were any Czech speakers is not clear, but the main (if not only) language used in Herrnhut, as in the adjacent villages, was German. The Moravian community in Teichnitz, however, and later in Kleinwelka, was overwhelmingly Wendish and referred to as 'die wendische Brüdergemeine'. From their centre in Kleinwelka they maintained contact with their brothers and sisters dispersed over a wide area, including Lower Lusatia (Knauthe 1767: 314).

The Moravians referred to themselves as an *ecclesiola* of the Lutheran Church (*ODCC* 1990: s. v. Moravian Brethren) and they had sympathizers among the Wendish Lutheran clergy, including Jan Pjech (1707–1741) and Johann Gottfried Kühn (1706–1763). Nor were they ever rejected by the official church. They nevertheless irritated some Lutherans and were referred to by the derogatory terms *mukarjo* 'bigots' and *štundarjo* (from *Betstunde* 'prayer meeting') (R. Jenč 1954: 182). Some pastors regarded them as a sect. Kleinwelka was almost adjacent to the parish of Neschwitz and here there was some friction. In 1741 Pastor Kaltschmidt recorded: 'Church assemblies were on the point of being disturbed by a few silly members of the Moravian Brethren who had gone to Herrnhut, whither some of our people had gone and afterwards held private conventicles, which was remedied by a royal decree.' In 1767 Pastor Jurij Mjeń noted: 'The good parish of Neschwitz has . . . for fifteen years been uncommonly assailed by the Herrnhuther . . . . In Kleinwelka they established a strong colony and in Saritsch [have held] special meetings and have had many emissaries in this parish.' But by 1810 Pastor Haenich was prepared to concede: 'The formerly despised Herrnhuter or Moravian Brethren, whose colony in Kleinwelka has grown enormously [promise] in the experience of all good and well-intentioned Christians [to become] a dam against the rising tide of disbelief and false enlightenment' (R. Jenč 1954: 182; M. Kral 1937: 14–15). In Lower Lusatia in 1778 a warning to all those who followed the Herrnhuters and 'consider them good and true Christians' was published in a little book entitled *Unterschejd jadnogo wernego Kscheszżana a jadnogo Herrnhutara* 'The Difference between a true Christian and a Herrnhuter'. It is thought to have been written by G. F. Gude (pastor of Lauban) and translated by Gotthelf Christlieb Fritze (Fryco) (R. Jenč 1954: 182).

The Leipzig Students' Society

A society for the cultivation of the Wendish language was founded by the Wendish students of theology at Leipzig University in 1716. It started with a small group which used to meet socially. They were aware that living in Leipzig, isolated from their Wendish element and immersed in German and Latin, they were at risk of forgetting their mother tongue or losing fluency in it. The total number of Upper Wendish printed books in existence was still less than twenty, so opportunities for keeping in touch with the language by reading were limited. The society's meetings were therefore not merely social, but had a practical purpose as well. Its members were all intending to work as pastors in Wendish parishes, where advantage would accrue not only from their colloquial command of the language, but also from their eloquence in it, for the sermon had become a central feature of a pastor's duties. Surprisingly, the Wendish language played no part in a pastor's training.

The Wendish students told their tutor Dr Pfeiffer about their meetings and he suggested that they might use them to practise composing and delivering sermons to one another. They agreed and applied to the Dean of the Theology Faculty Dr Schmiede for his approval to use the Leipzig Church of the Paulines (*Paulinerkirche*) for this purpose. It is reported that at this proposal he smiled (perhaps a rare occurrence), but gave them permission. They were allotted one hour a week on Sunday from 1 to 2 pm. The society's rules stated: 'The preacher must appear in the church at exactly one o'clock dressed in black. He may not preach for less than half nor more than three quarters of an hour. He shall not read his sermon but preach from memory' (*Kurzer Entwurf* 1767: 131–4, 139). The six founding members were:

1. Johannes Theophilus Ast (1695/1696–1719),
2. Adam Zacharias Schirach (1693–1758),
3. Johann Mosig (1693–1721),
4. Johann George Bär (1689–1724),
5. George Kneschke (?–1757), and
6. Johann Christian Bulitius (1696–1751).

The number of members was always small, and during the five years 1723–1728, there was no activity at all, but by 1767 there were ten current members, and the total number of current and previous members had reached 111. Of these thirty-three were dead, forty-four were holding priestly office, and seventeen were waiting for vacant livings. Only three had abandoned theology (*Kurzer Entwurf* 1767: 134–40). To mark the society's fiftieth anniversary a group of clergymen put their heads together to write a history of the church in Wendish Upper Lusatia, including the history of the society. The result was published in Budissin in 1767 as *Kurzer Entwurf einer Oberlausitz-wendischen Kirchenhistorie abgefaßt von einigen Oberl. wendischen evangel. Predigern* 'A Brief Outline of an Upper Lusatian Wendish Church History Written by Several Upper Lusatian Wendish Clergymen'. The unnamed authors are known to have been Johann Friedrich Lange (1738–1770), Deacon in Neschwitz, Petrus Pannach (1716–1785), pastor of Malschwitz, and Adam Gottlob Schirach (1724–1773), pastor of Kleinbautzen. The 1766 jubilee, including the publication of the *Entwurf*, was managed by Lange and Johann Wenzel (1737–1801), who at the time was a domestic tutor in Budissin but ended his life as pastor of Barut.

The *Entwurf* contains brief histories of all the Protestant Wendish churches in Upper Lusatia, including details of all the pastors that had held spiritual office in them since the Reformation. There follows a history of the Leipzig Society, including the names and biographical data of all the 111 men who were or had been members since its foundation in 1716. The original documents for this account had been inherited by Adam Gottlob Schirach from his father Adam Zacharias Schirach, one of the founder members. Many of the biographies appear to have been written by the subjects themselves (K. A. Jenč 1867: 481). They contain glimpses into the daily lives of a clearly defined social category in the first half of the century.

Noteworthy is the role played by scholarships in the education of a number of these Wendish students. The endowment of Gregor Mättig and the free places at the Electoral School in Meissen appear in several of the biographies. To judge by parental professions, however, the lowest economic level was not much in evidence. An exception is Christoph Petschke of Pommritz in the parish of Hochkirch, who worked for many years as a shepherd and was almost twenty-four years old before he went to school in Budissin. He was a member of the society from 1720 to 1723, but never became a pastor. Further details in his case are sparse (*Kurzer Entwurf* 1767: 144).

Of the 111 entrants in the list, 32 were pastors' sons. Some were also the grandsons of pastors. Town dwellers are well represented (Weißenberg, Wilthen, Kamenz, Hoyerswerda, Spremberg, and, particularly, Budissin). The profession recorded of rural students' fathers was only rarely *Gärtner* and never *Häusler*. Nevertheless, the entries do not shrink from reference to the poverty of their subjects. Christian Gottlob Schmidt, for example, later pastor of Ossling, who composed his own biography, alluded in his story of shivering starvation as a student in Leipzig to the delicate task of pouring a few drops of olive oil from his lamp into his watery gruel, while leaving enough oil in the lamp to escape sitting in the dark (*Kurzer Entwurf* 1767: 148). The usual course of action for new graduates waiting for ordination, it seems, was to find a place as domestic tutor in the household of a gentleman, where they might at least expect to be fed.

A constant problem for the society was the wish of Germans to join. The original statutes had stated that it consisted of members who understood Wendish (Musiat 2001: 21). Following revision in 1766, they said membership was restricted to those who were well versed in the language or were making serious efforts to learn it. Some German members went on to contribute substantially to the Wendish cause (such as Georg Körner), but some were tiresome. It was therefore decided in 1781 not to accept members who knew no Wendish at all; but the problem was endemic. By 1804 there were only eight members and of these only three were Wends (K. A. Jenč 1867: 492–5).

The Prague Wendish Seminary

There were no universities in Lower Lusatia or Upper Lusatia, and in Saxony and Brandenburg the universities were all Protestant, so Catholic Wends aspiring to enter the church were obliged to look elsewhere. This usually meant the Universities of Prague or Olmütz, or seminaries at Komotau, Krumau, or Leitmeritz (Zeil 1967: 19). Because most Wends were poor, they were usually dependent on scholarships. Opportunities for Catholic Wends to study in Prague improved dramatically in the eighteenth century, thanks to the actions of two brothers from Temritz, a village on the north-west edge of Budissin. They were Martin Norbert Schiman (Měrćin Norbert Šiman), born in 1637, and Georg Josef Schiman (Jurij Józef Šiman), born in 1646. Both studied theology in Prague and held clerical office in the Prague Archdiocese, but in 1673 Martin became a canon of the Cathedral Chapter in Budissin and died here in 1707, leaving his estate to endow a seminary to educate Wends preparing for the priesthood.

A hall of residence (*Konvikt*) for poor Wendish students in the Prague Kleinseite (Malá strana) had existed under Jesuit supervision since the 1690s in a building purchased by the brothers. In 1704 Josef Schiman, planning expansion, bought a building site near the Charles Bridge and built a single-storey house, registered in the name of the Budissin Chapter. Combining his brother's legacy with his own money he now set about erecting a substantial house on the same site, which was completed and came into use as the Wendish Seminary in 1728. Josef Schiman died the following year. The source of the brothers' wealth is not known.

Despite its name, the seminary (Wendisches seminar/Serbski seminar) was primarily a hall of residence rather than a place of instruction. Its residents, depending on age, attended either the local gymnasium or the university, but internal provision was made for training in Wendish grammar and public speaking in Wendish, German, and Latin. It was a bastion of the Wendish language in predominantly German-speaking Prague. The number of residents at the time of opening was nineteen and was to increase (Łusčanski 1892: 3–8; Zeil 1967: 17–22).

The 1710 hymnal

The Protestant Wends' need of a printed hymnal had been on the Upper Lusatian Estates' agenda since 1689, but it was only in 1703 that they agreed to engage competent persons to produce new translations of the hymns then in use in the Wendish parishes and have them published. In November 1703, it was reported that Archdeacon Paul Praetorius had agreed to take on the task, and that he had recommended the appointment of a committee consisting of Johann Ast of Budissin, Georgius Matthaei of Kollm, Johann Wauer of Hochkirch, and himself. He further suggested that every Protestant church in Upper Lusatia be enjoined by letters patent to have its schoolmaster copy out the texts of hymns then in use locally and send them in to the committee by Easter. The Estates approved but with the proviso that copies be requested only from the most populous parishes (Mětšk 1960d/1981: 28–31).

Praetorius and Matthaei were the most experienced members of the committee, having already participated in the translation of the *Catechism* (1693), the *Epistles and Gospels* (1695), and the *Agenda* (1696). The committee's first meeting began on 16 April 1704 and lasted several days. Each member was allotted his share of the task and in the course of the next eighteen months they met fourteen more times to discuss their work and allot further assignments, each meeting lasting three or four days. The final meeting (2–7 November 1705) brought the work to completion. The translators were paid a total fee of 200 thalers, including expenses of 73 thalers and 8 groschen incurred for subsistence during the meetings (*Gesangbuch* 1710: [xi], 32).

At this point the Northern War intervened and from September 1706 to September 1707 Upper Lusatia was again overrun by the Swedish armies of Charles XII. Budissin was particularly affected. On 26 February 1709, Praetorius died and on 22 April that year there was a great fire in Budissin, which destroyed three-quarters of the town. The first decade of the eighteenth century also brought plague, drought, unusually severe cold, 'and other scourges' (*Gesangbuch* 1710: [i–ii]). Despite everything, at the Oculi (23 March) diet in 1710 it was reported that the proofs were ready and it was resolved that, as soon as printing was complete, each parish should collect its copies from the printer, J. Willisch, and pay him from its own revenues. Each church was placed under an obligation to buy at least three copies of the hymnal at 8 groschen a copy. The churches were further instructed to get rid of all the old manuscript hymn books. Fortunately, not everyone complied.

With more than 950 pages, *Das Teutsche und Wendische Gesangbuch* 'The German and Wendish Hymnbook' (Budissin 1710) was the largest Wendish printed book to date. It contains 202 hymns, each in both languages, the German and Wendish versions facing each other. The Wendish versions are almost all translations from German originals. From the sixteen-page preface, signed by the three surviving committee members on 3 February 1710, it is clear that they took their prosody seriously, but at the same time they professed to adhere as closely as possible to the sense of the German originals. Although it had originally been thought that from the hymns sent in by the parishes the best versions could be selected and corrected by a little light editing, it was, in the event, found necessary to re-translate them all. But, as the revisers tell us:

> So that it may be known how far our new revised versions differ from the old, we have left a couple of old Easter hymns mainly in the old version which we consider probably the best. These are 'Gelobt sey Gott im höchsten Tron', p. 185, and 'Wjeselmy so wšitcy wěrni/Freu dich du ganze Christenheit' in the appendix, p. 856. The first of these we have been unable, after diligent searching, to find in any German hymn-book, and so have had to translate it from Wendish into German. Especially so, because it is one of the best-known Wendish Easter-hymns.

> (*Gesangbuch* 1710: [ix–x]).

It turns out, however, that the first of these two hymns does have a German original. It is the second ('Wjeselmy so wšitcy wěrni' ('Let us rejoice, all faithful')) that has a pure Wendish pedigree and so is probably the only such case among the entire 202 hymns.

The preface contains the first rudiments of a theory of Sorbian versification, which were to be continued and elaborated by Matthaei in his *Wendische Grammatica* (Budissin 1721). He seems to have been the leading light in matters of both grammar and metrics, and his grammar embodies the fruits of his experience on both Praetorius Committees. In the second edition of the hymnal, published in 1719, there were 42 more hymns. A third edition followed in 1726 and a fourth in 1732 (R. Jenč 1954: 156). In all of these, the German and Wendish texts were printed facing each other, but in 1733 a monolingual Wendish version appeared, edited by Jan Gotthelf Böhmer (1704–1743). Containing 322 hymns and with a format measuring 16 cm × 7 cm, it claimed to be cheaper and easier to carry than its predecessors (Figure 5.1).

Figure 5.1 Budissin, *c.* 1710.

Robert Hales

In 1704 (the year the hymn-book committee began its work) Praetorius had an unexpected visitor from England. This was Mr Robert Hales (c. 1675–1735), an emissary of the Society for Promoting Christian Knowledge (SPCK), the oldest Anglican mission agency (founded 1698) (Brock 1966: 452n.). Together Praetorius and Hales were to make an unusual contribution to the development of Wendish religious literature. Knauthe describes Hales as 'an eminent English lord, Baron von Hales' and 'an English royal envoy', who made a stop in Budissin while on his way from Vienna to Berlin. This matches the society's record that he was in Berlin on 23 February 1703/1704. Chancing to be in the vicinity of St Michael's Church one day, when the Wendish service had just ended, he was struck by the unusual dress of the people leaving the church on their way home. On enquiry he was told that they were 'a remnant of the old Sorbian Wends, who 1,000 years ago owned this land' (Knauthe 1767: 281–2).

Learning of the existence of the Wendish Archdeacon Praetorius, Hales arranged to meet him and from him sought information about the Christianity of the Wends and the 'condition of their souls'. He gave Praetorius a booklet in English, together with a German translation, and requested him to have it translated into Wendish, published, and distributed among the Wends. The printing costs were paid by Hales, who also gave Praetorius a fee for the translation. The English book in question was *The Necessity of Caring for the Soul* (Dublin, 1700) by Richard Allestree (1619–1681), canon of Christ Church, Oxford, and provost of Eton College. Before the year was out, the Wendish translation had been published. Although it bears the German title *Nothwendige Seelen-Sorge in eines Predigers Sendschreiben an seine Pfarrgenossen vorgestellt* ('Necessary care for the soul, presented in a pastor's letter to his fellow parishioners') (Budissin, 1704), the text is in Wendish (79 pages). The only surviving copy is in the Bautzen Municipal Library.

Hales was not a lord, but as a contemporary SPCK source notes, continental colleagues were prone to style him 'Baron after the title of his father' (McClure 1888: 355–6). Robert Hales was the fourth son of Sir Edward Hales Bart (1645–1695), who was ennobled by King James II in France on 3 May 1692 (after the king's deposition) (Ruvigny 1974, s.v. Tenterden; Stone 2002: 3). Nothing is known of the process whereby permission was obtained to publish the translation, but the intervention of a complete outsider in Lutheran affairs can hardly have failed to cause consternation.

The 1728 Bible

The decision to publish the whole Bible in Upper Sorbian appears not to have been discussed by the Estates, but to have resulted from the private initiative of four clergymen: Johann Lange (Jan Langa, 1669–1727), Matthaeus Jokisch (Matej Jokuš, 1668–1735), Johann Böhmer (Jan Běmar, 1671–1742), and Johann Wauer (Jan Wawer, 1672–1728). The first the Estates heard of it was a report at the *Oculi* (Lent) diet in 1728 that the translation was complete and had been dedicated to them (Mětšk 1960d/1981: 35–6). The four pastors had begun work on their translation on 14 April 1716 and had completed it on 27 September 1727. During that time they had held forty-five meetings to discuss their work. Before starting, they held a meeting in Budissin at which each of them was told what he was to translate. A period of working at home in their spare time would be followed by a meeting at which each translator read his version aloud, while the others listened. Of the listeners one checked the sources, one the German version of Luther, and the third other translations (*Biblia* 1728: [x–xi]).

The task they faced was not quite as daunting as it might seem, for by now substantial parts of the Bible had already been translated and published, including Michael Frentzel's version of the New Testament. There was a belief that certain further portions of the Old Testament had already been translated and that the manuscripts were lying undiscovered here and there in Upper Lusatian parsonages, but efforts to find them were unsuccessful. Wendish translations of the *Book of Psalms*, the *Book of Proverbs, Ecclesiastes*, the *Song of Solomon*, and *Jesus Sirach* already existed in printed form, but they required revision and this, the translators said, gave them 'a lot of trouble'. Even the New Testament gave them 'no less toil', for although Frentzel had translated and published the whole thing, there remained not only many typographical errors, but also places where the translation 'was not given in good Wendish, according to the true Budissin dialect' and these they corrected. The title page of the New Testament in the 1728 version, however, still shows Michael Frentzel as the translator.

Wendish soldiers

Wendish soldiers constituted significant components of both Saxon and Prussian armies, and served in the Silesian wars (1740–1742, and 1744–1745). In the second war, the Prussian army invaded Upper Lusatia (Bahlcke 2001: 166). In the Saxon army Wends were not allotted to separate units (for the Prussian *Wendenregiment*, see below) and were generally inconspicuous unless they had difficulty speaking or understanding German. Glimpses of them may be gained from chance references in memoirs of the time, such as those of Georg Körner (1717–1772). Born a German, in Zwickau, where as a schoolboy he learned Wendish from a Wendish soldier, he studied at Leipzig and joined the Wendish Students' Society there (NBS 1984, s.v.; Zwahr 1984: 54). On ordination in 1742 he became a military chaplain in the Saxon army (Körner 1979–1980, 1: viii).

He records an incident in the Kosel regiment at Runstock (probably Rohnstock) in Silesia in 1745 involving a Wendish grenadier, who had been sentenced to death. On arrival Körner found that the German chaplain to the Prinzgotha regiment had already been summoned and the proceedings were already under way. The regiment had its marching orders and was in a hurry, but as the chaplain was very conscientious and the grenadier could understand very little German, his spiritual preparation for death was proceeding very slowly. The grenadier had already been blindfolded, but the chaplain was still trying to convey to him the meaning of a funeral hymn, when unexpectedly the general arrived and 'from pity and in view of the state of his soul' decided to spare the man's life (Zwahr 1984: 56).

Körner relates another incident from the same year at Komotau in Bohemia, when, in the absence of the chaplain of the Schönberg Fusilier Regiment, he was asked to give communion to Drummer Lehmann, a Wendish soldier, sick from fever and dysentery. Lacking the authority to minister in Wendish, Körner first questioned the man in German but this evoked no response. Then he began to make his confession in Wendish, which Körner could understand, enabling him to identify the sick soldier as a *hajak* (Upper Wend), and when Körner, speaking Wendish, put questions to him from the Catechism, he replied with a joyful expression (Zwahr 1984: 56).

In Körner's own regiment too, the *Jasmundisches Regiment*, there were a number of Wends, most of whom could speak German. One day, after delivering a sermon, Körner questioned some of them about it and discovered that they had not understood it. They were quite open about it and explained that German was not their mother tongue.

Hereupon I invited one of them into my tent and read him a spiritual meditation from the book *Rozwučenje wot někotrych nuznych štukow teho křesćijanstwa* 'Instruction in Several Necessary Aspects of Christianity' and then I saw how this man was roused to quiet attention, was moved, and made happy. He told me straight away that, although he could speak German a bit, he had never understood the word of God properly since he had left his homeland for foreign parts. In 1746–1747 this regiment was transferred to the Dresden garrison and here I met this same man and other countrymen of his in the Bohemian Church of St. John, where it was easier for them to understand a Czech preacher than a German.

(Zwahr 1984: 57).

Körner, who was from 1746 himself a preacher of the Bohemian Church of St. John in Dresden, estimated that he now had about fifty Wendish parishioners. He deduced that in the whole Saxon Army, the Wends would add up to almost a battalion and so would have merited the provision of a special Wendish chaplain (Zwahr 1984: 54, 57).

Nathanael Gotfried Leske (1751–1786)

A valuable source of details of Wendish social conditions and everyday life, especially in the *Standesherrschaft* of Muskau, in the north-east of Upper Lusatia and bordering on Lower Lusatia, is Nathanael Gotfried Leske's *Reise durch Sachsen in Rüksicht der Naturgeschichte und Ökonomie* 'A Journey through Saxony Considering Natural History and Economy' (Leipzig, 1785), based on a journey undertaken in 1782, when the author was Professor of Economics at Leipzig. Although he was mainly interested in agricultural methods and natural history, he also had an anthropological bent. He was born in Muskau on 22 October 1751, the son of Gottfried Leske, pastor of the Wendish church in Muskau and archdeacon of the German church there. Five or six years after Nathanael's birth, the family moved to Königswartha on his father's installation as pastor there. As a child Nathanael suffered a permanent injury resulting from a fall, said to be the fault of a careless nanny. Despite his disability, he became a pupil first of the Budissin Gymnasium (1761–1765) and then of the orphanage school at Halle (1765–1766). He later studied at Leipzig University (1769–1773), where in 1773 he graduated as Bachelor of Medicine (Šołta 1981: 3). In addition to medicine, Leske studied philosophy, Greek, Latin, ethics, theology, physics, mineralogy, law, modern languages, and botany.

In 1774 or 1775 at the age of twenty-two or twenty-three, Leske was elected to a chair of natural history at Leipzig, and in 1778 to a chair of economics. In 1786 he unsuccessfully aspired to a chair of physics, which would have brought him a higher income, but the same year he was offered and accepted a post at the University of Marburg in Hessen as Professor of Finance and Economics. He set out from Leipzig on the journey to Marburg, travelling by coach, but on the way was victim of an accident. Though seriously injured, he reached his destination, but died there soon after arrival on 25 November 1786. He was thirty-five.

Though born in Muskau and brought up in Königswartha, Leske never describes himself as a Wend and does not say that he could speak Wendish. It is inconceivable, however, that he could have failed to learn the language of his childhood environment, particularly as his father was a pastor of Wendish parishes and is the author of several Wendish translations. In his short life, Nathanael Leske wrote and published several important books in the fields of natural science and economics. The *Reise durch Sachsen...* (Leipzig, 1785) stands apart from the others. In it he describes the places he passed through on his journey, including areas inhabited by Wends, especially his birth place Muskau, which continued to interest him, though he had left it at a tender age.

During his visit to Muskau he was accompanied by Johann George Vogel, superintendent of the Lutheran church there. His reports from Muskau are dated 12 and 16 June 1782. He writes:

The inhabitants are serfs (*Leibeigene*) or, to use the euphemized term preferred here, hereditary subjects (*Erbuntertanen*). They all live in extreme poverty; and as they can barely achieve subsistence from their land, they are very often obliged to seek refuge in the charitability of the *Standesherr* [...]. These inhabitants [...] are all Wends, with the single exception of the citizens of the town of Muskau. But the town too was probably once inhabited by Wends [...]. They are manifestly distinguished from the Germans living among them by their manners, dress, and differences in customs.

Referring to Johann Hortzschansky's articles in the *Provinzialblätter* in 1782, he notes:

The Wends, as Herr Hortzschansky shows (and I, who grew up among them, agree), are lacking in wordy compliments, but they are anything but discourteous. They drink like the Germans, are not malicious (as is alleged against them), unless their justified sensitivity to the insults of the Germans is considered such, but brave, stout-hearted, loyal (especially to each other), industrious, and impervious to the greatest hardships. In cleanliness they almost outdo the Germans; they practise hospitality, are always of a cheerful disposition, and religious [...].

Mainly for the purpose of making a pictorial record of natural phenomena, Leske was accompanied by Johann Salom Richter, an artist, who prepared the engravings which illustrate the *Reise*. In a limited number of copies they were coloured by hand. They include several Wendish scenes, whose impact as sources of ethnographic information is enhanced by Leske's circumstantial commentaries. The following is a good example (Figure 5.2):

The seventh copper etching shows the wedding of a Wendish couple, which took place during my presence in Muskau and was sketched on the spot by Herr Richter. Principally, the bride and bridegroom are worthy of special notice. The latter always has a sword slung over his shoulder, of which in the church, however, he divests himself before approaching the altar. Around his head he has a wreath plaited together from various flowers, leaves, and ribbons. The rest of his clothing is very simple and chosen at his own discretion. Beside him stands the match-maker (*Brautwerber*), who has a long double towel, adorned at the bottom with fringes, hanging down over his arm like a sash. Behind him stand the other wedding-guests of the male sex. The bride and all the wedding-guest of the female sex are dressed in black. The former and her two bridesmaids, who are standing immediately behind her, are wearing black velvet caps, slightly tapering upwards, which are open at the top and have a round knot at the back. Around the round knot goes a brass hoop, two fingers broad towards the top, from which often spangles or stars of brass hang. At the top of the velvet cap is wound a wreath of green and red, or only green, silk. The hair is drawn together firmly and smoothly, and plaited into two plaits at the back, where the bride's cap sits, so that when it is firmly wound round with a silk ribbon it looks as if a whole piece of ribbon were wound round together. The neck is bare. The women standing behind the bridesmaids have a white cloth tied round their caps, their neck is covered by a cloth, and they carry under the arm, as a decoration, a big white linen cloth rolled up, just as German women carry their fan or umbrella. Last of all stands the bride's maid, who does not wear a black dress, but just a white linen blouse that in front reaches to below the breast and on the arms to beneath the elbows.

(Leske 1785: 135–6).

Figure 5.2 A Wendish wedding in Muskau. Engraving by Schoenberg after a drawing by Johann Salomo Richter [1782]. From Nathanael Gotfried Leske, *Reise durch Sachsen in Rücksicht der Naturgeschichte und Ökonomie* (Leipzig 1785), p. [326].

A peasant writer: Hanso Nepila (1766–1856)

The existence in the eighteenth century of Wendish books, printed in hundreds of copies, implies that the ability to read was not uncommon among the Wends. The ability among them to write, however, was less common and largely restricted to the clergy. Peasant life, in any case, was not conducive to writing, and manuscripts written by laymen in Wendish are at this time still extremely rare. Outstanding among these rarities, however, are the writings of Hanso Nepila. He was born in 1766 in Rohne, near Schleife, in the *Standesherrschaft* of Muskau. Born a serf of the *Standesherr* of Muskau, he became the leaseholder of half a hide of land. During childhood he experienced utter destitution and the famine of 1772. Nevertheless, he went to school, though very irregularly, and learned to read and write. Following the death of his father, he took over the impoverished family smallholding and attempted to scratch a living. He married Marie Paulick in 1789 (Jahn 2010: 138, 344).

Though poor, Nepila was a man of parts. He carved furniture and even made himself a pair of wings with which he attempted to fly (Brijnen 2004: 16–17). But it was as a writer that he excelled. Commissioned by neighbours and friends who could read but not write, Nepila made manuscript copies of Bible texts and hymns. The dialect of Schleife straddles the border between Upper and Lower Lusatia (*SSA* 1: 48), and the people of Schleife, though living in Upper Lusatia, might well have opted, given the chance, for the Lower Wendish versions of the Bible and other sacred texts, but the decision was made for them. It was the books approved by the Upper Lusatian Estates that found their way into all Upper Lusatian churches, and it was from the Upper Wendish Bible that Nepila made his copies. He also wrote religious books of his own, and these too were in a variety based on the language of the Upper Wendish Bible. But his most important literary production is his autobiography, which includes many details of the changing scenes of life in the parish of Schleife in his time, and this, having no secular models to follow, he wrote in his native dialect. Nepila was a proud man and had ambitions, but as he grew older and saw his ambitions frustrated, his disappointment and sadness grew. He wrote his autobiography largely to get things off his chest, not expecting them to be read by anyone ever.

The number of Nepila's manuscripts was considerable, but when, in 1856 at the age of eighty-nine, he died, most of them were stuffed into his coffin and buried with him. The greater part of the surviving five manuscripts, three of which are autobiographical, was published by Matej Handrik (1864–1946), pastor of Schleife, at the end of the nineteenth century (Handrik 1896/1898/1899/1900). The remainder had to wait until 2004 (Brijnen 2004: 23–5). A German translation of all his manuscripts was published as an appendix to a monumental study of Nepila in 2010 (Jahn 2010: 629–805). His language is quite different from that of other Wendish texts and its largely paratactic or coordinated style probably reflects the style of his speech.

Nepila did not know the date of his own birth and mistakenly attributes to 1770 the events of the famine year 1772, which constitute his earliest childhood memories (Jahn 2010: 161–70). This is how he begins his story:

Of the famine year and of poverty and want and how great labour awaited me and I risked great trouble. Now then, your high and noble and good worships, you are appointed by God for authority and justice, and I too acknowledge that authority is very necessary and good too here in this world. I am the peasant Hanso Nepila, owner of half a hide, born in Rohne and my name is recorded in the baptismal books as Hanso Nepila in Rohne. Well now, you high and noble ladies and gentlemen, I am going to expound to you too a new story of the famine year then, when I was small, and of what I had to eat then, in that famine year, the year of hunger, and the date was 1770. It was a very wet year and a very lean year and a very hungry year. The rye would not grow at all but stayed all stunted in the ground and it was a failure and the buckwheat did not grow at all. In the hills the people were picking at it, and in the lowlands there was nothing of it [to be seen] for the knot-grass and couch-grass. And people carried it home in pieces of cloth or in bundles, so very little of it there was. And the millet scarcely crept out of the ground and nothing came of it at all.

The people threshed all the rye and they sowed it all again and then they ran short, and they had not sown all that should have been sown. And they bought it, wherever they could get it, so that they could sow a little. It was very dear. At that time a bushel of rye cost 18 thalers at sowing time; and later in the winter and until harvest a bushel of rye always cost 16 thalers. Oh that was very dear grain. Money had to be paid straight away, if the peasants wanted to buy a bushel of rye.

Oh, what a year of scarcity that was! Oh, it was a very hungry year too in the whole land of Saxony and in the whole land of the Emperor. In both these lands there was such a dearth that the people suffered from great hunger and had nothing to eat, so that they had to go to begging in Brandenburg just to get little bits of bread to keep them alive. And the number of people wandering around in the Cottbus region was very great. People went there from the Budissin region and from the Muskau region, and they were very numerous. The people [there] were unable to give them enough. Some there were among them that were so very weak and hungry that they just sat down by the roadside and could not go any further, so weak they were. But those that were on their way home, taking bits of bread with them, found the starving ones along the way, and they gave them pieces of the bread that they had begged themselves, so these could eat enough to continue on their way there to beg pieces of bread, to keep themselves alive. That is what old people have told me, and the begging had not been going on long before it was forbidden and watchmen were posted; they kept watch on it and no longer let anyone enter the village, and anyone they did find they threw out and chased away.

The area alluded to by Nepila variously as Cottbus, Brandenburg, and Prussia may be understood as the Cottbus Circle. He continues:

In Cottbus there were a lot of people wandering around and begging, but when the watchmen caught them, they shoved them around, beat them, and drove them away. There were Saxon people who went there intending to buy rye or actually did manage to buy rye, but if the Frenchmen met them, they took it all away. That was theirs. It was not worth anyone's while asking if they could have it back. The King of Prussia had certain people and they were called Frenchmen and it was their job to see what the Saxon people had bought in Cottbus, and from whomsoever they met they took everything away, that was theirs, and no one ever got anything back again. Prussia was rich. Everything had turned out very nicely there. They had [what they needed], but the King of Prussia had neither love nor mercy for the starving Saxon people. He was so malicious and unkind that he gave them nothing, not even for money, but took everything away from them that they had bought, and in Prussian Cottbus a bushel of rye cost 10 thalers and a little more. Later the peasants went to Muskau and turned to the gentry for rye. They had a bit, and they bought it from them or even borrowed it, so long as it lasted. So then the peasants took the chaff of rye or linseed or oats to the mills to be ground into flour and they baked bread from it and ate it. It was so wrinkly and prickly and dry that at first we could not moisten it in our dry, weak mouths, however much we wanted to swallow it, for we were so very hungry. The bread was so very dry and crumbly that the loaves did not hold together or remain whole, but they burst and bubbled apart. [...] I too ate it. I know what it was like and how good it was. I am not lying, the Lord God knows I am not lying, [when I say] I ate it and we still wanted more.

(Handrik 1899: 43–45).

Nepila's father eventually joined the beggars along the edge of the Cottbus Circle. He would usually be away for a fortnight at a time. In the meantime his wife and son stayed at home and had to make shift with anything edible they could find. Nepila lists the various leaves his mother would gather and boil to make a meal: hops, lime, plum, hedge-mustard, rape, potato, and nettles. But the staple fare was goose-foot (*atriplex*), which his mother managed to gather daily. She served it boiled, without (as Nepila repeatedly notes) salt or fat. One day after an absence of over three weeks Nepila's father returned home and shook out onto the table from his sack the fruits of his search: five crusts of bread, at which someone had already been nibbling:

That was a treat for the two of us. Mother soaked the crusts in water and we ate them, but they were so small they hardly helped to still our hunger. And mother wept because we had nothing to eat except the goose-foot without salt or fat, and even this she could not find anywhere in order to cook it. The goose-foot everywhere was torn bare and there was hardly any to be found, so my father stayed at home for two days and helped to pick the goose-foot and gather it until we had a little more of it and mother cooked it for us and we ate it. But my father did not eat much. He did not like it, for he said it was very bitter and not nice. He did not eat much of it, but mother and I we ate it gladly, for we were used to it. On the third day my father went off to Prussia again and he stayed there right up until the harvest. And at home no work was done; everything was left standing or lying there. Nor did the other people do much work. Everyone was searching for food, going round looking for leaves, picking them and gathering them; and they boiled goose-foot and ate it. But by now there was none left to be plucked and gathered. It had all been found and picked and left bare.

(Handrik 1899: 49).

Eventually Nepila resorted to eating clay:

My father had clay at home, so later I went up to it and sat down by it and tried to eat it. And I squeezed little pancakes from it, and bit them, and ate. I was still hungry, but I did not feel like eating it. It was not as bitter as the goose-foot, but had a sharper taste. And that time I did not eat much. I walked away from it and went to bed. And my God and Lord kept me alive, and in the morning I got up, fit again, thanks to the Lord almighty. He kept me alive and would not let me die from hunger.

(Handrik 1899: 50).

Saxon Lower Lusatia

Leuthen

Language policy in Saxon Lower Lusatia in the eighteenth century was still centred on promoting the use of German in the church and remained unchanged from the outline drawn in the Modest Admonition of 1668. Following the extinction of the Saxony–Merseburg line in 1738, the *Landesherr* of Lower Lusatia again became the Elector of Saxony, who was now Friedrich August II (also king of Poland), but there was no perceptible change in policy on Wendish matters (Mětšk 1969: 49, n. 118). The maintenance of public order, however, took precedence over linguistic matters, and the authorities were sometimes prepared to compromise. It was important, first of all, to avoid conflict with the landed gentry, some of whom at least understood Wendish, were conservative by temperament, and did not want to provoke their serfs into going on the rampage instead of getting the harvest in. There was also a spiritual side to the language question. So long as the Wends claimed they could not understand German, those who deprived them of access to the word of God bore a heavy responsibility. Many landowners, therefore, continued to appoint only Wendish-speaking pastors.

The parishioners of many Wendish parishes, for their part, continued to assert their ignorance of German and to claim their traditional role in confirming the presentation of new pastors. In 1725 Johann Adam Jar (1699–1762), on presentation to the living of Leuthen, fulfilled the traditional requirement of preaching a trial sermon in both languages, German and Wendish. He passed the test and was notified to that effect by means of a formula stating that the parish had 'found no fault in your person, life, doctrine, or language' (Mětšk 1970: 165n.).

On Jar's retirement twenty years later, the new owner of Groß Leine, Joachim Heinrich von Lang, who like his seventeenth-century predecessor von Zittwitz was also *Landesältester*, took advantage of the vacancy to complain to the Elector about the lack of German in the Gr. Leine church and to suggest that the arrival of a new incumbent might present an opportunity for reform. He appended to his letter outlines of the existing predominantly Wendish orders of service for both mattins and evensong and of his proposal for new predominantly German orders. The letter and appendix both survive (Mětšk 1969: 23–4). From them it seems that the main bone of contention was the sermon, which was still entirely Wendish at mattins and predominantly Wendish at evensong. Seeing he paid 'considerable tithes' to support the pastor, von Lang felt services should be so arranged that he and his family, who were 'unskilled in the Wendish language' could attend them. In any case, he said, both the village of Groß Leine and the whole parish, apart from a few old people, were so well versed in the German language that there was no longer any need to favour 'this barbaric language, on whose extermination the intentions of the *Landesherr* had anyway already been expressed previously' (Mětšk 1969: 22–3).

The Leuthen *Standesherr* Graf von Schulenburg zu Lieberose, however, saw fit to follow tradition and Christoph Fritz Schneider (born Trebitz 1719) held his electoral sermon in Wendish and German as usual and this (as the record states) was 'to the total satisfaction of the entire parish of Leuthen and Groß Leine' (Mětšk 1970: 165). Von Lang, in addition to writing to the Elector, had written directly to von Schulenburg, but in milder terms, suggesting merely that 'a little more German might be sung and preached in the Groß Leine church' (Mětšk 1970: 166). Otherwise, he did not interfere in the installation of Schneider, but remained 'quite calm', as one source puts it (Mětšk 1970: 166).

The circumstances of Schneider's installation show that the approval of the parishioners was more than a mere formality; but the record that his electoral sermon was 'to the total satisfaction of the entire parish of Leuthen and Groß Leine' does not tell the whole story. A Leuthen church warden (*kěbjetar*) Georg Richter and the village mayors of Dollgen and Groß Leine had reservations about Schneider's Wendish. He was born at Trebitz, near Lieberose, like his predecessor Jar, so must have been a native speaker, but Richter and his associates were stern judges. They made the parish's acceptance conditional on remedial measures ('...let it be remembered that the candidate still stumbled a little in the Wendish, which could be corrected with practice') and an appropriate assurance was given.

Schneider stayed only four years in Leuthen. In 1749 the living was again vacant and von Schulenburg was minded to install Eusebius Gottfried Roscius, who came from Vetschau. By now, four years of sermons that neither he nor his family could understand had taken their toll of von Lang's patience and he opposed the presentation vigorously. It seems likely that he had a candidate of his own who shared his linguistic preferences. When Roscius was due to visit the parish to give a trial sermon, von Lang forbade his serfs to attend on pain of a 5 pfennig fine. He told Roscius that he did not want him and threatened to deny him entry to the Groß Leine church. Von Schulenburg was evidently undismayed, and the sermons were given in time-honoured fashion and to the parishioners' satisfaction. Von Lang complained to the Consistory that von Schulenburg had not invited him as 'co-patron' to the trial sermons, but his claim to this office, as in the previous century, failed (Mětšk 1970: 165).

The Cottbus Circle

A New Testament for the Wends of Lower Lusatia (1709)

Among the main objectives of Spener and the Pietist Movement was an intensified study of the Bible, aiming at enhanced personal devotion (*ODCC* 1990: 1088), and their influence on the processes that brought the Bible to the Wends in Upper Lusatia has already been noted. The same intellectual currents, but a little later and from a different direction, were also instrumental in the publication of the Wendish Bible in Lower Lusatia. One of the most zealous adherents of Pietism in Lower Lusatia was *Oberjägermeister* Christian von Panwitz (1689–1703), lord of Kahren (Korjeń), a village a few kilometres south-east of Cottbus (Mětšk 1962a: 40). He corresponded with August Hermann Francke (1663–1727), also a leading Pietist and the founder of the Francke Foundations. Through Pietistic circles in Berlin von Panwitz came into contact with Baron Karl Hildebrand von Canstein, later founder of the Canstein Bible Institute in Halle. The von Panwitz family used to visit Berlin and it was here, through von Canstein, that von Panwitz made the acquaintance of Johann Gottlieb Fabricius (1679–1741), a young man who had been studying theology at Gießen and Halle. While at Halle, he had also acted as tutor in August Hermann Francke's Foundation (Mětšk 1940/1981: 15).

Von Panwitz held the right of presentation to the parish of Kahren and in 1701 he appointed Fabricius to the pastorate. Probably von Canstein was instrumental in this appointment, for he showed a continuing interest in Fabricius's progress in Kahren. On 3 July 1703, he wrote to Francke: 'I am not yet fully acquainted with the understanding between the Polish H[err] Fabricius and H[err] von Pannwitz. I think of him often [and wonder] when he will come here, so that I can hear of it from him and later from Fabricius' (Mětšk 1940/1981: 15). In the light of subsequent events, it seems likely that the understanding in question related to the translation and publication of Wendish books. Von Panwitz died in 1703, but he left Fabricius in a strong position to execute the publishing plans.

Fabricius was not a Wend. He was born in Skwierzyn (Schwerin an der Warthe), which from 1793 to 1945 was in Prussia, though in Fabricius's time it was still in Poland, as it has been again since 1945. Fabricius's father was the owner of a royal mill and a gentleman. His mother's maiden name was Deutsch. It is thought likely that his first language was German, but that he knew Polish too from an early age (Mětšk 1979: 3). That he knew no Wendish before his appointment to the living in Kahren is clear from an allusion in the introduction to his New Testament to being caused by God 'to get to know the fundamentals of this to me previously quite unknown language' (Schuster-

Šewc 1967a: 365). Following his appointment as pastor of Kahren, he set about learning Wendish, using a copy of Johann Chojnan's manuscript grammar and assisted by the pastor of Papitz (named Korn), a native speaker, in whose house he lived for a time. He lost no time in getting down to the task of producing religious books in Wendish.

Manuscript versions of the main devotional texts were already in circulation. It was now a matter of getting them into print. Von Panwitz had enabled Fabricius to set up a printing press in the school in Kahren, and there in 1706, assisted by Andreas Richter, a professional printer, he published his translation of Luther's Little Catechism (*D. Martin Luthers sel. kleiner Catechismus nebst einem christlichen Glaubensbekennniß [...] in die wendische Sprache übersetzt und nunmehr zum gemeinen Gebrauch der evangelischen Niederlausitzschen Kirchen [...]*). It is worth noting that, although Fabricius intended his Catechism to be used in parishes of Lower Lusatia (including the Cottbus Circle), he referred to its language simply as Wendish. It is based on the vernacular of the Cottbus area and would later be called Lower Wendish or Lower Sorbian.

The Elector Friedrich III (reigned 1688–1713) had exploited the difficulties faced by the Emperor Leopold I in the War of Spanish Succession to secure imperial consent to the promotion of Ducal Prussia to a kingdom, and on 18 January 1701, in Königsberg, he had been crowned Friedrich I king in Prussia. But it was his father, the Great Elector, Friedrich Wilhelm I (reigned 1640–1688), who had managed to reduce the power of the Brandenburg Estates and had begun to rule as an absolute monarch. Whereas in Lusatia the support of the Estates had been necessary to initiate a programme of Wendish publishing, in absolutist Prussia (including the Cottbus Circle) everything depended on the king (Scheuch 2001: 164–5).

King Friedrich I was an enlightened monarch, who was not hostile to the Wendish language. He was even prepared to assist the publication of the New Testament in Wendish. Somehow von Panwitz had managed to draw the king's attention to Fabricius's work and to induce him to take a sympathetic view. Although von Panwitz had died in 1703, six years before Fabricius was ready to publish his New Testament, King Friedrich's approval had already been assured and was announced in the foreword to the 1706 Catechism. The king allowed the New Testament to be dedicated to him and gave Fabricius financial assistance.

There is, however, a marked difference between the grovelling manner of Fabricius's dedicatory preface and the confident tone of Frentzel's prefaces:

> In former times the Slav Wends were not allowed to appear before the countenance of the most serene ruler of the land, for they would, from more than heathen blindness, be subjects of neither Jesus Christ nor the sovereign, but arrogantly expected to rule themselves. They sought not what was best for the country, but illegally to take possession of it. Therefore to a Christian and legitimate authority this nation could have been nothing but abominable.
>
> Now in all submissiveness I make so bold as to bring the aforementioned nation before Your Royal Majesty's Royal throne, but, thanks be to God, in another and better guise. It comes with the New Testament of our Lord Jesus Christ, who in

grace too has turned towards this otherwise hated people [and] from whom they derive not only the healing doctrine of salvation but also learn more and more to be submissive and obedient.

Your Royal Majesty may view it as a precious blessing from God Almighty that under your royal and happy reign the pure word of God has been revealed in many languages, its Godly power has been exercised over many, and that now too the new Covenant of Grace is being published for your Wendish subjects in the precincts of Cottbus, who can understand it in no other language.

The title page of the New Testament states that it was translated and printed by Gottlieb Fabricius, pastor in Kahren, and printed in Kahren in 1709 by Johann Gottlob Richter. A year earlier, however, Fabricius had moved to Peitz (also in the Cottbus Circle), where he remained as senior pastor until 1726, and the preface to the New Testament was signed in Peitz on 4 April 1709. From his introduction, however, it emerges that Fabricius was, strictly speaking, not a translator, but rather an editor of an older version, assisted by native speakers. As he tells us:

A written New Testament in the Wendish language was indeed already to hand, which, as one can see, had been translated piecemeal by various persons and subsequently written out as a whole by someone, though it is very little known or almost not known at all, and the sense of the German version is not always conveyed therein, let alone the sense of the original, so that obvious untruths are found therein. Yet the applied zeal of the toilers of old must be praised and the advancement of words recognized with many thanks.

(Schuster-Šewc 1967a: 365).

He goes on to say that in some cases he followed the original Greek, rather than the German, for 'it is known that its idioms can often be better expressed in Wendish than in German'. A crucial role in the work had been played by Christoph Ermelius, Archdeacon of the Wendish Church in Cottbus and a native speaker. He had read the whole text and had supplied Fabricius with his comments, 'which I willingly followed'.

According to a report of 1714 from Fabricius's successor as pastor of Kahren, Friedrich Lüderwaldt (1681–1739), the New Testament that was 'already to hand' (as the introduction puts it) had been lent to him by a neighbouring pastor on condition that he return it in a very short time. Realizing that he would not have time to make a copy of it himself in the time specified, he sent it by post to von Panwitz in Berlin. Von Panwitz engaged the assistance of an expert bookbinder, who unbound it gathering by gathering. The gatherings were then dispersed among local scholars and hastily copied. The original was then rebound and returned to Kahren, where Fabricius gave it back to its owner within the specified term. He now had his own copy, which formed the basis of the New Testament printed in 1709. There are also allusions in the sources to other seventeenth and early eighteenth-century manuscripts of the complete New Testament in the Wendish of Lower Lusatia, of which nothing further is known (Schuster-Šewc 1996: 10–12).

Fabricius stayed in Peitz until 1726, when he was moved to Cottbus as superintendent and school inspector, and here he died in 1741 (K. A. Jenč 1880: 132; Schuster-Šewc 1967a: 366). Fabricius's version was reissued in Cottbus in 1728 by the printer Richter, who had moved the press there following completion of his work on the first edition. It went through further editions in 1741, 1759, and 1770, each time (it is thought) with 1,500 copies (R. Jenč 1954: 169). In the 1759 edition, several readings from the Old Testament were added. In 1821 the Prussian Bible Society brought out a double edition, consisting of one bilingual version with parallel German and Wendish texts and one version in Wendish only. Of each version 3,000 copies were printed. The Spremberg publisher Säbisch brought out a further bilingual edition in 1848 (R. Jenč 1954: 170).

Rebellion (1715–1717)

Generally speaking, the status and condition of European peasants worsened the further east they lived, and east of the Elbe the law placed little restraint on the power of the serf-owner (Blum 1978: 38–9; Clark 2006: 160–7). The plight of the Wendish serf was exacerbated by an ethnic dimension (Blum 1978: 46). Writing in 1714, Friedrich Lüderwaldt, Fabricius's successor at Kahren, observed that the land-owning class

> behave towards their subjects with great harshness, because they are serfs, indeed in some places even with an old deep-rooted hatred and bitterness against them, as if they persistently harboured a rebellious mind and heart against their superiors. They burden, bleed, and debilitate these Wendish dogs (a name which, sadly, one often hears) with drudgery and hard punishments to such an extent that the poor people and their families live in extreme poverty, so that, for all their hard labour, they can barely get their daily bread and a linen smock.

(Zwahr 1984: 27).

In late 1707 there were rumours of impending revolt among the Wendish serfs in parts of the Cottbus Circle. Friedrich I sent the Cottbus *Amtshauptmann* Geheimrat Wilhelm von Gröben (Kunze 1969: 73) to investigate, and he reported on 11 February 1708 that all was quiet, 'although I have observed that the serfs of the Wendish nation are of a very rebellious and obstinate nature. To which I must add that many are to such an extent kept down and oppressed by their superiors that they can barely scrape a living' (Mětšk 1962a: 34). At the end of 1710, the village mayors of the entire circle submitted a complaint concerning the sums required of serfs to purchase their freedom. Although trouble was clearly brewing, Friedrich I, by the use of compromise and by restraining the nobility, managed to keep the lid on the unrest. His successor Friedrich Wilhelm I (r. 1713–1740), known as the 'Soldier King', however, adopted a new policy. In December 1714, realizing that the Wends could provide him with a supply of men for his expanding army, he founded the Wendish Regiment (*Wendenregiment*), number 26 in the Prussian army list, commanded by Major-General von Loeben (Mětšk 1962a: 60, n.2). Its recruiting area was mainly in the Cottbus Circle but also in parts of the Beeskow and Lebus regions.

There is a legend, which may not be entirely fanciful, that Friedrich Wilhelm in his youth had come into contact with the Wends on his estate at Wendisch Wusterhausen (later Königs Wusterhausen), south-east of Berlin, and had grown to like them. Later, following the discovery of a mutinous plot among the Wendish grenadiers at Potsdam, his liking had turned to hatred (Mětšk 1965a: 170). Whatever the truth of this story, the nobility, who had been dissatisfied with the policy of Friedrich I, certainly believed that in his son they had an ally against the Wends, and proceeded to impose new burdens on their serfs (Kunze 1969: 74–5).

In early 1715 *Landrat* von Klitzing, lord of the *Rittergut* of Schorbus, reported obstinacy and disobedience from the peasants of the Cottbus Circle. They were said to have been holding clandestine assemblies and one of their number, Lehmann, the mayor of Eichow, had been arrested. Subsequently, however, he had been rescued from custody by a mutinous crowd. On 3 February 1715, the serfs of the Cottbus Circle petitioned the king with a list of grievances against their feudal lords. Friedrich Wilhelm appointed a committee, consisting of *Landrat* von Klitzing, *Geheimrat* von Gröben, and the *Kreisfiskal* Johann Christian von Kirchhof, to investigate both the report of von Klitzing, including the rescue of Lehmann, and the peasants' complaints against the landowners (Mětšk 1962a: 42–3; Kunze 1969: 75). The committee, having summoned delegations from both the peasants and the nobility to a hearing in Cottbus on 27 March 1715, reported on 8 April:

> Whereas it now [...] clearly transpires that as Lehmann, former headman of Eichow, was about to be brought in custody to Peitz, the serfs blocked the road in such a way that the cart had to stop, and this Lehmann must have thereby gained the opportunity, despite having both hands and one foot in irons, to get off the cart, whereupon they surrounded him, struck off the irons, and led him away. And although the serfs in their submission take great pains to mitigate this violent act, it is de facto clear that they did carry out this outrage.

> (Mětšk 1962a: 42).

The instigators of the assemblies, apart from Lehmann, were identified as: Jürgen Quarow of Ressen, Dalitz of Werben, Jürgen Kochan of Eichow, and Hans Richter of Leeskow. The ringleaders of Lehmann's rescue were named as: Hans Dücke, Noack, Zerne, Mallusch, Janike, and Buslei (all of Eichow) and Muschler, Naue, mayor Stojan, Semisch, and Lalisch (of Krieschow). The committee recommended that the persons named be condemned to two or three months hard labour (*Festungsarbeit*) in Peitz, while the others be ordered to supply the convicts, during their imprisonment, with 'the usual scanty prison food' (Mětšk 1962a: 43) and to be commanded on pain of severe corporal punishment to refrain from all suspicious gatherings and collections of money, and to live in future peacefully and obediently (Mĕtšk 1962a: 43).

The committee also warned the king that the peasants had threatened, in the event of their punishment, to go in great numbers ('100 or 200 and, if that were not enough, 1,000 strong') to Berlin and to persist until they received a resolution from the king himself. But if they went unpunished (the committee warned), there was a risk they might be encouraged to attempt even more daring operations. The king agreed with the committee's recommendations and on 4 May 1715 ordered the arrest of the accused. However, the authorities had learned their lessons from the bungled attempt to arrest Lehmann in Eichow, and decided to change their methods. Instead of arresting the accused, they summoned them to appear on 6 July 1715 in the courtyard of Cottbus castle. Some of those summoned prudently decided not to appear, but most of them obeyed and on the day appointed, accompanied by several hundred supporters, made their way to the castle 'in a fairly tumultuous manner' to demand the revocation of the arrest warrant (Kunze 1969: 82). A detachment of thirty soldiers under a lieutenant, detailed by von Gröben, was silently lying in wait. During the confrontation the peasants 'adequately demonstrated by means of defiant words and gestures their tough attitude'. Seventeen of them were arrested: Jürgen Kochan, Hans Dücke, Noack, Zerne, Matuschk, Janike, and Buslei (from Eichow), Siedt, Muschler, Stojan, Semisch, Lalisch, and Schulze (from Krieschow), Jürgen Quarow (from Ressen), Dalitz (from Werben), Hans Richter (from Leeskow), and Jürgen Laust (from Gosda). Incensed by this treatment, both the prisoners and their sympathizers declared that from now on they would perform no feudal service for their masters (Kunze 1969: 82–3).

Hans Lehmann, following his escape, had briefly sought refuge across the border in Saxon territory, but by Sunday 24 July 1715, he was back in Eichow and attending a service at his parish church in Krieschow. Emerging from the church, he encountered Egidus Leonhard von Zabeltitz, the lord of the manor, who told the village bailiffs to take him into custody. When they refused, von Zabeltitz seized Lehmann himself, but Jürgen Golz from Eichow called on the bystanders to retaliate. Lehmann's father grabbed the squire by the throat, while the others held his hands and feet, enabling Lehmann to make his escape. He again found safety in Saxon territory (Kunze 1969: 83n.).

The committee instructed the wives of the men in custody to perform their husbands' feudal duties. When they refused, the commission declared that the villages in question would remain under military occupation until the recalcitrant peasants acknowledged their duties. The resistance continued, but on 28 August 1715, *Landrat* von Klitzing managed to arrest Lehmann. 'The gentry are not a little gratified that this arch rebel has at last fallen into the hands of his rightful judge', wrote the *Landrat* in a letter of 8 September. Lehmann was brought to the city gaol in Berlin, from where he should have been transferred to Peitz, but the authorities feared to move him through the open country, particularly as the Peitz garrison at the time was undermanned. The king therefore ordered him to be taken to the prison in Spandau. He and Martin Dalitz from Werben were regarded as the principal authors of the revolt, compared with whom the remaining prisoners were small fry. Whether by luck or good judgement on the part of the insurgents, the revolt and subsequent strike had occurred at the worst possible time for the landowners. If something were not done quickly, the harvest would be lost. Those arrested on 6 July did not serve the two or three months envisaged, but were soon released (Kunze 1969: 84). Mindful of the economic harm, the king ordered the committee to make sure that the peasants were not totally ruined.

Martin Dalitz, the only inhabitant of the parish of Werben to be named in the record, was regarded as sharing with Lehmann the highest degree of guilt and remained in prison with him, after all the others had been released. In February 1716 their wives appealed to the king for their release and he called for an assessment of the situation. He was informed that Lehmann and Dalitz had been the originators and ringleaders of the revolt. They had incited the serfs of both the Cottbus Circle and the neighbouring region, organized assemblies, and collected money. The unrest and insubordination were still continuing and it was impossible to say evil consequences might not follow, if they were released. Nevertheless, the king decided that both men should be required to promise on oath to be of good behaviour and set free. The nobility expressed their deep dissatisfaction 'for fear of new disturbances' (Kunze 1969: 84).

On 7 May 1716, the investigatory committee was relieved of its duties and further administration of the matter referred to the government of the Neumark. Dalitz took the oath on 29 June 1716, promising 'at all times to be quiet and peaceful, obey our superiors, abstain totally from all forbidden assemblies and collections of money, as well as incitement and instigation to rebellion, and also otherwise behave as is proper for a good and honest serf...' (Kunze 1969: 84n.). This apparently was not enough, for he remained in prison for seven more months and was only set free following a further petition from his wife. At the command of the king in February 1717, he was released immediately. Lehmann was treated similarly. He is reported in May 1716 to have been prepared to promise on oath to be of good behaviour, though he tried to make it conditional on the repeal of the royal ban on occupying deserted farms. After further discussion, in the course of which the nobility repeated their opposition to the release of the two rebels, Lehmann too was set free early in 1717.

It was not long before the nobility's fears were realized. Dalitz and Lehmann lost no time in summoning the disaffected peasants of the Cottbus Circle to rebellious assemblies. Lehmann told them they would be free of all feudal obligations only when the nobility had been driven from the land and advised them to take up arms to resist attempts to coerce them to carry out unpaid labour. On 9 July 1717, Lehmann was again taken into custody, but this only fanned the flames of the revolt. On 11 July a mass demonstration was held in the Cottbus woods, which took a decision to carry out no more labour obligations. The following day over 4,000 peasants gathered near the village of Raddusch to discuss their next steps (Kunze 1969: 85).

The nobility correctly foresaw that the rebels would again make their way to Berlin to petition the king, so they requested him to have them arrested. They also asked him for assistance in the Cottbus Circle. The king wrote to Lieutenant Colonel von Billerbeck on 14 July: 'My dear Lieutenant Colonel von Billerbeck, you will be aware that in that Circle a rebellion has broken out among the peasants; you are to do everything you can to control it to the best of your ability and to arrest the ringleaders, whom you are thereafter to send, all together, to Spandau.' Four days later von Billerbeck reported that the rebels had dispersed. Many were lying low in Saxon territory, waiting for the return of the deputation from Berlin. When it did return, its members were all arrested by von Billerbeck and taken not to Spandau but to Küstrin, because the nobility considered that peace would return more quickly, if they were taken as far away as possible (Kunze 1969: 86).

The number of peasants arrested in July 1717 was at least eight. No consideration seems to have been given to putting them on trial, but after they had been in prison for six months, they all petitioned for clemency and the matter was referred to the faculty of jurisprudence at the University of Rostock. The judgement was delivered on 5 March 1718. Lehmann was held to be the ringleader of the rebellion. Taking into account the fact that he had already been imprisoned once and had broken his oath to be of good behaviour, the faculty concluded that he was a hopeless case and recommended he be imprisoned for life with hard labour. The case of Martin Dalitz, who had also broken his oath and was accused of having conspired with Lehmann, was viewed with remarkable leniency. It was proposed that he, 'as an example to others', be sentenced to one year's hard labour. Mathias Denkel was to be imprisoned for six months. The sentence proposed for Mathias Britschke, Paul Rietze, and Jürgen Petsche was fourteen days imprisonment on bread and water. As the crimes of Jürgen Bogen and Mathias Hanusch were judged to be less heinous, their immediate release was recommended. The proposed sentences were all confirmed by the king (Kunze 1969: 87).

By the time the faculty reported, it seems, the accused had already been in gaol for at least seven months, but this fact seems not to have been taken into account. It is moreover difficult to reconcile the record with the faculty's observation, justifying leniency in the case of Jürgen Bogen, that he had 'already served seven weeks [in prison] in Spandau', seeing he appears from another source to have been incarcerated since July 1717. On 8 July 1718, the wives of Lehmann, Dalitz, and Denkel petitioned the king for their release. Even if pre-sentencing time were not taken into account, Denkel should by now in any case have been due for release. On 30 August the king ordered that Lehmann should stay in gaol, but that Dalitz and Denkel should be freed. Denkel was indeed set free, but Dalitz inexplicably stayed in gaol. He is next heard of in 1720, when his wife together with Hans Lehmann's wife jointly sent a petition dated 6 February to the king begging for the release of their husbands. There is no mention of the king's earlier release order of 30 August 1718.

The king now decided not to reprieve Lehmann, but he again ordered Dalitz to be freed. It emerges, however, that the commandant of Küstrin was not prepared to release him until he had paid for the cost of his keep. The bill, which survives, relates to the period from 12 September 1717 to 20 March 1720 and demands the not inconsiderable sum of 27 thalers, 4 groschen, and 8 pfennigs. Since his family was destitute there was no possibility of Dalitz paying. Finally, the king, who must by now have wondered whether anyone was listening to what he said, had to intervene again with an order for the costs to be borne by the authorities. Eventually, close to the end of the year, Dalitz was freed.

Lehmann is last heard of on 4 March 1721 in a letter from the king to *Geheimrat* von Gröben, denying a further appeal for his release (Kunze 1969: 88).

The new church at Burg

In 1725 Friedrich Wilhelm I settled some of his retired soldiers on land to the north-west of Burg, a village in the parish of Werben in the Cottbus Circle. The settlement was called Kauper. Burg itself lay to the north-west of Werben and was already a good distance from the parish church. Under Friedrich II 'the Great' (r. 1740–1786), the number of parishioners grew considerably. Travelling conditions in the Spree Forest were arduous. So far as possible, people made their journeys by boat, but some destinations could be reached only on foot, crossing waterways and swamps by paths known only to the initiated. Despite this and the remoteness of their parish church, the people of Burg and Kauper were compelled to make the journey to Werben. The Werben church was the nearest and they had no choice. Eventually, however, in 1745 the inhabitants of Burg, including Kauper, petitioned the feudal lord of Werben, von Schönfeldt, and the Consistory in Küstrin for permission to build their own church and break away from the Werben parish. Burg had no junker of its own but belonged directly to the king, so two peasants from Burg, named Natuška and Šemjel, set off for Berlin to petition the king (Krušwica 1915: 120–1).

At a hearing held in Küstrin on 9 January 1746, the plaintiffs (the people of Burg and Kauper) claimed that the journey from Burg to the Werben church took at least one hour in good weather and two hours in bad. The people of Kauper needed two or three hours. During floods, which were endemic in the Spree Forest, the paths were impassable. It was said that the people of Kauper and Burg, on arrival in church, would fall asleep from fatigue and sleep through the sermon. It was impossible to take children to church or for children to attend confirmation classes. The pastor was similarly prevented by the inaccessibility of these parts of his parish from visiting the sick and weak there. Moreover, the increase in numbers had made it impossible for everyone to fit into the church, and, to make matters worse, a pastor had been installed whose Wendish was minimal. Although with help he had managed to translate his sermons into Wendish, he was incapable of ministering to the sick and dying (Mětšk 1962a: 53). It was, however, part of the pastor's duties to visit Burg, and once every six weeks he would preach there in a big room. A glebe meadow beside the Spree was provided for him to pasture the horse that he needed to take him to Burg (Krušwica 1915: 120). In its reply the Consistory said that from Burg the Werben church could be reached in half an hour or, at most, three quarters of an hour. From the extreme end of Kauper the journey took two hours at most. As for the pastor's linguistic inadequacy, 'the Wendish language, according to edicts, is to be done away with, so it is no deficiency in Schindler if at first he was not fully conversant with it'. The petition was rejected (Mětšk 1962a: 52–5).

However, the validity of the edicts of the previous monarch had expired. Friedrich II 'the Great' followed his father's practice in looking after his old soldiers, and in creating new settlements to fill the land, but on the question of the Wendish language he was of a different mind. In May 1748 he appointed a committee of two men (Schwarz and

Mirdelius) to look more closely into the question of a church for Burg and, following their report favouring the petitioners, he decided that there should be a separate church in Burg with its own pastor. Schwarz and Mirdelius also reported that the pastor of Werben was indeed incapable of offering edification or comfort to his parishioners in their own language, 'for although according to the decrees the Wendish language was supposed to become extinct, it is hard for old people to abandon it and learn German; meanwhile, they should not forgo the necessary consolation and spiritual comfort in the hour of their death' (Mětšk 1962a: 56).

It was the case of Burg and its aspiration to have its own church that made the king realize that it would be beneficial to his other policies, if he renounced his father's decrees calling for the extinction of Wendish. The Royal Chancery consequently issued the following announcement:

> It is the most gracious intention of His Royal Majesty to renounce those edicts which concern the abolition of the Wendish language, at least in the Cottbus Circle. Whereas the foreigners from [the land of] Meissen and from Lower Lusatia are mostly Wends and are glad to leave the Margraviate in view of the bans on the Wendish language, they will therefore be all the more ready to move in as colonists and settlers. In order to attract as many of all conditions and kinds into the country as are prepared to come, His Majesty is pleased, for the present, once more to allow and protect the Wendish language for the subjects of the Cottbus Circle.

The location of this document in the archive makes it clear that it relates to the Burg case (Mětšk 1962a: 57). The qualifying 'at least in the Cottbus Circle' is significant. Friedrich's tolerance of the Wendish language did not extend to other parts of Prussia. An application to the king from colonists in the newly settled village Neulübbenau (Kreis Beeskow) for a Wendish-speaking pastor was denied with the note: 'it would be better for foreign Wends who do not understand German adequately to accept places in the Cottbus Circle' (Mětšk 1962a: 100–101n.). At Michaelmas 1751 Burg became a separate parish (Krušwica 1915: 120–2).

Except for the reign of Friedrich Wilhelm I (1713–1740), royal policy in the eighteenth century was broadly benevolent towards the Wends in the Cottbus Circle. The kings tolerated or even fostered the language. The Cottbus councillor K. Chr. Gulde was over optimistic, however, when in 1785 (the year before Friedrich the Great's death) he wrote of the Wends: 'They love their language, whatever intention there may have been to completely obliterate it in the Cottbus Circle. It has notwithstanding this survived to the present. And now that in recent times more has been learned of its utility, it is surely not likely that its suppression will ever be commanded again' (Mětšk 1962a: 64).

Fritze's Old Testament (1796)

It was not until 1796 that Fabricius's New Testament (1709) was complemented by a translation of the Old Testament into Wendish 'as it is found around Cottbus'. This was the work of Johann Friedrich Fritze, who was born on 20 September 1747, the son of Andreas Albert Fritze, pastor of Kolkwitz, a few kilometres west of Cottbus. Having been orphaned when he was not yet four, he was sent at the age of ten to the gymnasium in Cottbus, then in 1761 to the lyceum in Lübben. In 1766 he moved to Halle, where, as well as studying at the University, he was employed as a teacher at Francke's orphanage. He left Halle in 1768 and for a time lived with his elder brother, Gotthilf Christlieb, who was a deacon in Lübben. The next year he moved to Vetschau as an assistant pastor. Four and a half years later he was called to Kahren and remained here as pastor for five years, but in 1778 a call came from Kolkwitz, the parish of his birth, and here he served his flock for the remaining forty-one years of his life. He died on 15 January 1819 (Mětšk 1962a: 64-5n; NBS, s. v.).

Fritze began work on his translation in 1790, but his literary inclinations had been revealed long before that in two long poems or hymns, written to commemorate the tragic events of Monday 26 March 1781, when a large part of Kolkwitz was consumed by fire and two villagers died. When in 1858 the *Bramborski Serski Casnik* published an article on his achievements, there were still old people alive who could remember him supervising the printing of his Old Testament and his attention to detail was proverbial. He was said to have been in the habit of asking old people 'in the fields and meadows for the name of this or that thing or for words […] most pleasing to Wendish ears' (K. A. Jenč 1880: 134).

Unlike Fabricius, Fritze did not have access to an earlier translation, but had to translate the whole text himself. Also unlike Fabricius, he was a native speaker of Wendish. He took a great interest in his native language and corresponded on linguistic matters with the founder of Czech Slavonic studies Josef Dobrovský (1753–1829) (R. Jenč 1954: 172). His Wendish dictionary and grammar remained in manuscript. He lacked the personal contact with people in high places that Fabricius had enjoyed and had great difficulty in getting his translation published. On 1 July 1791, he wrote to von Gedicke, chairman of the Royal Supreme School Board (*Oberschulkollegium*), asking for approval for his translation and applying for financial support. Ignoring Upper Lusatia, he alluded to the opinion that the Wends were the only Protestant Christians not to have the whole Bible in their own language, thereby 'sharing partly the fate of Catholic Christians'. He estimated the cost of publishing the Old Testament at 2000 thalers and recalled that, when Fabricius had been in a similar situation, King Friedrich I, then reigning, had given his gracious assistance (Mětšk 1962a: 64–76).

King Friedrich Wilhelm II (reigned 1786–1797) was generally well disposed towards the Wends, as was his Minister of State Johann Christoph von Wöllner (1732–1800), but they were in no hurry to help. From Fritze's letter of 1 May 1792 we may deduce that the king's reply to Fritze's submission had been encouraging but cautious. Referring to 'Your Majesty's most gracious command that I should gradually begin the translation of the Old Testament into the Wendish language…', he reported that he had already translated eighteen books. This may have been less gradual than the king intended. Two months later Fritze was informed that the king was not yet ready to make a decision, but that the Supreme School Board would make a grant of 100 thalers. Fritze expressed his gratitude and suggested that some headway might be made by instructing all Wendish churches to subscribe in advance to his Old Testament, each church buying one copy for itself and three copies for its school. He estimated that this would cover the cost of 250 copies.

The Cottbus Superintendent Schmidt, in reply to a request from Berlin for his opinion, endorsed Fritze's project wholeheartedly, even though, as he said, 'I cannot really judge the value of the translation as such, because I can understand Wendish only a little. That, however, is not in the least to his prejudice, for many Wendish pastors have given me a credible assurance that he has a quite exceptional command of the Wendish language of this neighbourhood.' In February 1793 the king issued a decree assuring his support, commanding the Consistory of the Neumark to ensure that 'at least those churches that can afford it buy an appropriate number of copies, to recommend the book to church patrons, and to foster its distribution in every way possible' (Mětšk 1962a: 70). There was still no indication of the degree of financial help to be expected, but at least goodwill was in evidence.

Fritze naturally reckoned on selling his translation not only in parishes under the king of Prussia, but also in Saxon Lower Lusatia. He therefore sought the approval of the Consistory in Lübben and of the Elector Friedrich August III as *Landesherr* of Lower Lusatia. The Consistory replied: 'The distribution of the translation in question would be nothing less than an act of encouragement to the Wendish language, ... [which] with regard to the propagation of religious and practical principles and to the reduction of misbelief and superstition would not be advisable' (Mětšk 1962a: 70n.). This response highlights the clash between the Prussian policy of tolerance towards the Wendish language and the anti-Wendish policy of the margraviate, including its Consistory in Lübben.

Even within the circle there were opponents of the official line, as the tolerant Superintendent Schmidt discovered, when, in accordance with the king's command to foster the distribution of Fritze's translation, he broached the question with August Wilhelm von Rotberg, lord of Petershain from 1789 to 1811 and patron of the Petershain church. Petershain, about 6 kilometres south-west of Drebkau, was situated inside Prussian territory. Von Rotberg wrote in reply to Schmidt:

In Petershain the translation of the Old Testament would not be applicable. First, the church lacks the funds, secondly, Petershain is no longer to be reckoned among the Wendish villages. Apart from a few old people, more German than Wendish is spoken here. German is spoken by the parents to their children and by the children to each other. Since both before and after the Seven Years War various instructions have been published that schoolmasters teach the children the German language, every effort has been made here to cause the complete decline of the Wendish language. So there is neither in the entire village nor in the incorporated hamlets Allmosen, Bahnsdorf, and Lindchen a single person, old or young, who would be able to read the aforesaid work in the Wendish language, because young people receive instruction in reading German only.

(Mětšk 1962a: 70–1).

It is doubtful if Germanization was proceeding with the speed von Rotberg suggests, for nearly a century later, Ernst Muka found that the old people of the parish (about one third) still spoke Wendish. Muka also discovered that, although there had been a tradition of conflict with the von Rotbergs, Wendish had remained in use in the Petershain church until the death Pastor Johann Friedrich Dallwitz in 1842. The patron had then appointed a German pastor contrary to the parishioners' wishes, provoking resistance from the people of Bahnsdorf (Muka 1884a: 19–20, 90–1; Muka 1884b: 145).

The extent of support from the Prussian state for printing Fritze's Old Testament eventually amounted to 1500 thalers (Mětšk 1962a: 91, 101–2), but the funds were released in small instalments and only after repeated supplications. As well as receiving help with the printing costs, Fritze was expected to recuperate what money he could from actual sales. He appears thus to have been left with an unrealized capital sum in the form of several hundred copies of his work. As late as 1801 he wrote asking the king if he would, from the funds of the Supreme School Board, buy 200 copies at the agreed retail price of 16 groschen a copy and present one to each of the top pupils (one girl and one boy) in every Wendish school. This application was turned down (Mětšk 1962a: 91–2).

Pomerania

Dreger, Bernoulli, Brüggemann, and Haken

A long silence of the sources on the Wendish presence in Pomerania is broken only in 1748 by a note that 'beyond the river Stolpe the Wendish language is still used by the peasants and church services are held in it. This language is erroneously called Kashubian (*Cassubisch*), because although the Kashubs (*Cassuben*), Pomeranians, Poles, etc. had one language, the true Kashubian land was where now Belgard, Arnhausen, Polzin, Neu-Stettin, Dramburg, and Schievelbein lie' (Dreger 1748: 378). The First Partition of Poland (1772) brought Royal Prussia (as West Prussia) under Hohenzollern rule. Until then the bulk of the Kashub population had been subjects of the king of Poland, but now they were united with their western compatriots under Friedrich II the Great. Whether this unification provoked any celebrations is not known, just as nothing is known of any Kashubian activity whatsoever at that time. Seven years later, however, by a strange coincidence, two reports on the Kashubs appeared independently in the same year. In 1777 the Swiss Johann Bernoulli (1744–1807), astronomer royal in Berlin, as the guest of the Prussian minister Count Otto Christoph von Podewils, travelled from Wusterwitz (Ostrowiec) to the then Kashub village Zipkow (Szczypkowice), near Glowitz (Główczyce), south of Lake Leba (Łeba). In the first volume of his *Reisen...* (Leipzig, 1779) he has left a lively account of what he saw there. He had no hesitation in referring consistently to the Slavs of Pomerania as *Cassuben*. He distinguishes them from the Poles but reserves *wendisch* for reference to the Slavs of Lusatia. Of the Kashubs (*Cassuben*) he writes:

This little people still has its own language, which is used for preaching and in which devotional books are printed. [...] yet it is probably merely a decayed dialect of the Slavonic. The Kashubs understand the Poles fairly well, whereas the latter have some difficulty in understanding the Kashubs. The Count's cook, who had worked in Lusatia, where Wendish is widely spoken, could understand much of the Kashubian. Incidentally, the great difference between this language and German is inconvenient to the noblemen who have estates in Kashubia; so the estate-owners do everything possible, though so far without much success, to introduce German generally and to banish Kashubian. In the churches immediately after the Kashubian sermon they have another preached in German, which the serfs are also obliged to attend, but preaching the sermon in German alone is not yet possible, because as yet many understand nothing at all of this language. Yet probably the desired change will gradually take place, partly because the Kashubs are merging more and more with the Pomeranians, and partly too because, as the swamp and heathland is made arable, many German colonists are being settled in this area.

(Bernoulli 1779: 138–9).

The same year (1779) Ludwig Wilhelm Brüggemann (1743–1817), Court Preacher at the Schloßkirche in Stettin and a member of the Consistory, published the first volume of a comprehensive description of Pomerania. For the section on the Kashubs, he had solicited the assistance of two informants, one of whom was the senior pastor of Stolp and chairman of the Stolp Synod, Christian Wilhelm Haken, the other a Pastor Backe in Fritzow. Brüggemann observed: 'Although between the Dievenow and Lupow remnants of the old Wendish-Germans are still encountered, the true Wendish heritage is to be found among the peasants and country-folk between the Lupow and the Leba' (Brüggemann 1779: lxiii). A report published here on the peculiarities of the *Plattdeutsch* spoken by the semi-Germanized Wends located in the west of the Duchy between the Dievenow and the Lupow is attributed to Haken. This is followed by a detailed account of their clothing, character, customs, diet, and economy, which is attributed to Backe. Finally, Haken expounds on the people of undiluted Wendish ways who live between the Lupow and Leba (Brüggemann 1779: lxiii–lxxii).

In addition, a letter from Haken to Brüggemann survives, in which Haken shows that he had personal knowledge of life in some Kashubian villages, where the language survived:

For nearly 600 years now the Germans have been driving the Kashubs or Wends further and further eastwards out of their old habitations. In Pomerania formerly their border in the west was the Stolpe and in the east the Leba; subsequently however they have been driven so far that now they are all bounded by the Lupow and the Leba.

The great national pride of the Kashubs is the main reason why they have so long offered defiance against the total obliteration of their Sarmatian tribe. This pride prevents them from interbreeding in any way with the German race, the more so because they regard the Germans as usurpers of this their fatherland. This pride also leads them to reckon it shameful to speak the language of the Germans, which in their ears sounds so barbaric, assuming that they are familiar with it in order to express themselves in case of need.

There is an instruction in existence that pastors are to aim so far as possible at getting rid of the Kashubian language, to impose on them exclusively German schoolmasters, and not to confirm them unless they can read German. This, however, calls for wisdom and discretion, because, in the first place, care must be taken not to let them notice that the intention is to repress their language, otherwise the Kashubs would be roused to such proud anger that they would resist this plan with extreme violence. Secondly, because religion comes into consideration. It should not be thought that because Kashubs can in everyday life make themselves understood after a fashion in German, they can necessarily be capable of receiving religious instruction in German. In everyday life they form the correct understanding of words by looking at all the things they denote, but to handle abstract or unusual concepts their mother tongue must be used as an aid to clothe their ideas properly.

Both these reasons have combined to prevent, until now, the complete removal of the Kashubian language from my synod, but in my ten years here with the support of the pastors I have brought things to a point where in some places, when vacancies occur, provided the patrons are not obstinate, the prospective incumbent can manage without this language, because in five or six years, the remaining old people who cannot understand German, will be dead. In some parishes, however, a further fifty years will probably be necessary.

The parishes in which sermons are delivered in Kashubian may be divided into two classes:

1. Where the pastor simply must preach in Kashubian, because half to two thirds of his listeners cannot understand German well enough. They include the parishes of Garde, Rowe, Smolsin, Glowitz, Zetzenow, Stojentin, and Schurow.

2. Where the Kashubian language will soon disappear. They include the parishes of Dammen, Lupow, Mikow, Nossing, Budow.

Because the difference between the pure Polish and Kashubian languages is like that between High German and *Plattdeutsch*, the Kashubs generally understand Polish, though they do not speak it. Therefore, books for elementary education are Polish, just as no other Bible than the Polish is used.

Moreover, the pastor must resign himself to preaching and catechising in their dialect. If he does not do so, the Kashubs regard it as an affront to their language and will rather go miles away to another parish, will provoke factions against the pastor, and will persecute him with their own unique brand of vindictiveness. I witnessed the installation of a pastor who was not Kashubian enough for them; they locked him out of the church, were about to stone him, and almost killed him in the churchyard.

(*List* 1909: 205–7).

Lüneburg

Christian Hennig von Jessen

Our richest source of information on the Wendish language in the Duchy of Brunswick-Lüneburg is the *Vocabularium Venedicum* of Christian Hennig (1649–1719), pastor of Wustrow from 1679 until his death. During the 1680s he carried out observations of the folkways and customs of his parishioners, but his records were all destroyed by a fire in Wustrow in 1691. Shortly afterwards, stimulated by the interest of others, he began to study the language. In Johann Janieschge, a peasant from the village of Klennow, he found an excellent informant and teacher (Olesch 1989a: 138). The *Vocabularium* is the result of Hennig's work over the years around the turn of the century, steadily collecting Wendish words and phrases. The manuscript, which has survived undamaged to the present day, has been published (Olesch 1959). Hennig's preface was written in 1711 and his remarks evidently relate to that year, including the note:

> In these parts at the present time only a few of the old people speak Wendish, and they could scarcely do so in the presence of their children and other young people, for they thereby incur ridicule. The fact is that these, the young people, have such a horror of their mother tongue, that they cannot bear even to hear it, let alone learn it. Therefore, it cannot but be assumed that within twenty, or at most thirty, years, when the old people are no more, the language too will have gone, and then in these parts it will no longer be possible to get to hear a Wend speaking his language, however much money you are ready to spend.

These observations relate to the area between Uelzen, Lüchow, and Dannenberg, in the Ämter of Lüchow, Wustrow, and Dannenberg. Hennig's concept of the Drawehn restricts it to the land west of the Jeetzel. He puts the number of persons east of the river able to speak or understand Wendish at no more than ten (Olesch 1989a: 138–9).

Johann Parum Schultze

Accounts of the Lüneburg Wends are almost all written by Germans. There is in fact only one Lüneburg Wend who speaks to us directly. This is a peasant named Johann Parum Schultze who in the early 1720s began writing his memoirs of life in the Wendland and he continued writing them until his death in 1740. He was born in 1677 in the village of Süthen, near Lüchow. His artless frankness and attention to detail make his chronicle (as it is called) a mine of information on Wendish customs and language. He was a village mayor (*Schultheiss*), as was his father before him, and was both literate and moderately well educated. His text is written in what purports to be standard German (that is to say, not the local *Plattdeutsch*), but it clearly reveals the effects of Wendish interference. He was a little unsure in his use of initial *h-* and the German definite and indefinite the articles, for example, and the auxiliary verbs *haben* and *sein* are confused. The original manuscript has not survived. What we have is a copy and not a good one. It is sometimes difficult to understand Schultze's precise meaning.

He describes such events as hunting wolves, the destruction of the townlet Wustrow by fire in 1691, when he was fourteen, his dispute with the magistrate Spreyer, the success or failure of harvests, and various commercial transactions. He was married in 1710 to Cathrina Gröpcken, but she died in 1732 at the age of forty-three, having borne nine children. Schultze's chronicle in several respects bears out the assertions made in Hildebrand's report of the 1671 visitation. Describing conditions before the Thirty Years' War he writes:

> The people before the great war were very plain and simple in their Christianity. When the priest preached, they heard the sound, but they understood nothing of it. […] At that time there were no schools in the country. They knew nothing of writing, but they had the Catholic prayers about Mary, and they were in Wendish. I have heard from old women 'Out of the Holy Gospel', 'When Jesus was Twelve Years Old', and other such fine prayers, which they had learned from their ancestors.
>
> (Olesch 1967: 142–3).

Parum Schultze recalls that in his childhood a *Kreuzbaum* stood in every village, as testimony to belief in Christ crucified. By 1724, however, the last remaining specimen was in the village of Jabel and by 1729 even this one had fallen down and was trodden underfoot. 'What once claimed our respect', he laments, 'is now trampled with muddy feet' (Olesch 1967: 149).

The entries in Parum Schultze's chronicle were made over a long period of time and are irregularly dated. In 1725 he added a glossary of Wendish words, which he prefaced as follows:

> I have undertaken in this year 1725 to write for posterity of the Wendish language, for it is a very difficult language to speak, and also difficult to write. […] for I have often heard people name something, but when it was written down they could not read it, for my grandfather at one time spoke Wendish a great deal and my father knew the Wendish language perfectly, just as they both spoke German well. Some of the older people spoke half Wendish and half German, just as now when someone from France or a so-called Frenchman by birth mixes French with German, so it was with those born among the Wends, that the people said what should be at the end came in front, and the front part came behind; and there are still grandmothers like that today among us. I am a man of 47 years and when it is all over with me and three others in our village, no one will know what a dog is called in Wendish. In the Thirty Years' War the German language penetrated here. No one can say how widely this [Wendish] language was used in the surrounding area, for it is written in the description of the world that the Mecklenburg Land was Wendish, for their king was Wendish too. But when I have been there, in Wismar, Schwerin, Boizenburg,

Lübeck, Hamburg, I could not discover that there were Wends living there. Or, if they did once live there, the people must have been completely exterminated, because when I asked the names of their meadows or fields, they all sounded German to me. For if the fields had formerly had Wendish names, they would have remained, as here in this district as far as Ueltzen, Ahrendsee, Salzwedel...

(Olesch 1967: 165–6).

As mayor of Süthen, Parum Schultze was familiar with juridical and penal customs, and he reports on many cases of crime from the Wendish villages, leading to executions, imprisonment, flogging, or banishment. The gallows stood just outside the townlet of Lüchow, a couple of miles from Süthen. Death sentences were carried out by hanging, the sword, or burning at the stake (Olesch 1967: 153–60).

The king of England and the Hanover Wends

Ernst August, Duke of Brunswick-Lüneburg (1629–1698), in 1679 became Duke of Hanover and in 1692 was elevated to the rank of elector. Hanover became the ninth electorate. Ernst August was succeeded in 1698 by his son Georg Ludwig (1660–1727), who as George I Lewis succeeded in 1714 to the English throne, arriving in his new domain in September that year. He continued to rule Hanover simultaneously, however, and was sometimes alleged to be more concerned about Hanover than Britain. He resided mainly in England, but made a number of visits to Hanover, including one lasting thirty weeks (from June 1725 to January 1726), and his interest in Hanoverian matters, it appears, even extended into such fine detail as the fate of his non-German subjects the Lüneburg Wends. There are three pieces of evidence for this. The first comes from Johann Georg von Eckhard:

> Then the Wendish people living in the Lüchow and Wustrow Prefectures of the Duchy of Lüneburg has a Slavonic way of speaking which merits our attention. Men of this people, with their language, were formerly even treated with derision by our Saxons and, its use being prohibited under grave penalty by the officials, they mostly denied that they knew it, whereby it happened that it thrived only among old peasants. And we should in a short time have had a people ignorant of its native tongue, had not these Slavs of ours been roused again under the merciful guidance (*sub clementi regimine*) of Georg Ludwig, our most gracious Elector, to its preservation and use.

(Eckhard 1711: 267–8).

The second and third pieces of evidence are entries in the register of deaths at Wustrow parish church, which was searched by Reinhold Olesch in the 1960s and 1970s. Here entry No. 20 on page 16 under the year 1750 notes:

On the same day 21 March in the afternoon the death occurred in Dolgau from a disease of the chest of the old midwife Emerentz Jägers, wife of Hans Jürgen Jäger, and she was publicly interred in Passion week on 24 inst., aged 67. NB. She had the honour of speaking to his Majesty our sovereign lord in the old Wendish tongue, when she had been summoned to the Göhrde in 1727.

(Olesch 1989b: 149).

Another entry in the register under the year 1756 (page 37) reads:

Dolgau. Emerentz, nee Drausmans, widow of Johann Schultze, hereditary village mayor and landlord, died after enduring a protracted illness on 3 October the sixteenth Sunday after Trinity towards evening and was publicly interred on 5 inst., aged 88. P. S. This old widow is the last of those who could speak and sing Wendish perfectly, therefore she too was obliged to appear before his Royal Majesty our gracious Sovreign lord at the Göhrde, so that he could hear this language from her lips.

(Olesch 1989a: 147).

It seems likely that both these women appeared before George I on the same occasion in 1727, but his interest in Wendish appears to have been of long-standing to judge from Eckhard's note dated sixteen years earlier. However, the suggestion that George I was in the Göhrde in 1727 is not easily reconciled with what is known of his whereabouts that year. He appears to have spent the first part of the year in London and to have been on his way to Hanover on 11/22 June 1727 when he died unexpectedly near Osnabrück. He was succeeded by his son George II, who was then in England (*ODNB*, s.v.). The episode needs further research, beginning with a check on the date in the earlier entry.

The death of Emerentz Schultze in Dolgau on 3 October 1756 may be taken as the end of Wendish in the Lüneburg region, but even as late as the beginning of 1798 in the village of Kremlin (north-west of Dolgau) a man named Warratz died who was said to have been capable of reciting the Lord's Prayer in Wendish (Olesch 1962: 15). After this vestiges of the language could still be detected in the Lüneburg Wendland in the form of loanwords and certain other peculiarities of the local Low German (*Plattdeutsch*) that replaced it. Indeed, even while Wendish was still spoken here, one of the oddities of the area that attracted attention was the strange German spoken by the Wends.

In a letter dated 17 May 1691, Georg Friedrich Mithoff, magistrate of Lüchow, provided answers to a number of questions which had been sent to him by his brother-in-law Chilian Schrader on behalf of the philosopher and mathematician Gottfried Wilhelm Leibniz (1646–1716) concerning the Wends, their customs, and language (Olesch 1967: 50–5). In reply to a specific enquiry as to the Wends' distinctive way of speaking German, Mithoff provided a list of characteristic features and the texts of a prayer, a confession, and two passion hymns, all in the German dialect of the Wendland.

Both list and texts were later published by Leibniz (1717: 335–45). Mithoff noted, for example, that the Wends often omitted the sound *h* at the beginning of a word (e.g. *Ehre* for *Herr* 'gentleman') or, conversely, inserted *h* before a vowel (e.g. *haugen* for *Augen* 'eyes') (Olesch 1967: 53–5).

A Polabian folk song

In his records of the Wendish (Polabian) language Hennig von Jessen included the words and music of a folk song, accompanied by a German translation. This is the only known Polabian literary composition. From Hennig's manuscript it was published in 1711 by Johann Georg Eckhart, accompanied by Hennig's German translation. It begins:

Katy mês Ninka beyt?	Who is to be the bride?
Teelka mês Ninka beyt.	The owl is to be the bride.
Têlka ritzy	But the owl said
Wapak ka neimo ka dwemo:	To the two of them:
Goss giss wiltge grîsna Sena;	I am a very ugly woman;
Nemik ninka beyt:	I cannot be the bride;
Gos nemik Ninka beyt.	I cannot be the bride.

(Eckhart 1711: 269–70).

Stanzas 2, 3, 4, 5, and 6, in which the wren, crow, wolf, hare, and stork, one after the other, decline the positions of groom, best man, cook, barman, and musician, respectively, are similar in form to stanza 1. Finally, stanza 7:

Katy mês teisko beyt?	Who is to be the table?
Leisko mês teisko beyt.	The fox is to be the table.
Leiska ritzy	The fox said
Wapak ka neimo ka dwemo:	To the two of them:
Ris plast neitmo mia wapeis,	Spread out my tail;
Bungde woessa teisko:	That will be your table,
Bungd wôssa teisko.	That will be your table.

(Jugler 1809: 207).

In his manuscript Hennig described how the Wends sang the song: 'It should now be noted that when the fox has spoken, his behind is to be spread out, and all of them who are sitting at the table begin to pound on the table with their fists and end the song in this way' (Polański and Sehnert 1967: 220).

Through Eckhart's book of 1711 the German translation came to the notice of Johann Gottfried von Herder, who in volume one of his collection of folksongs (Leipzig, 1778), published a slightly revised version, as *Die lustige Hochzeit. Ein wendisches Spottlied* 'The

Merry Wedding. A Wendish Satirical Song' (Herder 1807: 139–40). It appeared again four years later, re-worked, as the closing song in Johann Wolfgang von Goethe's musical play *Die Fischerin* 'The Fisherwoman', which was first performed at Tiefurt on 22 July 1782, but published only in 1806. The play ends with the heroine Dortchen, who has previously agreed to marry her suitor the next day, saying: 'I am really tired of all this gossip and if you cannot produce something better tomorrow the owl can be the bride.' This is the cue for the closing song:

Wer soll Braut sein?	Who shall be the bride?
Eule soll Braut sein!	The owl shall be the bride!
Die Eule sprach zu ihnen	The owl then replied
Hinwieder, den beiden:	To the pair of them:
Ich bin ein sehr gräßlich Ding,	I am a very shocking thing,
Kann nicht die Braut sein,	I cannot be the bride,
Ich kann nicht die Braut sein!	I cannot be the bride!

In stanza 7 Goethe removed the reference to the fox's tail and added an eighth stanza, neatly bringing the play to an end:

Wer soll der Tisch sein?	Who shall be the table?
Fuchs soll der Tisch sein!	The fox shall be the table!
Der Fuchs, der sprach zu ihnen	The fox said to them
Hinwieder, den beiden:	In reply to the pair of them:
Sucht euch einen andern Tisch!	Find yourselves another table!
Ich will mit zu Tisch sein,	I too want to sit at table,
Ich will mit zu Tisch!	I too want to sit at table!
Was soll die Aussteuer sein?	What shall be the dowry?
Der Beifall soll die Aussteuer sein!	The applause shall be the dowry!
Kommt, wendet euch zu ihnen,	Come, turn and face the people,
Die unserm Spiele lächeln!	Who smile upon our play!
Was wir auch nur halb verdient,	What we have but half deserved
Geb' uns eure Güte ganz,	May your bounty give us in full,
Geb' uns eure Güte ganz!	May your bounty give us in full!

(Olesch 1968: 11; Goethe ([1902–1912]), 8: 90–2, 338–9).

CHAPTER 6
AWAKENING 1800–1900

Napoleon

On 20 April 1792, revolutionary France declared war on the Holy Roman Empire and, as the nineteenth century dawned, French military might threatened disaster for Prussia and Saxony. For the Lusatian Wends, however, it heralded emancipation– national as well as social. Nine out of ten of them were still servile peasants, concentrated fairly compactly in lands to the south-east of Berlin and north-east of Dresden. About 80 per cent of them (some 196,000) were under the Elector of Saxony, inhabiting parts of Upper and Lower Lusatia and of the counties (*Ämter*) of Stolpen, Großenhain, Senftenberg, and Finsterwalde. The remaining 20 per cent (about 49,000) were subjects of the king of Prussia and lived mainly in the Prussian exclave of Kreis Cottbus (surrounded by Saxon Lower Lusatia) but partly also in the Silesian Principality of Sagan and in the Prussian Kreis Beeskow-Storkow (Mětšk 1962b: 80–1; Kunze 1978: 10; Scheuch 2001: 72).

On 6 August 1806 Emperor Franz II abdicated and became Franz I of Austria, thus bringing the Holy Roman Empire to its end. In the twin battles of Jena and Auerstädt in October that year, the Prussian and Saxon armies suffered a catastrophic defeat at the hands of the French. One of the participant Prussian units in these engagements was the 26th regiment of musketeers and grenadiers, made up mainly of Wends from Kreis Cottbus and known as the *Wendenregiment*. Like the rest of the Prussian army, it suffered terrible casualties. The survivors were taken prisoner and the regiment was never re-formed. The Prussian state collapsed and its territory was occupied by French troops. Saxony submitted to Napoleon and joined the states of the Rhine Federation in accordance with the terms of the Peace of Posen, signed on 11 December 1806 (Liersch 1931: 3, 7, 20, 21; Scheuch 2001: 76).

For his submission the Saxon Elector Friedrich August III was rewarded by Napoleon, becoming King Friedrich August I of the new Kingdom of Saxony, which was enlarged by the inclusion (at Prussia's expense) of the Kreis Cottbus exclave. This was confirmed by the Treaty of Tilsit, whereby Prussia lost more than half its territory. Consequently, more than 95 per cent of all Lusatian Wends from 1807 to 1815 lived under the king of Saxony (Hartstock 1977: 13). They were thus unaffected by a decree issued on 9 October 1807 by King Friedrich Wilhelm III of Prussia putting an end to hereditary servitude.

On 17 July 1807 Napoleon visited Budissin (or Bautzen, as it was now commonly called) and in a song composed to celebrate the occasion, written in German but obviously by a Wend (probably Jan Dejka), he was thanked for the gift of Kreis Cottbus, which had brought about the unity of the Wends:

> And so our town extols your sway,
> Its deeds we Wends applaud and praise,
> The source of our uniting.

(Mětšk 1962b: 78)

At the Congress of Vienna in 1815, however, the map was again redrawn. Prussia regained Kreis Cottbus and received from Saxony the whole of Lower Lusatia and the north of Upper Lusatia. Saxony thus lost more than half its territory to Prussia (Kunze 1978: 52). Lower Lusatia, including Kreis Cottbus, now became part of the Prussian *Regierungsbezirk* Frankfurt (Oder) in the Province of Brandenburg. The part of Upper Lusatia ceded to Prussia came under *Regierungsbezirk* Liegnitz, Province of Silesia (Kunze 2003:14–15). The new border ran arbitrarily over the land, cutting through parishes. Eleven villages found that the new state border had cut them adrift from their parish churches (Kunze 2001: 288). Half the Upper Wends were now isolated from Budissin/Bautzen, their traditional capital. In post-1815 Prussia, neither Lower Lusatia nor the newly acquired northern part of Upper Lusatia had any administrative status. Church government and administration also changed. The Lübben Consistory was dissolved and its duties assumed partly by the Church and School Commission of the provincial government in Frankfurt (Oder) and partly by the Consistory of the Province of Brandenburg in Berlin. In Prussian Upper Lusatia, church matters were in the hands of the local government in Liegnitz and of the Consistory of Silesia in Breslau (Kunze 2003: 16).

The situation in which 95 per cent of the Wendish population had lived under Saxon rule was now reversed to one in which 80 per cent lived in Prussia. Many of the Wends who now became (or reverted to being) Prussians, assuming that the 1807 decree applied to them too, refused to perform their services. Attempts by landowners to compel them were resisted. On 12 March 1816, the king issued a statement addressed to the rural population of Lower Lusatia and Kreis Cottbus, explaining that the obligation for them to perform feudal services remained in force. It was not until 7 July 1821 that a decree abolishing feudal services in Prussia was published, but it still did not apply to all categories of peasant. It was only on 2 March 1850, that the remaining categories were released from their feudal obligations (Kunze 1978: 56–9; Clark 2006: 327–30). In the much reduced Kingdom of Saxony, serfdom was abolished in 1832. There were now only about 50,000 Saxon Wends. Yet it was among them that the idea of nationality flourished most freely in the mid-nineteenth century (Map 6.1).

Map 6.1 The rump of Saxony and Upper Lusatia after 1815.

'A deeply decayed language'

The Prussian Church and School Commission in Frankfurt issued an instruction to all the superintendents of Lower Lusatia on 11 November 1818, directing that in Wendish elementary schools in future the Wendish language was to have no more than an auxiliary role in teaching the youngest classes. For the older pupils teaching was to be carried out entirely in German. 'A so deeply decayed language', it was explained, 'barely serving to denote everyday objects of common life, cannot possibly be suitable for the kind of instruction of the young which our times demand'. Wendish church services too were to be reduced:

Preaching in Wendish alone may no longer be practised anywhere, with the possible exception of funeral sermons, or when it is expressly requested. Instead, gradually longer and longer parts of the sermons and the liturgy are to be written and delivered in German. The same applies to German hymns, which are to be gradually practised in the schools and introduced in the churches, if this has not already happened.

(Mětšk 1969: 32–3)

Between 1815 and 1830, despite repeated protests by the parishioners, Wendish church services were discontinued in the Prussian Upper Lusatian parishes of See, Kosel, and Hohenbocka, and in the Lower Lusatian parishes of Dollenchen, Göllnitz, Sacro, Eulo, Mulknitz, Krugau, Neu Zauche, Pritzen, Wendisch Sorno, Groß Leuthen, Straupitz, and Laasow (1830) (Kunze 2003: 18).

In 1823 a new pastor was introduced to the parish of Greifenhain in Lower Lusatia, near Calau. Franz Ludwig Blütchen was unable to speak Wendish, so the parishioners complained to the authorities in Frankfurt. Blütchen promised to learn Wendish. When he thought he had learned enough, he delivered a trial sermon, but the parish was not satisfied. He promised to work harder on his Wendish, but his flock was still dissatisfied and renewed their complaint. This time they wrote to Superintendent Fabrizius in Calau, saying they would not stop protesting until a Wendish-speaking pastor had been installed. They said any number of Wendish applicants had been rejected. They told the Superintendent: '...you have behaved unscrupulously towards us....If Blütchen once more ascends our pulpit with his pitiful speeches, we swear to you that we shall denounce you to His Royal Majesty'. Fabrizius, however, supported Blütchen and the parish lost the battle. There were similar rows in Wendisch Sorno, Laasow, Graustein, Groß Särchen, and other parishes of Upper and Lower Lusatia (Kunze 2003: 19).

In 1843, however, the Prussian Minister of Education, Johann Albrecht Friedrich Eichhorn (1779–1856), began to doubt the theological propriety of introducing German components to the traditional Wendish liturgical office. The new practice, most commonly, was to open with part of the Wendish liturgy, continue with the German, and finish with the rest of the Wendish service. When asked to report on present procedures, the Spremberg Superintendent Helmricht defended the directive of 11 November 1818, saying he found it 'very expedient, because by hearing both German and Wendish sermons, which are always the same...knowledge of the German language is also...increased, and understanding of the content of the sermon is facilitated and secured'. It was admitted that, given the chance, the Wends would not attend the German sermon, but so long as it was sandwiched between the two halves of the Wendish service, they could not avoid it (Kunze 1978: 131).

The Minister decided that, where a continuous Wendish service was still customary, it should 'so far as possible, everywhere and always, be held together in all its components in an uninterrupted entirety'. Germanization, however desirable, could not be pursued to the detriment of the 'religious satisfaction' and the 'ecclesiastical morality' of the population (Kunze 1978: 131–2). On 22 December 1845 a new directive was issued, based on an edict of the Ministry of Education, to the effect that 'until Wendish parishioners voluntarily forgo separate services...the aim be constantly kept in view' of holding uninterrupted Wendish services (Kunze 1978: 132, 140–1). A few Wendish school-books were printed and in 1856 optional instruction in Wendish was introduced at the Cottbus Gymnasium. This, it was said, was to help prospective candidates for the ministry in the Wendish area (Kunze 2003: 20–2).

In the Kingdom of Saxony there was a more tolerant policy, which had a tradition going back to the eighteenth century. In a petition dated 19 August 1834, submitted to the Saxon Estates Assembly, eighteen Wendish Lutheran clergymen requested that the Wendish language be used in elementary schools not only in religious instruction but also in other subjects, and that an express statement to that effect be included in the forthcoming law on elementary schools 'to reassure citizens of Wendish tongue'. The petitioners reinforced their request with the confessional argument that without the proposed provision the new law would put Protestant children at a disadvantage, because in Catholic schools there was no restriction on the use of the mother tongue (Hartstock 1977: 23).

In a sitting of the Second Chamber of the Saxon Diet in Dresden on 30 August 1834, Dr Klien, the member for Bautzen and a Wend, and Dr Müller, the Minister of Education, both spoke in support of the petition. Dr Müller said the Saxon government had no intention whatsoever of driving the Wendish language out of the schools of Wendish parishes, but only of continuing to ensure that in these schools the study of the German language and education in it would not be neglected (Hartstock 1977: 24, 169).

The *Oberamtsregierung* of the margraviate of Upper Lusatia on 10 November issued a statement, saying that 'even though it is in many respects to be wished that one day we shall attain a position where all citizens have a complete command of the German language, yet it cannot in any way be the intention of the authorities to compel the Wends, by direct or indirect means, to give up their national language'. This received the full agreement of the Saxon Government and the Saxon Elementary School Law of 1835 contained the following paragraph:

Instruction in all elementary schools is to be given in the German language; but children of the Wendish nation are to be taught to read both German and Wendish. Also, for as long as the church services in the parish remain completely Wendish, it shall be permitted not only for the memorizing of the principal parts of the Catechism, Bible texts, and hymns, and verses of hymns, but also for religious instruction and confirmation instruction to take place with the application of the Wendish language...

(Hartstock 1977:21, 46; Kunze 2002: 95)

However, in Bautzen at St Michael's Church in 1836 a small but ominous change took place, when it was decreed that henceforth German services would be held here five times a year. Until now, since 1619, all the services had always been held in Wendish. Later, as the century matured, the number of German services at St Michael's increased steadily (T. Malinkowa 1998: 255).

Literature and the Wendish press

Before the nineteenth century almost all Wendish books were devotional in content. Writing on secular subjects was generally part of the German domain, and the secular aesthetic of the Wends, both musical and verbal, found its expression in folklore. The first Wendish newspaper, *Měsačne pismo k rozwučenju a k wokřewjenju* 'A Monthly Record for Instruction and Amusement', came out in 1790, but it was banned after the first issue. The second was the *Serbski powědar a kurier* 'The Wendish Reporter and Courier', which was edited and published in Löbau by Jan Dejka (1779–1853), a master joiner, and appeared from 1809 to 1812. The number of readers was too small for it to succeed in the long term, but the fact that it survived for three years is significant and its distinctly national tone is an exceptionally early manifestation of the national awakening.

For thirty years after this the only sign of literary activity was in the manuscript newspapers run by students' societies, but in 1841 *Volkslieder der Wenden in der Ober- und Nieder-lausitz* 'Folk-songs of the Wends in Upper and Lower Lusatia', a remarkable annotated edition of 331 folksongs, was published in Grimma (Haupt and Schmaler 1841). This was almost entirely the work of its second author, Jan Ernst Smoler (Schmaler) (1816–1884). In 1842, a weekly newspaper called *Jutrnička* 'Morning Star' appeared, edited by Jan Pětr Jordan. It lasted only six months (January to June), but was seamlessly succeeded in July 1842 by *Tydźenska Nowina* 'Weekly News', edited by Handrij Zejler. Both *Jutrnička* and *Tydźenska Nowina* brought their readers not only news but also small literary offerings. Smoler's *Volkslieder* was highly influential, not only on the Wends but also among the other Slav nations. At the time of its publication Smoler, aged twenty-five, had completed his theological studies at Breslau University, but having decided against entering the church, was living with his parents in Lohsa. Later that year (1841) he returned to Breslau, where he became one of the first students of a new subject, the study of Slavonic languages. By the time he graduated here (1845), the second volume of the *Volkslieder* had appeared (1843), containing 200 songs from Lower Lusatia. He had also published a phrase-book and vocabulary called *Mały Serb* 'The Little Wend' in 1841 and a *Deutsch-Wendisches Wörterbuch* 'German-Wendish Dictionary' in 1843. In all these books he used a new orthography of his own creation, taking some letters from the Czech and Polish alphabets, and printed in Latin type. Hitherto everything had been in Gothic type. Smoler had broken away from both Protestant and Catholic literary traditions and created a secular, non-sectarian way of writing Wendish, but it was not popular. The main reason why Handrij Zejler was able to make a success of *Tydźenska Nowina* was his decision to stick to the spelling system with which most of his readers were familiar, the old system used in the Protestant Bible and hymn-books. Before the end of 1848 Zejler had handed over the editorship of *Tydźenska Nowina* to Smoler and from January 1849 its title was converted to the plural *Tydźenske Nowiny*. Smoler immediately set about increasing sales, and by 1850 the circulation had reached 1,000. In 1850 he opened his own bookshop and became the paper's publisher. From 1854 the title was *Serbske Nowiny* 'Wendish News' (Rauch 1959: 40, 57, 65).

Handrij Zejler (1804–1872) was pastor of Lohsa, in Prussian Upper Lusatia from 1835 to the end of his life. In 1830 he had published a *Kurzgefaßte Grammatik der Sorben-Wendischen Sprache nach dem Budissiner Dialekte* 'Concise Grammar of the Sorb-Wendish Language according to the Budissin Dialect', but even before this he had begun writing poetry, including poems which were to become classics of Wendish literature. In 1844 he met the young composer Korla Awgust Kocor (1822–1904) and together, inspired by Joseph Haydn's oratorio *Die Jahreszeiten* 'The Seasons' and James Thomson's *The Seasons* (on which Haydn's work is based), they conceived the idea of a Wendish oratorio celebrating the yearly progress of Nature and agriculture. The resulting five cycles of poems are collectively called *Počasy abo Boža stwórba a člowjeske žiwjenje* 'The Seasons or God's Creation and Human Life'.

Another newspaper, *Serbski Nowinkar*, first appeared in March 1848. By the end of May it had 600 subscribers, but on 12 August the same year it ceased publication (Völkel 1984: 38–9, 182). By the terms of the new press laws, which required only the registration of the paper and the name of the editor, it was not subject to censorship and was shockingly open in its condemnation of the feudal hierarchy and its support for the Frankfurt parliament. The first Wendish newspaper in Lower Lusatia also appeared in the revolutionary year 1848, but its arrival was facilitated by counter-revolutionary forces. The Cottbus district governor (*Landrat*) von Schönfeld, supported by the Prussian Ministry of the Interior, was its originator. *Bramborski serbski casnik* 'Brandenburg Wendish Newspaper', a political weekly, first appeared on 5 July 1848. Its editor was Matthias Nauke (Mato Nowka), pastor of Madlow, on the edge of Cottbus and its aim was to exert a calming influence in a time of revolutionary agitation. The editor's job was to support the status quo and it was October 1850 before it started to deal with news of real interest to the Wends, notably by reporting with approval the song festival in Bautzen. The number of readers was very small: 90 in 1863, 230–250 in 1867. Gradually news from the Wendish villages grew, and in 1864 Kito Šwjela took over as editor. It changed its name in 1881 to *Bramborske Nowiny* 'Brandenburg News' and in 1885 to *Bramborski Casnik* 'Brandenburg Newspaper' (Rauch 1959: 58–64; Völkel 1984: 43–8, 182–3).

Wendish song festivals (1845)

One of the signs of these turbulent times was the discovery and cult of folklore. There was an unprecedented interest in the folk-song. In September 1842 Handrij Zejler reported in *Tydźenska Nowina* on the great festivals of song being held Dresden and elsewhere. He proposed the organization of similar festivals for the Wendish people in both Upper and Lower Lusatia, suggesting that through song and music they might be helped in the 'improvement, retention, and unfolding of their love of life and its national Lusatian spirit' (quoted in Hartstock 1977: 54).

On 17 October 1845 the first Wendish Song Festival was held in the spacious hall of the Bautzen Rifle Club (*Schießhaus*) under the direction of K. A. Kocor. The choir was made up mostly of schoolmasters from the whole of Saxon and Prussian Upper Lusatia. Of the audience the weekly *Erzähler an der Spree* reported: 'They were not only Wends, in whose mother-tongue the singing was to take place there publicly, but mainly Germans [...]' Most of the songs performed were not folk-songs but new compositions by Kocor to texts by Zejler and Smoler (Zwahr 1984: 209).

The following year on 7 August a second festival was held, this time in the Bautzen 'Three Limes' Hotel (*Gasthof zu den Drei Linden*). The *Erzähler an der Spree* (14 August 1846) reported that there were now over 120 singers, both male and female. This showed 'that the love of the cause, nationality, is beginning to become more widespread, that gradually slumbering spirits, rousing each other into action, are waking to new life'. After the singing there was a banquet with toasts in Wendish and German, and at one o'clock in the morning the ball began, in which about a hundred couples participated. The ladies were wearing rosettes with the national colours. This is one of the earliest indications of the existence of Wendish national colours (Zwahr 1984: 211). A slightly later reference tells us that they were blue, white, and red (*Camenzer Wochenschrift*, 29 June 1848, quoted in Hartstock 1965: 132–3). The dancing went on till 5 o'clock.

A few months later the third Wendish Song Festival was held in Hoyerswerda (in Prussia). Ten further concerts of songs took place between 1845 and 1851, and two more in 1860 and 1861 (Hartstock 1977: 54–5). Of the sixth Wendish song festival, which took place on 11 October 1848 in Löbau, the *Sächsischer Postillon* (15 October 1848, p. 611) wrote: 'the high and the low, the rich and the poor, local people and people from afar, Germans and Wends were overcome by a feeling, a longing for brotherly concord' (Hartstock 1977: 104n.).

Old Lutherans

The Protestant churches early in the century were experiencing a growing enthusiasm for individual, private devotions or conventicles, with an emphasis on emotion. They were called, among other things, *erweckte Christen* 'awakened Christians'. At the same time, many believers were pre-occupied with questions of orthodoxy. The Consistory of the Lutheran Church in Saxony was in some circles regarded as excessively liberal. In Prussia a new crisis among the Lutherans arose, when on 27 September 1817, to mark the third centenary of the Reformation, King Friedrich Wilhelm III announced his intention to merge the Lutheran and Reformed (Calvinist) churches in his kingdom into a single church, and in 1830, on the 300th anniversary of the Augsburg Confession, a unified form of service was introduced throughout Prussia, including Wendish parishes (Clark 2006: 415). Some Prussian Lutherans, unable to accept the doctrinal compromise, broke away from the state church, and formed their own parishes. They were called the *Evangelisch-lutherische Kirche Altpreußens*, colloquially known as *Altlutheraner* 'Old Lutherans', and were especially numerous in Silesia. After suffering the imposition of fines, imprisonment, and other forms of persecution, some of them decided to emigrate overseas, and, even after 1845, when the Prussian state agreed to tolerate their existence, emigration continued. There were other reasons for emigrating. The 1840s were lean years and the land was overpopulated. There was widespread hunger.

Just inside Prussia following the 1815 adjustment of the frontier lay the Wendish village of Weigersdorf, forming part of the parish of Groß Radisch. When the new form of service was introduced here in 1830 no one seemed to notice. Then, one day, around 1841, the cobbler Andreas Urban, returning home from Spremberg after buying leather there, brought the people of Weigersdorf news of resistance to the unified church and the realization that Pastor Mischner in Groß Radisch by holding services according to the new united form had caused them unwittingly to stray from the true Lutheran doctrine. The village schoolmaster Andreas Dutschmann (born Purschwitz 1808) succeeded in persuading Pastor Mischner to return to the traditional Lutheran form. From somewhere Mischner must have received a reminder, however, and he soon reverted to the form prescribed by the state (T. Malinkowa 1999: 103).

Urban, to ease his conscience, began to attend services over the border in the nearby Saxon parish of Kotitz, where the pastor was Jan Kilian (1811–1884). The cobbler Urban and the schoolmaster Dutschmann studied the arguments of the Lutheran separatists and sought Kilian's advice. Kilian translated for Urban the articles of faith of the Old Lutherans into Wendish. Before long a group of people had decided to break with the Prussian State Church, to abandon the Groß Radisch parish, and to form a new, truly Lutheran parish (T. Malinkowa 1999: 103). Kilian made contact with the Prussian Old Lutherans and Pastor Geßner from Lower Silesia, who had just spent five years in gaol for his resistance, agreed to care for the new parish of Weigersdorf, which was founded on 1 May 1843 with fourteen members from the villages of Weigersdorf and Dauban. More members were admitted from the nearby Prussian village of Klitten. Pastor Geßner made quarterly visits and held services in the houses of Andreas Urban in Weigersdorf and the Lehnig family in Ölsa, near Klitten (T. Malinkowa 1999: 103). Kilian agreed to be the pastor of the new parish, but this meant he would have to leave Saxony and become a subject of the king of Prussia. His application to do so was at first rejected (1844), but in 1845 Friedrich Wilhelm IV defused the situation throughout Prussia by offering a general amnesty and granting Lutherans the right to establish themselves as autonomous church associations (Clark 2006: 419). In 1847 Kilian received official permission to serve the Weigersdorf parish as well as Kotitz. The movement had meanwhile spread, leading in 1846 and 1847 respectively to the construction of two new churches in Weigersdorf and Klitten. On 14 May 1848 Kilian was granted Prussian citizenship, and at Michaelmas he took leave of his Kotitz congregation and moved across the frontier to Dauban (T. Malinkowa 1999: 104).

In Saxony Wendish dissatisfaction with the state church was notably present in the village of Drehsa (in the parish of Gröditz), where the wheelwright Johann Zwahr (Jan Swora) and the blacksmith Johann Stosch (Jan Stoš) lived. They founded Lutheran societies representing conservative opinion in Rachlau, Purschwitz, Neschwitz, and Siebitz (T. Malinkowa 1999: 11). In Klilian's own parish, in the village of Särka in 1848, the 'awakened Christians' organized a petition against the proposed release of village schools from church supervision (T. Malinkowa 1999: 11). In both Prussia and Saxony many Wends feared that the pure Lutheran doctrine was under threat from the state churches.

Students' societies

The emancipation in Upper Lusatia was followed by an increase in the number of Wendish societies. Between 1838 and 1847 seven new societies sprang up, followed by twenty-five in one year in 1848 (Musiat 2001: 19–40). The statutes of a Wendish Society at the Bautzen Gymnasium with the title *Societas Slavica Budissinensis* 'The Bautzen Slav Society' received official recognition in 1839, but groups of Wendish boys are known to have held meetings there well before that. An informal society of this kind, led by Jan Ernst Smoler, used to meet between 1832 and 1836. When Smoler left in 1836 it became dormant until revived by Karl August von Aehrenfeld (Korla Awgust z Kłosopólski) in 1839 with statutes approved by the Rector (Figure 6.1).

The purpose of the society was simply to cultivate the Wendish language (K. A. Jenč 1865: 257), but its horizons were immediately broadened by a visit from Ľudovít Štúr (1815–1856), the future leader of the Slovak national movement, who at that time was a student at Halle and had travelled to Bautzen to find out if the Wends in Lusatia were still alive. He was delighted to discover that they were not only alive but also very active and had just founded their *Societas Slavica*. He made a stirring speech and gave them the

Figure 6.1 Jan Ernst Smoler (1816–1884).

names and addresses of other Slav activists. They thus began to correspond with (among others) Jan Kollár, the author of *Slavy dcera*, a work of Pan-Slav sentiments, in which the Wends make an appearance. He found ready ground among the Bautzen Wends for his doctrine of Slav reciprocity. In 1862–1863 the society was briefly closed down on grounds of supected Pan-Slav activity (Hartstock 1977: 52; K. A. Jenč 1865: 260–1; Musiat 2001: 50).

When Smoler arrived in Breslau as a student in 1836 he at once set about establishing a society among the Wendish students there, and was persuaded to open it to both Wends and Lusatian Germans. The *Akademischer Verein für lausitzische Geschichte und Sprache* 'Academic Society for Lusatian History and Language' was supported and encouraged by two of the University's professors, both Czechs, Jan Evangelista Purkyně (1787–1869), professor of physiology, and František Ladislav Čelakovský (1799–1852), professor of Slavonic philology. Further Wendish students' societies came into existence at the Bautzen Teachers' Seminary (*Verein wendischer Seminaristen*, founded 1839) and at the Wendish Seminary in Prague (*Serbowka*, founded 1846) (Musiat 2001: 42–5, 52–5, 57–64). Few of the Wends who later achieved prominence in the national movement did not pass through one of these societies. They were hotbeds of devotion to the Wendish cause. The predominance of Saxon Wends among the national leaders reflects the relative rarity of students' societies, indeed, of societies of any kind in Prussia (Musiat 2001: 7). The Breslau society was a significant exception, but it was disbanded in 1850. Rarest of all were Wendish societies in Lower Lusatia (Musiat 2001: 129–30).

Florian Ceynowa (1817–1881)

The Kashubs in the nineteenth century continued their traditional silence up to the 1850s, when, for the first time, an individual Kashub made himself heard. This was Florian Ceynowa, who attempted, single-handed, to follow the example of the Lusatian Wends in creating a national movement. He was born on 4 May 1817 in Slawoschin (Sławoszyno), near Putzig (Puck), the son of a free peasant. He entered the Catholic gymnasium at Konitz (Chojnice), where instruction was exclusively in German, though the school records show his native language as Polish (Roppel 1967: 5). The Konitz gymnasium had links with the University of Breslau and it was here that he matriculated in 1841 to study medicine. He joined the *Slavisch-literarische Gesellschaft* 'Slav literary society', whose activities were supervised by Jan Evangelista Purkyně (1787–1869), Dean of the Medical Faculty. Purkyně has already appeared in our narrative as a supporter of Smoler's Lusatian Society. The cult of Panslavism in Breslau had a profound effect on Ceynowa. He attended the lectures of Čelakovský and it is possible that his acquaintance with the Russian scholar I. I. Sreznevskij dates from this time (Karnowski 1921: 103). He also met Smoler (Szultka 2012: 54; Řezník 2012: 108–9, 119).

From 1843 he performed obligatory military service in Königsberg as an army surgeon in the Prussian artillery before continuing his medical studies at Königsberg University. In 1846 he participated in an unsuccessful uprising and following his arrest spent about eight months in prison in Graudenz (Grudziądz), awaiting trial. From here he was transferred to the Moabit Prison in Berlin and on 2 August 1847 the trial began against the 254 conspirators. As one of the ringleaders, Ceynowa was condemned to death. Before King Friedrich Wilhelm IV could confirm the sentence, however, in March 1848 revolution broke out in Berlin and the king was forced to grant an amnesty. Ceynowa was released (Neureiter 1978: 30–1).

Unable to continue his studies in Königsberg, he now spent some time with his sister and her husband in Putzig, continuing his field-work among the Kashubs, and in 1850 he sent to Sreznevskij a manuscript of his collection of Kashub words which, in his opinion, bore 'a greater similarity to Russian than to Polish' (Karnowski 1921: 103). In 1851 he gained the title of Doctor of Medicine from the University of Berlin on the basis of a thesis in which he examined various Kashubian folk customs in the medical field and argued against superstition (Neureiter 1978: 39). Newly qualified, he was appointed physician to the house of Count Hutten-Czapski in Bukowitz (Bukowiec) near Schwetz (Świecie), but a dispute over a question of professional confidentiality involving the Count's daughter led to his dismissal. He was deprived of the right to practise medicine. To keep the wolf from the door he acquired a small-holding and, despite threats and penalties, continued to practise. How he got away with this or whether his licence was restored is not known, but his medical skills were respected by his patients and he often gave his services free of charge to the poor (Neureiter 1978: 40). His Kashubian studies continued, and in 1856 he received a significant visit from the Russian scholar Alexandr Fedorovič Hilferding (1831–1872). In the summer of 1861 he undertook a long journey, first to Bautzen to visit his friend, Jan Ernst Smoler, and then to Prague to see the Czech poet, Karel Jaromír Erben (1811–1870) (Neureiter 1978: 40–2) (Figure 6.2).

In the years following the Polish uprising of 1863 against the Russians, Ceynowa was a frequent visitor to Konitz and Neustadt (Wejherowo). In these two towns the gymnasiums were attended by young men from the Kashub area, and Ceynowa made efforts to find among them supporters for his cause. They would meet in the house of one of the boys or a hotel, where beer, wine, cigars, and cakes would be provided. Songs would be sung, including his Kashubian translation of Fedor Ivanovič Tjutčev's Panslav poem 'Shall we forever separated be'. Ceynowa would then propound his message to the effect that the only hope of protection against Germanization was the friendly hand of the Russians. Most of those present rejected his views, but, undismayed, he would press copies of his pamphlets on them before taking his leave (Pobłocki 1908–1909: 136–7).

In 1867 an ethnographic exhibition was due to be held in Moscow and a group of Russians decided to organize, in conjunction with the exhibition, a conference of representatives of all the Slav countries. With Russian government support and funds at their disposal, committees were set up in St Peterburg and Moscow. Invitations were sent out, including the offer to pay for travel and maintenance. Most of the recipients accepted the invitation, but the Poles as a group decided to boycott it in protest against Tsarist oppression in Poland. The Lusatian Wends were represented by Jan Ernst Smoler and Pĕtr Dučman, the Kashubs by Florian Ceynowa. It was agreed that before proceeding

Figure 6.2 Florian Ceynowa (1817–1881).

to Russia the foreign participants would all meet in Warsaw and here they elected Smoler as their leader.

The group travelled first to St Petersburg, where the events included, for a select few, including Ceynowa, an audience with Tsar Nicholas II. At a reception in the Hotel Bellevue Ceynowa spoke, emphasizing the unity of the Slavs (Roppel 1968: 253). The correspondent of *Dziennik Poznański* (cited by Karnowski 1921: 107) reported that the Russians present looked on Ceynowa with suspicion, taking him for a Pole. Only when 'some great expert in ethnography explained that the Kashubs are not Poles and hate the Poles as the Russians do', did their hearts warm to him (Karnowski 1921:107). In Moscow, after the opening of the ethnographic exhibition, the Russian Professor Bessonov gave a lecture, in the course of which he praised Ceynowa's work.

On 2 June at a grand reception for almost 800 people in a marquee in Sokolniki Park the atmosphere changed. The poet Tjutčev read a long poem of welcome, but in the speeches by the Russians Pogodin, I. S. Aksakov, and V. Solovev comments were made on the absence of the Poles. Speaking for the Slav guests František Rieger (1818–1903), leader of the Czech group, tried to explain. He advocated peace between the Poles and the Russians and asked the Russians to extend the hand of reconciliation. There were signs of disapproval from the Russians, including shouts and whistling.

Count Vladimir Čerkasskij made an uncompromising speech, in which he accused the Poles of ingratitude. Reconciliation would come only when the Poles gave up the idea of independence and returned, in the role of the Prodigal Son, to the Slav family. At this point Ceynowa sprang up and passed a note to the chairman, requesting the right to speak, but this was denied him under the pretence of procedural niceties. Demonstratively, he walked out of the meeting and the next day left Moscow for home (Roppel 1968: 255; Neureiter 1978: 48–9).

The Moscow episode must have been a sobering experience. Ceynowa continued his literary activities, including the publication in Posen (Poznań) in 1879 of a Kashubian grammar, but nothing further is known of his contacts with his Russian friends, if any. He died in Bukowitz of a heart attack on 26 March 1881 (Neureiter 1978: 49–50).

Ceynowa was an eccentric in more ways than one. His single-handed attempts to create a Kashubian national movement were a signal failure, but he is the first Kashub we know who realized that his native speech was capable of becoming a literary language, separate from Polish. His arrest and trial in 1846–1847 qualify him as a Polish patriot, yet his sense of nationality was distinct from that of a Pole. The Kashubs having much in common with the Lusatian Wends thanks to their shared struggle against Germanization, he might have been expected to find common cause with Jan Ernst Smoler, but in fact little is known of their relationship. At Breslau they must have known each other through their links with Purkyně, Čelakovský, and others, but on what grounds Smoler is described as Ceynowa's friend (Neureiter 1978: 42; Kunze 1995: 75) is not known.

His attempts to create a Kashubian literary language earned him accusations from Poles of separatism. But the Slavophil precepts which he shared with Smoler and the other participants in the 1867 conference were based, not on the assertion of the individuality of Slav languages, but on the belief that there was really only one Slav language, which had many dialects (Brock 1992: 185). Smoler was on many occasions moved by accusations of Panslavism to declare his loyalty to Saxony and Germany. Ceynowa, on the other hand, was not loyal to the Prussian state, as he had shown in 1846–1847, and this may have been a barrier between him and Smoler. Thanks to Ceynowa we know that in his time the western limit of the Kashub language in Pomerania was the River Wipper (Wieprza). Writing in German, but eschewing the word *wendisch*, he used *kaschubisch* for the language which (he maintained) had been once 'spoken in the whole of Pomerania and perhaps in the land of the Obodriti too'; but he said a preferable term was *pommersch-slavisch* (Ceynowa 1850/2001: 170).

Slovincians

When the Russian scholar Alexandr Fedorovič Hilferding (1831–1872) arrived in West Prussia in 1856 to study the language and ethnography of the Kashubs, his guide was Ceynowa. They travelled together from Danzig as far as Bütow (Bytów), where Ceynowa left him. Hilferding then pursued his journey unaccompanied, finishing with the Hel (Hela) Peninsula (Gil´ferding 1862: 3). His trip included a visit to a number of Protestant villages in the extreme west, in the vicinity of Lake Garde (Gardna) and Lake Leba (Łeba), including Schmolsin (Smoldzino), Garde (Gardna), Virchenzin (Wierzchocino), and Klucken (Kluki). These villages, isolated by swamps from the main Kashubian area, had been part of the Duchy of Pomerania. He was interested to discover that the people here called their language *Slovinsko mova* or *szproka* (his transcription) (Gil´ferding 1862: 9n.). Although he also heard comments of the kind 'The Slovincian language (or the Kashubian language) and Polish are one and the same; we have Polish books, our church services are Polish', he noted that the word *polski* was applied only to language and only in the sense that they had Polish religious books. The Slovincians and Kashubs never called themselves Poles. In the village Giesebitz (Izbicy) he even heard a different word to describe the language of the Poles. 'We speak Polish,' they said, 'but *Polacka mova* is different'. In the same village he was told: 'Kashubs and Slovincians are the same' (Gil´ferding 1862: 21n.).

On the Kashubs generally Hilferding concluded that, with the exception of some on the borders of Great Poland, 'they do not feel and are not conscious of their connection with the Polish people' and 'do not feel in themselves any inner bond with the land of Poland', though they attend mass with a Polish missal and know their language is similar to Polish (Gil´ferding 1862: 14). From Ostend on 21 August (2 September) he wrote to Sreznevskij about his visit to the Leba and Gardener Lakes, reporting that he had found 'a new Slav dialect; not Kashubian, but Slovincian', located 'beyond the marshes (as they say of them), where the type of nationality is quite different from the Polish and Kashubian' and where the people called themselves 'Slovinstji ledze' (Bulakhov 1976: 70).

In his assessment of the Kashubs' inability or reluctance to identify with the Poles Hilferding says nothing of the unwillingness of many Poles to accept the Kashubs. Hieronim Derdowski (1852–1902), the second Kashubian writer of note after Ceynowa, in his humorous verse epic *O panu Czôrlińscim co do Pucka po sece jachoł* 'About Mr Czarlinski who rode to Putzig to get nets', represents those Kashubs who did think of themselves as Poles but found themselves rejected. His hero, Pan Czarlinski, recalling a visit to Warsaw, says:

When I was with the merchants in Warsaw about a year ago,
They would not believe that I was their compatriot.
They thought I belonged – may God forgive them! –
To the tribe from which the black rat-trap makers come,
And they would not offer me their hand in brotherhood,
Though I am a Pole, heart and soul, as they are.
We Kashubs still guard the coastal border of Poland,
But our brothers in Warsaw look down on us.
(*Ciéjm z kupcami we Warszawie bywôł tak przed rociem,*
Téj nie chcelë mnie tam wierzëc, że jem jëch rodôciem.
Liczëlë mnie – niechże za to Pón Bóg jëch nie kôrze! –
Do tij rózdżi, z chtórnyj wëszlë czôrni łapiczkôrze

I nie chcelë mnie téż wcôle podac bratnij dłoni,
A jô z dusz i ze sercem Polôk jem, jak oni.
Më Kaszubë, jesz strzeżemë Polscij morsciëch granic,
A w Warszawie naszy bracô mają naju za nic.)

(Derdowski 1960: 126)

The Maćica Serbska

At the instigation of Jan Ernst Smoler at Easter 1845 a meeting was held at an inn called the *Winica* (Vineyard), near Bautzen, to consider the foundation of a Wendish scholarly and scientific association, to be organized on the lines of such bodies already existing in other Slavonic countries. The first of them had appeared in Serbia in 1826 and was called the *Matica Srpska*, using the Serbian word *matica* 'queen bee' as a symbol of fecundity. Even before the meeting Smoler had drawn up a draft constitution, which was approved by a committee elected by the meeting. However, the *Maćica Serbska* 'Wendish Maćica', as it was to be called, had to wait for the approval of the authorities in both Saxony and Prussia, and it was therefore not until 7 April 1847, at a further meeting in Bautzen, that it was properly established with Adolf Klien as the first president and Smoler as a member of the committee.

The Maćica saw the publication of Wendish literature as one of its main tasks, partly to enlighten the general public and partly for scholarly purposes. It issued its own journal, the *Časopis Maćicy Serbskeje*, beginning in 1848, and organized meetings for the discussion of cultural and scientific matters. In the first year of its existence the membership was sixty-four and within seven years it had grown to 220. Gradually, separate sections were founded, each dealing with one particular branch of study. The linguistic section was created in 1853/4, and was followed by special sections for the study of natural history, literature, national economy, pedagogy, demography, music, etc. Over the years the Maćica was responsible for the publication of many books, ranging from dictionaries, grammars, and school-books to imaginative literature. It was predominantly middle class and non-sectarian, with a strong clerical contingent, both Protestant and Catholic. There were a number of foreign members, mostly from other Slavonic countries (Muka 1923: 37–42).

The question of premises for the Maćica was first discussed in 1861 (*Wućahi* 1862: 57), and by the time of the 1866 Easter meeting the need for a place to keep the library, antiquities, and other collections was said to be urgent. In 1869 the committee issued an appeal for contributions to a special fund for the purpose of buying a suitable building. The first contributor was Handrij Zejler, who immediately gave 50 thalers, and in 1870 the *Časopis Maćicy Serbskeje* 'Journal of the Wendish Maćica' began to publish lists of contributions and the names of contributors (Bryl-Serbin 1924: 20–2). In 1873 Smoler, at his own risk, purchased from a Bautzen farmer, an old house with a barn and large yard on the corner of Lauengraben and Äußere Lauenstraße. The price was 20,000 thalers (60,000 marks). He had a mortgage of 14,000 thalers, but the remaining 6,000 thalers had to be paid by the end of the year. An extraordinary general meeting in 1873 unanimously approved his action, resolved that the Maćica's home should be built on the site as soon as possible, and decided to step up efforts to raise money (Bryl-Serbin 1924: 23).

It was Smoler who decided on the name *Serbski Dom* 'Wendish House'. Having moved into the house himself together with his bookshop, he travelled to Moscow and St Petersburg in search of wealthy benefactors. By 1874 the mortgage had been significantly reduced; but only a few years later the Maćica found itself in serious financial trouble, when one of its Russian backers went bankrupt and it discovered that the house and its contents were at risk of being sold off to pay his debts (Bryl-Serbin 1924: 28). Smoler was sixty-five years old, but in the autumn of 1881 he set off for Russia again, still hoping to find benefactors there. The prospect of a Wendish House in the centre of Bautzen had by now caused displeasure in certain German circles, and Smoler's journeys to Russia roused accusations of a Panslav plot. The German press falsely accused him of accepting gifts from Russians for personal gain. While in Russia he fell ill. He was not fit to return home until 1883 and the following year he died.

The financial situation improved a little and by 1885 the Maćica was drawing a modest profit from letting the property, but this could make only a small contribution towards paying off the mortgage. Meanwhile, further small sums continued to come in steadily from collections made among the people, as the lists of thousands of contributors published at this time in *Serbske Nowiny*, *Łužica*, *Katolski Posoł*, and the *Časopis Maćicy Serbskeje* show. The individual contributions were sometimes in hundreds of marks, sometimes in pfennigs. Arnošt Muka (Karl Ernst Mucke), who had taken over as secretary of the Maćica in 1881, decided to launch a new appeal. In 1882 the new literary journal *Łužica* had been launched with Muka as editor, and he used it as a vehicle for encouraging contributions. In the first year it raised 764 marks, a remarkable achievement (Bryl-Serbin 1924:35).

The Wendish Ethnographic Exhibition, which took place in Dresden as part of the 1896 Exhibition of Saxon Trade and Artistic Endeavour, brought in 3,000 marks. The following year the Maćica celebrated its fiftieth anniversary and it was decided to mark the event by ceremonially laying the foundation stone of the Wendish House. The deed was performed by Jaroměr Imiš in the presence of numerous dignitaries, including the Mayor of Bautzen, Dr Kaeubler, who also spoke expressing good wishes. He was later heard to say that he expected any day to hear the project had gone bankrupt (Bryl-Serbin 1924: 51–2, 96). Once the foundation stone had been laid construction work began. In 1898 the debt on the original purchase was cleared and as the century ended a good part of the building was complete. The library and museum were already in use (Bryl-Serbin 1924: 56–8).

1848: The springtime of nations

In the fateful year of 1848, when in one country after another authority was challenged and set aside, the Wends did not fail to voice their demands. On 17 March 1848 a meeting took place in Lehndorf of peasants from villages belonging to the Marienstern Convent and on 31 March a deputation handed a list of thirteen demands to the Abbess. The tone of the demands was an odd mixture of deference and barely concealed threat: 'Now has the hour come, most honoured lady abbess, when you must show how you mean to treat your subjects [...]. In confidence that a deputation sent from our midst to your highly honoured ladyship will bring us your decisons, we remain in the, as yet, strictest obedience...' (Hartstock 1977: 63). The communities of Demitz, Prischwitz, and Wendischbaselitz refused to pay their dues to the Convent and in reply the Convent offered some minimal concessions, which the peasants did not find acceptable. A new deputation repeated their original demands on 27 April and further concessions were offered, which the peasants still regarded as inadequate.

In mid-May, peasants from the villages whose feudal lord had been the Bautzen Town Council (*Ratsdörfer*) assembled to form a peasant's society (*Bauernverein*). Further societies sprang up in Radibor, Großpostwitz, and Hochkirch. Though their concerns were not primarily ethnic, they usually had the word *serbski/wendisch* in their titles (*Hochkircher Wendischer Bauern-Verein*, etc.) and said in their statutes that anyone could join who could understand Wendish and agreed to follow the rules. The societies were seeking ways of coping with post-emancipation challenges, of getting rid of vestiges of the old order, and of increasing productivity. The need for education was universally felt and appears in all their statutes (Hartstock 1965: 125; Hartstock 1977: 69).

From the Radibor society came a proposal for a composite petition presenting all grievances from all the Wendish societies in Saxony. The secretary Jan Bartko submitted a draft to a meeting on 21 May at which several other villages were represented. Peter Ziesch (Pětr Cyž), on behalf of the villages whose feudal lord had been the Marienstern Nunnery, told the meeting that they too were planning a petition, so it was agreed to circulate the petition in its final version to all the Wendish villages in Saxony. Its twenty-eight demands included the abolition of the Upper Lusatian provincial constitution, of the separate status of the Upper Lusatian nobility, and of the privileges of the owners of manorial estates (*Rittergutsbesitzer*) and lords of the manor (*Grundherrn*). The version submitted bore the signatures of sixty-nine heads of communities (*Gemeinden*) representing at least 3,000 peasants, artisans, and rural proletarians (Hartstock 1977: 75).

Twenty-three Wendish peasant societies are known to have existed (Hartstock 1977: 75). The peasants' petition was directed not to the Government but to the Second Chamber of the Saxon Landtag. Their aim for Germany was, as they put it in *Serbski Nowinkar* of 5 August 1848 (p. 154), 'a democratic republic in which the whole people rule', an ideal which they believed to have been attained in Switzerland and North America. The question of a petition to raise the status of the Wendish language was raised among members of the Maćica, but there was opposition. Nor did everyone even share the opinion that the Wends were the victims of injustice. The opponents of the proposal, led by Friedrich Klien (Bjedrich Klin), were outvoted by a majority led by Smoler. Klien used the columns of *Tydźenska Nowina* to advise all Wends against any hasty action: 'Show your old love of the fatherland and of the king, who loves his faithful Lusatians. Show yourselves to be faithful and true Christians.' Klien, though a Wend, was a Bautzen town councillor, the police director, and the chief censor for the Bautzen Kreis. His opposition to anything that might be remotely considered rebellious was not surprising (Hartstock 1966: 4–5).

Smoler's followers, however, did not think of themselves as rebels. They were merely concerned about the linguistic and cultural inequality suffered by the Wends and understood themselves to have been given permission to make requests to the authorities. As they explained in their petition to the Saxon government led by the liberal Prime Minister, Alexander Braun: 'Since the roaring tempest has now passed and you have allowed the whole people to approach you with confident requests, we Wends too approach you to pour out our hearts before you' (Hartstock 1966: 6). The principal plea of the Maćica's petition was 'that our beloved nationality and mother tongue be not only protected against any restriction, but be much promoted so as to achieve its deserved status'. Specific proposals were made relating to the rights of the Wendish language in schools, churches, and the administration of justice. The petition was signed by almost 5,000 heads of household. This was an exclusively Saxon matter. Wends who lived in Prussia or were Prussian subjects, including Smoler and Handrij Zejler, were not qualified to sign. A delegation travelled to Dresden and handed the petition to Braun on 26 July 1848. His main concern being to calm the agitated masses, he naturally promised that everything necessary to the well-being of the Wends would be done (Hartstock 1966: 68).

Johann Miertsching

Since the 1730s the Moravians of Herrnhut had been sending missionaries to remote parts of the world (see Chapter 5) and they continued to do so throughout the nineteenth century. Although many of the missionaries were Wends, it is not always easy to distinguish them from Germans. The best known and best documented Wendish missionary is Jan August Miertsching (1817–1875), who achieved fame through his contribution as interpreter to an English Arctic expedition in 1850–1854. He was born at Gröditz on 21 August 1817 and at the age of fifteen was sent to Kleinwelka, where he learned the trade of a shoemaker. In 1844–1849 he spent five years with the Moravian mission in Labrador, assisting in a school for Eskimo children and learning their language. At the end of 1849 he had only recently returned to Kleinwelka, when the Mission Board of the Brethren told him of a request from the British Admiralty for the assistance of a missionary competent in the Eskimo language to join a voyage to the Canadian Arctic to renew the search for Sir John Franklin and his men, of whom there had been no news since 1845. The Admirality was of the opinion that the chances of Franklin's crew coming to the notice of the inhabitants of the Arctic were better than of their being found by their countrymen, which meant that the services of an interpreter were essential (Benham 1854: *passim*).

Miertsching arrived in London on 16 January 1850 and proceeded immediately to Plymouth, where he was only just in time to join the *Investigator*, commanded by

Captain Robert McClure, which on 20 January sailed from Plymouth Sound together with the *Enterprise* under the command of Captain Richard Collinson. Miertsching was to remain with the *Investigator* for the next five years. He had time on the voyage to learn English. On 12 April the ships entered the Strait of Magellan and with a fair wind reached Honolulu on 1 July. By 2 August they were in the Arctic Ocean and met their first ice. A few days later they made contact with a party of Eskimos and Miertsching's skill proved its value. From now on they had frequent and useful meetings with Eskimos, but could learn nothing of the fate of Franklin's crew. Proceeding eastwards overland, however, McClure on 26 October 1850 discovered he had reached a point on the shores of Barrow Strait close to the line previously marked on the charts by Sir Edward Parry, proceeding from the east. McClure had thus discovered the North-west Passage. If the ice melted, it would be possible to manoeuvre his ship through Barrow Strait and sail for England.

But the ice, even in the summer next year, allowed the *Investigator* very little mobility. By the end of September 1851 the ship was frozen in, never to move again. The crew waited in vain for summer 1852 to release them from the ice, and after a further year of immobility the situation was desperate. McClure in March 1853 decided to divide the crew into three parties, two of which would set out on foot – one heading for Port Leopold, the second aiming for Fort Good Hope. The remainder would stay with the ship and wait for another summer. By now everyone on board was suffering from scurvy.

On 7 April departure was imminent, when a sailor reported sighting in the distance a black moving object. Hopes rose that it might be an Eskimo. They had not seen a human stranger for twenty-one months. At length, a man appeared before them and said in English 'I am Lieutenant Pim of the ship "Resolute"'. They had been rescued by an expedition commanded by Captain H. Kellett approaching from the east. Kellett's ships the *Resolute* and *Intrepid*, however, were also frozen in and it was the end of August 1854 before Miertsching with McClure and other members of the crew of the *Investigator*, abandoning their ship, could set sail for England on the *North Star*, casting anchor at Sheerness on 7 October. On 11 November Miertsching left for Kleinwelka (Miertsching 1967: 239).

On 7 October 1856, Miertsching was married at Herrnhut to Clementina Auguste Erxleben and at the end of December that year left with her on further missionary service to South Africa. They returned safely in April 1869 to Kleinwelka, where the family settled and Miertsching died there on 30 March 1875 (Zubor 1975: 97). As a key member of the McClure expedition, a participant in the discovery of the north-west passage, and the author of a popular account of the voyage, Miertsching achieved a degree of fame unusual among the Wends. Yet the fact that he was a Wend is often overlooked. His entry in the *Dictionary of Canadian Biography* says only that he was born 'of German working-class parents' and his Wendish ethnicity is noticeably absent in the version of his arctic diary published in 1855 and re-printed in 1856 and 1864 (*DCB*, s.v.; Miertsching 1967: xii).

The diary's editor, L. H. Neatby, never refers to him as a Wend but calls him 'the young German' (Miertsching 1967: 246). Benham, however, whose biography includes facts and incidents communicated by Miertsching himself, was better informed. He knew that Miertsching's father was a 'Servian Vend' and that Kleinwelka was 'originally established for the religious and moral instruction of those Vends, who, though living in the midst of their German oppressors, are a distinct nation, with a language of their own, which is a dialect of the Sclavonic, and of which they are very tenacious' (Benham 1854: vi, 1). Miertsching himself evidently felt that his role in the discovery of the North-west Passage reflected credit on the Wends, for he wrote under the date 23 April 1853 (when his party was on the march to join the *Intrepid* and *Resolute*): '...all starved and wretched as I was, I could not suppress the proud thought that here in this polar region I was the only Wend from Germany, and that I had had a share in the North-west Passage, sought for 300 years, and now discovered by us' (Miertsching 1967: 195). The corresponding entry in the 1855 version lacks an equivalent for the words 'I was the only Wend from Germany' (Miertsching 1855: 144–5).

In July 2010, Canadian archaeologists found the wreck of HMS Enterprise in Mercy Bay, Northwest Territories. It lies partly buried in silt and the following July it was visited by divers (*Expedition* 2014) (Figure 6.3).

Figure 6.3 Jan Awgust Měrćink (Johann August Miertsching) (1817–1875).

Panslavs versus conservatives

The realization among the Wends that the various Slavonic languages were related goes back at least as far as Michael Frentzel in the seventeenth century, but linguistic kinship cannot have had much significance for the Wendish peasant, while he was illiterate and bound to the soil. Even after emancipation the Panslav idea had to be explained in simple terms:

> Far and wide throughout the great Austrian empire there live many peoples, who together with us Wends belong to one tribe and to one nation, who have the same blood as we Wends and almost the same language. These people live in Galicia, in Bohemia, in Moravia, in Slavonia, in Illyria, in Dalmatia, in Croatia, in the Bukovina, on the Adriatic Sea, and far away in Montenegro. All these peoples are called Slavs. We Wends are also Slavs.

(Serbski Nowinkar 1848: 75)

The omission of any reference here to the Russians or the Poles and the specific mention of Austria arises from the 1848 context, in which the first Slav Congress was being held in Prague, bringing the Panslav idea into the political arena. Some Lusatian Wends embraced it, but sidestepped its political implications. There were no thoughts of political autonomy. As Smoler said at the time of the Franco-Prussian War: 'Politically we are Germans' (R. Jenč 1960: 35), and few of his compatriots would have disagreed. In certain Wendish circles Russophile sentiments were expressed, and even the notion of the Tsar of Russia as the leader of all the Slavs occasionally put in an appearance (Fiedler 1868: 39; R. Jenč 1960: 35), but this way of thinking alarmed the vast majority and won them no friends among their German neighbours, for the spectre of Russian-led Panslavism haunted German public opinion and provoked a perception of the Wends as a Russian fifth column.

Panslavism also affected the Wendish language. In Upper Wendish literature, beginning with Smoler's *Mały Serb* (1841) and the editorial apparatus to his *Volkslieder* (1841), a policy of rejecting of Germanisms and substituting new Slavonic words is apparent. The main source of the new elements is Czech. For example, *lazować* (cf. Ger. *lesen*) 'to read' was replaced by the neologism *čitać* (cf. Czech *čítati*) and *štunda* (cf. Ger. *Stunde*) 'hour' made way for *hodźina* (cf. Czech *hodina*). This process, which was also extended to grammar, erected a barrier between the language of the new literature and the spoken language. It created a gulf between secular and devotional literature, and became a regular cause of discord.

Until the 1840s, Wendish literature was almost entirely devotional in content and its language followed orthographic traditions going back to Michael Frentzel and Ticin. There was still a separate Catholic spelling system, but all printing used Gothic type. As early as 1841, however, Smoler experimented with a new orthography, using letters taken from Czech and Polish and printed in Latin type. A new system which was neither

Protestant nor Catholic was a means of crossing the confessional divide. Readers, however, were set in their ways, so the Maćica provided them with books on secular themes but printed in the old Protestant orthography. The newspaper *Serbske Nowiny* too used the old system for fear of losing its readers.

Because it had been devised by analogy with Czech and Polish spelling conventions, the new system was called 'analogical' (*analogisch*). The old system used in devotional books was called the Bible system. Smoler and many members of the Maćica favoured the use of the analogical system for secular literature, but were aware of popular resistance to it. Therefore, in 1858, when Smoler introduced it to *Serbske Nowiny*, he did so unobtrusively in a monthly supplement. The previous year the first fascicle of a Wendish-German dictionary had appeared and this too, having the new reading public in mind, used the new orthography. The next part of the plan was the replacement in 1860 of the monthly supplement to *Serbske Nowiny* by a new monthly literary magazine called *Łužičan*, also printed in the new orthography. Though *Serbske Nowiny* was still printed in the old orthography, its readers would already have noticed in it the arrival of new, unfamiliar words, grammatical forms, and constructions taken from Czech. *Łužičan*, however, went further along this route, using the new vocabulary and grammar, as well as the new orthography. It made a point, moreover, of discussing these innovations and advocating their use.

There were also religious magazines. The Protestant monthly *Misionske Powěsće* appeared from 1844 to 1849, edited by Handrij Zejler. It was replaced by the weekly *Zernička* from 1849 to 1852 and this was succeeded from 1854 by the monthly *Missionski Posoł*. The Catholic monthly (later fortnightly) *Katolski Posoł* was only launched in 1863. All these naturally stuck to their traditional spelling systems and were printed in Gothic type. Advocates of the analogical spelling system not only saw it as a weapon to breach the wall between the confessions, they also wanted the Wends to be aware that they were Slavs. They hoped, furthermore, to attract the attention of other Slav peoples. The new spelling, however, had few supporters. They were mostly to be found in the Maćica, though even here support was not unanimous. Outside the Maćica most people were resistant to it. They were used to reading their Bibles, hymn-books, church magazines, and *Serbske Nowiny* all printed in the old system. It would be hard to make them change their ways, but the first editor of *Łužičan*, Michał Hórnik (a Catholic priest), made it clear that the popularization of the new spelling was one of his primary objectives, emphasizing its ecumenical function. He sought controversy and criticized the old spelling used in *Misionski Posoł* (Völkel 1984: 55).

Misionski Posoł had many more readers than *Łužičan*, but even among those that did not read *Łužičan* the word got around that there were plans to extend the use of the new orthography, possibly even to religious texts. This was disturbing; so to reassure his readers the editor of *Misionski Posoł*, Pastor Jan Rudolf Rychtar (1809–after 1886), announced in June 1863: 'I am certain that none of my brothers of the cloth will ever permit the Bible, the hymn-book, the Catechism or any of the edifying books promised by our book society to be printed for the Wendish people in any orthography other than that used hitherto' (Rychtar 1863: 86; J. Cyž 1977: 195). He was reacting to the views of readers who had noticed even in *Misionski Posoł* 'new, incomprehensible or unfamiliar Wendish words'. He told his readers that Wendish writing must avoid German words for which a good Wendish equivalent existed. His attitude to what he called 'new Wendish words' (i.e. mainly words borrowed from Czech) was not hostile, but he asked his contributors to gloss them with their German equivalents in brackets (Rychtar 1863: 87). Hórnik, however, condemned Rychtar's display of understanding for his readers' fears and his assurance that the new spelling would not be used in religious texts.

The Estates' Teacher Seminary in Bautzen (founded 1817) from 1834 had its own Wendish teacher. From 1849 the post was held by Smoler, who brought with him the distinction of having recently taught Prince (later king) Albert of Saxony. From 1858 it was taken over by Korla Awgust Fiedler, a follower of the reform movement. Here he was clearly in a position to influence orthographic developments. In 1863, the *Societas slavica Budissinensis* at the Bautzen Gymnasium was refounded and a teacher was appointed to instruct it members in Wendish. This was Jan Korla Mróz, Deacon at the Wendish church of St Michael in Bautzen and a traditionalist. He did not like Catholics and was known to have resigned from the Maćica because it admitted them. He had also excluded a Catholic from his Wendish lessons on sectarian grounds (J. Cyž 1977: 197).

In 1863 the issue of spelling reform was discussed in the columns of *Serbske Nowiny*, Mróz representing the conservative view, Fiedler the reformist. Smoler, who had the very rare distinction of having studied Slavonic languages at a university, was also a reformer. He even advocated the linguistic reform of Wendish religious texts and said the clergy should be educated in the philology of their native tongue. To prove his point, in 1864 he published a slim volume in which he argued that existing Wendish translations of a sentence from the Athanasian Creed (*Spiritus sanctus a Patre et Filio, non factus nec creatus nec genitus est, sed procedens* 'The Holy Ghost is from the Father and from the Son, neither made, nor created, nor begotten, but proceeding') were inaccurate (Schmaler 1864: 12–18).

Smoler's knowledge of Slavonic philology, however, was limited. Under Čelakovský at Breslau he appears to have gained the impression that perfective verbs are not capable of having a present tense. He found cases in the Wendish hymnal where 'est procedens' was conveyed as *wuńdźe* 'proceeds' (perfective present) and mistakenly condemned this as incorrect, asserting that it should be *je wuchadźacy*. Smoler's readers must have been confused by this assertion, which will surely have countered their native-speaker's intuition (not to mention his) (Wornar 1999: 169–70). The more talk there was of reform, the more alarmed the people became. In January 1864 it was reported that signatures were being collected for a petition to Rychtar, demanding that he retain the old spelling and that the authorities be asked to insist on its being taught. There were rumours that spelling had theological implications (J. Cyž 1977:198).

Four years later, signatures were again being collected for a petition, addressed this time to the Bautzen *Kreisdirektion* and requesting official support for the retention of the old orthography in religious books. Organized by the blacksmith Andreas Stosch (Handrij Stoš) of Drehsa in the parish of Gröditz to the east of Bautzen, the petition attacked Smoler, Fiedler, and the Maćica. Smoler reacted in the pages of *Serbske Nowiny* (April 1868), asserting that the petition was being masterminded surreptitiously by someone in Bautzen but that neither Stosch nor his anonymous backer was 'competent to decide how the Wendish language should be used, written, or taught'. The man behind the scenes was 'leading simple people astray in a diabolic manner'. In the parish of Gröditz alone in the month of June 1868, it proved possible to collect 252 signatures of adult males (J. Cyž 1977: 199).

The petitioners asked for the protection of the *Kreisdirektion* against the innovators in the Maćica Serbska, who (they said) wished to unite the Wends spiritually with the 'the Russian peoples as their Slav brothers'. They demanded that members of the Maćica (because it was confessionally mixed) should have no influence on the revision of Protestant religious books and that, because the new orthography was a link in the Panslav chain, anything published in it, especially *Łužičan*, should be banned in places of public education, particularly at the Estates' Teacher Seminary in Bautzen. The Wends (they argued) had no reason to enter any spiritual union with the Slav peoples and no intention of doing so. At the time of the Stosch campaign, a new edition of the Upper Wendish hymnal was in preparation and had reached the proof stage with the Bautzen printing firm Ernst Moritz Monse. The petitioners wished to be assured that Monse would not be permitted to print it in anything other than the traditional orthography, and that correction of the proofs would be entrusted to clergymen who were not members of the Maćica. There was also concern at the new *Prjenja Cžitanka* 'First Reader' which had recently been introduced to schools and contained passages in the new spelling. The petition requested that in any new edition these be removed and that the book's title be changed to *Knischki k prjenjemu Lasowanju* 'A Book for First Reading', eliminating the stigmatized Czech word *čítanka* 'reader' (J. Cyž 1977: 199-201).

The connection made in the petition between the new spelling and Panslavism was not an invention of Stosch and his followers. It had already been made by Fiedler in *Łužičan*. In the issue for December 1866 (187-8) he wrote: 'So let us assert above all that we should unite spiritually with our Slav brothers. Then we shall be a living branch on the mightly tree of Slavdom [...].' Fiedler's words had had the opposite of the effect intended. Spiritual unity with the other Slavs was not what the people of Gröditz wanted. Smoler responded to the petitioners in *Serbske Nowiny*, exhorting the signatories to withdraw their signatures and threatened those that did not do so with legal action for libel (J. Cyž 1977: 201). Stosch and company, however, flushed with success, now had further copies of the petition printed and distributed for signature. Smoler reacted with another booklet, *Die Schmähschrift des Schmiedmeisters Stosch gegen die sprachwissenschaftlichen Wenden, beleuchtet vom Standpunkt der Wissenschaft und Wahrheit* 'Master Blacksmith Stosch's Libel against the Philological Wends Illuminated from the Point of View of Learning and Truth' (Bautzen, 1868), defending Fiedler and alluding again to an anonymous author hiding behind Stosch. Although he does not name him, Smoler suspected Jan Korla Mróz, Deacon of St Michael's Church, Bautzen. In addition to the Gröditz petition, Stosch and his supporters collected more than 2,100 further signatures from fourteen parishes (J. Cyž 1977: 204-5).

On 16 October 1868, the *Kreisdirektion* asked Monse in what form he was proposing to print the new hymnal and requested a set of the proofs. Monse replied that the book would be printed in traditional form. The proofs had been read by several Lutheran clergymen and a few corrections made, mainly in the interest of consistency. The *Kreisdirektion* also wrote to I. G. W. Leuner, Director of the Estates' Seminary, asking for an explanation of the methods of teaching Wendish at the Seminary. Leuner, who knew no Wendish and was no friend of the Wends, used the opportunity in his reply to resume an old refrain, namely, the neglect by some Wendish teachers of the German language. He had asked Fiedler to explain his methods and appended Fiedler's report, which he considered satisfactory. Fiedler denied the charge that he taught only the new orthography and said that he taught both systems. In this, he said, he was following the *Kreisdirektion*'s instruction of 10 June 1864 (J. Cyž 1977: 206–8).

The *Kreisdirektion* on 23 October 1868 passed to Friedrich Heinrich Immisch (Jaroměr Hendrich Imiš), pastor of Göda, in his capacity as chairman of the Wendish Protestant Pastors' Conference, twelve fascicles of proofs of the new hymnal, enclosing the Stosch petition and asking for a committee of clergymen to consider whether certain alterations which had been detected in the hymns would make them difficult to sing. A week later, the *Kreisdirektion* informed Leuner that they hoped that his Wendish teacher would continue to follow its instruction of 10 June 1864 (J. Cyž 1977: 208–9).

The committee elected by the Wendish Protestant Pastors' Conference concluded that most of the changes made in the proofs were not unfamilar to the congregations and would cause them no difficulty, but they also thought that the hymnal should be printed unaltered in its traditional form, because the people were opposed to any change. In his report to the *Kreisdirection* Immisch said that the Conference of Wendish Pastors had approved a proposal by Pastor Rjeda of Baruth that the hymnal be printed in both the old and the new orthographies (J. Cyž 1977: 209–10, 212). The *Kreidirektion* informed Stosch and his followers on 7 December 1868 that the printing of the amended hymnal would proceed as planned, but that, seeing how attached Wendish worshippers were to the old version, a number of unamended copies would also be printed and they would be distinguished by a note on the title-page. Monse was instructed to proceed on these terms, including the provision for different title-pages (J. Cyž 1977: 210–11). There was no further mention of a proposal to print a version in the new orthography. As for Wendish teaching at the Estates' Seminary, the *Kreisdirektion* told the Stosch petitioners that the present practice of giving instruction in the use of both orthographies, old and new, would continue (J. Cyž 1977: 210–11).

The case of the Stosch petition shows how remote some members of the Maćica Serbska were from the concerns of the majority of the Wendish population. Between 1867 and 1878 the number of subscribers to *Łužičan* fell from 300 to 60–70 (Völkel 1984: 184). On 11 July 1870, the *Kreisdirektion* informed the Maćica that its decision had been approved by the Saxon Ministry for Religion and Public Education. After this Stosch wrote two more long letters requesting a reappraisal of the decision but without success, and that was the end of the matter (J. Cyž 1977: 213). Further editions in the old orthography and in Gothic type appeared in 1881, 1883, 1889, 1907, and 1920.

The hymnal was not printed in the new orthography and in Latin type until 1931 (Malink 2010: 4).

The Second Reich

On 18 January 1871, during the Franco-Prussian War, even before the Prussian victory was complete, the Second Reich was founded in the Hall of Mirrors at Versailles with King Wilhelm of Prussia as emperor of Germany (Scheuch: 90–1). Even after it became part of the German Empire, however, Saxony remained more tolerant of Wendish culture than Prussia. A new Saxon education act of 1873 specified that Wendish children were to be taught to read in both German and Wendish and that Wendish could be used in religious education in parishes where Wendish church services were still held (Kunze 2003: 35). That there were those in Prussia who disapproved of this tolerant treatment of the Wends in Saxony was revealed in the Prussian *Schlesische Zeitung* (published in Breslau/Wrocław) of 16 March 1882. It condemned the Wendish national movement for criticizing the authorities, alleged that Panslavism was rife among Wendish intellectuals, especially the clergy and that Bautzen was a centre of Panslav agitation. It attacked *Serbske Nowiny*, whose editor was said to be receiving Russian money to foster Russian sympathies among the Wends. 'This newspaper', the article alleged, 'notoriously owes its birth and partly, even today, its maintenance, to Russian finances. The editor's house in Bautzen was built and the printer's shop was procured with Russian money.' The allusion to Smoler is unmistakable. The movement is said to be led by 'a very clever and very active clergyman', whose 'influence is felt far into Prussian Lusatia'. This is a reference to Friedrich Heinrich Immisch (Jaroměr Hendrich Imiš) (Immisch 1884: 27–30).

The article was reported on or reproduced in many other German papers, mainly with approval. The *Bautzener Nachrichten* of 19 March and 26 March, however, rejected its assertions, saying it was 'teeming with falsehoods and laughable distortions' (Immisch 1884: 23). Though anonymous, it is known to have been instigated and framed by Pastor Kuhring of Lohsa and Archdeacon Wieder of Hoyerswerda and written by *Amtsrichter* Dr Andrä of Hoyerswerda. The impetus for writing and publishing it, however, came from *Schulrat* Eduard Bock, a Prussian official who in 1873 had been transferred from Königsberg to Liegnitz, where he held a supervisory position overseeing schools in Prussian Lusatia (Muka 1885: 115; *Stawizny*, 2: 158). Under his regime, the bilingual schoolbooks that had only been introduced into Prussian Upper Sorbian schools in 1862 were withdrawn. He is also reputed to have ordered Wendish girls to remove their traditional headdress (Šołćic 1967: 64). To Bock are attributed the legendary words (directed to a teacher in Prussian Upper Lusatia): 'You must help carry the Wendish language to its grave' (Immisch 1884: 106). In the late 1870s and the 1880s, Bock was the bane of the Wendish national movement. His leading opponents were Smoler and Imiš. The conflict had not only a Wendish-German but also a Saxon-Prussian dimension.

The *Schlesische Zeitung* was a regular mouthpiece for the anti-Wendish view. Responding to protests against the imposition of German in Wendish schools and churches, it told its readers on 5 June 1885: 'Wendish school instruction and Wendish church services in the middle of a region that is German to the core is, in the century of the nationality principle, an absurdity. The Wendish clergy lack through their Wendish endeavours the finest virtue of all times and peoples, love of the fatherland. They are cultural reactionaries' (No. 384) (quoted in Kunze 2003: 32). Allegations of Panslavism against prominent Wends, however, were not the prerogative of the Prussian press. Articles in the same vein appeared in the *Dresdner Zeitung* in 1882 and in the *Dresdner Nachrichten* in 1885 and 1886 (R. Jenč 1960: 36–7).

Pastor Kuhring and Archdeacon Wieder were among those present at a conference of Prussian Wendish pastors held in Horka in January 1881, when a petition was put forward by Pastor Julius Wjelan (1817–1892), pastor of Schleife. It had been composed as a result of complaints and pleas brought to the pastors by their congregations. Wjelan was born in Schleife on 1 February 1817, the only son of the pastor of that parish, Jan Wjelan. He attended the gymnasium in Bautzen, where he met Smoler. Together they founded the Wendish Society there and in 1836 went on to study theology together at the University of Breslau. In 1852, Wjelan succeeded his father as pastor of Schleife. He remained here in his native village and in this office until his death forty years later. Wjelan defiantly held all-Wendish services, disregarding the 1845 Prussian rule that they should be bilingual (Šołćic 1967: 63–4), but he was far from being a radical. He and his supporters were conservatives, who believed that the welfare of Wendish children was being 'endangered by instructions coming from the liberal era' (Immisch 1884: 121).

The petition was in due course sent to Robert von Puttkamer, Prussian Minister for Education, in Berlin. It complained that in some parishes schoolmasters were being appointed who knew no Wendish and that, as a result, the children, who knew no German, were not receiving proper religious instruction or even learning to read in their native tongue (Immisch 1884: 28–9; Muka 1885: 115). The signatories asserted that there existed 'pressure to ban the Wendish tongue altogether from our schools' (Immisch 1884: 121). The children, by being detached from their mother-tongue, were at the same time being detached from good morals and discipline 'of which the increasing arrogance and licentiousness of recent times clearly provide testimony'. The signatories therefore asked the minister to take action so that Wendish candidates for appointment as teachers in schools 'be given special consideration when necessary' and that 'in our Wendish schools at least religion, bible phrases, hymns and reading be taught in the mother tongue' (Immisch 1884: 121).

It was a year before a reply came. Von Puttkamer had meanwhile been replaced by Heinrich von Goßler, who on 16 January 1882 wrote to Wjelan with specious assurances: 'It is far from being the intention of the Royal Government to drive the Wendish language from the schools in question, nor has it any reason to do so. But it has the duty to ensure that non-German children are equipped with the knowledge of German to leave school and enter life.' The decision of the petitioners to set in train a campaign to defend the language, however, had (he said) caused surprise 'in view of the otherwise so loyal conduct' of the Wendish population (Immisch 1884: 122–3).

In 1872, of the seventy-one elementary schools in Kreis Cottbus, sixty-four were still using Wendish in the lowest classes (in addition to German). Ten years later, the figure had sunk to 53. In the 1870s also, a few schools in Kreis Calau and Kreis Spremberg were using Wendish, and one in Kreis Guben. In the forty-two years from 1858 to 1900, according to official figures, the number of Wends in Lower Lusatia fell from 76,400 to around 36,000, a drop of 53 per cent (Kunze 2003: 33–4). In Prussian Upper Lusatia in 1885, the Breslau Consistory prohibited the use of Wendish in instruction for confirmation. The number of schools under the Liegnitz Government using Wendish fell from 62 in 1847 to 50 in 1882. Between 1861 and 1910, according to official census figures, the Wendish population under Liegnitz fell by 14.1 per cent (from 31,962 to 27,474 individuals). Nevertheless, in 1884 there were here still twenty-one parishes with Wendish church services (Kunze 2003: 31–2).

In the course of the nineteenth century in Lower Lusatia as a whole, the number of parishes where Wendish church services were held fell from forty-nine to twelve. This was largely the result of installing pastors who were ignorant of Wendish. Superintendent Ebeling said in 1882: 'That clergymen whose mother tongue is not Wendish hold office in Wendish parishes is particularly desirable. They bring with them into the Wendish parishes all the spiritual assets which God has bestowed on the German nation...' Meanwhile qualified Wendish clergy were being sent to German parishes, while the authorities made fake claims that there were no Wendish applicants for vacancies in Wendish parishes. Eventually, many Wends came to see they had no future in the ministry, unless they were prepared to serve in German parishes. At the Cottbus Gymnasium, optional Wendish instruction was abolished in 1888 on the grounds that its task had been completed as there was no longer any demand for Wendish-speaking pastors. Protests, in which even the conservative *Bramborski Casnik* participated, fell on deaf ears (Kunze 2003: 30–3).

The 'Young Wends'

At the time of the foundation of the Second Reich, the generation of Wends that had led the national awakening was nearing its end. Zejler died in 1872, Smoler in 1884, Wjelan in 1892, and Hórnik in 1894. Imiš lived until 1897. Meanwhile, a new generation had appeared. In 1871, a new society called *Lubin* was founded for all Wendish students studying in Bautzen. Collaboration between *Lubin* and the societies in Leipzig and Prague led to the foundation of a union of all Wendish students' societies which was given the title *Schadźowanka serbskeje studowaceje młodźiny* 'Assembly of Wendish Student Youth'. It first met in Crostwitz in August 1875. Its leading lights were Karl Ernst Mucke (Arnošt Muka) (1854–1932) and Jan Ernst Holan (1853–1921), both studying at Leipzig, and Jakub Bart (1856–1909), who was in Prague preparing for the priesthood. Before long Assemblies were being held three times a year, the main one being in August (R. Jenč 1960: 48–9). The *Schadźowanka* encouraged the creation of further students' societies. The Wendish students training to become teachers at the Bautzen Estates'

Teachers' Seminary had had their own society since 1839, but in 1876 it was refounded with the title *Swoboda* 'Liberty' and contributed a strong musical element. In 1886, however, the authorities at the Seminary banned all student societies, including *Swoboda* (Musiat 2001: 52–5).

At the second *Schadźowanka* in 1876, it was decided to found a new journal to express the views of the younger generation and to publish their literary work. There was dissatifaction with *Łužičan* and a perception that it was a vehicle for the outdated ideas of the older generation. Mucke was chosen to be editor and it was decided that copy was to be submitted to him through the various local societies. The first number of *Lipa Serbska* 'The Wendish Lime Tree', with the sub-title *Časopis młodych Serbow* 'Journal of the Young Wends', appeared on 3 November 1876. There were immediately differences of opinion between the Leipzig and Prague societies over editorial policy. The Prague view, expressed by Jakub Bart, was that the contents of the journal should appeal to a wide readership and reflect the life and concerns of the rural population, so in 1877 the editorship was handed over to him for four years, though legal responsibility was retained by Mucke (Krječmar 1952: 5–28).

Bart lost no time in provoking controversy with an article in *Lipa Serbska* in 1878 attacking the puristic, bookish language of many writers, which discouraged ordinary Wends from reading literature in their own language. His article caused resentment among the older generation. Although no one was named, it was clear that the charges were directed at Christian Traugott Pfuhl (Křesćan Bohuwěr Pful) (1825–1889), author of the (at that time) definitive Upper Wendish-German dictionary (1866). Pfuhl's contemporaries rallied to his support and decided that he should, in their name, write and publish a riposte. It had been written and was at the printer's, when Smoler, anxious to avoid a rift in the national movement, intervened and publication was abandoned.

Bart again attacked the older generation in a play called *Stary Serb* 'The Old Wend', loosely based on a Czech original, published in 1881 and performed in Bautzen in March 1883 (R. Jenč 1960: 218–19). From 1882 a new literary journal called *Łužica* 'Lusatia' appeared, replacing both *Lipa Serbska* and *Łužičan*, and in its columns in May 1883 it carried an article by Bart deprecating the state of Wendish poetry, particularly a general lack of attention to the formal side of poetic composition. He expressed his views forcefully and wrote disparagingly of the works of Zejler. Bart insisted on greater rigour and on the application of rules taken from Czech versification. Not everyone agreed, so in the next issue of *Łužica* (June) Pfuhl, as the author of the only previous treatise on Wendish poetics, sprang to the defence of the old school (Topolińska 1962: *passim*; R. Jenč 1960: 220–1). Mucke, as editor, seems to have been concerned at the strength of feeling being expressed (Krječmar and Nowotny 1958: 46) but decided to publish both sides of the argument.

Bart now let the matter drop and the fact that he had decided to remain silent gave him the idea for his pen-name, Ćišinski (from *ćichi* 'quiet'), under which in 1884 he published his first collection of poems *Kniha sonetow* 'A Book of Sonnets'. The epigraph *Facta loquuntur* 'Deeds speak' meant that he considered the poems vindicated the principles he had expounded in his article. As he immodestly put it in a letter to his

Czech friend Adolf Černý: 'I think that with the *Book of Sonnets* a new epoch will open in our literature' (12 October 1886, Krječmar and Nowotny 1958: 370).

Jakub Bart-Ćišinski (as he was henceforth known in literary contexts) became pre-eminent among Wendish poets, but his career as a priest was stormy. In 1883, he was ordained in Bautzen and allocated to the Wendish Catholic parish of Ralbitz. From here he was moved the following year to Radibor, north of Bautzen, but was moved again three years later. Aware of his unbending commitment to the Wendish cause and his obstinate character, the Catholic authorities contrived henceforth to keep him away from Wendish parishes, which, considering the scarcity of German Catholic parishes in Saxony, took some ingenuity. He served consecutively in Schirgiswalde (south of Bautzen), Dresden, Chemnitz, and Radeberg. His friendship with the Czech opera singer Therese Saak and the love poems published in his third collection *Přiroda a wutroba* 'Nature and the Heart' (1889) roused the displeasure of his bishop, who forbade him to continue writing in that vein (Krječmar 1956/57a: 112). Shortly before his move to Chemnitz in 1896, he was sent to a monastery in Bohemia to do penance and his transfer from Dresden too seems to have been a punishment. In May 1901, he had to spend seven months in a sanatorium for alcoholics at Waldernbach in the Westerwald (Krječmar 1956/1957b: 127).

The rift between the generations was only one of the dichotomies found in Wendish society, including those between Protestants and Catholics, Saxons and Prussians, and Upper and Lower Lusatians. Although by European standards confessional conflict was minimal, there was a confessional aspect to the generational clash. Among the Young Wends the influence of the Prague *Serbowka* was strong. The old Wends they disparaged were all Protestants. The linguistic and aesthetic judgement of Catholic Wends was often conditioned by their close links with Prague, where the Catholic clergy were all trained. Since 1806, moreover, Prague had been in a foreign country, and after 1871 links between Wends and Czechs were liable to interpretation as manifestations of Panslavism. As a consequence of the robust policy adopted by the German state towards the Catholic Church in the 1870s the very presence of Wendish students at the Prague Seminary was regarded as suspicious. In 1902, the Berlin newspaper *Tägliche Rundschau* interpreted the presence of a few Czechs at the *Schadźowanka* in Lohsa as evidence of a Wendish demonstration hostile to the state (*Kirche* 2003: 43).

Following Smoler's death in 1884 the leader's mantle fell on the shoulders first of Michał Hórnik (1833–1894) and then, after his death, of Karl Ernst Mucke (Arnošt Muka) (1854–1932). The leadership role of Jakub Bart-Ćišinski too was considerable. All these men (there were no women) were Upper Wends and most of them were Saxons. Notably underrepresented in the leading circles were the Lower Wends. This may have been one of the reasons why Mucke decided to devote his efforts primarily to Lower Wendish affairs. He was born in Großhänchen on the south-west edge of the Wendish speech-area. At the age of fifteen he visited the Spree Forest for the first time and remained thereafter devoted to the study of Lower Wendish culture. Every year in the summer holidays he would travel around Lower Lusatia, often accompanied by a friend, observing and recording the life and language. From 1874 to 1879, he studied classics and Slavonic languages at Leipzig University. He then secured a post teaching classics at the Bautzen Gymnasium, an ideal location for him to pursue his Wendish activities, but, although he was always on good terms with the headmaster, Otto Kreußler, his Wendish enthusiasm attracted the hostile attention of the Mayor of Bautzen, Löhr, who was also chairman of the Gymnasium's governors. In 1883, on the occasion of the king of Saxony's birthday and at the invitation of Kreußler he gave a public lecture on the South Slav National Epic, in which he drew comparisons with Homer's Iliad and Odyssey. This was at the height of the excitement caused by the 1882 article in the *Schlesische Zeitung* and Löhr used the opportunity to complain to the Ministry of Education that the lecture constituted politically motivated Panslavic agitation. The defence that lectures on the South Slav Epic had been given several times at Leipzig University and that portions of it had been translated by Goethe was of no avail (Petr 1978: 28–9) and Mucke was transferred to Chemnitz, well away from the Wends. His entire teaching career from now on was to be spent outside the Wendish area, first in Chemnitz, then (from 1887) in Freiberg. His removal from Bautzen forced him to resign as secretary to the committee of the Maćica, but he continued to do all he could for the Wendish cause and to pursue his research in Lower Lusatia during the holidays (Figure 6.4).

Smoler's *Volkslieder* (1841 and 1843) contained not only folk-songs but also ethnographic material of all kinds, most of which the author had gathered himself.

Figure 6.4 Korla Ernst Muka (Karl Ernst Mucke) (1854–1932).

Mucke now continued Smoler's work. His first contribution to the field was published in the *Časopis Maćicy Serbskeje* in 1872, when he was eighteen and still at school. By 1894, he had published in instalments nearly 400 folk-songs and variants. He had many helpers, including the Czechs Adolf Černý and Ludvík Kuba. Mucke's interests focused on a comprehensive plan to describe and analyse the language of the Lower Wends in all its variations. First, however, he recorded the precise contemporary demographic situation, publishing it in extensive articles in the *Časopis Maćicy Serbskeje* in 1884–1900. Every Wendish parish was visited and described, including the names of past and present pastors and schoolmasters and their practices, language distribution, history, and statistics. Lower Lusatia and most of Prussian Upper Lusatia were visited by Mucke himself, but much of the data for Saxon Upper Lusatia was collected for him by others (Petr 1978: 70). The result is a unique source for the state of the Lusatian Wends in the late nineteenth century. His historical and comparative account of the Wendish language (*Laut- und Formenlehre*) was published in Leipzig in 1891 and won the Jablonowski Society's prize (Mucke 1891).

Emigration to Australia

Economic conditions in Germany following the end of the feudal order led to widespread emigration. In the course of the century, some five and a half million German emigrants left for overseas destinations. Among them were about five thousand Lusatian Wends. The primary destination was Australia. The prospect of owning land and knowing prosperity was the main attraction, but for those whose theological principles diverged from the official church, there was also the promise of religious freedom. Many emigrated in groups and planned to set up their own communities. Two Wendish groups sailed for Australia in 1848. The first, made up of Wends from both Upper and Lower Lusatia, left Hamburg on the *Victoria* on 15 June 1848 and docked at Adelaide, South Australia, on 6 November. On board was Andreas Kappler (1802–1877), accompanied by his large family, who until his departure had been pastor of the Wendish townlet of Weißenberg. The second group, which sailed on the *Alfred* on 15 August that year and arrived on 6 December, was led by Michael Deutscher, a miller from Zschorna. Numbering forty-six and all from Upper Lusatia, they intended to remain as a community in their new homeland. A third group, consisting of ten families and a few unattached young people, sailed on the *Pribislav* on 23 August 1849 and arrived in Melbourne on 2 February 1850 after a voyage that had included a five-week interlude in Rio de Janeiro. They planned to settle as a Wendish congregation and had engaged as their pastor Andreas Penzig from Ebendörfel, but he was taken ill and died in Berlin on his way to join his flock before their departure.

The largest single group heading for Australia, and the best organized, was led by Johann Zwahr of Drehsa. It sailed on the *Helena* in 1851. Numbering ninety-two, the Wends constituted the majority of the passengers. They were intent on joining up with those who had sailed on the *Alfred* in 1848 to form a Wendish colony with its own church and school, but attempts to recruit a pastor before departure failed. The *Alfred* group settled on a site on the River Gawler about twelve kilometres from Tanunda. They called their settlement Rosenthal (later it would be Rosedale). It was February 1849. The inhabitants of Rosenthal joined the German Lutheran parish of Hoffnungsthal, where there was a German pastor and with his approval they set up a school. The teacher was German. Rosenthal, the first Wendish settlement in Australia, was of short duration. Three years after its foundation, most of the families moved on (T. Malinkowa 1999: 39).

By the time the *Helena* group arrived in Adelaide on Christmas Eve 1851, the Wends at Rosenthal had already taken a decision to move out of South Australia into Victoria. Four families of the *Helena* group decided to go with them. The rest stayed in South Australia and founded a settlement which they called Ebenezer. They were still hoping to recruit a Wendish pastor (T. Malinkowa 1999: 60). There was already one Wendish pastor in South Australia. This was Andreas Kappler, once pastor of Weißenberg, who had arrived on the *Victoria* in 1848. He was available and willing to serve his countrymen, but the Ebenezer flock was not prepared to have him. They were orthodox Lutherans. He was too liberal for them and so destined to work only in German parishes (T. Malinkowa 1994a: 11). The only ordained minister known to have used Wendish in Australia as a liturgical language was Christoph Samuel Daniel Schondorf (1814–1898), a German member of the Herrnhut Moravian Brethren, who had spent some years in Kleinwelka, where he had learned Wendish.

Schondorf had been ordained deacon in 1853 and sent to preach among the Brethren in South Australia. In 1854 he met some Wends from Ebenezer, who asked him if he would be prepared to conduct services for them. In a letter of 20 October 1854, Schondorf describes Ebenezer as a community consisting wholly of Wends from the Bautzen region. Confessional differences between the strict Lutherans and the Moravians were not, it transpired, insurmountable, and Schondorf officiated regularly in Ebenezer from 1854 to 1859 (T. Malinkowa 1999: 62). He refers in another letter to being able to communicate with those Wends 'especially women, who understand no German, much less English' (T. Malinkowa 1994a: 16–17).

In 1856 in the school in Ebenezer teaching was being carried out in Wendish by a Johann Dallwitz (Malinkowa 1994a: 11n.). The school operated for about five years in the mid-1850s. Maria Zwahr (Johann Zwahr's daughter), who attended the school until she was ten, later recalled that she learned German only after it was closed (Zwar 1997: 11). Despite the absence of Wendish pastors and schools, there were a number of settlements in which the language survived for a time. In the German parishes the Wends were renowned for their exceptional piety and knowledge of the Bible. The number of Wendish entrants to the ministry in Australia was disproportionately large (Zwar 1997: 40). On 17 July 1885, shortly after arriving in Castlemaine, Pastor Simpfendörfer wrote a letter reporting on his first experiences in Australia. He said he had found devout congregations. 'Many of the colonists have a very good knowledge of the Bible, and one of these old fathers knows by heart the whole New Testament in Wendish, and a good part of it in German' (Wuchatsch 2004: 160).

Emigration to Texas

The other main destination of Wendish emigrants overseas was Texas and it was here that the largest single group settled. Numbering 541 and led by Jan Kilian, the group sailed from Liverpool on the *Ben Nevis* on 26 September 1854. Owing to an outbreak of cholera on board, they put into Queenstown (Cobh) in Ireland and were able to resume their voyage only on 23 October, arriving in Galveston on 15 December. The total number of deaths on the journey was eighty-one (Malinkowa 1999: 132). The group crossed Galveston Bay by steamer and reached Houston, where they met a German Lutheran pastor, who did what he could to accommodate them. They now split into family groups, which began individually to make their way into the interior. Many abandoned the main party, but twenty-five families continued under Kilian's leadership, living at first in tents and huts. On 11 February 1855 they were able to buy land in Bastrop County on Rabbs Creek about fifty kilometres from New Ulm. Their plots varied greatly in size depending on ability to pay. They set about building houses and on 26 February 1856 Kilian was able to open the school. He now had a house, part of which served as a church. By Whitsun 1857, a bell-tower was in operation (Malinkowa 1999: 133–9). In 1860 the settlement was registered in Washington for postal services with the name Serbin, derived from their own self-designatory term *Serb*.

Kilian was eager to make contact with other Lutherans who were already established in Texas, and it might have been convenient to join the Texas Lutheran Synod, but he knew it to be of an unacceptably liberal inclination; so, instead, in February 1855 he wrote to the Missouri Synod in St Louis, which he knew to be appropriately conservative in doctrine. In reply he received a message of welcome. When in 1866 the Serbin parish joined the Missouri Synod, it was the first Texas parish to do so (Malinkowa 1999: 135–6, 159). The conditions in Texas were unfamiliar to the Wendish farmers and the crops they were used to, such as rye, wheat, potatoes, and vegetables, were not particularly successful, so they began instead to cultivate maize and cotton (Malinkowa 1999: 140–1). Their standard of living was lower than that of their neighours, partly because their plots were relatively small and partly because their neighbours kept slaves, an expedient rejected by the Wends on religious grounds (Malinkowa 1999: 142).

Adversity had so far kept the community together, but once it became clear that its material needs were assured, bickering broke out. A revivalist faction, that had made contact with some Methodists in the vicinity, believed their own worship lacked a fervour which could be supplied by prayer meetings. Kilian disagreed but tried to compromise. Some of his flock nevertheless left and built a little church, which in June 1859 they dedicated to St Peter. This provoked Kilian's remaining parishioners, whose services hitherto had been held in his house, to build their own church, which was dedicated as 'the first Wendish Lutheran church in Texas' at Christmas that year (Malinkowa 1999: 144). The Wends of Serbin corresponded regularly with their kin in Lusatia, where their letters were eagerly awaited and read. They subscribed to *Serbske Nowiny* and ordered Wendish books. In 1867, for example, a consignment including thirty Bibles and seventy hymnals arrived (Malinkowa 1999: 204).

The American Civil War (1861–65) was a turning point for the Texan Wends. Hostilities barely impinged on Texan territory, but the Wends were compelled to serve in the Confederate Army and in 1863 Serbin mourned the death of five of its sons (Malinkowa 1999: 148). The war also brought benefits, for the Union's blockade of the South caused cotton prices to rise and the Wends were still able to export their cotton through Mexico. For the survival of the Wendish language in Serbin, however, the war was fatal. Being located away from the battle area, Serbin became a haven for refugees, most of whom were Germans (Malinkowa 1999: 149). They began to attend the Serbin church and sent their children to the school. Temporarily, their influence was countered by further Wendish migrants from Lusatia, who continued to arrive until the 1880s. From 1862 a church service in German was held every sixth Sunday for the refugees and before long the Wendish language was under threat. The Wends were the overwhelming majority, but they had retained their self-effacing ways from the old country. In 1869 of the 581 parishioners only eighty-eight were from German or mixed German-Wendish families (Malinkowa 1999: 187), yet a pro-German faction in 1867 had succeeded in persuading a majority to vote for a motion ruling that all parish meetings would in future be held in German. The pastor (Kilian) would translate for those whose German was inadequate. The opponents of the motion, led by Kilian, were outvoted (Malinkowa 1999: 160).

That same year (1867) the revivalist separatists of St Peter's disbanded themselves and returned to the main parish (Malinkowa 1999: 146), but there was now the threat of a new break between opposing factions, centred on the language question. The arrival in the parish in 1869 of Ernst Leubner, a German, as schoolmaster and cantor, quickly brought matters to head. He took an uncompromising pro-German stance, refused to adapt his organ accompaniment to the Wendish way of singing or to learn the Wendish liturgy (Malinkowa 1999: 161; Nielsen 2003: 67). It is not clear what constituted the Wendish way of singing, but allusions to it also occur in Haupt and Schmaler (1841: 25), Sykora (1936: 58), and Wićaz (1955: 13).

In 1870 the parish split into two. The break did not strictly follow linguistic lines. Though containing a vociferous pro-German element and taking Leubner with them as their teacher, the break-away parish was still half Wendish (Malinkowa 1999: 166) and still wished to have a Wendish pastor, so the Missouri Synod sent them Johann Pallmer, who arrived in December 1870. The new parish took over the land which had belonged to the previous St Peter's congregation and also its name. They built their own church. Kilian's parish retained most of the property and an unfinished stone church, which was completed the following year and on 3 December dedicated to St Paul (Nielsen 2003: 69–71). The two parishes were destined eventually to be reconciled, but not in Kilian's lifetime. His successor was his son Hermann, who had studied theology at the St Louis seminary and took over the parish in 1883. The following year Kilian died (Malinkowa 1999: 168–70). Before the end of the century Serbin had over a 1,000 inhabitants, several shops and businesses, and a post office (Malinkowa 1999: 172).

Not all Wendish emigrants overseas travelled in big groups. Apart from those who went to Australia and Texas, small parties also settled in Nebraska and other American states, in Canada, and in South Africa. Individuals, in addition, are known to have made their way to New Zealand and South America. A remarkable individual case was that of the Lower Wendish poet Mato Kosyk, who was born in Werben, fifty miles south-east of Berlin, in 1853. Having failed to take the school-leaving certificate (*Abitur*), he discovered that in Germany he would not be able to study to enter the church without it. After working for a time on the revision of the Lower Wendish hymnal, he heard that in America the lack of the *Abitur* was not a bar to theological study and sailed in 1883 to New York with a group of Wendish emigrants from Werben. On arrival he took his leave of them and travelled to Springfield, Illinois, where he enrolled at the Concordia Theological Seminary. In June 1885, he was ordained and served as pastor in German parishes in Nebraska and Oklahoma. Though he rarely made contact with other Wends in America, in 1890 he was astonished to meet several of his countrymen in Nebraska, in the little town of Sterling, where the Lutheran parish was half Wendish (Malinkowa 1999: 213). The juxtaposition of Wendish and American themes in the poems written in emigration make Kosyk's work unique in Wendish literature. He introduces American English words like *blizzard, cyclone, wigwam,* and *prairie* into his Wendish texts. He developed a life-long sense of affinity with the Indians, which is reflected in the poems. He died in Albion, Oklahoma, in 1940 (Stone 2006: *passim*).

Wendish domestic servants

New agriculture methods in Lusatia and the freeing of the serfs accelerated Wendish migration from the country to the towns. By the mid-nineteenth century there were Wendish communities in Dresden and Berlin, consisting predominantly of domestic servants. In Dresden Wendish hireing fairs were held every 2 January to facilitate their employment (Muka 1886: 177). In Berlin hireing fairs were replaced by agencies, supplying bourgeois families with Wendish cooks, wet-nurses, chamber-maids, and nannies, as well as footmen, coachmen, and grooms. The men were famous for their skill in dealing with horses. The proverbial Wendish diligence in religious observance imparted respectability. And they were cheap. Wendish women in service, however, were known for wearing their national dress, even when far from home. If a prospective employer objected, they were even known to demur and keep looking until they found one that did not (Michalk and Protze [1974]: 141). The Wendish national dress thus became a feature of the urban landscape in both Dresden and Berlin.

Women of the burgeoning bourgeoisie found that feeding babies hindered their social life and thought it ruined their figures. It was said to be reminiscent of animals and not ladylike. These aversions were complemented by the opportunity to demonstrate social superiority by employing a wet-nurse. It is estimated that in Berlin in 1900 there were still about 1,000 wet-nurses, although by then the institution was in decline (Noack 2008: 15–19). There was a traditional belief in the particular potency of the milk of Wendish women. In 1841 Smoler noted: 'Wendish wet-nurses are much sought after and many a German child since 1750 has had a Wendish wet-nurse to thank for his life and his strength' (Haupt and Schmaler 1841: 9). The choice of the year 1750 here suggests a reference to a case noted in the *Sachsenzeitung* in 1833:

> The fashion of regarding the Wendish race as a fount of vital energy for the sucklings of refined and wealthy parents began around 1750. It arose through a Swedish Lady von Stenn, then staying in Dresden, who lost her husband shortly after giving birth and whose grief was so great that she and her baby were close to death.

A Wendish wet-nurse was procured and 'the child so quickly recovered and became so strong and vigorous, that the mother granted the wet-nurse a pension for life' (Noack 2008: 21). The wet-nurses's degree of intimacy with the family employing her was shared with no other servant, and this was often to her long-term advantage.

The House of Wettin is said to have employed wet-nurses from the Wendish region as early as the eighteenth century, but the first and only documented case is that of Maria Bradel (nee Rolle) from Zescha on the outskirts of Neschwitz, north-west of Bautzen, who suckled the last king of Saxony, Friedrich August III (1865–1932). The junker of Neschwitz, Baron von Vietinghoff-Riesch, made the introduction, and Maria Bradel soon arrived in Dresden with her baby daughter. The only problem was that she could not understand German. The royal nurse, on the other hand, was in the habit of speaking French. These difficulties were overcome through the intervention of the other Wendish servants. Later, she also gave her royal suckling tuition in her native language and enjoyed lifelong royal favour (Noack 2008: 21; Rychtar 2013: 8).

The Hohenzollerns too had Wendish wet-nurses, beginning with Anna Cludi from Burg in the Spreewald who in 1884 was engaged to suckle the third child of the Kaiser Wilhelm II (1859–1941). The relationship between suckling and wet-nurse was often not unlike that of kin. A wet-nurse might continue for many years to enjoy the favour of the child she had suckled, and sometimes it would last for life. The case of Maria Jank (1864–1944) of Straupitz, for example, is well documented. She was married and after the birth of her first child took a position as wet-nurse of the twin sons of Wilhelm Fürst von Hohenzollern-Sigmaringen. Later her responsibility was limited to one twin, Franz Joseph Ludwig Maria Karl Anton Tassilo, Prince of Hohenzollern-Emden (1891–1964). He kept in touch with her to the end of her life, sending gifts, greetings-cards, and letters telling her about family events (Noack 2008: 33–5).

It was widely held that the wet-nurse custom had a corrupting influence on the lower classes. Pregnancies among single women were said to be wantonly or even deliberately arranged to facilitate employment. The socialist politician August Bebel in *Die Frau und der Sozialismus* 'Women and Socialism' (1879) wrote:

> It is well known, for example, that Wendish Lusatia (the Spreewald) is the region from which women of the Berlin bourgeoisie, who are unwilling or unable to suckle their new-born babies, get their wet-nurses. Wet-nurse production, whereby village girls get pregnant in order, after the birth of their child, to hire themselves to well-

to-do Berlin families as wet-nurses, is conducted on a commercial basis. Girls who have three or four illegitimate children as a means of obtaining employment as wet-nurses are not uncommon. [...] From the standpoint of middle-class morality this is an objectionable practice, but from the standpoint of the family interests of the bourgeoisie it seems praiseworthy and desirable.

(Noack 2008: 23)

Although this picture of carefree unmarried motherhood in the Wendish village is out of tune with most other sources, the commercial approach to the practice does find corroboration in individual biographies and is scarcely surprising. Sometimes funds were needed to meet particular needs. Marie Jank, for example, engaged herself to the house of Hohenzollern-Sigmaringen specifically with the intention of earning enough money to replace her family's thatched roof with tiles (Noack 2008: 33).

The inclination of Wendish servants to retain their national dress, even in Berlin, may once have been problematic, but before long it became an advantage, for it advertised and endorsed the genuine article, as used by the upper classes. Transition from wet-nurse to nanny or nursemaid was but a natural progression and before long the Lower Wendish national dress with its angular hood, worn by nannies and nursemaids pushing perambulators, had become part of the metropolitan scene. It was a status symbol, not so much for the wearer as for the bourgeois family that employed her. The Wendish nanny, appropriately attired, was much photographed and appeared on picture postcards. She raised the status of the family that employed her. It was, however, only a question of time before the livery became more important than the identity it represented. And so it came to be worn by nannies who were not Wendish at all and even by those who hailed from other parts of Germany. An extreme case is reported in the household of a colonial officer which in 1899 returned from German south-west Africa with a black wet-nurse, who did her best to conform to her new surroundings by donning the Wendish dress of the Spreewald. The attention she attracted as she pushed her pram along the Kurfürstendamm was noted in the press (Noack 2008: 31).

The fact that most wet-nurses were unmarried mothers was a cause of embarrassment only in the most fastidious families. Prince Louis Ferdinand (1907–94), the son of Crown Prince Wilhelm, recalled: 'To begin with I had a wet-nurse from the Spreewald. [...] My wet-nurse had only one tiny defect – she was an unmarried mother. When my grandmother the Empress, a stickler for morality, heard about this, she insisted on her being replaced immediately by another girl with a marriage certificate' (Noack 2008: 22). Employment as a wet-nurse in Berlin was, from the point of view of a Wendish girl, highly desirable. Her responsibilities were essentially transitory, it is true, but they might well to lead to something permanent. Though its lowest-ranking member, she became part of the comfortable bourgeois family, which she would accompany everywhere, even on holiday. In family photographs and paintings of the Berlin *fin de siècle* the Wendish nanny is a frequent participant. The hours of work, of course, were long and undefined, but board and lodging came automatically. There was homesickness to cope with, it is

Figure 6.5 Wendish Nannies in Berlin, *c.* 1909.

true, but there was always the chance of meeting other Wendish nannies while taking the baby for a walk. They seem to have made a practice of meeting one another in this way, to judge from photographs of the period showing clutches of them with their charges, pushing large-wheeled prams, sometimes in formation, or sitting on park benches in the Tiergarten and elsewhere (Figure 6.5).

Wendish church services in Dresden and Berlin

The sounds of her native language were not the only aspect of village life the Wendish servant-girl might sigh for. She missed the rural sense of community and, particularly, loss of religious observance and the traditional close contact with the church. By comparison with the Wendish village, Berlin and Dresden were godless places. The number of Wends living in or near Dresden by 1848 was great enough to motivate the foundation of a Wendish Lutheran parish there and this was followed a year later by a Catholic counterpart. Each confession held services four times a year – the Lutherans in the *Kreuzkirche*, the Catholics in the *Hofkirche*. In 1849–1850 the Wendish Lutheran parish had over a thousand parishioners, but by 1883 the figure had fallen to 860. Lutheran worshippers in the 1880s numbered around 500–800. For attendance at Catholic mass, the figure was about 300–400. By 1886 the hireing fairs were said to be in decline, probably owing to new methods of finding work (Muka 1886: 177).

Unlike Dresden, Berlin never had a Wendish parish, but the care of Wendish souls in the German capital was not overlooked. Thinking not only of servants but also of Wendish soldiers, in 1884 Pastor Pawoł Broniš from Cottbus promised to hold Wendish services annually in the Berlin Garrison Church, located centrally in the Neue Friedrichstrasse, and the first took place there on 16 October 1884. At the second, in spring 1885, over four hundred Berlin Wends were present and in 1886, 300 Wends plus many Germans. In 1887 the Brandenburg Consistory gave the annual event its official approval (Pful 1886: 52; Tuschling 2002: 267–8). From 1896 onwards Broniš was replaced by J. B. Krušwica, pastor of Werben, who in 1897 estimated the numbers at 140 and the same again the following year. Krušwica noted that 90 per cent of those present were women and that for some of them, it was the only occasion in the year when they could get leave to attend church (Tuschling 2002: 268; Janaš and Marti 2003, 3: 520).

In addition, in 1894 Jan Bogumił Nytška received permission to conduct Wendish services in Berlin in the hall of the Moravian Brethren at Wilhelmstrasse 136, and the first service there took place in December that year. Nytška's services (which may possibly be better described as prayer-meetings) were held about six times a year and were attended by an average of twenty-seven worshippers in 1895–1897, reaching over fifty at Christmas 1896. Here too women predominated (Tuschling 2002: 269–70). Seeing that even individual Wendish nannies in their national dress often attracted interest, it is not surprising that a whole multitude of them at their annual service in the Garrison Church merited the attention of the German press. In 1886 the *Reichsbote* noted: 'The Wendish women in our church presented a fine, lovely, and moving picture [...] We Germans, of whom there were many present, listened attentively to the pleasant sounds of the unfamiliar language' (Janaš and Marti 2003, 3: 520–1). It was, however, the relatively modest Wilhelmstrasse meetings that in 1897 caught the eye of a reporter for the Polish-language newspaper *Dziennik Berliński* 'Berlin Daily', which on 18 November that year carried an article on the Wends in Berlin:

Perhaps our readers will be interested in the news that the Wends on Sundays [...] conduct prayer meetings in the hall of the school at Wilhelmstrasse 136. We think that many of our countrymen may be curious enough to call in there to hear a kindred language. It would be good if they could make closer contact with the Wends. Up to now they do not know us at all and judge all our people by the few seasonal migrants who take the bread from their mouths in their own land. They are therefore a little sullen towards us. The writer of this article has had the chance in Saxony, near Bautzen, to get to know the Wends and made the unpleasant discovery that the Protestant Wends there dislike the Poles as much as they respect the Russians. It is hard to explain these feelings, but it would be good if this sullenness could be changed into friendship.

(Tuschling 2002: 270)

This article raised the spectre of Panslavism. It was brought to the notice of the Berlin chief of police and so even reached the High President of Brandenburg, Count Hue de Grais, who concluded that the services might 'be a base for getting Wends to participate in Slav ventures'. Asked to comment, the Wendish pastors all confirmed the purely religious nature of the services, emphasizing the preponderance of women. No distinction was made between the two locations, though the Polish article had mentioned only the Wilhelmstrasse services. The President of the Brandenburg Consistory said it had considered the prayer meetings a useful way of countering the threat of the Berlin environment to the religious life of the many Lower Lusatians here, mostly women, whose mother tongue was Wendish. He remained aware of 'the extremely serious character of Polish and Slav intentions' and the need to be constantly on the look-out 'to prevent any possible agitation', but for the time being he could see no danger in the present situation.

And so the annual Wendish service in the Garrison Church took place in 1899, led once more by Pastor Krušwica. But the Minister for Public Worship and Education, in agreement with the Minister for Home Affairs, did not agree with the Consistory and on 14 April 1899 wrote:

[...] in my opinion, it is advisable now, right from the start, to head off this movement, which may in the future be dangerous, and gradually do away with these services, for which a sufficient need cannot, in my opinion, be established. [...] In view of these grave concerns I should be greatly obliged to the Protestant Supreme Church Council, if [...] it would so act as to cause the Wendish services here to be first, if possible, restricted, without directly offending the participants, and at a convenient time in the future abolished.

(Tuschling 2002: 271)

The effect was immediate. In 1900 the annual service was held not in the Garrison Church but in the parish hall of the Moravian Brethren, where Nytška had held his prayer meetings. That was the last. The prayer-meetings too came to an end in 1900. Nytška took care, however, that his work was continued by the Berlin City Mission, founded by Adolf Stoecker (1835–1909), which was to a large extent independent of the state church, worked with social groups alienated from it, and had its own premises. The Mission appointed Měto Měsćan, who had been trained as a missionary but found unsuitable for service in India, to care for the Wends in Berlin as part of his duties as a town missionary. He continued Nytška's services, but they were now held on the City Mission's premises. Here in 1902, Matej Broniš (Pawoł's son) preached to a congregation of about 60. After 1902 there are no further references in the Berlin Mission's records to Wendish services, but the archive is incomplete and thereafter the trail disappears (Tuschling 2002: 271–2).

The Lüneburg Wendland

At the beginning of 1798 in Kremlin (north-west of Dolgow) in the Lüneburg Wendland, an old man called Warratz, who was said to be capable of reciting the Lord's Prayer in Wendish, died (Olesch 1962: 15). With that the Wendish language west of the Elbe appeared to have breathed its last. Consequently, something of a stir was caused in 1893 when the results of the Prussian census of 1890 were published, for they revealed that in *Kreis* Lüchow in response to the question as to their native language, 585 individuals (2.06 per cent of the population) had underlined the word *wendisch*.

Although it was thought unlikely that the language had really survived so long, the Cracow Academy of Arts (*Akademia Umiejętności*) commissioned Ernst Mucke to visit the Lüneburg Wendland to ascertain the facts at first hand (Muka 1904a: 313–14). He was able to confirm that Wendish here had indeed died out in the previous century but produced a report on various local peculiarities attesting the once Slav nature of the area. Not only the inclination of the local people to call their Low German dialect *wendisch* but also place names, surnames, customs, costumes, and about forty Slav loan-words in the German dialect betrayed their Wendish past. He commented briefly on traces of Wendish influence on the phonetics and grammar of the German dialect (Muka 1904b: 417–18) – features that had already attracted the attention of Georg Friedrich Mithoff, Magistrate of Lüchow, while the language still lived (cf. Chapter 5). Further evidence of the traces of Wendish left behind in the German of the Lüneburg Wendland (and of other formerly Slav areas) came to light in the *Deutscher Sprachatlas*, the result of a vast dialectological survey initiated in the winter of 1879–1880 by Georg Wenker (Stone 1994: *passim*).

CHAPTER 7
SELF-DETERMINATION 1900-1945

The Wendish House

By 1904 the construction of the Wendish House (*Serbski Dom*) in the Bautzen *Lauengraben* was complete. It was an unprecedented national symbol, much more than bricks and mortar. The ceremonial opening took place on 26 September in the presence of many distinguished guests, including *Landesältester* Graf von Lippe, representing the Upper Lusatian Estates, the Bautzen *Amtshauptmann* von Kirchbach, and the Mayor of Bautzen Dr Knaeubler. Among the foreign guests were Adolf Černý, Director of the Bohemian Anthropological Museum, and officials of the Serbian *Matica Srpska*. It was a picturesque occasion, enlivened by Wendish national costumes. On 26 April 1905 the *Maćica* for the first time held its annual general meeting in the Wendish House and the following month the Wends welcomed and paid homage to King Friedrich August of Saxony in a ceremony held in front of the building. It was decorated for the day in the Wendish colours (blue, red, and white), the sight of which enraged some of the more sensitive German citizens (Bryl-Serbin 1924: 82, 96).

It was an imposing building with a red roof, stretching 61 metres along the *Lauengraben* and 15 metres wide in the middle. Its roof ridges were 31 metres and 40 metres above street level. Most importantly, it housed the *Maćica*'s library and museum. In the middle on the ground floor was the Wendish Cafe. The Town Council steadfastly refused repeated applications for permission to open a restaurant. Otherwise, the ground floor was occupied by shops and a branch of the Löbauer Bank. Rents were now bringing in a substantial return and gradually paying off the debt. In 1922, by which time the debt had been reduced to M193,000, the life insurance policy which Mucke had given to the Maćica in 1894 matured. With the proceeds, augmented by gifts from his family, he paid off the remaining debt and set up the Mucke Foundation. The House was now able to use all its profits to 'contribute to the well-being of the nation', as Jan Bryl put it (Bryl-Serbin 1924: 93–4) (Figure 7.1).

Lusatia – Panslavism and politics

At the beginning of the twentieth century, the German government remained suspicious of the non-German nationalities within the Reich and was constantly on its guard. The Lusatian Wends were relatively innocuous, but it was feared they might be affected by Panslavism and become a disaffected foreign body in the state. The loyalty of Wends who

Figure 7.1 The Wendish House (*Serbski Dom*), Bautzen, 1920s.

had contact with either Czechs or Poles was suspect. The Prussian envoy in Dresden, Count Dönhoff, reported on 7 March 1906 to the Reich Chancellor in Berlin, Bernhard Fürst von Bülow, on an interview he had had with the Saxon Minister of Education and Culture, Richard von Schlieben, on the risk of Panslavic activity in Saxony. Von Schlieben had told him that a Wend, if in moments of resentment at injustices he imagined the German government had done him, were told by certain of his countrymen that a better future might be found in close union with his Slav brothers in Russia, 'the possibility could not be excluded that he would give a hearing to such promptings', but there was (said von Schlieben) at present no danger, because the leaders of the Wends were all loyal and reliable (Zwahr 1968: 47, no. 26).

Misgivings about contact between Wends and other Slavs were exacerbated by the confessional divide. On the specific question of the Wendish Seminary in Prague von Schlieben had told Dönhoff that almost without exception the Catholic priests of Saxony were educated there and that this was a matter in urgent need of adjustment. He hoped in his present position as Minister to find a solution 'in conformity with our German interests' (Zwahr 1968: 47, no. 26). The Prague Wendish Seminary was indeed a significant point of contact between Czechs and Wends. In the autumn of 1894 a 15-year-old Wend named Jan Bryl arrived there. He attended the German gymnasium in the *Malá Strana* and then went on to study law at the Charles University. After completing his military service at Dresden he returned to Prague to study classics, German, and Slavonic philology (1904–1907). Here he became a friend of Josef Páta (1886–1942), a Czech, who was also studying Slavonic philology. Their friendship and interests were to have long-term consequences. In 1901 the Charles University instituted a lectureship in Lusatian Wendish (Sorbian), held by Adolf Černý. The Wendish students founded a Lusatian-Wendish Society, named after him, because their activities centred round the topics introduced in his lectures (Petr and Tylová 1990: 5–6). Later it was called the Society of the Friends of Lusatia (*Společnost přátel Lužice*). Josef Páta and his brother František were members, and when the Czechoslovak state emerged in 1918, they both entered its civil service.

The industrialization of Lusatia proceeded steadily, and by 1911 it was estimated that more than half of all the Wendish children here were entering trades or industrial occupations rather than agriculture (Mětšk 1957: 455n.). The railway network was now fully developed, and brown coal was being mined in open-cast workings. There were stone-quarries. The textile industry flourished. Glass was being manufactured. All this was conducive to Germanization; but industry's thirst for cheap labour was satisfied not only by Wendish migration to local industrial centres but also by the immigration of Czechs and Poles, who in industrial relations began to exhibit a militancy unknown to the Wends. The Saxon authorities feared they would be a bad influence.

There were legal restrictions on the use of non-German languages at public meetings. In October 1907, by which time there were between four and five thousand Czechs working in industry in the Ostritz area, the linguistic issue was on the agenda. After the police had dispersed a riotous meeting of Czech workers who had insisted on using their mother tongue, the *Kreishauptmann*, von Craushaar, was forced to reconsider policy. He reported to the Ministry of the Interior in Dresden that he had in mind a new regulation stipulating German as the only language permitted at public meetings. He was, however, uncertain how to proceed, because at recent election meetings held in Wendish it had been thought prudent not to intervene, so as to avoid provoking resentment among the 'politically well-meaning Wends' (Zwahr 1968: 163 (no. 159), 281n.).

The Wends' demographic centre of gravity was still on the land, but here too there was dissatisfaction. Although capitalism and industrial methods were penetrating agriculture, vestiges of the feudal system survived and operated to the advantage of the owners or tenants of manorial estates (*Rittergüter*). Most significantly, the junkers retained the feudal right of pre-emption. Small-holders (usually Wends) found it hard to compete with their larger neighbours because if a small-holding failed and its owner went bankrupt, the land was bought up by the junker using his right of pre-emption. Big estates consequently grew steadily larger, while Wendish farmers were reduced to the state of farm-labourers (Rajš 1987: 9–10). The Wendish agricultural population, whether landed or landless, was united in its opposition to pre-emption.

Domowina (1912)

There were two Saxon constituencies which regularly returned Wendish deputies to the Second Chamber of the *Landtag*. One Wendish deputy at the beginning of the twentieth century was Michał Kokla (1840–1922), member for Rural Constituency No. 8. The other, Jan Awgust Zoba (1869–1911), represented Rural Constituency No. 5. They were both landowners and conservatives. For mutual protection and to help each other in the constant struggle to prevent Wendish land being swallowed up by huge manorial estates, Wendish farmers formed themselves into agricultural unions, such as the Rural Electoral Association (*Wjesne wólbne towarstwo/Ländlicher Wahlverein*), founded in 1903 and led by Michał Kokla (Kasper 1965: 208–11; Remes 1993: 133n.). There were agricultural unions in Ralbitz, Radibor, Kuckau, Crostwitz, Hochkirch, Hoyerswerda, Königswartha, Panschwitz, and elsewhere. From 1881 there was a farmers' periodical, the *Serbski Hospodar*, providing information on modern farming methods, stock-breeding, amelioration of soil, etc. From the 1890s, for financial defence against the power of German capital, mutual societies, credit unions, savings banks, and dairy cooperatives were formed (Rajš 1987: 10). Simultaneously, national consciousness among the Wends was maturing as a political force, and the authorities took steps to keep themselves informed. The Bautzen *Kreishauptmann* noted: 'From the occurrences of the year under review [1910] a remarkable manifestation deserving to be stressed is the strikingly intensified accentuation of the Wendish element in all areas of public life, particularly in the Wendish press, which is regularly read in the office of the *Kreishauptmann*' (Zwahr 1968: 188, no. 177).

In January 1911 Jan August Zoba died and was replaced as deputy for Rural Constituency No. 5 by Arnošt Bart (Ernst Barth) (1870–1945). Zoba had fought steadfastly for the Wends on linguistic issues and even gained a reputation as a Panslavist (Zwahr 1968: 186, no. 175), but Bart was more radical and there were signs, quite early in his career, that he would leave his mark on the political map. He was committed to the need for the Wends to present a united front, and it was from a group centred on him that the initiative came for the creation of a single union, aspiring to represent all Wendish associations of both Upper and Lower Lusatia. The group consisted of Bogumił Šwjela (1873–1948), Jurij Słodeńk (1873–1945), Jan Dwórnik (1871–1928), Franc Kral (1886–1915), and Bart (*Stawizny*, 2, 1975: 247–8). The foundation meeting was held at the headquarters of the Hoyerswerda Wendish Society on 13 October 1913 (Rajš 1987: 36–7). Sixty delegates attended, representing thirty-one associations with a joint membership of 2,890. From Saxony there were fourteen Catholic and ten Protestant associations and from Prussia, five Protestant and one Catholic. From Lower Lusatia there was only one: the *Maśica Serbska* (Mětšk 1957: 451n.).

The Union of Wendish Associations was given the name *Domowina* 'Homeland'. Its creation – a milestone in Wendish history – was immediately heralded as a great triumph, but from the account of the foundation meeting it is obvious that all was not well. In particular, the almost total absence of organizations from Lower Lusatia is striking (Mětšk 1957: 448–9). The frailty of the national movement in Lower Lusatia was also reflected in the state of literature and the press. In 1923 the Lower Wendish newspaper *Serbski Casnik* was selling only 200 copies, whereas sales of the Upper Wendish *Serbske Nowiny* had reached 6,000. In that year, however, the editorship of *Serbski Casnik* was taken over by Wilhelmina Wittka (Mina Witkojc), who by personal effort, travelling round Wendish villages and rousing interest, managed to lift the number of subscribers from 200 (1923) to 1,200 (1926). The style and contents of the paper changed (Völkel 1984: 182–3; Geskojc 1996a: 97; Pohontsch 2002: 74).

Witkojc (1893–1975) was born in Burg, in the Spree Forest. She left school at the age of fourteen and worked as a servant, in factories and in agriculture. In 1922 she came to Bautzen, where she was taught by Mucke to read and write her native language and found employment with the Smoler publishing house. The expansion in the number of readers of the *Casnik* suggests that the editor's views were not unpopular but they were controversial. She wrote in support of national minorities, condemned war, and wrote of Wendish kinship with other Slavs. These were provocative themes, which did not appeal to conservatives, of whom there not a few among the Lower Wends.

In *Casnik* no. 32 for 1929 she wrote: 'War is nothing less than murder, robbery, criminality, finally descending into paganism.... The people, being blinded, welcomed this mad activity with jubilation. That is not surprising, seeing that the German government before the War had for decades been preparing and rousing the people for war, particularly through the schools' (Geskojc 1996b: 260). This was too much for some readers, including Benjamin Bieger, a Lutheran pastor, who on 13 August wrote to cancel his subscription: 'I am extremely sorry that the *Casnik*'s sordid preaching of hatred against Germanity has driven me to this. [...] If the *Casnik* is not capable of safeguarding decently the Wendish cause which is close to our hearts, it is better that it should expire today rather than tomorrow' (Geskojc 1996b: 260). There was a confessional aspect to his displeasure: 'The Upper Lusatian and – even more far-fetched – partly Catholic content is totally alien to our Lower Wendish people' (Geskojc 1996a: 98).

With the issue dated 8 July 1933 *Serbski Casnik* ceased publication, but there is no evidence that it was closed by the authorities. In 1931 Mina Witkojc had been replaced by Fryco Rocha as responsible editor. For another two years after that, however, she continued to edit the Supplement and to irritate conservative readers until in April 1933 she was banned from all journalistic activity (see below). The last issue contained no announcement of the closure, but the issue for 17 June had already admitted that the paper was in financial difficulty (*Serbski Casnik* 1933: 120).

World war – an Easter truce (1915)

During the First World War Arnošt Bart was kept under police surveillance. From 8 February 1915 his mail was being opened, translated, and read (Zwahr 1968: 114, no. 94, and 281n.). The Wendish press was also under observation. As early as 28 November 1914 the *Amtshauptmann* Dr von Pflugk recorded that he had engaged *Oberlehrer* Johann Ernst Hantschke (Jan Arnošt Hančka) (1867–1928) to read *Serbske Nowiny*, *Łužica*, and *Katolski Posoł* and to translate for him any passages he regarded as suspicious. Hančka reported that Marko Smoler, editor of *Serbske Nowiny*, was pursuing a pro-Russian line. He also gave information on certain members of Bart's circle suspected of holding pro-Russian views (Zwahr 1968: 240, no. 240 [*sic*]). On 1 December von Pflugk tackled Smoler and cautioned him about his pro-Russian and pro-Serbian stance. Smoler denied the allegation but was given a warning, the first of several (Zwahr 1968: 241–2, no. 242; Völkel 1984: 35).

On 1 January 1915 a new law on censorship came into operation. Copy for *Serbske Nowiny* was now submitted to the police for approval in advance of publication. In April 1915 consideration was given to a letter sent to *Serbske Nowiny*, written by a Wendish soldier to his relatives in Rohne, in the parish of Schleife, describing events at the front at Easter 1915:

On Easter Day we lay in our trenches near the little Polish town of Łopuszno facing the Russians. It was a fine day and peacefully quiet around us. Suddenly a few Russians came running from their trench and placed a pot of Easter eggs in the middle between them and us, saying 'For the eggs – vodka'; then they went back again. It wasn't long before we had replaced the eggs with a bottle of a good schnapps. The Russians didn't wait, but quickly took it. After a little while we saw to our surprise a crowd of Russians coming up out of their trench, stopping in front of it, and starting to dance. We didn't need asking twice, but climbed out of the trench, with a concertina, of course, and twirled in competition with the Russians. When we had amused ourselves like that for quite a while, they offered us their hand to say goodbye, promising not to shoot at us that day, and went back to their trench. And they kept their promise too, for there wasn't a single shot the whole day and so we could continue to celebrate our Easter in peace. H. K.

The censor informed Smoler that accounts of 'so-called scenes of fraternization between friend and foe' were forbidden and that the letter could therefore not be published (Völkel 1984: 35–6).

Casualties

In a patently anti-German book on the Wends, Vierset claimed that during the War Germans deliberately sent Wendish soldiers, especially intellectuals, into the most dangerous positions at the front. To test this assertion Schmidt questioned several German officers, who attested that in the regiments under their command no distinction had been made between Wend and German and all soldiers conducted themselves with equal loyalty and bravery (Vierset 1923: 54; O. E. Schmidt 1926: 69–75). Vierset says more than 6,000 Wends were killed, constituting one-thirtieth of the Wendish population. Schmidt puts the total number of Wendish dead at between 2,000 and 3,000, concluding that Wendish losses were proportionally no worse than German losses (Schmidt 1926: 73). A proper statistical analysis has never been made and, in view of the uncertainty of the criteria for determining who was a Wend, any analysis would be difficult. Zwahr in *Stawizny Serbow*, however, estimates in round figures that the number of men killed constitutes between 3 and 4 per cent of the population of Lusatia (German and Wendish) (*Stawizny*, 2, 1975: 267). Among the prominent Wends that lost their lives were: Franc Kral, Secretary of the Domowina, Jurij Rječka, cantor and schoolmaster of the Bautzen Catholic parish, Jurij Delenk, editor of *Katolski Posoł*, and Hajno Jordan, cantor and schoolmaster in Schleife. The names of many others may been seen to this day on village war memorials throughout Wendish Lusatia and in the death notices published at the time in *Serbske Nowiny*.

Mistrust of Wendish soldiers in the army is exemplified by the case of Jurij Delenk, Catholic priest and editor of *Katolski Posoł*, who having been conscripted and selected to be an army chaplain, was waiting for appointment, when 'various letters arrived from Bautzen, slanderous and wounding letters, because certain of his Bautzen opponents considered his public Wendish activity sufficient cause not to entrust him with the honoured office of field-chaplain. Even in the last months of his life, when the possibility of his being promoted to reserve officer was under consideration, a dispatch arrived from Bautzen in response to the enquiry of his superiors at the front: politically unreliable'. Delenk had studied in Prague, and could speak Czech, but there is nothing in his biography (*NBS*, s.v.) to suggest that he was a radical. It is known, however, that following ordination in 1905 he was sent to Zittau, where he had pastoral responsibility for Czech immigrant workers, to whom it was his custom to preach in Czech. This was enough to attract the hostile attention of the authorities and the press (Delan 1918: 106–7).

November 1918: The Wendish National Committee

During the War the Allies exploited the disaffection of national minorities in the German and Austrian armies. Czech national consciousness was strong and Czech deserters from the Austrian army were formed into legions in Russia, France, and Italy. In February 1916, Thomas Masaryk and Edvard Beneš set up a Czechoslovak National Council in Paris, which the Allies recognized as a provisional government. On 11 November 1918 the Armistice was signed. Two days later in Bautzen about twenty men of various social strata met in the Wendish House to discuss how in the new political situation Wendish interests could best be represented. They elected the committee of a new national organization, called the Wendish National Committee (*Wendischer Nationalausschuß/Serbski narodny wuběrk*), with Arnošt Bart as chairman. The other members were: Jan Bryl, secretary, Božidar Dobrucky (1893–1957), treasurer, and Jurij Dučman. At a public meeting in Hochkirch a resolution was adopted, demanding that in the new German state full rights be granted to the Wendish language in church, school, and administration (Remes 1993: 126–8; Serbin 1920: 19; Scheuch 2001: 96, 204).

On 20 November a further mass meeting was held in Crostwitz. The resolution passed here was more specific and more ambitious than its predecessor:

> We Lusatian Wends, assembled in Crostwitz on 20 November, resolutely declare that on the basis of the right of self-determination of nations, recognized throughout the world, demand that we build our own future ourselves in a united Wendish Upper and Lower Lusatia and govern ourselves. Therefore a Wendish

Union of all Upper and Lower Wends has been created, which will support the Wendish National Committee, to secure autonomous development in the future for our two united Wendish Lusatias and the united Wendish nation. That this may be possible we demand that at the future peace conference there also be present a representative of the Wendish nation.

(Serbin 1920: 20; Völkel 1984: 37; Remes 1993: 128)

The Czechs too were interested in the Wendish question. *Národní listy* on 27 October 1918 had carried an article by Adolf Černý on 'Lusatia and the Peace Conference', in which he demanded that the Peace Conference grant the Wends self-administration in a united Lusatia and raised the question of uniting Lusatia to the Czechoslovak Republic, which was proclaimed the following day, 28 October 1918. Černý was now an official of the newborn Czech state, on whose behalf he travelled to Bautzen on 17 November, using a passport issued in the pseudonym Čornak (the Wendish equivalent of Černý). His mandate was to arouse Wendish national sentiment (Pata 1920: 49; Serbin 1920: 20; Zwahr 1968: 272; Zwahr 1970: 83, 151–2).

On 8 December 1918 the Wendish National Committee published its manifesto in *Serbske Nowiny* and *Katolski Posoł*. The next day in an interview for the Czech newspaper *Venkov*, the Saxon Minister of the Interior Lipinski declared his country's readiness to make concessions on the Wendish question, provided that the Czechs renounced interference in Saxon internal affairs. The National Committee did not react (Remes 1993: 133–4, 209, 334), but on 21 December they agreed on a memorandum to be submitted to the Preparatory Committee arranging the preliminaries for the Peace Conference. They claimed the right of the Wends to be represented at the Conference, to be regarded as an independent nation, and to be taken under the protection of the Allies. For their protection 'from the revenge of the Germans' they called for the occupation of Saxon and Prussian Lusatia. They asked for the immediate release of Wendish prisoners-of-war and for exemption from war reparations (Remes 1993: 135–6, 210).

The Memorandum of 21 December reveals a respectable degree of organization:

The members of the Committee are elected by the Wendish Union. The Wendish Union accepts any Wend, male or female. Each parish sends a delegate to the National Committee; each village attached to a parish elects a representative; all the representatives of a parish and the delegate form a Parish Committee, in charge of local propaganda and all political activity. By the end of 1918 22 parishes had been organized. The National Committee consequently consisted of 26 members, including its bureau. As soon as Wendish Lusatia has been recognized as an independent state, the National Committee will be transformed into a national assembly and elect a government.

(Raschhofer 1937: 224–5; Remes 1993: 137n.)

Bryl and Bart in Paris (1919)

It was not clear whether the Wends' leaders would be able to leave Germany to attend the Peace Conference. To be on the safe side, they decided to rely on the help of their Czech friends. On 20 December 1918, therefore, the National Committee sent Bryl (who had a passport) to Prague, where he met Černý. Arrangements were made for him to travel to Paris with the Czech delegation on 6 January. Czech Foreign Minister Beneš was already there before them. At the beginning of January Bart, who had no passport, crossed into the Czechoslovak Republic, where he was received by Páta, now a government adviser on the Lusatian question, and from Prague towards the end of January he travelled to Paris in an official train (Schmidt 1926: 80–2; Remes 1993: 143, 172n.) (Figure 7.2).

At a session of the Peace Conference on 5 February 1919, the Wendish memoranda were formally submitted by the Czech delegation. Edvard Beneš in his speech said: 'The Czechoslovaks consider it their sacred moral duty to present the demands of the Lusatian Wends to the Peace Conference. The Czechoslovaks do not demand the Lusatian Wends for themselves, but call on the Peace Conference not to let the non-German nations perish in a German sea. The question is equally political and moral' (Serbin 1920: 22; Remes 1993: 143n.). On 23 January, however, Beneš had been embarrassed to receive news that, without Allied agreement, Czech forces had occupied Teschen contrary to

Figure 7.2 Arnošt Bart (Ernst Barth) (1870–1956).

his express order not to do so. Under Allied pressure, they were promptly forced to withdraw; but the restraint with which he put his territorial claims on 5 February may have been conditioned by a feeling that the pugnacity shown by the Czechs in Teschen had weakened their case (Remes 1993: 165–6).

On 5 February, when the Wendish question, in the framework of Czech demands, came before the Peace Conference, Bart and Bryl were both still in Paris, but on 11 February Bart returned to Lusatia to keep the Wendish public informed. He addressed a meeting held in the Krone Hotel, Bautzen, on 22 February. Bryl, meanwhile, remained alone in Paris. The number of people attending the meeting, according to the Prussian Ambassador to Saxony, was something approaching 3,000 persons and the proceedings were conducted entirely in Wendish. The chairman was Jurij Dučman from Crostwitz (Serbin 1920: 22–3; Remes 1993: 157, 171, 173).

Bart told the meeting (according to *Bautzener Nachrichten*) that in Paris the Allies had assured him that the Wends would be allowed the right to national self-determination. Wilson and Lloyd George had shown the greatest sympathy to the Wendish cause. What had been said and written about annexation by Czechoslovakia was a fairy-tale; the Czechs had publicly and vehemently rejected the idea of occupying Lusatia. The existence of a Wendish state was perfectly feasible, but it would have to be joined to a larger economic unit. Bart spoke for an hour, during which there were frequent expressions of agreement from the floor. A motion proposed by a Lower Wend and passed by a large majority expressed the meeting's fullest trust in the Wendish National Committee and its resolve to 'stand determined and unhesitating behind them' (Serbin 1920: 23–4). A version of Bart's speech supplied to the Bautzen Attorney-General Dr Böhme, however, was more lurid. It said Bart had spoken of a Wendish independent state stretching from the Elbe to the Oder, covering 4,500 sq. km. Prussian Ambassador Reinhardt reported: 'The town [Bautzen], in which all the hotels […] were overflowing with Wendish guests from the country, makes a quiet and very German impression. It is said to contain 30 per cent Wends, but they are not obtrusive. In the streets I heard only German spoken, even by the peasants who were here for Bart's speech. The mood of most is quite against Wendish separatism […]. After singing the Wendish national anthem the participants dispersed' (Remes 1993: 157n., 157, 173).

Faced with the task of securing its borders, the German Republic recruited volunteers for this purpose from among the hordes of German soldiers returning home from the front, enrolling them into various units, including the Free Corps (*Freikorps*) and the Border Guard (*Grenzschutz*). The Czechs claimed and had occupied the whole of Bohemia, but its northern part (the Sudetenland) was German-speaking. The Sudeten Germans disputed and resisted Czech claims. Where Germany had once faced its friendly neighbour Austria, there was now a border with a new, hostile state which had contrived to align itself with the victorious Allies. Conscious of the possibility that the new Czechoslovak state would make incursions beyond the northern frontier of Bohemia into Lusatia, the German government began in late February to deploy units of its Border Guard (*Grenzschutz*) in Lusatia, not only along the border but also in Wendish villages. This aroused resentment (Remes 1993: 27; Scheuch 2001: 100–1).

Among the many Wendish places occupied were Brohna, Königswartha, Cunnewitz, Radibor, Ralbitz, and Weissenberg. Recruiting offices for the *Grenzschutz* were opened in the towns and on the big manorial estates. 'The fatherland is in peril. The Czechs are at the gates, eager to rob and burn our peaceful farmsteads', declared an announcement in the *Bautzener Nachrichten* on 8 March, placed by a unit of the *Grenzschutz* to attract volunteers (Serbin 1920: 41–2; *Stawizny*, 3, 1976: 28–9). At a meeting held on 5 March to express opposition to the Wendish National Committee, a speaker said: 'The Wendish movement is particularly promoted from the Catholic side. A glaring example took place in Ralbitz. There they refused to accept the German *Grenzschutz*: "We're not accepting any German army; we are Wends." For this the village had to pay a fine of 1,500 marks and accept a double occupation' (*Bautzener Tageblatt*, quoted by Serbin 1920: 26). The National Committee issued a statement, saying:

> We are able to expose all reports of an impending invasion of Saxony or Lusatia by the Czechs as a blatant lie. [...] We have evidence that the heavy military presence has come about on account of our Wendish movement. Why are villages situated some 20 or 30 km from the Czech frontier being overrun by soldiers, while the big barracks in Bautzen, barely 10 km from the Czech frontier, stand almost empty. [...]. More than ten days ago we sent a protest to all the ministers and requested that the army be withdrawn.

> (Serbin 1920: 30–1)

The protest was unsuccessful. The *Grenzschutz* also interfered in public meetings, where, with its help, the National Committee's opponents were applauded, while its supporters were silenced with shouts and abuse. The *Grenzschutz* was involved in incidents in Eutrich, Königswartha, and Marienstern, including rowdy behaviour, theft, and robbery. In Bautzen, a cabman named Symank was killed by a member of the *Grenzschutz* (Serbin 1920: 42).

On 13 March the Saxon *Volkskammer* passed a motion that the government take vigorous action against any incursion by Czech forces across the Saxon border. In reply to the question how it had been possible for the Wendish leaders to pass the border without passports, Minister Dr Gradnauer said: 'I cannot help thinking that the Wendish leaders travelled to Paris with passports from the Czech Government. They travelled in an official train.' In Paris they had succeeded in getting together with the leaders of the Entente, but 'Wilson's principles may not in any way be applied to the Wendish question.' Gradnauer said the Government was ready to compromise, but 'we want the Wends to remain inside the frontiers of Germany... There can be no question of the Wends being represented at the Peace Conference' (Serbin 1920: 31–3).

While the Commission for Czechoslovak Affairs was in session in Paris, Bart was in Lusatia. He was still there on 15 March, when a meeting of representatives of the Wendish Union was held in the Wendish House. It passed a resolution, including the following declaration:

We 400 elected representatives of the Lusatian Wends, having resorted here from all parts of Saxon and Prussian Upper and Lower Lusatia on 15 March 1919, hereby declare that all Lusatian Wends do truly stand behind the Wendish National Committee. We firmly declare that the proceedings in the Saxon Volkskammer on 13 March are the best proof that no German government and no German popular representatives will ever in the least way be able to give us the rights that belong to us according to the laws of God and man. [...] Therefore, we ask the Peace Conference to protect us.

(Serbin 1920: 24–5)

On 7 March Bart had made a brief journey to Prague, where he spoke to Páta and the president of the American Commission, complaining about the occupation of Wendish villages by German troops. He was advised to put his allegations in writing, which he did immediately on his return to Lusatia, setting them out in letters of 10 March to Páta and the American Commission (Schmidt 1926: 83; Remes 1993: 185). Later that day the letters were entrusted to a supporter named Jakub Hicka (Jakob Hitzke), a Catholic Wend from the village of Radibor, who had agreed to act as a courier for the National Committee. He immediately set off on foot for Prague, passing through the mountainous, forested region that divides Lusatia from Bohemia and intending to cross the border without the knowledge of the German authorities. He was already on Czech soil, when he was arrested by a German customs official (Serbin 1920: 43). This was a coup for the German police. They now had evidence of collusion between the Wendish leaders and Czech officials. From Hicka's interrogation and papers found in his possession they discovered that the main contact in Prague was Professor Josef Páta, but that three further officials of the Czechoslovak Foreign Office (Dr Machatý, Dr Veverka, and Dr Štěpánek) were also authorized to handle correspondence from the Wendish National Committee. Also confiscated was a letter from Dr Ernst Mucke (described in the police report as 'playing an important role behind the scenes') in which Páta was said to be as irreplaceable for the Wendish cause in Prague as Černý was in Paris. Hicka was kept under arrest for eight weeks (Serbin 1920: 43; Schmidt 1926: 83; Remes 1993: 174–5, 179–81).

It was only on 24 March that Bart for the second time left Bautzen en route to Paris. He travelled via Prague, Linz, and Basle. The date of his arrival is not known, but he was in Paris on Passion Sunday (6 April 1919). On arrival he was dismayed to hear from Černý that there had been no reaction to the Wendish question presented to the Conference by Beneš. On 11 April Bart and Bryl, as representatives of the Wendish National Committee, submitted a further memorandum to the Peace Conference, drawing attention to 'the German Government's preparations for war by assembling a substantial volunteer army in Lusatia (as well as in Silesia and other parts of East Germany)'. They restated their appeal for an independent Wendish state, preferably joined to Czechoslovakia. Alternative versions of independence were also stated, but it was emphasized that any kind of autonomy under the German Government would exist only on paper, because now that the Wends had shown their opposition through their national movement and had asked for help from the Allies, the Germans would redouble their efforts to Germanize them (Remes 1993: 218).

The April Memorandum also refers to numerous meetings and resolutions demanding independence and to a 'Proclamation of the National Committee in which this demand is formulated... signed by tens of thousands of Wends, men and women'. A new appeal to the Peace Conference was being 'circulated for signature in the whole of Lusatia'. Finally, in view of the known concern of the Allies at events in Russia, it was thought prudent to assure them that: 'The Serbo-Lusatian nation is in its entirety a firm barrier against Bolshevism' (Remes 1993: 219). Bart told Černý and Karel Kramář (the leader of the Czech delegation) about the military operations in Wendish Lusatia and said he believed Germany was preparing for war. Kramář arranged a meeting between Bart and a correspondent of the Paris newspaper *Le Matin*, which on 15 April carried an article under the headline 'Germany secretly mobilizing again'. It referred to the evidence of Czech delegates, who were said to have seen the military build-up in Lusatia, and referred by name to a witness named 'Broda'. This was to have consequences for Bart, when he returned to Germany (Serbin 1920: 25; Schmidt 1926: 83; Remes 1993: 178n., 186–7).

The Bautzen trial

On 12 April in Dresden, the Minister for War Neuring was assassinated and martial law was declared. The German authorities used the opportunity on Monday 14 April to raid and search the dwellings of Mucke, Bryl (though he was away in Paris), and Bryl's parents-in-law (Kerk by name) in Pirna. The German press reported on the success of these measures and said Bart had 'fled abroad'. News of Hicka's arrest, the police searches, and the allegation that Bart had fled soon reached Paris, and on 22 April Bart and Bryl issued a statement, reminding the world that Germany had signed the armistice conditions on which the Wendish National Committee's actions were based. In response to the threat of arrest and claims that they had fled they said 'We have not fled abroad, but are here to represent the interests of our nation at the Peace Conference... When we have completed our mission we shall return, whatever the outcome and whatever the situation, to our homeland' (Serbin 1920: 42–3).

On 3 May 1919 *Serbske Nowiny* (no. 18) reported that the Peace Conference had recognized Bart and Bryl as representatives of the Wendish nation and this was soon picked up by the German press. In retaliation, the Committee of Pro-Saxon Wends, together with equivalent organizations in Prussian Upper Lusatia, sent the following statement to the Peace Conference:

A loud protest is raised against the conduct of Messrs Bart and Bryl, who are acting before the Peace Conference like representatives of the Wendish people. The Wendish people has not given them a mandate for such actions and never would give them one. With their inflammatory propaganda they have been able to raise only a small minority in favour of their enterprise, which is hostile to

Germany and dangerous for the existence of their own people. The overwhelming majority of our people reject their plans vehemently and will not follow them.

Meanwhile, the Wendish Union was holding mass protest meetings in support of its leaders (Bryl 1920: 44).

At the beginning of May Bryl returned to Lusatia and was arrested on arrival. He was interrogated on 5 May but released. On 11 May, he spoke at a meeting in the Wendish House and said:

The Conference has accepted all the documents and resolutions of the Wendish people and is now examining the Wendish question. Bart and Bryl were sent to Paris by the Wendish Union to represent as delegates their national interests. The Wendish nation, organized in the Wendish Union, gave them its mandate. Because the German Government would not issue passports to them or to any Wend engaged in the service of the nation, the National Committee was obliged to seek contact with the Peace Conference by methods which the German authorities consider illegal. But where, we ask, after the signing of the Armistice and the great revolution of 1918 in Germany and Austria, were the political frontiers between those two neighbouring states and the Czechslovak Republic truly located? – What political view of this matter do the authorities take who invite Austrians and Bohemian Germans (who now belong to the Czechoslovak Republic) into German armies of volunteers, accept them, and register them? Where do they get these crowds of legionaries, who now in our Wendish villages have distinguished themselves with such heroic deeds of thievery and intimidation of our population? Where do these German newcomers get their passports, who issued and signed them, and in what names?

A motion put to the meeting called for the release of Hicka and for free access to the Peace Conference. It protested against judicial interference in the activities of the National Committee. It rejected the allegations sent to the Peace Conference by the Committee of Pro-Saxon Wends and confirmed its recognition of the Wendish National Committee as the only body authorized to represent Wendish interests at the Peace Conference. The motion also condemned the fact that the meeting was actually taking place in contravention of an official ban, whereas in that week alone thirteen German protest meetings had been allowed (Serbin 1920: 44–5; Remes 1993: 172n.).

Six days later German indignation at the Wendish presence in Paris was again excited, when on 17 May *Bautzener Nachrichten* under the heading 'Stupidity or Treason?' published a full translation of the article published a month earlier in *Le Matin*. This was embarrassing for Bryl, who had only recently been released from custody in Bautzen. He was now interrogated again by the German police and, confronted with the article, he decided to distance himself from Bart's allegations. He said Bart had spoken to the newspaper not as a delegate of the National Committee but in a personal capacity and in spite of his (Bryl's) attempts to dissuade him (Remes 1993: 189).

On 20 June 1919 the trial took place before the *Landesgericht* in Bautzen of seven members and supporters of the Wendish National Committee. The accused were: 1. Jakub Hicka sr., of Radibor, 2. Rev. Božidar Dobrucky, pastor of Kleinbautzen, 3. Jurij Dučman, of Crostwitz, 4. Pětr Pawoł Hantuš, of Radibor, 5. Michał Nawka, of Radibor, 6. Jakub Hicka jr., and 7. Dr Ernst Mucke. Hicka sr. was charged with illegally crossing the Saxon-Czech border without a passport; illegally carrying uncensored and unstamped letters and printed matter; and with smuggling money into Czechoslovakia. Dobrucky and Dučman were charged with inciting Hicka to commit the said acts, Hantuš and Hicka Jr with assisting him. Nawka was accused of sending 300 marks to Czechoslovakia. Although the public prosecutor recommended that Hicka Sr's time already spent in custody be regarded as sufficient punishment, the court sentenced him to four months imprisonment and a fine of 300 marks. Mucke and Dobrucky were each sentenced to four months imprisonment and a fine of 500 marks. Hicka Jr and Hantuš were given one month in prison, and Nawka had to pay a fine of 200 marks. Dučman was discharged without penalty. Bryl escaped prosecution. He was reported to have been extremely cooperative during his interrogation by the Bautzen examining magistrate. That was the end of his friendship with Bart (Serbin 1920: 52–3; Schmidt 1926: 86; Remes 1993: 175, 179).

The minorities clause

Oskar Trautmann was a diplomat and member of the German delegation to the Paris Peace Conference. He came from Muckwar in Lower Lusatia and believed himself to be of Wendish descent on his mother's side. He took an interest in Wendish affairs and was not anti-Slav, though he did not approve of the Wendish National Committee's aspirations. He had been a friend of Bogumił Šwjela since they were schoolboys and their friendship is attested in their correspondence over a period of fifty years (1896–1946). He eventually retired to his estate at Schlichow, near Cottbus, where he died after the Second World War (Mětšk 1959: 468–9). Šwjela was one of the founders of the Domowina and a loyal Wend, but he was a moderate, diplomatic, and capable of compromise. Occasionally Trautmann would consult Šwjela on Wendish matters. When in December 1918 he received report that a delegation of Wends was in Prague saying that in view of the abdication of the Hohenzollern and Wettin dynasties the Lusatias must by the terms of the Treaty of Vienna revert to the Czech Crown, he sent a telegram (from Berlin) asking Šwjela (in Dissen) if he knew anything about this (Mětšk 1959: 477–8). Šwjela's reply is not known, but on 27 December Trautmann sent him a further telegram, this time asking him to travel to Bautzen, discuss the current situation with the leaders of the Wends, and then travel to Berlin to report to him. The German Foreign Office would cover his expenses (Mětšk 1959: 478).

Three days later Trautmann was again in touch, thanking Šwjela for agreeing to travel but letting him know that, as he was being sent to Spa to meet the German Armistice Committee, Šwjela would not find him in Berlin. Nevertheless, Šwjela was (he said) expected at the Foreign Office. That the visit did take place is clear from a manuscript note of 2 January 1919 in Šwjela's hand on the back of Trautmann's letter. Šwjela wrote:

> In the opinion of the Secretary of State, the solution of the Wendish question by the creation of a Free State is possible. The Foreign Office looks with sympathy on a solution through which, in the framework of the future Reich Constitution, the oppression of the Wends could be ended. The wishes of the Wends laid before the Peace Conference could best be represented by the German Committee.

> (Mětšk 1959: 479 n.)

The presence of two Wends at the Conference and the presentation of their memorandum meant that, whatever the outcome of their submission, they would at least bring the Wendish question to the notice of the Press, and this was embarrassing for the German Government. Trautmann wrote to Šwjela on 9 March 1919: 'Have you seen the enclosed article from the *Frankfurter Zeitung* and can we not do something effective in the Wendish press too to counter and mitigate the apparently monomaniac ideas of Herr Barth?' It is not known whether Šwjela felt inclined to assist, but among the Wends too there was a reaction to the press reports. On 5 March 1919 a new movement appeared, which was opposed to the Wendish National Committee. It was not asking for independence but only for autonomy within the Reich. This was the Committee of Pro-Saxon Wends (*Wuběrk saksoswěrnych Serbow*) (Mětšk 1959: 483, 492). The Wendish question had also been influential in another respect. Trautmann on 22 June wrote:

> In the [Foreign] Office we are generally of the opinion that an annexation of Lusatia was never seriously desired by the Czechs. It was rather that Beneš in February this year wanted to use the Wendish business as a bargaining counter against a predictable step by our representatives on the question of the Bohemian Germans. And the Czechs were successful in this. Without the construction of the moral pressure of the Wendish question Count Brockdorff would, to judge from all appearances, have gained considerably greater concessions against the Allies' demands in the east.

> (Mětšk 1959: 495)

Trautmann also had an explanation for the Wends' failure to persuade the Allies to grant their wishes. He wrote:

> At any rate, the Wendish business has hereby been recognized finally as a German internal matter, which – if not altogether clearly – even Bart has finally admitted. In the Wendish matter it was, furthermore, of advantage to the German view of

things that Wilson and the English fear the spread of Bolshevism to Germany, and alongside the events in Bremen, Brunswick, and Munich the radical demands of the Wendish leaders against landed property did nothing to bolster trust in them in Allied circles.

(Mětšk 1959: 495)

The National Committee's claim to speak for all Wends was not unreasonable. The meeting of the Wendish Union in the Wendish House on 15 March was attended by '400 elected representatives...from all parts of Saxon and Prussian Upper and Lower Lusatia', implying an electorate of tens of thousands. The meeting had been called to counter the assertions, made by the Committee of Pro-Saxon Wends and in the debate in the Saxon Volkskammer on 13 March, that it was not representative. Secondly, there is the allusion in the April Memorandum to 'several tens of thousands' of signatures to the National Committee's Proclamation (Raschhofer 1937: 254–5). This, if it could be verified, would be a persuasive index of mass support among a total population numbering ostensibly about 200,000.

On 7 May 1919 the German delegation, headed by Foreign Minister Brockdorff-Rantzau, received the draft treaty and on 29 May, submitted counter proposals. In their reply of 16 June, the Allies rejected nearly all the German counter proposals. This reply evidently contained a clause on minorities which had not been there previously, for on 22 June Trautmann wrote to Šwjela:

The Allies' draft treaty of 7.5 having passed over the Wends in silence, the clause on minorities in the version of 16 [June], which definitely was formulated not wholly without Bart's agitation, will, in the opinion of most of the gentlemen of our delegation, scarcely have any application to them, as they cannot count as a minority in the legal sense.

(Serbin 1920: 49–51; Mětšk 1959: 494–5; Zwahr 1970: 90–1)

Bart, however, regarded the inclusion of the minorities clause as a triumph. *Serbske Nowiny* published a letter from him, written on 18 June:

The national rights of the Lusatian Wends in the basic agreements are now clear and firmly recognized. That is an achievement for the national movement and the national awakening of the Wends, whose far-reaching importance today scarcely anyone will understand. In the peace resolutions presented to the Germans on 7 May nothing of this kind was laid down. In the first half of June too, [in] the requirements relating to the rights of minorities, we found nothing favourable to us Wends. After unrelenting efforts we managed to re-direct the attention of the arbitrating circles to our Wendish question. The resolutions presented to the Germans on 16 June produced the paragraph relating to the protection of minorities in the final statements in such a way that it ensures us Wends comprehensive and precise guarantees for spiritual, religious, and cultural development.

(Serbin 1920: 48; Zwahr 1970: 91)

The Prague newspaper *Národní Politika* agreed. In a report from Paris published on 22 June it announced:

The Peace Conference has devised a basis for the solution of the Wendish question. This appeared in the reply given to the Germans on Monday 16 June in reply to their counter proposals. It includes in the first part the following decision: 'The United and Allied Powers are prepared to give German minorities a guarantee of their rights relating to the cultivation of religion and culture in territories annexed from the German Reich by the new states created by the Peace Treaty. This guarantee will be put under the protection of the League of Nations. The United and Allied Powers take cognizance of the German delegation's declaration that Germany is resolved to treat the national minorities on its territory in accordance with the same principles.'

(Serbin 1920: 50–1; Remes 1993: 183n.)

The paper would have taken a different view, had it known of the doctrine, already forming in the German delegation, that the Wends could not count as a national minority. Brockdorff-Rantzau was not prepared to sign the Versailles Treaty and on 20 June 1919 he resigned. The resulting crisis caused Scheidemann's cabinet to resign too, but on 28 June the Treaty was signed by representatives of a new government. Bart was present at the signing. There was no reference in the Treaty to the Wends, but there was in Part 1 of the Appendix an article on national minorities (Article III) (Mětšk 1959: 494 n.; Zwahr 1970: 93; Remes 1993: 183).

Bart's arrest

Following Bryl's return to Lusatia and arrest at the beginning of May, Bart had remained alone in Paris and had decided to make one last attempt at retrieving something from the Peace Treaty. Interpreting creatively the terms of the Treaty relating to national minorities (like the author of the as yet unpublished article in *Národní Politika*), he wrote from Paris on 17 June to Matthias Erzberger, who had just been appointed Finance Minister of the Reich, informing him that the Wendish National Committee had 'conclusively attained the objective it sought, seeing that at our instigation the necessary guarantees regarding education, religion, and the development of our national culture have been recognized for our nation too in the foundations of the Peace Treaty (Appendix, Part 1, Article III)'. He repeated the demands for the unification of the Wendish-speaking areas of Upper and Lusatia in an autonomous province, the use of Wendish at all levels of public administration, the election of a national administrative body, and unrestricted national autonomy. He stated that he was ready to start negotiations immediately and assumed that now was the time to present the demands to the Government of the Reich, because their later implementation by the League of Nations would cause more work and have 'disagreeable consequences' for the Government. He asked Erzberger to convey his demands to the German Government (Remes 1993: 220–1).

This strangely overconfident letter is dated 17 June 1919, the day after the date of the Allies' second draft treaty, constituting their reply to the German counter proposals. It was not until 20 June that Brockdorff-Rantzau resigned, so on 17 June the German delegation must still have been studying the new draft. To judge from Trautmann's words 'formulated not wholly without Bart's agitation', Bart was justified in thinking Article III had been added 'at our instigation' or partly so. But he was misinformed as to the precise terms of the Article (or deluding himself). In any case, the Treaty was not signed until 28 June; so on 17 June it was rash to make any assumption as to its final contents.

Both Bart and Bryl were convinced that the minorities clause was a result of their efforts. In old age Bart recalled: 'The peace negotiations were approaching their conclusion. And nothing for the Wends! I decided to ask generally for the protection of national minorities. I sent off eight telegrams with the same demand...' The recipients (he said) included Wilson, Lloyd George, Clemenceau, and the heads of the Chinese, Japanese, and Italian delegations. 'That evening the Paris newspapers reported that the Peace Conference had decided unanimously that Germany must accord the same rights to its minorities as it demanded for its German minorities abroad. The German representative Brockdorff-Rantzau also accepted this demand' (Zwahr 1970: 93–4).

Bart remained in Paris and did not return to Germany until 2 October 1919, when he was arrested as he crossed the border. His trial opened on Monday 19 January 1920. The principle charge was that in April 1919 in Paris, as a German, by assisting a foreign power, he had damaged the military power of the German state, this constituting attempted treason. He had committed the offence by informing the French newspaper *Le Matin* that Germany was secretly mobilizing. The trial lasted one day. Bryl's testimony was used against him. He was sentenced to three years in prison, minus the three months spent in custody awaiting trial (Serbin 1920: 76; Schmidt 1926: 85; Zwahr 1970: 96–7; Remes 1993: 189). There were protests from the Czechs and from the Swiss newspapers *Journal de Genève, Tribune de Lausanne, Democrat*, and *Suisse Liberale*, as well as from the Slav Institute in Paris. In reply to a parliamentary question the Czech Foreign Minister, Edvard Beneš, said:

The former Wendish parliamentary deputy Arnošt Bart was a member of the Czechoslovak delegation from the beginning of proceedings at the Peace Conference [...]. I myself had the opportunity, either alone or together with Arnošt Bart, to negotiate with President Wilson, with Secretary of State Lansing, with Foreign Ministers Balfour and Pichon, and with other French and English Ministers. [...] In a separate announcement it was specifically stated that the Allies with satisfaction note Germany's undertaking to give all national rights to national minorities. This passage refers particularly to the Lusatian Wends.

A petition, organized by the Wendish Union and signed by thousands, was sent to Berlin, but without result (Serbin 1920: 78–80).

Bart served the first part of his sentence in Leipzig, but on 26 May 1920 he was transferred to Gollnow, where the conditions were better. Here his letters were not censored, which meant he could write in his native language again. He continued to brood on Bryl's role in his conviction. On 2 June he wrote to his wife:

> For your suffering only Bryl is guilty. I am only unsure still how far he did it all from malice or stupidity. None of my friends, with the exception of Čornak [Černý], can believe the treachery he committed towards me. Without knowing anything for certain, he lied and lied, and the greater the nonsense he babbled against me the more they believed him...

After serving almost one year of his sentence Bart was reprieved and released on 16 September 1920. He immediately resumed office as President of the Domowina (Zwahr 1970: 97, 105, 110).

Young Kashubs (*Młodokaszubi*)

In both Habsburg and German Empires scholarly interest in the local Slav languages and folklore could not avoid having political implications. Impartiality was almost impossible. In 1907 in Karthaus (Kartuzy) (Pomerelia) Friedrich Lorentz and Izydor Gulgowski founded a *Verein für kaschubische Volkskunde* ('Society for Kashubian Folk-Studies') with the objective of collecting and making accessible 'everything to do with Kashubian folklore in the widest sense'. It published its own journal the *Mitteilungen des Vereins für kaschubische Volkskunde* (Proceedings of the Society for Kashubian Folk-Studies). By 1914 the number of members had grown to 196, including Kashubs, Poles, and Germans. The society was not very old before Lorentz was accused of having founded it to further Polish interests. In 1910, in an attempt to placate his accusers and to avoid further conflict, he resigned as chairman of the society and as editor of the *Mitteilungen*, and the statutes of the society were amended to make it clear that the object of its interest was the folklore of all peoples (German, Polish, Dutch, and Scandinavian) who had ever lived in Kashubia (Neureiter 1978: 75). Born in Mecklenburg in 1870, Lorentz lived for most of his life in the Kashubian region and from 1896 devoted himself to the study of the history and, above all, the language of the Kashubs. He is the author of numerous books and articles on these subjects, including a history of the Kashubs (1926) and a history of the Kashubian language (1925). What records remain of the language of the Slovincians are mainly his work, especially his Slovincian grammar (1903), two-volume Slovincian dictionary (1908–1912), and a collection of texts (1905). When Juliusz Koblischke (1910:

12–14) cast doubt on the testimony of Hilferding and Ceynowa regarding the Slovincians, Lorentz was ready to corroborate it up to a point: 'The adjective *slovinšti* is used by the Slavs in the parishes of Groß Garde and Schmolsin in *Kreis* Stolp to denote their language and only their language.' The nouns *Slovinc* and *Slovinka* (says Lorentz) were used only to denote the worshippers who attended the Slavonic Protestant church services in those parishes (Lorentz 1910: 15). The fact remains that commentators have needed a name for the people of those parishes and have chosen to call them *Slovinzen*, Slovincians, and the like. After many years of field-work among the Slovincians Lorentz spoke with unique authority when he estimated the number of speakers at between 200 and 250 (1903: 2).

Just as some Germans thought the *Verein* too Polish, so some Kashubs thought it too German, and it was to some extent as a reaction to it that the movement known as the Young Kashubs (*Młodokaszubi*) sprang up, led by Aleksander Majkowski. He was born on 17 July 1876 at Berent (Kościerzyna). He studied medicine at Berlin University from 1897 to 1900, when he transferred to Greifswald. He later recalled the impression made on him there by his first visit to the cloisters of the medieval university. He never forgot the portraits of the Pomeranian dukes carved in the walls with the often repeated title 'Dux Pomeranorum et Cassuborum' or 'et Cassubiae'. Another event that influenced his decision to take up the national cause was the unveiling of the Mickiewicz statue in Warsaw in 1898, which he witnessed. Owing to his membership of the Polish students' union *Adelphia*, which used to help the Polish seasonal workers on the surrounding estates to organize themselves, he was expelled from the university in 1901 for pro-Polish agitation. He was advised to continue his studies at a university where the Polish question did not arise. He chose Munich, which seemed far enough away for safety, and here in 1902 he founded the Polish students' alliance *Vistula*, which constituted the germ for the subsequent society of Young Kashubs.

Majkowski completed his medical studies in 1903 and qualified as a doctor in 1904. At the end of 1904 he returned to Kashubia and for a year worked at the Sankt- Marien-Krankenhaus in Danzig. While here he was approached by the owners of the *Gazeta Gdańska* and offered the position of chief editor, which he accepted (without telling his superiors at the hospital) and managed somehow to discharge his editorial and medical duties simultaneously. He introduced a Kashubian supplement to the paper under the title *Drużba* (the word for the master of ceremonies at a Kashubian wedding). It survived for six numbers from May to July 1905. At the end of the year, he moved back to his home town Berent and set up a private medical practice (Neureiter 1978: 82–4). Though well disposed towards the *Verein für kaschubische Volkskunde*, Majkowski was uneasy about its use of the German language. He therefore brought out his own monthly journal on Kashubian affairs, *Gryf*, which was printed mainly in Polish and partly in Kashubian and whose first number appeared in Berent in November 1908. At a meeting in Danzig on 20–21 June 1912, the Union of Young Kashubs (*Vereinigung der Jungkaschuben*) was founded. The political aspect of its work aroused hostility from sections of the Polish press and accusations of separatism. On the outbreak of war in August 1914 Majkowski was conscripted into the German army and served as a medical officer on the Rumanian and Western Fronts. He fell ill with rheumatism in July 1918 and was transferred to

Zoppot (Sopot), where in November he heard of the German collapse. He became deputy to the head of the Commission for determining the position of the northern section of the future German-Polish border (Neureiter 1978: 85–9).

The Kashubs at the Peace Conference (1919)

If the claims of the Lusatian Wends were a matter of minor importance to the Peace Conference, the same could not be said of Poland's claims to access to the Baltic, and central to this question was the status of the Kashubs. They were, in the words of Sir Robert Donald, 'the key people of the Corridor' and they had 'more natural claims to the territory which they occupy than any other race, as it has been their home from remote ages' (1929: 31). In view of posterity's acute interest in the Conference's handling of the Polish question, however, it is surprising how little is known of the Kashubian presence in Paris in 1919. The Polish National Committee, led by Roman Dmowski, had been in Paris during the War, and Dmowski was now on the spot to lead the Polish Delegation to the Peace Conference. He was joined by Ignacy Jan Paderewski, the Polish Prime Minister, to whom Woodrow Wilson had in January 1917 first mentioned Poland's right of access to the sea (Davies 1981, 2: 387). How this was to be achieved was a subject for negotiation, but in western Poland the people were taking matters into their own hands. On 27 December 1918 an anti-German revolt broke out in the Grand Duchy of Posen (Poznań). In West Prussia the German government was still in control, but Polish and Kashubian armed units were being organized, and Local People's Councils were springing up. In Poznań a Supreme People's Council (*Naczelna Rada Ludowa*) was formed, and a Sub-Committee thereof appeared in Danzig, led by Dr Józef Wybicki with Dr Franciszek Kręcki as his deputy. Kręcki was also chief of the OWP (Military Organization of Pomerania/*Organizacja Wojskowa Pomorza*), which was preparing for armed conflict. Involved in the OWP were the Kashubs Dr Aleksander Majkowski, Antoni Abraham of Oliwa, Antoni Miotk of Puck, and Fr Bolesław Witkowski of Mechowa (Bolduan 1970: 13).

Early in 1919 the Sub-Committee was preparing to take Danzig by force of arms but was restrained by the Supreme People's Council in Poznań. Hoping to achieve the same outcome by negotiation at the Peace Conference, Wybicki and his Sub-Committee decided to send a delegation of Kashubs to Paris to join the Polish Delegation there. This proposal was approved by the People's Councils and the Council for the Neustadt (Wejherowo) *Powiat* put forward its own chairman, Aleksander Majkowski, as a suitable delegate, but his candidature was frustrated by Łaszewski, the representative for Pomerania on the Supreme People's Council in Poznań. The reasons for his objection are not known. The other delegates, however, were approved – namely Antoni Abraham, Tomasz Rogala, and Dr Mieczysław Marchlewski. The inclusion of Antoni Miotk in the delegation, proposed by Abraham, was also approved (Bolduan 1970: 14).

At this point in the narrative, several uncertainties arise. There were obviously substantial logistical problems of the same kind as those faced by the Lusatian Wend delegates in travelling to Paris. Passports were needed and there was a risk that the German authorities would not let them leave Germany. Who of the four named delegates actually left Danzig and how many of them of them reached Paris are questions to which the sources offer various answers. Their departure took place on 14 April 1919 and their first destination is likely to have been Warsaw, where the newly independent Polish government probably issued them with passports. Abraham, Rogala, and Marchlewski arrived in Paris on 18 April and were received by the Polish National Committee. Miotk, it seems, was not with them, possibly having been delayed by passport problems. The three delegates remained in Paris until 29 April, when they left for Poland disguised in one of General Haller's military railway transports and returned to Danzig (Socha-Borzestowski 1975: 8).

One of the reasons for the uncertainty surrounding the Kashubian representatives' presence at the Peace Conference arises from their reluctance, while there, to disclose their names. This is revealed in a report of 3 May 1919 in a short-lived weekly newspaper, published in Paris:

> Three delegates of the Polish political organizations of West Prussia and the city of Gdańsk (Dantzig) have just arrived in Paris. A lawyer from Gdańsk, a farmer, and a fisherman from the land of the Kashubs to the west of Gdańsk are among the delegation. [...] When, after a few minutes of conversation, we start to take notes, they make a striking observation:
>
> – It would be better not to publish our names. We left our country secretly. It is impossible to obtain passports from the German authorities, who try hard to prevent the Polish population of West Prussia making any contact with the other parts of Poland and with the Allies. And we have left our families there. Why should we expose them to harassment or persecution? We shall give our names wherever we are received, but it would be unhelpful to publish them in the press.
>
> (*L'Indépendence Polonaise* 1919: 2)

Because no further reports from French sources are known, we are reduced to using second-hand accounts of what Antoni Abraham told his compatriots after he had returned home. These claim that the delegates were received by the Prime Minister Ignacy Paderewski and by Erazm Piltz, delegate of the National Committee to the French Government. They further claim that Abraham met Woodrow Wilson, Lloyd George, Orlando, and Marshall Foch and that together with representatives of the Mazurs and Silesians they gave evidence to the Conference's Commission for Polish Questions. One of their functions was to serve as living exhibits of the Polishness of the indigenous inhabitants of West Prussia (Socha-Borzestowski 1975: 7) or, at least, of their desire to be united with Poland. (Whether the question of the relationship between Poles and Kashubs arose is not known.) As further evidence of their claims the group brought with them copies of the journal *Gryf*, of the Gdańsk street directory, containing 9,250 surnames ending in *-ski*, *-ki*, or *-icz* and also numerous resolutions of individual People's

Councils demanding the incorporation of Pomerelia and Danzig into the Polish state (Bolduan 1970: 15). Very little of this can be corroborated from independent sources and it might, in any case, be objected that, while many Kashubs have surnames ending -*ski* or -*ki*, these are not typical and that -*icz* is a characteristically east Polish suffix.

A further detail was added to the story in 1957 by Włodzimierz Steyer in a letter to the journal *Kaszëbë* (no. 2, quoted in Bolduan 1970: 14). Referring to his meetings with Abraham in 1921–1923, Steyer said:

> ... [Abraham] mentioned as a co-participant in his chequered journey the name of Augustyn Kąkol. He asserted that thanks to proof in the possession of the latter that his ancestors had been living on the land along the western shore of Lake Zarnowitz/Żarnowo for 700 years, he so astonished Wilson and Lloyd George (the Celt who was so contemptuously disposed towards the Slavs) that they immediately corrected the border on the map to include the lake in accordance with Augustyn's demand.

Kashubs in the Second Polish Commonwealth

The new Polish-German border after 1920 brought by far the greater part of the Kashubs back to Poland after a century and a half of German rule. Although Germany kept the Slovincians, the villages between them and Lake Zarnowitz, and those further south surrounding Bütow, the new political boundary emphasized the fact that Polish access to the Baltic was realized exclusively through Kashubian territory (Lorentz 1925, map; Borzyszkowski et al. 1999: 60, map 14). Most of Kashubia had, in fact, become the Polish Corridor. As Aleksander Majkowski wrote in 1925: 'Perhaps those who in the pre-war period so feared the Young Kashub movement, the expression of the tribal sense of the Kashubs, will today pause to reflect, when in the language of diplomats there is talk no longer of Kashubia but of the Corridor' (Gryf 1925, no. 1, quoted by Borzyszkowski et al. 1999: 56).

But although Polish claims to an outlet to the Baltic were largely based on the Kashubian presence here, the Kashubs did not receive a warm welcome in the revived Polish state. The challenge of integrating the populations inherited from all three partitioning powers, in fact, presented itself constantly to successive governments in inter-war Poland. The ties of national solidarity between Poles from the various regions did not automatically take up where they had left off at the end of the eighteenth century. Roughly one-third of the Second Commonwealth's population was made up of non-Polish minorities (Germans, Ukrainians, etc.). Their status as minorities was at least unambiguous, but the Kashubs, according to the official Polish view, were not a national minority but Polish.

The former *Pommerellen*, now called *Pomorze Gdańskie*, needed 43,000 civil servants and officials, including teachers. This was far more than could possibly be supplied from the Kashub population, so swarms of officials from other parts of Poland descended on them. Owing to discrepancies between the policies of the partitioning powers there was a disproportionately copious supply of minor officials from the south-east (Galicia), who had previously known nothing of the Kashubs but easily adopted the German tradition of regarding them with contempt. The incomprehensible Kashubian language was often mistaken for German and the Kashubs were treated accordingly (Wańkowicz 1963: 91–2).

The Kashubs were no less hostile to the newcomers. Of the three partitions the German had had the highest standards of living and education. The Austrian had the lowest. It is therefore surprising to find that the Poles from central and eastern Poland who flooded into Pomerelia in the 1920s proceeded to take all the best jobs. Or so it was said. In the Kashubian popular perception, Kashubia was being taken over by uneducated people from the poorer parts of the country. They naturally looked down on them but were shocked to find they were moving into positions of authority. The Kashubs thought themselves superior culturally and materially, but they were probably inferior in one important respect – their command of Polish. The authorities regarded it as axiomatic that they were Poles and spoke Polish. Both the Versailles Treaty and the Polish Constitution guaranteed the rights of national minorities, but no one, it seems, ever considered this fact to be relevant to the Kashubian situation. A set of derogatory or contemptuous terms grew up to denote the stereotypical newcomer: *Antk* 'Tony' (a hypocoristic of *Anton* 'Anthony') meant a Pole from central Poland, *Galileusz* a Pole from Galicia, *Rusk* a Pole from the east. The adjective *bosi* 'barefoot(ed)' was used, alluding to the proverbial barefooted poverty from which they were supposed to have fled. Phrases noted at that time include: *Më momë terå bosêgo školnêgo* ('We've got a teacher from central Poland now', literally 'a barefooted teacher'); *On je z bosëχ strón* ('He comes from the barefooted parts', sc. 'central Poland') (Sychta 1967–1976, 1: 5, 60–1; Kutta 2003: 120–1).

The true state of public opinion among the Kashubs towards the end of the War, as it became increasingly clear that the German army was facing defeat, is hard to fathom. According to Polish sources they greeted the German collapse with joy. In Berent (Kościerzyna) in December 1918, the German mayor was ousted and replaced by the Kashub Klemens Lniski. The Kashubs responded to the growing uncertainty by arming themselves and forming home guard units (Kutta 2003: 57). Friedrich Lorentz, on the other hand, says the collapse of 9 November provoked no reaction in Kashubia other than curiosity (1926: 139–40). It is said that the Kashubs welcomed with enthusiasm the arrival of Polish troops in January 1920 (Donald 1929: 37–8), but eye-witness accounts are elusive. What is clear is that the Kashubs were soon disappointed by the new regime. There were several reasons for this. In the first place, partly owing to the new borders, there was a rapid decline in their already unhappy economic situation. A Polish military intelligence report of January 1922 noted: 'the state of the people in Kashubia is deteriorating. The poor Kashub population, which before the Great War used to migrate to foreign parts to make a living, usually into the depths of the Reich, stays at home without work and suffers want' (Kutta 2003: 106). The Kashub fishermen along the Baltic shore were cut off from their traditional markets in Danzig. Secondly, the Polish army treated the Kashub region as occupied territory. The natural reaction was to treat the army as occupiers. Thirdly, the space left by departing Germans was rapidly filled by an influx of Poles from the former Russian and Austrian partitions, who instead of adjusting to the sensitivities of the Kashubs, were inclined to mock them and their speech. The Polish-Kashub linguistic barrier was constantly obtrusive. A Grudziądz police report of 1925 observed: 'The opinion that we used to be oppressed by the Germans and today we are oppressed by Poles from other provinces, and especially from Little Poland, is heard more and more often. There is a special undercurrent of dissatisfaction in the Kashubian districts' (Kutta 2003: 130).

Among the German minority in the Polish Corridor, there were many who resented their new citizenship and hoped for a return of the Reich. They were supported by like-minded Germans inside the Reich. The Polish government was nervous and deployed police agents to detect any pro-German activity. It was feared that a pro-German rising might take place, giving the German government an excuse to intervene. The Corridor was of crucial importance to Poland's defence and economy. Its loss would have cut Poland off from the sea. In 1922 a German conspiracy was discovered. Emil Fenske and Oskar Krüger, both Pomerelian Germans, were arrested for planning a rebellion in the Kashub area. No Kashubs were involved. In 1925 rumours of a further German conspiracy, this time involving Kashubs, appeared in the local press. The *Gazeta Kaszubska* on 19 April demanded an investigation by the authorities and said 'If there are any Kashubs who have been aspiring to detach Kashubia from Poland, they should be exposed, their names published as traitors to the national cause, and the guilty punished' (Kutta 2003: 185). It later transpired that at the beginning of 1925, if not earlier, Franciszek Kruszyński, a Kashub, had been into touch with the German para-military organizations *Stahlhelm* and *Einwohnerwehr* and had gathered a group of fellow Kashubian conspirators. He had been encouraged in these plans by Dr Siegfried Wagner, director of the Danzig *Heimatdienst*. The day of action was to be 27 September 1925. At 9 pm the rebels intended to occupy certain public buildings in Wejherowo, Puck, and Kartuzy, cut off telephone and telegraph links, open prisons, release prisoners, arrest officials, and declare the separation of Kashubia from Poland. German forces were expected to cross the frontier and claim the land on behalf of Germany.

The date had been chosen because it would precede the Locarno Conference by a few days and give the conference something to think about (Kutta 2003: 186). The Polish police were well informed, however, and, shortly before zero-hour, intervened and arrested most of the conspirators. Those involved were all Kashubs: Franciszek Kruszyński, Józef Miszka, Augustyn Labuda, Wincenty Bojka, Józef Śladowski, Józef Ellwart, Jan Müller, Józef Pokorski, and Jan Schraeder. Kruszyński evaded arrest by fleeing to Germany. Śladowski fled to France. The Public Prosecutor's Office took nearly two years to prepare its case. When the accused were finally, in June 1927, taken before the Court in Starogard, Pokorski, Müller, Ellwart, and Schraeder were found not guilty. Another year passed before (in June 1928) the court passed sentence on the other three. Bojka and Labuda were released without further penalty. Miszka was sentenced to two and a half years imprisonment (Kutta 2003: 187).

On 1 September 1929 a Regional Association of Kashubs (*Zrzeszenie Regionalne Kaszubów*) came into existence with about forty members. It was immediately accused of separatism and treated by the authorities with suspicion and hostility (Kutta 2003: 244–5). Whereas in elections to the Reichstag the Kashubs had consistently voted for the Polish candidates, they now began to waver, and in the elections to the Sejm in the late 1920s, for the first time in their history, they returned a German (Donald 1929: 37–8). Official opinion on the Kashubian question was summed up in 1931 in a secret report prepared by the Pomeranian *Wojewoda* Stefan Kirtiklis:

> …hitherto among the generality of the Kashubs there has not existed a feeling of national separateness, nor has it even been established which of the numerous varieties of Kashubian is to play the role of a literary language. Hence the vast majority of Kashubs consider their speech a peasant dialect and cease to use it as soon as they acquire an education. These opinions and the passivity typical of the Kashubian popular masses have meant that the regional movement, at present organized by the Regional Association of Kashubs has not yet extended beyond the bounds of a meagre handful of activists, recruited mainly from among the intelligentsia. [...] Serious misgivings, however, are aroused by the activities of some young representatives of the Kashubian regional movement (Labuda, Trepczyk), who are even linked to the German camp (Lorentz) by the bonds of personal relations.

(Kutta 2003: 306)

Lusatian Wends in the Weimar Republic and Third Reich

Article 113 of the Constitution of the Weimar Republic guaranteed certain rights to national minorities, so in 1926 and again the following year the Communist Group in the Saxon Landtag pressed for its implementation in relation to the Wends. The Communists called for the training of Wendish teachers, financial support for the extension of teaching in Wendish, and the appointment of Wendish judges and officials. They also wished to make any social or political discrimination against the Wends a punishable offence. All these efforts failed. On 9 November 1920, the first group was set up in Bautzen of a Wendish sports organization named *Sokoł* 'Falcon'. It was followed by many further *Sokoł* groups in various Upper Lusatian villages, but the headquarters were in Bautzen. The Wendish *Sokoł* followed the example of similar bodies under the same name in other Slavonic countries. Its members were not solely concerned with sport and gymnastics but also strove to develop a strong national spirit and resist Germanization. Among Germans it was widely suspected that *Sokoł* groups were a manifestation of Czech infiltration.

After the shock of Wendish demands for independence in 1918–1919, the authorities never ceased to keep a watchful eye on the Wendish situation, and at the beginning of 1920 it was decided to set up a special department for that purpose with headquarters in Bautzen and under the direction of the *Kreishauptmann*. The proposed aims of the new Wendish Department (*Wendenabteilung*) were to include:

(i) strengthening the German element in the Wendish territories and effective opposition to the threat of Wendish irredentism in all spheres of public and private life,

(ii) emphasis on the treasonable nature of all Wendish national aspirations,

(iii) the exposure of all Wendish national consciousness as hostile to the Reich.

The *Wendenabteilung* actually came into existence only in 1923. Its name and activities were not made public (Mětšk 1967: 12–13, 159).

In the Weimar Republic all the national minorities organized themselves into associations for self-preservation. The Poles had their Union of Poles in Germany (*Związek Polaków w Niemczech*) and this organization proposed the foundation of a Federation of National Minorities in Germany (*Verband der nationalen Minderheiten in Deutschland*), standing for the interests of the Danish, Friesian, Lithuanian, Polish, and Wendish minorities and publishing its own journal called first *Kulturwille* and later *Kulturwehr*. For the whole life of this journal (1925–1936), its editor-in-chief was Jan Skala (1889–1945), a Catholic Wend from Nebelschütz. He was an important figure, not only for the Wends but for the other minorities too. By the time he took over *Kulturwille*, Skala was already an experienced journalist and an irritation to the authorities. In 1928, when he was sued for defamation, he protested, though without success, against the denial of his right to use his native language in court, as guaranteed by Article 113 of the Constitution.

When the Nazis came to power in January 1933, the minorities faced new dangers. In the columns of *Kulturwehr* Skala continued to resist oppressive policies. In May that year the first of many searches of his home were made by the police and much of his correspondence was confiscated. When, in September 1935, he received a letter from the Minister of Propaganda (Joseph Goebells) threatening him with imprisonment for criticizing officials, he replied by requesting not only that the threat be withdrawn but also that the cause of his criticism be remedied. The same year he exposed in his journal the true meaning of the Nuremberg Laws. In March 1936 Skala was banned from engaging in any further journalistic activity even under a pseudonym. That meant the end of his career and of *Kulturwehr*. Unemployed and impoverished, he continued the struggle by publishing anonymously abroad. He published an article in London in the *Slavonic and East European Review* under the pseudonym Sorabus, drawing attention to the plight of the Wends. Eventually, in January 1938, at the age of 48, he was arrested and taken to the Gestapo prison in Dresden to be interrogated. When he was released nine months later, he was suffering from deafness caused by rough treatment. He returned to his family in Berlin, where he found menial work (Kroh 2009: passim).

The banning of the Domowina

The *Ermächtigungsgesetz* of 23 March 1933 put an end to parliamentary democracy, and, with hindsight, one might think that now the writing was on the wall for the Wends, but to many that was not how it seemed at the time. Ota Wićaz, for example, took a sanguine view of Wendish prospects in the New Germany, to judge from a letter he wrote to Pawoł Nedo on 27 March: 'I am convinced that no harm is threatened to the Wends, if they remain true to the German state' (Bresan 2002: 48). There were soon signs to the contrary. In mysterious circumstances on 9 April 1933 the *Sokoł* dissolved itself, and two days later the daily *Serbske Nowiny* was banned for eight days. The ostensible reason for the ban was an article by Měrćin Nowak-Njechornski, published on 21 February, referring to the variety of the German language spoken in Bratislava in what was alleged to be a contemptuous manner, thereby 'threatening public order and security'. The real objective, however, was to purge the newspaper of certain individuals who were thought to harbour anti-German and pro-Czech sentiments. These were Marko Smoler, editor-in-chief, Gustaw Janak, managing director, Mina Witkojc, sub-editor of *Serbski Casnik*, Jakub Šajba and Pawoł Grojlich (both printers), and the following directors: Pawoł Lubjenski, Jakub Lorenc-Zalěski, Měrćin Nowak-Njechornski, Jurij Słodeńk, Arnošt Bart, and Jan Šěca. They were all forbidden to carry out any work for the newspaper, or enter its premises, or even to contribute to any other newspaper or magazine. When the paper began to appear again, the change in the editorial line was immediately obvious (Völkel 1984: 118–19).

On 28 April six leading Wendish activists, were arrested on 'urgent suspicion of posing a danger to the state': (1) Arnošt Bart, (2) Dr Jan Cyž, (3) Gustaw Janak, (4) Měrćin Nowak-Njechornski, (5) Jurij Słodeńk (Georg Melzer), and (6) Jakub Šajba. At the same time searches were made of the houses of (1) Arnošt Bart Jr, (2) Jan Haješ, (3) Herman Kóćka, (4) Bjarnat Krawc, (5) Pawoł Krjećmar, (6) Pawoł Lubjenski, (7) Měrćin Meltke, (8) Jan Meškank, (9) Gustaw Mjertin, (10) Maks Mjertin, (11) Michał Nawka, (12) Marko Smoler, (13) Jan Symank, (14) Křesćan Tawzynt, and a person named (15) Hernašt (no further details known) (Bresan 2002: 49). Jan Haješ's daughter Leńka later recalled the events in Lohsa that morning:

It was about 7.30 a.m. when they came tugging at the door and a mob of SA men rolled in. About 18 of them and three senior Nazis.... They surrounded the house holding loaded guns. They threatened to shoot anyone who left the house. I had a Wendish letter. They claimed it was Czech and seditious, hostile to the Nazis.... They tore up precious books.... Those SA men were like robbers. They said everything was treason. With their boots they tore the seats of chairs, suspecting secret things were hidden there. Above all they wanted to give us hell. The neighbours, hardened Nazis, shouted that they should hang us from the lampposts: 'Take them away.'

(Rajš 1987: 112)

On 6 May Nedo wrote to Wićaz: 'No one dares lift a finger for the Wendish cause. People are afraid to speak Wendish.... The Domowina is powerless and the leadership of the Maćica asleep.' If Wićaz shared these concerns, he certainly did not show it. He had just taken over as editor of the *Časopis Maćicy Serbskeje* and, putting on a brave face in his first editorial, he told his readers:

> With complete confidence [...] I acknowledge the new government established by the Volkskanzler Adolf Hitler, relying on his express promises that in the new Germany no nationality may be forcefully Germanized. And with confidence I hope that proper conservation of our nationality, based on loyalty to the state, will find total understanding from a state that intends to rebuild itself with the powers of the Aryan nationality. — One of the greatest gains pointing to the future that has grown out of the German revolution is a recognition of the singularity and the rights of every nationality.
>
> So let us all get to our work and may God bless us.

(Wićaz 1933: 15; Bresan 2002: 49)

The anti-Wendish measures of April 1933 attracted attention outside Germany. They were condemned in the Czech press and concern was expressed in the Czechoslovak parliament. The Society of Friends of Lusatia (*Společnost přátel Lužice*) held protest meetings and sent telegrams to Hitler. The German minorities outside the Reich were also worried, fearing retaliation (Huebner 1988: 255–6). On 17 May, in a speech to the Reichstag, Hitler said: 'While we cling with boundless love and loyalty to our own nationality, on the same principle we also respect the national rights of other peoples and wish from the innermost depths of our hearts to live with them in peace and friendship. The very concept of Germanization is unknown to us' (Bresan 2002: 50n.).

In early June five of the six Wendish prisoners were released, followed three weeks later by the sixth. Protest letters were sent to the League of Nations, but, despite the provisions of the Peace Treaty, it would not accept responsibility. Outside Germany there were protest meetings, at one of which, near Mnichovo Hradiště in northern Bohemia, more than 30,000 people were present (Hartstock 1964: 211–13; Huebner 1988: 256). There were puzzling inconsistencies in Nazi policy. In June 1933 the Gauleiter of Brandenburg, Wilhelm Kube, issued a message of reassurance to the Wends, saying that National Socialism would always defend them (Huebner 1988: 257–8). Towards the end of July, however, the Nazi *Kreisleitung* in Kamenz put a ban on the use of Wendish at a forthcoming meeting of Wendish students, saying there was 'no place for the Wendish language...in the new Germany', but this was overruled by the Bautzen *Amtshauptmannschaft*, possibly recalling what Hitler had said in May. On 28 July the Bautzen *Sturmabteilung* asked for permission to lock up Arnošt Bart again for mocking the Nazi salute, but the public prosecutor could not find an appropriate law to charge him (Zwahr 1970: 124–5; Huebner 1988: 256–7). This legislatory defect was made good only in December 1934 (Huebner 1988: 257n.).

Concerns at the plight of German minorities abroad and the memory of Hitler's speech in May continued to moderate anti-Wendish action. The report dated 4 September 1933 of a discussion between representatives of the Reich, Saxony, and Prussia recorded: 'The representatives of the Reich's Ministries and of the Prussian departments took the view that in the interests of the German minorities in Europe a tolerant policy towards the Wends too is necessary' (Kašpor 1958: 140). In accordance with this milder policy Dr Johannes Sievert, the Bautzen *Amtshauptmann* and head of the *Wendenabteilung*, on 20 September issued an official declaration in which, while condemning the actions of the National Committee in 1919, promised the Wends that they would be permitted to continue to cultivate their language and culture. This, coming so soon after Hitler's repudiation of Germanization, was reassuring (Huebner 1988: 257, 270n.).

On 31 October 1933, the Domowina held its first general assembly under the new regime and agreed in principle with the proposal that it should be a unified national organization, able to speak for the Wends as a whole, and not be merely an umbrella structure of smaller associations. A resolution was passed protesting against the transfer of Wendish teachers to locations outside the Wendish area (Huebner 1988: 258; *Stawizny*, 3: 134–6). Attempts were made to adjust to the new regime. In October the Wends piously enquired whether the greeting 'Heil Hitler' might have a Wendish equivalent, such as 'Sława Hitlerej' or 'Zdar Hitlerej' (the answer was 'no') and, unlike the Polish and Danish minorities, they did not fail to participate in Hitler's plebiscite in November. In December the district school inspector in Kamenz wrote in reply to the Domowina's protest at the expulsion of Wendish teachers from the Wendish area, saying they had not been removed from their homeland because they were still in Germany and anyone who regarded 'Russia or some other country' as his homeland had no right to be treated as a German citizen. When read out at the Domowina's extraordinary assembly on 27 December, the letter provoked an uproar. The 25-year-old schoolmaster Pawoł Nedo was elected president. The Domowina now declared itself to be 'the sole representative of the Wendish people' (Huebner 1988: 258–9).

Continuing the search for an accommodation with the Nazis, the Domowina's leaders frequently quoted Hitler's speech of 17 May, claimed they were imbued with the same nationalist spirit as the Nazis, and adopted much of the Nazi paraphernalia, including the *Führerprinzip*. The Nazis were only momentarily taken aback by these protestations of orthodoxy. Three days after the Domowina had published particulars of its new organization with regional units called *Gaue* and with Pawoł Nedo as *Führer*, the Saxon State Chancellery prohibited the use of Nazi terminology by private bodies (Huebner 1988: 259 and 27). The *Wendenabteilung* had seen through the revitalized Domowina's lip service to Nazi ideas and was unmoved by allusions to Hitler's 'deliberately misunderstood' speech of 17 May (Kašpor 1958: 143). In any case, the Domowina did not even look Fascist. The *Führerprinzip* was compromised by the continued existence of the executive committee and Nedo lacked the dictatorial manner. Though he was never a member of the Nazi Party, in July 1933 he became a candidate for the SA. In June 1934, however, he was expelled for 'indifference and lack of discipline' as well as for his Wendish activities (Huebner 1988: 160n.; Bresan 2002: 126).

Nedo was already known to the Nazis, because, through his knowledge of Wendish folklore, he had some years earlier met and attempted to enlighten Walther Frenzel (1892–1941), a local Nazi historian, who in July 1933, having attained a position of influence, had had Nedo appointed adviser to the Bautzen Nazi Party on Wendish cultural matters. The Nazis now intended to use Nedo in his new office of President of the Domowina, but he had other ideas. Treading a fine line, pretending to be a supporter of the New Order, he managed to delay disaster for four years. In 1934 in Lower Lusatia, according to a report from the *Regierungsbezirk*, National Socialism had 'made an especially strong impression in the Wendish villages', but in Saxony it was the Domowina that was gaining in strength. Even Sievert could not help admitting it had been a successful year for the Wends. In January 1935 a new monthly supplement to *Serbske Nowiny* was launched with the title *Naša Domowina* 'Our Homeland'. It was skilfully edited by Nedo to enable Wends to air their views with an Aesopian ambiguity that generally got the better of the censor (Huebner 1988: 261–2).

Disappointed to see the Wends prospering, Sievert in September 1935 began to issue a series of regulations making life more difficult for them. On 18 December he informed Nedo that a new law had made the black, white, and red swastika banner the only German national flag. Displaying any other flags or colours, including the Wendish tricolour, was forbidden (Hartstock 1967: 184–5; Huebner 1988: 264). New Year 1936 brought the Wends a new set of regulations forcing them to get permission from three separate authorities for meetings open to the public. Full translations had to be submitted for theatrical and choral events. In January too Sievert handed to the Domowina for their approval the draft of a new constitution, renaming it 'Domowina: Union of Wendish-Speaking Germans' and restricting their activities to certain cultural matters 'within the framework of the German people and state' (Huebner 1988: 264). On 19 January a gathering of local representatives of the Domowina unanimously rejected it and passed a resolution condemning the attempts of the authorities 'to abolish the independent existence of our people […] through decrees and directives'.

On 18 February Nedo was summoned to the *Amtshauptmann*'s office. He reported to Sievert that the Domowina Committee had rejected the demand that it disband its youth groups (Hartstock 1967: 179). Expressing his disappointment at the Government's Wendish policy and at the discussions regarding the new constitution, he enquired: '... so do the authorities think that we have no national sense of honour at all?' Sievert replied that, as matters stood, it would surely be very hard to find a way to an understanding. With that the discussion was at an end (Bresan 2002: 135). Having received no response to their ultimatum, the Saxon State Chancellery on 16 March ordered the *Amtshauptmann* to prohibit all public and private meetings of the Domowina and affiliated associations. He again summoned Nedo on 18 March and announced the decision. The ban was communicated to him only orally, not in writing, and publication of it in the Wendish press was forbidden. Faced with the problem of conveying news of the ban to his members without using the press and without holding a meeting, Nedo invited the local representatives of the Domowina to what he called 'a private conversation' in the Wendish House on 22 March. Leaflets explaining the negotiations and their outcome were printed and distributed with *Serbske Nowiny*. Two days later, Nedo was informed by his education authority that he was being transferred far away from the Wendish area to a school in the Province of Hanover (Bresan 2002: 136).

Rather than submit to his transfer, however, Nedo decided to resign from teaching altogether and, with the help of Jan Skala, found a training post in the Polish bank *Unia* in Berlin (Bresan 2002: 145). From here he could easily visit Lusatia. He knew his correspondence was being read by the police and that communication by letter was therefore risky. However, from Bautzen he issued circulars to Domowina members, reassuring them. 'And when you are Bautzen, go into the Domowina office or the Wendish shop. There you can learn the latest news, there you can always find people ready and willing to advise and help you. Keep in touch with each other, then we can come to no harm', he wrote in a circular of 7 June 1937 (Bresan 2002: 140).

There were still three Wendish organizations that were not affiliated to the Domowina and thus not subject to the ban: the Maćica Serbska, the Cyril and Methodius Society, and the Society for the Support of Wendish Students. The Maćica held its annual assembly in Bautzen on 31 March 1937. This gave Nedo an opportunity to speak and explain recent events to a large number of Wends. His speech here was noted by the *Wendenabteilung*, but no action was taken against him. Less than three months later, all activities of the Maćica were banned (10 June 1937) (Bresan 2002: 142). On 25 August 1937 the Gestapo raided the Wendish House, closed down the offices of *Serbske Nowiny*, and arrested its publisher Dr Jan Cyž. That was the end of Wendish publishing for the duration of the Third Reich, with the exception of *Katolski Posoł* and the Catholic annual *Krajan*, both of which, thanks to the Concordat with the Vatican, continued to appear until 1939 (Rauch 1959: 149; Völkel 1984: 126–7; Huebner 1988: 269; Bresan 2002: 144).

Even after the outbreak of war in 1939, however, the property of the Domowina and the Maćica Serbska was still protected by legality. The *Landrat* Dr Eckhardt on 5 December 1940 wrote to *Regierungsrat* Dr Werner Essen: 'It has […] not yet proved possible to confiscate the property of the Maćica Serbska, consisting principally of the Wendish House here, a fairly extensive and probably valuable library, and the Wendish Ethnographic Museum.' At this time, a group of members of the Maćica was still trying to save its holdings. Precious books, manuscripts, pictures, and other objects, which remained in the as yet unsealed museum, were gradually being removed and entrusted to private individuals (Šěn 1999: 24). The legal veneer still protecting the Maćica's property was, however, too good to last. On 4 February 1941, *Regierungsrat* Dr Essen ordered its expropriation and entrusted the execution of the order to the security police in Berlin and Dresden. The expropriated material was to be handed over to an organization under his control, known as the *Publikationsstelle* at Berlin-Dahlem, a society founded by a group of Prussian historians in 1933 to award scholarships and publish the results of research into East European, especially Polish, history. Since 1938, however, it had been directly subordinate to the State Ministry of the Interior (Burleigh 1988: 90–1; Šěn 1999: 25). In late spring 1938 Sievert had been replaced as Bautzen *Amtshauptmann* and head of the *Wendenabteilung* by Dr Hermann Eckhardt. In 1939 the *Amtshauptmannschaft* became a *Kreis* and Eckhardt became a *Landrat* (Huebner 1988: 270 and 58).

The formal distraint on the Maćica's property occurred in April 1941, but it was nearly a year before it was put into effect. On 8 December that year the Saxon Minister of the Interior handed over the Wendish House, the Wendish Museum, and their entire contents to the Mayor of Bautzen. He made an appropriate amendment to the record in the land registry. On 21 January 1942 Bautzen *Landrat* Dr Eckhardt wrote to the *Publikationsstelle* saying he had received orders to put the possessions of the Maćica Serbska at their disposal and in February the librarian of the *Publikationsstelle*, Dr Harald Cosack, came to Lusatia for a fortnight to organize the Library's transfer to Berlin. He had repeated meetings with Dr Eckhardt (Šěn 1999: 25–6). In February 1942, approximately 18,000 volumes from the Maćica's Library were conveyed to the *Publikationsstelle* in Berlin. Here they languished until November 1943, when to escape Allied bombing they were moved to a manor house at Lehn, near Löbau (Šěn 1999: 27).

Wendish support for Nazis

In the elections of 1932 and 1933 in *Landkreis* Cottbus, where the Wends made up something approaching half the electorate, the Nazi share of the vote was considerably higher than the average for Germany as a whole. The Nazi Gauleiter Wilhelm Kube could not conceal his approval of the Wends, 'since they have voted National Socialist in much higher percentages [than the Germans]'. At the other extreme, in the predominantly Wendish Catholic villages in the eastern part of the *Amtshauptmannschaft* Kamenz, the NSDAP in July 1932 received less than 15 per cent of the vote. Even in the following March, although the Nazis now polled 24 per cent, this was still less than half what they attained in the rest of the *Amtshauptmannschaft*. Rural Catholics generally throughout Germany tended to reject the NSDAP and vote for the Centre Party, but Catholics who were Wends were twice as likely to do so. According to the census of 1933, conducted under the Nazis, the total number of Wendish-speakers had dropped to 57,167 (Huebner 1988: 251–4).

Before coming to power the Nazis seem to have given little thought to the Wendish question, but there were local officials who were members of the Nazi Party and had their own views. When it came to votes, however, the Nazis had no prejudices and the NSDAP placed advertisements in *Serbske Nowiny* for the November 1932 election (Huebner 1988: 254–5). Wendish teachers felt an overriding duty to contribute to the maintenance of the language, but they could do so only if they were working in schools in the Wendish area. They were thus under pressure to join the Party or its associated organizations, such as the SA, for a teacher who did not do so drew attention to himself and thereby, in the case of a Wendish teacher, increased the risk of being posted outside his native region. Joining the Party seemed to offer a defence. Moreover, those teachers who did not join, whether German or Wendish, ran the risk of dismissal. The number who managed to survive without doing so was very small (Schurmann 1998: 95, 38n.). On 26 September 1940 Reinhard Heydrich (1904–1942), Chief of the Reich Security Services and the Security Police, reported to the Reich Ministry of Education, that the Wends were still busily pursuing their cultural work and preventing 'the final solution of the Wendish problem' (Schurmann 1998: 95). The worst offenders were teachers and priests. He therefore proposed to deprive nine teachers in Saxony and sixteen in

Brandenburg of the opportunity for pro-Wendish activity by having them transferred from Lusatia to West Germany. Regardless of whether they were in the Party or not, Heydrich considered them all politically unreliable (Schurmann 1998: 38, 72n., 95, 178).

Wendish resistance

After August 1937 the only refuge of the public use of the Wendish language was provided by the churches. Otherwise, Wendish history from now until 1945 comes down to the personal experiences of individuals. For official purposes the Wends, whether they liked it or not, were Germans. Men of military age were conscripted into the German armed forces. There were, however, still a number of Wends who had never accepted the defeat suffered by their representatives at Versailles and whose determination to gain independence from Germany was only strengthened by the Nazi takeover. As relations between Germany and the new Slav states became polarized, the Wends were further constrained to decide which side they were on, and some saw Czechoslovakia and Poland as their potential protectors. Anticipating a repeat of the German defeat, some Wends envisaged the reappearance of the Wendish question on the international agenda and made plans accordingly. One of those who resisted the Nazis was Jurij Cyž, a Catholic, who was born in Säuritz on 6 October 1904, the son of a smallholder. In 1928 he entered the Charles University to study law, but after one year transferred to the University of Leipzig and graduated there in 1935. In both Prague and Leipzig he was active and prominent in Wendish student societies. On 30 August 1938 in Ostro he was married to Marija Dundová, a citizen of Czechoslovakia. In January 1937 in Warsaw Cyž met a Pole who revealed that he was an officer of the Polish intelligence service and was looking for reliable anti-Nazis among the Wends. He used the code-name 'Michał' (his identity as Captain Wojciech Lipiński was to remain a secret until the twenty-first century). Cyž discussed the matter with Nedo and they agreed that the Domowina would not assist in recruiting agents, but that in certain circumstances would undertake collaboration with the Poles. At his next meeting with Michał, Cyž supplied him with information on German fortifications on the Czech border (or the lack of them), reinforcements of the Bautzen garrison, and public morale in Germany (Woźny 2010: 236–7; Pałys 2013: 119).

The Poles were building a fifth column among the Polish minority in Germany and regarded Wends too, if they were ethnically conscious, as potentially useful. Jurij Cyž introduced compatriots he knew to be ready to work against the Nazi regime. They were mainly Wends who were already in Poland or connected to Poland in one way or another, and included his wife Marka, Pawoł Nedo, Pawoł Nowotny (a student at the University of Poznań), Nowotny's fiancée Hilda Balzer, Wójćech Kóčka, Jurij Brězan, and Pawoł Cyž (Jurij's brother). Měrćin Nowak, though not in Poland, was also somehow involved. There is conflicting evidence as to the participation of Pawoł Dudźik. It is possible, but unlikely, that Dr Jan Cyž was implicated (Marciniak 1995: 247).

At the beginning of April 1937 at the priest's house in Crostwitz a meeting was held, at which Fr Jan Wjenka, Pawoł Nedo, Dr Jan Cyž, Franc Natuš, and Jurij Brězan were present. It was resolved to set up a network of trusted persons based on Domowina leaders. According to Polish sources, it was understood that the Wends would collaborate in measures aimed at defeating Germany and achieving independence. They would receive material and logistical help. The contact man was to be Pawoł Nowotny. It was planned that Jurij Cyž would set up a branch of the Domowina in the Netherlands, so that in case of war he could move to France or Great Britain to continue to represent the Wendish cause. On 1 September 1939, Germany invaded Poland and ten days later the Gestapo came to Jurij Cyž's flat in Berlin and took him to their headquarters in the Alexanderplatz, where he was interrogated and tortured. Within a few days he was moved to Sachsenhausen Concentration Camp. Here he met his younger brother Pawoł, who had been arrested earlier at home in Säuritz. Jurij Cyž was released on 3 February 1940 and returned to his wife and daughter in Berlin. In November that year he was conscripted and served on various Luftwaffe stations. In May 1944 he was in a military hospital in Dresden, using the opportunity to gather information on the air defences of the city. Here he made contact with a resistance group and, it is thought, with the British Special Operations Executive (SOE) (B. Cyž 2004: 366–7; Pałys 2013: 122). On 6 November 1944 Dr Jan Cyž, Jan Meškank, Jurij Cyž, Marka Cyžowa and several former officials of the Domowina, were simultaneously arrested. Jurij Cyž and his wife Marka were taken first to the prison in Dresden, then to Berlin, where under torture he revealed some details of the Wendish opposition. On 20 February 1945 the pair were taken before a court in Potsdam. Jurij was sentenced to death, Marka to eight years imprisonment (B. Cyž 2004: 362–4; Pałys 2013: 118–19).

Also involved in the Wendish resistance was the student Jurij Měrćink, though his precise role remains uncertain. On 16 August 1937 he was returning to his studies in Prague from a visit to Lower Lusatia (L. Kola 1984: 156). At the border, as he was crossing into Czechoslovakia, he was searched and arrested. He was found to be in possession of certain circulars and invoices emanating from the Domowina. What they were or how their discovery compromised the Wendish leadership is not known, but news of his arrest alarmed Pawoł Nedo, who at the time was in Berlin. He immediately travelled to Upper Lusatia and somewhere near Bautzen met Dr Jan Cyž. The same evening the most important Domowina documents were smuggled out of the Wendish House and taken to a safe place in Hochkirch. Nedo, who obviously knew what Měrćink was carrying, had realized the seriousness of the situation and foreseen that the offices of the Domowina were to be raided. This was shortly before the Gestapo raid of 25 August 1937, when Dr Jan Cyž was arrested and the Domowina offices searched and sealed (Šěn 1999: 23; Bresan 2002: 143n.).

The Gestapo mulled over the expediency of arresting Nedo, but postponed action (Bresan 2002: 143). Měrćink was to spend the next eight years (except for six months in 1940) in various kinds of incarceration, first in prison in Dresden and Leipzig and later in Sachsenhausen Concentration Camp (Žur 1977: 191–2). Dr Jan Cyž remained in custody for one year. Pawoł Nedo, following his resignation from the teaching profession, had found a job as a book-keeper on a nobleman's estate near Wilmersdorf, 90 kilometres north of Berlin. Here in November 1939 he was arrested and taken to the

Gestapo prison in Potsdam. A month later he was released (Bresan 2002: 154). Eventually he was conscripted and at the end of November 1944 found himself in Budapest in the ranks of the retreating Wehrmacht. At this point he was again arrested and taken this time to a military prison in Lehrter Str. in Berlin. His misfortune this time had resulted from the arrest of Jurij Cyž, who had broken down under interrogation and given the Gestapo a list of names (Nowotny 1996: 13; Bresan 2002: 159). After interrogation Nedo was charged with preparing to commit high treason, and in mid-February 1945 he was transferred to the prison of the *Volksgericht* in Potsdam. Here he saw his fellow prisoners being taken out to be executed or dying from the brutal conditions of their detention, but there was news of the advancing Red Army. In view of the general practice of the *Volksgerichtshof* at that time and of the death sentence already passed on Jurij Cyž, Nedo expected the same fate, but on 27 April he was freed by advancing Soviet troops (Nedo 1960: 129–32; Bresan 2002: 160).

On Monday 6 November 1944, the main day of Wendish arrests, Dr Jan Cyž went to work in Bautzen as usual, but just before 9 o'clock the Gestapo came for him and took him to Bautzen police station. That evening he was transferred under escort to Dresden by train. At Gestapo Headquarters in Dresden it was mid-December before his interrogation started. His interrogator, whom, it turned out, he had already met during his imprisonment in 1937–1938, wanted to know about Michał, but Cyž genuinely knew very little about it (J. Cyž 1955: 35). Shortly before Christmas, hearing that the prisoners Jurij Cyž, Pawoł Cyž, and Marka Cyžowa were being transferred to Berlin, and that Józef Nowak and Cicilija Cyžec were being released, he deduced that he and Jan Meškank were the only remaining Wends (J. Cyž 1955: 37).

In the night of Shrove Tuesday 13 February 1945, Dresden was the target of one of the biggest air-raids of the War. The prisoners were terrified of being burned or buried alive in the ruins of their gaol. From his cell window Cyž could see Dresden burning. The prisoners were constantly snuffing out sparks to prevent their palliasses from igniting. It was becoming unbearably hot and they could not see for smoke. Eventually, at about half past three, there was the sound of a key scraping in a lock and their door opened. They were being released by a prisoner, who had managed to break out and take the keys from a guard. There was shouting in a variety of languages, as prisoners tried to find their friends and countrymen. He found Jan Meškank, who pointed to pools of water left by the firemen's hoses and told Cyž to soak his overcoat in the water and run to freedom between the burning houses down to the Elbe. A moment later Cyž saw his friend moving rapidly down towards the Elbe, but the flames were so hot that he could not follow him (J. Cyž 1955: 40). Later, having survived a further air raid, Cyž climbed into the back of a lorry that took him to a railway station, where he boarded a train for Kamenz. Back in Wendish territory, he rested for a time in Nebelschütz but feared discovery. One night he received a warning to escape while he could, so he went to the hospital in Wittichenau, where, with the help of a trusted doctor, he was admitted to the contagious diseases ward. Here, with three other Wends, he awaited the arrival of the Red Army (J. Cyž 1955: 42).

Jan Meškank's experiences on that same fatal Monday 6 November 1944 and in the prison in Dresden were similar to those of Cyž. In his memoir he recalls having seen Cyž twice briefly in the prison but being unable to talk to him. Cyž, on the other hand, does not recall seeing Meškank until the mayhem following the air raid (Meškank 1955: 49). On the night of 13 February 1945, Meškank was sharing his cell with two other prisoners. After hours of bombing smoke and sparks were penetrating the cell, and the palliasses were beginning to smoulder, but he managed to escape and found Cyž. Together the two men looked down a narrow street in which every building was on fire. Twice they tried to pass down it, but were driven back by the heat (Meškank 1955: 52–3). Having lost touch with Cyž, Meškank ran down to the Elbe and crossed a bridge. He set out on a long walk through the Dresden woods to Radeberg and Pulsnitz, where he was able to board a train. Before long, he was standing in the Wendish village of Cannewitz and could see his sister-in-law's house, where he found refuge (Meškank 1955: 55). On 4 March he was moved by friends to a new refuge, in a hayloft with a bed and table and here he was fed well and left undisturbed. During the next few weeks he read all the works of Handrij Zejler and Jakub Bart-Ćišinski (Meškank 1955: 80). From his hayloft hide-out on Friday 20 April he saw two horsemen in unfamiliar uniforms ride into the farmyard, he rushed out from his lair to welcome them. One aimed his rifle, but he said in Russian 'I'm from a concentration camp – prison' and all was well. They were soldiers of the Polish Second Army, part of the Red Army's First Ukrainian Front, commanded by Marshall Ivan Konev.

The situation was still very dangerous with hostilities continuing in the vicinity, so he decided on the evening of the following day (Saturday) to go to Crostwitz. On Sunday he went to mass in Crostwitz and was moved to hear the Lord's Prayer, spoken by the German parish priest Lucius Teichmann (see below), but in Wendish again after five years of compulsory German in the Crostwitz church. On 25 April (St Mark's Day) he went to mass in Storcha and, coming out of church, noticed that the Polish forces were retreating. On Thursday the Germans returned (Meškank 1955: 81). It was not until the morning of Tuesday 8 May that the Polish troops returned to Crostwitz, and the Divisional Commander, a Soviet Colonel, set up his headquarters in the house where Meškank had had his hiding place (Meškank 1955: 82–3). Two days later, in Crostwitz on Ascension Day, 10 May 1945, Meškank and Dr Jan Cyž were both present at the revival of the Domowina (Schurmann 1998: 57).

Wendish martyrs

Many Wends suffered persecution, imprisonment, or death at the hands of the Nazi police and Gestapo. Others served and died in the German armed forces. The Wendish inmates of prisons and concentration camps were there, ostensibly at least, not simply because they were Wends but for some other reason, though the reasons were often trivial. Because the German Democratic Republic had its own criteria for assessing anti-Nazi activity, the fates of some of the following have been revealed only since 1990 (Rajš 1992: 447).

Alojs Andricki (1914–1943), born in Radibor, was from 1939 to 1941 a Catholic chaplain at the Hofkirche in Dresden. In 1941 he was arrested in Dresden and charged with uttering 'malignant, slanderous, and malicious utterances about leading personalities of the state and the NSDAP'. He was taken to Dachau concentration camp and here shortly after Christmas 1942 he fell ill, probably with typhus. He reported to the sick-bay and on 3 February 1943 was killed by means of a poisoned injection. His ashes were buried in Dresden on 15 April 1943. In 2011 Andricki was beatified (*NBS*, s.v.; Andricki 1998; Andritzki 2013).

Marja Grólmusec (1896–1944), born in Leipzig, was the daughter of a Catholic Wend. She worked first as a teacher and later as a journalist. In 1933 she returned to her father's native village Radibor and here in 1934 she was arrested for anti-Nazi activities. After five years in prison she was moved to Ravensbrück Concentration Camp, where she died on 6 August 1944 (*NBS*, s.v.).

Jakub Korjeńk (1884–1945), born in Ralbitz, worked in the kaolin factory in Caminau (Kamjenej), nr. Königswartha. He did not vote in the Nazi elections and was known to use the slogan 'Who votes for Hitler, votes for war'. He gave Soviet prisoners-of-war food and clothing, and helped two of them to escape. One of these was recaptured and found to be wearing clothing that was traced to Korjeńk. In November 1944, he was arrested and taken to the concentration camp in Neumünster. On 25 March 1945 his family received a telegram saying he had died there on 25 February (Rajš 1992: 447).

Pawlina Krawcowa (1890–1941) was born into a poor family in Dalitz in the parish of Kolkwitz on 18 December 1890 and learned German only when she started school. She was trained in tailoring in Berlin. With her husband Reinhold Krautz (Krawc), a weaver, she moved to Cottbus, where she worked as a dress-maker on her own account and opened a little shop in Sandower Straße. She used to make dolls, clothed in authentic Lower Sorbian national dress, which gained her a reputation beyond the bounds of Lusatia. She made friends in Prague and visited Prague frequently. One day in April 1938, she was travelling in a train to Burg and got into conversation with someone whom she asked: 'Why are they giving new names to the villages and rivers in the Spree Forest?' The next day the Gestapo arrested her. By the time she was released eleven months later, she was an invalid. She died on 16 September 1941.

As the Gestapo report noted, neither she nor her husband was politically active, but her trips to Prague had attracted attention. 'Are the dolls camouflage, behind which she hides Panslavic aims or even espionage?' they asked themselves. 'The frankness with which she speaks to total strangers of her experiences in Czechoslovakia is astounding…so she can only attribute to herself her arrest through reckless talk in the Spree Forest train…' (Hančka 1971: 8; Horýnová 1971: 8; Nowakojc 1993: 150–1).

Marja Meškankec (1923–1944) was born on 4 June 1923 in Hoske, near Wittichenau. She came from an agricultural family and worked for the village inn-keeper in Hoske. When it was discovered that she had been involved in secretly supplying Polish forced workers with food, she was arrested and interrogated on 19 June 1942. Because she refused to give the names of others who had been involved, she was taken to Ravensbrück Concentration Camp, where she died in July 1944 (*NBS*, s.v.; Wornar 1997: 134–5).

Alfred Möller (Młynk) (1914–1944), born in Schönau, was a potter like his father before him. When the call-up came to join the German army, he refused and fled to

Czechoslovakia. When the Germans occupied Czechoslovakia, Möller for a while found refuge in a monastery before making his way to Vienna. Here he was arrested and taken to the Moabit prison in Berlin, where he was tortured. In February 1944, his parents received news that he had died there (Rajš 1992: 448)

Pawoł Njek (1891–1944), born in Bautzen, was a soldier in the First World War and seriously wounded. He then returned to his profession of teacher, working in schools in Wendish Catholic villages and elsewhere. He was a Communist and following the Nazi takeover in 1933 was arrested and spent six months in prison. After his release, he was unable to find employment. His anti-Nazi activities again led to his arrest in Bautzen in 1942 and after a trial in Dresden he was taken to Buchenwald Concentration Camp, where he died in an air raid on 24 August 1944 (*NBS*, s.v.).

The three Petrik sisters, Lejna Kieschnik (Chěžnikowa), nee Petrick (1900–1942), Marta Petrick (1904–1942), and Mina Schulze (Šołćina), nee Petrick (1909–1942) were all born in Kringelsdorf but found work in domestic service in Brösa. They were active in Wendish organizations. Lejna drew attention to herself by refusing to participate in Nazi elections and quoting the slogan 'Who votes for Hitler, votes for war'. She spent a year in prison in Bautzen in 1934–1935. Mina was known for arguing against the Nazis, using the Biblical quotation 'Father, forgive them, for they know not what they do.'

They were all persuaded in 1936 to become Jehovah's Witnesses and were at a meeting of the sect, when it was raided by the police. Because they refused to renounce the Jehovah's Witnesses, they were sentenced in Cottbus to terms of imprisonment. On release they were required to sign certain undertakings, including a promise to use the 'Heil Hitler!' greeting. They refused and were sent first to prison and then, separately, to Auschwitz, where they all died in 1942 – Marta in September, Mina in October, and Lejna in November (Rajš 1992: 445–6).

Magdalena Rychtarowa, nee Rozmijec (1908–1944), was born in Schleife. In 1944 she was offered work in a munitions factory, which she declined 'so as not to help prolong the war'. She was arrested and her four children were taken to distant orphanages. Her relatives knew she had been taken to Auschwitz on 1 March and later heard she had died there on 4 September of heart failure. They were sent a cigar box containing what were said to be her ashes (Rajš 1987: 159–60; 1992: 448).

Pawoł Thomas was born on 6 March 1898 in Trebendorf. He worked in a weaving mill in Spremberg and joined the Social Democratic Party. As a result of his contributions to the newspaper *Märkische Volksstimme*, he was arrested in 1933 and sent to Sachsenhausen Concentration Camp, where he died from the effects of torture on 27 April 1942 (*NBS*, s.v.).

Slav place names Germanized

The year 1936 saw the beginning of a policy in the east of the Reich to replace German place names suspected of being of Slav origin with names of unambiguously German derivation. This affected not only names in areas, where there were still Wendish, Kashubian, or Polish inhabitants but also of locations where the last Slavs had died out centuries earlier. In a confidential circular letter dated 14 June 1937, the *Oberpräsident* of Brandenburg explained:

> For national-political reasons it is urgently desirable that, wherever it is in any way capable of consideration, the existing Wendish names and designations of villages, locations, rivers, and streams, as well as especially of rivulets in the Spree Forest, should gradually disappear and be replaced by purely German names and designations. The same applies to field-names where such still exist.
>
> I therefore request you in the first place to establish what designations of this kind still exist in your region and to record them in an exhaustive list. Simultaneously, in each case it is to be noted whether a Germanization is advisable or, alternatively, why it is not. If feasible, at the same time, an appropriate German designation may be proposed...

> (Förster 1996: 26).

The policy was not restricted to Brandenburg. In 1936 *Torga*, north-west of Görlitz, was given the new name *Kleeberg, Leschwitz*, south of Görlitz, was converted into *Weinhübel, Lipsa*, south of Ruhland, was transformed as *Lindenort*, and *Zschornegosda*, north of Ruhland, became *Schwarzheide*. *Presehna*, north of Finsterwalde, was changed in 1937 to *Birkwalde*. The same year *Byhleguhre*, south-east of Lübben, became *Geroburg*, while nearby *Byhlen* became *Waldseedorf*. *Dlugy*, north-east of Calau, became *Fleißdorf*. *Weissagk*, south-south-east of Calau became *Märkischheide* (Eichler 1975: 77), *Dobristroh*, north-west of Senftenberg, was renamed *Freienhufen* (Eichler 1985–2009, s.v.), and *Tätzschwitz*, north-west of Hoyerswerda, became *Vogelhain* (Pečikowa 1995: 216).

Those responsible for the reforms sometimes showed a modest philological acumen. The etymological sense of *dub* 'oak' in *Dubrau* and *Dubring* was successfully identified and conveyed in their substitutes *Eichenwald* and *Eichenhain* respectively. In *Jetscheba*, the etymon *jatřob* 'hawk' was detected and reproduced in the new *Habichtau*. No such subtlety can be observed in the conversion of *Weißagk* to *Märkischheide* or *Publik* to *Wildfelde*. The conversion of *Lausa*, north-east of Dresden, to *Weixdorf* in 1938 may have been unconnected with the anti-Slav campaign. The adjectival element 'Wendisch' was also subject to removal and even the word 'Deutsch', if it drew attention to the non-German character of the surroundings. *Wendischsohland*, south of Bautzen, became *Frühlingsberg*. *Wendischbaselitz* in the Catholic region became *Kleinbaselitz*, while *Deutschbaselitz* became *Großbaselitz*. *Wendisch Drehna*, south-west of Luckau, became *Walddrehna*. Meschgang gives a list of fifty-six place names in Upper Lusatia that were replaced in the course of this fairly inconsistent and piecemeal policy (1973: 167–8).

Meanwhile in Australia and Texas

By the 1930s the Wendish language in Australia was on its last legs. Recording his first impressions of the small rural congregation of Thomastown, Victoria, which had been founded by settlers from Germany in the 1850s, Pastor Ewald Steiniger wrote in his diary on 28 May 1935: 'Of the formerly thriving German community there are only one or two left who still speak German. A few elderly Wendish people still speak Wendish. Otherwise everything is in English' (Steiniger 2004: 293, 613).

In Texas, where the Wendish settlement was more compact than in Australia, the language was better preserved, but here too, in Serbin, Jan Kilian's parish, German and English had by this time replaced Wendish as the everyday languages. The last confirmation service in Wendish took place in 1906, conducted by Hermann Kilian, who had succeeded his father in 1883. In the last years before Hermann's death in 1920 Wendish church services were still held monthly, mainly for old people, but with his death they came to an end. His successor, Hermann Schmidt, was a competent Wendish-speaker, who used the language in many situations, but the congregation no longer felt the need for Wendish church services. In domestic life too Wendish was gradually being replaced, first by German, then by English. In 1926 eight families were known to be using Wendish in the home.

Wendish national consciousness and an attachment to the language remained, however, and on solemn occasions, such the anniversary of the parish's foundation, a Wendish sermon would be preached and Wendish hymns sung. This happened in 1929, 1936, 1954, and 1979. Until it ceased publication in 1949, the local newspaper *Giddings Deutsches Volksblatt*, still carried occasional items in Wendish. Jan Kilian's children had all spoken Wendish, but his grandchildren grew up speaking German (Malinkowa 1999: 170, 190–4).

The Lutheran Church under the Nazis

In October and November 1940, some twenty-three Wendish teachers were dismissed from their posts and expelled beyond the bounds of the Wendish area. The Wendish clergy, both Protestant and Catholic, were also prone to expulsion, but the position of Protestants was complicated by the movement known as *Deutsche Christen* 'German Christians', which supported Hitler and sought a synthesis of Nazism and Christianity (*ODCC*, s.v.). By the 1940s they dominated more than half the German *Landeskirchen*. Opposed to them and to National Socialism was the *Bekennende Kirche* 'Confessing Church'. The Wends were affected by both these movements. Two Wendish pastors were members of the *Bekennende Kirche* (BK). The first of these was Gottfried Rösler (Rejsler), pastor of Milkel and (from 1935) of Schleife. The second was his successor in Milkel Gerhard Lazer (Lazar). Known to have been BK sympathizers but not members, were Hinc Šolta and Gerhard Wirth (both curates) and Awgust Mikela, pastor of Malschwitz (Malinkowa 1996: 271n.).

The *Deutsche Christen* (DC) gained many supporters among the Wends. Six Wendish pastors became members of both the NSDAP (Nazi Party) and the DC. These were: Gerhard Böttger (Großpostwitz), Pawoł Albert (Malschwitz), Julius Riotte (Riota) (Königswartha), Jan Kapler (Neschwitz), Ernst Wjezar (Göda), and Curt Handrik (Purschwitz). After the War Albert and Handrik were judged to have been 'harmless hangers-on'. At the other extreme were the convinced National Socialists Riota, Kapler, and Wjezar (Malinkowa 1996: 267). As early as 1934 Wjezar reduced Wendish services in Göda to alternate Sundays. In the same year, Kapler with increasing frequency was failing to hold Wendish services in Neschwitz. In Königswartha, Riota abolished confirmation instruction in Wendish and reduced the number of services. Apart from these three parishes, however, traditional Wendish church activities continued normally until 1937 (Malinkowa 1996: 267).

On 10 May 1937, the church authorities announced that Pastor Kapler had been made deputy superintendent of Bautzen and senior Wendish pastor. His Party membership had put him in a position where he could operate easily against Wendish interests. The same year he was commissioned to inspect Wendish churchyards and advise on the removal of headstones with inscriptions in Wendish. He was instrumental in the appointment of a Nazi curate against the wishes of the parishioners in Malschwitz (Malinkowa 1996: 268). On 17 July 1937 Gustav Mürbe (Gustaw Mjerwa), pastor of Hochkirch, chairman of the Wendish pastors' Main Conference, was notified that no further activity of the Conference would be tolerated. For nearly two years he strove to have the ban lifted but in vain. The general ban on publishing in Wendish put an end to the Lutheran newspapers *Pomhaj Bóh* (banned 22 August 1937) and *Nowy Missionski Posoł* (banned in June that year). It was also the end of the book-series *Serbska Lutherska Knihownja* (Malinkowa 1996: 268).

Action against the church continued in November 1940, when the four Pastors Pawoł Kapler of Bautzen (brother of the Nazi Kapler), Mjerwa of Hochkirch, Lazar of Milkel, and Wirth of Klein Bautzen were individually summoned to Dresden and in the offices of the *Landeskirche* told to find new parishes outside the Wendish area. They were told that the *Landeskirche* had been forced to take this action by *Reichskirchenminister* Kerrl and the *Reichsführer* SS. The pastors protested that there was no reason why they should leave their present parishes and took no action, but early in 1941, Kapler and Lazar were both compelled to move. Wirth had meanwhile been called up into the Wehrmacht, so the question of his transfer was now only theoretical (Malinkowa 1996: 268–9). Mjerwa meanwhile stayed put for over a year. A new, German pastor was moved into Hochkirch, but he had to take up lodgings in the village, while Mjerwa continued to reside in the parsonage. Mjerwa was offered a German parish, which he declined. He was offered another and another but still declined. Finally, he accepted the fourth offer and on 21 January 1942 he moved with his family to Oelsa near Dippoldiswalde, where he was warmly received by his new flock (Malinkowa 1996: 269).

In 1938 the *Bund deutscher Osten* (BDO) told the Minister for Home Affairs that the government should ban the practice of holding church services in the Wendish language. The Minister took a pragmatic view: 'I expect bans of that kind in the church sphere either to fail or to be counter-productive. I think it would be better, if Wendish church services were restricted to the true extent of linguistic need.' On 26 February 1941, however, the Bautzen Superintendent (a German) called the Wendish clergy to a meeting, at which they were told to reduce the frequency of services in Wendish to once a month and to hold them, if possible, at unusual times, such as in the afternoon. On 29 March, he summoned two church wardens from each Wendish parish and gave them the same instructions. Baruth, Kleinbautzen, and Purschwitz complied with the order and went over to holding Wendish services only once a month. Klix and Gröditz decided to hold them fortnightly. In these five parishes these arrangements remained in operation until the end of the War. In Göda all Wendish services came to an end at the beginning of 1941. In Wilthen their frequency was reduced to once every three months. A most unusual case was that of Oßling, where Pastor Pawoł Wićežk throughout the whole duration of the Third Reich continued to hold Wendish services and to preach in Wendish every Sunday. In Königswartha Pastor Kapler-Njeswačanski, who was a German, continued to celebrate Wendish services until December 1941, when he was arrested. After his release in spring 1942 he made no attempt to resume them (Malinkowa 1996: 270).

In Lower Lusatia by the end of the 1930s Dissen was the only parish where services were still being held in Wendish. They came to an end in May 1941, when Pastor Bogumił Šwjela was forbidden to continue by the Brandenburg Consistory. On 7 April 1941 Pastor Mjerwa at Hochkirch received a visit from a Gestapo official and a local policeman, who told him that at 10 am that day all Wendish associations in Saxony and Prussia had been dissolved, including the Wendish Main Pastors' Conference. They confiscated the Conference's documents and assets of 1,600 Reichsmarks.

Expulsion of Catholic priests

The Catholic Wends were, with good reason, suspected of particular recalcitrance. By the end of 1940, only two of the ten Catholic Wendish parishes were in the care of Wendish priests. On 27 November 1940 Lucius Teichmann, a German Franciscan in Breslau, was told to travel with four other Franciscans to Bautzen, where they would receive instructions from the Bishop. On arrival in Bautzen on 30 November, they were told by Bishop Petrus Legge that he had received from the Gestapo a list of names of Wendish priests who were to be forced to give up their parishes and moved to German-speaking parts of his diocese. The incumbents of the parishes concerned (Crostwitz, Ostro, Radibor, Ralbitz, Nebelschütz, Sdier, and Storcha) had accepted their fate. They were accused of being active in the Wendish national movement. The Franciscans were asked to take over in the parishes shortly to be deprived of their parish priests. He also conveyed to them the following instructions from the Gestapo: (1) They were forbidden to learn Wendish. If by any chance any of them already knew Wendish he must not use it either officially or privately. (2) Religious instruction in their new parishes must be given in German. It could not be delegated to Wends. (3) The language of hymn-singing must gradually be changed to German. The Gestapo intended to make checks to ensure that these stipulations were being observed (L. Teichmann 1984: 158–9; *Wosady* 1984: passim).

On arrival in their Wendish parishes the Franciscans were apprehensive. They expected and got a frosty reception. Fr Teichmann, who replaced Fr Jan Wjenka in Crostwitz, opened his first sermon by explaining: 'I have come to you not from the state or the Gestapo but from your bishop' (L. Teichmann 1984: 160). In time the outsiders were grudgingly accepted. By the beginning of 1942 the expulsion of priests and teachers from Lusatia was still not complete, but on 2 February 1942 the Reich Minister of Education was informed: 'The removal of the Wendish priests and teachers is […] to be postponed until after the war' (Kasper 1961: 132–3; Schurmann 1998: 38).

Soon after the outbreak of hostilities in 1939, large numbers of prisoners of war and forced labourers from Poland and elsewhere were brought into Lusatia. After 1941, more followed from the Soviet Union. The Wends discovered that they had much in common with these unfortunates, first of all simply on the linguistic plane, particularly with the Poles, but they also shared a sense of solidarity with victims of Nazi oppression. Often it was simply on humanitarian grounds that they gave them help, even enabling them to escape and then remain hidden until the arrival of the Soviet army in 1945.

CHAPTER 8
FROM LIBERATION TO EUROPEAN UNION
1945–1990

The liberation

In mid-April 1945, as the Second Polish Army, fighting under Soviet command as part of the First Ukrainian Front, reached Lusatia, most of the civilian population was fleeing westwards in fear of the invaders. Expectations varied, however, and many Lusatian Wends, especially the Catholics, seeing the defeat of Germany as their liberation, stayed put. The Jewish academic Victor Klemperer and his wife Eva, forced to leave Dresden after the air-raid of 13 February, had even chosen to flee eastwards and seek refuge in the Catholic Wendish village of Piskowitz. Here, the Klemperers made their way to the house of Hańža Šołćina, who had been their maid in the 1920s. Though they had kept in touch after she had left their service, it was now many years since their last meeting, but she immediately welcomed them with open arms. Opinions here were strongly anti-Nazi and stories of Russian atrocities treated with disbelief. Although they could not understand the Wendish conversations going on around them, the Klemperers felt safe (Rajš 1987: 160; Klemperer 1999: 51).

The resistance of the retreating German forces was fierce and losses among Soviet and Polish troops were heavy. After taking Bautzen on 21 April, the Soviet-Polish forces were driven back by a German counter-offensive, causing them to relinquish some of their gains, including Bautzen and Kamenz. It was 7 May 1945 before Kamenz was again taken by the Soviet Army and only the following day (the date of German capitulation) that the whole of Upper Lusatia was finally liberated (B. Cyž 1965: 25 1969: 75; Schurmann 1998: 23, 32). Some of the troops engaged in the operation had been told in advance that they were entering territory where a Slav population might be encountered. Many Wends stayed in their homes and greeted the advancing Soviet soldiers by hanging out white flags. It is claimed that they also flew again for the first time in years their own flag – the blue, red, and white flag of the Wends (*Die Sorben* 1964: 56; J. Cyž 1965: 148–50).

This idealized picture, however, created for consumption in the German Democratic Republic (GDR), of joyful Wendish people coming out of their houses to greet the victors, many of the women wearing their national dress, is open to qualification. Photographs of these scenes are hard to find and personal testimonies of the Wends that were there remained elusive for many years. Although in the GDR, evidence of violence inflicted on civilians by the liberators was suppressed, an unusually frank and credible account has been left by Fr Teichmann, the Franciscan who was imposed as parish priest in Crostwitz in 1940 in place of Fr Jan Wjenka. Teichmann saw the entry of Russian and Polish troops into his parish and heard accounts of eye-witnesses from other parishes. On Sunday, 15 April 1945 (as he recalled in 1979), he warned his parishioners of the approaching danger and told them to prepare themselves spiritually for the possibility of sudden death. 'After mass a woman told me that speaking Wendish she would be able to communicate with the Russians and would greet them with coffee and cake. I warned her to be careful.'

On 20 April 1945, the liberators arrived in Crostwitz. The first Soviet soldier Fr Teichmann encountered came straight up to him and, without speaking, took his watch. Then, general plundering began. Everything of value, including horses, was taken. Some of the Polish and Russian forced labourers employed on local farms established solidarity with their armed countrymen and shared in the looting. Farm carts were taken and driven off loaded with booty (Teichmann 1984: 185–91). On 25–26 April, there was renewed fighting and the Soviet forces were compelled to retreat from Crostwitz, but on 7 May they returned and resumed looting. They broke into the church, where some of the villagers, in the vain hope that it would provide security, had hidden their valuables. The liberators took everything. 'For understandable reasons, I do not know all the women and girls who were raped. The number of cases known just to me from the limited area of the Crostwitz parish is breathtaking' (Teichmann 1984: 189). The victims included the woman who a few weeks earlier had promised to meet the victors with coffee and cake.

Fr Teichmann records meticulously the names of seventeen Crostwitz Wends killed by the Soviet forces during late April and early May 1945 (1984: 190–1). As parish priest he is likely to have been better informed than most on the incidence of death. On 22 April, he buried simultaneously eight victims of shooting. The Crostwitz parish record of burials shows that twenty-two civilians were killed during the last weeks of the War. The total number of burials for the year 1945 was 134 compared with 66 in 1944 (*Wosady* 1984: 100).

In April 1945 Kata Cyžec of Storcha was nearly 14 years old. Fifty years later, she recalled:

We did not believe the propaganda about atrocities of the Red Army, but the atrocities of German soldiers against other nations were known and discussed in our family. Anyone who says he did not know about that either had his ears and eyes closed or he did not want to know about it.

On 20 April Polish soldiers arrived in our village and we welcomed them and told them we were Wends, Slavs, and that there were no German soldiers among us. Everything remained fairly calm. But the next day it was different. New soldiers arrived and began stealing. They said my father was a German officer and took him away. In the evening I went to look for him and one of the Poles working for the farmers in Storcha introduced me to one of his countrymen, saying: 'This is the daughter of the man that was shot.' Worse was to come, for on 25 April the German army returned. There was fighting and many soldiers were killed on both sides. Large numbers of Poles were taken prisoner. They were all shot and their bodies buried between Weidlitz and Pannewitz. At least, that is what people said. Today they are in a cemetery at Görlitz. [...]

[R]elations between the Polish and Soviet army and the inhabitants were not as pleasant as they seem from various reports in the past. In our little village the liberators shot six men and a woman. I know of at least six such cases in Crostwitz, one in Quoos, thirteen in Kleinwelka, and recently I read in *Serbske Nowiny* of four in Camina. And most of them were Wends. The greatest atrocity of all against civilians was in Niederkaina, where on 22 April 195 people were locked in a barn which was then burned. Today there is a tablet there to commemorate the fact, put up since re-unification. [...]

(Malinkowa 1995: 242–3)

Mikławš Cyž, Kata's father, was the village schoolmaster, choirmaster, and church-organist in Storcha. In 1937, after much soul-searching, he joined the NSDAP. He was not a Nazi by conviction but joined in order to avoid being transferred away from the Wendish area, where he felt his duty lay. He took this fateful step because, after consulting his parish priest, Jurij Delan, he concluded that the right thing was to stay in his village. Party membership, he believed, was likely to protect him from deportation (*Serbske šulstwo* 1993: 142).

In 1943, made homeless by the bombing of Berlin, the family of Jan Skala moved to Silesia and by 1945 they were living there in a village then called Erbenfeld (until 1939 Dzieditz, now Dziedzice), which was taken by Soviet forces on 19 January. The German population had fled, leaving only a few Poles and the Skalas to welcome the liberators. Skala had every reason to believe that his anti-Fascist credentials would stand him in good stead, but on 22 January, a drunken Soviet soldier entered the Skalas' kitchen and threatened them with his sub-machine gun. Skala, speaking Russian, tried to calm him, but the soldier fired an indiscriminate burst and Skala fell dead. Skala's two daughters and his eleven-month-old grandson were unharmed.

To the new authorities who subsequently emerged in the GDR, Skala's fate was a cause of embarrassment. They honoured him as an anti-Fascist and a victim of the Gestapo, but the circumstances of his death did not fit their rose-tinted vision of the liberation. The only acceptable formula to describe his death was the equivocal 'perished in a tragic way following the arrival of the Soviet Army' (*NBS*, s.v.). Only in 2009 was the truth revealed when Peter Kroh, who at the age of eleven months had been present at his grandfather's death, published the above version of events, as related to him by his mother (Kroh 2009: 307–8).

The horrors experienced by the Lusatian Wends in the spring and summer of 1945 left deep wounds. A natural reluctance to recall the trauma was reinforced for the next forty-five years by restraints on freedom of speech, especially on critical assessments of the liberation. Nevertheless, accounts by those brave enough to voice their memories (though often wishing to remain anonymous) were being carefully recorded over the years and were to be eventually published (Budar 2013: *passim*).

Revival

On 29 April 1945, American forces liberated Dachau Concentration Camp, where Fr Jan Cyž Hajničanski and Fr Beno Šołta had managed to survive for over four years. Fr Cyž, on 5 May, in his capacity as Chairman of the pre-war Wendish People's Council (*Serbska ludowa rada/Wendischer Volksrat*), sent a telegram to the exiled President Edvard Beneš of Czechoslovakia, asking him to take the Wends under his protection and represent their interests to the victorious Allies. He sent a further telegram on 9 May (Delan 1992: 137; Schurmann 1998: 44). Fr Cyž also wrote to the Domowina leadership, urging the organization at the parish and district levels of local Wendish committees – referred to as *Nationalausschüsse* 'national committees' – which could carry out administrative functions and form the basis of a state apparatus. He took his administrative model from the Czechoslovak state apparatus, intending to create conditions for a smooth integration of Lusatia into Czechoslovakia, if things turned out that way (Pronjewič 1995: 273).

In the second half of January, in anticipation of the liberation, a Committee of Lusatian Wends (*Komitej Łužiskich Serbow*) had been formed in Nucknitz, near Crostwitz, consisting of Dr Jurij Ješki (1896–1970), Franc Natuš (1898–1950), Jan Rjenč (1878–1971), and Jan Wawrik (Schurmann 1998: 33). On 24 April, a meeting of the *Komitej* was held in Crostwitz. Natuš and Ješki were now joined by Dr Jan Cyž (1898–1985), Jan Lipič (1885–1971), Jurij Mencl (1903–1951), and Jan Zarjeńk. It was decided to make contact as soon as possible with the Soviet command and to obtain official approval for the re-establishment of the Domowina (Schurmann 1998: 36). Dr Jan Cyž has described how this mission was carried out. On 9 May 1945, accompanied by Jurij Cyž, he visited the Soviet commandant in Kamenz. In what language the interview was conducted we are not told, but the difficulties of communication seem to have been insurmountable, for he writes: 'We introduced ourselves as Lusatian Wends. We were given a friendly reception, but despite all explanations as to who the Wends were and what they wanted, we could not make ourselves understood. We received a pass to travel to Yugoslavia and as far as he was concerned that was that' (J. Cyž 1957: 340). (The misunderstanding must have arisen from the Sorbian word *Serb* 'Sorb/Wend' or its corresponding adjective *serbski* 'Sorbian/Wendish'.) Despite this setback, later the same day the Domowina was refounded without Soviet permission. Present at the ceremony were fifteen pre-1937 members of the organization. Dr Jan Cyž was elected temporary president until Pawoł Nedo, who had been the president at the time of the Domowina's dissolution, should return from captivity to resume office. Aware that it was still incumbent upon him to get official approval and to inform the Soviet forces about the Wends, Cyž went to Bautzen with his son, also named Jan. Their journey took them through scenes of desolation and destruction. In Bautzen, buildings were still burning and they found the Wendish House in ruins, having being blown up by the retreating German forces.

The officer in charge of the Bautzen Kommandatura, Captain Kuzmenko, already knew about the Wends and was glad of the opportunity to obtain up-to-date information. But he was unable at first to assume the responsibility for approving the reorganization of the Domowina. On 17 May, however, he officially informed Cyž that the Domowina might resume its activities on the same lines as before its dissolution. On 25 May 1945 the Bautzen Kommandatura, on behalf of the Control Commission in Berlin, appointed Cyž to the post of District Governor (*Landrat*) for the Bautzen district, entrusting him with the task of establishing a new democratic administration for the whole population, not only the Wends (J. Cyž 1957: 342). This was an unprecedented distinction for a Wend and must have raised some German hackles. As *Landrat* he replaced Dr Hermann Eckhardt, formerly also head of the *Wendenabteilung*, who was now held in custody pending his trial.

During the last days of fighting, Pawoł Nedo and Jurij Cyž were both in prison in Potsdam under sentence of death. Despite raids by American bombers, the prison had remained unscathed, but the arrival of the Soviet forces on 27 April secured the prisoners' release. Nedo immediately returned to his family in Groß Rietz and a month later, he set out for Bautzen by motorcycle. When he reached Commerau, near Königswartha, he stopped at the house of a Domowina activist, and here he unexpectedly met Dr Jan Cyž. It was a joyful reunion. Nedo, having been introduced by Cyž to the Soviet military authorities as the President of the Domowina, resumed office forthwith, and at the beginning of June was appointed by the Soviets to the post of District Education Officer (*Kreisschulrat*) for the northern division of the Bautzen school district. He thus became responsible for putting into practice a new school system which for the first time ever took the existence of the Wendish language fully into account. Nedo's work began at a juncture when the language had just suffered a decade of unprecedented malice –during which children had been forbidden to speak their mother tongue (Bresan 2002: 160–5) (Figure 8.1).

Figure 8.1 Pawoł Nedo (1908–1984).

Prague had been liberated on 9 May 1945 by units of the Red Army commanded by General Rybalko (Schurmann 1998: 42), and there on the same day a Lusatian-Wendish National Committee (*Łužiskoserbski Narodny Wuběrk*) had been set up, claiming to be the successor of the committee which at Versailles in 1919, headed by Arnošt Bart, had demanded independence for the Wends (Barker 1996: 39–40). It was independent of the Domowina but had similar aims and was composed of Wendish concentration camp survivors and other Wends who had spent the war in Czechoslovakia, namely: 1. Dr Mikławš Krječmar, 2. Dr Ivan Smoler, 3. Korla Kóčka, 4. Jan Grofa, and 5. Pawoł Krječmar. They were joined on 25 May by: 6. Fr Beno Šołta and 7. Fr Jan Cyž (Schurmann 1998: 43).

Several leading Wendish figures at this time were bearers of the common surname *Cyž/Ziesch(e)*, some related, some not. Care should be taken, in particular, to distinguish between Dr Jan Cyž (recently escaped from the Gestapo in Dresden, and now Bautzen *Landrat*) and Fr Jan Cyž (recently released from Dachau Concentration Camp). The latter is sometimes also known as Cyž Hajničanski, from the name of his parish Hainitz/Hajnicy. Before the end of May, two representatives of the newly reconstituted Domowina arrived in Prague. These were the Deputy Chairman Jan Meškank (recently escaped from the Gestapo in Dresden) and Jurij Cyž (until recently under sentence of death in Potsdam). Their mission was to make contact with the National Committee and with Czech politicians (Schurmann 1998: 43). In June 1945, the pre-war Czech Society of Friends of Lusatia (*Společnost přátel Lužice*) was revived (Pałys 2013: 124).

Between May 1945 and December 1947, the Domowina and the National Committee sent a stream of telegrams and memoranda to the victorious Allies and the United Nations, demanding the creation of an independent Wendish state, either under UN guarantee or under the protection of Czechoslovakia or Poland (Barker 1996: 40). Experience under the Nazis had radicalized the Wendish leaders. They wanted to break away from Germany completely. As the National Committee put it in a memorandum sent to Stalin and Beneš in June 1945: 'For hundreds of years the Lusatian Serbs have seen nothing good from the Germans…. It is no wonder, then, that the nation today has but one wish: that they should never again in the future be under the domination of the Germans, who have shown nothing but enmity' (quoted in Barker 1996: 40). The situation seemed providential. The Wends had received favourable treatment from the Soviet authorities in their early recognition of the Domowina and the preferment of Dr Jan Cyž and Pawoł Nedo. But all this was soon to be changed by the privileged status given first to the German Communist Party (KPD) and then to its successor, the Socialist Unity Party (SED), formed in April 1946 by merging the KPD with the Social Democratic Party (SPD). Many of the German Communists who now moved into key positions had spent the War in the Soviet Union (Barker 1996: 41). Prominent among the Wendish leaders, on the other hand, were former concentration camp prisoners and victims of the Gestapo (Dr Jan Cyž, Fr Jan Cyž, Pawoł Nedo, Fr Beno Šołta, Jan Meškank, Jurij Cyž, and others).

At the end of August 1945 the National Committee moved to Bautzen. Jurij Cyž, however, as the Committee's secretary general, remained in Prague, continuing to represent it there (Pałys 2013: 123). On 17 September, a joint meeting of the National

Committee and the Domowina agreed to set up a *Łužiskoserbska Narodna Rada* (Lusatian-Wendish National Council) as the executive arm of the two organizations (Barker 1996: 42). Between 2 and 10 January 1946, under the auspices of the Domowina and the National Committee, many Wendish villages and some administrative regions (*Kreise*) elected local *Nationalausschüsse* 'national committees', intended to provide grass-roots support for the National Council rather than (as in the proposal of Fr Jan Cyž in May 1945) to prepare for annexation by Czechoslovakia. The National Council was now no longer calling for union with Czechoslovakia but for the creation of an independent Sorbian state under international protection (B. Cyž 1969: 87; Barker 1996: 42–3).

A twenty-page booklet in French, English, and Russian versions, entitled *1500 Years of Struggle for National Existence: Memorandum of the Lusatians, the Last European Nation still Fighting for its Independence*, was published by the National Council in Prague. Signed and dated 'Bautzen 7 January 1946' by the four members of the Council (Fr Jan Cyž, as chairman, Dr Jan Cyž, Pawoł Nedo, and Dr Jurij Cyž), it contained a map of Lusatia stretching from the south-east outskirts of Berlin to the Czech border and a summary of Wendish politics, history, and economics. The booklet alluded to 'innumerable [Wendish] victims in German concentration camps and prisons' and '[Wendish] soldiers in the ranks of the allied armies' as indications of their democratic credentials. (Evidence of Wends in the ranks of the allied armies has so far proved elusive.) The National Council was demanding: 1. that the Wends be admitted to the United Nations, 2. that the National Committee be recognized as the government of an independent Lusatia, 3. that their claims be put before the peace conference, 4. that the Allies guarantee the independence of Lusatia, and 5. that the Wends be immediately exempted from the regulations relating to defeated Germany (*Memorandum* 1946: 6–7).

On 9 January a mass rally, organized by the National Council, was held in the Hotel 'Krone' in Bautzen. A resolution was passed that: 'Only elected Sorbs can represent the Sorbs. A decision as to the claim of the Sorbs will be taken exclusively by international bodies and the Soviet Military Administration. We know that all Slavonic nations support the Sorbs' claim. We have confidence that the Western powers too will help us' (B. Cyž 1969: 87). The campaign to elect *Nationalausschüsse* provoked indignation and hostility from the Germans, especially from those who had just arrived in Lusatia either as refugees or having been expelled from the Sudetenland and Silesia. A meeting of members of the elected local *Nationalausschüsse* was held in the Krone Hotel in Bautzen on 27 January 1946, at which Fr Cyž announced that the National Committee had sent Marka Cyžowa as a delegate to the UN conference in London and had submitted an indictment of twenty-four war criminals to the Nuremberg Military Tribunal. Fr Cyž was elected chairman of the National Committee, which consisted of twenty-five members, and three leading officials of the Domowina were elected to the National Council (B. Cyž 1969: 89). A commission was set up 'for the creation of a completely independent Wendish state'. According to a report of the Krone meeting, made by Max Duschmann (a KPD member), Nedo said: 'The Communists have made great promises to the Wends, but up to now they have not kept any of them.... A German is a German, whether Fascist or Communist, and we want nothing to do with them' (quoted in Barker 1996: 43).

Pawoł Cyž

In April 1946, Jurij Cyž met the Polish Deputy Foreign Minister Zygmunt Modzelewski in Prague. It was agreed that the Poles would receive a Wendish representative and on 30 April, Pawoł Cyž arrived in Warsaw in that role. He had been incarcerated at the same time as his brother Jurij at Potsdam and released by Soviet forces on 27 April 1945 (Pałys 2013: 123–5). The costs of his stay in Poland in summer 1946 were borne by the Polish Foreign Ministry and he was given a warm welcome. Among the slogans displayed at one of the events arranged in his honour, a Czech diplomat noted 'Lusatia belongs to Poland.' Nevertheless, his discussions with officials in Poland were unproductive. In July, the Poles received from Jurij Cyž on behalf of the Wendish National Council a request to persuade the Soviet occupation authorities to prevent further placement of German refugees in the Wendish area and to remove those that had already been settled there. There was no reaction (Pałys 2013: 127–8).

On 22 September 1946 Pawoł Cyž was married in Opole to Anna Knosała, the sister of his friend Ryszard Knosała, who had perished in Dachau. By now, he no longer had any official status as a representative of the Wends but stayed on in Opole. In January 1947 elections were held in Poland, disregarding the provisions of the Yalta and Potsdam agreements and resulting in victory for the pro-Soviet bloc. In March 1947, notwithstanding the increasingly hostile environment for those who did not conform, Cyž protested to the Polish Western Union (PZZ) in Poznań against Polish support for Soviet policy on the Wendish question. This was a risky step. As late as July that year, he had a meeting with Deputy Premier Stanisław Mikołajczyk, who was now totally powerless and must have been thinking about his own safety, for in October he had to flee for his life and return to London (Davies 1981, 2: 570–1; Pałys 2013: 133).

In September 1948 the Domowina decided to recall Pawoł Cyž from Poland, together with its other members, Anton Nawka and Arnošt Černik. It was not until the end of January 1949, however, that Cyž complied. Back in Bautzen, he practised as a lawyer and renewed contact with Jurij Rjenč. His alienation from the Domowina, which was now completely under SED control, attracted attention and he escaped the clutches of the Security Police only by jumping from a first floor window, while the policemen who been sent to arrest him were still standing at the front door. Through West Berlin he made his way with his family to West Germany, where he pursued a successful career until his retirement in 1975 and death in 1977. His associates Jurij Rjenč and Bjarnat Rachel were later imprisoned for having been connected with the National Council (Pałys 2013: 135–7). In the GDR, the name Pawoł Cyž was deleted from history.

Taming the Domowina

One of the methods used by the KPD to discredit the Sorbs and Wends was to allege that Nazi Party membership had been disproportionately high among them. This theme was exploited in a speech made by Wilhelm Pieck, Co-Chairman of the Central Committee, in Hoyerswerda on 26 February 1946 (Barker 1996: 43–4), and in March Nedo wrote to Pieck asking for clarification. In reply Pieck wrote: 'You have been accurately informed about my remarks, in fact I am astonished at your temerity in daring to dispute them. I have in my possession a long list of Domowina activists who were members of the NSDAP. Amongst them is a certain *Kreisschulrat* Nedo from Bautzen, who [...] was a member of the SA' (Barker 1996: 44). Nedo had not been a member of the NSDAP. Nor had he, strictly speaking, even been a full member of the SA, though he was a candidate member from October 1933 to June 1934 (see above). As a holder of a public office (elementary school teacher), he had been unable to avoid this, but by being uncooperative he had quickly engineered his own expulsion (Schurmann 1998: 57n.). That Nedo, despite this stigma, had been appointed Director of Education for Bautzen District by the Soviet military authorities must have riled Pieck (who had spent the War in Russia). In this letter, as in his speech, Pieck said that the policy of the KPD was 'to support the Wendish people in the maintenance of their culture and to oppose any restrictions on their rights and liberties', but it would oppose their struggle for autonomy (Barker 1996: 44).

At about the same time (March 1946), the KPD in Bautzen set about depriving the Domowina of its ability to act as a political organization. On 17 May the previous year, it had been authorized by the Soviet military authorities as 'the political, antifascist, and cultural body representing the whole of the Wendish people' (Barker 1996: 44), but the Germans (dominated by the KPD) now taking over local administration from the Russians were irked by the Domowina's political activities, especially its organization of *Nationalausschüsse* in Sorbian villages, which they correctly saw as an attempt to supplant the existing administration (Barker 1996: 45). Probably under Russian pressure, the Domowina now changed its course towards greater cooperation with the KPD and accepted that it was mainly a cultural organization, thereby distancing themselves from the National Committee in Prague. The Soviet military authorities, at the instigation of the KPD, refused to approve the 120 or so *Nationalausschüsse* scattered throughout the Upper Sorbian villages, which were intended to give the Domowina a popular base (Schurmann 1998: 185).

In April 1946 in Berlin, the KPD and the SPD were nominally united as the SED (B. Cyž 1969: 94). The SPD was in fact taken over by the KPD, and this changed the political situation fundamentally. The Wends were faced with new difficulties. On 1 September 1946 local elections were held in the Soviet Zone. The Domowina had hoped that it would be able to put up its own candidates, but the Soviet authorities, following the emergence of the SED, ruled that only existing political parties would be allowed to stand (Barker 1996: 46). In June or July, the SED had decided to discriminate between active and nominal members of the Nazi Party, so as to bring the latter into the democratic system. This was a popular move and it persuaded some Wends to support them (Schurmann 1998: 117).

The CDU, meanwhile, had not formulated its policy on the Wendish question (Schurmann 1998: 117). The Domowina therefore negotiated an agreement with the SED, whereby the Domowina gave its support to the SED, in return for which Domowina candidates who were not SED members could be placed on the SED list. However, there were occasions when the SED offended the Domowina by striking its candidates from the list, which led to complaints. The SED also complained, when it discovered that some members of the Domowina were members of other parties or even standing as candidates for them. Consequently, Domowina members were prohibited from standing for other parties (Schurmann 1998: 119). For the Wends, the arrangement was advantageous in so far as it resulted in many of their members being elected to local councils in the Wendish area. For the SED, it meant their share of the vote in this area was much higher than in the purely German parts of Lusatia (Schurmann 1998: 118).

The agreement was extended for the Saxon Land and Kreis elections on 20 October. This time, however, none of the Domowina candidates was high enough on the list to have any chance of winning a seat (Barker 1996: 46). There was one Wend, Gusta Mertin from Uhyst/Spree, Kr. Hoyerswerda, among the deputies elected to the Landtag, but he stood as an SED candidate (Schurmann 1998: 122). Wendish voting patterns were erratic. In Protestant areas support for the SED was strong, but in the Catholic villages in Kreis Kamenz it was weak (B. Cyž 1969: 10). In mid-September, before the Land and Kreis elections, Fr Jan Cyž, Chairman of the National Committee and National Council, revealed that he was opposed to Wendish participation. He argued that, as a separate nation, the Wends should not tolerate any German government. A similar view was expressed by the General Secretary of the National Council, Jurij Cyž. The Domowina could not accept this rejection of their agreement with the SED and feared the views expressed by the officials of the National Council might be regarded by the Soviet Military Administration as sabotage (Schurmann 1998: 121).

The Soviet Military Administration had already made it clear to the Domowina officials that the only way forward was in close cooperation with the SED, so on 15 October 1946 Nedo, Dr Jan Cyž, and Arnošt Černik resigned from the National Council, saying Domowina officials could not simultaneously be members of either the National Council or the National Committee (Schurmann 1998: 124–5). Three days earlier, on 12 October, the Domowina had withdrawn from the National Council. Yet, despite having had its own way in everything, the SED was still suspicious of the Domowina. Kurt Krenz told the Party's District leadership in Dresden that the Domowina had only joined the agreement with the SED 'to put itself in a good light with the occupation authorities' and he said the split with the National Committee was 'just play-acting' intended 'to pull the wool over our eyes by leading us to believe that there has been a split between the leading forces in the Wendish movement' (Barker 1996: 47). The split, however, was real.

The end of the National Council

The National Council was simultaneously planning a more radical way of achieving their aspirations. In late August or early September 1946 in their office in Prague, Jurij Rjenč had been introduced by Jurij Cyž to a Czech using the name Jan Knotek (his real name was Václav Moravec). Knotek claimed to have been a Czech partisan and said that with him in the partisans had been a Lower Wend named Fryco Marak from Schmogrow

Knotek wished to use his experience to help the Wends to effect their union with Czechoslovakia. He said he intended to visit Rjenč in Bautzen and to make contact with Marak. Cyž asked Rjenč to give Knotek assistance, and in the second half of October Knotek visited Rjenč in Bautzen, accompanied by Jan Wjacławk (born 1924) (B. Cyž 2010b: 17–18).

At a later meeting Knotek proposed the formation of a unit of young Wends to be trained in police work. At the right moment they would by force of arms oust the German police and take power. Knotek was also introduced to Nedo and he told him he had been commissioned by Jurij Cyž to organize partisan activities among the Wends. He said he was to take his instructions from Jurij Rjenč. Nedo, however, decided that the projected partisan activities would harm the Wends' national interests, and two days later he went to the Soviet Kommandatura in Bautzen and revealed Knotek's plans to Major Chaplin. He also spoke to Fr Jan Cyž and urged him to investigate the matter and take preventive action. This exacerbated the conflict between the National Council and the Domowina, which now regarded the Council as a 'little clique of political fanatics' and was especially hostile to Jurij Cyž and his wife Marka. Surprisingly, the Russians took no action, so in December Nedo informed the Czech police, and they at the beginning of 1947 arrested Knotek. Nedo was above all anxious to avoid any kind of row which would endanger the Wendish cause (B. Cyž 2011: 11–13).

The rift was now complete. The leaders of the Domowina knew that if they did not reach a compromise with the SED, they risked losing all they had gained. The National Council, however, was not prepared to compromise and continued to hold out for independence under the protection of Czechoslovakia or Poland. The resignation from the National Council of Nedo and Dr Jan Cyž weakened it critically. The death of its General Secretary Jurij Cyž on 28 September 1947 was a further blow (Schurmann 1998: 161), and the following year on 8 August the Chairman Fr Jan Cyž-Hajničanski also died, bringing the National Council's activities to an end (B. Cyž 2010b: 17).

Saxon Law for the Protection of Sorbian Rights (1948)

Signs that traditional attitudes towards the Wends had not changed were revealed by the first post-war census, taken on 29 October 1946 throughout the Soviet Occupation Zone. In agreement with the Domowina, the Military Government had issued a leaflet of 'Directions on the Census for the Wendish (Sorbian) Population'. The census aimed to correct the falsification that had taken place under the Nazis and before them, when Sorbs were routinely threatened or tricked into declaring themselves Germans (Schurmann 1998: 131). The 'Directions' warned that infringements of the rules designed to achieve an accurate figure would incur punishment by fine or imprisonment. Nevertheless, the Domowina received many complaints of irregularities from practically all parts of Upper and Lower Lusatia and submitted them attached to its own letter of protest to General Vladimir S. Semenov of the Military Government, claiming that the data on language and nationality collected by the census were unreliable. Employers had attempted to persuade their Wendish workers to enter themselves as Germans. The police had confiscated copies of the 'Directions', creating the impression that they were illegal. Forms in which inhabitants had entered themselves as Wends had been declared invalid and returned for correction. In some cases the tellers had even decided to complete the 'language' and 'nationality' questions themselves without considering the opinion of the individuals concerned. Despite all these obstacles, 25,213 inhabitants of Saxony alone managed to record themselves as Sorbs by language and nationality (Schurmann 1998: 131–2).

In his report to the SED District leadership mentioned above, Krenz also reported Sorbian dismay at the lack of any mention of the Wends in the draft constitution for Saxony. He was himself among those Sorbian leaders who signed a telegram to the Saxon government on 7 February 1947 expressing their consternation, but, when a delegation of Sorbian SED members travelled to Dresden on 27 February, it learned that the draft constitution had already been finalized for presentation to the *Landtag* and the Sorbs would have to wait for a special law (Barker 1996: 47).

In Moscow in March 1947, a conference of the foreign ministers of the four war-time allies met. The Domowina and the National Committee sent separate memoranda, both repeating demands for separation from Germany. There was a Yugoslav delegation present and the Wendish demands received its support. The western allies feared that the Soviet Union might support them too, but in the event it did not. At a further foreign ministers' conference in London in December 1947, the Domowina again submitted a memorandum, which again produced no result. In the meantime, dismayed at the prospect of being abandoned to the mercies of the German authorities in the Soviet Occupation Zone, they set about cutting their losses and facing the task of forcing Saxony to grant them some kind of legal status (Barker 1996: 48). They could not do this without the support of the SED.

The Domowina wrote to the Central Committee of the SED in Berlin, setting out its concerns and making a series of proposals. Foremost among these were: 1. the recognition of a Sorbian nation; 2. the formation of a single Sorbian administrative area; and 3. the formation of a separate Sorbian section of the SED. A Domowina delegation met the SED leadership on 21 November 1947, but Otto Grotewohl, formerly chairman of the East German SPD and now joint chairman of the SED, said the Sorbs could not be a nation, because they lacked the necessary defining features, as laid down by Stalin. He also rejected the demands for a Sorbian administrative unit and a Sorbian SED section but conceded that the SED favoured the protection of national minorities. The other joint chairman, Wilhelm Pieck (formerly KPD) concurred, describing the Sorbs as 'the remnants of a national group which are no longer in possession of a Slav native soil'. Wilhelm Koenen, representing Saxony, did not disagree but showed a sliver of sympathy for the Sorbian position. Outright hostility came from Friedrich Ebert, representing Brandenburg. He said there were in Brandenburg 'no visible signs of a living Sorbian culture' and considered it 'inappropriate to start a campaign to bring the Sorbian nation back to life' (Barker 1996: 50). However, the SED did take the Domowina seriously and did not want to make enemies unnecessarily. Before the meeting ended it said that in

Saxony procedures towards making a law to protect and promote Sorbian cultural rights would be expedited. The consent of the Soviet Military Authority having been obtained, the Saxon Law for the Protection of the Rights of the Sorbs was passed on 23 March 1948. It was not until September 1950, however, that a similar piece of legislation was passed in Brandenburg (Barker 1996: 49–52).

In the first post-war years, the German terms *Wenden* and *wendisch* were still in common use both colloquially and officially. Gradually, however, they were replaced by *Sorben* and *sorbisch*. Neither the reason for this nor the mechanism whereby the innovatory forms were introduced are known, but the change can be dated to late 1947 or early 1948. The law of 23 March 1948 finally put the official seal of approval on *Sorben* and *sorbisch*. Henceforth, in all official publications *Wenden* and *wendisch* were avoided. The neologisms gradually gained favour in Upper Lusatia and by the 1960s, the balance was tipping in their favour. In Brandenburg, however, *Sorben* and *sorbisch* came to be associated with the Upper Sorbs and official policy. Here unofficially (and in West Germany), *Wenden* and *wendisch* lived on. In the West German press the change in terminology (and the reinstatement of Slav place names) were ridiculed (*Der Spiegel*, 14 February 1948: 7).

The trial of Dr Hermann Eckhardt, formerly *Landrat* of Kreis Bautzen and head of the *Wendenabteilung*, opened in Bautzen on 30 November 1948. He was accused of instigating the expulsion and arrest of Sorbian priests, abolishing the Sorbian language from schools, confiscating and destroying Sorbian libraries, and of responsibility for the imprisonment and death of Sorbian, Czech, and Polish antifascists by denouncing them to the Gestapo. Evidence was given of the sufferings of Fr Jan Cyž (1883–1948), whose death three months earlier was attributed to his ordeal in Dachau, and of Alojs Andricki, who had died there in 1943. Eckhardt, it was reported, had passed the names of 103 Sorbian activists to the Gestapo, thereby incurring complicity in their suffering or death. In his defence he said he had regarded the Sorbian movement as a threat to the security of Germany and that he could not have avoided collaborating with the Gestapo. He was convicted of crimes against humanity and sentenced to fifteen years imprisonment (Zwahr 1984: 454–60). This is the only known war-crimes trial in which the victims were Wends/Sorbs.

Yugoslav support

Support for the Lusatian Wends in their post-war aspirations had been declared by Marshal Tito in November 1945 and the Sorbian National Council from 1 January appointed Jurij Rjenč as their plenipotentiary representative in Yugoslavia. He took up his position in the spring and met Tito and the other main political figures. Yugoslavia began to release Sorbian prisoners of war (Pałys 2012: 216). In summer 1946 at a ceremony in Schleife in honour of the Red Army a representative of the Yugoslav Military Mission in Berlin made a speech, declaring that Yugoslavia would ensure the liberation of the Sorbian people. This was repeated at a rally in Radibor. The Soviet occupation authorities were irritated. In December that year, members of the Military Mission visited Bautzen and repeated Yugoslavia's support in the course of talks with representatives of both the Domowina and the National Council. Yugoslavia was also a source of material aid. When officials of Sorbian organizations had occasion to visit Berlin, the Yugoslavs provided board, lodging, and fuel. The Domowina received a Yugoslav motor-car as a gift. General Jaka Avšič, a Slovene, head of the Military Mission, obtained permission from the Soviet administration for 800 Sorbian children to attend summer camps organized by the Czechoslovak Red Cross. Yugoslav aid was also given in setting up the new Sorbian printing press (Pałys 2012: 218).

24 August 1947 was the centenary of the foundation of the Maćica Serbska and the day appointed for laying the foundation stone of the new House of the Wends/Sorbs (*Serbski Dom*) in Bautzen. The victorious Slav states were represented at the ceremony, alongside the Soviet delegate, and on 11 June 1948 the Sorb building brigades took delivery of thirty tonnes of Yugoslav cement. To facilitate the early release of Sorbian prisoners, the Domowina provided the Yugoslavs with lists of names. The number freed exceeded 119 (of whom at least twenty-one were Lower Sorbs/Wends) (Pałys 2012: 218–19).

In May 1946 the World Federation of Democratic Youth called for the formation of brigades of volunteers to help in the reconstruction of Yugoslavia. General Avšič proposed that Sorbian young people should participate. The task of forming a Sorbian brigade was passed to Jan Nalij, who had the group assembled and ready within two weeks. The flag-ship project of the first year of the Yugoslav Five-Year Plan for 1947–1951 was the construction of the Šamac-Sarajevo railway line. The participation of the young Sorbs was a great success and on 28 February 1948, the 'shock brigade' of the Sorbian youth movement *Serbska Młodźina* was ceremonially awarded the insignia of the order *Rad i Red* 'Work and Order' First Class. Their leader Jurij Brězan was personally decorated with the same distinction Second Class.

Early in March 1948 the *Serbska Młodźina* received an invitation for fifty young Sorbs to work on the construction of the Belgrade-Zagreb motorway in the period 15 June to 1 August 1948. Led by Jurij Brězan again, the Sorbian group left on schedule in early June, but during their stay in Yugoslavia the political climate changed. On 28 June 1948 the Cominform published its resolution expelling the Communist Party of Yugoslavia. The rift between Yugoslavia and the other Cominform countries was to have grave implications for the Sorbs, for Yugoslavia had been the only country to support on an international level Sorbian claims for independence, and Sorbian organizations had cultivated Yugoslav links. In the autumn of 1948 *Nowa Doba*, simple-mindedly and alone among the newspapers appearing in the Soviet Occupation Zone, published an article devoted to the fifth anniversary of the foundation of the new Yugoslavia as well as a congratulatory letter from the Sorbian Slavonic Committee (Pałys 2012: 225–7).

In August the Sorbian brigade returned home to discover they had been compromised by their Yugoslav involvement. They were forced to publish a condemnation of Tito and return their medals. While in Yugoslavia in 1947 Jan Nalij had made arrangements for himself and his brother Pawoł to study in Ljubljana. Now, following Tito's fall from grace, they decided it would be prudent to return home, but to make the journey they needed documents. At home in Bautzen, their brother Korla appealed on their behalf to Dr Jan Cyž, the Bautzen *Landrat*, but he said that, in view of the Nalij brothers' known political position (they were CDU supporters), he feared they might be regarded as counter-revolutionaries and traitors. Therefore, he could not help. Eventually, with the help of CDU officials, they returned in spring 1950. Titoism now became a convenient label with which to mark any claim to national rights made by Sorbs without official approval. Many who later made such claims were made to suffer accordingly (B. Cyž 1969: 126, 136, 142; M[alinkowa] 1990: 3; Malink 1992: 23–4; *Serbja pod stalinistìskim socializmom* 1992: 73).

Jurij Rjenč, who from spring 1946 had been the Sorbian representative in Yugoslavia, had also found time to open his law practice in Bautzen, where, as a successful defence lawyer and a member of the National Council, he attracted hostile attention. On 8 July 1948 the Domowina, whose hostility to the National Council had grown in step with its dependence on the SED, expelled him. On 30 September 1950 he was arrested at home in Bautzen and taken to Dresden, where he was interrogated by a Soviet officer, Lieutenant F. Samochin. The Soviet writ still ran in the GDR, even though since 1949 it had purported to be a sovereign state. From the record of his interrogation, however, found in the archives of the Lyubyanka by Benedikt Cyž in 1999, it seems that it was not his activity as a lawyer nor even his work in Yugoslavia that had led to his arrest but his role in the National Council and, especially, his link with Václav Moravec and other participants in the 1946–1947 partisan fiasco (B. Cyž 2010a, 2010b, 2011). He was sentenced to twenty-five years imprisonment, but thanks to an amnesty declared after Stalin's death in March 1953, he was released on 21 January 1954 (not 1953, as stated in Cyž 2010a: 19).

The Domowina in Lower Lusatia

On 27 May 1945, on resuming office as president of the Domowina, Nedo issued a circular to Domowina representatives with the news 'The Domowina is functioning again' (Bresan 2002: 161–3) and a few days later he wrote to Franz Saisowa, the newly appointed Cottbus *Landrat*, with the same news and to inform him that the Domowina's representative in Lower Lusatia was Bjedrich Fryco Latk (Friedrich Lattke) (1890–1983), living in Neundorf, near Peitz (Schurmann 1998: 175 and 10). There was no response. Saisowa, though a Wend himself (Zajźěwa/Saischowa), was a renegade, ready to use strong-arm methods against the Wendish movement (*Serbja pod stalinistiskim socializmom* 1992: 60). It was not until August that a second attempt was made to re-assert the Wendish presence in Brandenburg, when three members of the Maśica Serbska – Benjamin Běgař (1873–1945), Awgust Neumann (1884–1963), and Karlo Jordan (1885–1967) – wrote to Major Ivan Savkin, the Commandant of the Soviet Military Administration in Cottbus and the Cottbus District, with a list of requests, including the restitution of the Maśica's library, access to its assembly room in the Wendische Volksbank, and the appointment of 'Slavophile' officials and Wendish-speaking teachers. There is no evidence, however, that the Commandant ever reacted to the letter or even received it. A month later, Běgař died.

There were signs that attitudes in Brandenburg were still not ready for a renewal of Wendish initiatives. When, at the beginning of 1946, Karlo Jordan tried to enlist the support of an old Maśica member called Hussok in Skadow, Kr. Cottbus, he declined, saying the SPD had threatened to seize his land and evict him, if he resumed his Wendish activities. In January 1946, therefore, Jordan travelled alone to the Soviet Military Administration at Berlin-Karlshorst to deliver the letter drawn up the previous August. It was accepted, but there was no reply and he was told to deal in future with the Kommandatura at Potsdam (Schurmann 1998: 180–1). The Domowina leaders in Bautzen were kept informed of events in Lower Lusatia and on 25 February 1946, they appointed Albert Wjelk (Wölk) as their representative there. There was an immediate result. A letter from Cottbus to the Domowina in Bautzen, dated 27 February 1946, reported: 'From today the Domowina exists in Cottbus. We the undersigned this morning visited the Russian Commandant in Cottbus and submitted to him our concerns. The Domowina was given his approval and tomorrow our chairman Theodor Pehla of Schlichow will be given the decree. At the same time the Commandant will provide us with a building.' The signatories were Wjelk, Pehla, and Fryco Morling (b. 1894). The report also alluded, though without details, to recent difficulties encountered by Wends in the Cottbus area. The German police had been intending to make arrests but had been restrained by the Russians (Schurmann 1998: 182–3).

These achievements, however, were all short-lived, for a few days later Pehla and Morling received an invitation to visit the Cottbus Kommandatura, where on 5 March they were seen by Captain Strongin, the officer responsible for political affairs. He told them they would have to wait for ratification from Potsdam. Until then, the approval for Domowina activity was rescinded. Steps already taken in Döbbrick, Kr. Cottbus, to form a Domowina group with about fifty members led by Wylem Neumann, the village mayor, were condemned by Strongin as premature (Schurmann 1998: 184). Strongin's revocation of approval was now interpreted by enemies of the Wends as a ban on Wendish activities. The SPD chairman in Döbbrick had told Morling 'that he must report immediately all activity of the Wendish movement and that I [Morling], as a separatist or Czech agent, would be arrested'. Anti-Wendish propaganda was rife, concentrating on the generalization that the Wends had been Nazis. In April 1946 in Schlichow, a notice was displayed in the mayor's office saying: 'Wendish meetings are strictly prohibited. If two Wends are talking together, that is regarded as separatist activity and they are to be arrested' (Schurmann 1998: 186–9).

When Błažij Nawka, an Upper Sorbian student, visited Lower Lusatia at the end of June to collect information for the Domowina leadership, he learned that the Wends were being intimidated by the police and other officials. Captain Strongin was openly proclaiming that Wends were Fascists (Schurmann 1998: 190–1). The police action against Wendish activists was being instigated by Friedrich Greschenz (Grešeńc), the Cottbus Director of Education and a Wendish renegade (*Serbja pod stalinistiskim socializmom* 1992: 60). On 12 July the Domowina leadership sent the lawyer Jurij Rjenč to explore the situation in Lower Lusatia. Armed with the intelligence gathered by Nawka and using his forensic skills, he told Colonel Vakulenko, the Cottbus town

Commandant, that the Wends in Upper Lusatia were committed to the socialist path. In an interview with Strongin he questioned the action of the police and said the Wends were expecting help from the Military Administration. Strongin now showed understanding, but said the Wends in Lower Lusatia were 'reactionary and not progressive'. Nevertheless, Strongin was now prepared to help and he agreed with Rjenč that Theodor Pehla of Schlichow, an SED member, should be spokesman for the Lower Wends (Schurmann 1998: 191).

The meeting in the Kommandatura was only the start of a busy day for Rjenč, who now moved on to the Cottbus SED offices, where he was received by the Deputy Town Chairman, Willy Finzelberg, and the District Chairman, Albert Brämigk. Brämigk, who was of Wendish descent, rejected all cooperation with the Domowina. The use of the language was unnecessary, he said, because all Wends felt themselves to be German. Those who were not Germans could go to live in Czechoslovakia. Both he and Finzelberg said the Wends were separatists. After all, they said, only three months earlier their representatives had advocated the annexation of both Lusatias by Czechoslovakia. Wends in large numbers had been in the NSDAP, and now they had their agents in Paris and London openly negotiating for the separation of Lusatia from Germany (Schurmann 1998: 192). At a later stage the meeting was joined by the SED Town Chairman Willy Pröllop, who, unlike Brämigk, did not conceal his Wendish identity and said he was ready to work with Wendish socialists. Brämigk maintained his opposition.

Later still that day (12 July 1946), Rjenč and Theodor Pehla returned to the Kommandatura for further discussions with Captain Strongin. Pehla complained about the persecution of Wends by the police and questioned the policy of regarding any conversation between two Wends as separatist activity (Schurmann 1998: 193). Strongin agreed that this particular decision was excessive and condemned it (Schurmann 1998: 199n.). He was now in a conciliatory mood. Wendish activities in Lower Lusatia, it was agreed, would be led by Pehla (Schurmann 1998: 193). Strongin's change of heart, however, had no effect. Wends continued to be criminalized, and in August 1946 Werner Schlierike, a teacher from Byleguhre near Straupitz and an SED official, was arrested merely for discussing the Domowina with other Wends (Schurmann 1998: 195n.).

Local elections were now imminent, so the Domowina, seeing that in Brandenburg there was no prospect of its standing separately, decided to hold three rallies in Heinersbrück, Dissen, and Werben to explain their intentions (Schurmann 1998: 196). Preparations were entrusted to Wends free of Nazi stigma, notably Theodor Pehla (SED), Měto Laški/Martin Laschki (SED), Awgust Neumann (CDU), and Fryco Kitlař (unaffiliated). On 15 August Laški had a further meeting with Strongin, who now insisted on having written accreditation for the Domowina from the Military Government in Potsdam before he would authorize its activities.

On Sunday, 8 September 1946, nineteen Wends met in Měto Laški's house in Werben. Laški himself was absent, having been arrested two days previously by the police in Cottbus, but officers for a Lower Wendish Domowina were elected, with Laški as chairman and Kito Šmogeŕ and Theodor Pehla as deputy chairmen. Resolutions passed included demands for the immediate release of Laški, the unification of Upper and Lower Lusatia in an administrative unit under the protection of the Soviet Union, the establishment of Wendish schools, and the formation of a Wendish socialist party. Following an appeal to the Cottbus Kommandatura, Laški was released the next day (Schurmann 1998: 198–9, 199n.). The meeting had called for a Wendish socialist party but provisionally the newly elected officers of the Lower Wendish Domowina were ready to support the SED. Some in fact were members, but the SED had rejected Wendish proposals for cooperation. On 12 September Mina Witkojc was arrested and held by the police for a few hours, because, together with Jurij Rjenč, she had been putting up election posters with the words (in Wendish) saying 'Wends vote for List 1', that is, for the SED. Two days later, however, on the day before the elections, officers of the Lower Wendish Domowina, with the agreement of Strongin, participated in an SED meeting in Döbbrick, at which Mina Witkojc, speaking in Wendish, told her countrymen and women to vote SED, because as yet there was no Wendish party (Schurmann 1998: 200–1).

As chairman of the Domowina in Lower Lusatia, Laški had a meeting on 27 January 1947 with Albert Brämigk, seeking reconciliation. He told Brämigk he hoped the SED would not overlook the human rights of minorities and reminded him of the Germanization policies of successive German governments, especially under the Nazis. Brämigk's reaction is not recorded, but police action against Wendish activists continued (Schurmann 1998: 205). A week later Kito Smogeŕ, Deputy Chairman of the Domowina in Lower Lusatia, complained to the Kommandatura that in Schmellwitz an official named Günther with two policemen had searched the card-index of Domowina members held by Morling and declared membership cards to be invalid. On complaining to the Kommandatura two days later, Morling was told that Domowina activities were not permitted and that even registering members was forbidden. He therefore sent his membership records to Bautzen, informing the leadership of the circumstances (Schurmann 1998: 206–7).

Reacting to the information received from Morling, the Bautzen leadership wrote to the SED leadership in Cottbus on 27 February offering cooperation and to the Soviet Military Administration in Berlin-Karlshorst on 8 March pointing out that, if the population of Lower Lusatia had not yet 'joined the progressive course to a sufficient degree', it was due to the refusal of the Cottbus SED to cooperate with the Domowina. This offer appears to have been listened to, because on 3 May a conference took place in Werben, attended by SED members of the Domowina and officials of the Brandenburg, Cottbus, and Bautzen SED. Kurt Krjeńc (SED) spoke and said that the responsibility for the lack of cooperation lay with the SED. The meeting agreed that cooperation between the Domowina and the SED in Lower Lusatia should be expedited (Schurmann 1998: 210, 289).

Nevertheless, the Brandenburg SED continued to drag its feet. Even after 23 March 1948, when the Saxon Landtag passed its law guaranteeing the rights of the Sorbs, Friedrich Ebert, leader of the Party in Brandenburg, was still assuring the central leadership that no sign of a Wendish movement in Brandenburg had been detected (8 April) (Schurmann 1998: 216). In July Nedo visited Lower Lusatia and spoke to Albert

Brämigk, who was now more cooperative, but Saisowa was as contemptuous as ever (Schurmann 1998: 219). At the end of September 1948, Brämigk told the Bautzen SED that the Brandenburg SED was in favour of a unified policy on the Wendish question, and finally, on 20 January 1949, the government of Brandenburg approved the Domowina's application for permission to operate in Lower Lusatia (Schurmann 1998: 222). It was only on 18 September 1950 that Brandenburg passed a decree of similar content to the Saxon legislation (Schönfeld and Holder 1966: 33–4).

Place names

At various times in the late 1940s, some of the German place names which had been imposed by Nazi administrators on Wendish villages were removed and the traditional names (i.e. German names of Wendish origin) reinstated. A law restoring the old names in the Hoyerswerda, Niesky, and Kamenz Districts was published on 12 January 1948. Among the names in question were *Brischko* (Birkenhain), *Nardt* (Elsternhorst), *Sabrodt* (Wolfsfurt), *Spohla* (Brandhofen), *Tätzschwitz* (Vogelhain), *Wendischbaselitz* (Kleinbaselitz), *Horka* (Wehrkirch), *Tschelln* (Nelkenberg), and *Wunscha* (Wildfelde) (B. Cyž 1969: 366–7). This piece of legislation was one of the last to use the variant *wendisch* (for *sorbisch*). The timing and details of similar procedures in other areas, if any, have yet to be established. *Weinhübel*, near Görlitz, however, which from 1305 to 1936 had been *Leschwitz*, remained unchanged and was incorporated into Görlitz. Meschgang reminded his readers that this relic of the Third Reich had been overlooked (1973: 144). The following also escaped denazification: *Bergheide* (until 1937 *Gohra*), *Buchholz* (until 1936 *Krischa*), *Schwarzheide* (until 1936 *Zschornegosda*), *Freienhufen* (until 1937 *Dobristroh*), *Birkwalde* (now part of Sonnewalde; until 1937 *Presehna*), *Walddrehna* (until 1937 *Wendisch Drehna*).

The eastern part of Lusatia was now in Poland, but the number of Sorbs east of the Neisse was very small. Almost all of the Sorbian speech-area lay to the west of the new frontier. Proof that the 'recovered lands' had once been populated by Slavs (though not necessarily by Poles) was provided by thousands of place names. There were also, however, many place names that were not of Slav origin, and even those whose Slav pedigree was impeccable were rarely suitable for immediate official use in Polish. In January 1946, a committee was set up to supervise the composition of a Polish gazetteer for all the 'recovered lands' (the *Komisja Ustalania Nazw Miejscowości* 'Committee for Establishing the Names of Localities'). To enable the new Polish state administration to function without referring to places by their German names, some 30,000 new Polish forms were necessary. It was a matter of urgency and the Committee set to work at once. Their procedures varied from reviving forgotten Slavonic names to inventing totally new ones. In the case of eastern Lusatia, there were a number of towns and villages which already had Sorbian names in addition to the official German version (*Commission* 2014).

Wójćech Kóčka

One of the most active participants in the post-1945 independence movement was Wójćech Kóčka (or Kučka) (Albert Kutschke), who was born at Oehna (Wownjow), just north of Bautzen, on 13 October 1911. He attended the Catholic High School in Bautzen and later studied archaeology, anthropology, and ethnography at Poznań University (1932–1936), where on graduation became an assistant in the department of pre-history. In 1938 he became a naturalized citizen of Poland. In the 1930s, when German historians were attempting to rewrite the history of Central Europe, Kóčka was working in a highly politicized sphere (Pałys 2006). He was one of the small group of Wends linked to an officer of the Polish secret service operating under the codename 'Michał' (Nowotny 1996: 13; cf. Chapter 7 above).

Kóčka spent the War in Poland in hiding, working in a horticultural cooperative. Following allied victory, he worked ceaselessly for the Wendish cause. From October 1945 he was a member of the Wendish National Committee, who in early 1946 sent him to Poland, where he persuaded the Prime Minister Edward Osóbka-Morawski to receive a delegation from the Committee, as representatives of the Sorbian people, and to accept a copy of its memorandum. On 22 February 1946, he applied to the Polish Ministry of Foreign Affairs for the early release of Wendish prisoners-of-war held on Polish territory (Pałys 2006: 388). Between 15 and 21 May Kóčka and Ernst Černik had discussions with representatives of various ministries in Warsaw. They were received by Władysław Gomułka, Deputy Prime Minister of Poland and Minister for the Recovered Territories, but were disappointed to hear that the demands of the National Committee were held to be unrealistic. Gomułka said that for Poland at that time the main objective was to secure its western borders and expel the Germans from the new Poland. Only when these problems had been settled, would there be a chance of considering a solution to the Wendish question (Mieczkowska 1993: 103; Pałys 2006: 388–9).

In order to persuade the Slavonic states to demand at least a high degree of autonomy for Lusatia, he attempted to obtain a hearing at a plenary meeting of the Pan-Slav Committee in Warsaw in June 1947, but despite his accreditation from the Slav Committee in Bautzen, he was denied entry to the plenary sessions (Pałys 2006: 389). In a discussion with the secretary of the Pan-Slav Committee Moczałow, however, he gained an assurance that Wendish cultural development was guaranteed but was again told that there could be no further discussion until the Polish frontier on the Oder and Neisse was firmly established (Šurman 1991: 270–1; Pałys 2006: 389).

Applications made by Kóčka, Anton Nawka, and other Wends in Poland resulted in the handing-over of twenty-one POWs from a camp in Jaworzno to a representative of the PZZ on 3 June 1947. On release they were sent for convalescence to Wrocław, where Kóčka took them into his care. Following further requests, another thirty-six Wendish POWs were released on 9 October and allowed to return home (Palys 2006: 389). In January 1947, Kóčka secured permission from the authorities for all Wends who, as a result of hostilities or expulsion had been forced to leave their homes in what was now Polish territory, to return to Poland (Pałys 2006: 389). He thought it would be best, if they could settle somewhere near Muskau and establish contact with the Wends on the left bank of the Neisse. They should be joined, he said, by a Wendish pastor, a Wendish teacher, and a number of nationally conscious Wends from the Hoyerswerda and Schleife areas to revive the Wendish psyche of those who had been Germanized. In this way a Wendish base could be established on Polish soil, which might be 'a substitute for Wendish statehood'. In May 1947, the Ministry for Recovered Territories promised to offer material assistance to those thus resettled. There were attempts by the Domowina to compile a register of Wendish-speakers who had been expelled from Poland, but by the beginning of 1948 it had been abandoned (Mieczkowska 1993: 103–4; Pałys 2006: 389).

Kóčka also made plans for the foundation of a Wendish gymnasium with boarding facilities in the part of Görlitz which was now in Poland (i.e. Zgorzelec), and in spring 1946 the Polish authorities in Zgorzelec made preparations for its construction. Financial provision for the project was approved. In January 1948, a date was fixed for the opening of the school in the autumn that year, but the acceptance by the Saxon parliament on 23 March 1948 of the Law for the Protection of the Rights of the Sorbs deprived the project of its impetus, and the plans were abandoned (Pałys 2006: 390). Another of Kóčka's efforts to enable young Sorbs to study in Poland, however, was crowned with success. In autumn 1947, a group of four Sorbian students began their studies at the new University of Wrocław with scholarships provided by the Polish Ministry of Education. Kóčka personally supervised the conversion of a building belonging to the Silesian Institute into a hostel for the Sorbian students (Młynk 1967: 68). In January 1948, the Domowina requested Kóčka to arrange for the acceptance by Wrocław University of a further group, which arrived in March 1948.

In 1947 and 1948 Kóčka had talks with Gomułka and other ministers in an attempt to obtain economic aid for Lusatia, but without success. Meanwhile, he was managing to pursue his academic career and in 1948 he received the degree of doctor, having written a thesis on the early historical anthropology of the western Slavs. In 1955, he returned to Poznań University and here in 1960 he was elected to the Chair of Archaeology (Pałys 2006: 391). He died on 18 November 1965 at the age of 54.

Sorbian schools

Many of the expelled Germans stayed in the Sorbian area, where they were shocked to find they were now in a part of Germany inhabited by Slavs. The Wends too were shocked. They discovered that their recently restored linguistic freedom was now impaired by a huge influx of Germans. The linguistic situation had altered. In villages that had recently been Wendish-speaking, the vernacular was now German. This was a watershed in Wendish history (Keller 2005: *passim*). Failure to realize the extent of this change was to have implications for the unprecedented expansion of the Wendish school-system which was now initiated. Schools in the Soviet Occupation Zone opened again on 1 October 1945, but conditions for a time remained chaotic. There was at first no official curriculum

(Barker 2000: 43–4). There was a general shortage of Wendish teachers, owing primarily, as we have seen, to the disqualification of former Nazi Party members. Many teachers, moreover, were not available because they had been forcibly transferred to other parts of Germany. In neighbouring Czechoslovakia, however, the rule disqualifying former party members did not apply, so it proved possible to open schools there attended by Wendish children and employing Wendish teachers who had been in the Party.

In January 1946 a teacher training institute was set up in the manor-house in Radibor, directed by Michał Nawka, at which Sorbian teachers could be trained on intensive three-month courses. In its first year it trained 282 new teachers, of whom 170 were Sorbs. Nevertheless, two years after the resumption of school activity the Domowina complained to the SED Central Committee (4 October 1947): 'Despite incessant reminders and petitions by the Sorbs to the competent German authorities, to this day no Sorbian schools for Sorbian children have been organized. The language of instruction is German. Sorbian is permitted as a subject of study for three hours a week in a few scattered districts of Saxon Upper Lusatia. In the schools of the area inhabited by the Sorbs Sorbian is treated as a foreign language for Sorbian children' (Schurmann 1998: 273; Barker 2000: 44).

The Saxon Law for the Protection of the Rights of the Sorbs, passed on 23 March 1948, was implemented very slowly. Bureaucratic skill in prevarication makes it hard to assess the extent to which the delay resulted simply from anti-Sorbian sentiments, but that prejudice was part of official policy emerges clearly from a letter written by the Dresden SED to the Central Committee on 5 September 1949: '... we will delay handling the matter in order to let certain extreme desires fade away'. The extreme desires in question included the wish to have a Sorbian youth movement, independent of the Free German Youth (FDJ), which those who knew no better thought was one of the rights the new law was meant to protect (Barker 2000: 40).

On 7 October 1949, the GDR came into existence, replacing the Soviet Occupation Zone. Article 11 of the Constitution of the GDR stated:

> The parts of the Republic's population speaking foreign languages are by legislation and administration to be encouraged in their free ethnic development; in particular, they may not be hindered in the use of their mother-tongue in education, in internal administration, and in legal processes.

> (Krahl 1972: 3).

The March Law had been passed despite opposition within the SED and doubts about it persisted. In 1950 the Chairman of the Saxon SED Lohagen said: '... today we would never make the Sorb Law in the form in which it was passed' and his message for the Sorbs was: 'Remember, in fifty years nobody will speak Sorbian any longer' (Ela 1993: 23–4). The increasing centralization in the GDR was not advantageous to the Sorbian educational system. Responsibility for education was transferred from the *Land* level to a central ministry in Berlin, which in the directives and timetables it issued for the school year 1951–1952 forgot about the position of Sorbian in Sorbian schools. Sorbian teachers were forced to improvise (Ela 1993: 24; Barker 2000: 55).

In 1951 Fred Oelsner, a member of the Politburo was given responsibility for the Sorbian question and in April 1952 a new set of directions was issued, bringing a stability and legal structure to the Sorbian school system which Sorbian teachers welcomed. Sorbian became an obligatory subject for all Sorbian children, but the precise status of Sorbian in schools was to vary locally. In schools described as B-schools the language of instruction remained German, but Sorbian was to be taught as a compulsory subject. In A-schools, on the other hand, all subjects were to be taught in Sorbian, German being introduced as a subject in the second year. Some schools of this type had been operating already, but in 1952 their number was increased to nine. The same year, seventy-two B-schools were set up. A-schools were located exclusively in parts of the Bautzen and Kamenz *Kreise* in areas where Sorbian speakers were still in a majority. In Lower Lusatia there were only B-schools, even in areas where Sorbs were in a majority (Ela 1993: 26; Barker 2000: 55; Schulwesen 2012).

By 1955 there were in Lower Lusatia twenty-two Sorbian elementary schools of type B and one Sorbian secondary school (gymnasium). In that year in Upper Lusatia there were seventy-three B-schools, eleven A-schools, and one secondary school (gymnasium). Plans to convert ten B-schools in both Upper and Lower Lusatia into A-schools never came into effect. The number of pupils in Sorbian schools grew throughout the 1950s and in 1960 reached a highpoint of 22,435. The production of Sorbian schoolbooks also reached new heights. The official slogan was 'Lusatia is becoming bilingual' (*Die Lausitz wird zweisprachig*). The status of the language in the school system was enhanced and there was a new sense of confidence. In some quarters, however, there was opposition to the promotion of the Sorbian language and, especially, resistance by some parents to its position in schools. German newcomers, who had been expelled from beyond the Oder-Neisse line, were particularly hostile (Schulwesen 2012).

It was all too good to last, and the fact remained that the Sorbs were outnumbered. In February 1958 Fred Oelsner was relieved of all his state and party functions. Achim Handrik, head of the government's Sorbian Department, stated in a speech: 'The slogan "Lusatia is becoming bilingual" is wrong. It is confusing. The slogan must be "Lusatia is becoming socialist". The nationalities policy must play a role subordinate to socialist construction' (Ela 1993: 31). In the early 1960s, there were ominous changes in government policy. First, in 1962 Sorbian was replaced by German as the language of instruction in science subjects in A-schools. Then, in 1964 participation in Sorbian lessons in B-schools was made optional. Pupil numbers sank drastically. In the 1970s, however, they revived (Ela 1993: 32–3; Schulwesen 2012).

State support for Sorbian culture

Article 40 of a new GDR Constitution, which came into force in 1968, stated: 'Citizens of the German Democratic Republic of Sorbian nationality have the right to foster their mother-tongue and culture. The state supports the exercise of this right' (*Zusammenstellung* 1982: 2). If this is less categorical than the corresponding article in the Constitution of 1949, that may be to reflect the changes in the school-system in the early 1960s. State support, however, continued to manifest itself in many other ways. Throughout the Sorbian speech-area (and often beyond its limits) sign-posts, street-names, traffic-signs, and other public notices were written in Sorbian as well as German. For the first time in history a professional Wendish (Sorbian) theatre was founded. In 1963 it was combined with the Bautzen Municipal Theatre to produce the German-Sorbian People's Theatre, sharing a historic building in Bautzen and with a repertoire of both German and Sorbian plays. Sorbian radio programmes were instituted in 1949 and from 1964 transmitting time was extended to 290 minutes weekly. At the University of Leipzig degrees in Sorbian language, literature, and history were introduced. In Bautzen the Institute for Sorbian Ethnography (*Institut für sorbische Volksforschung*) was set up, housing the Sorbian Central Library and Archive.

There was generous support for Sorbian publishing. The total number of Sorbian books published in the twenty years ending 1967 exceeded one thousand. That over half of these were text-books of one kind or another reflects the changes which had taken place in the school system. Most books were published in editions of 800–1000. By the 1960s it had become clear that the most popular Sorbian publication was the annual calendar, called *Protyka* in Upper and *Pratyja* in Lower Sorbian, containing literary contributions and illustrations. Issued at a time to take advantage of the Christmas rush, it sometimes achieved annual sales of 6,000 copies.

The Domowina People's Press (*Ludowe Nakładnistwo Domowina*) was founded in 1947 and became a state undertaking in 1958. It became responsible for almost all publishing in the Sorbian language. Many Sorbs, who before the War had been barely literate in their own language, became avid readers. To foster this tendency a book club was founded, called 'The Circle of Friends of the Sorbian Book' (*Koło přećelow serbskeje knihi*). The new Upper Sorbian daily newspaper *Nowa Doba* 'New Times' first appeared on 6 July 1947. The nearest thing to a Lower Sorbian equivalent was the weekly *Nowy Casnik* 'New Newspaper'. Its first issue came out on 5 March 1956.

The publishing business was one of several new fields offering employment for Sorbian-speakers and requiring their linguistic skills. All publications were subject to state censorship, however, and journalism, in particular, had its risks, as the case of Hinc Šołta shows.

Press freedom and the Stasi

Hinc Šołta was born into a Lutheran family in Neudorf near Königswartha on 10 December 1937, the son of an agricultural labourer. He left school at the early age of sixteen and found work with the Upper Sorbian daily newspaper *Nowa Doba*. In January 1956, he became the paper's local editor. Aged nineteen, he had rapidly reached a remarkably high position on the editorial staff and was supervising the work of colleagues much older than himself, one of whom was secretly working for the Ministry of State Security (*Stasi*). His young enquiring mind was naturally excited by the cracks in the Stalinist monolith that began to appear in 1956. The Twentieth Congress of the Communist Party of the Soviet Union in February that year, at which Stalin was denounced by Khrushchev, was followed in June by riots in Poznań and by the Hungarian Uprising. It would have been surprising if he had not reacted to these events, and his comments on them, made orally to his colleagues at *Nowa Doba*, were reported to the security services. He was particularly interested in political developments in Poland, was studying Polish, and corresponding occasionally with a Pole in Warsaw. They exchanged books and magazines.

The Sorbian-speaking agents of the security police were keeping an eye on the contents of *Nowa Doba*, which on 10 April 1957 carried a brief notice on the king of the Yemen:

Ahmed, the present king of the Arab state of Yemen, had twelve brothers. The life-stories of these brothers reveal that relationships in the Yemeni royal family are not what they might be. The careers of these twelve brothers ended as follows: Mohammed was drowned. Hassan was deported. Hussein was murdered. Ali does not get on with his brother Ahmed. Abdullah's life came to an end on the scaffold. Quazim was deported. Mutahir's life ended in Cairo in unexplained circumstances. Ibrahim disappeared without trace. Yahia also lost his life in an unexplained way. Abbes and Muhsin were murdered, and Abdurahman has been excluded from public life by his brother the present king.

This information had been extracted by Šolta from a copy of the Polish illustrated magazine *Dookoło Świata*. Unfortunately for him, however, the Yemen was regarded by the GDR as an ally, because its king was hostile to America. In Poland the thaw had set in, but not in the GDR.

The chief editor of *Nowa Doba* enquired as to the source. Following the advice of an older colleague, Šolta said it came from *Trybuna Ludu*, the mouthpiece of the Polish United Workers' Party. The Stasi checked and found that this was not true. Šolta came to their notice again later in 1957, when *Nowa Doba* on 5 September reported, first, that the son of John Foster Dulles (U.S. Secretary of State) was studying for the priesthood and attending a ten-month course at the Jesuit College in Münster (West Germany) and, secondly, that the son of Konrad Adenauer (West German Chancellor), a Catholic priest, was studying at Münster University. The Stasi noted that the report would strengthen the opinion of the Sorbian Catholics that 'Adenauer and Dulles are really not bad people, if their children are such good Christians' (Schulze-Šolta 2003: 46).

Early on Friday, 30 May 1958, Šolta left his house in Bautzen and set out to walk to his office, less than a mile away. But he had gone only a few yards when a man sprang from the passenger seat of a parked car, barring his way, and said: 'Police. Come with us. We want to ask you a few questions.' Šolta was pushed into the back seat of the car where he found himself between two men. His surprise increased when he recognized one of them as a school-friend from the Sorbian High School in Bautzen. He was driven a short distance to a department of the Ministry for State Security.

From now on Šołta had no contact with the outside world. From Bautzen he was taken to Dresden and interrogated. As late as October his father, who could only surmise that he had fallen foul of the *Stasi*, was still desperately seeking official information as to his whereabouts. In October he appeared before a judge and was sentenced to fourteen months imprisonment for 'propaganda endangering the state and malicious defamation'. His sentence was served in Bautzen, and on 29 July 1959 he was released. While in prison, Šołta had been informed that he had been dismissed from his job with *Nowa Doba*. Following his release he looked for employment, first with the printers of the Domowina press, later with *Nowa Doba*, but without success. After further similarly unsuccessful applications he left Lusatia and eventually found work as an administrator with the Lutheran Church in Werdau. Only in 1992 were the verdict and sentence of the Dresden court annulled (Schulze-Šołta 2003: 40).

Demolition

The GDR aimed to be self-sufficient in the production of energy and Lusatia was destined to be its energy centre. It possessed brown coal resources in abundance, so in the middle of Lusatia, in the heart of the Wendish homeland between Spremberg and Hoyerswerda, the Black Pump (*Schwarze Pumpe*) Combine was built. It was to become the world's largest plant for processing brown coal and producing gas and electricity. The new town of Neu-Hoyerswerda was built specially to house the combine's workers, together with their families. The Sorbian character of the central Lusatian area was eroded. It was no longer simply a question of Germanization. A new population had arrived.

The business of mining and processing brown coal was not new to the Wends. From small beginnings in the nineteenth century it had grown steadily, meeting the needs of the new industries. The mining was at first confined to central Lusatia and the first miners came from the surrounding Wendish villages. In fact, there was a time when the German supervisors would refer to the miners indiscriminately as *Wenden*, regardless of ethnicity (Förster 1996: 11). In the early twentieth century, however, the proportion of Wends was steadily decreasing, as they were joined by workers from other areas (Förster 1996: 13).

The first Wendish village to be demolished to make accessible the coal that lay beneath it was Neu-Laubusch (Nowy Lubuś), west-north-west of Hoyerswerda. That was in 1924. Most of the inhabitants, for whom the mine by now was the main local employer, moved to the neighbouring works estate. They numbered 125. During the next twenty years three further villages were demolished, leading to the eviction and resettlement of a total of 785 people. This degree of destruction, however, was trivial by comparison with the havoc which followed between 1945 and 1989, when, to help satisfy the GDR's energy demands, seventy-one further villages in Lusatia were demolished. During these forty-five years 22,296 people, predominantly from Wendish/Sorbian villages, were evicted and re-housed. This figure does not include the number of people who moved on their own initiative once they had heard that their community was doomed or who were thereby indirectly constrained to do so. Those displaced by these events were usually rehoused in nearby conurbations, where individual Wends were dispersed among the German majority. The 1948 Law for the Protection of the Rights of the Sorbs provided no protection from the consequences of brown-coal mining.

Meanwhile, agricultural activity in the mining areas suffered. The water table was affected and the land became increasingly infertile. Crop yields were reduced. Nor was the devastation restricted to villages located above coal deposits. In 1972–1973 Nimschütz (Hněwsecy) and Malsitz (Małsecy), on the outskirts of Bautzen, were submerged under a great reservoir, needed to provide water for the coal-fired power station's cooling systems (Förster 1996: 125–7, 144–6). Most of the villages and their churches dated from the Middle Ages, some from as early as the thirteenth century. In some cases they were villages which had significance in Wendish history or where, in the nineteenth century, folklorists had gathered folk-songs, tales, and traditions. Jan Ernst Smoler's birthplace, Merzdorf (Łućo), south-south-west of Weißwasser, together with its church and manor house, was demolished in 1978–1979. The name is first recorded in c. 1400 as Lucze and in 1418 as Merteinsdorf. One of the folk-songs he wrote down here mentions the village by name:

Łućo, jedna mała wjeska,
tu ja wostać njemóžu.
'Łućo is a little village,
here I can no longer stay.'

(Förster 1996: 127–33)

The history of Stradow (Tšadow), north-west of Spremberg, first recorded in 1350 as Strodou, came to an end in 1983–1984. The pastor here from 1812 to his death was Johann Georg Zwahr (1785–1844), author of the first Lower Wendish dictionary (*Niederlausitz-wendisch-deutsches Handwörterbuch*), which was published from his manuscript by his son in Spremberg in 1847 (Förster 1996: 241–7).

German unification in 1990 brought about changes in the demand for energy but did not reduce it. Under new management Black Pump has continued to operate and Wendish villages have continued to be demolished. The rate of destruction has, however, moderated. In 1990 there were seventeen mines in operation. By 1993 the number had fallen to ten and of these only five were expected to survive. This resulted in large-scale unemployment. The destruction of Wendish villages slowed but did not stop. In 1992–1993 Wolkenberg (Klěsnik), south-south-east of Drebkau, and Mocholz (Mochowc), south-south-east of Weißwasser were demolished (Förster 1996: 19). A campaign, started in 1986 by the villagers of Klitten (Klětno) to save their home from the bulldozers, was crowned in February 1990 with success. Attempts to preserve Horno (Rogow), on the other hand, including an appeal under Article 25 of the Brandenburg constitution (which guarantees Wendish rights), failed. The village met its end in 2004–2005. Further demolition is expected.

The Kashubs in People's Poland (PRL)

By the terms of the Potsdam Agreement (August 1945) the Oder-Neisse line became Poland's provisional western frontier, but even before this huge numbers of Germans had already crossed the line. Later, millions more crossed it after being expelled. The frontier between Germany and Czechoslovakia was restored to its 1938 position and the Germans inhabiting the area to the south of it – the Sudetenland – were also expelled. By 1950, there were about 12.5 million refugees in the four occupation zones (Keller 2005: 6). Although the decision to relocate the frontier on the Oder-Neisse line had been taken at the Teheran and Yalta Conferences without Polish agreement, the new Polish authorities were left with the task of explaining it to the Polish public. The explanation that the western territorial gains were compensation for the losses in the east was not acceptable, so they called the gains (with varying degrees of plausibility) 'recovered lands' (*ziemie odzyskane*) (Davies 1981, 2: 501, 509; Mieczkowska 2006: 35n.). The fact remained, however, that some of the pre-German inhabitants of Pomerania and Lusatia would have been better designated as Wends, Sorbs, or Kashubs than as Poles.

By May 1945, most of the German inhabitants of the Kashubian region had fled. The Kashubs were able as early as January 1946 to re-assert their existence at the first post-war Kashubian Congress in Wejherowo. Most of them had already resided within Poland before 1939, but many, under varying degrees of compulsion, had signed the *Deutsche Volksliste* and these had now to undergo the judicial process of Rehabilitation (Bykowska 2012: 10). Those whose habitations before 1939 had been in Germany and who were consequently German citizens were now faced with the process of Verification. This was designed to separate the 'natives' or 'aboriginals' (*autochtonowie*) from the Germans and expedite the expulsion of the latter. To remove any doubts the Kashubs may have had, on 5 July 1945 an edict was published in Lębork (Lauenburg) advising citizens of the Reich of Kashubian origin now residing in the Lębork *powiat* that they were 'considered to be Poles and citizens of the Polish Commonwealth' (Bykowska 2012: 351). The Verification procedure began with investigation by a committee and, if successful, culminated in a ceremonial declaration of loyalty to the Polish state. One of the main criteria was command of Polish, though paradoxically it was expressly envisaged that 'even those who with the passing of the years had succumbed to Germanization should be returned to Poland'. With few exceptions, anyone who had not applied for Verification by August 1946 was assumed to be German and deported (Bykowska 2012: 9, 159, 455). Many Kashubs had contributed substantially to the victory over Nazi Germany, but some had shared the fate of the Sorbs and Wends in Lusatia in being compelled to serve in the German armed forces. They were now exposed to accusations of collaboration.

Kashubian resistance to the German occupiers had been centred on the underground resistance formation *Gryf Pomorski*, which remained loyal to the Polish Government in London. It attempted to protect Polish citizens, gathered intelligence, and carried out raids on German military installations in the Pomeranian region.

It included many Kashubs. *Gryf Pomorski* was preceded by *Gryf Kaszubski*, founded in 1939 in Czarlino, near Sulęczyno, at the instigation of Józef Dambek. It changed its name in 1941 to reflect its wider field of activity following unification with other resistance units.

The last commander was the Kashub Augustyn Westphal (1884 or 1885–1946). He had been in the German army in the First World War. Immediately after the occupation of Pomerania by German troops in 1939, he went into hiding and began to organize the resistance. By May 1944 he was the commander of 'Gryf Pomorski' and on 21 March 1945, faced by the advancing Red Army and realizing that to resist them was unrealistic, he disbanded *Gryf Pomorski* and surrendered. Nevertheless, at the end of 1945 he was arrested by the Security Police (UB) and falsely accused of collaborating with the Germans and spying. For two months he was imprisoned and interrogated under torture. On release, though severely injured, he managed to participate in the Kashubian Congress in Wejherowo in January 1946 and to deliver a solemn speech. He died on 27 September 1946 from the damage done to his kidneys during interrogation. Many other members of *Gryf Pomorski* were arrested or killed by the newly installed UB. Some were sent to camps in the USSR. Among those killed was the former commander Grzegorz Wojewski. In 1947 117 former members of *Gryf Pomorski*, believing that legality had returned to Poland, sent a letter of protest at the treatment of their organization to the Minister for Justice, the Procurator General, and others, but without result (Westphal 2012).

The post-war years, which brought a further and increasing influx to the Kashubian region of newcomers from other parts of Poland, saw no reduction in the level of mutual suspicion and lack of understanding. The Kashubs were still officially regarded as Poles, not as a national minority, and the sounds of Kashubian speech were still prone to be mistaken for German (Wańkowicz 1963: 91, 94). At the end of 1960 a number of Kashubs, suspected of separatism and revisionism, were being kept under observation by the Polish security services. The real reasons why the authorities took a dislike to them, it seems, were their love of their native language, their stubbornness in using it whenever possible, and their habitual complaints about the linguistic discrimination they suffered. In Operation Pomerania the political police (UB) decided to keep observation on a number of suspects, including Aleksander Labuda, Stefan Bieszk, Jan Rompski, Marceli Łukowicz, Jan Trepczyk, Feliks Marszałkowski, Franciszek Grucza, Damroka Majkowska, Wojciech Kiedrowski, and Edmund Kamiński, who were all well known for their Kashubian cultural activities, mainly as writers. In December the homes of Labuda, Bieszk, and Rompski were raided by the police. Photographs and manuscripts were confiscated. They were later summoned individually by the public prosecutor in Gdańsk and interrogated. As the official record reveals, they were neither intimidated nor contrite. Bieszk responded to the accusations by saying that attempts were being made to stigmatize him as a criminal, when all he was doing was promoting Kashubian culture. He told his interrogators that the Kashubs were accustomed to persecution and that the authorities were intent on destroying the Kashubian intelligentsia (Paczoska 2004).

The last of the Slovincians

Kashubian territory to the west of the River Leba (Łeba), in 1945 for the first time since the Middle Ages, came under Polish rule. These were the villages where forty years earlier Friedrich Lorentz had found between 200 and 250 speakers of Slovincian. In the meantime, Germanization had progressed. That the villagers had not yet been fully Germanized, however, was demonstrated, for one thing, by the fact that most of them had stayed put and had no intention of leaving their homeland. A number of the inhabitants of the village of Klucken (Kluki) successfully applied for Verification and took the oath of allegiance to Poland (Figure 8.2). The population of the village in 1939 had numbered 618, but by 1947 it had fallen to 418. It fell still further in September that year, after the expulsion of 184 inhabitants, leaving 234 of the original population. Before the end of 1945 new settlers from eastern Poland (now annexed by the USSR) had begun to arrive, looking for loot and evicting the villagers from their houses. In September 1948 a further ninety-two inhabitants, having been found deficient in aboriginality, were deported to Germany. By 1950, there were 142 natives in the village and thirty-eight new settlers from the east (Bolduan 1992: 10–13; Bykowska 2012: 384–8).

Knowledge of the Slovincian language among the inhabitants of Kluki was fragmentary. Ludwig Zabrocki during a visit in July 1946 was able to observe how an old man named Otto Kirk, using his vestigial competence in the language of his fathers, managed to communicate after a fashion with Russian soldiers. He had a reasonably large vocabulary but was unable to form sentences grammatically (Zabrocki 1975: 101,

Figure 8.2 Slovincians at their Verification ceremony, c. 1946.

105). By 1950, when the Kashubian journalist Tadeusz Bolduan visited Kluki, Kirk had been deported. Bolduan found that from the moment of their arrival the newcomers had terrorized the natives, constantly harassing them and subjecting them to abuse. Complaints to the authorities, even when supported by Bolduan and others, brought no redress (Bolduan 1992: 14–16). When Feliks Rogaczewski, the new village schoolmaster, arrived in August 1947, he found that the main language of most of the inhabitants was German, and this was the language he used in everyday dealings with them. In the school he introduced Polish. A fair number of the older inhabitants could still remember fragments of the Slav language which they had learned imperfectly from their parents, but they did not acknowledge the name *Slovinzen* or the adjective *slovinzisch*. They maintained that they were *Kaschuben*, whereas the Catholic *Kaschuben* to their east were, according to them, not *Kaschuben* but *Polen* (Zabrocki 1975: 105).

Rogaczewski, who spoke fluent German and a little Kashubian, was responsible for introducing the Polish language, but he also encouraged the villagers to recall, if they could, and use their ancestral language. Occasionally whole sentences would unexpectedly emerge, but no one ever regained real fluency (Rogaczewski 1975: 74–5; Bolduan 1992: 13). In 1951 he facilitated a visit to the village by Zenon Sobierajski, a dialectologist from the University of Poznań, who made gramophone recordings from some of the oldest inhabitants (Sobierajski 1964: 109–27). By 1970 those that had escaped deportation had, in most cases, learned Polish and been integrated into Polish life, but now only eighty of the original inhabitants remained. The aggressive behaviour of their new neighbours, the intention of which was to drive them out and appropriate their property, had not abated. After 1970 it was possible for citizens of Poland, who had relatives in West Germany, to obtain permission (on payment of a fee) to join them. Family members of the Kluki Slovincians were already in the West and urging them to come, and so they eventually agreed By 1974 only five Slovincians remained in Kluki. The last one committed suicide in 1987 (Bolduan 1992: 26–7). In West Germany the people of Kluki did their utmost to stay together and mostly settled in the same neighbourhoods in Hamburg. Their assimilation into West German society was limited, and they remained emotionally attached to Kluki, which they continued to visit, whenever possible. In 1996 the first of a series of reunions was held there (Filip 2012: 198–9).

After 1990: Reconstruction

In 1990, the Polish People's Commonwealth ceased to exist and was replaced within the same borders by the Third Polish Commonwealth. The GDR also expired and its territory was united with the German Federal Republic. These changes were of great significance for both the Kashubs and the Lusatian Wends and Sorbs. Much of the secrecy that had concealed important aspects of their lives was lifted.

The emotions aroused among the Sorbs by the mass demonstrations that began with Mikhail Gorbachev's visit to mark the GDR's fortieth birthday on 7 October 1989 were different from those felt by other GDR citizens. Unlike Germany, the Sorbian homeland was not politically divided. Relatively few Sorbs had ties with West Germany. Some felt they had more in common with their Slav neighbours to the south and east. In particular, those who could remember life in a united Germany were not enthusiastic about the prospect of German re-unification.

Nevertheless, resigned to their vulnerability in the turbulence of German history, the Sorbs began to discuss their hopes for the future. For this purpose on 11 November 1989 a hastily assembled Sorbian People's Assembly (*Serbska ludowa zhromadźizna/Sorbische Volksversammlung*) met for the first time. The Assembly opposed the SED-dominated Domowina and called for the creation of a Sorbian Round Table (*Serbske kulojte blido*), which, consisting of representatives of the Domowina, the Sorbian People's Assembly, the Cyril-Methodius Union, and the editorial board of *Nowa Doba*, met on 19 December. From 3 January 1990 the existence of the Sorbian Round Table was acknowledged by the Round Table of the GDR, but it was accorded only observer status.

On 17 March 1990 an extraordinary congress of the Domowina was held at which the statutes were reformed and a new praesidium elected. By this time the SED had changed into the PDS. Candidates for the chairmanship of the praesidium were the Protestant clergyman Jan Malink, put forward by the Sorbian People's Assembly, and the previous First Secretary Jurij Grós. A proposal was made, however, that the new chairman should not be a member of any political party. The candidature of Jurij Grós, a member of the PDS, thereby became questionable, so he withdrew. At this point a new candidate appeared and was elected. This was the previous cultural secretary of the Domowina, Bjarnat Cyž, a Catholic. It was evident that confessional factors had played a role. The extraordinary congress also ratified a document, previously passed by the Sorbian Round Table, in which it was recalled that Sorbian experience of united German statehood had not been good. Among the demands made were:

1. A guarantee of the rights of the Sorbian people to be recorded in the new constitution.

2. Continuing state financial support for Sorbian cultural and educational institutions.

3. New administrative units to be arranged so as to avoid dividing the Sorbian people.

4. The development of relations between Sorbs and Germans on the basis of trust, tolerance, and respect, while honouring the Sorbian traditions of friendship with other Slav peoples.

On 18 March, the day after the extraordinary Domowina congress, free and secret elections were held throughout the GDR. Among the 400 delegates elected to the new *Volkskammer* there were six Sorbs. They were (from Kreis Bautzen) Marja Michałkowa (CDU), Jurij Grós (PDS), and Jurij Čornak (*Demokratische Bauernpartei Deutschlands*); (from Kreis Kamenz) Ludwig Nowak (CDU) and Stanisław Tilich (CDU); and (from Kreis Cottbus) Werner Maruš (DBD) (C. Kola 1990: 129–31; *Šěsć Serbow* 1990: 156; *Volksversammlung* 2012).

After 1990: Taking stock

The reluctance of the GDR authorities to face facts and their obsession with secrecy had for a long time obscured the demographic reality. One of many rude awakenings that came with the new freedom was the revelation that the statistics on the Sorbian population given in East German reference books were false. The people who actually lived in Sorbian (or ostensibly Sorbian) villages were of course aware of the pace of the Germanization that had occurred between the end of the War and the end of the GDR, but they could not write about it and probably thought it better not even to talk about it. Anyone that did so was liable to be accused of nationalism. In the early 1990s, Sorbian publications, relieved of their inhibitions, began to carry reports on the true state of affairs. The new editor of the monthly *Rozhlad* encouraged people with local knowledge to write accounts of their villages and so a series of articles was published, revealing many details of the kind that had previously been suppressed, including the extent of Germanization in individual parishes.

From Hochkirch, south-east of Bautzen, a parish which had figured prominently in Sorbian history over the centuries, Pawoł Grojlich reported in 1992: 'In Hochkirch Sorbian is now the everyday language across all generations in only five houses.' The number of houses in which the use of the language would have been, in his opinion, still capable of being prodded back into life was twelve. In the village school the number of children participating in Sorbian instruction was twenty-two (P. Grojlich 1992: 85). Yet in some other Protestant parishes the language-shift had gone so much further that Hochkirch had acquired the reputation of a Sorbian stronghold (M. Grojlich 1992: 86). And indeed, by comparison with them, the language in Hochkirch was still fairly strong. A relatively high proportion of Sorbian speakers was also found in Quoos, where, out of 150 inhabitants, there were still about forty-five with a command of Sorbian. A further ten to fifteen could understand it. The informant added: 'To declare yourself Sorbian now takes courage' (Grofa 1994: 366–7).

Likewise in Tätzschwitz, north-west of Hoyerswerda, the Sorbian-speaking element in 1995 was still appreciable, but here too the age of the speakers foretold the language's extinction. There were still nine women in the village who wore the Sorbian national dress every day; but the youngest of them was 73 years old. About forty villagers were users of Sorbian, although many more could understand it. In the primary school in Laubusch fourteen pupils were studying Sorbian, but in the middle school the number was down to four, and from the new school year it was planned to drop it altogether (Pečikowa 1995: 218).

On the western periphery of the Sorbian speech-area, in the parish of Uhyst am Taucher, lies the village of Großhänchen, famous in Sorbian history as the birthplace of Karl Ernst Mucke (1854–1932) and the subject of his poem 'Elegija na Wosyk' (1873). From a distant relative of Mucke in 1992 came the news that the last Sorbian-speaker in the village, Oto Pěčka, had died in 1983 (Šěrakec 1992: 391). On the southern periphery too extinction seemed to be imminent. Here in Groß Postwitz, where the pastorate at the end of the seventeenth century had been held by Michael Frentzel, there was still in 1992 a Domowina group, but it had at most nine members. Sorbian services for a small congregation were still occasionally held in Frentzel's church, though the minister officiating had to come from another parish (Brycka 1992: 437). In Gröditz, the birthplace of Warichius, author of the first Sorbian printed book, there were in 1994 five people capable of speaking Sorbian, all aged over seventy. A few more could understand it (Malinkowa 1994b: 209).

Many of *Rozhlad*'s correspondents attributed the decline in the number of native-speakers to the influx since 1945 of German refugees from the Sudetenland and east of the Oder-Neisse Line. That this might be a cause of Germanization had been a delicate subject in the GDR. On the other hand, there are also occasional accounts of the newcomers' children being assimilated linguistically to their new Sorbian environment, but this seems to have happened only in Catholic villages. As a teacher from Crostwitz noted:

> After the War the German refugee children quite quickly learned to understand Sorbian and before long they were even speaking it. We have right up to the present day, thank God, parents from ethnically mixed marriages who loyally send their children to the Sorbian school in Crostwitz. After all, they had all learned Sorbian in the nursery and the play-group.

(Mikławšk 1992: 316)

The experience in most other Catholic villages appears to have been similar. A teacher from Ostro recalled that in 1947 forty-two German families arrived, representing 60 per cent of the total village population:

> The grandfathers, grandmothers, and mothers of the refugees readily allowed their children and grandchildren, playing with the village children, to speak Sorbian and to use Sorbian among themselves. [...] In the school [...] the language of conversation was mainly Sorbian. Mr J[an] Meškank [the teacher] regarded that as quite normal and so it became established.

By 1992 the inhabitants of Ostro were almost all Sorbs (97 per cent) (Nawka 1992: 162–3).

A correspondent from Storcha, another Catholic village, wrote: 'Today as you walk through Storcha you can still in almost every household speak Sorbian, but in a number of Sorbian families now they use German among themselves' (Krawc 1993: 124). In Schönau, also Catholic, there was a similarly strong Sorbian presence:

> In the village centre our Sorbian mother tongue is still dominant, especially in conversations between neighbours and villagers. Without exception all church events in our chapel take place in Sorbian. [...] Because many of our youngest people speak Sorbian, I am convinced that our mother tongue will survive for

another fifty years in our village and I hope that will be so in many families. And another thing about the young people. When our Sorbian youngsters gather together, Sorbian is spoken.

(Langa 1994: 51)

Despite the generally optimistic outlook conveyed by these accounts from Catholic parishes, the overall picture is one of a drastic decline. It is a picture that cannot be reconciled with the entries for 'Sorbs', 'Sorben' etc. in most twenty-first-century encyclopaedias, such as Wikipedia, which in its German and English versions assesses the number of Sorbs/Wends at 60,000 (*Sorben* 2012; *Sorbs* 2012). The Sorbian Wikipedia, on the other hand, makes a clear distinction between its figures for Sorbs/Wends (60,000) and for speakers of the Sorbian/Wendish language (between 20,000 and 30,000) (*Serbja* 2012).

Kashubs in the Third Polish Commonwealth

In Poland, following the wave of free public discussion and consultation that followed the semi-free elections of June 1989, the Sejm appointed a Committee for National and Ethnic Minorities, which on 13 March 1990, led by the Deputy Speaker Olga Krzyżanowska, visited the Kashubian area and held meetings in Gdańsk and Wieżyca. Not only the *Zrzeszenie Kaszubsko-Pomorskie* but also individual Kashubs were at last able to have their say. It was pointed out that the *Zrzeszenie*, as a society operating outside state structures and sometimes in defiance of them, had no official financial support (J[anke?] 1990: 18–19). There were complaints about the intolerance the Kashubs had encountered in People's Poland, especially in schools. Former pupils recalled their experience of corporal punishment inflicted in school in the 1950s and 1960s for speaking Kashubian. One witness (Franciszek Okuń) said: 'The teachers did everything to stamp out Kashubian. They not only forbade the children to speak it but even told the little girls to report on boys who spoke Kashubian during break and count how many Kashubian words they used. Afterwards, on returning to the classroom, they were punished with blows from a rubber cable or a cane.'

How rare or typical such attitudes were in People's Poland is hard to judge, but they were certainly in marked contrast to the exhortation in the 1960 Kashubian-Polish and Polish-Kashubian pocket dictionary of Aleksander Labuda: 'Kashubian today is only spoken in a small area, so we should foster it carefully and treat it with appropriate respect' (A. Labuda 1960: 6). The very existence of this book, published by a state publisher of schoolbooks (*Państwowe Zakłady Wydawnictw Szkolnych*) to assist teachers new to the Kashub area, is evidence of enlightened views among at least some elements in the teaching profession at that time.

At the 1990 session in Wieżyca the specific, separate nature of Kashubian was emphasized and it was significantly dignified by the term *język* 'language'. Demands were made for special provision for Kashubian in the education system. Witold Bobrowski observed: 'In the school where I teach there are children in the reception class and class one who know only the Kashubian language. For them Polish is a new language and they need special textbooks' (J[anke?] 1990: 20). Since then conditions in the Third Polish Commonwealth have been auspicious for the Kashubs. They have been favourably affected by new legislation and they have not been slow to seize new opportunities. In 1991 a Kashubian secondary school was opened in Brusy and a primary school in Głodnica, near Linia. By 2003 the language was being taught in no less than eighty-one schools to 4,780 pupils, and the numbers were continuing to rise. At the end of 2005 the number of pupils learning Kashubian in about one hundred primary schools was 5,196, while in twenty-seven middle schools it was 1,345. While all this activity may be assumed to have pleased Kashubian activists, there appears to have been a degree of opposition from some educational administrators, some teachers, and some parents (Obracht-Prondzyński and Wicherkiewicz 2011: 166–7). Details are still elusive.

The 1992 Law on Radio and Television Broadcasting recognized a general obligation to meet the needs of national and ethnic minorities, and the rights of Polish citizens belonging to such minorities were enshrined in a new Constitution in 1997. Under local government reorganization introduced in 1999 the whole of Kashubia came under the new *Województwo Pomorskie*, divided into *powiats*. There is a Kashubian population in the *powiats* of Puck, Wejherowo, Kartuzy, Lębork, Bytów, and Kościerzyna, in the northern part of the *powiat* of Chojnicy, and in the eastern part of the *powiat* of Słupsk. A Polish Language Act of 1999 said that in areas with large non-Polish populations minority languages might be used in bilingual place names, in personal names, and in the local administration (Obracht-Prondzyński and Wicherkiewicz 2011: 146–9).

The National Census of 2002 was the first since 1931 to include questions on nationality and language. The category of nationality (*narodowość*) is entirely a matter of individual choice and is quite separate from citizenship. The results were surprising. Only 5,062 Polish citizens gave their nationality as Kashubian, but 52,665 reported themselves as users of the Kashubian language in domestic situations. The 2002 Census also revealed that there were ten Kashubian *gminy* in which Kashubian-speakers constituted more than 20 per cent of the inhabitants: Przodkowo (49 per cent), Sulęczyno (48.6 per cent), Stężyca (43.2 per cent), Sierakowice (39.9 per cent), Somonino (30.8 per cent), Chmielno (34.8 per cent), Linia (35.5 per cent), Szemud (26.3 per cent), Parchowo (22.3 per cent), and Puck (30.9 per cent) (Obracht-Prondzyński and Wicherkiewicz 2011: 151–6).

In 2003, Poland signed the Council of Europe's European Charter for Regional or Minority Languages and ratified it in 2009. Meanwhile (2005) an act had been passed according Kashubian legal status as a 'regional language'. Article 19, paragraph 2, of the 2005 Act on National and Ethnic Minorities and Regional Language states: 'The Kashubian language is a regional language within the meaning of the act' (*Językiem regionalnym w rozumieniu ustawy jest język kaszubski*). The act also states that a *gmina* where no less than 20 per cent of the residents are users of the regional language may be registered as a *gmina* 'where an auxiliary language (*język pomocniczy*) is used', meaning that Kashubs may, in dealings with the local authority, use Kashubian in 'written or oral form' and, on request, receive a reply in like form (Obracht-Prondzyński and Wicherkiewicz 2011: 155–6). By 2012 the *gminy* of Linia, Parchowo, and Sierakowice had registered under this provision (*Gminy* 2012). In registered *gminy*, moreover, official signs displaying the names of villages, streets, etc. may, in addition to the Polish name, also carry the Kashubian equivalent (Obracht-Prondzyński and Wicherkiewicz 2011: 156–7).

In the Polish National Census of 2011 there were again questions relating to language and nationality, but this time they were formulated differently. 229,000 citizens of Poland (in round figures) now stated their nationality as Kashubian. Of these 213,000 said they were simultaneously of Polish nationality, but 17,000 described themselves as exclusively Kashubian. The census form also asked about languages used in domestic contexts (it being taken for granted that the only language used in formal contexts would be Polish). In the replies the languages most often named apart from Polish were Silesian (509,000) and Kashubian (106,000) (*Raport z wynikow* 2012: 106–8).

Social mobility – political prominence

The social obstacles which down the centuries ensured the survival of the Wends and Kashubs in enclaves served simultaneously to inhibit social mobility. Very few Wends or Kashubs ever achieved positions of wealth, influence, or power, and they could only do so by being totally assimilated to the majority surrounding them. A prerequisite for advancement was always a faultless command of the majority language, and it still is, but two prominent cases from the twenty-first century suggest that something has changed.

The first is that of Stanislaw Tillich, Minister President (Prime Minister) of Saxony. He was born in the Sorbian village of Neudörfel (Nowa Wjeska), near Kamenz, in 1959, and his native language is Sorbian. He learned German at the age of five. He was educated at the Sorbian Gymnasium in Bautzen before studying engineering in Dresden. He has worked both as a civil servant and as a businessman. Even before the end of the GDR he was a member of the CDU and 1990 in the first free elections he was elected to the *Volkskammer*. He was first elected to the Saxon Landtag in 2004 and in 2008 became Minister President. He was re-elected to this office in 2014. No Sorb or Wend before him had ever held such an exalted position. Moreover, his political success has not entailed abandoning his Sorbian roots. On his personal website he states: 'I was born in 1959 in a Sorbian family and I cherish the Sorbian language and culture. I have remained true to my homeland.' His Wikipedia entry records his citizenship as German and his nationality as Sorbian (*Ministerpräsident* 2014; *Tillich* 2014). His membership of the Sorbian minority seems not to have damaged his political career, nor has the fact that, though Prime Minister of Saxony, the most Protestant of all the *Länder* and the birthplace of the Lutheran Reformation, he is a Catholic.

Sorbs who thought Tillich might exert political influence to their advantage, however, may have been disappointed. When interviewed for the Sorbian journal *Rozhlad* in

2010, Tilich was asked how far it was possible for him to act on behalf of the Sorbs in his official position. He replied carefully: 'I am the Minister President of all Saxons, but the new state agreement for the Foundation for the Sorbian People, for example, would probably have turned out differently, had I not been there' (*Maćerna rěč* 2010: 14–15).

The second case is that of Donald Tusk, Prime Minister of Poland from 2007 to 2014 and since then President of the European Council. Born in Gdańsk in 1957, he is a Kashub and makes no secret of the fact. Although it has formed the subject of comment by his opponents, there is no sign of it having harmed his political career. He is the only Prime Minister of the Third Commonwealth to have been re-elected (in 2011) and also the longest serving holder of that office so far.

In the past the question of the loyalty of the Kashubs to the Polish state has often been raised, as we have seen, and it is still not dead. It has been occasionally raised in the case of Donald Tusk. It was discovered, for example, that Tusk's grandfather had been a soldier in the Wehrmacht during the Second World War. In 2005 Tusk's political opponent Jacek Kurski tried to make capital out of this fact, but it appears to have carried little weight. Tusk was then a candidate for the presidency of Poland. It transpired that Józef Tusk, as a citizen of the Free City of Danzig, had been conscripted and after a few months had deserted and joined the Polish forces in the West. Donald Tusk was narrowly defeated in this election, but surveys suggest that the allegation was not a material factor in his defeat. The winner, Lech Kaczyński, issued an apology for the defamatory claims and Kurski was expelled from his party *Prawo i Sprawiedliwość* (*Kurski* 2014; *Tusk* 2014).

The criteria for ethnicity vary a good deal, but it is clear that Kashubian ethnicity is not dependent on the ability to speak Kashubian. Donald Tusk in 2011, while on a visit to Canada, met a group of emigre Kashubs. Their leader made a speech in English and Kashubian, but Tusk replied in Polish, saying: 'My Kashubian is not as good as that of the Ontario Kashubs' (*Dziennik* 2014).

Not the last chapter

It is only too easy to fall into the trap of thinking of the European past against a mental template supplied by the present-day map of Europe. Those so entrapped are prone to overlook groups like the Wends, Sorbs, and Kashubs, which have never had their own political geography. Although the sources have often recorded their existence only grudgingly, much of their history can, with perseverance, be retrieved. Submerged in political formations over which they had no control, they have seen political borders adjusted many times. In the course of well over a millennium they have watched duchies, kingdoms, empires, and republics come and go, but they have never governed themselves.

Today they are an endangered species. Confined to three tiny ethnic islands in remote corners of north-east Europe, only a few successors of the medieval Wends are still there in their ancestral homelands. Though once numerous, they have never been powerful, but they have shown surprising resilience over the centuries. Now they may appear to be on the brink of extinction. The number of speakers of the languages continues to fall, but many inhabitants of Germany and Poland (not to mention Texas, Ontario, and Australia) have not forgotten that their ancestors were Wends, Sorbs, or Kashubs. The languages may dwindle and fade, but their history and the history of the people that once spoke them will remain. Without their participation, the history of Central Europe is incomplete.

SOURCES

Akta (1844), 'B. V. Akta weřejná i sněmovní w Čechách i w Morawie od r. 1414 do 1428', in *Archiv český*, ed. František Palacký, Part 3 (Prague).

Andree, Richard (1874), *Wendische Wanderstudien. Zur Kunde der Lausitz und der Sorbenwenden* (Stuttgart).

Andricki, Alojs (1998[?]), *Kapłan Alojs Andricki* (Bautzen).

Andritzki, Alois (2013), <http://de.wikipedia.org/wiki/Alois_Andritzki> [accessed 28 June 2013].

Annales (1895), *Annales Regni Francorum inde ab a. 741, usque ad a. 829 qui dicuntur Annales Laurissenses maiores et Einhardi*, ed. G. Pertz and F. Kurze (Hannover).

Bahlcke, Joachim (ed.) (2001), *Geschichte der Oberlausitz: Herrschaft, Gesellschaft und Kultur vom Mittelalter bis zum Ende des 20. Jahrhunderts* (Leipzig).

Balthasar, Jakub Heinrich (1725), *Erste Sammlung einiger zur Pommerschen Kirchenhistorie gehörigen Schriften* (Greifswald).

Barker, Peter (1996), 'The Birth of Official Policy towards the Sorbian Minority in the Soviet Zone of Occupation in Germany (1945–1948)', *German History: The Journal of the German History Society*, 14: 38–54.

Barker, Peter (2000), *Slavs in Germany – the Sorbian Minority and the German State since 1945* (Lampeter).

Bartoš, F. M. (1933), 'Manifesty města Prahy z doby husitské', in *Sborník přispěvků k dějinám hlavního města Prahy*, ed. V. Vojtíšek, díl 7, 253–311.

Bauer, Max (1911), *Soldan-Heppe/Geschichte der Hexenprozesse*, neu bearbeitet und herausgegeben von Max Bauer, vols. 1–2 (München) (undated reprint, c. 2000).

Benham, Daniel (1854), *Sketch of the Life of Jan August Miertsching, Interpreter of the Esquimaux Language to the Arctic Expedition on Board H.M.S. 'Investigator', Captain McClure, 1850, 1851, 1852, 1853* (London).

Berghaus, Heinrich (1867), *Landbuch des Herzogthums Pommern und des Fürstenthums Rügen*, Teil III, Bd. I (Berlin).

Bernoulli, Johann (1779), *Reisen durch Brandenburg, Pommern, Preußen, Curland, Rußland und Pohlen in den Jahren 1777 und 1778*, 1. Band (Leipzig).

Biblia (1728), *Biblia, to je zyłe szwjate pißmo … *(Budissin).

Bielfeldt, Hans Holm (1982), *Die slawischen Wörter im Deutschen: Ausgewählte Schriften 1950–1978* (Leipzig).

Blaschke, Karlheinz (1961), 'Zur Siedlungs- und Bevölkerungsgeschichte der Oberlausitz', in *Oberlausitzer Forschungen*, ed. Martin Reuther (Leipzig), 60–80. Here cited from reprint in Blaschke 2000: 21–49.

Blaschke, Karlheinz (ed.) (1967), 'Bevölkerungsgeschichte von Sachsen bis zur industriellen Revolution (Ausschnitte für die Oberlausitz)', *Bevölkerungsgeschichte von Sachsen bis zur industriellen Revolution* (Weimar), 204–17. Here cited from reprint in Blaschke 2000: 114–37.

Blaschke, Karlheinz (1994a), 'Das Markgraftum Oberlausitz und das sorbische Volk. Eine regionale und ethnische Einheit seit 1400 Jahren', in *Nationale, ethnische Minderheiten und regionale Identitäten im Mittelalter und Neuzeit*, ed. Anton Czacharowski (Toruń), 17–29. Here cited from reprint in Blaschke 2000: 9–20.

Blaschke, Karlheinz (1994b), 'Das Markgraftum Oberlausitz – Eine Ständerepublik im sächsischen Staatsverband', in *700 Jahre politische Mitbestimmung in Sachsen. Begleitheft aus Anlaß der Ausstellung zur Eröffnung der Neubauten des Sächsischen Landtags im Bürgerfoyer des Elbflügels* (Dresden), 71–4. Here cited from reprint in Blaschke 2000: 108–13.

Blaschke, Karlheinz (1997), 'Der Oberlausitzer Sechsstädtebund als bürgerlicher Träger früher Staatlichkeit', in *650 Jahre Oberlausitzer Sechsstädtebund 1346–1996. Mitteilungen des Zittauer Geschichts- und Museumvereins*, 25: 17–27. Here cited from reprint in Blaschke 2000: 50–60.

Blaschke, Karlheinz (1998), 'Landschaft und Geschichte um Hoyerswerda', *Sächsische Heimatblätter*, 44, H. 4: 189–92. Here cited from reprint in Blaschke 2000: 226–33.

Blaschke, Karlheinz (1999a), 'Der Übergang des Markgraftums Oberlausitz von der Krone Böhmen an den Kurfürsten von Sachsen während des Dreißigjährigen Krieges', in *350 rocznica Pokoju Westfalskiego na terenach Euroregionu NYSA 1648–1998*, ed. Przemislaw Wiater (Jelenia Góra), 15–27. Here cited from reprint in Blaschke 2000: 93–107.

Blaschke, Karlheinz (1999b), 'Der Pönfall der Oberlausitzer Sechsstädte von 1547', in *Pönfall der Oberlausitzer Sechsstädte 1547*, ed. Kamenzer Geschichtsverein (Kamenz), 41–50. Here cited from reprint in Blaschke 2000: 87–92.

Blaschke, Karlheinz (2000), *Beiträge zur Geschichte der Oberlausitz. Gesammelte Aufsätze* (Görlitz-Zittau).

Blaschke, Karlheinz (2003), 'Die geschichtliche Leistung des sorbischen Volkes im germanisch-slawischen Berührungsraum Ostmitteleuropas', in *Im Wettstreit der Werte. Sorbische Sprache, Kultur und Identität auf dem Wege ins 21. Jahrhundert*, ed. herausgegeben von Dietrich Scholze (Bautzen), 61–81.

Blum, Jerome (1978), *The End of the Old Order in Rural Europe* (Princeton).

Bocatius, Ioannes (1990), *Opera quae exstant omnia. Poetica*, ed. Franciscus Csonka, vols 1–2 (Budapest).

Bogusławski, Wilhelm (1861), *Rys dziejów Serbo-łużyckich* (St Petersburg).

Bogusławski, Wilhelm and Michał Hórnik (1884), *Historija serbskeho naroda* (Budyšin).

Bolduan, Tadeusz (1970), *Apostoł narodowej sprawy – o Antonim Abrahamie* (Wejherowo-Gdańsk).

Bolduan, Tadeusz (1992), 'Losy społeczne i polityczne Słowińców w Klukach w latach 1945–1975. Próba oceny', in *Studia Kaszubsko-Słowińskie. Materiały z II Konferencji Słowińskiej (Łeba 11–13.05.1992)*, ed. Jerzy Treder (Łeba), 9–30.

Borzyszkowski, J. (ed.) (2012), *Życie i dzieła Floriana Ceynowy (1817–1881)* (Gdańsk).

Borzyszkowski, J., J. Mordawski and J. Treder (1999), *Historia, geografia, język i piśmiennictwo Kaszubów* (Gdańsk).

Brankačk, Jan (1964), *Studien zur Wirtschaft und Sozialstruktur der Westslawen zwischen Elbe-Saale und Oder aus der Zeit vom 9. bis zum 12. Jahrhundert* (Bautzen).

Bresan, Annett (2002), *Pawoł Nedo (1908–1984)* (Bautzen).

Briefsammlung (1837), 'IX. Briefsammlung', *Jahrbücher des Vereins für Mecklenburgische Geschichte und Altertumskunde*, 2: 197–210.

Brijnen, Hélène B. (2004), *Die Sprache des Hanso Nepila. Der niedersorbische Dialekt von Schleife in einer Handschrift aus der 1. Hälfte des 19. Jahrhunderts* (Bautzen).

Brock, Peter (1966), 'Daniel Ernst Jablonski and Education in Lower Lusatia', *Slavonic and East European Review*, 44: 444–53.

Brock, Peter (1992), *Folk Cultures and Little Peoples. Aspects of National Awakening in East Central Europe* (New York).

Brückner, Alexander (1911), *Jakuba Teodora Trembeckiego Wirydarz poetycki*, vol. 2 (Lwów).

Brüggemann, Ludwig Wilhelm (1779), *Ausführliche Beschreibung des Gegenwärtigen des Königl. Preußischen Herzogthums Vor- und Hinterpommerns*, 1. Teil (Stettin).

Brycka, Jurij (1992), 'Radna wjes Budestecy', *Rozhlad*, 42: 434–7.

Sources

Bryl-Serbin, Jan (1924), *Serbski Dom w Budyšinje. Stawizny jeho nastaća a wuwića* (Bautzen).

Buchwald, Georg (1894), *Wittenberger Ordiniertenbuch 1537–1560* (Leipzig).

Buchwald, Georg (1895), *Wittenberger Ordiniertenbuch 1560–1572* (Leipzig).

Budar, Beno (2013), *Sym měła tajki strach* (Bautzen).

Bugenhagen, Johannes (2008), *Pomerania. Faksimiledruck und Übersetzung der Handschrift von 1517/18*, ed. Norbert Buske (Schwerin).

Bulakhov, M.G. (1976), *Vostočnoslavjanskie jazykovedy. Biobibliografičeskij slovar´*, tom I (Minsk).

Burleigh, Michael (1988), *Germany Turns Eastwards. A Study of Ostforschung in the Third Reich* (Cambridge).

Bykowska, S. (2012), *Rehabilitacja i weryfikacja narodowościowa ludności polskiej w województwie gdańskim po II wojnie światowej* (Gdańsk).

Bystroń, Jan Stanisław (1960), *Dzieje obyczajów w dawnej Polsce. Wiek XVI–XVIII*, vol. I (Warsaw).

Cameron, Euan (1991), *The European Reformation* (Oxford).

CDB, *Codex diplomaticus Brandenburgensis. Sammlung der Urkunden, Chroniken und sonstigen Quellenschriften für die Geschichte der Mark Brandenburg und ihrer Regenten* herausg. von Adolph Friedrich Riedel, 41 vols (Berlin, 1838–68).

CDLS, *Codex diplomaticus Lusatiae superioris*, 6 vols (Görlitz, 1856–1931)

CDS, *Codex diplomaticus Saxoniae regiae*, Hauptteil 2, Band 3 Urkunden des Hochstifts Meissen 1423–1581 (Leipzig, 1864ff.).

Ceynowa, Florian (1850), *Eine kleine Sammlung kaschubischer Wörter, welche eine größere Ähnlichkeit mit der rußischen als mit der polnischen Sprache haben* (Danzig). Cited here from reprint in Ceynowa (2001):167–206.

Ceynowa, Florian (2001), *Uwagi o kaszubszczyźnie*, ed. Jerzy Treder, [...] Hanna Popowska-Taborska (Wejherowo-Rumia-Pelplin).

Chadwick, Owen (1984), *The Reformation* (Harmondsworth).

Christiansen, Eric (1997), *The Northern Crusades* (London).

Chronik (1905), *Die Dresdner Handschrift der Chronik des Bischofs Thietmar von Merseburg. Mit Unterstützung der Generaldirektion der Kgl. Sächs. Sammlungen für Kunst und Wissenschaft, der König-Johann-Stiftung und der Zentraldirektion der Monumenta Germaniae historica in Faksimile herausgegeben* (Dresden, 1905).

Chytraeus, David (1593), *Chronicon Saxoniae* (Leipzig).

Clark, Christopher (2006), *Iron Kingdom. The Rise and Downfall of Prussia, 1600–1947* (London).

Cologne (2014), <http://en.wikipedia.org/wiki/Demographics_of_Cologne> [accessed 16 October 2014].

Commission (2014), <http://Wikipedia.org/wiki/Commission_for_the_Determination_of_Place_Names> [accessed 12 August 2014].

Cramer, Reinhold (1858), *Geschichte der Lande Lauenburg und Bütow*, 2 vols (Königsberg).

Croll[e], David (1586), *Eine kurtze Predigt Zur Einweihunge der newen Kirchen zu Schmolsyn/in hinter Pommern [...]* (Stettin).

Cromer, Martin (1577), *Polonia sive de situ, populis, moribus, magistratibus et Republica regni Polonici libri duo* (Cologne).

Cyž, Benedikt (2004), 'Narodowc, wšosłowjan a spjećowar dr. Jurij Cyž před 100 lětami so narodźił', *Rozhlad* 54: 362–7.

Cyž, Benedikt (2010a), 'Z MGB-akty Jurja Rjenča. Před 50 lětami bu serbski prawiznik zajaty', *Rozhlad* 60, 10: 18–20.

Cyž, Benedikt (2010b), 'Z MGB-akty Jurja Rjenča (2)', *Rozhlad* 60, 12: 16–19.

Cyž, Benedikt (2011), 'Z MGB-akty Jurja Rjenča (3)', *Rozhlad* 61, 10: 11–14.

Cyž, Beno (1965), *Časowa dokumentacija k najnowšim serbskim stawiznam 1945–1960* (Bautzen).

Cyž, Beno (1969), *Die DDR und die Sorben. Eine Dokumentation zur Nationalitätenpolitik in der DDR* (Bautzen).

Cyž, Jan (1955), 'Drježdźanske póstnicy před dźesać lětami', *Rozhlad* 5: 33–43.

Cyž, Jan (1957), 'Sowjetske wójsko a Serbja', *Rozhlad* 7: 338–42.

Cyž, Jan (1965), 'Bitwa niže Budyšina 1945', *Rozhlad* 15: 97–108 and 141–50.

Cyž, Jan (1977), 'Wojowanje přećiwo prawopisnej reformje serbskeje rěče w druhej połojcy 19. lětstotka', *Lětopis. Jahresschrift des Instituts für sorbische Volksforschung*, B 24: 194–215.

Czok, Karl (1961), 'Die Auswirkungen des Bautzener Aufstandes von 1405', *Lětopis Instituta za serbski ludospyt*, B 8: 108–26.

Daenell, Ernst (2001), *Die Blütezeit der deutschen Hanse. Hansische Geschichte von der zweiten Hälfte des XIV. bis zum letzten Viertel des XV. Jahrhunderts*, 2 vols (Berlin-New York). Reprint of Berlin 1905 edition.

Davies, Norman (1981), *God's Playground. A History of Poland in Two Volumes* (Oxford).

Davies, Norman (2011), *Vanished Kingdoms. The History of Half-Forgotten Europe* (London).

DCB, *Dictionary of Canadian Biography* (2003–14) (Toronto), <http://www.biographi.ca> [accessed 4 September 2014].

Delan, Jurij (1918), 'Nekrolog LXXXV: Jurij Deleńk', *Časopis Maćicy Serbskeje*, 106–10.

Delan, Šćepan (1992), 'Farar Jan Cyž: swěrny syn serbskeho naroda', in *Serbska Protyka 1993* (Bautzen), 134–7.

Derdowski, Jarosz (1960), *O Panu Czôrlińscim co do Pucka po sece jachoł*, ed. Leon Roppel (Gdańsk).

Die Sorben (1964), 1 ed. (Bautzen).

Die Sorben ([1970]), 3 ed. (Bautzen).

Dobozy, Maria (1999), *The Saxon Mirror. A 'Sachsenspiegel' of the Fourteenth Century* (Philadelphia).

Dobschütz (2013), <http//de.wikipedia.org/wiki/ElisabethvonDoberschütz> [accessed 3 December 2013].

Donald, Robert (1929), *The Polish Corridor and the Consequences* (London).

Dreger, Friderich von (1748), *Codex Diplomaticus, oder Urkunden, so die Pommersch-Rugianisch- und Caminsche auch andere benachbarte Lande angehen*, 1 (Stettin).

Dresden (2014), <http://de.wikipedia.org/wiki/Einwohnerentwicklung_von_Dresden> [accessed 16 October 2014].

Duden (1974), *Duden Aussprachewörterbuch*, 2. Auflage (Mannheim-Wien-Zürich).

Dziennik (2014), <www.dziennik.com/wiadomosci/artykul/tusk_u_kanadyjskich-kaszubow> [accessed 30 November 2014]

Eckhart, Johann Georg von (1711), *Io. Georgii Eccardi Historia studii etymologici* (Hanover).

Eichler, Ernst (1960), 'Zachodniosłowiańskie *chyža, chyča*', *Język polski*, 40: 218–20.

Eichler, Ernst (1963), 'Die Bedeutung der Oberlausitzer Grenzurkunde und anderer Grenzbeschreibungen für die slawische Sprachgeschichte', *Lětopis instituta za serbski ludospyt*, 10: 20–83.

Eichler, Ernst (1975), *Die Ortsnamen der Niederlausitz* (Bautzen).

Eichler, Ernst (1985–2009), *Slawische Ortsnamen zwischen Saale und Neiße. Ein Kompendium*, 4 vols (Bautzen).

Einhardi Vita (1911), *Einhardi Vita Karoli magni* (1911), in *Scriptores rerum germanicarum in usum scholarum*, ed. G. H. Pertz and G. Waitz (Hannover-Leipzig).

Ela, Ludwig (1993), 'Městno serbskeho šulstwa w narodnostnej politice – přinošk do diskusije', in *Serbske šulstwo (1945–1970). Mjez socialistiskej ideologiju a narodnej zamołwitosću*, ed. Jurij J. Šołta and Trudla Malinkowa (Bautzen), 20–37.

Sources

Expedition (2014), <http://en.wikipedia.org/wiki/McClure_Arctic_Expedition> [accessed 22 October 2014].

Fiedler, K. A. (1868), 'Alexander Cesarewič, ruski wulkowjerch-naslědnik', *Łužičan*, 9: 39–41.

Filip, M. (2012), *Od Kaszubów do Niemców. Tożsamość Słowińców z perspektywy antropologii historii* (Poznań).

Förster, Frank (1996), *Verschwundene Dörfer. Die Ortsabbrüche des Lausitzer Braunkohlenreviers bis 1993* (Bautzen).

FRA (1859), *Fontes rerum austriacarum. Oesterreichische Geschichts-Quellen* [...] Zweite Abteilung. Diplomataria et Acta. XIX. Band. Quellen zur Geschichte der böhmischen Brüder [...] (Wien 1859), hrsg. Anton Gindely.

Frankfurt (2014), <http://www.de.wikipedia.org/wiki/Bevölkerungsentwicklung_von _Frankfurt(Oder)> [accessed 25 November 2014].

Fredegar (1888), 'Chronicarum quae dicuntur Fredegarii scholastici libri IV. cum continuationibus', in *Monumenta Germaniae historica. Scriptores rerum Merovingicarum*, vol. 2, ed. B. Krusch (Hannover), 1ff.

Frentzel, Michael (1670), *S. Matthæus und S. Marcus/Wie auch die drey allgemeinen Haupt-Symbola In die Wendische Sprache mit Fleiß übersetzet* [...] (Bautzen).

Friedrich, Karin (2000), *The Other Prussia. Royal Prussia, Poland and Liberty 1569–1772* (Cambridge).

Frinta, A. (1952), 'Sławny C. Peucer běše Serb', *Lětopis Instituta za serbski ludospyt*, A 1: 146–8.

Frinta, A. (1955), *Lužičtí Srbové a jejich písemnictví* (Prague).

Fröde, T. (1999), *Abraham Frenzelii Collectaneorum Lusaticorum. Sammlung Lausitzer Sachen des Abraham Frenzel. Findbuch mit Stichwort-, Personen- und Ortsregister* (Olbersdorf).

Gerlach, Jan (1959), 'Język polski w obradach i korespondencji urzędowej w Prusach Królewskich w XVI–XVIII w', in ed. Gerard Labuda, *Szkice z dziejów Pomorza, 2. Pomorze nowożytne*, 163–86.

German Church (2004), *A German Church in the Garden of God. Melbourne's Trinity Lutheran Church 1853–2003*, ed. Herbert D. Mees (Melbourne).

Gesangbuch (1710), *Das neue Teutsche und Wendische Gesangbuch* (Budissin).

Geskojc, Anja (1996a), 'Mina Witkojc ako redaktorka Serbskego Casnika', *Rozhlad*, 46: 97–8.

Geskojc, Anja (1996b), 'Poměr casnikarki M. Witkojc k dolnoserbskej inteligency a jeje pśisud za cas nacionalsocializma', *Rozhlad*, 46: 259–62.

Geuenich, Dieter (2004), 'Karl der Große, Ludwig „der Deutsche" und die Entstehung eines „deutschen" Gemeinschaftsbewußtseins', in *Zur Geschichte der Gleichung „germanisch-deutsch"*, ed. Heinrich Beck, Dieter Geuenich, Heiko Steuer, Dietrich Hakelberg (Berlin), 185–99.

Gil´ferding, A. F. (1862), 'Ostatki Slavjan na južnom beregu Baltijskogo morja', *Etnografičeskij sbornik*, vyp. 5: 1–191.

Gindely, Ant. (1859), *Quellen zur Geschichte der böhmischen Brüder* (Vienna).

Gminy (2012), <http://pl.wikipedia.org/wiki/Gminy_dwujęzyczne_w_Polsce> [accessed 1 August 2012].

Göda tausendjährig. Hodźij tysaclětny (2006), Festschrift zum Jubiläum, hg. von der Gemeindeverwaltung Göda beim Lusatia Verlag Bautzen (Bautzen).

Goethe, Johann Wolfgang von (1902–12), *Goethes sämtliche Werke. Jubiläums-Ausgabe in 40 Bänden* (Stuttgart-Berlin).

Górnicki, Łukasz (1566), *Dworzanin polski* (Kraków).

Grimm, Jacob and Wilhelm Grimm (1854–1961), *Deutsches Wörterbuch*, 16 vols (Leipzig), http://woerterbuchnetz.de/DWB/.

Grofa, Arnošt (1994), 'Chasow, wjes bohatych stawiznow', *Rozhlad*, 44: 363–7.

Grojlich, Marko (1992), 'Dońt serbskeje narańšeje wsy', *Rozhlad*, 42: 85–7.

Grojlich, Paweł (1992), 'Bukecy—něhdy a dźensa', *Rozhlad*, 42: 82–5.

Habel, E. and F. Gröbel (1989), *Mittellateinisches Glossar* (Paderborn-München-Wien-Zürich).

Hančka, G. (1971), 'K 30. posmjertninam Pawliny Krawcowej. Ludowa wuměłča sta so z antifašistku', *Předźenak*, 11 December, p. 8.

Handrik, M. (1896), 'Rukopisy Hansa Nepile-Rowniskeho', *Časopis Maćicy Serbskeje*, 73–89.

Handrik, M. (1898), 'Rukopisy Hansa Nepile-Rowniskeho', *Časopis Maćicy Serbskeje*, 65–74.

Handrik, M. (1899), 'Rukopisy Hansa Nepile-Rowniskeho', *Časopis Maćicy Serbskeje*, 42–55, 88–115.

Handrik, M. (1900), 'Rukopisy Hansa Nepile-Rowniskeho', *Časopis Maćicy Serbskeje*, 14–41.

Hartstock, Erhard (1964), 'Dokumente der ehemaligen "Wendenabteilung" zur faschistischen Unterdrückungspolitik gegenüber der Domowina (1933–1937)', *Lětopis. Jahresschrift des Instituts für sorbische Volksforschung*, B 11: 204–16.

Hartstock, Erhard (1965), 'Zur Bauernbewegung im sorbischen Gebiet der sächsischen Oberlausitz 1848–1849', *Lětopis. Jahresschrift des Instituts für sorbische Volksforschung*, B 12: 117–43.

Hartstock, Erhard (1966), 'Die sorbische kleinbürgerliche Intelligenz in der Revolution von 1848/49', *Lětopis. Jahresschrift des Instituts für sorbische Volksforschung*, B 13: 1–20.

Hartstock, Erhard (1967), 'Dokumente der ehem. "Wendenabteilung" zur faschistischen Unterdrückungspolitik gegenüber der sorbischen Bevölkerung (1935–1936)', *Lětopis. Jahresschrift des Instituts für sorbische Volksforschung*, B 14: 170–86.

Hartstock, Erhard (1977), *Die sorbische nationale Bewegung in der sächsischen Oberlausitz 1830–1848/49* (Bautzen).

Haupt, Leopold and Johann Ernst Schmaler (1841), *Volkslieder der Wenden in der Ober- und Nieder-Lausitz*, vol. 1 (Grimma).

Helbig, Herbert and Lorenz Weinrich (eds.) (1968), *Urkunden und erzählende Quellen zur deutschen Ostsiedlung, Erster Teil. Mittel- und Norddeutschland, Ostseeküste* (Darmstadt).

Helmold (1963), Helmold von Bosau, *Slawenchronik*, trans. and with commentary by Heinz Stoob (Darmstadt).

Henry the Fowler (2014), <en.wikipedia.org/wiki/Henry_the_Fowler> [accessed 20 August 2014].

Herder, Johann Gottfried von (1807), *Stimmen der Völker in Liedern* (Tübingen).

Herrmann, Joachim (ed.) (1970), *Die Slawen in Deutschland: Geschichte und Kultur der slawischen Stämme westlich von Oder und Neiße vom 6. bis 12. Jahrhundert. Ein Handbuch* (Berlin).

Herrmann, Joachim (ed.) (1985), *Die Slawen in Deutschland: Geschichte und Kultur der slawischen Stämme westlich von Oder und Neiße vom 6. bis 12. Jahrhundert. Ein Handbuch. Neubearbeitung* (Berlin).

Hesselbacher, Karl (1999), *Paul Gerhardt. Sein Leben – Seine Lieder*, 11 ed. (Neukirchen-Vluyn).

Heydenreich, Tobias (c. 1635), *Leipzigische Cronicke/Und zum Theil Historische Beschreibung der fürnehmen und weltberühmten Stadt Leipzig [...] bis auf das Jahr 1635* (Leipzig).

Hickel, Helmut (1967), *Sammlung und Sendung. Die Brüdergemeine gestern und heute* (Berlin).

Hoffmeister, Joachim (1964), *Der Kantor zu St. Nikolai. Beschreibung des Lebens von Johann Crügern* (Berlin).

Hopp, Dora Grete (1954), *Die Zunft und die Nichtdeutschen im Osten, insbesondere in der Mark Brandenburg* (Marburg).

Hórnik, Michał (1863), 'Z Budyšina a z Łužicy', *Łužičan*, 111–12.

Hórnik, Michał, see also Bogusławski, Wilhelm and Michał Hórnik.

Horýnová, Zdeňka (1971), 'Klanki wot ćety Pawliny', *Předźenak*, 11 December, p. 8.

Huebner, Todd (1988), 'Ethnicity Denied: Nazi Policy towards the Lusatian Sorbs', *German History. The Journal of the German History Society*, 6: 250–77.

Sources

Huth, Johann Ernst (1829), *Geschichte der Stadt Altenburg zur Zeit ihrer Reichsunmittelbarkeit bis zum endlichen Anfall an das Haus Meißen, am 23. Junius 1329, zum Gedächtnis dieses Tages aus Urkunden und bewährten Nachrichten dargestellt* (Altenburg).

Immisch, H. (1884), *Deutsche Antwort eines sächsischen Wenden. Der Panslavismus unter den sächsischen Wenden mit russischem Geld betrieben und zu den Wenden in Preussen hinübergetragen* (Leipzig).

Irmscher, Johannes (1983), 'Der sorbische Humanist Jan Rak', *Lětopis. Instituta za serbski ludospyt*, A 30: 41–5.

Jacobi, V. (1856), *Slaven und Deutschtum in kultur- und agrarhistorischen Studien* (Hanover).

Jahn, Peter Milan (2010), *Vom Roboter zum Schulpropheten: Hanso Nepila (1766–1856). Mikrohistorische Studien zu Leben und Werk eines wendischen Fronarbeiters und Schriftstellers aus Rohne in der Standesherrschaft Muskau* (Bautzen).

Janaš, Pětš and Roland Marti (eds.) (2000, 2001, 2003, 2004, 2006), *Mato Kosyk. Spise. Cełkowny wudawk*, 4 vols (vol. 3 in two parts) (Budyšin).

J[anke?], S[tanisław?] (1990), 'Pozwolće nam być sobą. Komisja sejmowa wśród Kaszubów', *Pomerania*, 18–20.

Jatzwauk, J. (1912), *Die Bevölkerungs- und Vermögensvergältnisse der Stadt Bautzen zu Anfang des 15. Jahrhunderts* (Bautzen).

Jecht, Richard (1911), *Der Oberlausitzer Hussitenkrieg und das Land der Sechsstädte unter Kaiser Sigmund*, I. Teil (Görlitz).

Jecht, Richard (1914), 'Der Oberlausitzer Hussitenkrieg und das Land der Sechsstädte unter Kaiser Sigmund, II. Teil', *Neues Lausitzisches Magazin*, 90: 31–146.

Jenč, K. A. (1849–50), 'Stawizny serbskeje ryčje a narodnosćje', *Časopis Maćicy Serbskeje*, 61–82 [I.] and 117–38 [II.].

Jenč, K. A. (1865), 'Serbske gymnasijalne towaŕstwo w Budyšinje wot 1839–1864', *Časopis Maćicy Serbskeje*, 253–310.

Jenč, K. A. (1867), 'Serbske prědarske towarstwo w Lipsku wot lěta 1716–1866', *Časopis Maćicy Serbskeje*, 465–540.

Jenč, K. A. (1875), 'Spisowarjo hornjołužiskich evangelskich Serbow, wot 1597 hač 1800', *Časopis Maćicy Serbskeje*, 3–42.

Jenč, K. A. (1880), 'Pismowstwo a spisowarjo delnjołužiskich Serbow', *Časopis Maćicy Serbskeje*, 73–154.

Jenč, R. (1954), *Stawizny serbskeho pismowstwa* [I.] (Bautzen).

Jenč, R. (1960), *Stawizny serbskeho pismowstwa. II. dźěl* (Bautzen).

Jugler, Johann Heinrich (1809), *Vollständiges Lüneburgisch-Wendisches Wörterbuch*. See Olesch (1962).

Kantzow, Thomas (1897), *Des Thomas Kantzow Chronik von Pommern in hochdeutscher Mundart*, Bd. I. Letzte Bearbeitung, Hg. Georg Gaebel (Stettin).

Kantzow, Thomas (1908), *Pomerania. Eine pommersche Chronik aus dem sechzehnten Jahrhundert*, Hg. Georg Gaebel (Stettin).

Karnowski, Jan (1921), W[ôś] B[udzysz], 'Dr. Florjan Ceynowa', *Gryf*, 5: 56–62, 103–18.

Kasper, Martin (1961), 'Ein faschistischer Plan zur Aussiedlung sorbischer Lehrer', *Lětopis Instituta za serbski ludospyt*, B 8: 127–33.

Kasper, Martin (1965), 'Zu den historischen Grundlagen für die Bewegung der Oberlausitzer werktätigen Bauern nach dem ersten Weltkrieg', *Lětopis Instituta za serbski ludospyt*, B 12: 207–30.

Kašpor, Měrćin (1958), 'Rozprawa wo diskusiji wo charakterje serbskeho narodneho hibanja za čas knježenja němskeho fašizma', *Lětopis Instituta za serbski ludospyt*, B 5: 131–49.

Katheder (2002), *Zwischen Katheder, Thron und Kerker. Leben und Werk des Humanisten Caspar Peucer 1525–1602* (Bautzen).

Kavka, František (1978), 'Karl IV. und die Oberlausitz', *Lětopis Instituta za serbski ludospyt*, B 25: 141–60.

Keller, Ines (2005), '*Ich bin jetzt hier und das ist gut so.' Lebenswelten von Flüchtlingen und Vertriebenen in der Lausitz. Lětopis.* Sonderheft. Gesamtband 52 (Bautzen).

Kienle, Richard von (1960), *Historische Laut- und Formenlehre des Deutschen* (Tübingen).

Kind-Doerne, Christiane (1973), 'Sorbischer Buchdruck in Bautzen vom Ausgang des 16. bis zum Beginn des 18. Jahrhunderts', *Archiv für Geschichte des Buchwesens*, 13, 4: 934–1020.

Kirche (2003), *Eine Kirche – zwei Völker. Deutsche, sorbische und lateinische Quellentexte und Beiträge zur Geschichte des Bistums Dresden-Meißen. Von der Wiedererrichtung 1921 bis 1929* (Bautzen-Leipzig).

Klemperer, Victor (1999), *Tagebücher 1945*, 3. Auflage (Berlin).

Kluge, Friedrich (1963), *Etymologisches Wörterbuch der deutschen Sprache*, 19 ed. (Berlin).

Knauthe, Christian (1767), *Derer Oberlausitzer Sorberwenden umständliche Kirchengeschichte* (Görlitz). Reprint, publ. by R. Olesch (Köln-Wien, 1980).

Knothe, Hermann (1885), 'Die Stellung der Gutsuntertanen in der Oberlausitz zu ihren Gutsherrschaften', *Neues Lausitzisches Magazin*, 61: 159–308.

Köbler, Gerhard (1999), *Historisches lexikon der deutschen Länder*, 6 ed. (München).

Koblischke, Julius (1910), 'Der Name', *Mitteilungen des Vereins für kaschubische Volkskunde*, 1: 12–14.

Kola, Cyril (1990), 'Wjeršk-wuchadźišćo...', *Rozhlad*, 40: 129–31.

Kola, Ludwig (1984), 'Jedyn, před kotrymž so čerty bojachu. K sydomdźesaćinam antifašistiskeho wojowarja Jurja Měrćinka', *Rozhlad*, 34: 156–8.

Kolberg, Oskar (1965), *Pomorze oraz Aleksander Hilferding: Ostatki Słowian na południowym brzegu Bałtyckiego morza* (Wrocław-Poznań).

König, Werner (1985), *dtv-Atlas zur deutschen Sprache. Tafeln und Texte*, 2 ed. (München).

Körner, Georg (1979–80), *Wendisches oder slavonisch-deutsches ausführliches und vollständiges Wörterbuch. Eine Handschrift des 18. Jahrhunderts*, 2 vols in 5 parts, publ. by R. Olesch (Köln-Wien).

Kötzschke, Rudolf (1935), vol. I of Kötzschke, Rudolf and Hellmut Kretzschmar ([1935]).

Kötzschke, Rudolf and Hellmut Kretzschmar ([1935]), *Sächsische Geschichte*. I. Rudolf Kötzschke, *Vor-und Frühgeschichte, Mittelalter und Reformationszeit* (Dresden), II. Hellmut Kretzschmar, *Geschichte der Neuzeit seit der Mitte des 16. Jahrhunderts* (Dresden).

Krahl, Dr Gerhard (1972), *25 Jahre Gesetz zur Wahrung der Rechte der sorbischen Bevölkerung*. Schriftenreihe für Lehrer und Erzieher im zweisprachigen Gebiet, Heft 6/1972 (Bautzen).

Kral, Jurij (1927), *Serbsko-němski słownik hornjołužiskeje rěče. Wendisch-deutsches Wörterbuch der oberlausitzer Sprache* (Bautzen).

Kral, M[ěrćin] (1937), *Stawizniske powěsće z našich serbskich wsow* (Bautzen).

Krausch, Hans-Dieter (1978), 'Beiträge zur Lebensgeschichte von Albin Moller', *Lětopis Instituta za serbski ludospyt*, A 25: 159–82.

Krautz, Alfred (1974), *Sorbische bildende Künstler* (Bautzen).

Krawc, Jan (1993), 'Baćoń – wjes na wyšinje', *Rozhlad*, 43: 122–4.

Krječmar, Mikławš (1952), 'Lipa Serbska', *Lětopis Instituta za serbski ludospyt*, A 1: 5–60.

Krječmar, Mikławš (1956/1957a), 'Wokoło přirody a wutroby', *Lětopis Instituta za serbski ludospyt*, A 4: 107–26.

Krječmar, Mikławš (1956/1957b), 'K Ćišinskeho skutkowanju w Radeberku a k jeho zažnemu pensionowanju', *Lětopis Instituta za serbski ludospyt*, A 4: 127–33.

Krječmar, Mikławš and Pawoł Nowotny (eds.) (1958), *Ćišinskeho listowanje z Muku a Černym* (Bautzen).

Krofey, Simon (1586), *Duchowne piesnie D. Marcina Luthera y ynßich naboznich męzow. Zniemieckiego wSlawięsky ięzik wilozone Przez Szymana Krofea sługę Bozego WBytowie* (Gdańsk), reprinted in Olesch (1958).

Sources

Kroh, Peter Jan Joachim (2009), *Nationalistische Macht und nationale Minderheit. Jan Skala (1889–1945): ein Sorbe in Deutschland* (Berlin).

Kromer, Marcin (1984), *Polska czyli o położeniu, ludności, obyczajach, urzędach, i sprawach publicznych Królestwa Polskiego księgi dwie* (Olsztyn). Translation of Cromer (1577).

Krušwica, J. B. (1915), 'Ze stawiznow Wjerbańskeje cyrkwje we Wjerbnje w Błotach', *Časopis Maćicy Serbskeje*, 34–48, 89–126.

Kühne, Heinrich (1983), 'Kaspar Peuker. Leben und Werk eines großen Gelehrten an der Wittenberger Universität im 16. Jahrhundert', *Lětopis. Jahresschrift des Instituts für sorbische Volksforschung*, B 30: 151–61.

Kunze, Peter (1969), 'Bauernunruhen im Kreis Cottbus 1715–1717', *Lětopis. Jahresschrift des Instituts für sorbische Volksforschung*, B 16: 70–90.

Kunze, Peter (1978), *Die preußische Sorbenpolitik 1815–1847: eine Studie zur Nationalitätenpolitik im Übergang vom Feudalismus zum Kapitalismus* (Bautzen).

Kunze, Peter (1993), 'Aus der Geschichte der Lausitzer Sorben', in Scholze (1993), 7–56.

Kunze, Peter (1995), *Jan Arnošt Smoler. Ein Leben für sein Volk* (Bautzen).

Kunze, Peter (2001), 'Geschichte und Kultur der Sorben in der Oberlausitz. Ein kulturhistorischer Abriß', in *Geschichte der Oberlausitz: Herrschaft, Gesellschaft und Kultur vom Mittelalter bis zum Ende des 20. Jahrhunderts*, ed. Joachim Bahlcke (Leipzig), 267–314.

Kunze, Peter (2002), *Sorbisches Schulwesen. Dokumentation zum sorbischen Elementarschulwesen in der sächsischen Oberlausitz des 18./19. Jahrhunderts* (Bautzen).

Kunze, Peter (2003), 'Die Sorbenpolitik in der Ober- und Niederlausitz vom Wiener Kongress bis zum Ersten Weltkrieg', in *Zwischen Zwang und Beistand: Deutsche Politik gegenuber den Sorben vom Wiener Kongress bis zur Gegenwart*, ed. Edmund Pech and Dietrich Scholze (Dresden) 13–38.

Kurski (2014), <www.pl.wikipedia.org/wiki/Jacek_Kurski> [accessed 30 November 2014].

Kurzer Entwurf (1767), *Kurzer Entwurf einer Oberlausitz-wendischen Kirchenhistorie abgefaßt von einigen Oberl. wendischen evangel. Predigern* (Budißin).

Kutta, Janusz (2003), *Druga Rzeczpospolita i Kaszubi 1920–1939* (Bydgoszcz).

Labuda, Aleksander (1960), *Słownik kaszubski* (Warsaw).

Labuda, Gerard (1949), *Pierwsze państwo słowiańskie. Państwo Samona* (Poznań).

Labuda, Gerard (2006), *Historia Kaszubów w dziejach Pomorza, I. Czasy średniowieczne* (Gdańsk).

Langa, Alois (1994), 'Šunow – wjes serbskich swjedźenjow', *Rozhlad*, 44: 49–53.

Lauenburg (2014), <http://de.wikipedia.org/wiki/Lande_Lauenburg_und_Bütow> [accessed 25 November 2014].

Lehmann, Rudolf (1968), *Urkundeninventar zur Geschichte der Niederlausitz bis 1400* (Köln-Graz).

Leibniz (1717), *Godofr. Gvilielmi Leibnitii Collectanea etymologica, Pars 2* (Hanover).

Lemmer, Manfred (2002), 'Münch ze Toberlû. Anmerkung zu Walther L76, 21', in *Röllwagenbüchlein. Festschrift für Walter Röll zum Geburtstag* (Tübingen), 43–50.

Leske, Nathanael Gotfried (1785), *Reise durch Sachsen in Rüksicht der Naturgeschichte und Ökonomie* (Leipzig).

Leszczyński, Józef (1963), *Stany Górnych Łużyc w latach 1635–1697* (Wrocław).

Liersch, F. K. (1931), *Das Wendenregiment* (Cottbus).

L'Indépendence Polonaise (1919), 'Dans le pays de Gdansk', *L'Indépendence Polonaise*, No. 15, 3 May 1919: 2–3.

Lippert, Woldemar (1894), 'Über die Anwendung des Namens Lausitz auf die Oberlausitz im 14. Jahrhundert', *Neues Archiv für Sächsische Geschichte und Altertumskunde*, 15: 41–62.

Lisch, G. C. F. (1837), 'Die letzten Wenden in Meklenburg auf der Jabelhaide', *Jahrbücher des Vereins für Mecklenburgische Geschichte und Altertumskunde*, 2: 177–8.

Lisch, G.C.F. (1841), 'Vater Unser der Wenden in Meklenburg im 16. Jahrhundert', *Jahrbücher des Vereins für Mecklenburgische Geschichte und Altertumskunde*, 6: 59–65.

List (1909), 'List pastora Hakena', *Gryf*, 1: 203–7.

Liška, P. (1876), *K stawiznam Hodźija a hodźijskeje wosady* (Bautzen).

Lorentz, F. (1898), 'Zur älteren kaschubischen Literatur', *Archiv für slavische Philologie*, 20: 556–577.

Lorentz, F. (1903), *Slovinzische Grammatik* (St Petersburg).

Lorentz, F. (1905), *Slovinzische Texte* (St Petersburg).

Lorentz, F. (1908–12), *Slovinzisches Wörterbuch*, vols 1–2 (St Petersburg).

Lorentz, F. (1910), 'Nochmals der Name', *Mitteilungen des Vereins für kaschubische Volkskunde*, 1: 14–16.

Lorentz, F. (1925), *Geschichte der pomoranischen (kaschubischen) Sprache* (Berlin-Leipzig).

Lorentz, F. (1926), *Geschichte der Kaschuben* (Berlin).

Ludat, Herbert (1936), *Die ostdeutschen Kietze* (Bernburg). Reprinted 1984 (Hildesheim-Zürich-New York).

Ludecus, Matthäus (1586), *Historia von der Erfindung, Wunderwercken und Zerstörung des vermeinten heiligen Bluts zur Wilsnagk* (Wittenberg). http://BayrischeStaatsbibliothekreader.digitale-sammlungen.de

Ludwig, Ulrike and Insa Christiane Hennen (2002), 'Peucer – Student und Professor in Wittenberg', in *Katheder*, 33–9.

Łusčanski, Jurij (1892), 'Serbski seminar s. Pětra w Prazy', *Časopis Maćicy Serbskeje*, 3–24.

Maćerna rěč (2010), 'Interview. "Maćerna rěč je dźěl mojeje wosobiny". Rozmołwa z ministerskim prezidentom Sakskeje Stanisławom Tilichom', *Rozhlad*, 60, 12: 14–15.

Magirius, Heinrich and Siegfried Seifert (1982), *Kloster St. Marienstern*, 2 ed. (Leipzig).

Magocsi, Paul Robert (1993), *Historical Atlas of East Central Europe* (Seattle and London).

Mahling, Jan (2002), 'Die evangelische Kirche – Gemeindegeschichte seit 1523', in *Von Budissin nach Bautzen. Beiträge zur Geschichte der Stadt Bautzen*, ed. Manfred Thiemann (Bautzen), 122–33.

Malink, Jan (1983), 'Die Beziehungen Martin Luthers zu den Sorben', *Lětopis. Jahresschrift des Instituts für sorbische Volksforschung*, B 30: 54–70.

Malink, Jan (1992), 'Mjez spěchowanjom, spjećowanjom a přesćěhowanjom – Serbske stawizny 1945-1960', in *Serbja pod stalinistiskim socializmom (1945–1960)* (Bautzen), 18–28.

Malink, Jan (2010), 'Krótke stawizny našich spěwarskich', *Pomhaj Bóh*, 6: 3–4.

Malinkowa, Kata (1995), '1945 – lěto wulkich přećiwnosćow', *Rozhlad*, 45: 242–4.

M[alinkowa], T[rudla] (1990), 'Naša swójbna tragedija. Interview z Korlu Nalijom', *Pomhaj Bóh*, 12: [3–4, 7–8].

Malinkowa, Trudla (1994a), 'Christoph Samuel Daniel Schondorf – Pfarrer sorbischer Auswanderer in Südaustralien', *Lětopis*, 41, 2: 11–24.

Malinkowa, Trudla (1994b), 'Hrodźišćo', *Rozhlad*, 44: 206–9.

Malinkowa, Trudla (1996), 'Wuskutki nacionalsocializma na cyrkwinske žiwjenje ewangelskich Serbow w Sakskej', *Rozhlad*, 46: 267–72.

Malinkowa, Trudla (1998), 'Narodne wuwiće ewangelskich Serbow w Sakskej w zašłym połdra lětstotku', *Rozhlad*, 48: 254–8.

Malinkowa, Trudla (1999), *Ufer der Hoffnung. Sorbische Auswanderer nach Übersee*, 2 rev. ed. (Bautzen).

Manecke (1858), *Topographisch-historische Beschreibung der Städte, Ämter und adligen Gerichte im Fürstentum Lüneburg* (Celle).

Marciniak, Stanisław (1995), 'Serbska konspiracija w druhej swětowej wójnje – wumyslenje a wěrnosć', *Rozhlad*, 45: 244–8.

Martini, Gregorius (1627), *Die Sieben Bußpsalmen des Königlichen Propheten Davids. Windisch und Deutsch* (Budissin). See Schuster-Šewc (2001).

Sources

McClure, Edmund (1888), *A Chapter in English Church History: Being the Minutes of the Society for Promoting Christian Knowledge for the Year 1698–1704 together with Abstracts of Correspondents' Letters during Part of the Same Period* (London).

Mecklenburg (2014), <http://en.wikipedia.org/wiki/Mecklenburg> [accessed 23 August 2014].

Memorandum (1946), *1500 Years of Struggle for National Existence: Memorandum of the Lusatians, the Last European Nation Still Fighting for Its Independence* (Prague).

Merbach, J. F. (1833), *Geschichte der Kreis-Stadt Calau* (Lübben).

Meschgang, Jan (1973), *Die Ortsnamen der Oberlausitz* (Bautzen).

Meškank, Jan (1955), 'A žiwjenska wola tola je dobyła', *Rozhlad*, 5: 47–55, 79–83.

Mětšk, Frido (1940), 'Lusatica aus dem Anfang des 18. Jahrhunderts. Ein Beitrag zur Geschichte des Pietismus in der Lausitz', *Zeitschrift für slavische Philologie*, 17: 123–42. Here cited from reprint in Mětšk 1981: 10–23.

Mětšk, Frido (1957), 'Založenje a skutkowanje Domowiny 1912–1914', *Lětopis Instituta za serbski ludospyt*, B 4: 438–78.

Mětšk, Frido (1958), 'Serbsko-pólska rěčna hranica w 16. a 17. lětstotku', *Lětopis Instituta za serbski ludospyt*, B 5: 3–25.

Mětšk, Frido (1959), 'Wonkowny zarjad Němskeho mócnarstwa a serbske hibanje (1918–1919)', *Lětopis* B 6: 463–501.

Mětšk, Frido (1960a), 'Wo bywšim archiwje Maćicy Serbskeje a wo jeho rekonstrukciji w archiwje Instituta za serbski ludospyt', *Lětopis Instituta za serbski ludospyt*, A 7: 106–16.

Mětšk, Frido (1960b), 'Zur Frage der deutsch-sorbischen Sprachgrenzen des 16. Jahrhunderts im Markgraftum Oberlausitz und im Amte Stolpen', *Lětopis Instituta za serbski ludospyt*, B 7: 83–132.

Mětšk, Frido (1960c), 'Verschiebungen der deutsch-sorbischen Sprachgrenze in den meißnischen Ämtern Großenhain und Mühlberg von 1500 bis zum Erlöschen der sorbischen Sprache', *Die Welt der Slaven*, 5: 155–90. Cited here from reprint in Mětšk (1981): 117–41.

Mětšk, Frido (1960d), 'Der Anteil der Stände des Markgraftums Oberlausitz an der Entstehung der obersorbischen Schriftsprache (1668–1728)', *Zeitschrift für slavische Philologie*, 28: 122–48. Here cited from reprint in Mětšk 1981: 24–44.

Mětšk, Frido (1962a), *Die brandenburgisch-preussische Sorbenpolitik im Kreise Cottbus vom 16. Jahrhundert bis zum Posener Frieden (1806)* (Berlin).

Mětšk, Frido (1962b), 'Einige Erwägungen über die Auswirkungen der territorialen Veränderungen zu Beginn des XIX. Jh. auf die sorbische Nationalität', *Lětopis Instituta za serbski ludospyt*, B 9: 60–87.

Mětšk, Frido (1962c), 'Die Sorben und die Universität Wittenberg', *Wiener Slavistisches Jahrbuch*, Bd. 9: 32–62. Here cited from reprint in Mětšk 1981: 95–116.

Mětšk, Frido (1962d), 'Über den Hinteren Wendischen Zirkel des sächsischen Kurkreises', *Die Welt der Slaven*, 9: 185–213, 225–45. Here cited from reprint in Mětšk 1981:142–76.

Mětšk, Frido (1963), 'Der Beitrag Abraham Frencels (1656–1740) zur sorbischen Demographie in der Zeit des Spätfeudalismus', *Zeitschrift für Slawistik*, 8: 229–58. Cited here from reprint in Mětšk (1981): 70–94.

Mětšk, Frido (1965a), *Der Kurmärkisch-wendische Distrikt. Ein Beitrag zur Geschichte der Territorien Bärwalde, Beeskow, Storkow, Teupitz und Zossen unter besonderer Berücksichtigung des 16. bis 18. Jahrhunderts* (Bautzen).

Mětšk, Frido (1965b), 'Zur Sorabität der Niederlausitzer Kreisstadt Calau und zum Widerstand ihrer Bürger gegen die Germanisierungsmaßnahmen der feudalabsolutistischen Landesgewalt', *Lětopis. Jahresschrift des Instituts für sorbische Volksforschung*, B 12: 67–88.

Mětšk, Frido (1966a), 'Zur sorbischen Siedlungs- und Namenkunde der Umgebung von Dahme', in *Orbis scriptus. Festschrift für Dmitrij Tschiževskij zum 70. Geburtstag* (München), 551–7. Here cited from reprint in Mětšk 1981: 196–202.

Mětšk, Frido (1966b) 'Zur Frage der ehemaligen sorbischen Bevölkerung des meißnischen Amtes Finsterwalde', *Die Welt der Slaven*, 11: 148–71. Here cited from reprint in Mětšk 1981: 177–95.

Mětšk, Frido (1967), *Bestandsverzeichnis des Sorbischen Kulturarchivs in Bautzen. Teil III: Das Depositum Wendenabteilung* (Bautzen).

Mětšk, Frido (1968), *Die Stellung der Sorben in der territorialen Verwaltungsgliederung des deutschen Feudalismus. Ein Beitrag zur Rechts- und Verfassungsgeschichte des deutschen Feudalismus im Sorbenland* (Bautzen, 1968).

Mětšk, Frido (1969), *Verordnungen und Denkschriften gegen die sorbische Sprache and Kultur während der Zeit des Spätfeudalismus. Eine Quellensammlung* (Bautzen).

Mětšk, Frido (1970), 'Bój poddanow Lutolskeho knjejstwa za wuchowanje serbskeje maćeršćiny wot kónca 17. do započatka 19. lětstotka', *Lětopis Instituta za serbski ludospyt*, A 17: 153–71.

Mětšk, Frido (1976), 'Frankobrodska „Viadrina" – Universitas Serborum', *Předźenak*, 11 September, p. 3.

Mětšk, Frido (1976–7), 'Zur urkundlichen und zur volkskundlichen Tradition des Uckroer Aufstandes', *Luckauer Heimatkalender*, 46–51. Reprinted in Mětšk 1981: 237–42.

Mětšk, Frido (1979), 'Pućrubar spisowneje delnjoserbskeje rěče', *Předźenak*, 14 April, p. 3.

Mětšk, Frido (1981), *Studien zur Geschichte sorbisch-deutscher Kulturbeziehungen* (Bautzen).

Mětškowa, Ludmila (1987), 'Bě Jan Krygař Serb?', *Pomhaj Bóh* 37, 7: [1].

Michałk, Frido (1985), 'Vorwort zum fotomechanischen Neudruck', *Ticinus 1679*: 5–40.

Michałk, Frido (1986), 'Aus der Korrespondenz J. X. Ticins (I)', *Lětopis Instituta za serbski ludospyt*, A 33: 52–69.

Michałk, Frido (1987), 'Aus der Korrespondenz J. X. Ticins (II)', *Lětopis Instituta za serbski ludospyt*, A 34: 57–78.

Michałk, Frido (1988a), 'Aus der Korrespondenz J. X. Ticins (III)', *Lětopis Instituta za serbski ludopsyt*, A 35: 41–69.

Michałk, Frido (1988b), Foreword to Swětlik (1721).

Michałk, Frido (1989), 'Aus der Korrespondenz J. X. Ticins (IV)', *Lětopis Instituta za serbski ludopsyt*, A 36: 63–91.

Michałk, Frido (1990), 'Aus der Korrespondenz J. X. Ticins (V)', *Lětopis Instituta za serbski ludopsyt*, A 37: 60–93.

Michałk, Frido (1991), 'Aus der Korrespondenz J. X. Ticins (VI)', *Lětopis Instituta za serbski ludopsyt*, A 38: 51–75.

Michałk, Frido (1992), 'Neue Erkenntnisse aus der Korrespondenz J. X. Ticins (1678–1693)', *Lětopis. Časopis za sorabistiku*, 39, 2: 69–74.

Michałk, Frido (1994), 'Aus der Korrespondenz J. X. Ticins (VII)', *Lětopis. Časopis za rěč, stawizny a kulturu Łužiskich Serbow*, 41, 1: 29–73.

Michalk, Siegfried and Helmut Protze (1967), *Studien zur sprachlichen Interferenz I. Deutsch-sorbische Dialekttexte aus Nochten, Kreis Weißwasser* (Bautzen).

Michalk, Siegfried and Helmut Protze ([1974]), *Studien zur sprachlichen Interferenz II. Deutsch-sorbische Dialekttexte aus Radibor, Kreis Bautzen* (Bautzen).

Mieczkowska, Malgorzata (1993), 'Łużyce a polska opinia publiczna w latach 1945–1949', *Lětopis. Zeitschrift für sorbische Sprache, Geschichte und Kultur*, 40, 1: 97–105.

Mieczkowska, Małgorzata (2006), *Polska wobec Łużyc w drugiej połowie XX wieku: wybrane problemy* (Szczecin).

Miertsching, Johann (1855), *Reise-Tagebuch des Missionars Joh. Aug. Miertsching, welcher als Dolmetscher die Nordpol-Expedition zur Aufsuchung Sir John Franklins auf dem Schiff Investigator begleitete. In den Jahren 1850 bis 1854* (Gnadau).

Miertsching, Johann (1967), *Frozen Ships. The Arctic Diary of Johann Miertsching 1850–1854*. Translated and with introduction and notes by L. H. Neatby (Toronto).

Sources

Mikławšk, Beno (1992), 'Wjes ze sylnej tradiciju', *Rozhlad*, 42: 313–16.

Ministerpräsident (2014), <www.ministerpraesident.sachsen.de/index.html> [accessed 30 November 2014].

Młynk, Jurij (1967), 'Před dwaceći lětami we Wrocławskiej Lusatii', *Protyka 1967*, 64–73.

Mokoschinus, Leonhardus (1599), *Historiarum Veteris Testamenti heroico carmine redditarum libri* (Witebergae) (quoted in Bocatius 1990, 1: 41 and Bocatius 1990, 2: 847).

Moller, Albin (1959), *Albin Moller. Niedersorbisches Gesangbuch und Katechismus. Budissin 1574.* Foreword by H. H. Bielfeldt and H. Schuster-Šewc (Berlin).

Montelius, O. (1899), 'Die Einwanderung der Slawen in Norddeutschland', *Correspondenz-Blatt der deutschen Gesellschaft für Anthropologie, Ethnologie und Urgeschichte*, 30: 127–8.

MPH, Bielowski, August (1960–1), *Monumenta Poloniae Historica/Pomniki dziejowe Polski*, vols 1–6 (Warsaw). Reprint of Lwów-Kraków ed. (1864–93).

MSHP, Mały słownik historii Polski (1967), ed. Tadeusz Łepkowski (Warsaw).

MUB, Mecklenburgisches Urkundenbuch, vols. 1–25 (Schwerin, 1863–1977).

Mucke, Karl Ernst (1891), *Historische und vergleichende Laut- und Formenlehre der niedersorbischen (niederlausitzisch-wendischen) Sprache* (Leipzig). Reprinted Leipzig 1965.

Muka, Ernst (1882), 'Frenceliana [IV]', *Časopis Maćicy Serbskeje*, 22–52.

Muka, Ernst (1884a), 'Delnjołužiske Serbowstwo w lěće 1880', *Časopis Maćicy Serbskeje*, 3–110.

Muka, Ernst (1884b), 'Statistika Serbow', *Časopis Maćicy Serbskeje*, 129–59.

Muka, Ernst (1885), 'Statistika hornjołužiskich Serbow pruskeho kralestwa', *Časopis Maćicy Serbskeje*, 3–120.

Muka, Ernst (1886), 'Statistika Serbow sakskeho kralestwa', *Časopis Maćicy Serbskeje*, 3–241 and map.

Muka, Ernst (1896), 'Přinoški k staršim serbskim cyrkwinskim a narodopisnym stawiznam', *Časopis Maćicy Serbskeje*, 112–33.

Muka, Ernst (1897a), 'Přinoški k staršim serbskim cyrkwinskim a narodopisnym stawiznam', *Časopis Maćicy Serbskeje*, 45–57.

Muka, Ernst (1897b), 'Přinoški k staršim serbskim cyrkwinskim a narodopisnym stawiznam', *Časopis Maćicy Serbskeje*, 128–47.

Muka, Karol Ernest (1904a), 'Szczątki języka połabskiego Wendów Lüneburskich. Zebrane i opracowane w latach 1901–1902', in *Materiały i Prace Komisji Językowej Akademii Umiejętności w Krakowie*, 1 (Kraków), 313–18.

Muka, Arnošt (1904b), 'Slované ve vojvodství Lüneburském', *Slovanský přehled*, 6: 417–18.

Muka, Arnošt (1923), 'Zapiski Maćicy Serbskeje', *Časopis Maćicy Serbskeje*, 3–54.

Müller, Ernst (1912), *Die evangelischen Geistlichen Pommerns [. . .], II. Theil: Der Regierungsbezirk Köslin [. . .]* (Stettin).

Münzverein (2014), <de.wikipedia.org/wiki/Wendischer Münzverein> [accessed 25 August 2014].

Musiat, Siegmund (2001), *Sorbische/Wendische Vereine 1716–1937* (Bautzen).

Myconius, Friedrich (1543), *Historia reformationis* (Wittenberg).

Najstarši (2011), 'Najstarši dopokaz delnjoserbšćiny', *Rozhlad*, 61, 7–8: 45.

Nawka, Cyril (1992), 'My tu hišće smy', *Rozhlad*, 42: 162–5.

NBS, Nowy biografiski słownik k stawiznam a kulturje Serbow (1984), ed. Pětr Kunze Jan Šolta and Franc Šěn (Bautzen).

NC (1994), 'Wažne słowa k wotworjenju Serbskego muzeja', *Nowy Casnik*, 18 June 1994, p. 4.

Neander [Nowak, Jakub] (1920), *Wobrazy z cyrkwinskich stawiznow* (Bautzen).

Nedo, Pawoł (1960), 'Wuswobodźenje k nowemu žiwjenju. Horšć dopomnjenkow na nalěćo 1945', *Rozhlad*, 10: 129–32.

Needon, Richard (1930), 'Der Verrat des Bautzener Stadtschreibers Peter Preischwitz im Jahre 1429/30', *Neues Archiv für Sächsische Geschichte und Altertumskunde*, 51: 11–19.

Neureiter, Ferdinand (1978), *Geschichte der kaschubischen Literatur. Versuch einer zusammenfassenden Darstellung* (Munich).

Nielsen, George (2003), *Johann Kilian, Pastor. A Wendish Lutheran in Germany and Texas* (Serbin, Texas).

NLM, *Neues Lausitzisches Magazin* (1822–1943).

Noack, Martina/Nowakojc, Martina (2008), *'Nach Berlin! Spreewälder Ammen und Kindermädchen in der Großstadt'/'Do Barlinja! Serbske seśelnice a źiśarki we wjelikem měśće'* (Cottbus).

Nowakojc, Martina (1993), 'Herbstwo Pawliny Krawcoweje w Serbskim muzeju w Choćebuzu', *Protyka 1994*, 150–1.

Nowotny, Pawoł (1996), 'K stawiznam ilegalneho antifašistskeho spjećowanje Serbow', *Rozhlad*, 46: 12–17.

Obracht-Prondzyński, Cezary and Tomasz Wicherkiewicz (eds.) (2011), *The Kashubs Past and Present* (Oxford-Bern, etc.).

OCEL, *The Oxford Companion to English Literature* (1985).

ODCC, *Oxford Dictionary of the Christian Church* (1990), ed. F. L. Cross (Oxford).

ODNB, *Oxford Dictionary of National Biography* (2004).

Odyniec, Wacław (1959), 'Stosunki społeczno-gospodarcze w starostwach kaszubskich Województwa pomorskiego w XVII I XVIII w', in *Szkice z dziejów Pomorza*, 271–312.

Odyniec, Wacław (1961), *Starostwo Puckie 1546–1678* (Gdańsk).

Olesch, Reinhold (1958a), *S. Krofey, Geistliche Lieder D. Martin Luthers und anderer frommer Männer* (Köln-Graz).

Olesch, Reinhold (1958b), *M. Pontanus, Der kleine Catechißmus D. Martini Lutheri. Deutsch vnnd Wendisch gegen einander gesetzt. Mit anhange der Sieben Bußpsalmen König DAVIDS Danzig 1643 und Passiongeschichte Danzig 1643* (Köln-Graz).

Olesch, Reinhold (1959), *Vocabularium Venedicum von Christian Hennig von Jessen* (Köln-Graz).

Olesch, Reinhold (1962), *Juglers Lüneburgisch-wendisches Wörterbuch* (Köln-Graz).

Olesch, Reinhold (1967), *Fontes lingvae Dravaenopolabicae minores et Chronica venedica J. P. Schvltzii* (Köln-Graz).

Olesch, Reinhold (1968), *Bibliographie zum Dravänopolabischen* (Köln-Graz).

Olesch, Reinhold (1989a), 'Finis lingvae Dravaenopolabicae', reprinted in Olesch (1989c), 134–48. Originally in *Festschrift für Friedrich von Zahn*. Bd. 1. *Zur Geschichte und Volkskunde Mitteldeutschlands*. Hg. W. Schlesinger (Köln-Graz, 1968), 623–37.

Olesch, Reinhold (1989b), 'Zur geographischen Verbreitung des Dravänopolabischen', reprinted in Olesch (1989c), 149–60. Originally in *Festschrift für Friedrich von Zahn*. Bd. 2. *Zur Sprache und Literatur Mitteldeutschlands*, Hg. R. Olesch u. L. E. Schmitt (Köln-Wien, 1971), 126–37.

Olesch, Reinhold (1989c), *Gesammelte Aufsätze I: Dravenopolabica*, Hg. Angelika Lauhus (Köln-Wien).

Ostrowska, Róża and Izabella Trojanowska (1974), *Bedeker Kaszubski* (Gdańsk).

Paczoska, Alicja (2004), 'Oskarżeni o separatyzm. Działania tajnych służb PRL wobec działaczy kaszubskich w latach 1945–1970', *Pamięć i Sprawiedliwość*, nr.2. Republished 19 February 2005 at <http://naszekaszuby.pl/modules/artykuly/article.php?articleid=149> [accessed 14 July 2012].

Pałys, Piotr (2006), 'Prof. dr. hab. Wójćech Kóćka (13. 10. 1911–18. 11.1965)', *Rozhlad*, 56: 387–91.

Pałys, Piotr (2012), 'Misja Wojskowa Federacyjnej Ludowej Republiki Jugosławii przy Międzysojuszniczej Radzie Kontroli Niemiec wobec spraw łużyckich w latach 1946–1949', in Szewczyk (2012): 215–28.

Pałys, Piotr (2013), 'Jurij i Pawoł Cyżowie w serbołużyckim ruchu narodowym', *Lětopis*, 60, 1: 118–37.

Sources

Paris (2014), <http://en.wikipedia.org/wiki/Demographics_of_Paris> [accessed 16 October 2014].

Pata, J. (1920), *Łužica* (Bautzen).

Pech, Edmund and Dietrich Scholze (eds.) (2003), *Zwischen Zwang und Beistand: Deutsche Politik gegenüber den Sorben vom Wiener Kongress bis zur Gegenwart* (Dresden).

Pečikowa, Martina (1995), 'Ptačecy – wjes na kromje jamow', *Rozhlad*, 45: 216–18.

Petr, Jan (1967), 'Přinoški k stawiznam serbskeje rěče a kultury', *Lětopis Instituta za serbski ludospyt*, A 12: 1–17.

Petr, Jan (1978), *Arnošt Muka* (Bautzen).

Petr, Jan (1989), *Abraham Frencel* (Bautzen).

Petr, Jan and Milena Tylová (1990), *Josef Páta. Bibliografický soupis publikovaných prací a přehledem jeho činnosti* (Praha).

Peucer, Caspar (1594), *Idyllium patria* (Bautzen). Reproduced in *Jahresschrift 2001*, 7. Jahrgang, Hg. Stadtmuseum Bautzen, 7–114.

Pful, [K. B.] (1886), 'Starinki z Budyšina a z Lipska. VII.', *Łužica*, 5: 51–3.

Pietsch, Karl (2006), 'Göda, seine historischen Anfänge bis hin zur Reformation', in *Göda tausendjährig*, 34–45.

Phillips, W. (2004), 'Germans: Arriving, Settling, Worshipping', in *German Church* (2004), 30–5, 580.

Pobłocki, Gustaw (1908–9), 'Doktor Cejnowa', *Gryf*, 1: 128–38, 149–64.

Pohontsch, Anja (2002), *Der Einfluss obersorbischer Lexik auf die niedersorbische Schriftsprache* (Bautzen).

Polański, Kazimierz and James Allen Sehnert (1967), *Polabian-English Dictionary* (The Hague-Paris).

Pölitz, Karl Heinrich Ludwig (1809), *Geschichte der Statistik des Königreiches Sachsen und des Herzogthums Warschau, für Selbstbelehrung und Jugendunterricht. Zweiter Teil* (Leipzig).

Pommern (2014), <http://de.wikipedia.org/wiki/Herzogtum_Pommern> [accessed 18 October 2014].

Popowska-Taborska, Hanna (1997), 'Krzysztof Celestyn Mrongowiusz o związkach kaszubsko-łużyckich', *Lětopis*, 44: 198–201.

Popowska-Taborska, Hanna (2001), 'Szymon Krofey i Michał Pontanus – niełatwa kwestia autorstwa kaszubskich zabytków', *Studia z filologii polskiej i słowiańskiej*, 37: 89–97. Cited here from reprint in Id., *Szkice z kaszubszczyzny* (Gdańsk 2001), 305–14.

Pronjewič, Aleksej Stanislawowič (1995), 'Stejišćo ZSSR při rozrisanju serbskeho narodneho prašenja po 2. swětowej wójnje', *Rozhlad*, 45: 272–9.

PUB, Pommersches Urkundenbuch, vols. 1–11 (Stettin-Köln, 1868–1990).

Rajš, Franc (1987), *Stawizny Domowiny we słowje a wobrazu* (Bautzen).

Rajš, Franc (1992), 'Tři dotal njeznate wopory fašizma', *Rozhlad*, 42: 445–8.

Raport z wyników. Narodowy spis powszechny ludności i mieszkań 2011 (2012), <http://stat.gov.pl/cps/rde/xbcr/gus/lud_raport_z_wyników_NSP2011.pdf> [accessed 9 September 2014].

Raschhofer, Hermann (1937), *Die tschechoslowakischen Denkschriften für die Friedenskonferenz von Paris 1919/1920*, Beiträge zum ausländischen öffentlichen Recht und Völkerrecht, Heft 24 (Berlin).

Rauch, Walter J. (1959), *Presse und Volkstum der Lausitzer Sorben* (Würzburg).

Raupp, Jan (1978), *Sorbische Musik*, 2 ed. (Bautzen).

Remes, Friedrich W. (1993), *Die Sorbenfrage 1918/1919. Untersuchung einer gescheiterten Autonomiebewegung* (Bautzen).

Reuther, Martin (1953a), 'Beiträge zur Geschichte des deutschen und sorbischen Elementarschuwesens der Stadt Bautzen bis zum Jahre 1873', *Lětopis Instituta za serbski ludospyt*, B 1: 121–153.

Reuther, Martin (1953b), 'Die Oberlausitz im Kartenbild des 16. bis 18. Jahrhunderts mit besonderer Berücksichtigung der deutsch-sorbischen Sprachgrenzenkarten von Scultetus und Schreiber', *Lětopis Instituta za serbski ludospyt*, B 1: 154–72.

Reuther, Martin (1955/1956), 'Der Görlitzer Bürgermeister, Mathematiker, Astronom und Kartograph Bartholomäus Scultetus (1540–1614) und seine Zeit', *Wissenschaftliche Zeitschrift der Technischen Hochschule Dresden*, 5 (Heft 6):1133–61.

Reymann, Richard (1902), *Geschichte der Stadt Bautzen* (Bautzen).

Řezník, M. (2012), 'Czeskie kontakty Floriana Ceynowy', in Borzyszkowski (2012), 101–30.

Rogaczewski, Feliks (1975), *Wśród Słowińców. Pamiętnik nauczyciela* (Gdańsk).

Roggan, Alfred (2011), 'Das sorbische (wendische) Lieberose/Luboraz. Die andere Geschichte einer Kleinstadt und der älteste sorbische (wendische) Bürgereid der Niederlausitz', *Lětopis*, 58, 2: 62–9.

Roppel, Leon (1967), *Florian Ceynowa. Twórca regionalizmu kaszubskiego* (Gdańsk).

Roppel, Leon (1968), 'Arnošt Smoler a Florian Ceynowa na Słowjanskim zjězdźe w Ruskej l. 1867', *Rozhlad*, 18: 251–9.

Röseberg, Dr. (1930), 'Leben und Wirken Michael Frentzels, Übersetzter des Neuen Testaments in das Wendische (Obersorbische)', *Beiträge zur sächsischen Kirchengeschichte*, 39: 30–112.

Ruske, Michael (2002), 'Verrat an den Feind? Die Bekenntnisse des Peter Preischwitz (1430/31)', in *Eide, Statuten und Prozesse. Ein Quellen- und Lesebuch zur Stadtgeschichte von Bautzen 14–19 Jahrhundert*, ed. Alexander Kästner (Bautzen).

Ruvigny (1974), Melville Henry Massue Marquis de Ruvigny & Raineval, *The Jacobite Peerage […]* (London and Edinburgh). Facsimile of the original edition of 1900.

Rychtar, Helmut (2013), 'Wosebitostka ze Šešowa. Serbowka Marja Bradlowa ćěšerka poslednjeho sakskeho krala była', *Pomhaj Bóh*, 5: 8.

Rychtar, Rudolf (1863), 'Njeschto wot ßerbskeho prawopißa k smjerowanju mojich lubych lasowarjow', *Misionski Posoł*, 85–7.

Sachße, Carl (1848), *Sachsenspiegel oder Sächsisches Landrecht zusammengefaßt mit dem Schwäbischen nach dem Cod. Pal. 167, unter Vergleichung des Cod. pict 164, mit Übersetzung und reichhaltigem Repertorium von Dr. Carl Sachße, Prof. d. R. in Heidelberg* (Heidelberg).

Schelz, Th. (1842), 'XVIII. Beschreibung der hauptssächlichsten lausitzischen u. der Lausitz benachbarten Städte, in die Zeit von 1530 gehörig, aus dem Monachus Pirnensis bei Mencken, Scriptores Rerum Saxon. Tom III. col. 1527 sqq. mit Anmerkungen', *Neues Lausitzisches Magazin*, 20: 291–357.

Scheuch, Manfred (2001), *Historischer Atlas Deutschland* (Augsburg). First publ. Vienna 1997.

Schiller, Karl and August Lübben (1875–81), *Mittelniederdeutsches Wörterbuch*, 6 vols. (Bremen).

Schlesinger, Walter (1962), *Kirchengeschichte Sachsens im Mittelalter*, 2 vols (Cologne-Graz).

Schlimpert, Gerhard (1978), *Slawische Personennamen in mittelalterlichen Quellen zur deutschen Geschichte* (Berlin).

Schmaler, J. E. (1864), *Welches ist die Lehre des athanasianischen Symbolums von der dritten Person in der Gottheit und wie wurde sie von wendischen Theologen sprachlich aufgefasst?* (Bautzen).

Schmidt, Otto Eduard (1926), *Die Wenden* (Dresden).

Schmidt, Tobias (1656), *Chronici Cygnei Pars Posterior oder Zwickauscher Chronicken Anderer Theil.*

Schneeweis, Edmund (1953), *Feste und Volksbräuche der Sorben vergleichend dargestellt* (Berlin).

Schneider, F. (1864), 'Duchowny J.F. Serbin a kulowske bratstwo', *Katolski Posoł*, 2: 4–6, 27–8.

Schneider, Johannes (1961), 'Materialien zur Geschichte des Bautzener Weichbildes und seiner Ratsdörfer 2. Teil: Von 1547 bis 1648', *Lětopis Instituta za serbski ludospyt*, B 8: 183–99.

Scholze, Dietrich (ed.) (1993), *Die Sorben in Deutschland. Sieben Kapitel Kulturgeschichte* (Bautzen).

Sources

Schönfeld, Rudolf and Karl Holder (1966), *Grundzüge der Nationalitätenpolitik und deren Verwirklichung in der DDR. Schriftenreihe für Lehrer und Erzieher im zweisprachigen Gebiet* (Bautzen).

Schrage, Gertraud Eva (2001), 'Die Oberlausitz bis zum Jahr 1346', in Bahlcke 2001, 55–97.

Schulwesen (2012), <http://de.wikipedia.org/wiki/Sorbisches_Schulwesen> [accessed 4 August 2012].

Schulze, Eduard Otto (1896), *Die Kolonisierung und Germanisierung der Gebiete zwischen Saale und Elbe* (Leipzig).

Schulze, Hans K. (1980), 'Slavica lingua penitus intermissa. Zum Verbot des Wendischen als Gerichtssprache', in *Europa slavica – Europa orientalis: Festschrift für Herbert Ludat zum 70. Geburtstag*, ed. Grothusen, Klaus-Detlev and Klaus Zernack (Berlin), 354–67.

Schulze-Šołta, Heinz (2003), *Mundtot gemacht. Ein sorbischer Redakteur in den Fängen der Staatssicherheit* (Bautzen).

Schurmann, Peter (1998), *Die sorbische Bewegung 1945–1948 zwischen Selbstbehauptung und Anerkennung* (Bautzen).

Schuster-Šewc, H. (1967a), *Sorbische Sprachdenkmäler. 16–18. Jahrhundert* (Bautzen).

Schuster-Šewc, H. (1967b), *Das niedersorbische Testament des Miklawuš Jakubica 1548* (Berlin).

Schuster-Šewc, H. (1986), 'Die älteste Schicht der slawischen sozialökonomischen und politisch-institutionellen Termini und ihr Schicksal im Sorbischen', *Lětopis Instituta za serbski ludospyt*, A 33: 1–19.

Schuster-Šewc, H. (1993), *Michael Frentzel:Postwitzscher Tauff-Stein oder christliche und einfältige teutsch-wendische Predigt von der heiligen Taufe. Ein sorbisches Sprachdenkmal aus dem Jahre 1688* (Köln-Weimar-Wien).

Schuster-Šewc, H. (1996), *Das Neue Testament der niedersorbischen (Berliner) Handschrift. Ein Sprachdenkmal des 17. Jahrhunderts* (Bautzen).

Schuster-Šewc, H. (2001), *Die ältesten Drucke des Obersorbischen: Wenceslaus Warichius und Gregorius Martini. Eine sprachwissenschaftliche Analyse. Mit Faksimiledruck, Transliteration und Transkription* (Bautzen).

Schwebe, Joachim (1960), *Volksglaube und Volksbrauch im Hannoverschen Wendland* (Cologne-Graz).

Scribner, R. W. and C. Scott Dixon (2003), *The German Reformation*, 2 ed. (Basingstoke-New York).

Sehling, E. (1902), *Die evangelischen Kirchenordnungen des XVI. Jahrhunderts*, 1 (Leipzig).

Seifert, Siegfried (2002), 'Die katholische Kirche nach der Reformation', in *Von Budissin nach Bautzen. Beiträge zur Geschichte der Stadt Bautzen*, ed. Manfred Thiemann (Bautzen), 110–21.

Šěn, Franc (1999), 'Wobstatki a wosud knihownje a archiwa Maćicy Serbskeje', *Lětopis*, 46, 2: 19–32.

Šěrakec, Lubina (1992), 'Na wopominanje. Elegija na Wosyk', *Rozhlad*, 42: 390–1.

Serbin, Jan [=Jan Bryl] (1920), *Serbske stawizny w zańdźenosći a přitomnosći z podrobnym rozpominanjom serbskeho hibanja a wojowanja wo kulturnu samostatnosć łužiskich Serbow* (Bautzen).

Serbja (2012), <http://hsb.wikipedia.org/wiki/Serbja> [accessed 14 November 2012].

Serbja pod stalinistiskim socializmom (1945–1960) (Bautzen, 1992).

Serbske šulstwo (1993)=*Serbske šulstwo (1945–1970). Mjez socialistiskej ideologiju a narodnej zamołwitosću* (Bautzen, 1993).

Serbski Nowinkar (1848) (Bautzen).

Šěsć Serbow (1990), 'Šěsć Serbow zapósłancy Ludoweje komory', *Rozhlad*, 40: 156.

Šewc, Hinc (1997), 'Mikławša Jakubicowy přełožk Noweho zakonja do serbšćiny z lěta 1548. Pospyt noweho hladanja na wosobinu přełožowarja a jeho rěč', *Lětopis*, 44, 2: 31–52.

Siebert, Richard (1904), 'Elf ungedruckte Urkunden aus einem im Herzoglichen Haus- und Staatsarchiv in Zerbst befindlichen Nienburger Copiale', *Mitteilungen des Vereins für Anhaltische Geschichte und Altertumskunde*, 9: 181–94.

Siebke, Johannes (1940), *Die Gegenreformation im Lande Bütow* (Greifswald).

Ślaski, Kazimierz (1959), 'Polskosć Pomorza Zachodniego w świetle źródeł XVI–XVIII', *Szkice z dziejów Pomorza*, 2: 34–74.

Słownik staropolski, vols 1–11 (Kraków, 1953–2003).

Sobierajski, Zenon (1964), *Polskie teksty gwarowe z ilustracją dźwiękową, IV. Lubawskie – Ostródzkie – Kaszuby* (Poznań).

Socha-Borzestowski, Bronisław (1975), 'Kaszubscy delegaci na konferencji pokojowej w Paryżu w 1919 roku', in *Panorama kaszubsko-pomorska*, ed. Br. Socha-Borzestowki, 7–9 (London).

Šołćic, Wórša (1967), 'Narodny wojowar, basnik a wumělc', *Rozhlad*, 17: 62–9.

Šolta, Jan (1976), *Abriß der sorbischen Geschichte* (Bautzen).

Šolta, Jan (1981), 'K 230. róčnicy narodnin a 195. róčnicy posmjertnin. Wuznamny wučenc, rozswětler a doprědkar Nathanael Bohumer Leska', *Předźenak*, 14 November 1981, 3.

Sorben (2000), *Die Sorben in Bautzen. Serbja w Budyšinje* (Bautzen).

Sorben (2012), <http://de.wikipedia.org/wiki/Sorben> [accessed 14 November 2012].

Sorbs (2012), <http://en.wikipedia.org/wiki/Sorbs> [accessed 21 November 2012].

Spangenberg, Cyriacus (1572), *Mansfeldische Chronica. Der Erste Theil* (Eisleben).

SSA, Sorbischer Sprachatlas, vols 1–15 (Bautzen, 1965–96).

SSS, Słownik starożytności słowiańskich, vols 1–6 (Wrocław-Warszawa-Kraków, 1961–77).

Stawizny, Stawizny Serbow, vols. 1–4 (Bautzen, 1975–9).

Steiniger, D. (2004), 'The Ministry of Pastor Ewald Steiniger:1935-64', in *German Church* (2004), 292–3, 613.

Stone, Gerald (1972), *The Smallest Slavonic Nation: the Sorbs of Lusatia* (London).

Stone, Gerald (1986), 'The First Sorbian Sentence', in *Festschrift für Wolfgang Gesemann*, Band 3. *Beiträge zur slawischen Sprachwissenschaft und Kulturgeschichte*, 337–43 (Neuried).

Stone, Gerald (1991), 'Porjedźenki k dotalnymaj wudaćomaj A. Molleroweje zběrki lěkarskich zelow z lěta 1582', *Lětopis Instituta za serbski ludospyt*, A 38: 19–29.

Stone, Gerald (1994), 'Vestiges of Polabian in Wendland Platt', in *Res Slavica. Festschrift für Hans Rothe zum Geburtstag*, ed. Pieter Thiergen and Ludger Udolph in collaboration with Wilfried Potthoff (Paderborn-München-Wien- Zürich), 627–37.

Stone, Gerald (2002), 'Serbsko-jendźelske zetkanje w lěće 1704', *Pomhaj Bóh*, 8: 3.

Stone, Gerald (2006), 'Ten poems of Mato Kosyk (1853–1940) translated and introduced', *Slavonica*, 12: 25–39.

Šurman, P. (1991), 'Zajimawy list z Pólskeje. K 80. posmjertnym narodninam Wójćecha Kóčki 13. oktobra', *Rozhlad*, 41: 270–1.

Swětlik, Jurij Hawštyn (1721), *Vocabularium latino-serbicum*. Facsimile reprint with a foreword by Frido Michałk (Bautzen).

Sychta, Bernard (1967–76), *Słownik gwar kaszubskich na tle kultury ludowej*, Vols 1–7 (Wrocław-Warszawa- Kraków- Gdańsk).

Sykora, August (1936), *W Malešecach před sto lětami* (Bautzen).

Szewczyk, Grażyna Barbara (ed.) (2012), *Serbołużyczanie wobec tradycji i wyzwań współczesności* (Katowice).

Szkice z dziejów Pomorza (1959), ed. Gerard Labuda, I. *Pomorze średniowieczne*, II. *Pomorze nowożytne*, III. *Pomorze na progu dziejów najnowszych* (Warsaw).

Szultka, Zygmunt (1991), *Język polski w Kościele ewangelicko-augsburskim na Pomorzu Zachodnim od XVI do XIX wieku* (Wrocław-Warsaw-Cracow).

Szultka, Zygmunt (2012), 'Ceynowy droga ze Slawoszyna do Bukowca', in Borzyszkowski (2012), 25–100.

Sources

Taylor, A.J.P. (1945), *The Course of German History* (London).

Teichmann, Doris (1998), *Studien zur Geschichte und Kultur der Niederlausitz im 16. und 17. Jahrhundert* (Bautzen).

Teichmann, Lucius (1984), *Steinchen aus dem Strom. Vom Dritten Reich und unseren Nachbarn im Osten*, 2 ed (Cologne).

Tetzner, F. (1899), *Die Slovinzen und Lebakaschuben* (Berlin).

Tharaeus, Andreas (1990), *Enchiridion Vandalicum. Ein niedersorbisches Sprachdenkmal aus dem Jahre 1610*. Hg. Heinz Schuster-Šewc (Bautzen).

Thiemann, Manfred, *Von Budissin nach Bautzen* (Bautzen, 2002).

Thietmar (1992), Thietmar von Merseburg, *Chronik*, neu übertragen und erläutert von Werner Trillmich (Darmstadt).

Ticinus, Jakub Xaver (1679), *Principia linguae wendicae, quam aliqui wandalicam vocant* (Pragae). Facsimile reprint, ed. F. Michałk (Bautzen, 1985).

Tillich (2014), <http://www.de.wikipedia.org/wiki/Stanislaw_Tillich> [accessed 30 November 2014].

Tollius, Jacobus (1700), *Epistolae Itinerariae ex auctoris schedis postumis recensitae suppletae, digestae annotationibus, observationibus et figuris adornatae, cura et studio Henrici Christiani Henninii* (Amsteloedami).

Topolińska, Zuzanna (1962), 'Stejišćo a róla Ćišinskeho w stawiznach hornjoserbskeje wersifikacije', *Lětopis Instituta za serbski ludospyt*, A 9: 62–71.

Trautmann, R. (1948), *Die Elb- und Ostseeslavischen Ortsnamen*, 1 (Berlin).

Trautmann, R. (1949), *Die Elb- und Ostseeslavischen Ortsnamen*, 2 (Berlin).

Trautmann, R. (1950), *Die slavischen Ortsnamen Mecklenburgs und Holsteins* (Berlin).

Trautmann, R. (1956), *Die Elb- und Ostseeslavischen Ortsnamen*, 3. Register, compiled by H. Schall, including contents of Trautmann (1950) (Berlin).

Treder, Jerzy (ed.) (1999), *Tragedia o bogaczu i Łazarzu* (Gdańsk-Gdynia).

Treder, Jerzy (2003), 'Komu może przeszkadzać etnonim Słowińcy?', in *Obrazy Ziemi Słupskiej. Społeczeństwo – administracja – kultura*, VII Konferencja Kaszubsko Pomorska, ed. A. Czarnik (Słupsk), 59–70.

Treder, Jerzy (ed.) (2006), *Język kaszubski. Poradnik encyklopedyczny* (Gdańsk).

Tuschling, Steffen (2002), 'Serbske namše w Barlinju', *Rozhlad*, 52: 266–72.

Tusk (2014), <www.pl.wikipedia.org/wiki/Donald_Tusk> [accessed 30 November 2014]

Udolph, Ludger (ed.) (2004), *Basnje humanistow*. Serbska poezija 50 (Bautzen).

Urban, Zdeněk (1993), 'Marginalie k biografii a literární činnosti Albina Mollera', *Lětopis*, 40, 2: 89–97.

Veckenstedt, Edmund (1880), *Wendische Sagen, Märchen und abergläubische Gebräuche* (Graz).

Vierset, Auguste (1923), *Un peuple martyr. La question des Wendes devant l'opinion publique* (Bruxelles).

Vitzk, Matthäus Joseph (1857), 'VII. Chronicon reverandi capitali et collegiatae ecclesiae Budissinensis auctore Matth. Jos. Vitzk Decano nec non Administratore Ecclesiastico utramque per Lusatiam', *Neues Lausitzisches Magazin*, 33: 186–251.

Vogel, Johann Jacob (1714), *Leipzigisches Geschicht-Buch Oder Annales. Das ist: Jahr- und Tage-Bücher Der Weltberühmten Königl. und Churfürstlichen Sächsischen Kauff- und Handels-Stadt Leipzig* (Leipzig).

Vogel, Werner (1960), *Der Verbleib der wendischen Bevölkerung in der Mark Brandenburg* (Berlin).

Völkel, Měrćin (1984), *Serbske nowiny a časopisy w zašłosći a w přitomnosći* (Bautzen).

Volksversammlung (2012), <http://de.wikipedia.org/wiki/Sorbische_Volksversammlung> [accessed 14 August 2012].

Wańkowicz, Melchior (1963), *Walczący gryf* (Warsaw).

Weber, Max (1906/1974), 'XIV. Capitalism and Rural Society in Germany', in *From Max Weber: Essays in Sociology*, trans. and ed. H. H. Gerth and C. Wright Mills (London and Boston, 1974), 363–85. Reprint of a version first published in 1906.

Wedgwood, C. V. (1961), *The Thirty Years War* (Harmondsworth).

Wehler, Hans-Ulrich (1985), *The German Empire 1871–1918*, trans. Kim Traynor (Leamington Spa-Hamburg-New York).

Weiss, Christianus Henricus (1727), *Antiquitatum Misnico-Saxonicarum singularia duobus libris exposita, quorum alter antiquissimorum misniae incolarum, Hermundorum, Thuringorum ac Venedorum; alter Saxonum veterum [...] auctore M. Christiano Henrico Weissio, Gymnasii Altenburgensis Directore* (Chemnitz).

Wenzel, Walter (1987–94), *Studien zu sorbischen Personennamen*, 4 vols. (Bautzen).

Westphal (2012), <http.//pl.wikipedia.org/wiki/Augustyn Westphal> [accessed 14 July 2012].

Westphalen, Ernst Joachim de (1740), *Monumenta inedita rerum Germanicarum praecipue Cimbricarum et Megapolensium*, Bd. 2 (Leipzig).

Wićaz, Ota (1922), *[1] Wo serb. ludowym basnistwje. [2] Serbja jako misionarojo Bratrowskeje Jednoty. [3] Serbowka w Surinamje* (Bautzen, 1922).

Wićaz, Ota (1933), 'We wěcach redakcije', *Časopis Maćicy Serbskeje*, 86: 14–15.

Wićaz, Ota (1955), 'Kak sym Probstec Hanje wosušk njesł', in idem, *Serb ze złotym rjapom* (Budyšin), 12–18 (reprinted from *Předźenak* 1927, 89).

Widu. Gesch. (1935), *Widukind. Geschichte des deutschen Volkes* (Leipzig).

Widukind (1971), 'Die Sachsengeschichte des Widukind von Korvei', in *Quellen zur Geschichte der sächsischen Kaiserzeit*, ed. Albert Bauer Reinhold Rau und (Darmstadt), 1–183.

Wielopolski, Alfred (1954), 'Polsko-pomorskie spory graniczne w latach 1536–1555', *Przegląd Zachodni*, 10, tom 2 (nos. 5–8): 64–111.

Winarjec-Orsesowa, Hańža (1996), *Radwor. Starodawna cyrkwinska wjes* (Radibor).

Wölkowa, Sonja (2007), *Gregoriusowe kěrlušowe knižki a jich pozicija mjez najstaršimi hornjoserbskimi rěčnymi pomnikami* (Bautzen).

Wölkowa, Sonja and Franc Šěn (2001), 'Rukopisne hornjoserbske spěwarske w 17. lětstotku. (Pospyt kulturnohistoriskeje a rěčespytneje analyzy)', *Lětopis* 48, 1: 44–70.

Wornar, Jan (1997), 'Wopor njesebičneje pomocy. Marja Meškankec z Hózka', *Serbska protyka 1998* (Bautzen), 134–5.

Wornar, Edward (1999), 'Analytiski futur perfektiwnych werbow w hornjoserbšćinje', *Lětopis* 46, Wosebity zešiwk: 168–72.

Wornar, Edward (2011), 'Serbska sada w rukopisnej zběrce z lěta 1510' *Lětopis*, 58, 2: 135–7.

Wornar, Edward (2012), 'Kak serbska je Budyska přisaha?', *Lětopis*, 59, 2: 114–21

Wosady (1984), *Wosady našeje domizny: Krajan 3* (Leipzig).

Woźny, Aleksander (2010), *Łużyce w planie dywersji polskiego wywiadu wojskowego w latach 1931–1939* (Opole).

Wućahi (1862), 'Wućahi z maćičnych protokollow. Wot spočatka lěta 1861 do augusta 1862', *Časopis Maćicy Serbskeje*, 55–60.

Wuchatsch, Robert (2004), 'The Travelling Ministry 2: Pastor Gottlob Simpfendoerfer', in *German Church* (2004), 159–62 and 600.

Wukasch, Charles (2004), *A Rock against Alien Waves. A History of the Wends* (Austin, Texas).

Zabrocki, Ludwig (1975), 'O Słowińcach i Kaszubach nadłebskich', in: Rogaczewski (1975), 100–9. Originally published 1947.

Zeil, Wilhelm (1967), *Bolzano und die Sorben. Ein Beitrag zur Geschichte des „Wendischen Seminars" in Prag zur Zeit der josefinischen Aufklärung und der Romantik* (Bautzen).

Zitzewitz, Georg (1927), *Geschichte der ersten und zweiten Linie des Geschlechts von Zitzewitz (1312–1926) nach dem hinterlassenen Manuskript des verstorbenen Generalleutnants Wedig von Zitzewitz, aus dem Hause Budow. Im Auszuge herausgegeben von dem Familien-Vorstande. Bearbeitet durch Georg v. Zitzewitz aus dem Hause Beßwitz* (Stettin).

Zubor, A. (1975), 'Jan Awgust Měrćink. K jeho 100. posmjertninam 30. měrca 1975', *Serbska Protyka*, 94–7.

Zusammenstellung (1982), *Zusammenstellung einiger ausgewählter schulpolitischer Dokumente für Schulen im zweisprachigen Gebiet (1982)*. Schriftenreihe für Lehrer und Erzieher im zweisprachigen Gebiet, Heft 4 (Bautzen).

Zwahr, Hartmut (1968), *Sorbische Volksbewegung. Dokumente zur antisorbischen Staatspolitik im preußisch-deutschen Reich, zur Oberlausitzer Bauernbewegung und zur sorbischen nationalen Bewegung 1872–1918. Quellenauswahl* (Bautzen).

Zwahr, Hartmut (1970), *Arnošt Bart-Brězynčanski – žiwjenje a skutkowanje založićela Domowiny* (Bautzen).

Zwahr, Hartmut (1984), *Meine Landsleute. Die Sorben und die Lausitz im Zeugnis deutscher Zeitgenossen* (Bautzen).

Zwar, Heidi (1997), *The Loss of Wendish Ethnicity in Australia 1848–1919*. B.A. thesis ([Melbourne]).

Žur, Hubert (1977), *Komuž muza pjero wodźi*, 2 ed. (Bautzen).

INDEX

Index

Index

Index

Index

Index

Index

Index

Index